TURTLE MOUNTAIN RESERVATION CHIPPEWA INDIANS 1932 CENSUS WITH BIRTHS & DEATHS 1924-1932

TRANSCRIBED BY
JEFF BOWEN

NATIVE STUDY
Gallipolis, Ohio
USA

Copyright © 2016
by Jeff Bowen

ALL RIGHTS RESERVED
No part of this publication may be reproduced
or used in any form or manner whatsoever
without previous written permission from the
copyright holder or publisher.

Originally published:
Baltimore, Maryland
2016

Reprinted by:

Native Study LLC
Gallipolis, OH
www.nativestudy.com

Library of Congress Control Number: 2020915602

ISBN: 978-1-64968-034-1

Made in the United States of America.

Other Books and Series by Jeff Bowen

1901-1907 Native American Census Seneca, Eastern Shawnee, Miami, Modoc, Ottawa, Peoria, Quapaw, and Wyandotte Indians (Under Seneca School, Indian Territory)

1932 Census of The Standing Rock Sioux Reservation with Births And Deaths 1924-1932

Census of The Blackfeet, Montana, 1897- 1901 Expanded Edition

Eastern Cherokee by Blood, 1906-1910, Volumes I thru XIII

Choctaw of Mississippi Indian Census 1929-1932 with Births and Deaths 1924-1931 Volume I

Choctaw of Mississippi Indian Census 1933, 1934 & 1937, Supplemental Rolls to 1934 & 1935 with Births and Deaths 1932-1938, and Marriages 1936-1938 Volume II

Eastern Cherokee Census Cherokee, North Carolina 1930-1939 Census 1930-1931 with Births And Deaths 1924-1931 Taken By Agent L. W. Page Volume I

Eastern Cherokee Census Cherokee, North Carolina 1930-1939 Census 1932-1933 with Births And Deaths 1930-1932 Taken By Agent R. L. Spalsbury Volume II

Eastern Cherokee Census Cherokee, North Carolina 1930-1939 Census 1934-1937 with Births and Deaths 1925-1938 and Marriages 1936 & 1938 Taken by Agents R. L. Spalsbury And Harold W. Foght Volume III

Seminole of Florida Indian Census, 1930-1940 with Birth and Death Records, 1930-1938

Texas Cherokees 1820-1839 A Document For Litigation 1921

Choctaw By Blood Enrollment Cards 1898-1914 Volumes I thru XVII

Starr Roll 1894 (Cherokee Payment Rolls) Districts: Canadian, Cooweescoowee, and Delaware Volume One

Starr Roll 1894 (Cherokee Payment Rolls) Districts: Flint, Going Snake, and Illinois Volume Two

Starr Roll 1894 (Cherokee Payment Rolls) Districts: Saline, Sequoyah, and Tahlequah; Including Orphan Roll Volume Three

Other Books and Series by Jeff Bowen

Cherokee Intruder Cases Dockets of Hearings 1901-1909 Volumes I & II

Indian Wills, 1911-1921 Records of the Bureau of Indian Affairs Books One thru Seven

Native American Wills & Probate Records 1911-1921

Visit our website at **www.nativestudy.com** to learn more about these and other books and series by Jeff Bowen

This book is dedicated to
Jordan Trimble,
a great friend with vision.

TABLE OF CONTENTS

Chippewa Delegation	vi
Turtle Mountain Reservation family	vii
1932 Census Cover	viii
Introduction	ix
Census Instructions	xiii
1932 Census	3

BIRTHS

July 1, 1924 – June 30, 1925	239
July 1, 1925 – June 30, 1926	242
July 1, 1926 – June 30, 1927	246
July 1, 1927 – June 30, 1928	250
Additional Names 1927 – 1928	254
July 1, 1928 – June 30, 1929	255
Additional Names 1928 – 1929	260
July 1, 1929 – June 30, 1930	261
Additional Names 1929 – 1930	266
April 1, 1930 – March 31, 1931	267
Additional Names 1930 – 1931	271
April 1, 1931 – March 31, 1932	272
Additional Names 1931 – 1932	278

DEATHS

July 1, 1924 – June 30, 1925	281
July 1, 1925 – June 30, 1926	282
July 1, 1926 – June 30, 1927	283
July 1, 1927 – June 30, 1928	284
July 1, 1928 – June 30, 1929	285
July 1, 1929 – June 30, 1930	287
April 1, 1930 – March 31, 1931	289
April 1, 1931 – March 31, 1932	290
Index	293

Chippewa Delegation, ca 1871
In center, wearing white shirt, is well-known Chippewa Chief Little Shell III, who was the last of the Little Shell line of hereditary chiefs. He is known for his participation in The McCumber Agreement or "The Ten Cent Treaty".

Turtle Mountain Reservation family, ca 1943

CENSUS.
Turtle Mountain, North Dakota.
April 1, 1932.

This is an image of the front cover taken from the Turtle Mountain Census of 1932.

INTRODUCTION

These records have been transcribed from the National Archival film roll M-595 Roll 604, Indian Census Rolls 1885-1940, (Turtle Mountain) Chippewa Indians 1932 with Birth and Death rolls, 1924-1932. On page v of this book is a set of instructions explaining how to read the census and the key at the top of each page. The original 1932 Census was typed using a columnar set form with labels at the top of each column. This transcription has been revised using semicolons to separate each column due to size.

The birth and death records transcribed for this book were originally published by the author in a separate publication in July of 1996. Their inclusion here completes the transcription of M-595 Roll 604, and offers researchers the opportunity to examine its contents in one place.

Each census, in the original, is in alphabetical order but in a few instances a name has been inserted that disrupts the sequence and has created the need for a limited index in the back of the book. Researchers should check the table of contents for each census division or location.

In all cases, the author has been careful to copy the names and dates exactly as indicated on these microfilm records. It is his hope that these pages will be of great value to those seeking their heritage among the Turtle Mountain Chippewa and that this work will honor the people of this tribe and their ancestors.

Below are quoted a few paragraphs from Roland Marmon's book, *Last Card Played*, covering some of his tribe's history and relationship with the Métis in Canada.

"As a group, the Turtle Mountain Chippewa are the most prominent of the Plains Chippewa tribes in America with a membership of nearly eighty thousand people. The Turtle Mountain Chippewa were also affiliated with the ethnically European and Indian mixed Métis people, who constitute the largest Indigenous group in Canada, and were caught between national identities and Canadian and United States Federal policy."[1]

"The Federal Government sought treaties in an effort to prevent the Chippewa tribes in Minnesota from joining the Dakota and to insure the allegiance of the Chippewa to the United States. In 1863, when Governor of Minnesota Territory Alexander Ramsey and his delegation was sent by President Lincoln to negotiate a new treaty with the Minnesota Chippewa arrived at the forks of the Red Lake River and the Red River, bands of Chippewa and a large number of Metis were waiting. However, Ramsey could not begin negotiations until the Pembina or Plains Chippewa had arrived. Finally, three days later, the Pembina group consisting of about three hundred followers came in. The Pembina were led by two principal chiefs: Red Bear and a young man named Little Shell, who would also be called Little Chief by Ramsey at the Treaty Crossing. At this treaty council, the Pembina group ceded the Red River Valley (approximately eleven million acres) to the United States but retained the land north and west of Spirit Lake in present

---

[1] *Last Card Played*, Roland Marmon pg. 3, para. 2

day North Dakota (approximately ten million acres), which included the Turtle Mountains. Included in the treaty was the right of the Pembina Chippewa to live at the White Earth Reservation, which Little Shell refused, but approximately one hundred of his followers chose to. The Pembina Chippewa who moved to the White Earth Reservation were led by Chief Red Bear and accepted the provisions of the treaty in doing so. However, the plains-dwelling Pembina Chippewa, who refused to locate with the other Pembina Chippewa on the White Earth Chippewa Reservation were led by Aissance or Little Shell I, would become known as the Turtle Mountain Chippewa because of their preferred summer and winter hunting location in the Turtle Mountains of north central Dakota Territory."[2]

"Members of the Turtle Mountain Band of Chippewa belong primarily to the Pembina Band of Chippewa (Ojibwe) Nation. The Anishinaabe, the "Original People," or the Ojibwe have resided in North America since approximately 900. The people originated on the Island of La Pointe in the Great Lakes region and migrated in various directions as the bands dispersed. Members of the Ojibwe Nation include the present-day Ojibwe, Ottawa, and Potawatomi tribes of Canada, Michigan, Minnesota, Wisconsin, North Dakota, and Montana. The Ojibwe language is a member of the Algonquian linguistic family. The Ojibwe encountered Jesuit missionaries and French traders in 1640 along the shores of Lake Superior and became heavily involved in trade; their interactions with Cree and French traders forged strong relationships among those groups. Near the end of the 1700s the Mikinakwastsha -Anishinaabe Band of the Ojibwe separated from the tribe and established a community in the Turtle Mountains of North Dakota. The separation was primarily an economic move, as well as an attempt to find refuge from encroaching Euro-American settlement in Wisconsin. In North Dakota, the Ojibwe engaged in conflict with members of the Dakota tribe. Skirmishes over territorial rights continued for about 50 years, until the 1858 Sweet Corn Treaty defined tribal lands for both groups and mandated numerous resolutions for the tribes."[3]

This volume contains material that could tie numerous researchers to their Canadian heritage within the Métis people. "In Canada, the Métis, as defined by the Constitution Act 1982, are Aboriginal people. They are descendants of specific mixed First Nations and European ancestry who self-identify as Métis, and are accepted into their current community. The Métis people are the modern descendants of Indigenous women in Canada and the colonial-era French, Scottish and English trappers and fur traders they married. The descendants of these unions formed communities, first around hunting, trapping and fur trading, that to this day have a unique and specific culture. The term "Métis" does not mean any white person who believes they also have some Native ancestry. It refers to specific, intact communities of Aboriginal people and their culture. The majority of Métis people have combined Algonquian and French ancestry."[4]

Throughout their history, the Turtle Mountain Chippewa have always been synonymous with the Métis people. For example, references to Canadian places of

---

[2] *Last Card Played*, Roland Marmon pgs. 24-25 para. 3
[3] *National Geographic Indian Nations of North America* pg. 187 para 1 and para 1 pg. 191
[4] *Métis Aboriginal Peoples in Canada*, Wikipedia

residence appear among these records time and again (e.g., from Boggy Creek, Manitoba to Yorkton, Saskatchewan). Geographical references in the United States extend from Morgantown, WV, to Arizona, to Long Beach, California. In fact, this diverse tribe continues to assimilate during trying times and show strength no matter what roadblocks it has faced.

Jeff Bowen
Gallipolis, Ohio
NativeStudy.com

INSTRUCTIONS

(*A*) A separate roll is to be made of each reservation; also, of each *rancheria* or reserve, and a separate roll of Indians allotted on the public domain or homesteading. The roll is to be based on enrollment and not on residence.

(*B*) Persons are to be listed by families alphabetically; that is, not only by the first letter of the surname, but also by the second and subsequent letters when the first letter or letters are the same. For example: Ab*a*lon, Ab*b*ott, Ab*c*on, Ab*e*nd, Ab*i*ct; B*a*ll, B*e*ll, B*i*ll, B*o*ll, B*u*ll; ...etc. Families having the same surname are also to be listed in this way, e.g.; Brown, *A*nson; Brown, *B*ill; Brown, *C*harles; Brown, *D*avid. In the case of English translations of Indian names, such as John *Flying-Elk*, Flying-Elk is the surname and is to be listed under F. In such cases the first word of the translated Indian name determines the alphabetical position. The best way to accomplish this will be to write the names of each family group on a separate card; then, arrange the cards alphabetically and type the names therefrom onto the census roll.

Members of a family are to be listed in the following order: Head, first; wife, second; then children, whether sons or daughters, *in the order of their ages*; and lastly, all other relatives and persons living with the family who do not constitute another family group.

Annuity and per capita payment rolls are also to be prepared in the same manner.

(*C*) A family is composed of the following members:
1. Both parents and their unmarried children, if any, living with them; all other relatives and persons living with the family who do not constitute another family group.
2. Either parent and the unmarried children, if the other parent is dead; all other relatives and persons living with the family who do not constitute another family group.
3. A single person over 21 years of age, not living with a relative.

(*D*) For each person the following information is to be furnished:
1. NUMBER. – A number is to be assigned in serial order. Thus, the first person listed is to be numbered as "1," the second, as "2," and so on until the census is completed.
2. NAME. – If there are both an Indian and an English name, the allotment or annuity roll name is to be given. First, the last or surname; then, the given name in full. Ditto marks are to be used under the surname of the head for the surnames of the other members of one family.
3. SEX. – "M" for male; "F" for female.
4. AGE AT LAST BIRTHDAY. – Age in completed years at last birthday is to be shown. For infants under 1 year, age in completed months, expressed as twelfths of a year. Thus, 3 months as 3/12 yr.
5. TRIBE. – Care is to be taken that tribe, not band or local name, is given. Thus, Ute tribe, not Pahvant, which is a band of Ute. Likewise, Hupa tribe, not Bear River, which is a local name for the members of the Hupa tribe living near Bear River.

INSTRUCTIONS

6. DEGREE OF BLOOD. – "F" for full blood; "1/4+" for one-fourth or more Indian blood; "-1/4" for less than one fourth Indian blood.
7. MARITAL STATUS. – "S" for a single or unmarried person; "M" for a married person; and "Wd" for widowed of either sex.
8. RELATIONSHIP TO HEAD OF FAMILY. – The head, whether husband or father, widow or unmarried person of either sex, is to be designated as such. For the other members, the appropriate term which designates the particular relationship the person bears to the head is to be used.
9. RESIDENCE. –
    (a) At *jurisdiction* where enrolled: Yes or no. The term jurisdiction includes all reservations and public domain allotments under the agency.
    (b) *Or* at another jurisdiction. The name of the jurisdiction is to be given.
    (c) *Or* elsewhere:
        1. Post office: Both the proper name of the post office and the class by which it is known (city, town, village, etc.) are to be given. Thus, Lewiston, city.
        2. County.
        3. State.
10. WARD. – Yes or no. Wardship depends primarily upon the ownership of individual property held in trust or upon membership in a tribe living on a Federal reservation.

11. ALLOTMENT, ANNUITY, AND IDENTIFICATION NUMBERS. —"Al", for allotment; "An", for annuity; and "Id", for identification, before the appropriate number or numbers. All numbers are to be shown.

(*E*) Rolls not prepared in strict conformity with the above instructions will be returned for correction.

1932 Census Roll
Turtle Mountain Reservation

Turtle Mountain Reservation
1932 Census Roll

Key: Number; Surname, Given; Sex; Age at Last Birthday, Birthdate (if given); Tribe (Chippewa, unless stated otherwise); Degree of Blood; Marital Status; Relationship to Head of Family, Last Year Census Number; At Jurisdiction Where Enrolled (Yes/No); Elsewhere - Post Office, County, State; Ward (Yes/No); Allotment [Al.], Annuity [An.] and/or Identification [Id.] Numbers

NE   Abraham, Albert;   Head
1   "   Justine (Alberts); f; 28; ¼+; m; wife B-11; no; Lake Williams, Kidder, ND; yes; Id.64b, Al.DL11

2   Aiken, John; m; 60; ¼+; wd; Head B-1; no; Rolla, Rolette, ND; no; Id.62, Al.R3
Died   Virginia;   B-2   (Died 10-8-31)
3   "   Agnes; f; 19; ¼+; s; dau B-3; no; Rolla, Rolette, ND; no; Id.62e
4   "   Francois; m; 17; ¼+; s; son B-4; no; Rolla, Rolette, ND; no; Id.62f
5   "   Eva; f; 16; ¼+; s; dau B-5; no; Rolla, Rolette, ND; no; Id.62g
Died   Raymond   (Born 8-11-31 and died 11-26-31)

6   Aiken, Margaret; f; 51; ¼+; s; Head; no (Left out last census); Unknown; no; Id.63a, Al.H-010523

7   Akenensi, Old Man; m; 62; f; wd; Head B-9; no; Dunseith, Rolette, ND; yes; Id.2, Al.DL45

8   Akenensi, Thomas; m; 24; F; m; Head B-6; no; Dunseith, Rolette, ND; yes; Id.2b, Al.G-011730
9   "   Rose (Green Feather); f; 25; F; m; wife B-7; no; Dunseith, Rolette, ND; yes; Id.11c, Al.G363
10   "   Iron Thunder; f; 4; F; s; dau B-8; no; Dunseith, Rolette, ND; yes; none

NE   Alberts, George;   Head
11   "   Agnes (Warren); f; 24; ¼+; m; wife B-10; no; Dunseith, Rolette, ND; yes; Id.1002f, Al.GF-14920
12   "   Emma; f; 4 12-3-27; ¼+; s; dau ------; no; Dunseith, Rolette, ND; yes; none

13   Alberts, Wm Joseph; m; 32; ¼+; s; Head B-12; no; Glasgow, Mont; no; Id.64e

NE   Alick, Albert;   Head
14   "   Marie (Lavallie); f; 36; ¼+; m; wife A-1; yes; yes; Id.63e, Al.G-0340
15   " LeClaire, Delia; f; 11 11-18-20; ¼+; s; step-dau A-2; yes; yes; none
Died   "   Frank;   A-3 (Died 11-26-31); yes; none
16   "   Albert, Jr; m; 4 3-15-27; ¼+; s; son A-4; yes; yes; none
17   "   Morris; m; 3 3-29-29; ¼+; s; son A-5; yes; yes; none

NE   Alick, Asmael;   Head
18   "   Eva (Alberts); f; 24 10-30-07; ¼+; m; wife A-6; yes; yes; Id.64d, Al.H-030863
19   "   Donald; m; 5 2-21-27; ¼+; s; son A-7; yes; yes; none
20   "   Raymond; m; 3 6-1-28; ¼+; s; son A-8; yes; yes; none

Turtle Mountain Reservation
1932 Census Roll

Key: Number; Surname, Given; Sex; Age at Last Birthday, Birthdate (if given); Tribe (Chippewa, unless stated otherwise); Degree of Blood; Marital Status; Relationship to Head of Family, Last Year Census Number; At Jurisdiction Where Enrolled (Yes/No); Elsewhere - Post Office, County, State; Ward (Yes/No); Allotment [Al.], Annuity [An.] and/or Identification [Id.] Numbers

NE Alick, Joseph;   Head
21   "   Veronica (McCloud); f; 38; ¼+; m; wife B-13; no; Bonetrail, ND; no;
                                                                 Id.389a, Al.GF-88
22   "   Selma; f; 5 8-21-26; ¼+; s; dau B-14; no; Bonetrail, ND; no; none
23   "   Blanch; f; 3 5-31-28; ¼+; s; dau B-15; no; Bonetrail, ND; no; none
24   "   Ramona; f; 1 4-1-31; ¼+; s; dau ------; no; Bonetrail, ND; no; none

NE   Allard, Alexander; m;
25   "   Louise (Davis); f; 45; ¼+; m; wife A-9; yes; no; Id.70a, Al.H-010480
26   "   Lawrence; m; 23; ¼+; s; son A10; yes; yes; Id.70b, Al.H-010481
27   "   John B; m; 17; ¼+ s; son A12; yes; yes; Id.70d
Dead "   Mary Louise;   A11   (Died 4-9-28)
28   "   Georgeline; f; 15; ¼+; s; dau A13; yes; yes; Id.70e
29   "   Joseph E; m; 11 10-15-19; ¼+; s; son A14; yes; yes; Id.70f
30   "   Napoleon; m; 9 10-29-22; ¼+; s; son; A15; yes; yes; Id.70g
31   "   Louis; m; 7; ¼+; s; son A16; yes; yes; Id.70h
32   "   Elmer; m; 4; ¼+; s; son A17; yes; yes; Id.70i

33   Allard, Alfred; m; 33; ¼+; m; Head A-18; yes; yes; Id.65b, Al.H-040627
34   "   Cecelie (Keplin); f; 34; ¼+; m; wife A-19; yes; yes; Id.535b, Al.G-0520
35   "   Alfred; m; 6 4-19-25; ¼+; s; son A-20; yes; yes; none
36   "   Irene; f; 4 10-18-27; ¼+; s; dau A-22; yes; yes; none
37   "   Florence; f; 2 6-18-29; ¼+; s; dau A-21; yes; yes; none
38   "   Clarence; m; 1; 2-3-31; ¼+; s; son A-23; yes; yes; none

39   Allard, Arthur; m; 23; ¼+; s; Head A-24; yes; yes; Id.66c, Al.H-010485
40   "   Mary Rose; f; 19; ¼+; s; sis A-25; yes; yes; Id.66e

NE   Allard, Ezear;   Head
41   "   Elsie (Laverdure); f; 42; ¼+; m; wife A-26; yes; no; Id.67a, Al.g-)115[sic]
42   "   John; m; 10 11-19-11; ¼+; s; son A-28; yes; no; Id.67c
43   "   Marie; f; 8 9-19-23; ¼+; s; dau A-27; yes; no; Id.67b
44   "   Rita; f; 2 8-25-29; ¼+; s; dau A-29; yes; no; Id.67d

NE   Allard, Joe;   wd; Head
45   "   Frank; m; 15 4-19-16; ¼+; s; son A-30; yes; no; Id.68b
46   "   John; m; 14 6-13-17; ¼+; s; son A-31; yes; no; Id.68c
47   "   Mary; f; 13 2-28-13; ¼+; s; dau A-32; yes; no; Id.68d
48   "   Clifford; m; 10 7-30-21; ¼+; s; son A-33; yes; no; Id.68e
49   "   Eugene; m; 9; ¼+; s; son A-34; yes; no; Id.68f
50   "   Roy; m; 6; ¼+; s; son A-35; yes; no; Id.68g

Turtle Mountain Reservation
1932 Census Roll

Key: Number; Surname, Given; Sex; Age at Last Birthday, Birthdate (if given); Tribe (Chippewa, unless stated otherwise); Degree of Blood; Marital Status; Relationship to Head of Family, Last Year Census Number; At Jurisdiction Where Enrolled (Yes/No); Elsewhere - Post Office, County, State; Ward (Yes/No); Allotment [Al.], Annuity [An.] and/or Identification [Id.] Numbers

NE Allard, Joseph;   Head
51   "   Frezene (Falcon); f; 1/4+; m; wife A-36; yes; yes; Id.65a, Al.r-7

NE Allard, Michael;   Head
52   "   Agnes (Grandbois); f; 22; 1/4+; m; wife B-981; yes; yes; Id.442g
53   "   Patrice; m; 3 10-12-28; 1/4+; s; son ------; yes; yes; none
54   "   Michael, Jr; m; 1 6-18-30; 1/4+; s; son ------; yes; yes; none
55   "   Sylvester; m; 3/12 12-21-31; 1/4+; s; son ------; yes; yes; none

NE Allard, William;   Head
Died "   Josephine;   A-37   (Died 1931)
56   "   Morris; m; 21; 1/4+; s; son A-38; yes; no; Id.69b

57 Allery, Abraham; m; 65; 1/4+; Head A-39; yes; yes; Id.71, Al.R-9
58   "   Margaret (Lenoir); f; 70; 1/4+; m; wife A-40; yes; no; Id.71a, Al.G-311

59 Allery, Alexander; m; 32; 1/4+; s; Head B-16; no; Dunseith, Rolette, ND; yes;
                                                                    Id.81c, Al.G-09275
60   "   Sarah; f; 30; 1/4+; s; sis B-17; no; Dunseith, Rolette, ND; yes;
                                                                    Id.81d, Al.G-09279
Died "   Frank;   B-18   (Died 9-25-31)
61   Samuel; m; 22; 1/4+; s; bro B-19; no; Dunseith, Rolette, ND; yes;
                                                                    Id.81f, Al.G-026322

62 Allery, Baptiste; m; 77; 1/4+; wd; Head B-20; no; Dunseith, Rolette, ND; yes;
                                                                    Id.77, Al.DL-25

63 Allery, Ernestine (Lafurnais); f; 21; 1/4+; wd; Head B-22; no; Dunseith, Rolette, ND;
                                                                    yes; Id.569e, Al.none
Died "   Fred;   B-21   (Died 6-15-31)
64   "   Fred, Jr; m; 5/12 10-18-31; 1/4+; s; son; B-23; no; Dunseith, Rolette, ND;
                                                                    yes; none
Died "   Donald .... (Died 1-25-31)

65 Allery, Henry; m; 48; 1/4+; s; Head B-24; no; Unknown; yes; Id.86, Al.H-024482

66 Allery, Isadore; m; 45; 1/4+; s; Head B-26; no; Whitewater, Phillips, Mont; no;
                                                                    Id.83, Al.G09274

67 Allery, Jos oph[sic]; m; 48; 1/4+; wd; Head B-27; no; Unknown; no; Id.85, Al.G0688
68   "   Charles; m; 25; 1/4+; s; son B-28; no; Unknown; no; Id.85b, Al.---
69   "   Lillie; f; 19; 1/4+; s; dau B-29; no; Unknown; no Id.85c

Turtle Mountain Reservation
1932 Census Roll

Key: Number; Surname, Given; Sex; Age at Last Birthday, Birthdate (if given); Tribe (Chippewa, unless stated otherwise); Degree of Blood; Marital Status; Relationship to Head of Family, Last Year Census Number; At Jurisdiction Where Enrolled (Yes/No); Elsewhere - Post Office, County, State; Ward (Yes/No); Allotment [Al.], Annuity [An.] and/or Identification [Id.] Numbers

70 Allery, Joseph; m; 45; ¼+; m; Head B-30; no; Dunseith, Rolette, ND; yes; Id.79, Al.GF188
71 " Marie (Nadeau); f; 43; ¼+; m; wife B-31; no; Dunseith, Rolette, ND; no; Id.79a, Al.M271
72 " Marie; f; 18; ¼+; s; dau B-32; no; Dunseith, Rolette, ND; yes; Id.79b
73 " Eliza; f; 14 6-23-17; ¼+; s; dau B-33; no; Dunseith, Rolette, ND; yes; Id.79c
74 " Ernestine; f; 13 3-29-19; ¼+; s; dau B-34; no; Dunseith, Rolette, ND; yes; Id.79d
75 " Rose D; f; 10 10-25-21; ¼+; s; dau B-35; no; Dunseith, Rolette, ND; yes; Id.79e
76 " Josephine; f; 7 5-7-24; ¼+; s; dau B-36; no; Dunseith, Rolette, ND; yes; Id.79h

77 Allery, Josette (Daignon); f; 78; ¼+; wd; Head B-37; no; Malta, Phillips, Mont; yes; Id.73a, Al.GF135

78 Allery, Louis; m; 38; ¼+; m; Head B-38; no; Dunseith, Rolette, ND; yes; Id.78, Al.CF-190
NE " Ogila (Delorme); f; wife
79 " Catherine; f; 11 10-12-20; ¼+; s; dau B-39; no; Dunseith, Rolette, ND; yes; Id.78b
80 " Ernestine; f; 8 4-7-23; ¼+; s; dau B-40; no; Dunseith, Rolette, ND; yes; Id.78c
81 " Nicholas; m; 7 12-1-24; ¼+; s; son -----; no; none
82 " John; m; 1 5-1-30; ¼+; s; son -----; no; none

83 Allery, Louis; m; 44; ¼+; m; Head B-41; no; Dunseith, Rolette, ND; no; Id.84, Al.G-09272
NE " Josephine (Lemere); f
84 " Alvin; m; 15 7-16-16; ¼+; s; son B-42; no; Dunseith, Rolette, ND; no; Id.84b
85 " Francis; m; 11 5-23-20; ¼+; s; son B-43; no; Dunseith, Rolette, ND; no; Id.84c
86 " Georgeline; f; 3 1-9-29; ¼+; s; dau B-44; no; Dunseith, Rolette, ND; no; Id.84d

NE Allery, Mary (Lemire), Head
87 " Leo; m; 20; ¼+; s; son B-45; no; Tokio, Benson, ND; no; Id.75b

88 Allery, Martin; m; 35; ¼+; m; Head B-46; no; Tokio, Benson, ND; yes; Id.87b, Al.M-180
89 " Mary (Azure); f; 31; ¼+; m; wife B-47; no; Tokio, Benson, ND; yes; Id.120c, Al.G-564

Turtle Mountain Reservation
1932 Census Roll

Key: Number; Surname, Given; Sex; Age at Last Birthday, Birthdate (if given); Tribe (Chippewa, unless stated otherwise); Degree of Blood; Marital Status; Relationship to Head of Family, Last Year Census Number; At Jurisdiction Where Enrolled (Yes/No); Elsewhere - Post Office, County, State; Ward (Yes/No); Allotment [Al.], Annuity [An.] and/or Identification [Id.] Numbers

90 Allery(cont), Leo Ernest; m; 9 8-13-22; ¼+; s; son B-48; no; Tokio, Benson, ND; yes; Id.81e
91 " Willard; m; 5 3-10-27; ¼+; s; son -----; no; Tokio, Benson, ND; yes; none
92 " Clifford; m; 3 3-7-29; ¼+; s; son -----; no; Tokio, Benson, ND; yes; none

93 Allery, Napoleon; m; 67; ¼+; wd; Head b-49; no; Tokio, Benson, ND; no; Id.87, Al.DL-32

94 Allery, Patrick; m; 38; ¼+; s; Head B-50; no; Unknown; no; Id.82, Al.G-09280

95 Allery, Phillip; m; 40; ¼+; m; Head A-41; yes; Id.72, Al.R-11
NE " Betsey (Patnaud)
96 " Joseph A; m; 20; ¼+; s; son A-42; yes; Id.72e
97 " John P; m; 18; ¼+; s; son A-43; yes; Id.72f
98 " St.Ann; f; 15 2-8-17; ¼+; s; dau A-44; yes; Id.72g
99 " Rosalie; f; 13; ¼+; s; dau; A-45; yes; Id.72i
100 " Alfred; m; 9 4-18-22; ¼+; s; son A-46; yes; Id.72k
101 " Margaret; f; 5 6-7-26; ¼+; s; dau A47; yes; Id.72-l
102 " Louis ; m; 3 11-3-28; ¼+; s; son A48; yes; Id.72m
103 " Dorothy J; f; 8/12 7-3-31; ¼+; s; dau -----; yes; Id.72n

104 Allery, Rosalie (Belgarde); f; 48; ¼+; wd; Head B-51; no; Malta, Phillips, Mont; no; Id.88, Al.G0622
105 " Alfred; m; 29; ¼+; s; son B-52; no; Malta, Phillips, Mont; yes; Id.88d, Al.G25
106 " Jerome; m; 23; ¼+; s; son B-53; no; Malta, Phillips, Mont; yes; Id.88b
107 " Emelia; f; 18; ¼+; s; dau B-54; no; Malta, Phillips, Mont; yes; Id.88e
108 " Joseph; m; 14; ¼+; s; son B-55; no; Malta, Phillips, Mont; yes; Id.88f
109 " Christine; f; 11; ¼+; s; dau B-56; no; Malta, Phillips, Mont; yes; Id.88g

NE Allery, Sam; m; 44; ¼+; m; Head
110 " Mary B (Langer); f; 44; ¼+; m; wife A-49; yes; no; Id.80a, Al.G108
111 " Rosalie; f; 22; ¼+; s; dau A-51; yes; yes; Id.80c, Al.G012603
112 " Marie; f; 21; ¼+; s; dau A-52; yes; yes; Id.80d, Al.H024481
113 " John; m; 18; ¼+; s; son A-53; yes; no; Id.80e
114 " Frank; m; 15 3-18-17; ¼+; s; son A-54; yes; no; Id.80f
115 " Laura J; f; 12 5-17-19; ¼+; s; dau A-55; yes; no; Id.80g
116 " George C; m; 11 3-12-21; ¼+; s; son A-56; yes; no; Id.80h
117 " Emil; m; 10 2-24-22; ¼+; s; son A-57; yes; no; Id.80i
118 " Marie J; f; 8 9-13-23; ¼+; s; dau A-58; yes; no; Id.80j
119 " Gladys; f; 6 9-26-26; ¼+; s; dau A-59; yes; no; Id.80k
120 " Ida; f; 3 6-29-28; ¼+; s; dau A-60; yes; no; Id.80-l
121 " Evelyn; f; 2 11-6-29; ¼+; s; dau A-61; yes; no; Id.80m
122 " Doris; f; 1 10-29-30; ¼+; s; dau -----; yes; no; Id.80n

Turtle Mountain Reservation
1932 Census Roll

Key: Number; Surname, Given; Sex; Age at Last Birthday, Birthdate (if given); Tribe (Chippewa, unless stated otherwise); Degree of Blood; Marital Status; Relationship to Head of Family, Last Year Census Number; At Jurisdiction Where Enrolled (Yes/No); Elsewhere - Post Office, County, State; Ward (Yes/No); Allotment [Al.], Annuity [An.] and/or Identification [Id.] Numbers

NE Allery, William; m;   Head
123   "   Mary J (Lafountain); f; 26; ¼+; m; wife B57; no; Dunseith, Rolette, ND;
                                                              yes; Id.550e, Al.GF155
124 Allery, George; m; 7 4-15-24; ¼+; s; son B58; no; Dunseith, Rolette, ND; yes; none

125 Allery, William; m; 52; ¼+; s; Head B-59; no; Unknown (Canada); yes; Id.74, Al.GF136

126 All Still; m; 46; F; m; Head A-62; yes; yes; Id.20, Al.R167
127   , Daisy (Bonnaup); f; 35; F; m; wife A-63; yes; yes; Id.9b

NE Amundson, Anton;   Head
128   "   Rose (Belgarde); f; 23; ¼+; m; wife A64; yes; yes; Id.174e, Al.none
129   "   Dolores; f; 1 10-19-30; ¼+; s; dau A65; yes; yes; none

130 Amyott, Daniel; m; 43; ¼+; wd; Head B60; no; Unknown Canada; no; Id.91, Al.G-07786

131 Amyott, Francois; m; 49; ¼+; m; Head B61; no; Canton, Lincoln, SD; yes;
                                                              Id.92, Al.H-040625
132   "   Eme rse[sic] (Decoteau); f; 36; ¼+; m; wife B62; no; Canton, Lincoln, SD;
                                                              Id.92a, Al.G-416

133 Amyott, Joseph; m; 47; ¼+; m; Head B63; no; Dunseith, Rolette, ND; yes;
                                                              Id.89, Al.H-012498
NE   "   Victoria (Laroque); f; wife
134   "   Frank; m; 19; ¼+; s; son B64; no; Dunseith, Rolette, ND; yes; Id.89b

135 Amyott, Joseph; m; 32; ¼+; m; Head B65; no; Dunseith, Rolette, ND; yes;
                                                              Id.96b, Al.GF-185
136   "   St.Ann (Vivier); f; 27; ¼+; m; wife B66; no; Dunseith, Rolette, ND;
                                                              yes; Id.990e, Al.G-010062
137   "   (Hoff) Daniel; m; 7; ¼+; s; step son B67; no; Dunseith, Rolette, ND; yes; none
138   "   (Marsden) Raymond; m; 6; ¼+; s; step son B68; no; Dunseith, Rolette, ND; yes; none
139 Amyott, Leonard; m; 4; ¼+; s; step son B69; no; Dunseith, Rolette, ND; yes; none

140 Amyott, Louis, Jr; m; 60; ¼+; m; Head B70; yes; no; Id.96, Al.H039317
141   "   Mary (Lafountain); f; 50; ¼+; m; wife B71; yes; yes; Id.96a, Al.GF186
142   "   Francois; m; 21; ¼+; s; son B72; yes; yes; Id.96g, Al.G016825
143   "   Cecilia; f; 19; ¼+; s; dau B73; yes; yes; Id.96h, Al.H024485
144   "   Ernest; m; 17; ¼+; s; son B74; yes; yes; Id.96i, Al.H030437
145   "   Michael; m; 15; ¼+; s; son B75; yes; no; none
146   "   Theodora; m; 14; ¼+; s; son B 76; yes; no; none
147   "   Gladys; f; 13; ¼+; s; dau B77; yes; no; none
148   "   John P; m; 7 4-20-24; ¼+; s; son B78; yes; no; none

Turtle Mountain Reservation
1932 Census Roll

Key: Number; Surname, Given; Sex; Age at Last Birthday, Birthdate (if given); Tribe (Chippewa, unless stated otherwise); Degree of Blood; Marital Status; Relationship to Head of Family, Last Year Census Number; At Jurisdiction Where Enrolled (Yes/No); Elsewhere - Post Office, County, State; Ward (Yes/No); Allotment [Al.], Annuity [An.] and/or Identification [Id.] Numbers

149 Amyott, Peter; m; 60; ¼+; m; Head B-79; no; Dentaluta, Sask, Canada; no;
    Id.97, Al.G430
150 Amyott, Louise (Allery); f; 60; ¼+; m; wife B-81; no; Dentaluta, Sask, Canada; no;
    Id.97a, Al.H012499

151 Amyott, Riel; m; 34; ¼+; m; Head B-81; no; Erickson, Manitoba, Canada; no;
    Id.95b, Al.G431
NE "   Mary (Belgarde); wife
152 "   William; m; 17 4-16-14; ¼+; s; son B-82; no; Erickson, Manitoba,
        Canada; no; Id.95b
153 "   Ralph; m; 16 7-15-31; ¼+; s; son B-83; no; Erickson, Manitoba, Canada;
        no; Id.95c
154 "   Rosa; f; 14 4-15-17; ¼+; s; dau -----; no; Erickson, Manitoba, Canada;
        no; none
155 "   Norman; m; 12 4-17-19; ¼+; s; son -----; no; Erickson, Manitoba, Canada
        no; none
156 "   George; m; 10 4-21-21; ¼+; s; son -----; no; Erickson, Manitoba, Canada;
        no; none
157 "   Catherine; f; 8 5-29-23; ¼+; s; dau -----; no; Erickson, Manitoba, Canada;
        no; none
158 "   Dorothy; f; 84[sic] 1-15-28; ¼+; s; dau -----; no; Erickson, Manitoba, Canada
        no; none

159 Amyott, Wm. Alfred; m; 30; ¼+; m; Head B-84; no; Belcourt, Rolette; ND; yes;
    Id.96c, Al.G184
160 "   Clara (Lavallie); f; 28; ¼+; m; wife B-85; no; Belcourt, Rolette, ND; yes;
    Id.631c, Al.G0341
161 "   Fred; m; 8 8-23-23; ¼+; s; son B-86; no; Belcourt, Rolette, ND; yes; none
162 "   Norbert; m; 7 2-23-25; ¼+; s; son B-87; no; Belcourt, Rolette, ND;
        yes; none
163 "   Mary Cecilia; f; 2 9-2-29; ¼+; s; dau B-88; no; Belcourt, Rolette, ND;
        yes; none

NE Anderson, Andrew;   Head
164 "   Mary (Montriel); f; 34; ¼+; m; wife B-89; no; St.Paul, Ramsey, Minn;
        no; Id.739c, Al.W0647

NE Anderson, Henry;   Head
165 "   Louise (Herman); f; 30; ¼+; m; wife B-90; no; Devils Lake, Ramsey,
        ND; yes; Id.477c, Al.G-132
166 "   Adeline; f; 5 11-26-26; ¼+; s; dau B-91; no; Devils Lake,
        Ramsey, ND; yes; none
167 "   John Henry; m; 3 1-11-29; ¼+; s; son B-92; no; Devils Lake, Ramsey,
        ND; yes; none

Turtle Mountain Reservation
1932 Census Roll

Key: Number; Surname, Given; Sex; Age at Last Birthday, Birthdate (if given); Tribe (Chippewa, unless stated otherwise); Degree of Blood; Marital Status; Relationship to Head of Family, Last Year Census Number; At Jurisdiction Where Enrolled (Yes/No); Elsewhere - Post Office, County, State; Ward (Yes/No); Allotment [Al.], Annuity [An.] and/or Identification [Id.] Numbers

168   Anderson(cont), Irene V; m[sic]; 1   10-2-30; ¼+; s; dau B-93; no; Devils Lake, Ramsey, ND; yes; none

NE   Andriff, Evan;   Head
169   "   Josephine (Decoteau); f; 30; ¼+; m; wife B-94; no; Dunseith, Rolette, ND; yes; Id.286b, Al.GF-96
170   "   Frank; m; 9   8-22-22; ¼+; s; son B-95; no; Dunseith, Rolette, ND; no; none
171   "   Bernadine; f; 8   12-24-23; ¼+; s; dau B-96; no; Dunseith, Rolette, ND; no none
172   "   Martha; f; 6   6-7-25; ¼+; s; dau B-97; no; Dunseith, Rolette, ND; no; none
173   "   Lawrence; m; 5   8-23-26; ¼+; s; son B-98; no; Dunseith, Rolette, ND; no; none
174   "   Dorothy; f; 2   6-18-29; ¼+; s; dau -----; no; Dunseith, Rolette, ND; no; none

NE   Arnold, Loren;   Head
175   "   Marguerite (Jerome); f; 30; ¼+; m; wife B-99; no; Kansas City, Wyandotte, Kan; yes; Id.519c, Al.M85

176   Azure, Abraham; m; 33; ¼+; m; Head B-100; no; Devils Lake, Ramsey, ND; yes; Id.101b, Al.H-010433
NE   "   Delia (Lagimodiere);   wife
177   "   Raymond; m; 5   1-23-27; ¼+; s; son B-101; no; Devils Lake, Ramsey, ND; yes; none
178   "   Doris; f; 4   2-22-28; ¼+; s; dau B-102; no; Devils Lake, Ramsey, ND; yes; none
179   "   Ruby May; f; 3   3-14-29; ¼+; s; dau B-103; no; Devils Lake, Ramsey, ND; yes; none

180   Azure, Alexander; m; 77; ¼+; m; Head A-66; yes; yes; Id.100, Al.DL 04985
181   "   Virginia (Enno); f; 64; ¼+; m; wife A-67; yes; yes; Id.100a, Al.G-0678

182   Azure, Alexander; m; 57; ¼+; m; Head B-104; no; Devils Lake, Ramsey, ND; no; Id.101, Al.H 010436
NE   "   Elise (Martin);   wife
183   "   Eugene; m; 18   11-26-13; ¼+; s; son B-105; no; Devils Lake, Ramsey, ND; yes; Id.101f, Al.H-030240

184   Azure, Alphonse; m; 23   4-1-08; ¼+; m; Head B-106; yes; yes; Id.120g, Al.013021
185   "   Rose (Lafontain); f; 23   1-27-09; ¼+; m; wife B-107; yes; no; Id.557b
186   "   Peter; m; 3   2-10-29; ¼+; s; son B-108; yes; yes; none
187   "   Raymond; m; 3/12   12-3-31; ¼+; s; son; yes; yes; none

Turtle Mountain Reservation
1932 Census Roll

Key: Number; Surname, Given; Sex; Age at Last Birthday, Birthdate (if given); Tribe (Chippewa, unless stated otherwise); Degree of Blood; Marital Status; Relationship to Head of Family, Last Year Census Number; At Jurisdiction Where Enrolled (Yes/No); Elsewhere - Post Office, County, State; Ward (Yes/No); Allotment [Al.], Annuity [An.] and/or Identification [Id.] Numbers

188	Azure, Andre; m; m; 52; ¼+; m; Head A-68; yes; no; Id.107, Al.G-233f	
NE	" Clara (Gerally); ¼+; wife	
189	" Maxim; m; 20; ¼+; s; son A-69; yes; yes; Id.107b, Al.H-024480	
190	" Sylvester; m 18; ¼+; s; son A-70; yes; no; Id.107c	
191	" Ernestine; f; 14 7-7-17; ¼+; s; dau A-71; yes; no; Id.107d	
192	" Raymond; m; 8 10-29-23; ¼+; s; son A-72; yes; no; Id.107e	
193	" David; m; 4 7-2-27; ¼+; s; son A-73; yes; no; Id.107f	
Died	Mary Lola A-74; (Died 9-28-30) Id.107g	
194	" Rose Marie; f; 11/12 4-6-31; ¼+; s; yes; no; Id.107h	

195 Azure, Andre #2; m; 61; ¼+; m; Head A-75; yes; yes; Id.103, Al.R15
196   " Emily (Vivier); f; 75; ¼+; m; wife A-76; yes; no; Id.103a, Al.M312

197 Azure, Antoine; m; 68; ¼+; m; Head B-110; no; Devils Lake, Ramsey, ND; no; Id.140, Al.DL-02055
NE   Virginia (Dubbis); wife
198   " Eudora; f; 18 7-4-13; ¼+; s; dau B-113; no; Devils Lake, Ramsey, ND; no; Id.140e
199   " Joseph; m; 17 1-8-15; ¼+; s; son B-114; no; Devils Lake, Ramsey, ND; no; none

200 Azure, Antoine; m; 43; ¼+; s; Head B-109; no; Cheyenne River; no; Id.131, Al.G-0103021

201 Azure, Benoit; m; 26 7-31-05; ¼+; m; Head A-78; yes; yes; Id.130b, Al.G-08285
NE   " Madeline (Roy); wife
202   " Donald; m; 2 5-10-29; ¼+; s; son A-79; yes; yes; none
Died   " Mary Ann; A-80 (Died 12-3-31)
203   " Mary J; f; 1 7-17-30; ¼+; s; dau A-81; yes; yes; none

204 Azure, Claude; m; 52; ¼+; m; Head A-82; yes; no; Id.109, Al.R-17
205   " Julia (Brunnell); f; 47; ¼+; m; wife A-83; yes; no; Id.109a, Al.W33

206 Azure, Claude; m; 24 9-26-07; ¼+; m; Head B-112; no; Devils Lake, Ramsey, ND; yes; Id.140d, Al.G-07108
207   " Rose Ann (Smith); f; 24 10-22-07; ¼+; m; wife B2345; no; Devils Lake, Ramsey, ND; yes; Id.922b, Al.W-36

208 Azure, Elie; m; 53; ¼+; s; Head A-84; yes; yes; Id.110, Al.G-0151

209 Azure, Eliza (Delorme); f; 65; ¼+; wd; Head B-115; no; Dunseith, Rolette, ND; no; Id.120a, Al.G-656

Turtle Mountain Reservation
1932 Census Roll

Key: Number; Surname, Given; Sex; Age at Last Birthday, Birthdate (if given); Tribe (Chippewa, unless stated otherwise); Degree of Blood; Marital Status; Relationship to Head of Family, Last Year Census Number; At Jurisdiction Where Enrolled (Yes/No); Elsewhere - Post Office, County, State; Ward (Yes/No); Allotment [Al.], Annuity [An.] and/or Identification [Id.] Numbers

210 Azure, Fabian; m; 23; ¼+; m; Head A-85; yes; yes; Id.136b
211 " Agnes (Decoteau); f; 20; ¼+; m; wife A-86; yes; yes; Id.295c, Al.H-024544

Died Azure, Francois; A-87 (Died 12-25-31)
212 " Julia (Peltier); f; 76; ¼+; wd; Head A-88; yes; yes; Id.113a, Al.G-598
213 " Alphonsine; f; 30; ¼+; s; dau A-89; yes; yes; Id.113c, Al.G-08162

214 Azure, Frederick; m; 50; ¼+; m; Head A-90; yes; no; Id.142, Al.M-267
215 " Mary (Lucier); f; 63; ¼+; m; wife A-91; yes; no; Id.142a, Al.M-161
216 " Louise; f; 19; ¼+; s; dau A-92; yes; no; Id.142c
217 " Leo; m; 16 7-8-15; ¼+; s; son A-93; yes; no; Id.142d

218 Azure, Frederick; m; 25; ¼+; m; Head A-94; yes; yes; Id.100b, Al.G-0679
219 " Rose Delia (Lafontain); f; 22 6-27-09; ¼+; m; wife A-95; yes; yes;
                                                              Id.553b, Al.H-012657
220 " Mary Rose; f; 3 3-21-29; ¼+; s; dau A-96; yes; yes; Id.100c
221 " Cecelia; f; 2 2-24-30; ¼+; s; dau A-97; yes; yes; none

222 Azure, Frederick; m; 32; ¼+; m; Head A-98; no; Globe, Ariz; yes; Id.116b, Al.GF-29
NE   " Marceline (McGillis); wife
223 " Fred, Jr; m; 2 2-16-30; ¼+; s; son A-99; no; Globe, Ariz; yes; none

224 Azure, Gabriel; m; 54; ¼+; m; Head A-100; yes; yes; Id.116, Al. R-20
225 " Mary Rose (Houle); f; 42; ¼+; m; wife A-101; yes; no; Id.116a, Al.G-011726
226 " Josephine; f; 26; ¼+; s; dau A-102; yes; yes; Id.116c, Al.G-580
227 " Edna; f; 5 1-13-27; ¼+; s; dau A-103; yes; yes; none

228 Azure, George; m; 33 5-10-98; ¼+; m; Head B-116; no; Boggy Creek, Manitoba,
                                                              Can; no; Id.120b, Al.G-565
229 " Clarice (LaFontain); f; 28; ¼+; m; wife B-117; no; Boggy Creek, Manitoba,
                                                              Can; no; Id.550d, Al.GF-174
Dead " Rose; B-118 (Died 1924)
230 " Frank; m; 6 8-11-25; ¼+; s; son B-119; no; Boggy Creek, Manitoba, Can;
                                                              no; none
231 " Bertha; f; 2 7-29-29; ¼+; s; dau; no; Boggy Creek, Manitoba, Can; no; none

232 Azure, Isidore; m; 71; ¼+; m; Head A-104; yes; yes; Id.117; Al.R-21
NE   " Rosina (Dubois); wife
233 " Frederick; m; 24 12-23-07; ¼+; s; son A-105; yes; yes; Id.117b, Al.G-011
234 " Mary Jane; f; 20; ¼+; s; dau A-106; yes; yes; Id.117d, Al.H-024489
235 " Benjamin; m; 16 9-20-15; ¼+; s; son ------; yes; yes; none
236 " Lawrence; m; 15 3-19-17; ¼+; s; son ------; yes; yes; none
237 " Flora A; f; 11 1-26-21; ¼+; s; dau A-107; yes; yes; Id.117e
238 " Helen; f; 8 11-27-23; ¼+; s; dau A-108; yes; yes; Id.117f

Turtle Mountain Reservation
1932 Census Roll

Key: Number; Surname, Given; Sex; Age at Last Birthday, Birthdate (if given); Tribe (Chippewa, unless stated otherwise); Degree of Blood; Marital Status; Relationship to Head of Family, Last Year Census Number; At Jurisdiction Where Enrolled (Yes/No); Elsewhere - Post Office, County, State; Ward (Yes/No); Allotment [Al.], Annuity [An.] and/or Identification [Id.] Numbers

239 Azure(cont), Mabel; f; 4 5-27-27; ¼+; s; dau A-109; yes; yes; Id.117g

240 Azure, Israel; m; 48; ¼+; m; Head A-110; yes; no; Id.136, Al.M-313
241   "   Beatrice (Marion); f; 47; ¼+; m; wife A-111; yes; yes; Id.136a, Al.M-315
242   "   Stella (Lasota); f; 10; ¼+; f[sic]; dau adpt B1481 A-112; yes; (Counted twice last year) no; none

243 Azure, Jean; m; 24; ¼+; m; Head A-113; yes; yes; Id.126b, Al.G-014945
NE   "   Octavia; f;   wife   (Maiden name not known)

244 Azure, Jerome; m; 68; ¼+; m; Head A-114; yes; yes; Id.124, Al.R-24
245   "   Margaret (Allard); f; 68; ¼+; m; wife A-115; yes; yes; Id.124a, Al.H-012501

246 Azure, John B #1; m; 45; ¼+; m; Head A-116; yes; no; Id.126, Al.R-22
247   "   Josephine (Pepin); f; 38; ¼+; m; wife A-117; yes; no; Id.126a, Al.GF-89
248   "   Frank; m; 23; ¼+; s; son A-118; yes; no; Id.126c
249   "   Henry; m; 17; ¼+; s; son A-120; yes; no; Id.126e

250 Azure, John B #2; m; 62; ¼+; m; Head A-121; yes; yes; Id.127, [Al.] GF-182
251   "   Mary Jane (Belgarde); f; 52; ¼+; m; wife A-122; yes; yes; Id.177a, Al.R-218

252 Azure, John B #3; m; 54; ¼+; m; Head A-123; yes; no; Id.128, Al.G-07320
253   "   Mary Jane (Dauphinais); f; 40; ¼+; m; wife A-124; yes; yes; Id.128a, Al.GF-288
254   "   Ernest; m; 19; ¼+; s; son A-125; yes; yes; Id.128b
255   "   Mary Celine; f; 18; ¼+; s; dau A-126; yes; yes; Id.128c
256   "   Dominic; m; 15 6-1-16; ¼+; s; son A-127; yes; yes; Id.128d
257   "   Edward; m; 14 2-28-18; ¼+; s; son A-128; yes; yes; Id.128e
258   "   Irene M; f; 9 2-10-23; ¼+; s; dau A-129; yes; yes; Id.128g
259   "   Martin; m; 5 4-21-26; ¼+; s; son A-130; yes; yes; Id.128i
260   "   Florence; f; 4 3-6-28; ¼+; s; dau A-131; yes; yes; Id.128h
261   "   Frances; f; 6/12 9-7-31; ¼+; s; dau -------; yes; yes; none

262 Azure, John B #4; m; 78; ¼+; m; Head A-132; yes; yes; Id.129, Al.R 23
263   "   Mary (Marcellais); f; 66; ¼+; m; wife A-1509 A-133; yes; (Counted twice last year) yes; Id.689a, Al.G-354

264 Azure, John Louis; m; 45; ¼+; m; Head A-134; yes; no; Id.112, [Al.] GF-15
NE   "   Catherine (Laverdure);   wife
265   "   Mary A; f; 24; ¼+; s; dau A-135; yes; yes; Id.112b, Al.G-0152
266   "   Mary M; f; 19; ¼+; s; dau A-136; yes; yes; Id.112c
267   "   Dora E; f; 16 11-17-15; ¼+; s; dau A-137; yes; yes; Id.112d
268   "   Rita M; f; 13 5-10-18; ¼+; s; dau A-138; yes; yes; Id.112e
269   "   Alvina; f; 11 5-14-20; ¼+; s; dau A-139; yes; yes; none
270   "   Lawrence; m; 9 5-30-22; ¼+; s; son A-140; yes; yes; none

Turtle Mountain Reservation
1932 Census Roll

Key: Number; Surname, Given; Sex; Age at Last Birthday, Birthdate (if given); Tribe (Chippewa, unless stated otherwise); Degree of Blood; Marital Status; Relationship to Head of Family, Last Year Census Number; At Jurisdiction Where Enrolled (Yes/No); Elsewhere - Post Office, County, State; Ward (Yes/No); Allotment [Al.], Annuity [An.] and/or Identification [Id.] Numbers

271 Azure(cont), Peter; m; 7 12-24-24; ¼+; s; son A-141; yes; yes; none
272 " Rose; f; 5 12-23-26; ¼+; s; dau A-142; yes; yes; none
Dead " James; A-143 (Died 9-24-30)

273 Azure, Joseph J; m; 43; ¼+; m; Head B-120; no; Dunseith, Rolette, ND; yes;
Id.123, Al.H-039324
274 " Madeline (Decoteau); f; 43; ¼+; m; wife B-121; no; Dunseith, Rolette, ND; yes; Id.948a, Al.H-010488
275 " Elvina; f; 11 9-15-20; ¼+; s; dau B-122; no; Dunseith, Rolette, ND; yes; none
276 " Geraldine; f; 5 5-11-26; ¼+; s; dau -------; no; Dunseith, Rolette, ND; yes; none
277 " Cecelia; f; 3 12-25-28; ¼+; s; dau -------; no; Dunseith, Rolette, ND; yes; none
278 " Clarence; m; 1 4-28-30; ¼+; s; son B-123; no; Dunseith, Rolette, ND; yes; none

279 Azure, Joseph; m; 43; ¼+; m; Head B-124; no; Rolla, Rolette, ND; no;
Id.114, Al.G-08160
280 " Earnestine (Houle); f; 35; ¼+; m; wife B-125; no; Rolla, Rolette, ND; no;
Id.191b, Al.M 8
281 " Felix; m; 13; ¼+; s; son B-126; no; Rolla, Rolette, ND; no; none
282 " Flora; f; 12 1-26-20; ¼+; s; dau B-127; no; Rolla, Rolette, ND; no; none
283 " Mary E; f; 6 3-3-26; ¼+; s; dau B-128; no; Rolla, Rolette, ND; no; none

284 Azure, Joseph; m; 48; ¼+; m; Head B-129; no; Nishu, Ward, ND; no; Id.132, Al.R-29
NE " Adeline (Duboius); wife
285 " Edwin; m; 8 3-24-24; ¼+; s; son B-130; no; Nishu, Ward, ND; no; Id.132h
286 " Ernest; m; 4 1-2-28; ¼+; s; son B-131; no; Nishu, Ward, ND; no; Id.132i

287 Azure, Joseph; m; 50; ¼+; s; Head B-132; no; Unknown; no; Id.139, Al.G-28
288 " Arthur; m; 18; ¼+; s; son B-133; no; Boggy Creek, Manitoba, Can; no; Id.139b
289 " Ida; f; 15; ¼+; s; dau A-1416; yes; no; Id.139c

290 Azure, Joseph; m; 52; ¼+; wd; Head B-134; no; Promise, Dewey, ND; no;
Id.141, Al.M-266
291 " Fred; m; 21; ¼+; s; son B-135; no; Promise, Dewey, ND; no; Id.141b
292 " August J; m; 18; ¼+; s; son B-136; no; Promise, Dewey, ND; no; Id.141c
293 " Ellen; 15; ¼+; s; dau B-137; no; Promise, Dewey, ND; no; Id.141f
294 " Isadore; m; 12 1-31-20; ¼+; s; son B-138; no; Promise, Dewey, ND; no; Id.141e
295 " Emma; f; 11; ¼+; s; dau B-139; no; Promise, Dewey, ND; no; Id.141g

Turtle Mountain Reservation
1932 Census Roll

Key: Number; Surname, Given; Sex; Age at Last Birthday, Birthdate (if given); Tribe (Chippewa, unless stated otherwise); Degree of Blood; Marital Status; Relationship to Head of Family, Last Year Census Number; At Jurisdiction Where Enrolled (Yes/No); Elsewhere - Post Office, County, State; Ward (Yes/No); Allotment [Al.], Annuity [An.] and/or Identification [Id.] Numbers

296 Azure, Louis; m; 26 7-4-05; ¼+; m; Head B-140; yes; yes; Id.1034c, Al.G-07882
NE   "   Catherine (Bercier);   wife
297   "   Lazarus; m; 1 11-8-30; ¼+; s; son B-141; yes; yes; none

298 Azure, Louis; m; 36; ¼+; s; Head B-143; yes; no; Id.102, Al.H-010435

299 Azure, Martin; m; 34; ¼+; s; Head B-142; no; Ft.Berthold, ND; no; Id.216, Al.M 265

300 Azure, Margaret (Sampion); f; 75; ¼+; wd; Head A-144; yes; yes; Id.1034a, Al.G08163
301   "   Veronica; f; 32; ¼+; s; dau A-145; yes; yes; Id.1034b, Al.G 08166

302 Azure, Moses; m; 36; ¼+; s; Head B-145; no; Dunseith, Rolette, ND; no;
                                                                        Id.118, Al.G 09

303 Azure, Norman; m; 25; ¼+; m; Head A-147; yes; yes; Id.129c
304   "   Emma (Allery); f; 22; ¼+; m; wife A-148; yes; yes; Id.72d, Al.H-102496
305   "   Marie Louise; f; 2 2-5-30; ¼+; s; dau A-149; yes; yes; none
306   "   Florence; f; 6/12 9-9-31; ¼+; s; dau -----; yes; yes; none

307 Azure, Orvilla; f; 42; ¼+; s; Head B-146; no; Morgantown, Monongalia, WV; no;
                                                                 Id.121, Al.G-567

308 Azure, Omar; m; 32; ¼+; m; Head B-111; no; Devils Lake, Ramsey, ND; yes;
                                                               Id.140c, Al.G-07106
309   "   Mary Eliza (Dejarlais); f; 22; ¼+; m; wife B-650; no; Devils Lake, Ramsey,
                                            ND; yes; Id.317e, Al.G-036563

310 Azure, Patrice; m; 43; ¼+; s; Head A-150; yes; yes; Id.119, Al.G-010

311 Azure, Patrice; m; 44; ¼+; m; Head A-151; no; Devils Lake, Ramsey, ND; no;
                                                               Id.135, Al.G-08122
312   "   Caroline (Decoteau); f; 48; ¼+; m; wife A-152; no; Devils Lake, Ramsey,
                                                 ND; no; Id.295a

313 Azure, Pierre; m; 50; ¼+; wd; Head B-147; no; Devils Lake, Ramsey, ND; no;
                                                               Id.115, Al.G-015571
314   "   Roy A; m; 24 11-24-07; ¼+; s; son B-148; no; Devils Lake, Ramsey, ND;
                                                               yes; Id.115b, Al.G-0194
315   "   Caroline; f; 22; ¼+; s; dau B-149; no; Devils Lake, Ramsey, ND; yes;
                                                               Id.115d, Al.G-08277
316   "   Frank; m; 14 11-8-17; ¼+; s; son B-150; no; Devils Lake, Ramsey, ND;
                                                               no; Id.115e

Turtle Mountain Reservation
1932 Census Roll

Key: Number; Surname, Given; Sex; Age at Last Birthday, Birthdate (if given); Tribe (Chippewa, unless stated otherwise); Degree of Blood; Marital Status; Relationship to Head of Family, Last Year Census Number; At Jurisdiction Where Enrolled (Yes/No); Elsewhere - Post Office, County, State; Ward (Yes/No); Allotment [Al.], Annuity [An.] and/or Identification [Id.] Numbers

317 Azure(cont), Martin; m; 12 3-17-20; ¼+; s; son B-151; no; Devils Lake, Ramsey, ND; no; Id.115f
318   "   Raymond; m; 10 10-24-21; ¼+; s; son B-152; no; Devils Lake, Ramsey, ND; no; Id.115g
319   "   Margaret M; f; 1 2-19-31; ¼+; s; grand dau -----; no; (Dau of Caroline) Devils Lake, Ramsey, ND; no; none

320 Azure, Pierre; m; 58; ¼+; m; Head B-153; no; Devils Lake, Ramsey, ND; yes; Id.138, Al.R 27
321   "   Ellen (Dejarlais); f; 50; ¼+; m; wife B-154; no; Devils Lake, Ramsey, ND; no; Id.138a, Al.08286

322 Azure, Raphael; m; 25; ¼+; m; Head B-155; no; Devils Lake, Ramsey, ND; yes; Id.101e, Al.H 010434
323   "   Eugenia (Bercier); f; 29; ¼+; m; wife A-225; no; Devils Lake, Ramsey, ND; yes; Id.1167d, Al.M-13

324 Azure, Robert; m; 48; ¼+; m; Head A-153; yes; no; Id.130, Al.R 28
325   "   Mary (Vandal); f; 49; ¼+; m; wife A-154; yes; no; Id.130a, Al.G 08282
326   "   Eva; f; 21; ¼+; s; dau A-156; yes; yes; Id.130d, Al.016472
327   "   Simeon; m; 16 4-25-15; ¼+; s; son A-157; yes; no; Id.130e
328   "   Nora; f; 9 11-23-22; ¼+; s; dau A-158; yes; no; none
329   "   Edna; f; 7 2-23-26; ¼+; s; dau A-159; yes; no; none

330 Azure, Stanislaus; m; 34; ¼+; m; Head B-156; no; Devils Lake, Ramsey, ND; no; Id.140b, Al.G-07107
NE   "   Sarah Jane (Lohnes);   wife
331   "   Francois; m; 11 2-3-21; ¼+; s; son B-157; no; Devils Lake, Ramsey, ND; no; none
332   "   Clement; m; 10 1-7-22; ¼+; s; son B-158; no; Devils Lake, Ramsey, ND; no; none
333   "   Alma; f; 8 1-12-24; ¼+; s; dau B-159; no; Devils Lake, Ramsey, ND; no; none

334 Azure, William; m; 42; ¼+; m; Head B-160; no; Rolla, Rolette, ND; no; Id.105, Al.M-310
NE   "   Beatrice (Jerome);   wife
335   "   Louise; f; 10 8-17-21; ¼+; s; dau B-161; no; Rolla, Rolette, ND; no; none
336   "   Elizabeth; f; 8 11-9-23; ¼+; s; dau B-162; no; Rolla, Rolette, ND; no; none
337   "   Roger; m; 5 6-30-26; ¼+; s; son; no; Rolla, Rolette, ND; no; none
338   "   Mildred; f; 4 2-23-28; ¼+; s; dau; no; Rolla, Rolette, ND; no; none
339   "   John J; m; 6/12 9-21-31; ¼+; s; son; no; Rolla, Rolette, ND; no; none

Turtle Mountain Reservation
1932 Census Roll

Key: Number; Surname, Given; Sex; Age at Last Birthday, Birthdate (if given); Tribe (Chippewa, unless stated otherwise); Degree of Blood; Marital Status; Relationship to Head of Family, Last Year Census Number; At Jurisdiction Where Enrolled (Yes/No); Elsewhere - Post Office, County, State; Ward (Yes/No); Allotment [Al.], Annuity [An.] and/or Identification [Id.] Numbers

340 Azure(cont), William; m; 40; ¼+; m; Head B-163; no; Dunseith, Rolette, ND; no; Id.122, Al.G 568
341 " Josephine (Dumont); f; 42; ¼+; m; wife B-164; no; Dunseith, Rolette, ND; no; Id.368, Al.G 0439
342 " Matilda; f; 15 4-3-16; ¼+; s; dau B-166; no; Dunseith, Rolette, ND; no; none
343 " Max; m; 14 11-18-17; ¼+; s; son B-165; no; Dunseith, Rolette, ND; no; none
344 " Harry; m; 12 2-27-20; ¼+; s; son B-167; no; Dunseith, Rolette, ND; no; none
345 " Lyman; m; 9 6-4-22; ¼+; s; son B-168; no; Dunseith, Rolette, ND; no; none
346 " Peter; m; 6 6-5-25; ¼+; s; son B-169; no; Dunseith, Rolette, ND; no; none

347 Azure, William; m; 27; ¼+; m; Head B-170; no; Devils Lake, Ramsey, ND; yes; Id.109b, Al.L-034151
348 " Mary (Azure); f; 23; ¼+; m; wife B-171; no; Devils Lake, Ramsey, ND; yes; Id.115c, Al.G-08277
349 " (Jacqmaret[sic]), Louis; m; 8 2-10-24; ¼+; s; step son B-172; no; Devils Lake, Ramsey, ND; yes; none

350 Azure, Xavier; m; 27; ¼+; m; Head ----; yes; (This family left off of last census, error); yes; Id.120c, Al.G-562
351 " Emily (Parisien); f; 28; ¼+; m; wife A-1719; yes; yes; Id.791d
352 " Clarence; m; 1 4-7-30; ¼+; s; son ----; yes; yes; none
353 " Fred S; m; 10/12 6-5-31; ¼+; s; son ----; yes; yes; none

NE Bahach, John;   Head
354 " Emma (Falcon); f; 24; ¼+; m; wife B-173; no; Milwaukee, Milwaukee, Wis; yes; Id.385c, Al.G-095
355 " Peter; m; 2 8-12-29; ¼+; s; son B-174; no; Milwaukee, Milwaukee, Wis; yes; none

NE Baker, Francis;   Head
356 " Eliza (Dejarlais); f; 29; ¼+; m; wife B-175; no; Dunseith, Rolette, ND; yes; Id.315c, Al.G 101
357 " Mary Jane; f; 8 12-18-23; ¼+; s; dau B-176; no; Dunseith, Rolette, ND; yes; none
358 " Emma; f; 5 10-6-26; ¼+; s; dau B-377; no; Dunseith, Rolette, ND; yes; none

359 Baker, Josette (Frederick); f; 70; ¼+; wd; Head B-178; no; Devils Lake, Ramsey, ND; no; Id.144a, Al.DL-19

360 Baker, Moses; m; 38; ¼+; m; Head B-179; no; Ft.Totten, Ramsey, ND; no; Id.146, Al.M-340
361 " Marceline (Montour); f; 29; ¼+; m; wife B-180; no; Ft.Totten, Ramsey, ND; yes; Id.584, Al.G-264
362 " Mary Flora; f; 10 10-26-21; ¼+; s; dau B-181; yes; yes; none

Turtle Mountain Reservation
1932 Census Roll

Key: Number; Surname, Given; Sex; Age at Last Birthday, Birthdate (if given); Tribe (Chippewa, unless stated otherwise); Degree of Blood; Marital Status; Relationship to Head of Family, Last Year Census Number; At Jurisdiction Where Enrolled (Yes/No); Elsewhere - Post Office, County, State; Ward (Yes/No); Allotment [Al.], Annuity [An.] and/or Identification [Id.] Numbers

363 Baker(cont), George; m; 7 10-28-24; ¼+; s; son B-182; no; Ft.Totten, Ramsey, ND; yes; none
364 " Clemence; f; 6 2-3-26; ¼+; s; dau B-184; no; Ft.Totten, Ramsey, ND; yes; none
365 " Cecil R; m; 4 2-15-28; ¼+; s; son; no; Ft.Totten, Ramsey, ND; yes; none
366 " Moses, Jr; m; 1 12-17-30; ¼+; s; son B-183; no; Ft.Totten, Ramsey, ND; yes; none

367 Baker, Napoleon; m; 44; ¼+; m; Head B-185; no; Ft.Totten, Ramsey, ND; no; Id.147, Al.M-372
NE " Syphrine (Dubois); wife
368 " Rosanna; f; 17 5-13-15; ¼+; s; dau B-186; no; Ft.Totten, Ramsey, ND; no; none
369 " Joseph; m; 15 11-19-16; ¼+; ; son B-187; no; Ft.Totten, Ramsey, ND; no; none
370 " Josephine; f; 13 1-26-19; ¼+; s; dau B-188; no; Ft.Totten, Ramsey, ND; no; none
371 " Alvina; f; 10 3-17-22; ¼+; s; dau -----; no; Ft.Totten, Ramsey, ND; no; none
372 " Margaret; f; 5 6-26-27; ¼+; s; dau -----; no; Ft.Totten, Ramsey, ND; no; none
373 " Francis; m; 5 1-13-27; ¼+; s; son ------; no; Ft.Totten, Ramsey, ND; no; none
374 " Veronica; f; 4 1-17-28; ¼+; s; dau ------; no; Ft.Totten, Ramsey, ND; no; none
375 " M. Elizabeth; f; 1 6-25-30; ¼+; s; dau ------; no; Ft.Totten, Ramsey, ND; no; none

376 Baker, Patrick; m; 46; ¼+; m; Head A-160; yes; no; Id.145, Al.M-339
NE " Louise (Trothier); wife
377 " Edna Mabel; f; 14 1-31-18; ¼+; s; dau A-161; no; Unknown; no; none
Died " Annie; A-162 (Died 5-11-24)
378 " Agnes; f; 1-10-24; ¼+; s; dau A-163; yes; no; none
379 " Helen B; f; 1 7-12-30; ¼+; s; dau A-164; yes; no; none

380 Baston, Antoine; m; 39; ¼+; s; Head B-189; no; Trenton, Williams, ND; no; Id.150, Al.M 390

381 Baston, Charles; m; 67; ¼+; m; Head B-190; no; White Earth, Mountrail, ND; no; Id.149, Al.M-225
382 " Justine (Parisien); f; 64; ¼+; m; wife B-191; no; White Earth, Mountrail, ND; no; Id.149a, Al.M-223
383 " Peter; m; 31 2-1-01; ¼+; s; son B-192; no; White Earth, Mountrail, ND; yes; Id.149b, Al.M-388
384 " Fred; m; 23 6-1-18; ¼+; s; son B-193; no; White Earth, Mountrail, ND; yes; Id.149c, Al.G-05387
385 " Laura; f; 20 11-1-11; ¼+; s; dau B 194; no; White Earth, Mountrail, ND; no; Id.149e

NE Baston, Frank; Head
386 " Josephine (Dejarlais); f; 25; ¼+; m; wife B-195; no; yes; Fort Berthold; yes; Id.315d, Al.G07879

Turtle Mountain Reservation
1932 Census Roll

Key: Number; Surname, Given; Sex; Age at Last Birthday, Birthdate (if given); Tribe (Chippewa, unless stated otherwise); Degree of Blood; Marital Status; Relationship to Head of Family, Last Year Census Number; At Jurisdiction Where Enrolled (Yes/No); Elsewhere - Post Office, County, State; Ward (Yes/No); Allotment [Al.], Annuity [An.] and/or Identification [Id.] Numbers

387 Baston(cont), Mary R; f; 5 5-26-26; ¼+; s; dau B-196; no; yes; Fort Berthold; no; none
388 " Robert; m; 2 8-28-29; ¼+; s; son ----; no; yes; Fort Berthold; no; none
389 " Wilfred; m; 3/12 12-13-31; ¼+; s; son -----; no; yes; Fort Berthold; no; none

390 Baston, Joseph; m; 43; ¼+; m; Head B-197; no; Dunseith, Rolette, ND; no; Id.151, Al.M224
NE " Margaret (Sheperd); f; wife
391 " Mary; f; 15 4-10-15; ¼+; s; dau B-198; no; Dunseith, Rolette, ND; no; Id.151b

392 Baston, Patrice; m; 39; ¼+; s; Head B-199; no; Fort Berthold; no; Id.153a, Al.226

NE Bauer, Fred; Head
393 " Eliza (Houle); f; 38; ¼+; m; wife B200; no; Homestead, Roosevelt, Mont; no; Id.153a, Al.G07831
(Two children of this family, William and May, said to enrolled at Fort Peck, Mont.)

NE Bauer, John; Head
394 " Justine (Houle); f; 37; ¼+; m; wife B-201; no; Brocton, Mont; no; Id.152a, Al.G-05752
395 " Charles; m; 19; ¼+; s; son B-202; no; Brocton, Mont; no; Id.152b
396 " Catherine; f; 15 3-26-17; ¼+; s; dau ------; no; Brocton, Mont; no; none
397 " Lydia; f; 12 8-24-19; ¼+; s; dau ------; no; Brocton, Mont; no; none
398 " Rose; f; 10 10-18-21; ¼+; s; dau ------; no; Brocton, Mont; no; none
399 " John; m; 6 3-8-26; ¼+; s; son -----; no; Brocton, Mont; no; none
400 " Joseph; m; 2 2-12-30; ¼+; s; son ------; no; Brocton, Mont; no; none

NE Beaman, Jack; Head
401 " Mary (Laverdure); f; 29; ¼+; m; wife B-203; no; Dooley, Sheridan, Mont; yes; Id.644d, Al.M-270

NE Beaton, Donald J; Head
402 " Rachel (Flowers); f; 21; ¼+; m; wife B-856; no; Port Ludlow, Wash; no; Id.392c
403 Beauchman, Ernest; m; 32 1-12-10; ¼+; m; Head B-210; no; Wolf Point, Roosevelt, Mont; no; Id.157e
NE Lucille (Day); wife

404 Beauchman, Gabriel; m; 53 1-29-79; ¼+; m; Head B206; no; Wolf Point, Roosevelt, Mont; no; Id.157 Al.R31
405 " Celina (Turcotte); f; 49 2-22-83; ¼+; m; wife B207; no; Wolf Point, Roosevelt, Mont; no; Al.GF25
406 " Michael; m; 20 11-30-11; ¼+; s; son B211; no; Wolf Point, Roosevelt, Mont; no; Id.157f

Turtle Mountain Reservation
1932 Census Roll

Key: Number; Surname, Given; Sex; Age at Last Birthday, Birthdate (if given); Tribe (Chippewa, unless stated otherwise); Degree of Blood; Marital Status; Relationship to Head of Family, Last Year Census Number; At Jurisdiction Where Enrolled (Yes/No); Elsewhere - Post Office, County, State; Ward (Yes/No); Allotment [Al.], Annuity [An.] and/or Identification [Id.] Numbers

407 Beauchman(cont), Joseph Louis; m; 18 7-25-13; ¼+; s; son B212; no; Wolf Point, Roosevelt, Mont; no; Id.157g
408 " Edna V; f; 16 5-11-15; ¼+; s; dau B213; no; Wolf Point, Roosevelt, Mont; no; Id.157h
409 " Rose Alvina; f; 15 9-5-16; ¼+; s; dau B214; no; Wolf Point, Roosevelt, Mont; no; Id.157i
410 " Martin Julius; m; 13 11-4-18; ¼+; s; son B215; no; Wolf Point, Roosevelt, Mont; no; Id.157j
411 " Daniel Phillip; m; 11 7-15-20; ¼+; s; son B216; no; Wolf Point, Roosevelt, Mont; no; Id.157k
412 " Viola Marguerite; f; 9 2-14-23; ¼+; s; dau B217; no; Wolf Point, Roosevelt, Mont; no; Id.157l
413 " Mary Jane; f; 3 9-22-28; ¼+; s; dau B218; no

414 Beauchman, Gabriel; m; 83; ¼+; m; Head B204; no; Wolf Point, Roosevelt, Mont; no; Id.154, Al.H039321
415 " Margaret (Azure); f; 72; ¼+; m; wife B205; no; Wolf Point, Roosevelt, Mont; no; Id.154a, Al.GF 21

416 Beauchman, Raphael; m; 26 1-27-06; ¼+; m; Head B209; no; Wolf Point, Roosevelt, Mont; yes; Id.157d, Al.G07292
NE " Alvina M (Lafreniere); f; wife
417 " Herman; m; 5 7-18-26; ¼+; s; son ----; no; Wolf Point, Roosevelt, Mont; yes; none

418 Beauchman, Sarah (Turcott); f; 39; ¼+; wd; Head B-219; no; Wolf Point, Roosevelt, Mont; no; Id.156a, Al.G-038628
419 " Francis; m; 20; ¼+; s; son B-220; no; Wolf Point, Roosevelt, Mont; no; Id.156c
420 " Lawrence; m; 18; ¼+; s; son B-221; no; Wolf Point, Roosevelt, Mont; no; Id.156b
421 " Ralph; m; 15 1-7-17; ¼+; s; son B-222; no; Wolf Point, Roosevelt, Mont; no; Id.156d
422 " Melvin; m; 12 5-24-19; ¼+; s; son B-223; no; Wolf Point, Roosevelt, Mont; no; Id.156e
423 " John; m; 10 4-27-21; ¼+; s; son B-224; no; Wolf Point, Roosevelt, Mont; no; Id.156f
424 " Donald; m; 9 1-7-23; ¼+; s; son B-225; no; Wolf Point, Roosevelt, Mont; no; Id.156g
425 " Agnes; f; 6; ¼+; s; dau B-226; no; Wolf Point, Roosevelt, Mont; no; Id.156h

Turtle Mountain Reservation
1932 Census Roll

Key: Number; Surname, Given; Sex; Age at Last Birthday, Birthdate (if given); Tribe (Chippewa, unless stated otherwise); Degree of Blood; Marital Status; Relationship to Head of Family, Last Year Census Number; At Jurisdiction Where Enrolled (Yes/No); Elsewhere - Post Office, County, State; Ward (Yes/No); Allotment [Al.], Annuity [An.] and/or Identification [Id.] Numbers

426 Beauchman, Thomas; m; 29 3-21-03; ¼+; m; Head B-227; no; Wolf Point, Roosevelt, Mont; yes; Id.156c, Al.GF-27
NE " Victoria (Laroque); wife
427 " Robert; m; 8 3-30-24; ¼+; s; son B-228; no; Wolf Point, Roosevelt, Mont; yes; none
428 " James; m; 6 6-8-25; ¼+; s; son B-229; no; Wolf Point, Roosevelt, Mont; yes; none
429 " John; m; 7-8-26; ¼+; s; son B-230; no; Wolf Point, Roosevelt, Mont; yes; none
430 " Marie P; f; 2 10-24-29; ¼+; s; dau -----; no; Wolf Point, Roosevelt, Mont; yes; none
431 " Ramona S; f; 11/12 4-8-31; ¼+; s; dau ------; no; Wolf Point, Roosevelt, Mont; yes; none

NE Beaudry, Alfred; Head; no; Malta, Phillips, Mont
432 " Virginia (Delorme); f; 28; ¼+; m; Div. wife B-231; no; Fort Belknap, Mont; yes; Id.331b, Al.G-04761
433 " Marie A; f; 10 3-12-22; ¼+; s; dau B-232; no; Fort Belknap; yes; none
434 " Louis Neil; m; 8 9-15-23; ¼+; s; son B-233; no; Malta, Phillips, Mont; yes; none
435 " Sanford W; m; 6 9-1-25; ¼+; s; son ------; no; Malta, Phillips, Mont; yes; none

NE Beaudry, Victor; Head
436 " Florence (Dejarlais); f; 25; ¼+; m; wife B-234; no; Malta, Phillips, Mont; no; Id.318f
437 " Rose Helen; f; 4 5-18-27; ¼+; s; dau ------; no; Malta, Phillips, Mont; no; none
438 " Theresa D; f; 3 3-10-29; ¼+; s; dau ------; no; Malta, Phillips, Mont; no; none
439 " Victor A; m; 3-30-32; ¼+; s; son ------; no; Malta, Phillips, Mont; no; none

NE Bell, William; Head
440 " Winifred (Schindler); f; 36; ¼+; m; wife B-502; no; Semans, Sask, Can; no; Id.221a, Al.G-0189
441 " Viola; f; 7 7-18-24; ¼+; s; dau -----; no; Semans, Sask, Can; no; none
442 " Fred; m; 5 5-15-26; ¼+; s; son -----; no; Semans, Sask, Can; no; none
443 " Lloyd; m; 3 7-11-28; ¼+; s; son ----; no; Semans, Sask, Can; no; none
444 " Robert J; m; 9/12 6-14-31; ¼+; s; son ------; no; Semans, Sask, Can; no; none

Died Belander, Pete; B-235 (Died 4-9-31)
445 " Flying Ring; f; 58; v; wd; Head B-236; no; Dunseith, Rolette, ND; yes; Id.57a, Al.G-014915

Turtle Mountain Reservation
1932 Census Roll

Key: Number; Surname, Given; Sex; Age at Last Birthday, Birthdate (if given); Tribe (Chippewa, unless stated otherwise); Degree of Blood; Marital Status; Relationship to Head of Family, Last Year Census Number; At Jurisdiction Where Enrolled (Yes/No); Elsewhere - Post Office, County, State; Ward (Yes/No); Allotment [Al.], Annuity [An.] and/or Identification [Id.] Numbers

446   Belgarde, Albert; m; ¼+; m; Head B237; no; Elphinstone, Sask, Can; no; Id.189, Al.G-016813
NE   "   Mary (Peltier);   wife
447   "   Martha; f; 17 9-5-14; ¼+; s; step dau B238; no; Elphinstone, Sask, Can; no; Id.189b
448   "   John; m; 16 2-1-16; ¼+; s; son B239; no; Elphinstone, Sask, Can; no; Id.189c
449   "   Freeman; m; 14 3-7-18; ¼+; s; son B240; no; Elphinstone, Sask, Can; no; Id.189d
450   "   Cuthbert; m; 11 1-8-21; ¼+; s; son B241; no; Elphinstone, Sask, Can; no; Id.189e
451   "   Joe; m; 9; ¼+; s; son B242; no; Elphinstone, Sask, Can; no; Id.189f
452   "   Mabel; f; 7; ¼+; s; son[sic] B243; no; Elphinstone, Sask, Can; no; Id.189g
453   "   Frank; m; 4; ¼+; s; son B244; no; Elphinstone, Sask, Can; no; Id.189
454   "   Collin; m; 1 2-8-31; ¼+; s; son B245; no; Elphinstone, Sask, Can; no; Id.189i

NE   Belgarde, Alex;   Head
455   "   Adele (Lenoir); f; 63; ¼+; m; wife B246; no; Ft.Totten, Ramsey, ND; no; Id.663a, Al.G-011733

456   Belgarde, Alexander; m; 29; ¼+; m; Head A165; yes; yes; Id.174c, Al.G-016545
457   "   Catherine (Charette); f; 46; ¼+; m; wife A166; yes; Id.237a, Al.G 420

458   Belgarde, Alexander; m; 33; ¼+; m; Head A167; yes; yes; Id.168e, Al.G 152
459   "   Sarah Jane (Gourneau); f; 24; ¼+; m; wife A168; yes; yes; Id.434e, Al.H-012595

460   Belgarde, Alexis; m; 62; ¼+; m; Head B247; no; Dunseith, Rolette, ND; no; Id.158, Al.DL 54
NE   "   Mary (Swan);   wife
461   "   Rosalie; f; 28; ¼+; s; dau B248; no; Dunseith, Rolette, ND; yes; Id.158c, Al.M 112

462   Belgarde, Alfred; m; 34; ¼+; s; Head B249; no; Unknown; yes; Id.182, Al.M 28

463   Belgarde, Alfred; m; 33; ¼+; m; Head A169; yes; yes; Id.168d, Al.G 15[?]
464   "   Rosalie (Morin); f; 32; ¼+; m; wife A170; yes; yes; Id.755b, Al.M202
465   "   Amelia; f; 11 5-28-21; ¼+; s; dau A171; yes; yes; none
466   "   Marveline; f; 8 6-6-23; ¼+; s; dau A172; yes; yes; none
467   "   Patrice; f; 5; ¼+; s; son A173; yes; yes; none
468   "   Raymond R; m; 10/12 5-10-31; ¼+; s; son A174; yes; yes; none

Turtle Mountain Reservation
1932 Census Roll

Key: Number; Surname, Given; Sex; Age at Last Birthday, Birthdate (if given); Tribe (Chippewa, unless stated otherwise); Degree of Blood; Marital Status; Relationship to Head of Family, Last Year Census Number; At Jurisdiction Where Enrolled (Yes/No); Elsewhere - Post Office, County, State; Ward (Yes/No); Allotment [Al.], Annuity [An.] and/or Identification [Id.] Numbers

469 Belgarde, Antoine; m; 43; ¼+; m; Head B250; no; Jamestown, Stutsman, ND; yes; Id.164, Al.M-333

470 " Clemence (Enno); f; 26; ¼+; m; wife B251; no; Bainville, Roosevelt, Mont; yes; Id.372e, Al.G-5

471 " Alexander; m; 16; ¼+; s; son B252; no; Bainville, Roosevelt, Mont; yes; none

472 " Dominick; m; 13; ¼+; s; son B253; no; Bainville, Roosevelt, Mont; yes; none

473 " Ernestine; f; 6 8-2-25; ¼+; s; dau B254; no; Bainville, Roosevelt, Mont; yes; none

474 Belgarde, Antoine; m; 69; ¼+; m; Head B255; no; Bainville, Roosevelt, Mont; no; Id.159, Al.R-32

475 " Julia (Amyott); f; 65; ¼+; m; wife B256; no; Bainville, Roosevelt, Mont; no; Id.159a, Al.M-282

476 " Laura; f; 39; ¼+; s; dau B1793; no; Bainville, Roosevelt, Mont; no; Id.162, Al.G-07961

477 " Roderick; m; 29; ¼+; s; son B257; no; Bainville, Roosevelt, Mont; yes; Id.159c, Al.M-334

478 " Emily; f; 25; ¼+; s; dau B258; no; Bainville, Roosevelt, Mont; yes; Id.159e, Al.G-265

479 " Martin; m; 24; ¼+; s; son B259; no; Bainville, Roosevelt, Mont; yes; none

480 Belgarde, Augustine; m; 23; ¼+; m; Head A187; yes; yes; Id.168h, Al.H-010532
NE " Rosella (Langan); wife
1992 " Ella; f; 3/12 11-20-31; ¼+; s; dau; yes; yes; Id.168h

481 Belgarde, Basil; m; 71; ¼+; m; Head A175; yes; no; Id.165, Al.R-33

482 " Virginia (Patnaud); f; 56; ¼+; m; wife A176; yes; no; Id.165a, Al.M-264

483 Belgarde, Basil, Jr; m; 37; ¼+; m; Head A177; no; Ft.Totten, ND; no; Id.166, Al.M-262

484 " Josephine; f; 20; ¼+; m; wife B1110; no; Ft.Totten, ND; yes; Id.475c, Al.G-023468

485 " Eugene; m; 3-15-32; ¼+; s; son -----; no; Ft.Totten, ND; yes; none

486 Belgarde, Baptiste; m; 43; ¼+; wd; Head B260; no; Dunseith, Rolette, ND; no; Id.173, Al.M-36

487 " Rose Laura; f; 11 7-24-20; ¼+; s; dau B261; no; Dunseith, Rolette, ND; yes; none

488 " Mary A; f; 10 1-24-22; ¼+; s; dau B262; no; Dunseith, Rolette, ND; yes; none

489 " Dorothy; f; 8 10-11-23; ¼+; s; dau B263; no; Dunseith, Rolette, ND; yes; none

Turtle Mountain Reservation
1932 Census Roll

Key: Number; Surname, Given; Sex; Age at Last Birthday, Birthdate (if given); Tribe (Chippewa, unless stated otherwise); Degree of Blood; Marital Status; Relationship to Head of Family, Last Year Census Number; At Jurisdiction Where Enrolled (Yes/No); Elsewhere - Post Office, County, State; Ward (Yes/No); Allotment [Al.], Annuity [An.] and/or Identification [Id.] Numbers

490 Belgarde(cont), Angeline; f; 3 6-28-28; ¼+; s; dau B264; no; Dunseith, Rolette, ND; yes; none

491 Belgarde, Elie; m; 26; ¼+; m; Head A178; yes; yes; Id.167d, Al.G-235
NE " Laura (Lambert); wife

492 Belgarde, Emery; m; 37; ¼+; s; Head B266; no; Medicine Lake, Sheridan, Mont; no; Id.161, Al.M-332

493 Belgarde, Emil; m; 28; ¼+; s; Head B265; no; Unknown; yes; Id.222, Al.G-035

494 Belgarde, Francois; m; 23 8-14-08; ¼+; m; Head B270; no; Dunseith, Rolette, ND; yes; Id.188f, Al.G-016808
NE " Rose (Gunville); f; wife
495 " No name; m; 2; ¼+; s; son B271; no; Dunseith, Rolette, ND; yes; none
496 " Jane; f; 4/12 11-7-31; ¼+; s; dau; no; Dunseith, Rolette, ND; yes; none

497 Belgarde, Frank; m; 23; ¼+; m; Head B267; no; Dunseith, Rolette, ND; no; Id.174d
498 " Eliza (Lattergrass); f; 28; ¼+; m; wife B268; no; Dunseith, Rolette, ND; yes; Id.620b, Al.H-038921
499 " Louis; m; 2 12-22-28; ¼+; s; son B269; no; Dunseith, Rolette, ND; yes; none
500 " John S; m; 8/12 7-17-31; ¼+; s; son; no; Dunseith, Rolette, ND; yes; none

NE Belgarde, Fred; Head
501 " Rose E (Poitra); f; 37; ¼+; m; wife B272; no; Dunseith, Rolette, ND; no; Id.191a, Al.H-010493
502 " Ida B; f; 19 9-8-12; ¼+; s; dau B273; no; Dunseith, Rolette, ND; no; Id.191b
503 " Martin; m; 16 8-28-16; ¼+; s; son B274; no; Dunseith, Rolette, ND; no; Id.191d
504 " Agnes; f; 13 11-21-18; ¼+; s; dau B275; no; Dunseith, Rolette, ND; no; Id.191e
505 " James; m; 11 1-9-21; ¼+; s; son B276; no; Dunseith, Rolette, ND; no; Id.191c
Died " Clarence; B277 (Died 1924) Dunseith, Rolette, ND; no; Id.191f

506 Belgarde, Freeman; m; 64; ¼+; m; Head B278; no; Elbowoods, ND; no; Id.188, Al.G-016814
NE " Pauline (Lenger); wife
507 " Robert; m; 25 8-15-06; ¼+; s; son B279; no; Elbowoods, ND; yes; Id.188e, Al.G-016809
508 " Ernest; m; 20 4-7-12; ¼+; s; son B280; no; Elbowoods, ND; no; Id.188g
509 " Agnes; f; 15 8-7-16; ¼+; s; dau B282; no; Elbowoods, ND; no; Id.188i
510 " Alice; f; 13 8-13-18; ¼+; s; dau B283; no; Elbowoods, ND; no; Id.188j

Turtle Mountain Reservation
1932 Census Roll

Key: Number; Surname, Given; Sex; Age at Last Birthday, Birthdate (if given); Tribe (Chippewa, unless stated otherwise); Degree of Blood; Marital Status; Relationship to Head of Family, Last Year Census Number; At Jurisdiction Where Enrolled (Yes/No); Elsewhere - Post Office, County, State; Ward (Yes/No); Allotment [Al.], Annuity [An.] and/or Identification [Id.] Numbers

511 Belgarde(cont), Alex; m; 9 6-7-22; ¼+; s; son B284; no; Elbowoods, ND; no; Id.188k
512 " John; m; 7 7-3-24; ¼+; s; son B285; no; Elbowoods, ND; no; Id.188l
513 " Alfred; m; 6 1-7-26; ¼+; s; son B286; no; Elbowoods, ND; no; Id.188m

514 Belgarde, Gabriel; m; 41; ¼+; m; Head B287; no; Ft.Berthold, ND, no; Id.186, Al.G-08295
NE " Alvina (Zache); wife
515 " Theodore; m; 9 8-7-22; ¼+; s; son B288; no; Ft.Berthold, ND; no; none
516 " Edward; m; 7 7-23-25; ¼+; s; son B289; no; Ft.Berthold, ND; no; none

Died Belgarde, Gilbert; A179 (Died 2-23-32)
517 " Sarah (Premeau); f; 60; ¼+; wd; Head A180; yes; no; Id.167a, Al.G-447
518 " Joseph; m; 33; ¼+; s; son A181; no; Chicago, Cook, Ill; yes; Id.. 167b, Al.M-106
519 " John; m; 29; ¼+; s; son A182; yes; yes; Id.167d, Al.M-108
520 " Dominic; m; 19; ¼+; s; son A184; yes; yes; Id.167h
Died " Alfred; A185 (Died 2-25-21)

521 Belgarde, Israel; m; 35; ¼+; s; Head B291; no; Unknown, Minn; no; Id.181, Al.M-301

522 Belgarde, Jacques; m; 64; ¼+; m; Head A186; yes; yes; Id.168, Al.R-35
NE " Helen (Trothier); wife
523 " Delia M; f; 20 4-25-11; ¼+; s; dau A188; yes; yes; Id.168i, Al.H-012505
524 " Phillip; m; 20 4-25-11; ¼+; s; son A189; yes; yes; Id.168j, Al.H-012506

525 Belgarde, James; m; 37; ¼+; m; Head B291; no; Dunseith, Rolette, ND; no; Id.176, Al.B-9
526 " Cecelia (Allery); f; 20; ¼+; m; wife B292; no; Dunseith, Rolette, ND; yes; Id.168j, Al.H-012506

527 Belgarde, John B; m; 36; ¼+; m; Head A190; yes; no; Id.192, Al.M-38
528 " Mary V (Gourneau); f; 32 3-22-00; ¼+; m; wife A191; yes; yes; Id.192a, Al.G-062
529 " Mary M; f; 16 2-6-16; ¼+; s; dau A192; yes; yes; Id.192b
530 " Elmer; m; 12 10-1-19; ¼+; s; son A193; yes; yes; Id.192c
531 " Joachim; m; 10 8-21-21; ¼+; s; son A194; yes; yes; Id.192d
Died " Marie R; A195; (Died 4-6-26)
532 " Martha; f; 3 8-12-28; ¼+; s; dau A196; yes; yes; Id.192f

533 Belgarde, Joseph; m; 29 12-18-02; ¼+; m; Head B293; no; Nishu, ND; yes; Id.188c, Al.G-016811
NE " Laura (St.Pierre); wife
534 " Mary Rose; f; 4 12-22-27; ¼+; s; dau B294; no; Nishu, ND; yes; none
535 " Louie; m; 2 9-4-29; ¼+; s; son B295; no; Nishu, ND; yes; none

Turtle Mountain Reservation
1932 Census Roll

Key: Number; Surname, Given; Sex; Age at Last Birthday, Birthdate (if given); Tribe (Chippewa, unless stated otherwise); Degree of Blood; Marital Status; Relationship to Head of Family, Last Year Census Number; At Jurisdiction Where Enrolled (Yes/No); Elsewhere - Post Office, County, State; Ward (Yes/No); Allotment [Al.], Annuity [An.] and/or Identification [Id.] Numbers

536	Belgarde, Louis; m; 55; ¼+; m; Head B296; no; Ft.Totten, Benson, ND; no Id.174, Al.H-024502	
NE	"	Celina (Oadotte); wife
537	"	Joseph; m; 30; ¼+; s; son B297; no; Ft.Totten, Benson, ND; no; Id.174b, Al.H-024504
538	"	Mary R; f; 21; ¼+; s; dau B298; no; Ft.Totten, Benson, ND; no; Id.174f
539	"	Henry; m; 17 11-5-14; ¼+; s; dau B300; no; Ft.Totten, Benson, ND; no; Id.174g
540	"	Elizabeth; f; 15; ¼+; s; dau B301; no; Ft.Totten, Benson, ND; no; none
541	"	Delia; f; 12; ¼+; s; dau B302; no; Ft.Totten, Benson, ND; no; none
542	"	Clara; f; 10; ¼+; s; dau B303; no; Ft.Totten, Benson, ND; no; none
543	"	Louisa; f; 7; ¼+; s; dau B304; no; Ft.Totten, Benson, ND; no; none
544	"	No name (Christenson); f; 3 5-9-28; ¼+; s; grand dau B299; no; Ft.Totten, Benson, ND; no; none
Died	"	Irene; B305 (1-18-30)

545 Belgarde, Louis; m; 49; ¼+; m; Head A197; yes; no; Id.184, Al.H031169
546 " Philomeme (Vivier); f; 52; ¼+; m; wife A198; yes; yes; Id.184a, Al.H031170
547 " Patrice; m; 21 6-6-10; ¼+; s; son A199; yes; yes; Id.184b
548 " Bartholemew; m; 17 6-26-14; ¼+; s; son A201; yes; yes; Id.184d
549 " Alex; m; 15 5-15-16; ¼+; s; son A202; yes; yes; Id.184e
550 " Fred; m; 13 12-29-18; ¼+; s; son A203; yes; yes; none
551 " Rebecca; f; 11 4-21-20; ¼+; s; dau A204; yes; yes; Id.184f
552 " Ralph; m; 5 3-30-27; ¼+; s; son A205; yes; yes; Id.184g
No Such Person   Joseph;   A200

553 Belgarde, Louise; f; 71; ¼+; wd; Head A206; yes; no; Id.185a, Al.G-08299
554 " Elie; m; 32; ¼+; s; son A207; yes; yes; Id.185b, Al.G-08298

555 Belgarde, Marcial; m; 42; ¼+; m; Head A208; yes; no; Id.178, Al.G-10
556 " Philomeme (Lafontain); f; 32; ¼+; m; wife Aa09[sic]; yes; yes; Id.558b, Al.G-289
557 " Marcial; m; 11 3-11-21; ¼+; s; son A210; yes; yes; Id.178b
558 " Louise A; f; 9 4-1-22; ¼+; s; dau A211; yes; yes; Id.178c
559 " Andrew; m; 6 4-30-25; ¼+; s; son A212; yes; yes; none
560 " Daniel; m; 4 3-26-28; ¼+; s; son A213; yes; yes; none
Died " Alice   (Died 4-14-30)
Died " Dorothy;   A214   (Born 4-22-31 and died 6-9-31)

561 Belgarde, Martin; m; 27; ¼+; m; Head A215; yes; yes; Id.168f, Al.G-153
NE " Elizabeth (Martin); wife
562 " Margaret; f; 2 7-1-29; ¼+; s; dau A216; yes; yes; none
563 " Stanley; m; 11/12 4-8-31; ¼+; s; son A217; yes; yes; none

Turtle Mountain Reservation
1932 Census Roll

Key: Number; Surname, Given; Sex; Age at Last Birthday, Birthdate (if given); Tribe (Chippewa, unless stated otherwise); Degree of Blood; Marital Status; Relationship to Head of Family, Last Year Census Number; At Jurisdiction Where Enrolled (Yes/No); Elsewhere - Post Office, County, State; Ward (Yes/No); Allotment [Al.], Annuity [An.] and/or Identification [Id.] Numbers

564 Belgarde, Norbert; m; 68; ¼+; m; Head B306; no; Froid, Roosevelt, Mont; no; Id.175, Al.R-37
565   "   Octavia (Azure); f; 48; ¼+; m; wife B307; no; Froid, Roosevelt, Mont; no; Id.175a, Al.G-11
566   "   Robert; m; 26; ¼+; s; son B308; no; yes; Froid, Roosevelt, Mont; yes; Id.175b, Al.G-12
567   "   Arthur; m; 21; ¼+; s; son B310; no; Froid, Roosevelt, Mont; no; Id.175d
568   "   Ernest; m; 19; ¼+; s; son B311; no; Froid, Roosevelt, Mont; no; Id.175e
569   "   Herman; m; 16; ¼+; s; son B312; no; Froid, Roosevelt, Mont; no; Id.175f

570 Belgarde, Pierre; m; 50; ¼+; m; Head B313; no; Dunseith, Rolette, ND; no; Id.179, Al.M-40
571   "   Cecile (Wilkie); f; 42; ¼+; m; wife B314; no; Dunseith, Rolette, ND; no; Id.179a, Al.G-229
572   "   Frank; m; 20; ¼+; s; son B315; no; Dunseith, Rolette, ND; yes; Id.179b, Al.H-024669
573   "   Joseph; m; 17; ¼+; s; son B316; no; Dunseith, Rolette, ND; no; Id.179c
574   "   Mary Rosina; f; 13 8-20-18; ¼+; s; dau B317; no; Dunseith, Rolette, ND no; Id.179c
575   "   Dorothy M; f; 12; ¼+; s; dau B318; no; Dunseith, Rolette, ND; no; Id.179e
576   "   Lawrence; m; 9 11-30-22; ¼+; s; son B319; no; Dunseith, Rolette, ND; no; Id.179f

577 Belgarde, Riel; m; 41; ¼+; m; Head B320; yes; no; Id.163, Al.G-07962
578   "   Victoria (Morin); f; 35; ¼+; m; wife B321; yes; no; Id.163a, Al.GF-108
579   "   Emma; f; 17 12-30-14; ¼+; s; dau B322; yes; no; Id.163b
580   "   Agnes; f; 14 11-28-17; ¼+; s; dau B323; yes; no; Id.163c
581   "   Nora; f; 12 9-23-19; ¼+; s; dau B324; yes; no; Id.163d
582   "   Marie; f; 11 11-25-20; ¼+; s; dau B325; yes; no; Id.163e
583   "   Harold; m; 2 10-12-29; ¼+; s; son B326; yes; yes; Id.163f

584 Belgarde, Virginia (Dunchain); F; 47; ¼+; wd; Head B327; no; Dunseith, Rolette, ND; no; Id.172e, Al.M-400

585 Belgarde, William; m; 52; ¼+; m; Head A218; yes; yes; Id.190, Al.R-39
586   "   Mary T (Lavallie); f; 50; ¼+; m; wife A219; yes; no; Id.190a, Al.G-660
587   "   Patrice; m; 21; ¼+; s; son A220; yes; yes; Id.190e
588   "   Cecelia; f; 18; ¼+; s; dau A221; yes; yes; Id.190f
589   "   Alexander; m; 14 11-6-17; ¼+; s; son A222; yes; yes; Id.190g
590   "   Francis; m; 12 5-2-19; ¼+; s; son A223; yes; yes; Id.190h

591 Belgarde, William; m; 21 5-17-10; ¼+; s; Head; no; Elbowoods, McLean, ND; no; Id.188n

Turtle Mountain Reservation
1932 Census Roll

Key: Number; Surname, Given; Sex; Age at Last Birthday, Birthdate (if given); Tribe (Chippewa, unless stated otherwise); Degree of Blood; Marital Status; Relationship to Head of Family, Last Year Census Number; At Jurisdiction Where Enrolled (Yes/No); Elsewhere - Post Office, County, State; Ward (Yes/No); Allotment [Al.], Annuity [An.] and/or Identification [Id.] Numbers

NE Belgarde, Antoine; m;   Head
592   "   Elise, (McCloud); f; 43; ¼+; m; wife B330; no; Rolla, Rolette, ND; no; Id.194a, Al.GF-148
593   "   Delia; f; 23; ¼+; s; dau B331; no; Rolla, Rolette, ND; yes; Id.194c, Al.H-010464
594   "   Henry; m; 22; ¼+; s; son B332; no; Rolla, Rolette, ND; yes; Id.194d, Al.H-010463
595   "   Mary E; f; 21; ¼+; s; dau B333; no; Rolla, Rolette, ND; yes; Id.194e, Al.H-024512
596   "   Florence; f; 17 10-9-14; ¼+; s; dau B334; no; Rolla, Rolette, ND; no; Id.194g
597   "   Elvina; f; 14 5-3-17; ¼+; s; dau B335; no; Rolla, Rolette, ND; no; Id.194h
598   "   Agnes; f; 13 11-24-18; ¼+; s; dau B336; no; Rolla, Rolette, ND; no; Id.194i
599   "   Adeline; f; 12; ¼+; s; dau B337; no; Rolla, Rolette, ND; no; Id.194j
600   "   Russell; m; 10; ¼+; s; son B338; no; Rolla, Rolette, ND; no; Id.194k

601 Bercier, David; m; 26; ¼+; m; Head A226; yes; yes; Id.1167a, Al.G-272
602   "   Annie (Azure); f; 23; ¼+; m; wife A126; yes; no; Id.1034d

603 Bercier, Elise (Lafrombois); f; 57; ¼+; wd; Head B339; no; Rolla, Rolette, ND; no; Id.195a, Al.R-41
604   "   Patrice; m; 34; ¼+; s; son B340; no; Rolla, Rolette, ND; no; Id.195b, Al.G-0851
605   "   Simeon; m; 28; ¼+; s; son B341; no; Rolla, Rolette, ND; yes; Id.195e, Al.G-0850
606   "   John B; m; 24; ¼+; s; son B342; no; Rolla, Rolette, ND; yes; Id.195g, Al.G-08
607   "   St.Ann; f; 20; ¼+; s; dau B343; no; Rolla, Rolette, ND; no; Id.195i
608   "   George; m; 15 3-29-17; ¼+; s; son B344; no; Rolla, Rolette, ND; no; Id.195j
609   "   Alexander; m; 13 1-10-19; ¼+; s; son B345; no; Rolla, Rolette, ND; no; Id.195k

610 Bercier, Emil; m; 35; ¼+; m; Head B347; yes; no; Id.1169a, Al.M-59
611   "   Delphine (Warren); f; ¼+; m; wife A2154; yes; yes; Id.1002h
612   "   Sylvester; m; 10/12 5-15-31; ¼+; m; step son ------; yes; yes; none

NE Bercier, Francis;   Head
613   "   Justine (Lafournais); f; 64; ¼+; m; wife A224; yes; yes; Id.1167a, Al.R-42
614   "   Albert; m; 25; ¼+; s; son A227; yes; yes; Id.1167f, Al.G-99
615   "   Mary Jane; f; 22; ¼+; s; dau A228; yes; yes; Id.1167g, Al.H-0130 8

616 Bercier, Joseph; m; 37; ¼+; m; Head A229; yes; no; Id.1171, Al.M-54
617   "   Rosalie (Langer); f; 37; ¼+; m; wife A230; yes; yes; Id.1171a, Al.G-116

Turtle Mountain Reservation
1932 Census Roll

Key: Number; Surname, Given; Sex; Age at Last Birthday, Birthdate (if given); Tribe (Chippewa, unless stated otherwise); Degree of Blood; Marital Status; Relationship to Head of Family, Last Year Census Number; At Jurisdiction Where Enrolled (Yes/No); Elsewhere - Post Office, County, State; Ward (Yes/No); Allotment [Al.], Annuity [An.] and/or Identification [Id.] Numbers

618 Bercier(cont), Joseph; m; 13 12-5-18; ¼+; s; son A231; yes; yes; Id.1171b
619 " Sylvia; f; 10 3-12-22; ¼+; s; son A232; yes; yes; Id.1171c
620 " Charley; m; 6 4-29-25; ¼+; s; son A233; yes; yes; none
621 " Louis; m; 3; 3-16-29; ¼+; s; son A234; yes; yes; none

622 Bercier, Julia; f; 36; ¼+; s; Head A235; yes; yes; Id.1168, Al.M-16

NE Bercier, Lawrence;   Head
623 " Sarah (Azure); f; 38; ¼+; m; wife A236; yes; yes; Id.187a, Al.G-08275
624 (Belgarde), Eva; f; 18; ¼+; s; step dau A238; yes; yes; Id.187d
625 (Belgarde), Victoria; f; 12 12-29-19; ¼+; s; step dau A240; yes; yes; Id.187d[sic]
626 Bercier, Gilbert; m; 9 10-12-22; ¼+; s; son A241; yes; yes; Id.187e
627 " Prudent; m; 9 10-12-22; ¼+; s; son A242; yes; yes; Id.187f
628 " Norman; m; 5 10-12-26; ¼+; s; son A243; yes; yes; Id.186g
629 " Marian; f; 3; ¼+; s; son A244; yes; yes; Id.186h

NE Bercier, Louis; m;   Head
630 " Marie R (Lafournais); f; 60; ¼+; m; wife B346; no; Rolla, Rolette, ND; no; Id.1169a, Al.H010466
631 " Albert; m; 30; ¼+; s; son B348; no; Rolla, Rolette, ND; yes; Id.1189g, Al.M59
632 " Mary; f; 20; ¼+; s; dau B349; no; Rolla, Rolette, ND; no; Id.1189h
633 " Arthur; m; 16; ¼+; s; son B350; no; Rolla, Rolette, ND; no; Id.1189i

634 Bercier, Mary M (Demontigny); f; 32; ¼+; wd; Head A245; yes; yes; Id.341c, Al.G08149
635 " George; m; 2 3-9-30; ¼+; s; son A246; yes; Id.341d

NE Bercier, Mike;   Head
636 " Jane (Vallie); f; 31; ¼+; m; wife B351; no; Bottineau, Bottineau, ND; yes; Id.975c, Al.GF226
637 " Ernestine; f; 11 9-1-20; ¼+; s; dau B352; no; Bottineau, Bottineau, ND; yes; Id.(None)
638 " Lillian; f; 9 9-23-221; ¼+; s; dau B353; no; Bottineau, Bottineau, ND; yes; none

639 Bercier, Norman; m; 36; ¼+; wd; Head A247; yes; no; Id.1172, Al.H010490
640 " Lorria; f; 11; ¼+; s; dau A248; yes; no; none

641 Bercier, Theodore; m; 36; ¼+; s; Head B354; no; Rolla, Rolette, ND; no; Id.1172, Al.H010490

Turtle Mountain Reservation
1932 Census Roll

Key: Number; Surname, Given; Sex; Age at Last Birthday, Birthdate (if given); Tribe (Chippewa, unless stated otherwise); Degree of Blood; Marital Status; Relationship to Head of Family, Last Year Census Number; At Jurisdiction Where Enrolled (Yes/No); Elsewhere - Post Office, County, State; Ward (Yes/No); Allotment [Al.], Annuity [An.] and/or Identification [Id.] Numbers

NE Bercier, Tobey;   Head --
642 " Celina (Lafountain); f; 58; ¼+; m; wife; yes   (Omitted from census last year by mistake); yes; Id.1170a, Al.G01313

643 Bercier, William; m; 48; ¼+; m; Head A249; yes; no; Id.193, Al.H012507
644 Bercier, Virginia (Bonneaup); f; 34; F; m; wife A250; yes; no; Id.193a, Al.G014926
645 " Paul; m; 14 5-20-17; ¼+; s; son A251; yes; no; Id.193b
646 " Francis; m; 11 9-4-20; ¼+; s; son A252; yes; no; Id.193c
647 " Victoria; f; 5 1-13-27; ¼+; s; dau A253; yes; no; Id.193d
648 " Angeline; f; 3 1-11-29; ¼+; s; dau A254; yes; no; Id.193e
649 " Agnes; f; 2 3-21-30; ¼+; s; dau A255; yes; no; Id.193f

650 Bergier, Eliza (Grandbois); f; 44; ¼+; wd; Head B355; no; Froid, Roosevelt, Mont; no; Id.1173b, Al.G013145
651 (Page [48])
652 " Edmund; m; 24; ¼+; s; son B356; no; Froid, Roosevelt, Mont; yes; Id.1173b, Al.G01314
653 " Rosalie; f; 20; ¼+; s; dau B357; no; Froid, Roosevelt, Mont; yes; Id.1173c, Al.--
654 " David; m; 19; ¼+; s; son B358; no; Froid, Roosevelt, Mont; yes; none
655 " Peter; m; 16 11-30-15; ¼+; s; son B359; no; Froid, Roosevelt, Mont; yes; Id.1173e
656 " Joseph; m; 14 3-2-18; ¼+; s; son B360; no; Froid, Roosevelt, Mont; yes; Id.1173f
657 " Alice; f; 12; ¼+; s; dau ---; no; Froid, Roosevelt, Mont; yes; none
658 " Francis; m; 9; ¼+; s; son ---; no; Froid, Roosevelt, Mont; yes; none
659 " Mary; f; 8 1-7-24; ¼+; s; dau B361; no; Froid, Roosevelt, Mont; yes; Id.1173f
660 " Laurine; f; 5 4-3-26; ¼+; s; dau B362; no; Froid, Roosevelt, Mont; yes; Id.1173g
661 " John R; m; 4 10-30-27; ¼+; s; son B363; no; Froid, Roosevelt, Mont; yes; Id.1173h

NE Bergie, Martin;   Head
662 " Marie (Poitra); f; 33; ¼+; m; wife B364; no; Poplar, Roosevelt, Mont; no; Id.871c, Al.H010454
No such " Joseph;   B365
child
663 " Madeline; f; 12 11-14-19; ¼+; s; dau B366; no; Poplar, Roosevelt, Mont; no; none
No such " Francis   B367
child
664 " Marie; f; 4 10-27-27; ¼+; s; dau B368; no; Poplar, Roosevelt, Mont; no; none

Turtle Mountain Reservation
1932 Census Roll

Key: Number; Surname, Given; Sex; Age at Last Birthday, Birthdate (if given); Tribe (Chippewa, unless stated otherwise); Degree of Blood; Marital Status; Relationship to Head of Family, Last Year Census Number; At Jurisdiction Where Enrolled (Yes/No); Elsewhere - Post Office, County, State; Ward (Yes/No); Allotment [Al.], Annuity [An.] and/or Identification [Id.] Numbers

NE Betosh, Jim;   Head
665   "   Ellen (Sayers); f; 49; ¼+; m; wife B369; no; Medicine Lake, Sheridan, Mont; no; Id.1178a, Al.G-0708

666 Bird, Ekos; m; 64; F; m; Head B370; no; Dunseith, Rolette, ND; yes; Id.7; Al.DL-23
667   "   Sun Woman; f; 69; F; m; wife B371; no; Dunseith, Rolette, ND; no; Id.7a, Al.G-326

NE Black Cloud, Francis;   Head
668   "   Elizabeth (Houle); f; 22; ¼+; m; wife; no; (Left out thru error); Wakpala, Corson, SD; no; Id.485b

669 Blue, Alfred; m; 30; ¼+; m; Head A258; yes; yes; Id. 1174B, Al.H-030414
670   "   Virginia (Toupin); f; 30 4-6-02; ¼+; m; wife A259; yes; yes; Id.962, Al.G-08310
671   "   Patrick; m; 13 12-15-18; ¼+; s; son A260; yes; yes; none
672   "   Genevieve; f; 10 5-8-21; ¼+; s; dau A261; yes; yes; none
673   "   Martin; m; 9 10-29-22; ¼+; s; son A262; yes; yes; none
674   "   Vivian; f; 8 1-22-24; ¼+; s; dau A263; yes; yes; none
675   "   Elsie S; f; 6 10-21-25; ¼+; s; dau B264; yes; yes; none
676   "   Marie A; f; 4 5-29-27; ¼+; s; dau A265; yes; yes; none
Died "   Raphael   (Born 4-27-31 and died 10-19-31)

677 Blue, Virginia (Demarais); f; 56; ¼+; wd; Head A256; yes; yes; Id.1174a, Al.H-032205
678   "   Charles E; m; 20; ¼+; s; son A257; yes; yes; Id.1174d, Al.H-024514

NE Boe, Ralph;   Head
679   "   Josephine (Thifault); f; 24; ¼+; m; wife B372; no; Long Beach, Los Angeles, Cal; yes; Id.947d
680   "   William; m; 4 12-11-27; ¼+; s; son; no; Long Beach, Los Angeles, Cal; yes; none
681   "   Ralph; m; 2 7-29-29; ¼+; s; son; no; Long Beach, Los Angeles, Cal; yes; none

682 Bonnaup, Joe; m; 76; F; m; Head A268; yes; yes; Id.9, Al.G-01495
NE   "   Sarah (Fagnant); wife

683 Bonneau, Emily (Jerome); f; 49; ¼+; wd; Head B373; no; Madoc, Daniels, Mont; yes; Id.1177a, Al.G-08418
684   "   Eugene; m; 22 5-24-09; ¼+; s; son B375; no; Madoc, Daniels, Mont; yes; Id.1177c
685   "   Dominique; m; 18 5-13-13; ¼+; s; son B376; no; Madoc, Daniels, Mont; yes; Id.1177d
686   "   Regina; f; 16 7-20-15; ¼+; s; dau B377; no; Madoc, Daniels, Mont; yes; Id.1177e
687   "   Madie; f; 15 3-26-17; ¼+; s; dau B378; no; Madoc, Daniels, Mont; yes; Id.1177f

Turtle Mountain Reservation
1932 Census Roll

Key: Number; Surname, Given; Sex; Age at Last Birthday, Birthdate (if given); Tribe (Chippewa, unless stated otherwise); Degree of Blood; Marital Status; Relationship to Head of Family, Last Year Census Number; At Jurisdiction Where Enrolled (Yes/No); Elsewhere - Post Office, County, State; Ward (Yes/No) Allotment [Al.], Annuity [An.] and/or Identification [Id.] Numbers

688 Bonneau(cont), Eva; f; 13 3-19-19; ¼+; s; dau B379; no; Madoc, Daniels, Mont; yes; Id.1177g
689 " Elmira; f; 11 8-24-21; ¼+; s; dau B380; no; Madoc, Daniels, Mont; yes; Id.1177h
690 " Jean Frank; m; 8 9-9-23; ¼+; s; son B381; no; Madoc, Daniels, Mont; yes; Id. 1177i

Died Bonneau, LaGloire;   A266   (Died 5-28-31)
691 " Victoria (Decoteau); f; 77; ¼+; wd; Head A267; yes; yes; Id. 1175a, Al. DL-03725

NE Bottineau, Israel;   B382   (Counted last year error)

693 Bottineau, Joseph; m; 68; ¼+; m; Head B383; no; Dunseith, Rolette, ND; yes; Id.1179, Al. DL 27
694 " Mary Rose (Amyott); f; 67; ¼+; m; wife B384; no; Dunseith, Rolette, ND; no; Id.1178a, Al. GF-197
695 " Frederick; m; 34; ¼+; s; son B385; no; Dunseith, Rolette, ND; yes; Id.1179b, Al.GF-194
692 on page [36]

696 Bottineau, Phillip; m; 37; ¼+; m; Head B386; no; Dunseith, Rolette, ND; yes; Id.1179e, Al.GF-196
NE " Elizabeth (Peltier); wife
697 " Napoleon; m; 7 7-26-24; ¼+; s; son B387; no; Dunseith, Rolette, ND; yes; Id.1179f, Al.---
698 " Ruth; f; 5 7-22-26; ¼+; s; dau 388; no; Dunseith, Rolette, ND; yes; Id. 1179g
699 " Alice; f; 2 8-6-30; ¼+; s; dau ---; no; Dunseith, Rolette, ND; yes; ---

NE Bouvais, Harry; m;   Head
700 " Emily (Lafournais); f; 34 3-24-98; ¼+; m; wife B389; no; San Clara, Manitoba, Canada; no; Id.564c, Al.M52
701 " Henry; m; 13 3-10-19; ¼+; s; son B390; no; San Clara, Manitoba, Canada; no; none
702 " Alice; f; 10 22-29-21; ¼+; s; dau B391; no; San Clara, Manitoba, Canada; no; none
703 " Jean; m; 7 5-20-24; ¼+; s; son B392; no; San Clara, Manitoba, Canada; no; none
704 " Verna; f; 3/12 12-28-31; ¼+; s; dau -------; no; San Clara, Manitoba, Canada; no; none

Turtle Mountain Reservation
1932 Census Roll

Key: Number; Surname, Given; Sex; Age at Last Birthday, Birthdate (if given); Tribe (Chippewa, unless stated otherwise); Degree of Blood; Marital Status; Relationship to Head of Family, Last Year Census Number; At Jurisdiction Where Enrolled (Yes/No); Elsewhere - Post Office, County, State; Ward (Yes/No); Allotment [Al.], Annuity [An.] and/or Identification [Id.] Numbers

NE Bouvier, Ed;   Head
705   "   Rosanna (Dumont); f; 31 12-22-00; ¼+; m; wife B393; no; Boggy Creek, Manitoba, Canada; yes; Id.367d, Al.G0442

706   Boyer, Alfred; m; 33; ¼+; m; Head B396; no; Culbertson, Roosevelt, Mont; no; Id.118c, Al.G092
707   "   Laura (Davis); f; 33; ¼+; m; wife B582; no; Culbertson, Roosevelt, Mont; yes; Id. 270c, Al.GF66
708   "   Joseph A; m; 8 5-15-23; ¼+; s; son ---; no; Culbertson, Roosevelt, Mont; no; none
709   "   Mary Rose; f; 7 7-11-24; ¼+; s; dau ----; no; Culbertson, Roosevelt, Mont; no; none
710   "   Corinne J; f; 4 8-8-27; ¼+; s; dau ----; no; Culbertson, Roosevelt, Mont; no; none
711   "   Selina; f; 1 11-25-30; ¼+; s; dau ----; no; Culbertson, Roosevelt, Mont; no; none

712   Boyer, Alexander; m; 43; ¼+; m; Head A269; yes; no; Id.1183, Al.H030415
713   "   Flora (Nadeau); f; 33 4-15-98; ¼+; m; wife A270; yes; no; Id.1183a, Al.M216
714   "   Madeline; f; 15 808016; ¼+; s; dau A271; yes; no; Id.1183c
715   "   George; m; 14 11-3-17; ¼+; s; son A272; yes; no; Id.1183d
716   "   Annie; f; 11 2-5-21; ¼+; s; dau A273; yes; no; Id.1183e
717   "   Veronica; f; 9 7-12-22; ¼+; s; dau A274; yes; no; Id.1183f
718   "   Marie; f; 7 8-1-24; ¼+; s; dau A275; yes; no; none
Dead   "   May;   A276   (Died Nov. 8, 1930.)
719   "   Gordon; m; 11/12 4-5-31; ¼+; s; son -----; yes; no; none

720   Boyer, Celina (Belgarde); f; 55; ¼+; wd; Head B394; no; Culbertson, Roosevelt, Mont; no; Id.1185a, Al.G16
721   "   Peter; m; 35; ¼+; s; son B395; no; Culbertson, Roosevelt, Mont; no; Id.1185b, Al.G08085
722   "   Alexander; m; 31; ¼+; s; son B397; no; Culbertson, Roosevelt, Mont; yes; Id.1185d, Al.G17
723   "   Adele; f; 21; ¼+; s; dau B398; no; Culbertson, Roosevelt, Mont; no; Id.1185h
724   "   Ernestine; f; 19; ¼+; s; dau B399; no; Culbertson, Roosevelt, Mont; no; Id.1185i
725   "   Vitalline; f; 17; ¼+; s; dau B400; no; Culbertson, Roosevelt, Mont; no; Id.1185j

NE Boyer, Gus;   Head
726   "   Sarah (Azure); f; 36; ¼+; m; wife B401; no; Sidney, Richland, Mont; no; Id.845a, Al.GF19

Turtle Mountain Reservation
1932 Census Roll

Key: Number; Surname, Given; Sex; Age at Last Birthday, Birthdate (if given); Tribe (Chippewa, unless stated otherwise); Degree of Blood; Marital Status; Relationship to Head of Family, Last Year Census Number; At Jurisdiction Where Enrolled (Yes/No); Elsewhere - Post Office, County, State; Ward (Yes/No); Allotment [Al.], Annuity [An.] and/or Identification [Id.] Numbers

727 Boyer, Joseph; m; 49; ¼+; m; Head A277; yes; yes; Id.1184, Al.H-030416
728 " Josephine (Baker); f; 42; ¼+; m; wife A278; yes; no; Id.1184a, Al.M-303
729 " Rose A; f; 22 5-10-09; ¼+; s; dau A279; yes; yes; Id.1184c
730 " Flora C; f; 19 4-3-12; ¼+; s; dau A280; yes; yes; Id.1184d
731 " Delphine; f; 16 10-30-15; ¼+; s; dau A281; yes; yes; Id.1184e
732 " Louie R; m; 14 10-3-17; ¼+; s; son A282; yes; yes; Id.1184f
733 " Lucy; f; 12 1-28-20; ¼+; s; dau A283; yes; yes; Id.1184g
734 " Robert; m; 9 6-4-22; ¼+; s; son A284; yes; yes; Id.1184g[sic]
735 " Stanley; m; 7 7-7-24; ¼+; s; son A285; yes; yes; none
736 " Maggie; f; 5 12-15-26; ¼+; s; dau A286; yes; yes; none
737 " Lloyd; m; 3 12-30-28; ¼+; s; son A287; yes; yes; none
738 " Irene; f; 5/12 10-10-31; ¼+; s; dau; yes; yes; none

Dead Boyer, Julia;   A288   Died Nov. 12, 1931

NE Boyer, Napoleon;   Head
739 " Theresa (Champagne); f; 56; ¼+; m; wife B402; no; Culbertson, Roosevelt, Mont; no; Id.1186a, Al.R-45
740 " Edward; m; 34; ¼+; s; son B403; no; Culbertson, Roosevelt, Mont; yes; Id.1186b, Al.G-275
741 " Pascal; m; 20; ¼+; s; son B404; no; Culbertson, Roosevelt, Mont; no; Id.1186c
742 " Joseph; m; 11 8-5-20; ¼+; s; son B405; no; Culbertson, Roosevelt, Mont; no; none

NE Boyer, Thomas;   Head
743 " Mary (Davis); f; 45; ¼+; m; wife B406; no; Culbertson, Roosevelt, Mont; no; Id.1187a, Al.M252
744 " Joseph; m; 23; ¼+; m; son B407; no; Culbertson, Roosevelt, Mont; yes; yes; Id.1187b, Al.G08291
745 " Joseph; f; 21; ¼+; s; dau B408; no; Culbertson, Roosevelt, Mont; no; Id.1187c
746 " George; m; 18 6-21-13; ¼+; s; son B409; no; Culbertson, Roosevelt, Mont; no; Id.1187d
747 " Helen; f; 17 6-11-14; ¼+; s; dau B410; no; Culbertson, Roosevelt, Mont; no; Id.1187e
748 " Emily; f; 16 8-18-15; ¼+; s; dau B411; no; Culbertson, Roosevelt, Mont; no; Id.1187f
749 " Agnes; f; 14 12-8-17; ¼+; s; dau B412; no; Culbertson, Roosevelt, Mont; no; Id.1187g
750 " Mary R; f; 11 5-21-20; ¼+; s; dau B413; no; Culbertson, Roosevelt, Mont; no; Id.1187h

Turtle Mountain Reservation
1932 Census Roll

Key: Number; Surname, Given; Sex; Age at Last Birthday, Birthdate (if given); Tribe (Chippewa, unless stated otherwise); Degree of Blood; Marital Status; Relationship to Head of Family, Last Year Census Number; At Jurisdiction Where Enrolled (Yes/No); Elsewhere - Post Office, County, State; Ward (Yes/No); Allotment [Al.], Annuity [An.] and/or Identification [Id.] Numbers

751 Bradford, Ernest; m; 28; ¼+; m; Head A289; yes; yes; Id.1186g, Al.H010425
752 " Amy (Malaterre); f; 26; ¼+; f[sic]; wife A290; yes; yes
753 " Stanley; m; 2 7-23-29; ¼+; s; son A291; yes; yes

NE Bradford, Frank;   Head   This couple said to be divorced.
754 " Mary (Vallie); f; 44; ¼+; m; wife B414; no; Dunseith, Rolette, ND; yes;
                                                                             Id.1188e, Al.H010423
755 " George; m; 23; ¼+; s; son B415; no; Dunseith, Rolette, ND; yes;
                                                                             Id.1188b, Al.H010424
756 " Frank; m; 21; ¼+; s; s-son B416; no; Dunseith, Rolette, ND; yes;
                                                                          Id.1188c, Al. G016317
757 " Alice; f; 16 9-21-15; ¼+; s; dau B---; no; Dunseith, Rolette, ND; yes;
                                                                                    Id.1188e

NE Braugh, Donald D;   Head
758 " Margaret (Rolette); f; 22; ¼+; m; wife B417; no; PO address unknown;
                                                       Oklahoma, Okla; yes; Id.894d, Al.H012630
759 " Donald, Jr; m; 1 1-11-31; ¼+; s; son B-418; no; Unknown, Okla; no; none

NE Brave, Joseph; m;   Head
760 " Margaret (Grant); f; 40; ¼+; m; wife B419; no; Rosebud; no; Id.1189a,
                                                                                      Al.M-238

NE Breland, Alex;   Head
NE " Ella (Demontigny); f;   wife
761 " Joseph; m; 27; ¼+; s; son A292; yes; yes; Id.1190B, Al.H-010517
762 " Robert M; m; 24; ¼+; s; son A293; yes; yes; Id.1190c, Al.H-010511
763 " Alex, Jr; m; 23; ¼+; s; son A294; yes; yes; Id.1190d, Al.H-010510
764 " Rose; f; 19; ¼+; s; dau A295; yes; yes; Id.1190e

765 Brien, Albert; m; 33; ¼+; s; Head B420; no; Nishu, ND; no; Id.202c, Al.G-08265
766 " Ernest; m; 31; ¼+; s; bro B421; no; Unknown; yes; Id.202d, Al.G-08262
767 " Frederick; m; 28; ¼+; s; bro B422; no; Unknown; no; Id.202c

768 Brien, Alexander; m; 56; ¼+; m; Head A296; yes; No; Id.197, Al.G-483
769 " Mary Jane (Belgarde); f; 49; ¼+; m; wife A297; yes; no; Id.169a, Al.M-201
770 " Marceline; f; 30 3-30-02; ¼+; s; dau A299; yes; yes; Id.197b, Al.G-08141
771 " Marie Elise; f; 21 10-29-10; ¼+; s; dau A300; yes; yes; Id.197f, Al.H-013033
772 Belgarde, Ernestine; f; 16 5-29-15; ¼+; s; step dau A301; yes; yes; Id.169b
773 Belgarde, Nora; f; 14 12-2-17; ¼+; s; step dau A302; yes; yes; Id.169c
774 Brien, Patrick; m; 14 4-24-17; ¼+; s; son A303; yes; yes; Id.197g
775 " Rosalie; f; 8 5-27-23; ¼+; s; dau A304; yes; yes; Id.197f
776 " Josephine; f; 5 6-29-26; ¼+; s; dau A305; yes; yes; Id.197j
777 " Adele; f; 3 5-3-28; ¼+; s; dau A306; yes; yes; Id.197k

Turtle Mountain Reservation
1932 Census Roll

Key: Number; Surname, Given; Sex; Age at Last Birthday, Birthdate (if given); Tribe (Chippewa, unless stated otherwise); Degree of Blood; Marital Status; Relationship to Head of Family, Last Year Census Number; At Jurisdiction Where Enrolled (Yes/No); Elsewhere - Post Office, County, State; Ward (Yes/No); Allotment [Al.], Annuity [An.] and/or Identification [Id.] Numbers

778 Brien, Alfred; m; 36; ¼+; s; Head B431; no; Unknown; no; Id.199, Al.G-540

779 Brien, Alfred; m; 53; ¼+; m; Head B423; no; Medicine Lake, Sheridan, Mont; no; Id.201, Al.G-07905

780 " Sarah (Morin.Harrison); f; 48; ¼+; m; wife B424; no; Medicine Lake, Sheridan, Mont; no; Id.201a, Al.G-07903

781 " Riel; m; 22 12-25-09; ¼+; s; son B425; no; Medicine Lake, Sheridan, Mont; yes; Id.201b, Al.G-07844

782 " Virginia; f; 19 4-20-13; ¼+; s; dau B427; no; Medicine Lake, Sheridan, Mont; no; Id.201d

783 " Mary Rose; f; 17 11-20-14; ¼+; s; dau B428; no; Medicine Lake, Sheridan, Mont; no; Id.201e

784 " Clemence; f; 13 1-2-19; ¼+; s; dau B429; no; Medicine Lake, Sheridan, Mont; no; Id.201f

785 " Victoria; f; 11 11-8-20; ¼+; s; dau B430; no; Medicine Lake, Sheridan, Mont; no; Id.201g

786 " Russell; m; 1- 7-26-121; ¼+; s; son; no; Medicine Lake, Sheridan, Mont; no; none

787 Brien, Edward; m; 40; ¼+; m; Head B432; no; Chicago, Cook, Ill; no; Id.200, Al.G-541

788 " Lucy (Gardner.Godon); f; 51; ¼+; m; wife B433; no; Phoenix, Maricopa, (Said to be divorced) Ariz; no; Id.424e, Al.H-038896

789 Brien, Gregoire[sic]; m; 70; ¼+; m; Head A307; yes; yes; Id.198b, Al.R-47
NE " Betsey (Cardinal); wife
790 " William; m; 23; ¼+; s; son A309; yes; yes; Id.198c, Al. H-013031
791 " Mary St.Ann; f; 21; ¼+; s; dau A310; yes; yes; Id.198e
792 " (Grant) Madeline; f; 16 1-31-17; ¼+; s; adpt dau A311; yes; yes; Id.460g

793 Brien, Gregory; m; 36; ¼+; s; Head B435; no; Chicago, Cook, Ill; no; Id.11193, Al.M-187

794 Brien, Joseph; m; 53; ¼+; m; Head B436; no; Medicine Lake, Sheridan, Mont; no; Id.1191, Al.M 721
NE " Adeline (Morin.Lafrance); wife
3031 " Mary; f; 27 11-17-04; ¼+; s; dau B437; no; Medicine Lake, Sheridan, Mont; yes; Id.1191b, Al.G05237
796 " Julius; m; 23; ¼+; s; son B438; no; Medicine Lake, Sheridan, Mont; no; Id.1191d
797 " Rose D; f; 20; ¼+; s; dau B439; no; Medicine Lake, Sheridan, Mont; no; Id.1191d
798 " John L; m; 17 7-1-14; ¼+; s; son B440; no; Medicine Lake, Sheridan, Mont; no; Id. 1191e

Turtle Mountain Reservation
1932 Census Roll

Key: Number; Surname, Given; Sex; Age at Last Birthday, Birthdate (if given); Tribe (Chippewa, unless stated otherwise); Degree of Blood; Marital Status; Relationship to Head of Family, Last Year Census Number; At Jurisdiction Where Enrolled (Yes/No); Elsewhere - Post Office, County, State; Ward (Yes/No); Allotment [Al.], Annuity [An.] and/or Identification [Id.] Numbers

799 Brien(cont), Marie; f; 8 6-25-23; ¼+; s; dau B441; no; Medicine Lake, Sheridan, Mont; no; Id. 1191f

800 Brien, Joseph; m; 37; ¼+; m; Head B442; no; Trenton, Williams, ND; no; Id.1194, Al.M183
801 " Mary Rose (Gooseline); f; 28; ¼+; m; wife B443; no; Trenton, Williams, ND; yes; Id.427b, Al.H-12542
802 " Peter; m; 7 10-27-34; ¼+; s; son B444; no; Trenton, Williams, ND; no; Id.427c
803 " Frank M; m; 5 8-18-26; ¼+; s; son B445; no; Trenton, Williams, ND; no; none

795 Brien, Alice; f; 31 11-22-00; ¼+; s; Head A298; yes; no; Id.197b
5524 " (Montriel) Albert; m; 12; ¼+; s; son B1787; yes; no; none

804 Brien, Joseph A; m; 38; ¼+; m; Head B446; no; Bainville, Roosevelt, Mont; no; Id.202b, Al.M-190
805 " Elise (Lavia); f; 40; ¼+; m; wife B447; no; Bainville, Roosevelt, Mont; no; Id.651, Al.M-130
806 " Wilfred; m; 12 11-9-19; ¼+; s; son B448; no; Bainville, Roosevelt, Mont; no; none
807 " Marion; f; 10 3-27-22; ¼+; s; dau B449; no; Bainville, Roosevelt, Mont; no; none
808 " Esther; f; 7 4-20-24; ¼+; s; dau B450; no; Bainville, Roosevelt, Mont; no; none
809 " Gloria; f; 5 10-3-26; ¼+; s; dau B451; no; Bainville, Roosevelt, Mont; no; none
810 " Albert Verne; m; 2 7-10-29; ¼+; s; son B452; no; Bainville, Roosevelt, Mont; no; none

811 Brien, Joseph Wm; m; 26 8-29-05; ¼+; m; Head A312; yes; yes; Id.197e, Al.G-485
812 " Rose (Lafrombois); f; 24; ¼+; m; wife A313; yes; yes; Id.575c, Al.G-0413
813 " Aloysius; m; 1 6-30-30; ¼+; s; son A314; yes; yes; none

814 Brien, Louis; m; 29; ¼+; m; Head A308; yes; yes; Id.198b, Al.G-543
815 " Mary (Dejarlais); f; 22; ¼+; m; wife A631; yes; yes; Id.312f, Al.H-010521
816 " Gordon; m; 7/12 8-30-31; ¼+; s; son; yes; yes; none

NE Brien, Mitchell; m;   Head
817 " Rose (McGillis); f; 40; ¼+; m; wife B453; no; St.John, Rolette, ND; no; Id.203a, Al.H-013038
818 " John; m; 15 3-12-17; ¼+; s; son B454; no; St.John, Rolette, ND; no; none
819 " Rosalie; f; 12 8-2-19; ¼+; s; dau B455; no; St.John, Rolette, ND; no; none
820 " Elizabeth; f; 9 7-23-22; ¼+; s; dau B456; no; St.John, Rolette, ND; no; none
821 " Laureat F; m; 1 2-18-31; ¼+; s; son; no; St.John, Rolette, ND; no; none

Turtle Mountain Reservation
1932 Census Roll

Key: Number; Surname, Given; Sex; Age at Last Birthday, Birthdate (if given); Tribe (Chippewa, unless stated otherwise); Degree of Blood; Marital Status; Relationship to Head of Family, Last Year Census Number; At Jurisdiction Where Enrolled (Yes/No); Elsewhere - Post Office, County, State; Ward (Yes/No); Allotment [Al.], Annuity [An.] and/or Identification [Id.] Numbers

NE Brien, Paul;   Head
822   "   Delia (St.Pierre); 31; ¼+; m; wife B457; no; Dunseith, Rolette, ND; yes; Id.942c, Al.G-507
823   "   Clara; f; 9 3-10-23; ¼+; s; dau; no; Dunseith, Rolette, ND; yes; none
824   "   Angus; m; 7 4-27-24; ¼+; s; son; no; Dunseith, Rolette, ND; yes; none
825   "   George; m; 6 12-19-25; ¼+; s; son; no; Dunseith, Rolette, ND; yes; none
826   "   Susanna; f; 4 8-27-27; ¼+; s; dau; no; Dunseith, Rolette, ND; yes; none
827   "   Alvina; f; 3 2-4-29; ¼+; s; dau; no; Dunseith, Rolette, ND; yes; none
828   "   Mary Celina; f; 1 12-11-30; ¼+; s; dau; no; Dunseith, Rolette, ND; yes; none

692 Brien, Phillip; m; 42; ¼+; s; Head B458; no; Unknown; yes; Id.1195, Al.G-08142

829 Brien, Pierre; m; 26; ¼+; m; Head A315; yes; yes; Id. 198e, Al.G-544
830   "   Agnes (Lattergrass); f; 21; ¼+; m; wife A316; yes; yes; Id.620f
831   "   John Verlin; m; 3 6-8-28; ¼+; s; son A317; yes; yes; none

832 Brien, Robert; m; 45; ¼+; s; Head B459; no; Unknown; no; Id.196, Al.M-184

833 Brien, Theodore; m; 75; ¼+; wd; Head B460; no; Medicine Lake, Sheridan, Mont; no; Id.1192, Al.M-188

NE Briere, Gregory;   Head
834   "   Alphonsine (Allery); f; 54; ¼+; m; wife B461; no; White Mound, Sask, Canada; yes; Id.204a, Al.GF-138
835   "   Anna; f; 30; ¼+; s; dau B462; no; White Mound, Sask, Canada; yes; Id.204c, Al.GF-140
836   "   William; m; 25; ¼+; s; son B463; no; White Mound, Sask, Canada; yes; Id.204d, Al.G-0425
837   "   Rose; f; 22; ¼+; s; dau B464; no; White Mound, Sask, Canada; yes; Id.204e, Al.G-014240
838   "   Mary Louise; f; 21; ¼+; s; dau B465; no; White Mound, Sask, Canada; yes; Id.204f
839   "   Alvina; f; 18; ¼+; s; dau B466; no; Hays, Blaine, Mont; yes; Id.204g
840 " (Adams) Tracey; m; 2-2-32; ¼+; s; grandson; no; (Illeg. Son of Alvina) Hays, Blaine, Mont; yes; none
5519 " (Talimentes) Frank; m; 3 7-3-28; ¼+; s; grandson; no; (Illeg. son of Alvina) Hays, Blaine, Mont; yes; none

841 Briere, Joseph; m; 35; ¼+; m; Head B467; no; Unknown; yes; Id.204b, Al.GF-130
NE   "   Louise (Doney);   wife
842   "   Albert D; m; 7 1-17-25; ¼+; s; son B468; no; Unknown; yes; none

Turtle Mountain Reservation
1932 Census Roll

Key: Number; Surname, Given; Sex; Age at Last Birthday, Birthdate (if given); Tribe (Chippewa, unless stated otherwise); Degree of Blood; Marital Status; Relationship to Head of Family, Last Year Census Number; At Jurisdiction Where Enrolled (Yes/No); Elsewhere - Post Office, County, State; Ward (Yes/No); Allotment [Al.], Annuity [An.] and/or Identification [Id.] Numbers

NE Brinkman, Fred;   Head
843   "   Rosalie (Grandbois); f; 23; ¼+; m; wife B469; no; Dagmar, Sheridan,
                                        Mont; yes; Id.442f, Al.G-07326
844   "   June; f; 7 6-28-24; ¼+; s; dau; no; Dagmar, Sheridan, Mont; yes; none
845   "   Erma; f; 6 1-14-26; ¼+; s; dau; no; Dagmar, Sheridan, Mont; yes; none

846 Bruce, Alfred; m; 30; ¼+; m; Head A318; yes; yes; Id.209c, Al.G-08375
847   "   Elizabeth (Smith); f; 29; ¼+; m; wife A319; yes; yes; Id.924b, Al.G-280
848   "   Joseph A; m; 9 8-27-22; ¼+; s; son A320; yes; yes; none
849   "   Ernest M; m; 6 11-15-25; ¼+; s; son A321; yes; yes; none
850   "   Raymond; m; 3 6-27-28; ¼+; s; son A322; yes; yes; none
851   "   Lawrence; m; 1 8-7-30; ¼+; s; son A323; yes; yes; none
852   "   Irene; f; 4/12 11-30-31; ¼+; s; dau; yes; yes; none

853 Bruce, Frederick; m; 43; ¼+; s; Head B470; no; Unknown; no; Id.442f, Al.G-04723

854 Bruce, Joseph; m; 83; ¼+; m; Head B471; no; Froid, Sheridan, Mont; no; Id.205,
                                                                    Al.G-04721
855   "   Rosalie (Ducept); f; 72; ¼+; m; wife B472; no; Froid, Sheridan, Mont; no;
                                        Id.205a, Al.G-04722

856 Bruce, Joseph; m; 28; ¼+; m; Head A324; yes; yes; Id.209d, Al.G-08396
857   "   Matilda (Smith); f; 27; ¼+; m; wife A325; yes; yes; Id.924c, Al.G-219
858   "   Cecile; f; 7 9-5-24; ¼+; s; dau A326; yes; yes; none
859   "   Edna; f; 4 12-13-27; ¼+; s; dau A327; yes; yes; none
860   "   William; m; 2 1-13-30; ¼+; s; son A328; yes; yes; none

NE Bruce, Louis;   Head
861   "   St.Ann (Morin); f; 43; ¼+; m; wife B473; no; Bottineau, Bottineau, ND;
                                        no; Id.210a, Al.GF-11
862   "   Joseph; m; 18; ¼+; s; son B474; no; Bottineau, Bottineau, ND; no;
                                        Id.210b, Al. none
863   "   Emily; f; 16 4-12-15; ¼+; s; dau B475; no; Bottineau, Bottineau, ND; no;
                                        Id.210c
864   "   Alexander; m; 15 8-19-16; ¼+; s; son B476; no; Bottineau, Bottineau, ND;
                                        no; Id.210d
865   "   Louis; m; 14 12-29-17; ¼+; s; son B477; no; Bottineau, Bottineau, ND; no;
                                        Id.210e
866   "   George; m; 12 1-18-20; ¼+; s; son B478; no; Bottineau, Bottineau, ND; no;
                                        Id.210f

867 Bruce, Robert; m; 40; ¼+; m; Head B482; yes; no; Id.206, Al.G-04723
NE   "   Dorothy (Neil);   wife

Turtle Mountain Reservation
1932 Census Roll

Key: Number; Surname, Given; Sex; Age at Last Birthday, Birthdate (if given); Tribe (Chippewa, unless stated otherwise); Degree of Blood; Marital Status; Relationship to Head of Family, Last Year Census Number; At Jurisdiction Where Enrolled (Yes/No); Elsewhere - Post Office, County, State; Ward (Yes/No); Allotment [Al.], Annuity [An.] and/or Identification [Id.] Numbers

Died Bruce, Virginia; B480 (Died 11-21-31)

868 Brunnell, Edward; m; 25; ¼+; m; Head A329; yes; yes; Id.217a, Al.W-31
869 " Alice (Grant); f; 27; ¼+; m; wife A330; yes; yes; Id.475d, Al.G-0111
870 " Corinne; f; 1 8-1-30; ¼+; s; dau A331; yes; yes; none

871 Brunnell, Ernest; m; 41; ¼+; m; Head A332; yes; no; Id.213, Al.GF-158
872 " Betsey (Delorme); f; 39; ¼+; m; wife A333; yes; yes; Id.213a, Al.G-08095
873 " William P; m; 18; ¼+; s; son A334; yes; yes; Id.213b
874 " Rachel; f; 16 4-12-15; ¼+; s; dau A335; yes; yes; Id.213c
875 " Cecilia; f; 15 10-18-16; ¼+; s; dau A336; yes; yes; Id.213d
876 " Evelyn; f; 12 1-3-20; ¼+; s; dau A337; yes; yes; Id.213e
877 " Stella; f; 10 3-17-22; ¼+; s; dau A338; yes; yes; Id.213f
878 " Marie; f; 8 8-20-23; ¼+; s; dau A339; yes; yes; Id.213g
879 " Theresa; f; 3 6-12-23; ¼+; s; dau A340; yes; yes; Id.213h
880 " Peter R; m; 3 2-12-29; ¼+; s; son A341; yes; yes; none

881 Brunnell, Frederick; m; 30; ¼+; m; Head A342; yes; no; Id.217b, Al.M-376
882 " Virginia (Patnaud); f; 30; ¼+; m; wife A343; yes; yes; Id.803c, Al.G-0474
883 " Beulah; f; 4 10-12-27; ¼+; s; dau A344; yes; yes; none
884 " Bernealia; f; 1 3-28-31; ¼+; s; dau; yes; yes; none

885 Brunnell, John, Jr; m; 63; ¼+; m; Head A345; yes; yes; Id.216, Al.DL-02423
Died " Claudia (Thomas); A346 (Died 12-1-31)
886 " Delia C; f; 21; ¼+; s; dau A347; yes; yes; Id.217f
887 " Alexander; m; 18; ¼+; s; son A348; yes; yes; Id.217g
888 " (Cook) John Faye; m; 3 7-23-28; ¼+; s; grandson A349; yes; (Illeg. of Delia) yes; none
889 Brunnell, Julia; f; 84; ¼+; wd; Head A350; yes; yes; Id.211a, Al.R-50
890 " (Paul) Barton; m; 13 2-17-19; ¼+; s; adpt son A351; yes; yes; Id.811c

891 Brunnell, Louis; m; 46; ¼+; m; Head A352; yes; no; Id.215, Al.R-51
892 " Mary (Turcott); f; 43; ¼+; m; wife A353; yes; no; Id.215a, Al.W-27
893 " Ernest Wm; m; 16 10-15-15; ¼+; s; son A355; yes; no; Id.215f
894 " Celina; f; 14 1-18-18; ¼+; s; dau A356; yes; no; Id.215g
895 " Caroline; f; 12 12-1-19; ¼+; s; dau A357; yes; no; Id.215h
896 " John; m; 10 2-24-22; ¼+; s; son A358; yes; no; Id.215i
897 " Roger; m; 7 5-8-24; ¼+; s; son A359; yes; no; Id.215j
898 " Martha; f; 5 8-24-26; ¼+; s; dau A360; yes; no; Id.none
899 " Edna; f; 3 10-29-28; ¼+; s; dau A361; yes; no; none
900 " Theresa; f; 1 11-28-30; 1;4; s; dau; yes; no; none

Turtle Mountain Reservation
1932 Census Roll

Key: Number; Surname, Given; Sex; Age at Last Birthday, Birthdate (if given); Tribe (Chippewa, unless stated otherwise); Degree of Blood; Marital Status; Relationship to Head of Family, Last Year Census Number; At Jurisdiction Where Enrolled (Yes/No); Elsewhere - Post Office, County, State; Ward (Yes/No); Allotment [Al.], Annuity [An.] and/or Identification [Id.] Numbers

901 Brunnell, Patrice; m; 35; ¼+; m; Head A363; yes; no; Id.212, Al.GF159
902 " Mary Jane (Perronteau); f; 32; ¼+; m; wife A364; yes; yes; Id.832b, Al.G0408
903 " Patrick; m; 14 3-16-18; ¼+; s; son A365; yes; yes; Id.212b
904 " Marie; f; 10 4-4-21; ¼+; s; dau A366; yes; yes; Id.212c
905 " Amanda; f; 9 12-22-22; ¼+; s; dau A367; yes; yes; Id.212d
906 " Ellen; f; 6 3-11-25; ¼+; s; dau A368; yes; yes; Id.212e
907 " Phillip; m; 1 5-3-30; ¼+; s; son A369; yes; yes; Id.212f

908 Brunnell, Peter; m; 50; ¼+; m; Head A370; yes; no; Id.214, Al.GF160
Dead " Louise (Grant); A371 (Died 11-27-26)
909 " Frank; m; 11 12-19-20; ¼+; s; son A372; yes; no; Id.214c
910 " Gloria; f; 10 3-11-22; ¼+; s; dau A373; yes; no; Id.214d
911 " Paul; m; 7 9-4-24; ¼+; s; son A374; yes; no; Id.214e

NE Brunnell, Phillip; m; Head B483
912 " Adele (Perronteau); f; 27; ¼+; m; wife A1800; yes; yes; Id.832d, Al.G-0406

913 Brunnell, Robert; m; 28; ¼+; m; Head A375; yes; yes; Id.217c, Al.M-328
914 " Louise (Peltier); f; 26; ¼+; m; wife A376; yes; yes; Id.820d, Al.H-010443
915 " Marie; f; 8 9-20-23; ¼+; s; dau A377; yes; yes; none
916 " Jessica; f; 6; ¼+; s; dau A378; yes; yes; none
917 " Louise; f; 2 6-4-29; ¼+; s; dau A379; yes; yes; none

NE Bursness, Oscar; Head
918 " Rosalind (Morin); f; 27; ¼+; m; wife B484; no; Medicine Lake, Sheridan, Mont; yes; Id.744d, Al.G-473
Dead " Bernice; B485 (Died 11-3-30)
919 " Gladys C; f; 1 10-26-30; ¼+; s; dau B486; no; Medicine Lake, Sheridan, Mont; yes; none

920 Cadott, Peter; m; 59; ¼+; m; Head B487; no; Dunseith, Rolette, ND; no; Id.219, Al.WHE
NE " Harriet; wife (Maiden name is not known)
921 " Veronica; f; 28; ¼+; s; dau B488; no; Dunseith, Rolette, ND; no; none
922 " Joseph; m; 27; ¼+; s; son B489; no; Dunseith, Rolette, ND; no; none
923 " Catherine; f; 25; ¼+; s; dau B490; no; Dunseith, Rolette, ND; no; none
924 " John C; m; 23; ¼+; s; son B491; no; Dunseith, Rolette, ND; no; none
925 " William; m; 21; ¼+; s; son B492; no; Dunseith, Rolette, ND; no; none

926 Cadott, Pierre; m; 89; ¼+; wd; Head B493; no; Dunseith, Rolette, ND; no; Id. 218

Turtle Mountain Reservation
1932 Census Roll

Key: Number; Surname, Given; Sex; Age at Last Birthday, Birthdate (if given); Tribe (Chippewa, unless stated otherwise); Degree of Blood; Marital Status; Relationship to Head of Family, Last Year Census Number; At Jurisdiction Where Enrolled (Yes/No); Elsewhere - Post Office, County, State; Ward (Yes/No); Allotment [Al.], Annuity [An.] and/or Identification [Id.] Numbers

927 Caldwell, Rachel (Belgarde); f; 48; ¼+; wd; Head B494; no; Strool, Perkins, SD; yes; Id.220a, Al.LEM-01784
929   "   Charles; m; 22; ¼+; s; son B496; no; Strool, Perkins, SD; yes; Al.LEM024758
930   "   Eugene; m; 20; ¼+; s; son B497; no; Strool, Perkins, SD; yes; Id.220d
931   "   Nellie; f; 18; ¼+; s; dau B498; no; Strool, Perkins, SD; yes; Id.220e
932   "   Freda; f; 15; ¼+; s; dau B499; no; Strool, Perkins, SD; yes; Id.220f
933   "   Rita; f; 11; ¼+; s; dau B500; no; Strool, Perkins, SD; yes; Id.220g
934   "   Nina; f; 8; ¼+; s; dau B501; no; Strool, Perkins, SD; yes; Id.220h

NE Cannery, Thomas;   Head   (Divorced from wife who is #440 on this roll)
935   "   John E; m; 16 6-23-15; ¼+; s; son B504; no; Semans, Sask, Canada; no; Id.221a
936   "   Rebecca; f; 13 10-14-18; ¼+; s; dau B505; no; Semans, Sask, Canada; no; none
937   "   Lucille; f; 12 3-1-20; ¼+; s; dau B507; no; Semans, Sask, Canada; no; none
938   "   William; m; 9 10-10-22; ¼+; s; son B506; no; Semans, Sask, Canada; no; none

939 Caplette, Elvina; f; 18 8-10-13; ¼+; s; alone A380; yes; yes; Id.224c, Al.H-024526

940 Caplette, Rose (Lacerte); f; 66; ¼+; wd; Head B508; no; Devils Lake, Ramsey, ND; no; Id.223a, Al.G-343

NE Cardigan, Walter;   Head
941   "   Irene (Martell); f; 19; ¼+; m; wife B722; no; Kansas City, Wyandotte, Kan; yes; Id.703b, Al.H-030389

NE Caribou, James;   Head
942   "   Agnes (Laverdure); f; 25; ¼+; m; wife B509; no; Cando, Towner, ND; yes; Id.647c, Al.G-07870
943   "   Edward H; m; 8 10-17-23; ¼+; s; son B510; no; Cando, Towner, ND; yes; none
944   "   Peggy; f; 7 3-20-25; ¼+; s; dau; no; Cando, Towner, ND; yes; none

NE Carmer, William;   Head
945   "   Nora (Gunderson); f; 29; ¼+; m; wife B1049; no; St.Paul, Ramsey, Minn; no; Id.462b
946   "   David; m; 11 6-9-20; ¼+; s; son ------; no; St.Paul, Ramsey, Minn; no; none
947   "   Vernon; m; 9 4-12-22; ¼+; s; son ------; no; St.Paul, Ramsey, Minn; no; none
948   "   Sidney; m; 8 2-19-24; ¼+; s; son -----; no; St.Paul, Ramsey, Minn; no; none
949   "   Lewis; m; 5 12-20-26; ¼+; s; son -----; no; St.Paul, Ramsey, Minn; no; none

Turtle Mountain Reservation
1932 Census Roll

Key: Number; Surname, Given; Sex; Age at Last Birthday, Birthdate (if given); Tribe (Chippewa, unless stated otherwise); Degree of Blood; Marital Status; Relationship to Head of Family; Last Year Census Number; At Jurisdiction Where Enrolled (Yes/No); Elsewhere - Post Office, County, State; Ward (Yes/No); Allotment [Al.], Annuity [An.] and/or Identification [Id.] Numbers

NE Carter, J E;   Head
950   "   Virginia (Bercier); f; ¼+; m; wife B511; no; Devils Lake, Ramsey, ND; yes; Id.195c, Al.G-0846
951   "   Violet; f; 10 2-14-22; ¼+; s; dau B513; no; Devils Lake, Ramsey, ND; yes; none
952   "   John; m; 8 2-8-24; ¼+; s; son ----; no; Devils Lake, Ramsey, ND; yes; none
953   "   Frances; f; 3; ¼+; s; dau -----; no; Devils Lake, Ramsey, ND; yes; none
Dead " (Beson) Mary;   B512   (Died Aug. 1919)

NE Cartnell, Harry;   Head
954   "   Mary (Boyer); f; 24; ¼+; m; wife B514; no; Sidney, Richland, Mont; no; Id.1185g, Al.G-07902
955   "   Marion B; f; 4/12 11-5-31; ¼+; s; dau ----; no; Sidney, Richland, Mont; no; none

NE Cartwright, Bert;   Head
956   "   Harriet (Desjarlais); f; 29; ¼+; m; wife B515; no; St.John, Rolette, ND; yes; Id.316b, Al.W-02926
957   "   Irene May; f; 1 3-10-31; ¼+; s; dau B516; no; St.John, Rolette, ND; yes; none

NE Cecil, Donald;   Head
958   "   Jessie (Caldwell); f; 24; ¼+; m; wife B495; no; Rapid City, Pennington, SD; yes; Id.220b, Al.LEM017853

NE Cedrilly, Ernest;   Head
959   "   Mary (Latrail); f; 34; ¼+; m; wife B517; no; Unknown; no; Id.1003a, Al.H-012557

NE Challender, Arthur M;   Head
960   "   Angeline (Lafrombois); f; 21; ¼+; m; wife B1376; no; Devils Lake, Ramsey, ND; yes; Id.592h, Al.H-012567

961 Champagne, Charles; m; 48; ¼+; m; Head A381; yes; no; Id.233, Al.G-08384
962   "   Josephine (Renville.Poitra); f; 65; ¼+; m; wife A382; yes; no; Id.233a, Al.G-082

963 Champagne, John M; m; 58; ¼+; m; Head B519; no; Unknown; no; Id.227, Al.G554
964   "   Josephine (Parisien); f; 52; ¼+; m; wife B520; no; Unknown; Id.227a, Al.G-554

965 Champagne, J B; m; 74; ¼+; m; Head A389; yes; yes; Id.230, Al.R-60
966   "   Adele (Poitra); f; 71; ¼+; m; wife A390; yes; no; Id. 230a
967 " (Davis) Elise; f; 16 6-18-15; ¼+; s; adpt dau A391; yes; yes; Id.262b

Turtle Mountain Reservation
1932 Census Roll

Key: Number; Surname, Given; Sex; Age at Last Birthday, Birthdate (if given); Tribe (Chippewa, unless stated otherwise); Degree of Blood; Marital Status; Relationship to Head of Family, Last Year Census Number; At Jurisdiction Where Enrolled (Yes/No); Elsewhere - Post Office, County, State; Ward (Yes/No); Allotment [Al.], Annuity [An.] and/or Identification [Id.] Numbers

968 Champagne, Louis; m; 32; ¼+; m; Head A397; yes; yes; Id.234c, Al.G-277
969   "   Victoria (Vallie); f; 29; ¼+; m; wife A384; yes; yes; Id.975b, Al.GF-218
970   "   Rita; f; 6 10-9-25; ¼+; s; dau A385; yes; yes; none
971   "   Helen; f; 5 1-8-27; ¼+; s; dau A386; yes; yes; none
972   "   Joseph P; m; 3 9-5-28; ¼+; s; dau A387; yes; yes; none
973   "   Frank; m; 2 1-29-30; ¼+; s; son A388; yes; yes; none

974 Champagne, Louis N; m; 38; ¼+; m; Head A392; yes; Id. 231
975   "   Catherine (Poitra); f; 32; ¼+; m; wife A393; yes; yes; Id. 231a, Al.G-016583
976   "   Louise; f; 8 8-17-23; ¼+; s; dau A394; yes; yes; none
977   "   Willard; m; 6 10-30-25; ¼+; s; son A395; yes; yes; none

978 Champagne, Marie (Poitra); f; 56; ¼+; wd; Head B521; no; Unknown; yes;
                                                                              Id.225a, Al.R-62

979 Champagne, Mary P; f; 23; ¼+; s; Head B522; no; Glasgow, Valley, Mont; yes;
                                                                         Id.232d, Al.L-014446
980   "   Joseph; m; 21; ¼+; s; bro B523; no; Glasgow, Valley, Mont; yes;
                                                                         Id.232e, Al.G-016816

981 Champagne, Mary Rose (Poitra); f; 56; ¼+; wd; Head A396; yes; yes; Id.234a,
                                                                                           Al.G-276
982   "   John B T; m; 26; ¼+; s; son A398; yes; yes; Id.234d, Al.G-403
983   "   Charles R; m; 21; ¼+; s; son A399; yes; yes; Id.234f
984   "   Collin A; m; 18; ¼+; s; son A400; yes; yes; Id.234g
985   "   Josephine; f; 16; ¼+; s; dau A401; yes; yes; Id.234h
986   "   Mary F; f; 12; ¼+; s; dau A402; yes; yes; Id.234i
No Such   Louis   A403
Person

987 Champagne, St.Pierre; m; 32; ¼+; wd; Head B524; no; Unknown; yes; Id.226b
                                                                            Al.G-283

988 Champagne, Wm. Jerome; m; 40; ¼+; m; Head A404; yes; no; Id.229, Al.F-70
989   "   Pauline (Bonneau); f; 38; ¼+; m; wife A405; yes; no; Id.229a, Al.G-08423
990   "   Oscar; m; 16 8-29-16; ¼+; s; son A406; yes; no; Id.229b
991   "   Fred; m; 13 4-20-18; ¼+; s; son A407; yes; no; Id.229c
992   "   Ernest; m; 13 1-24-19; ¼+; s; son; yes; no; Id.229d
993   "   Vivian; f; 10 1-21-22; ¼+; s; dau A408; yes; no; Id.229e
994   "   Edna; f; 6; ¼+; s; dau A409; yes; no; Id.229f
995   "   Gilbert; m; 3; ¼+; s; son A410; yes; no; Id.229g

Turtle Mountain Reservation
1932 Census Roll

Key: Number; Surname, Given; Sex; Age at Last Birthday, Birthdate (if given); Tribe (Chippewa, unless stated otherwise); Degree of Blood; Marital Status; Relationship to Head of Family, Last Year Census Number; At Jurisdiction Where Enrolled (Yes/No); Elsewhere - Post Office, County, State; Ward (Yes/No); Allotment [Al.], Annuity [An.] and/or Identification [Id.] Numbers

996 Charbonneau, Antoine; m; 78; ¼+; m; Head B518; no; Unknown; no; Id.236, Al.G-038625
NE " Mary (Bailey); wife
NE " Rosina step dau

997 Charbonneau, Robert; m; 68; ¼+; m; Head B525; no; Ft.Totten, Benson, ND; no; Id.235, Al.G-0306
NE " Mary (Bouvier); wife
998 " Anthony; m; 22; ¼+; s; son B526; no; Ft.Totten, Benson, ND; yes; Id.235c, Al.H-012659
999 " Clarence; m; 20; ¼+; s; son B527; no; Ft.Totten, Benson, ND; no; Id.235d
1000 " Elise C; f; 17 8-19-14; ¼+; s; dau B528; no; Ft.Totten, Benson, ND; no; Id.235g
1001 " Rose Agnes; f; 14 2-1-18; ¼+; s; dau B529; no; Ft.Totten, Benson, ND; no; Id. 235e
1002 " Stephen; m; 13; ¼+; s; son B530; no; Ft.Totten, Benson, ND; no; Id.none
1003 " Frank L; m; 23; ¼+; s; son B531; no; Ft.Totten, Benson, ND; no; Id.none
1004 " Charlie G; m; 10; ¼+; s; son B532; no; Ft.Totten, Benson, ND; no; Id.none
NE Charboyes; Head
1005 " Ellen (Latraille); f; 28; ¼+; m; wife B533; no; Minot, Ward, ND; yes; Id.624c, Al.H-012559

1006 Charette, Fabian; m; 19 12-12-12; ¼+; s; Head B411; yes; yes; Id.237d, Al.H-016388
1007 " Mary Rose; f; 18 2-28-14; ¼+; s; sis A412; yes; no; Id.237e
1008 " Joseph; m; 17 2-6-15; ¼+; s; bro A413; yes; no; Id.237f
1009 " Edna M; f; 14 6-30-17; ¼+; s; sis A414; yes; no; Id.237g

1010 Charette, Peter Wm; m; 23; ¼+; m; Head B537; no; Medicine Lake, Sheridan, Mont; yes; Id.239d, Al.G012799
NE " Phyllis (Wormbecker); wife
1011 " George; m; 3 10-28-28; ¼+; s; son ----; no; Medicine Lake, Sheridan, Mont; yes; none
1012 " Eugene; m; 7/12 7-3-31; ¼+; s; son ----; no; Medicine Lake, Sheridan, Mont; yes; none

1013 Charette, Simeon; m; 63; ¼+; m; Head A417; yes; yes; Id.238, Al.R64
1014 " Mary (Morin); f; 54; ¼+; m; wife A418; yes; no; Id.238a, Al.M245
1015 " Adele; f; 29; ¼+; s; dau A419; yes; yes; Id.238c, Al.M236
1016 " Philbert; m; 27; ¼+; s; son A420; yes; yes; Id.238d, Al.G489
1017 " Alexander; m; 26; ¼+; s; son A421; yes; yes; Id.428e, Al.G490
1018 " Ernest; m; 24; ¼+; s; son A422; yes; yes; Id.428f, Al.H010513

Turtle Mountain Reservation
1932 Census Roll

Key: Number; Surname, Given; Sex; Age at Last Birthday, Birthdate (if given); Tribe (Chippewa, unless stated otherwise); Degree of Blood; Marital Status; Relationship to Head of Family, Last Year Census Number; At Jurisdiction Where Enrolled (Yes/No); Elsewhere - Post Office, County, State; Ward (Yes/No); Allotment [Al.], Annuity [An.] and/or Identification [Id.] Numbers

1019 Charette, (cont), Caroline; f; 22; ¼+; s; dau A423; yes; yes; Id.238g, Al.H013025
1020 " John; m; 20; ¼+; s; son A424; yes; yes; Id.238b. Al.H023027
1021 " Simeon; m; 18; ¼+; s; son A425; yes; yes; Id.238i, Al.G036598
1022 " Michael; m; 15; ¼+; s; son A426; yes; yes; Id.238j

1023 Charette, Telesphore; m; 27 3-16-05; ¼+; m; Head A415; yes; yes; Id.237b, Al.G-182
1024 " Delia (Morin); f; 22; ¼+; m; wife A416; yes; yes; Id.770d, Al.H013053

NE Charette, William;   Head
1025 " St.Ann (Lagimodiere); f; 43; ¼+; m; wife B534; no; Medicine Lake, Sheridan, Mont; no; Id.239a, Al.GF-76
1026 " Louis; m; 27; ¼+; s; son B535; no; Medicine Lake, Sheridan, Mont; yes; Id.239b, Al.G-59
1027 " Thomas; m; 25; ¼+; s; son B536; no; Medicine Lake, Sheridan, Mont; yes; Id.239c, Al.G-60

NE Chargee, Emmet;   Head
1028 " Dora (Plante); f; 29; ¼+; m; wife B538; no; St.Paul, Ramsey, Minn; yes; Id.840d, Al.G-61

NE Charles, Jesse
1029 " Antoinette (Plante); f; 31; ¼+; wd; Head B2073; no; St.Paul, Ramsey, Minn; yes; Id.840b, Al.G-69
1030 " Raymond V; m; 7 9-29-24; ¼+; s; son; no; St.Paul, Ramsey, Minn; yes; none

NE Christenson, Walter;   Head
1031 " (Peltier) Albert; m; 16; ¼+; s; adpt son B539; no; Unknown; yes; Id.825, Al.H-013054

NE Christenson;   Head
1032 " Rose (Lambert); f; 34; ¼+; m; wife B540; no; Unknown; no; Id.596b. Al.M-177

NE Constance, Clarence;   Head
1033 " Mary Ann (Sayers); f; 35; ¼+; m; wife B541; no; Independence, Jackson, Mo; yes; Id.909b, Al.G-0713
1034 " Ruth; f; 11 12-22-22; ¼+; s; dau -----; no; Independence, Jackson, Mo; yes; none
1035 " Lloyd; m; 7 8-1-24; ¼+; s; son -----; no; Independence, Jackson, Mo; yes; none
1036 " Dean; m; 6 3-24-26; ¼+; s; son ------; no; Independence, Jackson, Mo; yes; none
1037 " Edward; m; 4 8-23-27; ¼+; s; son -----; no; Independence, Jackson, Mo; yes; none

Turtle Mountain Reservation
1932 Census Roll

Key: Number; Surname, Given; Sex; Age at Last Birthday, Birthdate (if given); Tribe (Chippewa, unless stated otherwise); Degree of Blood; Marital Status; Relationship to Head of Family, Last Year Census Number; At Jurisdiction Where Enrolled (Yes/No); Elsewhere - Post Office, County, State; Ward (Yes/No); Allotment [Al.], Annuity [An.] and/or Identification [Id.] Numbers

1038 Constance(cont), Albert; m; 2 5-12-29; ¼+; s; son ------; no; Independence, Jackson, Mo; yes; none

NE Cotterell, Carl Jay; Head
1039 " Flora (Bradford.Faine); f; 36; ¼+; m; wife B817; no; Kalispell, Flathead, Mont; yes; Id.1188f, Al.H-010426
Died " (Faine) Ella; B818 (Died 8-3-1921)
1040 " (Faine) Irene; f; 10 11-26-22; ¼+; s; step dau B819; no; Kalispell, Flathead, Mont; yes; none
1041 " (Faine) Joseph; m; 7 4-23-24; ¼+; s; stepson -------; no; Kalispell, Flathead, Mont; yes; none
1042 " Carl R; m; 2 1-10-30; ¼+; s; son ------; no; Kalispell, Flathead, Mont; yes; none
1043 " Violet; f; 3/12 11-6-31; ¼+; s; dau ------; no; Kalispell, Flathead, Mont; yes; none

NE Counts, Thomas; Head
1044 " Helen (McCloud); f; 24 10-28-07; ¼+; m; wife B1748; no; Dunseith, Rolette, ND; no; Id.722b
1045 " Thomas; m; 5 3-30-27; ¼+; s; son ------; no; Dunseith, Rolette, ND; no; none
1046 " Mary L; f; 3 8-25-28; ¼+; s; dau ------; no; Dunseith, Rolette, ND; no; none
1047 " Lloyd; m; 2 1-30-30; ¼+; s; son ------; no; Dunseith, Rolette, ND; no; none
1048 " Roy; m; 1 2-28-31; ¼+; s; son ------; no; Dunseith, Rolette, ND; no; none

NE Crawford, R J; Head
1049 " Lucille (LeCompt); f; 25 12-10-06; ¼+; m; wife B1576; no; Portland, Multonmah[sic], Ore; yes; Id.655d, Al.G-558

1050 Cree, Charles; m; 38; F; m; Head B542; no; Dunseith, Rolette, ND; yes; Id.9½a, Al.G-558
1051 " Rose (St.Claire); f; 25; ¼+; m; wife B543; no; Dunseith, Rolette, ND; yes; Id.935g, Al.H-030467
1052 " Celia; f; 8; ¼+; s; dau B544; no; Dinseith[sic], Rolette, ND; yes; none

1053 Cree, Charles; m; 57; F; m; Head B545; no; Dunseith, Rolette, ND; yes; Id.43, Al.DL-46
NE " Celia (Allery); wife
1054 " Israel; m; 21; ¼+; s; son B546; no; Dunseith, Rolette, ND; yes; Id.43d, Al.H-024469
1055 " Francis; m; 12; ¼+; s; son B547; no; Dunseith, Rolette, ND; yes; none
1056 " Louis; m; 9 11-8-22; ¼+; s; son B548; no; Dunseith, Rolette, ND; yes; none
1057 " Rosina; f; 4 2-24-28; ¼+; s; dau B549; no; Dunseith, Rolette, ND; yes; none
1058 " Jerome; m; 1 9-24-40; ¼+; s; son; no; Dunseith, Rolette, ND; yes; none

Turtle Mountain Reservation
1932 Census Roll

Key: Number; Surname, Given; Sex; Age at Last Birthday, Birthdate (if given); Tribe (Chippewa, unless stated otherwise); Degree of Blood; Marital Status; Relationship to Head of Family, Last Year Census Number; At Jurisdiction Where Enrolled (Yes/No); Elsewhere - Post Office, County, State; Ward (Yes/No); Allotment [Al.], Annuity [An.] and/or Identification [Id.] Numbers

1059 Cree, Thomas; m; 33; F; m; Head B550; no; Dunseith, Rolette, ND; yes; Id.43b, Al.H-012574
Died   Julia;   B551   (Died May 1929)
1060   "   Catherine (Bonnaup); f; 30; F; m; wife; no; Dunseith, Rolette, ND; yes; Id.9c
1061   "   Laura; f; 7 5-18-24; F; s; dau B552; no; Dunseith, Rolette, ND; yes; none
1062   "   Nice Sounding; f; 2; F; s; dau B553; no; Dunseith, Rolette, ND; yes; none

NE Crissler, Allen;   wd; Head
1063   "   Elvina; f; 29 3-11-03; ¼+; s; dau B554; no; St.John, Rolette, ND; yes; Id.242b, Al.G-065
1064   "   Alfred Wm; m; 27 3-32-05; ¼+; s; son B555; no; St.John, Rolette, ND; yes; Id.242c, Al.G-066
1065   "   Elsie; f; 20 1-14-12; ¼+; s; dau B557; no; St.John, Rolette, ND; no; none
1066   "   Charles; m; 17 1-2-15; ¼+; s; son B558; no; St.John, Rolette, ND; no; none

NE Crissler, Cary;   Head
1067   "   Eliza (Lafournais); f; 59 10-28-72; ¼+; m; wife B559; no; Scandinavia, Manitoba, Can; yes; Ifd.241a, Al.G-068
1068   "   Moses; m; 29 11-6-02; ¼+; s; son B560; no; Scandinavia, Manitoba, Can; yes; Id.241b, Al.G069
1069   "   Eva; f; 27 10-20-04; ¼+; s; dau B561; no; Scandinavia, Manitoba, Can; yes; Id.241c, Al.G070
1070   "   Emily; f; 25 12-21-06; ¼+; s; dau B562; no; Scandinavia, Manitoba, Can; yes; Id.241c, Al.G071
1071   "   Mary; f; 24 9-14-07; ¼+; s; dau B563; no; Scandinavia, Manitoba, Can; yes; Id.241d, Al.G067
1072   "   Elise; f; 20 2-21-12; ¼+; s; dau B565; no; Scandinavia, Manitoba, Can; yes; Id.241f
1073   "   Frederick; m; 18 10-20-13; ¼+; s; son B566; no; Scandinavia, Manitoba, Can; yes; Id.241i

1074 Crissler, Claude; m; 23; ¼+; m; Head B556; no; St.John, Rolette, ND; yes; Id.242d, Al.H030247
1075   "   Ida (Azure); f; 18 11-11-13; ¼+; m; wife A119; no; St.John, Rolette, ND; yes; Id.126d, Al.H030247

NE Croteau;   Head
1076   "   Lillian (LeBrun); f; 33; ¼+; m; wife A427; yes; yes; Id.653c, Al.M-220
1077   "   Leo; m; 5; -¼+; s; son A428; yes; yes; none
1078   "   Marie L; f; 11/12 5-14-31; -¼+; s; dau; yes; yes; none

NE Dahlstrom, Mangus H;   Head
1079   "   Virginia (Jerome); f; 58; ¼+; m; wife A429; yes; no; Id.244a, Al.DL-5
1080   "   Marie; f; 16 3-2-16; ¼+; s; dau A430; yes; no; none

Turtle Mountain Reservation
1932 Census Roll

Key: Number; Surname, Given; Sex; Age at Last Birthday, Birthdate (if given); Tribe (Chippewa, unless stated otherwise); Degree of Blood; Marital Status; Relationship to Head of Family; Last Year Census Number; At Jurisdiction Where Enrolled (Yes/No); Elsewhere - Post Office, County, State; Ward (Yes/No); Allotment [Al.], Annuity [An.] and/or Identification [Id.] Numbers

1081 Daignault, Gregory; m; 50; ¼+; m; Head B567; no; St.John, Rolette, ND; no; Id.245, Al.H-058856
NE   "   Genevieve (Allery);   wife
1082   "   John A; m; 23; ¼+; s; son B568; no; St.John, Rolette, ND; no; Id.245b
1083   "   Mary J; f; 18; ¼+; s; dau B569; no; St.John, Rolette, ND; no; Id.245c
1084   "   Joseph; m; 12; ¼+; s; son B570; no; St.John, Rolette, ND; no; none
1085   "   George; m; 6 8-8-25; ¼+; s; son B571; no; St.John, Rolette, ND; no; none

1086 Daignault, John B; m; 49; ¼+; s; Head B572; no; St.John, Rolette, ND; yes; Id.246, Al.H-030356

1087 Dauphinais, Antoine; m; 45; ¼+; s; Head B573; no; Thorne, Rolette, ND; Id.254, Al.G-186

1088 Dauphinais, David; m; 57; ¼+; m; Head A431; yes; yes; Id. 250, Al.R-67
NE   "   Mary (Martin);   wife
1089   "   Roy J; m; 17; ¼+; s; son A433; yes; yes; Id.250f
1090   "   Fred; m; 15; ¼+; s; son A434; yes; yes; Id.250g
1091   "   Louis; m; 13; ¼+; s; son A435; yes; yes; Id.250h
1092   "   Ethel; f; 11; ¼+; s; dau A436; yes; yes; Id.250i
1093   "   Hyles E; m; 8 12-30-23; ¼+; s; son A437; yes; yes; Id.250j
1094   "   Peter; m; 5 2-10-27; ¼+; s; son A438; yes; yes; Id.250k

1095 Dauphinais, Ezear; m; 47; ¼+; s; Head B574; no; Devils Lake, Ramsey, ND; no; Id.253, Al.G-185

1096 Dauphinais, John B; m; 51; ¼+; wd; Head A439; yes; yes; Id.247, Al.H-032212

1097 Dauphinais, Madeline; f; 79; ¼+; wd; Head B575; no; Canton (Insane Asylum), Lincoln, SD; yes; Id.252a, Al.DL-37

651 Dauphinais, Norman; m; 54; ¼+; s; Head A440; yes; no; Id.249, Al.R-69

1098 Davis, Adele (Laverdure); f; 46; ¼+; wd; Head A441; yes; no; Id.258a, Al.G-0338
1099   "   Peter; m; 24; ¼+; s; son A442; yes; yes; Id.258c
1100   "   John P; m; 22; ¼+; s; son A443; yes; yes; Id.258d
1101   "   Mary D; f; 20; ¼+; s; dau A444; yes; yes; Id.258e
Dead   "   Ernestine;   A445   (Died Jan. 27, 1922([sic])
1102   "   William; m; 15; ¼+; s; son A446; yes; yes; Id.258g
1103   "   Emilda; f; 13 7-31-18; ¼+; s; dau A447; yes; yes; Id.258i
1104   "   Joseph; m; 12; ¼+; s; son A448; yes; yes; Id.258h
1105   "   Marie; f; 9 2-21-23; ¼+; s; dau A449; yes; yes; Id.258j
Dead   "   Romeo;   A450;   (Died Apr. 17, 1929)
Dead   "   Delima; f;   A451   (Died May 18, 1929)

Turtle Mountain Reservation
1932 Census Roll

Key: Number; Surname, Given; Sex; Age at Last Birthday, Birthdate (if given); Tribe (Chippewa, unless stated otherwise); Degree of Blood; Marital Status; Relationship to Head of Family, Last Year Census Number; At Jurisdiction Where Enrolled (Yes/No); Elsewhere - Post Office, County, State; Ward (Yes/No); Allotment [Al.], Annuity [An.] and/or Identification [Id.] Numbers

1106 Davis(cont), Gilbert; m; 3 3-26-29; ¼+; s; son A452; yes; yes; Id.258m

1107 Davis, Alexander; m; 22; ¼+; m; Head A481; yes; no; Id.261d
1108   "   Elizabeth (Gourneau); f; ¼+; m; wife A913; yes; yes; Id.432h

1109 Davis, Edward; m; 27; ¼+; m; Head A453; yes; yes; Id.266e, Al.G-212
1110   "   Mary E (Malaterre); f; 19; ¼+; m; wife A454; yes; yes; Id.683b, Al.H-024636

1111 Davis, Emerize (Lavallie); f; 69; ¼+; wd; Head A455; yes; no; Id.260a, Al.G-600
1112   "   Paul; m; 22; ¼+; s; adpt son A456; yes; no; Id.260b

1113 Davis, Francois; m; 29; ¼+; m; Head B576; no; Sidney, Sheridan, Mont; yes; Id.270d, Al.GF-67
1114   "   Josephine (Decoteau); f; 23; ¼+; m; wife B577; no; Sidney, Sheridan, Mont; yes; Id.290d, Al.G-012930
1115   "   Leon F; m; 2 9-11-29; ¼+; s; son B578; no; Sidney, Sheridan, Mont; yes; none
1116   "   Mary A. J; f; 7/12 8-25-31; ¼+; s dau; no; Sidney, Sheridan, Mont; yes; none

1117 Davis, Francois; m; 59; ¼+; m; Head A457; yes; no; Id.259, Al.R-72
1118   "   Angelique (Turcotte); f; 56; ¼+; m; wife A458; yes; no; Id.259a, Al.GF-103
1119   "   Joseph E; m; 23; ¼+; s; son A460; yes; no; Id.259e
1120   "   J Elie; m; 21; ¼+; s; son A461; yes; yes; Id.259f, Al.G-016822
1121   "   Riel; m; 17 7-9-14; ¼+; s; son A462; yes; yes; Id.259g
1122   "   Daniel; m; 13; ¼+; s; son A463; yes; yes; Id.259h

1123 Davis, Francis; m; 46; ¼+; s; Head A466; yes; no; Id.264, Al.M60

1124 Davis, Frank; m; 29; ¼+; m; Head A474; yes; no; Id.276c
1125 Davis, Eliza (Decouteau); f; 26; ¼+; m; wife A475; yes; yes; Id.282d, Al.G08086
1126 Davis, Flora; f; 3 11-2-28; ¼+; s; dau A476; yes; yes; none
1127 Davis, Maggie B; f; 1 4-6-30; ¼+; s; dau A477; yes; (Counted twice last year) yes; none

1128 Davis, Frank C; m; 33; ¼+; m; Head A467; yes; no; Id.266b, Al.M64
1129   "   Mary (Parisien); f; 38; ¼+; m; wife A468; yes; no; Id.801, Al.H039318
1130   "   Mary Emily; f; 11 5-1-20; ¼+; s; dau A469; yes; no; none
1131   "   Mary Anna; f; 9 12-23-22; ¼+; s; dau A470; yes; no; none
1132   "   Frank Wm; m; 8 12-20-23; ¼+; s; son A471; yes; no; none
1133   "   Benedict; m; 6 10-10-25; ¼+; s; son A472; yes; no; none
1134   "   Raymond; m; 4 12-23-27; ¼+; s; son A472[sic]; yes; no; none
1135   "   Roy Jerome; m; 1 3-2-31; ¼+; s; son -----; yes; no; none

Turtle Mountain Reservation
1932 Census Roll

Key: Number; Surname, Given; Sex; Age at Last Birthday, Birthdate (if given); Tribe (Chippewa, unless stated otherwise); Degree of Blood; Marital Status; Relationship to Head of Family, Last Year Census Number; At Jurisdiction Where Enrolled (Yes/No); Elsewhere - Post Office, County, State; Ward (Yes/No); Allotment [Al.], Annuity [An.] and/or Identification [Id.] Numbers

1136 Davis, Gregory; m; 24; ¼+; m; Head A493; yes; yes; Id.266f, Al.G190
1137 " Alvina (Davis); f; 25; ¼+; m; wife A459; yes; yes; Id.259d, Al.G208
1138 " John Lloyd; m; 3 6-11-28; ¼+; s; son A464; yes; yes; none
1139 " Vernon; m; 2 9-21-29; ¼+; s; son A465; yes; yes; none
1140 " Doloros[sic]; f; 3-12 12-12-31; ¼+; s; dau ---; yes; yes; none

1141 Davis, John Baptiste; m; 47; ¼+; m; head A478; yes; yes; Id.261, Al.R74
1142 " Margaret (Laverdure); f; 47; ¼+; m; wife A479; yes; yes; Id.261a, Al.G0344
1143 " Frank; m; 26; ¼+; s; son A480; yes; yes; Id.261b, Al.G0345
1144 " John; m; 18; ¼+; s; son A482; yes; yes; Id.261e
1145 " William; m; 16 10-11-15; ¼+; s; son A483; yes; yes; Id.261f
1146 " Michael; m; 13 7-6-18; ¼+; s; son A484; yes; yes; Id.261g
1147 " Emma; f; 10 11-4-21; ¼+; s; son[sic] A485; yes; yes; Id.261h
1148 " Stella; f; 7 8-3-24; ¼+; s; dau A486; yes; yes; Id.261j
1149 " Lillian; f; 5; ¼+; s; dau A487; yes; yes; Id.261k

1150 Davis, Joseph; m; 31; ¼+; m; Head A488; yes; yes; Id.266c, Al.M67
1151 " Mary (Gladue); f; 42; ¼+; m; wife A489; yes; Id.417, Al.GF81

1152 Davis, Louis; m; 40; ¼+; s; Head A490; yes; yes; Id.256, Al.GF-075844

1153 Davis, Mary Rose; f; 60; ¼+; wd; Head A491; yes; no; Id.266a, Al.G-187
1154 " Joseph J; m; 19; ¼+; s; son A493; yes; no; Id.266h
1155 " Fred; m; 18; ¼+; s; son A494; yes; no; Id.266i

1156 Davis, Maxim; m; 45; ¼+; wd; Head A495; yes; no; Id.277, Al.GF-69
1157 " Louis; m; 20; ¼+; s; son A497; yes; no; Id.277c
1158 " Julius; m; 19; ¼+; s; son A498; yes; no; Id.277d
1159 " Harry; m; 17; ¼+; s; son A499; yes; no; Id.277e
Dead " Clemence A500 (Died 7-10-25)

1160 Davis, Michael; m; 79; ¼+; m; Head B579; no; Camperville, Manitoba, Can; no; Id.270, Al.R-77
1161 " Flavis (Allery); f; 69; ¼+; m; wife B580; no; Camperville, Manitoba, Can; no; Id.270a, Al.G-019613
1162 " Michael; m; 50; ¼+; s; son B583; no; Camperville, Manitoba, Can; no; Id.273, Al.W-2

1163 Davis, Norbert; m; 35 4-22-96; ¼+; m; Head B581; no; Camperville, Manitoba, Can; no; Id.270b, Al.GF-66
NE " Christine (Flette); wife Cam[sic]
1165 " Marie; f; 10 3-8-22; ¼+; s; dau ----; no; Camperville, Manitoba, Can; no; none
1166 " Michael; m; 7 5-3-24; ¼+; s; son ----; no; Camperville, Manitoba, Can; no; none
1167 " Annie; f; 5 7-20-26; ¼+; s; dau ----; no; Camperville, Manitoba, Can; no; none

Turtle Mountain Reservation
1932 Census Roll

Key: Number; Surname, Given; Sex; Age at Last Birthday, Birthdate (if given); Tribe (Chippewa, unless stated otherwise); Degree of Blood; Marital Status; Relationship to Head of Family, Last Year Census Number; At Jurisdiction Where Enrolled (Yes/No); Elsewhere - Post Office, County, State; Ward (Yes/No); Allotment [Al.], Annuity [An.] and/or Identification [Id.] Numbers

1168   Davis(cont), David; m; 3 5-24-28; ¼+; s; son ----; no; Camperville, Manitoba, Can; no; none
1169   "   Arthur; m; 2 3-4-30; ¼+; s; son -----; no; Camperville, Manitoba, Can; no; none

1170   Davis, Patrice; m; 46; ¼+; m; Head B584; no; Reedy Creek, Manitoba, Can; no; Id.272, Al.GF-63
NE   "   Louise (Flette);   wife
1171   "   Mary Rose; f; 8 5-5-23; ¼+; s; dau ------; no; Reedy Creek, Manitoba, Can; no; none
1172   "   Doris A; f; 6 5-12-24; ¼+; s; dau ------; no; Reedy Creek, Manitoba, Can; no; none
1173   "   Josephine; f; 4 10-2-17; ¼+; s; dau ------; no; Reedy Creek, Manitoba, Can; no; none
1174   "   Lucy; f; 1 8-25-30; ¼+; s; dau ------; no; Reedy Creek, Manitoba, Can; no; none

1175   Davis, Robert; m; 37; ¼+; m; Head A501; yes; no; Id.267, Al.M-66
1176   "   Mary Jane (Keplin); f; 32; ¼+; m; wife A502; yes; yes; Id.535e, Al.G09521
1177   "   Russell; m; 11 11-19-20; ¼+; s; son A503; yes; yes; none
1178   "   Ruth Mae; f; 6 5-7-25; ¼+; s; dau A504; yes; yes; none
1179   "   Elmer; m; 4 9-15-27; ¼+; s; son A505; yes; yes; none
1180   "   Dolores M; f; 6/12 9-6-31; ¼+; s; dau ----; yes; yes; none

1181   Davis, St.Pierre; m; 26; ¼+; s; Head B586; no; Unknown; no; Id.869c

1182   Davis, William; m; 35; ¼+; m; Head A506; yes; no; Id.268, Al.M-65
1183   "   Virginia (Delorme); f; 34; ¼+; m; wife A507; yes; no; Id.322b, Al.GF-102
1184   "   Ethel M; f; 13 4-26-18; ¼+; s; dau A508; yes; no; Id.268b
1185   "   Helen V; f; 12 10-31-19; ¼+; s; dau A509; yes; no; Id.268c
1186   "   William P; m; 10 10-8-21; ¼+; s; son A510; yes; no; Id.268a
1187   "   Sylvester; m; 8 11-1-23; ¼+; s; son A511; yes; no; Id.268e
1188   "   Vinier J; m; 6 12-16-25; ¼+; s; son A512; yes; no; Id.268f
1189   "   Stella J; f; 4 1-15-28; ¼+; s; dau A513; yes; no; none
Died   "   Finley;   A514   (Died 12-31-31)

1190   Davis, William; m; 87; ¼+; m; Head A515; yes; no; Id.274, Al.R-78
1191   "   Sarah (Nolin); f; 67; ¼+; m; wife A516; yes; no; Id.274a, Al.GF-68
1192   "   Ernestine; f; 12 8-8-19; ¼+; s; grand dau A517; yes; (Counted twice on last census) no; Id.586c, none

1193   Day, Fred; m; 36; F; m; Head A518; yes; yes; Id.57b, Al.G-01888
1194   "   Laura (Little Girl); f; 27; F; m; wife A519; yes; yes; 39b, Al.G-380
1195   "   James; m; 8 12-5-23; F; s; son A520; yes; yes; none
1196   "   George; m; 6 11-1-25; F; s; son A521; yes; yes; none

Turtle Mountain Reservation
1932 Census Roll

Key: Number; Surname, Given; Sex; Age at Last Birthday, Birthdate (if given); Tribe (Chippewa, unless stated otherwise); Degree of Blood; Marital Status; Relationship to Head of Family; Last Year Census Number; At Jurisdiction Where Enrolled (Yes/No); Elsewhere - Post Office, County, State; Ward (Yes/No); Allotment [Al.], Annuity [An.] and/or Identification [Id.] Numbers

1197 Day(cont), Evelyn; f; 4 12-4-27; F; s; dau A522; yes; yes; none
1198 " Henry; m; 2 11-22-29; F; s; son A523; yes; yes; none

1199 Day, John; m; 35; F; m; Head B587; no; Dunseith, Rolette, ND; yes; Id.57c, Al.G-01891S
1200 " White Hair; f; 32; F; m; wife B588; no; Dunseith, Rolette, ND; yes; Id.42b, Al.G-037044
1201 " Donald; m; 10 3-25-22; F; s; son B589; no; Dunseith, Rolette, ND; yes; none
1164 " Mary; f; 4 3-22-28; F; s; dau B590; no; Dunseith, Rolette, ND; yes; none

NE Decoteau, Adele (Azure); F; ¼+; wd; Head
1202 " Frederick; m; 12 8-4-19; ¼+; s; son B591; no; Cheyenne River; yes; Id.285b

1203 Decoteau, Alexander; m; 38; ¼+; m; Head A527; yes; yes; Id.283, Al.GF-91
1204 " Cecila M (Malaterre); f; 30; ¼+; m; wife A528; yes; yes; Id.680c, Al.G-0197
1205 " Gilbert; m; 10 2-13-22; ¼+; s; son A529; yes; yes; Id.283b
1206 " Oliver; m; 5 6-12-26; ¼+; s; son A530; yes; yes; Id.283c
1207 " Raphael; ; 3 12-7-28; ¼+; s; son A531; yes; yes; Id.283d

1208 Decoteau, Alexander; m; 28; ¼+; m; Head A524; yes; yes; Id.278e, Al.MC-026515
1209 " Nora (Wilkie); f; 24; ¼+; m; wife A525; yes; yes; Id.1014d
1210 " Lorraine; f; 3 9-13-28; ¼+; s; dau A526; yes; yes; none
1211 " Mary; f; 2 2-24-30; ¼+; s; dau -----; yes; yes; none

1212 Decoteau, Alfred; m; 28; ¼+; m; Head A532; yes; yes; Id.282b, Al.G-07047
1213 " Maggie (Morin); f; 27; ¼+; m; wife A533; yes; yes; Id.751c, Al.G-210
1214 " Louis; m; 4 9-5-27; ¼+; s; son A534; yes; yes; none
1215 " Rita; f; 3; ¼+; s; dau A535; yes; yes; none

1216 Decoteau, Andrew; m; 56; ¼+; m; Head A536; yes; no; Id.279, Al.R-80
1217 " Philomeme (Langer); f; 39; ¼+; m; wife A537; yes; no; Id.279a, Al.CF-183
1218 " Mary Ann; f; 27; ¼+; s; dau A538; yes; yes; Id.279c, Al.G-91
1219 " Mary Rose; f; 27; ¼+; s; dau A539; yes; yes; Id.279d, Al.G-92
1220 " Louise A; f; 23; ¼+; s; dau A540; yes; no; Id.279f
1221 " Victoria; f; 16 4-10-15; ¼+; s; dau A542; yes; no; Id.279i
1222 " Edward; m; 15 11-15-16; ¼+; s; son A543; yes; no; Id.279j
1223 " Roderick; m; 13 12-7-18; ¼+; s; son A544; yes; no; Id.279k
1224 " Michael; m; 11 10-21-20; ¼+; s; son A545; yes; no; Id.279l
1225 " Marie; f; 9 3-1-23; ¼+; s; dau A546; yes; no; Id.279m
1226 " Ambrose; m; 7 8-11-24; ¼+; s; son A547; yes; no; Id.279n
1227 " Frank; m; 5 10-1-26; ¼+; s; son A548; yes; no; Id.279o
1228 " June; f; 1/12 2-17-32; ¼+; s; dau; yes; no; Is[sic].279p

Turtle Mountain Reservation
1932 Census Roll

Key: Number; Surname, Given; Sex; Age at Last Birthday, Birthdate (if given); Tribe (Chippewa, unless stated otherwise); Degree of Blood; Marital Status; Relationship to Head of Family, Last Year Census Number; At Jurisdiction Where Enrolled (Yes/No); Elsewhere - Post Office, County, State; Ward (Yes/No); Allotment [Al.], Annuity [An.] and/or Identification [Id.] Numbers

1229 Decoteau, Andrew; m; 31; ¼+; m; Head B603; no; Devils Lake, Ramsey, ND; yes; Id.278d, Al.M-306
1230 " Rose (Slater); f; 23; ¼+; m; wife B2322; no; Devils Lake, Ramsey, ND; yes; Id.921d, Al.H-012637
1231 " Mary Jane; f; 6 5-22-25; ¼+; s; dau; no; Devils Lake, Ramsey, ND; yes; none

1232 Decoteau, Daniel; m; 60; ¼+; m; Head A549; yes; no; Id.280, Al.R81
1233 " Judith (Smith); f; 74; ¼+; m; wife A550; yes; no; Id.280a, Al.H010478

1234 Decouteau, Edmund; m; 30; ¼+; m; Head B592; no; Rosebud; yes; Id.291c, Al.H08381
1235 " Rosina (Belgarde); f; 26 7-25-05; ¼+; m; wife B593; no; Rosebud; yes; Id.188d, Al.G016810
1236 " Name unknown; m; 2; ¼+; s; son B594; no; Rosebud; yes; none

1237 Decouteau, Elie; m; 36; ¼+; m; Head A551; yes; yes; Id.290b, Al.G406
1238 " Margaret (Lavallie); f; 30; ¼+; m; wife A552; yes; yes; Id.631b, Al.G0342
1239 " Bruno; m; 6 9-12-25; ¼+; s; son A553; yes; Rosebud, yes; none
1240 " Albert; m; 5 1-24-27; ¼+; s; son A554; yes; yes; none
1241 " Ethel; f; 2 7-26-29; ¼+; s; dau A555; yes; yes; none
1242 " Lucy D; f; 1 9-4-30; ¼+; s; dau A---; yes; yes; none

1243 Decouteau, Ezear; m; 71; ¼+; m; Head A556; yes; yes; Id.282, Al.R82
1244 " Mary Rose (Lafontain); f; 60; ¼+; m; wife A557; yes; yes; Id.282a, Al.06040
1245 " Theodore; m; 24; ¼+; s; son A559; yes; Id.282e, Al.G08088
1246 " Josephine; f; 20; ¼+; s; dau A560; yes; yes; Id.282g, Al.H024541
1247 " Rose; f; 16 10-5-15; ¼+; s; dau A561; yes; yes; Id.282h
1248 " Julian; m; 15 3-1-17; ¼+; s; son A562; yes; yes; Id.282i
1249 " Armand; m; 10 7-11-21; ¼+; s; son A563; yes; yes; Id.282j

1250 Decoteau, Erancosi; m; 39; ¼+; m; Head A 564; yes; yes; Id.284, Al.GF-92
1251 " Eliza (Vallie); f; 36; ¼+; m; wife A565; yes; yes; Id.284a, Al.G-08197
1252 " Alexander; m; 16 4-8-15; ¼+; s; son A566; yes; yes; Id.284b
1253 " Belle Rose; f; 15; ¼+; s; dau A567; yes; yes; Id.284c
1254 " Joan D'Arc; f; 13; ¼+; s; dau A568; yes; yes; none
1255 " Francois; m; 11 1-3-21; ¼+; s; son A569; yes; yes; none
1256 " Anna; f; 9 3-1-23; ¼+; s; dau570; yes; yes; none
1257 " Walter; m; 6; ¼+; s; son A571; yes; yes; none
1258 " Elmer; m; 4 12-29-27; ¼+; s; son A572; yes; yes; none
1259 " Sylvester; m; 2; ¼+; s; son A573; yes; yes; none
1260 " Jeannette; f; 3/12 12-5-31; ¼+; s; dau; yes; yes; none

Turtle Mountain Reservation
1932 Census Roll

Key: Number; Surname, Given; Sex; Age at Last Birthday, Birthdate (if given); Tribe (Chippewa, unless stated otherwise); Degree of Blood; Marital Status; Relationship to Head of Family, Last Year Census Number; At Jurisdiction Where Enrolled (Yes/No); Elsewhere - Post Office, County, State; Ward (Yes/No); Allotment [Al.], Annuity [An.] and/or Identification [Id.] Numbers

1261 Decoteau, Frank; m; 64; ¼+; m; Head B595; no; Dunseith, Rolette, ND; no; Id.285, Al.R-83
NE   "   Emma (Plant);   wife

Died Decoteau, Fred   (~~Died 12-13-31~~)
1262   "   Philomeme (Azure); f; 39; ¼+; wd; Head A574; yes; no; Id.289a, Al.G-036562
1263   "   Norman; m; 21; ¼+; s; son A575; yes; no; Id.289b
1264   "   Rose P; f; 18; ¼+; s; dau A576; yes; no; Id.289c
1265   "   Benjamin; m; 14 7-17-27; ¼+; s; son A577; yes; no; Id.289d
1266   "   Frank; m; 13; ¼+; s; son A578; yes; no; Id.289e
1267   "   Collin; m; 10; ¼+; s; son A579; yes; no; Id.289f
1268   "   Ida; f; 10; ¼+; s; dau A580; yes; no; Id.289g
1269   "   Henry; m; 7 7-9-24; ¼+; s; son A581; yes; no; Id.289h
1270   "   Stella; f; 4 5-12-27; ¼+; s; dau A582; yes; no; none
1271   "   Charley; m; 2 3-15-30; ¼+; s; son A583; yes; no; none

1272 Decoteau, Frederick; m; 31; ¼+; wd; Head A584; yes; yes; Id.296b, Al.M-322
Died   "   Mary L (Blue);   A585   (Died 9-24-31)
1273   "   Lorraine; f; 1 5-10-30; ¼+; s; dau A586; yes; yes; none

1274 Decoteau, Israel; m; 23; ¼+; m; Head A590; yes; yes; Id.282g, Al.G-08259
1275   "   Marie (Duchain); f; 23; ¼+; m; wife A591; yes; yes; Id.364a, Al.H-10477

1276 Decoteau, James; m; 61; ¼+; m; Head B596; no; Dunseith, Rolette, ND; no; Id.286, Al.R-84
1277   "   Emily (Peltier); f; 50; ¼+; m; wife B597; no; Dunseith, Rolette, ND; no; Id.286a, Al.GF-95
1278   "   Antoine; m; 22; ¼+; s; son B598; no; Dunseith, Rolette, ND; no; Id.286c
1279   "   Flora; f; 18; ¼+; s; dau B599; no; Dunseith, Rolette, ND; no; Id.286d
1280   "   James; m; 15 12-19-16; ¼+; s; son B600; no; Dunseith, Rolette, ND; no; Id.286e

1281 Decoteau, John B; m; 35; ¼+; s; Head B601; no; Fort Yates; no; Id.291b, Al.H-09961

1282 Decoteau, John B; m; 39; ¼+; m; Head A592; yes; yes; Id.281, Al.H-010479
1283   "   Mary Jane (Vandal); f; 39; ¼+; m; wife A593; yes; yes; Id.281a, Al.GF-162
1284   "   Josephine; f; 16 11-9-15; ¼+; s; dau A594; yes; yes; Id.281b
1285   "   Joseph; m; 14 10-3-17; ¼+; s; son A595; yes; yes; Id.281c
1286   "   Clifford; m; 11 4-13-21; ¼+; s; son A596; yes; yes; Id.281d
1287   "   John Fred; m; 7 8-15-24; ¼+; s; son A597; yes; yes; Id.281e
1288   "   Ernest; m; 5 1-17-27; ¼+; s; son A598; yes; yes; Id.281f
1289   "   Cecelia; f; 2 8-24-29; ¼+; s; dau A599; yes; yes; Id.281g
1290   "   Florus; f; 1/12 3-21-32; ¼+; s; dau -----; yes; yes; none

Turtle Mountain Reservation
1932 Census Roll

Key: Number; Surname, Given; Sex; Age at Last Birthday, Birthdate (if given); Tribe (Chippewa, unless stated otherwise); Degree of Blood; Marital Status; Relationship to Head of Family, Last Year Census Number; At Jurisdiction Where Enrolled (Yes/No); Elsewhere - Post Office, County, State; Ward (Yes/No); Allotment [Al.], Annuity [An.] and/or Identification [Id.] Numbers

1291 Decouteau, Joseph; m; 19; ¼+; m; Head A541; yes; yes; Id.279g, Al.H024540
1292 " Marie (St Pierre); f; 20; ¼+; m; wife ---; yes; no; Id.939e

1293 Decouteau, Joseph A; m; 27; ¼+; m; Head A558; yes; yes; Id.282c, Al.G07047
1294 " Marian (Dauphinais); f; 20; ¼+; m; wife A432; yes; yes; Id.250d

1295 Decouteau, Joseph; m; 37; ¼+; m; Head A600; yes; yes; Id.294, Al.G418
1296 " Margaret (Wilkie); f; 23; ¼+; m; wife A601; yes; yes; Id.294a

1297 Decouteau, Margaret (Frederick); f; 89; ¼+; wd; Head A602; yes; no; Id.287a, Al.G408

1298 Decouteau, Mary Ann (Lafontain); f; 53; ¼+; wd; Head B602; no; Devils Lake, Ramsey, ND; no; Id.278a, Al.G01855
1299 " Marie; f; 16 9-22-15; ¼+; s; dau B604; no; Devils Lake, Ramsey, ND; no; Id.278i

No such child Decouteau, Gilbert; B605 (Error last year's census. No such child)

1300 Decouteau, Mary Louise; f; 18; ¼+; s; Head A588; yes; yes; Id.295d
1301 " Henry; m; 15; ¼+; s; bro A589; yes; yes; Id.295e

1302 Decouteau, Napoleon; m; 31; ¼+; m; Head B606; no; Devils Lake, Ramsey, ND; yes; Id.289b, Al.M354
1303 " Rosina (Langer); f; 31; ¼+; m; wife B607; no; Devils Lake, Ramsey, ND; no; Id.608b
1304 " Paul; m; 3 3-11-29; ¼+; s; son B608; no; Devils Lake, Ramsey, ND; yes; Id.none

1305 Decouteau, Patrice; m; 22; ¼+; m; Head B609; no; Devils Lake, Ramsey, ND; no; Id.278h
1306 " Eva (Wilkie); f; 22; ¼+; m; wife B620; no; Devils Lake, Ramsey, ND; no; Id.1014e

NE Decouteau, Peter; Head
1307 " Zilda (Poitra); f; 51; ¼+; m; wife A603; yes; yes; Id.298a, Al.G172
1308 " Napoleon; m; 19 9-28-12; ¼+; s; son A604; yes; yes; Id.298c
1309 " Laura; f; 13 3-8-19; ¼+; s; dau A605; yes; yes; Id.298d
1310 " Roger; m; 11 2-9-21; ¼+; s; son A606; yes; yes; Id.298e
1311 " John; m; 9 9-8-22; ¼+; s; son A607; yes; yes; Id.298f
1312 " Daniel; m; 7 4-25-24; ¼+; s; son A608; yes; yes; Id.298g
1313 " George; m; 5 5-2-25; ¼+; s; son A609; yes; yes; Id.298h
1314 " Mabel; f; 3 7-1-28; ¼+; s; dau A620; yes; yes; Id.298i

Turtle Mountain Reservation
1932 Census Roll

Key: Number; Surname, Given; Sex; Age at Last Birthday, Birthdate (if given); Tribe (Chippewa, unless stated otherwise); Degree of Blood; Marital Status; Relationship to Head of Family, Last Year Census Number; At Jurisdiction Where Enrolled (Yes/No); Elsewhere - Post Office, County, State; Ward (Yes/No); Allotment [Al.], Annuity [An.] and/or Identification [Id.] Numbers

1315 Decouteau(cont), Charles; m; 11/12 5-17-31; ¼+; s; son ------; yes; yes; Id.298j

1316 Decouteau, St Pierre; m; 56; ¼+; m; Head B611; no; Bottineau, Bottineau, ND; no; Id.297, Al.G06

1317 " Mary (Gladue); f; 43; ¼+; m; wife B612; no; Bottineau, Bottineau, ND; no; Id.297a, Al.G0444

1318 " Victoria; f; 23; ¼+; s; dau B613; no; Bottineau, Bottineau, ND; yes; Id.297c, Al.G01834

1319 " Peter; m; 20l ¼+; s; son B614; no; Bottineau, Bottineau, ND; yes; Id.297d, Al.G023430

1320 " Maximus; m; 19; ¼+; s; son B615; no; Bottineau, Bottineau, ND; yes; Id.297e, Al.H02920

1321 " Albert; m; 16 4-29-15; ¼+; s; son B616; no; Bottineau, Bottineau, ND; yes; Id.297f

Dead " Pat; B617 (Died 11-8-27)

1322 " Louis; m; 14; ¼+; s; son B618; no; Bottineau, Bottineau, ND; no; Id.297h

1323 " George; m; 11 9-7-20; ¼+; s; son B619; no; Bottineau, Bottineau, ND; no; Id.297i

1324 " Stanley; m; 7 9-2-24; ¼+; s; son B620; no; Bottineau, Bottineau, ND; no; Id.297g

NE Decouteau, Toussant; m; Head
1325 " Larose (Champagne); f; 54; ¼+; m; wife A611; yes; yes; Id.290a, Al.R86
1326 " Joseph; m; 21; ¼+; s; son A612; yes; yes; Id.290b, Al.H024543
1327 " Agnes A; f; 17 2-4-15; ¼+; s; dau A613; yes; yes; Id.290c
1328 " Albert; m; 14 9-29-17; ¼+; s; son A614; yes; yes; Id.290d

1329 Decouteau, Wilfred; m; 27; ¼+; m; Head A615; yes; yes; Id.278f, Al.G07852
1330 " Adele (Wilkie); f; 26; ¼+; m; wife A616; yes; yes; Id.1014c
1331 " John; m; 3 8-23-28; ¼+; s; son A617; yes; yes; none
1332 " Mary Ann; f; 1 3-14-31; ¼+; s; dau A618; yes; yes; none

1333 Decouteau, William; m; 29; ¼+; s; Head B621; no; Address unknown; yes; Id.293d, Al.G136

1334 Decouteau, William; m; 49; ¼+; m; Head B622; no; Address unknown; no; Id.1035, Al.GF11
NE " Madeline R (Bleff); wife

1335 Dejarlais, Alfred; m; 25; ¼+; m; Head B639; no; St.John, Rolette, ND; no; Id.316c, Al.W-02928
NE " Celia (Bercier); wife

Turtle Mountain Reservation
1932 Census Roll

Key: Number; Surname, Given; Sex; Age at Last Birthday, Birthdate (if given); Tribe (Chippewa, unless stated otherwise); Degree of Blood; Marital Status; Relationship to Head of Family, Last Year Census Number; At Jurisdiction Where Enrolled (Yes/No); Elsewhere - Post Office, County, State; Ward (Yes/No); Allotment [Al.], Annuity [An.] and/or Identification [Id.] Numbers

1336 Dejarlais(cont), Elsie Rose; f; 8/12 7-10-13; ¼+; s; dau ----; no; St.John, Rolette, ND; no; none

1337 Dejarlais, Antoine; m; 71; ¼+; m; Head B624; no; Address unknown; yes; Id.302, Al.W07990
1338 " Ursula (Martin); f; 74; ¼+; m; wife B625; no; Address unknown; no; Id.302a, Al.M178
1339 " John; m; 31; ¼+; s; son B626; no; Address unknown; yes; Id.302h, Al.M176

1340 Dejarlais, Calus; m; 60; ¼+; m; Head A619; yes; yes; Id.304, Al.H030425
NE " Adele (Swain); wife

1341 Dejarlais, Charles; m; 34; ¼+; m; Head A620; yes; yes; Id.305b, Al.DL-22
1342 " Felicite (Bercier); f; 31; ¼+; m; wife A621; yes; yes; Id.1169d, Al.M-57
1343 " Rachel; f; 8 11-19-23; ¼+; s; dau A622; yes; yes; Id.305b
1344 " Ernest; m; 3 5-16-28; ¼+; s; son A623; yes; yes; Id.305e
1345 " Antoine; m; 1 4-9-30; ¼+; s; son A624; yes; yes; Id.305f

1346 Dejarlais, Elise (McDonald.Schindler); f; 59; ¼+; wd; Head A625; yes; yes; Id.311a, Al.R-291

1347 Dejarlais, Francois; m; 67; ¼+; m; Head A627; yes; no; Id.310, Al.R-91
1348 " Marie (Gourneau); f; 62; ¼+; m; wife A628; yes; no; Id.310a, Al.M-20

1349 Dejarlais, Frank; m; 42; ¼+; m; Head B627; no; Buford, Williams, ND; no; Id.303, Al.M-250
NE " Margaret (Harrison); wife
1350 " Francis; m; 13 10-26-18; ¼+; s; son B628; no; (By former wife) Buford, Williams, ND; no; Id.303b
1351 " Edward L; m; 8 8-21-23; ¼+; s; son ------; no; Buford, Williams, ND; no; none
1352 " Russell F; m; 7 1-29-25; ¼+; s; son ------; no; Buford, Williams, ND; no; none
1353 " Blanch P; f; 5 3-18-27; ¼+; s; son ------; no; Buford, Williams, ND; no; none
1354 " Alma Rose; f; 1 7-19-30; ¼+; s; dau -----; no; Buford, Williams, ND; no; none
DEAD " Grace M (Died 7-28-29)

1355 Dejarlais, John; m; 61; ¼+; m; Head A629; yes; yes; Id.312, Al.R92
NE " Marie (Paul); wife
1356 " Michael; m; 29; ¼+; s; son A630; yes; yes; Id.312d, Al.M98
1357 " Lucy; f; 19; ¼+; s; dau A632; yes; yes; Id.312g, Al.H030229

1358 Dejarlais, Joseph H; m; 31; ¼+; m; Head A633; yes; yes; Id.612c, Al.M111
1359 " Lillian (Poitra); f; 27; ¼+; m; wife A634; yes; yes; Id.312½a, Al.G174
1360 " Paul; m; 10 10-12-21; ¼+; s; son A635; yes; yes; none

Turtle Mountain Reservation
1932 Census Roll

Key: Number; Surname, Given; Sex; Age at Last Birthday, Birthdate (if given); Tribe (Chippewa, unless stated otherwise); Degree of Blood; Marital Status; Relationship to Head of Family, Last Year Census Number; At Jurisdiction Where Enrolled (Yes/No); Elsewhere - Post Office, County, State; Ward (Yes/No); Allotment [Al.], Annuity [An.] and/or Identification [Id.] Numbers

1361 Dejarlais(cont), Flora; f; 5 8-5-26; ¼+; s; dau A636; yes; yes; none
1362 " Roman; m; 5/12 10-30-31; ¼+; s; son -----; yes; yes; none

1363 Dejarlais, Joseph; m; 48; ¼+; m; Head B629; no; Williston, William, ND; no; Id.308, Al.G08303
NE " Josephine; wife (Maiden name is not known)

1364 Dejarlais, Leander; m; 49; ¼+; s; Head B630; no; Address unknown; no; Id.299, Al.H010533

1365 Dejarlais, Louis; m; 56; ¼+; m; Head B631; no; Trenton, Williams, ND; no; Id. 315, Al.D03718
1366 " Mary L (Turcotte); f; 50; ¼+; m; wife B632; no; Trenton, Williams, ND; no; Id.315a, Al.G07878
1367 " Alexander; m; 23; ¼+; s; son B633; no; Trenton, Williams, ND; yes; Id.315e, Al.G09782
1368 " Julia; f; 17; ¼+; s; dau B634; no; Trenton, Williams, ND; no; Id.315f
1369 " Louis; m; 16 1-20-17; ¼+; s; son B635; no; Trenton, Williams, ND; no; Id.315g
1370 " Andrew; m; 13 1-18-19; ¼+; s; son B635; no; Trenton, Williams, ND; no; Id.315h
1371 " Gabriel; m; 9 4-20-20; ¼+; s; son B637; no; Trenton, Williams, ND; no; Id.315i
1372 " Benedict; m; 8 3-1-23; ¼+; s; son B638; no; Trenton, Williams, ND; no; Id.315j

1373 Dejarlais, Louis John; m; 36; ¼+; m; Head A637; yes; no; Id.314, Al.M96
1374 " Margaret (Charette); f; 31; ¼+; m; wife A638; yes; yes; Id.314a, Al.M244
1375 " Lawrence; m; 11 10-3-20; ¼+; m s; son A639; yes; yes; Id.314b
1376 " Ida; f; 10 12-30-21; ¼+; s; dau A643; yes; no; Id.none
No such child " Peter A640 (To correct error last census)
1377 " Joseph; m; 8 2-25-24; ¼+; s; son A641; yes; no; Id.314c
1378 " Marguerite; f; 5 7-18-26; ¼+; s; dau A642; yes; yes; Id.314c
1379 " Norabelle; f; 11/12 4-25-31; ¼+; s; dau ----; yes; yes; Id.314d

1380 Dejarlais, Louis; m; 24; ¼+; s; Head B640; no; St.John, Rolette, ND; yes; Id.316d, Al.W02927
1381 " Alice; f; 19; ¼+; s; sis B641; no; St.John, Rolette, ND; yes; Id.316e, Al.H030245
1382 " Emma; f; 15; ¼+; s; sis B642; no; St.John, Rolette, ND; no; Id.316f
1383 " Joseph L; m; 11 1-26-21; ¼+; s; bro B643; no; St.John, Rolette, ND; no; Id.316g

Turtle Mountain Reservation
1932 Census Roll

Key: Number; Surname, Given; Sex; Age at Last Birthday, Birthdate (if given); Tribe (Chippewa, unless stated otherwise); Degree of Blood; Marital Status; Relationship to Head of Family, Last Year Census Number; At Jurisdiction Where Enrolled (Yes/No); Elsewhere - Post Office, County, State; Ward (Yes/No); Allotment [Al.], Annuity [An.] and/or Identification [Id.] Numbers

1384 Dejarlais, Moses; m; 54; ¼+; m; Head B644; no; Dunseith, Rolette, ND; no;
Id.313, Al.H012533
NE " Caroline; wife (Maiden name not known)

1385 Dejarlais, Patrice; m; 31; ¼+; m; Head A644; yes; no; Id.310c, Al.M18
1386 " St Ann (Belgarde); f; 32; ¼+; m; wife A645; yes; yes; Id.170b, Al.M1835
1387 " Edna; f; 8 8-28-23; ¼+; s; dau A646; yes; no; none
Dead " Florestine; A647 (Died 10-27-27)
1388 " Gregory; m; 7 8-18-24; ¼+; s; son A648; yes; no; none

1389 Dejarlais, Patrice; m; 41; ¼+; m; Head B645; no; Devils Lake, Ramsey, ND; no;
Id.301, Al.G037079
1390 Dejarlais, Rosalie (St Germain); f; 39; ¼+; m; wife B646; no; Devils Lake,
Ramsey, ND; no; Id.301a, Al.M254
1391 " Andrew; m; 6 8-2-25; ¼+; s; son B647; no; Devils Lake, Ramsey, ND;
no; Id.301b
1392 " Jacob; m; 4; ¼+; s; son B648; no; Devils Lake, Ramsey, ND; no; Id.301c

1393 Dejarlais, Patrice; m; 51; ¼+; m; Head B649; no; Devils Lake, Ramsey, ND; no;
Id.317, Al.R95
NE " Jessie (Martin); f; wife
1394 " Alfred; m; 23; ¼+; s; son B623; no; Devils Lake, Ramsey, ND; no;
Id.317b
1395 " Raymond; m; 19; ¼+; s; son B652; no; Devils Lake, Ramsey, ND; no;
Id.317e
Dead " Lena; f; B653 (Died Apr. 26, 1922)
1396 " James E; m; 14 12-19-17; ¼+; s; son B654; no; Devils Lake, Ramsey,
ND; no; Id.317g
1397 " Joseph; m; 12 3-7-20; ¼+; s; son B655; no; Devils Lake, Ramsey, ND;
no; Id.317h
1398 " Alexander; m; 11 1-5-21; ¼+; s; son B656; no; Devils Lake, Ramsey,
ND; no; Id.317i
1399 " Ida Rose; f; 9 8-15-22; ¼+; s; dau ----; no; Devils Lake, Ramsey, ND;
no; Id.none
1400 " Christine; f; 7 4-22-24; ¼+; s; dau ---; no; Devils Lake, Ramsey, ND; no; none

1401 Dejarlais, Rose (Champagne); f; 33; ¼+; wd; Head A649; yes; yes; Id.234b, Al.G-404
1402 " Lucy Nora; f; 5 10-4-26; ¼+; s; dau A650; yes; yes; none
1403 " Mary Flora; f; 2; ¼+; s; dau A651; yes; yes; none

1404 Dejarlais, Victor; m; 39; ¼+; m; Head B657; no; Dunseith, Rolette, ND; no;
Id.306, Al.G81
NE " Rose (Peltier); wife
1405 " Maggie; f; 16 11-7-15; ¼+; s; dau B658; no; Dunseith, Rolette, ND; no; none

Turtle Mountain Reservation
1932 Census Roll

Key: Number; Surname, Given; Sex; Age at Last Birthday, Birthdate (if given); Tribe (Chippewa, unless stated otherwise); Degree of Blood; Marital Status; Relationship to Head of Family, Last Year Census Number; At Jurisdiction Where Enrolled (Yes/No); Elsewhere - Post Office, County, State; Ward (Yes/No); Allotment [Al.], Annuity [An.] and/or Identification [Id.] Numbers

1406 Dejarlais(cont), Joseph; m; 15 3-13-17; ¼+; s; son B659; no; Dunseith, Rolette, ND; no; none

1407 Dejarlais, William; m; 55; ¼+; m; Head B660; no; Trenton, Williams, ND; no; Id.318, Al.R-96
1408 " Mary (Bercier); f; 62; ¼+; m; wife B661; no; Trenton, Williams, ND; no; Id.318a, Al.G-038624
1409 " Roger; m; 23; ¼+; s; son B662; no; Trenton, Williams, ND; no; Id.318d
1410 " John B; m; 22; ¼+; s; son B663; no; Trenton, Williams, ND; no; Id.318e, Al.H-023535
1411 " Arthur; m; 19; ¼+; s; son B664; no; Trenton, Williams, ND; no; Id.318g

1412 Delonais, Francis; m; 56; ¼+; m; Head A652; yes; yes; Id.319, Al.R97
1413 " Mary Rose (Belgarde); f; 51; ¼+; m; wife A652; yes; yes; Id.319a, Al.GF47
1414 " George E; m; 23; ¼+; s; son A655; yes; yes; Id.319c, Al.G49
1415 " Norbert; m; 21; ¼+; s; son A656; yes; yes; Id.319d, Al.G08307
1416 " Mary A; f; 19; ¼+; s; dau A657; yes; yes; Id.319g
1417 " Ernestine; f; 14 10-11-17; ¼+; s; dau A658; yes; yes; Id.319h
1418 " Alexander; m; 10 3-12-22; ¼+; s; son A659; yes; yes; Id.319i
1419 " Mary Adele; f; 6 7-11-25; ¼+; s; dau A660; yes; yes; Id.319j

1420 Delonais, Theodore; m; 30; ¼+; m; Head A661; yes; yes; Id.319b, Al.G51
1421 " Eliza (Lafrombois); f; 27; ¼+; m; wife A662; yes; yes; Id.585f, Al.GF210
1422 " Peter; m; 10 3-24-22; ¼+; s; s-son A1273; yes; yes; none

NE Delong, Lee; Head
1423 " Harriet (Allery); f; 39; ¼+; m; wife A663; yes; no; d.320a, Al.G313
1424 " Mary E; f; 20 4-10-11; ¼+; s; dau A664; yes; no; Id.320b
1425 " Nancy A; f; 15 7-17-16; ¼+; s; dau A666; yes; no; Id.320d
1426 " George; m; 13 9-15-18; ¼+; s; son A667; yes; no; Id.320e
1427 " John; m; 12 4-11-19; ¼+; s; son A668; yes; no; Id.320f
1428 " Ernest J; m; 8 8-17-23; ¼+; s; son A669; yes; no; Id.320g
1429 " Rose; f; 6 3-2-26; ¼+; s; son A670; yes; no; Id.320h
1430 " Leona; f; 3 12-2-28; ¼+; s; dau A671; yes; no; Id.320i
1431 " Elizabeth; f; 5/12 10-28-31; ¼+; s; dau ----; yes; no; Id.320j

1432 Delorme, Angelique; f; 50; ¼+; s; Head B665; no; Address unknown; no; Id.325a, Al.G126

1433 Delorme, Bernard; m; 76; ¼+; m; Head A572; yes; yes; Id.324, Al.R98
NE " Christine (Robinson); wife

1434 Delorme, Francis; m; 61; ¼+; m; Head A675; yes; yes; Id.322, Al.R99
1435 " Cleophile (Gladue); f; 61; ¼+; m; wife A676; yes; yes; Id.322a, Al.GF100

Turtle Mountain Reservation
1932 Census Roll

Key: Number; Surname, Given; Sex; Age at Last Birthday, Birthdate (if given); Tribe (Chippewa, unless stated otherwise); Degree of Blood; Marital Status; Relationship to Head of Family, Last Year Census Number; At Jurisdiction Where Enrolled (Yes/No); Elsewhere - Post Office, County, State; Ward (Yes/No); Allotment [Al.], Annuity [An.] and/or Identification [Id.] Numbers

1436 Delorme, Francois; m; 38; ¼+; m; Head A677; yes; no; Id.323, Al.GF101
1437 " Margaret (Jollie); f; 42; ¼+; m; wife A678; yes; no; Id.323a, Al.M296
1438 " Blanche; f; 16 11-24-15; ¼+; s; dau A679; yes; no; Id.323b
1439 " David; m; 14 3-31-18; ¼+; s; son A680; yes; no; Id.323c
1440 " Estelle; f; 11 8-17-20; ¼+; s; dau A681; yes; no; Id.323d
1441 " Alma; f; 4 2-27-28; ¼+; s; dau A682; yes; no; Id.323e
1442 " Lucy Reah; f; 2 2-26-30; ¼+; s; dau A683; yes; no; Id.323f

1443 Delorme, John; m; 25; ¼+; s; Head A684; yes; yes; Id.321c, Al.G040

1444 Delorme, Joseph Jr; m; 64; ¼+; m; head A685; yes; no; Id.326, Al.M251
1445 " Julia (Grant); f; 45; ¼+; m; wife A686; yes; yes; Id.326a, Al.R102
1446 " Anthony; m; 24; ¼+; s; son A687; yes; yes; Id.326b, Al.H031155
1447 " Josephine; f; 17; ¼+; s; dau A688; yes; yes; Id.326e
1448 " Joseph; m; 16; ¼+; s; son A----; yes (Omitted from last years[sic] census by mistake) yes; Id.323f

1449 Delorme, Louis; m; 26; ¼+; m; Head A689; yes; yes; Id.326c, Al.H031169
1450 " Jane (Jaste); f; 21; ¼+; m; wife A690; yes; yes; Id.500g
1451 " Rita Marie; f; 4/12 11-18-31; ¼+; s; dau ----; yes; yes; Id.none

1452 Delorme, Louis; m; 56; ¼+; m; Head B666; no; Malta, Phillips, Mont; no; Id.331, Al.GF133
1453 " Virginia (Allery); f; 46; ¼+; m; wife B667; no; Malta, Phillips, Mont; no; Id.331a, Al.GF142
1454 " Alfred; m; 16 10-18-15; ¼+; s; son B670; no; Malta, Phillips, Mont; no; Id.331f
1455 " Beulah; f; 14 1-26-18; ¼+; s; dau B671; no; Malta, Phillips, Mont; no; Id.331h
1456 " Edwin; m; 10 3-12-22; ¼+; s; son B672; no; Malta, Phillips, Mont; no; Id.none

1457 Delorme, Patrice; m; 42; ¼+; m; Head B674; no; Langdon, Cavalier, ND; no; Id.330, Al.M-026707
NE " Emma (Monette); wife
1458 " Eva; f; 16 11-4-15; ¼+; s; dau B675; no; Langdon, Cavalier, ND; no; Id.330b
1459 " Blanche; f; 14 2-8-18; ¼+; s; dau B676; no; Langdon, Cavalier, ND; no; none

1460 Delorme, Patrice; m; 68; ¼+; m; Head A691; yes; yes; Id.328, Al.R-103
1461 " Madeline (Lafrombois); f; 67; ¼+; m; wife A692; yes; no; Id.328a, Al.MC-026705

1462 Delorme, Peter; m; 28; ¼+; m; Head A693; yes; yes; Id.328d, Al.G-08091
1463 " Ida Rose (Decoteau); f; 25; ¼+; m; wife A694; yes; yes; Id.296c, Al.G-08089
1464 " Peter C; m; 5 3-20-27; ¼+; s; son A695; yes; yes; none

Turtle Mountain Reservation
1932 Census Roll

Key: Number; Surname, Given; Sex; Age at Last Birthday, Birthdate (if given); Tribe (Chippewa, unless stated otherwise); Degree of Blood; Marital Status; Relationship to Head of Family, Last Year Census Number; At Jurisdiction Where Enrolled (Yes/No); Elsewhere - Post Office, County, State; Ward (Yes/No); Allotment [Al.], Annuity [An.] and/or Identification [Id.] Numbers

1465 Delorme(cont), Eugene E; m; 3 8-10-28; ¼+; s; son A696; yes; yes; none
1466 " Genevieve; f; 1 4-11-30; ¼+; s; dau A697; yes; yes; none

NE Delorme, William; Head
1467 " Mary L (Fagnant); f; 42; ¼+; m; wife B677; no; Medicine Lake, Sheridan, Mont; yes; Id.332a, Al.DL-43
1468 " Louis; m; 24; ¼+; s; son B678; no; Medicine Lake, Sheridan, Mont; yes; Id.332c, Al.H-012532
1469 " Victoria; f; 20; ¼+; s; dau B679; no; Medicine Lake, Sheridan, Mont; yes; Id.332d
1470 " Joseph; m; 19; ¼+; s; son B680; no; Medicine Lake, Sheridan, Mont; yes; Id.332e
1471 " Michael; m; 16 2-17-16; ¼+; s; son B681; no; Medicine Lake, Sheridan, Mont; yes; Id.332f

1472 Delorme, William; m; 32; ¼+; m; Head A698; yes; yes; Id.328c, Al.G-08092
1473 " Mary (Warren); f; 32; ¼+; m; wife A699; yes; no; Id.1002c, Al.G-285
1474 " Lorraine; f; 9 4-29-22; ¼+; s; dau A700; yes; yes; none
1475 " Aurelia; f; 8 12-7-23; ¼+; s; dau A701; yes; yes; none
1476 " Dolores; f; 6 6-30-25; ¼+; s; dau A702; yes; yes; none
1477 " Madeline; f; 4 11-2-27; ¼+; s; dau A703; yes; yes; none
1478 " William; m; 3 7-1-28; ¼+; s; son A704; yes; yes; none
1479 " Wendell J; m; 2 3-21-30; ¼+; s; son A705; yes; yes; none
1480 " Beatrice A; f; 1/12 2-16-32; ¼+; s; dau; yes; yes; none

1481 Delorme, William; m; 36; ¼+; m; Head A706; yes; yes; Id.327, Al.M-69
NE " Eliza (Allard); wife
1482 " Alfred; m; 12 4-26-19; ¼+; s; son A707; yes; yes; Id.327b
1483 " Catherine; f; 9 5-30-22; ¼+; s; dau A708; yes; yes; none
1484 " Leona; f; 7 4-14-24; ¼+; s; dau A709; yes; yes; none
1485 " Gladys; f; 4 11-23-27; ¼+; s; dau A710; yes; yes; none
Died " Calixte[sic]; A711 (Died 9-21-30)

NE Demarais, Joe; Head
1487 " Edna May (Standing); f; 26; F; m; wife B682; no; Dunseith, Rolette, ND; yes; Id.53b, Al.G-323

NE Demarais, John; Head
1488 " Clara (Belgarde); f; 17 6-27-14; ¼+; m; wife B281; no; Dinseith[sic], Rolette, ND; no; Id.188h
1489 " Eli; m; 3/12 1-15-32; ¼+; s; son; no; Dunseith, Rolette, ND; no; none

Turtle Mountain Reservation
1932 Census Roll

Key: Number; Surname, Given; Sex; Age at Last Birthday, Birthdate (if given); Tribe (Chippewa, unless stated otherwise); Degree of Blood; Marital Status; Relationship to Head of Family, Last Year Census Number; At Jurisdiction Where Enrolled (Yes/No); Elsewhere - Post Office, County, State; Ward (Yes/No); Allotment [Al.], Annuity [An.] and/or Identification [Id.] Numbers

NE Demarais, John F;   Head
1490   "   Delia (Azure); f; 27 1-22-05; ¼+; m; wife B683; yes; no; Id.129b
1491   "   Ernest J; m; 9 3-30-23; ¼+; s; son B684; yes; no; none
1492   "   Josephine; f; 7 7-7-24; ¼+; s; dau; yes; no; none
1493   "   Lillian; f; 6 5-6-25; ¼+; s; dau; yes; no; none
1494   "   Victoria; f; 2 5-1-29; ¼+; s; dau; yes; no; none
1495   "   John; m; 7/12 7-4-31; ¼+; s; son; yes; no; none

1496 Demarais, Julia; f; 29; ¼+; s; Head; no; Omitted from Cen sus last year Unknown; yes; Id.334, Al.G-83

NE Demarais, Robert;   Head
1497   "   Celina (Thomas); f; 51; ¼+; wife B685; no; Malta, Phillips, Mont; no; Id.335a, Al.G-389
1498   "   Joseph; m; 28; ¼+; s; son B686; no; Malta, Phillips, Mont; yes; Id.335b Al.G01759
1499   "   John E; m; 22; ¼+; s; son B687; no; Malta, Phillips, Mont; yes; Id.335c, Al.G028712
1500   "   Peter; m; 19; ¼+; s; son B688; no; Malta, Phillips, Mont; yes; Id.335f
1501   "   Catherine; f; 16 7-28-16; ¼+; s; dau B689; no; Malta, Phillips, Mont; no; Id.335h
1502   "   Rachel; f; 12 4-19-19; ¼+; s; dau B690; no; Malta, Phillips, Mont; no; Id.335i
1503   "   Mary; f; 10 2-10-22; ¼+; s; dau B691; no; Malta, Phillips, Mont; no; Id.335j
1504   "   Edward; m; 7 2-19-25; ¼+; s; dau B692; no; Malta, Phillips, Mont; no; Id.335k

1505 Demarais[sic], Robert L; m; 26; ¼+; m; Head B693; no; Malta, Phillips, Mont; yes; Id.335, Al.G391
1506   "   Caroline (Allery); f; 26; ¼+; m; wife B694; no; Malta, Phillips, Mont; yes; Id.88c
1507   "   Russell; m; 5 8 8-5-26; ¼+; s; son B695; no; Malta, Phillips, Mont; yes; Id.335-l
Dead   "   Delmar;   B696   (Died Dec. 1927)
1508   "   Edward; m; 4 12-15-27; ¼+; s; son ----; no; (Not on last years[sic] census) Malta, Phillips, Mont; yes; Id.none
1509   "   Ernest; m; 2; ¼+; s; son B697; no; Malta, Phillips, Mont; yes; Id.335n

NE Demo, Alphonse;   Head
1510   "   Philomene (Lafontain.Champagne); f; 45; ¼+; m; wife B698; no; Glasgow, Valley, Mont; no; Id.336a, A.L0304
1511   "   Joseph; m; 15 3-7-17; ¼+; s; son B699; no; Glasgow, Valley, Mont; no; none
1512   "   John; m; 14 3-18-18; ¼+; s; son B700; no; Glasgow, Valley, Mont; no; none

Turtle Mountain Reservation
1932 Census Roll

Key: Number; Surname, Given; Sex; Age at Last Birthday, Birthdate (if given); Tribe (Chippewa, unless stated otherwise); Degree of Blood; Marital Status; Relationship to Head of Family; Last Year Census Number; At Jurisdiction Where Enrolled (Yes/No); Elsewhere - Post Office, County, State; Ward (Yes/No); Allotment [Al.], Annuity [An.] and/or Identification [Id.] Numbers

1513 Demo(cont), Ida Rose; f; 11 7-2-20; ¼+; s; dau B701; no; Glasgow, Valley, Mont; no; none
1514 " Henry W; m; 10 10-20-21; ¼+; s; son B702; no; Glasgow, Valley, Mont; no; none
1515 " Lilly M; f; 9 10-31-22; ¼+; s; dau B703; no; Glasgow, Valley, Mont; no; none
Dead " Jerry; B704 (Died in 1927)
1516 " Robert; m; 6 5-30-25; ¼+; s; son ----; no; Glasgow, Valley, Mont; no; none

1517 Demontigny, Alfred; m; 35; ¼+; m; Head A712; yes; no; Id.341b, Al.G08246
1518 " Ellen (Vivier); f; 33; ¼+; m; wife A713; yes; no; Id.992b
Dead " Elmer; A714 (Died 4-7-19)
1519 " Martin; m; 12 2-13-20; ¼+; s; son A715; yes; no; none
1520 " Ruth; f; 10 4-30-21; ¼+; s; dau A716; yes; no; none
1521 " Alexander; m; 9 8-28-22; ¼+; s; son A717; yes; no; none
1522 " Harry; m; 7 7-28-24; ¼+; s; son A718; yes; no; none
1523 " Wilfred; m; 5 8-18-26; ¼+; s; son A719; yes; no; none

NE Demontigny, Ambrose; wd; Head
1524 " Ferdinand; m; 22; ¼+; s; son A720; yes; yes; Id.340b, Al.H010516
1525 " Patrick; m; 20; ¼+; s; son A721; yes; yes; Id.340c, Al.H024299
1526 " Emil; m; 18 2-2-18; ¼+; s; son A722; yes; yes; Id.340d, Al.H024728
1527 " Joseph; m; 16; ¼+; s; son A723; yes; yes; Id.340e
1528 " Ellen Ruth; f; 14; ¼+; s; dau A724; yes; yes; Id.340f
1529 " Louis D; m; 11; ¼+; s; son -----; yes; yes; Id.340g

1530 Demontigny, Gabriel; m; 37; ¼+; m; Head A725; yes; yes; Id.339, Al.GF206
NE " Dorothy (Halliday); f; wife
1531 " Lloyd; m; 6 1-17-26; ¼+; s; son A727; yes; yes; Id.none
1532 " James; m; 4 9-1-27; ¼+; s; son A728; yes; yes; none
1533 " Hazel; f; 7 11-3-24; ¼+; s; dau A726; yes; yes; none

NE Demontigny, Hermance; Head
1534 " Julia (Azure); f; 79; ¼+; m; wife A729; yes; yes; Id.338a, Al.R104
1535 " Elizabeth; f; 32; ¼+; s; dau A730; yes; yes; Id.338c, Al.GF204
1536 " Raphael; m; 30; ¼+; s; son A731; yes; yes; Id.338d, Al.GF203

1537 Demontigny, John Louis; m; 35; ¼+; m; Head A732; yes; no; Id.338b, Al.GF205
1538 " Clara (Wilkie); f; 32; ¼+; m; wife A733; yes; no; Id.1008b, Al.M101
1539 " John, Jr; m; 3 1-1-29; ¼+; s; son A734; yes; no; none

1540 Demontigny, Theresa; f; 55; ¼+; wd; Head B705; no; Rolla, Rolette, ND; no; Id.341a, Al.R105
1541 " Mary Adele; f; 26; ¼+; s; dau B706; no; Rolla, Rolette, ND; no; Id.341e

Turtle Mountain Reservation
1932 Census Roll

Key: Number; Surname, Given; Sex; Age at Last Birthday, Birthdate (if given); Tribe (Chippewa, unless stated otherwise); Degree of Blood; Marital Status; Relationship to Head of Family, Last Year Census Number; At Jurisdiction Where Enrolled (Yes/No); Elsewhere - Post Office, County, State; Ward (Yes/No); Allotment [Al.], Annuity [An.] and/or Identification [Id.] Numbers

NE De Sentel, Frank;   Head
1542   "   Maria (Marion); f; 18 7-23-13; ¼+; m; wife A1518; no; Fargo, Cass, ND; no; Id.699d

NE Deschamp, Louis;   Head;   no; Yorkton, Sask, Canada
1543   "   Mary; f; 8; ¼+; s; dau; no; Dunseith, Rolette, ND; yes; Id.882c
1544   "   Evelyn; f; 6; ¼+; s; dau; no; Dunseith, Rolette, ND; yes; Id.882d

NE Dionne, Alexander;   Head
1545   "   Rosalie (Lizotte); f; 28; ¼+; m; wife A735; yes; yes; Id.675b, Al.G-408
1546   "   Charlie; m; 11 11-12-21; ¼+; s; son A736; yes; yes; none
1547   "   Maurice; m; 8 4-22-23; ¼+; s; son A737; yes; yes; none
1548   "   Frank; m; 7 10-24-24; ¼+; s; son A738; yes; yes; none
1549   "   Blanche; f; 5 4-25-26; ¼+; s; dau A739; yes; yes; none
1550   "   Eva Marie; f; 4 7-11-27; ¼+; s; dau A740; yes; yes; none
1551   "   Alice Marie; f; 10-4-28; ¼+; s; dau A741; yes; yes; none
1552   "   Edward; m; 2 12-5-29; ¼+; s; son A742; yes; yes; none
1553   "   Joseph; m; 11/12 4-22-31; ¼+; s; son A743; yes; yes; none

NE Dionne, Frank;   Head
1554   "   Mary Jane (Bonneau); f; 47; ¼+; m; wife B707; no; Plentywood, Sheridan, Mont; no; Id.343a, Al.H-08997
1555   "   Harness; m; 22; ¼+; s; son B708; no; Plentywood, Sheridan, Mont; no; Id.344d, Al.010538
1556   "   Harry; m; 20; ¼+; s; son B709; no; Plentywood, Sheridan, Mont; no; Id.343e
1557   "   Marie; f; 17; ¼+; s; dau B710; no; Plentywood, Sheridan, Mont; no; Id.343f
1558   "   Alice; f; 14 7-4-17; ¼+; s; dau B711; no; Plentywood, Sheridan, Mont; no; Id.343g
1559   "   Frank; m; 12 8-27-19; ¼+; s; son B712; no; Plentywood, Sheridan, Mont; no; Id.343h
1560   "   Inez; f; 10 7-27-21; ¼+; s; dau B713; no; Plentywood, Sheridan, Mont; no; Id.343i

NE Dionne, John;   Head
1561   "   Mary R (Grandbois); f; 36; ¼+; m; wife B714; no; Medicine Lake, Sheridan, Mont; no; Id.345a
1562   "   Mary Sarah; f; 12 6-1-19; ¼+; s; dau B715; no; Medicine Lake, Sheridan, Mont; no; Id.345c
1563   "   Clarence; m; 8 1-18-24; ¼+; s; son; no; Medicine Lake; no; none
1564   "   Andrew; m; 6 3-29-26; ¼+; s; son; no; Medicine Lake; no; none
1565   "   Edward; m; 3 9-22-28; ¼+; s; son; no; Medicine Lake; no; none
1566   "   Dorothy; f; 1 2-24-31; ¼+; s; dau B716; no; Medicine Lake; no; none

Turtle Mountain Reservation
1932 Census Roll

Key: Number; Surname, Given; Sex; Age at Last Birthday, Birthdate (if given); Tribe (Chippewa, unless stated otherwise); Degree of Blood; Marital Status; Relationship to Head of Family, Last Year Census Number; At Jurisdiction Where Enrolled (Yes/No); Elsewhere - Post Office, County, State; Ward (Yes/No); Allotment [Al.], Annuity [An.] and/or Identification [Id.] Numbers

1567 Dionne, Joseph; m; 40; ¼+; m; Head A744; yes; yes; Id.344, Al.M-298
1568   "   May Julia (Kanick); f; 31; F; m; wife A745; yes; yes; Id.12b, Al.G-360
Died   "   Marie;   A746   (Died 12-26-31)
1569   "   Lizzie; f; 11 3-12-21; ¼+; s; dau A747; yes; yes; Id.344b
1570   "   Rena; f; 9 1-15-23; ¼+; s; dau A748; yes; yes; Id.344e
1571   "   Joseph; m; 7 4-15-24; ¼+; s; son A749; yes; yes; Id.344f
1572   "   Julia; f; 6 8-16-25; ¼+; s; dau A750; yes; yes; none
1573   "   Mary; f; 5 11-20-26; ¼+; s; dau A751; yes; yes; none
1574   "   Rose; f; 2 8-10-29; ¼+; s; dau A752; yes; yes; none
1575   "   Robert; m; 7/12 8-18-31; ¼+; s; son; yes; yes; none

1576 Dionne, Joseph Wm; m; 28; ¼+; m; Head A754; yes; yes; Id.342b, Al.H-024552
1577   "   Winifred (Premeau); f; ¼+; m; wife A1916; yes; yes; Id.880f, Al.H-010522
1578   "   Dorothy M; f; 10/12 5-26-31; ¼+; s; dau; yes; yes; none

NE Dionne, Louis;   Head
1579   "   Rose (Thomas); f; 48; ¼+; m; wife A753; yes; yes; Id.342a, Al.R-107
1580   "   Louis A; m; 21; ¼+; s; son A755; yes; yes; Id.342d, Al.H-01303
1581   "   John L; m; 18 12-27-13; ¼+; s; son A756; yes; yes; Id.342e
1582   "   Aflfred[sic] m; 15 1-6-17; ¼+; s; son A757; yes; yes; Id.342f
1583   "   Mary e; f; 13 6-14-19; ¼+; s; dau A758; yes; yes; Id.342g
1584   "   Lillian; f; 10 10-7-21; ¼+; s; dau A759; yes; yes; Id.342h
1585   "   Russell Roy; m; 8 2-27-24; ¼+; s; son A760; yes; yes; none
1586   "   Clarence; m; 5 5-3-26; ¼+; s; son A761; yes; yes; none
1587   "   Benedict; m; 3 10-7-28; ¼+; s; son A762; yes; yes; none
1588   "   Mary Alma; f; 1 12-7-30; ¼+; s; dau -----; yes; yes; none

1589 Dionne, Moses; m; 29; ¼+; s; Head B717; no; Froid, Roosevelt, Mont; no; Id.346b,
                                                          Al.M-299

NE Dionne, Peter;   Head
1590   "   Delia (Jaste); f; 27; ¼+; m; wife A763; yes; yes; Id.500d, Al.H-10420
1591   "   Mabel; f; 4 11-15-27; ¼+; s; dau A764; yes; yes; none
1592   "   Mary Delima; f; 3 2-2-29; ¼+; s; dau A765; yes; yes; none
1593   "   Theresa Mae; f; 1 2-24-31; ¼+; s; dau; yes; yes; none

1594 Dionne, Simon P; m; 26; ¼+; m; Head A766; yes; yes; Id.342c, Al.G-0296
1595   "   Josephine (Azure); f; 25; ¼+; m; wife A767; yes; yes; Id.117c
1596   "   Marguerite; f; 10/12 5-23-31; ¼+; s; dau; yes; yes; none

NE Doney, Alfred;   Head
1597   "   Elizabeth (Allery); f; 40; ¼+; wife B718; no; Malta, Phillips, Mont; no;
                                                     Id.348a, Al.G-09282
1598   "   Joseph; m; 17; ¼+; s; son B719; no; Malta, Phillips, Mont; no; Id.348b

Turtle Mountain Reservation
1932 Census Roll

Key: Number; Surname, Given; Sex; Age at Last Birthday, Birthdate (if given); Tribe (Chippewa, unless stated otherwise); Degree of Blood; Marital Status; Relationship to Head of Family, Last Year Census Number; At Jurisdiction Where Enrolled (Yes/No); Elsewhere - Post Office, County, State; Ward (Yes/No); Allotment [Al.], Annuity [An.] and/or Identification [Id.] Numbers

1599 Doney(cont), Charles; m; 12; ¼+; s; son; no; yes; none
1600 " Walter; m; 9; ¼+; s; son; no; yes; none
1601 " Martin; m; 6; ¼+; s; son; no; yes; none

NE Doney, John;   Head
1602 " Elizabeth (Allery); f; 43; ¼+; m; wife B720; no; Harlem, Blaine, Mont; no; Id.347a, Al.G-413
1603 " Wm John; m; 20 2-15-12; ¼+; s; son B722; no; Harlem, Blaine, Mont; no; Id.347d
1604 " Clara; f; 16 11-8-15; ¼+; s; dau B723; no; Harlem, Blaine, Mont; no; none
1605 " Florence; f; 13 6-6-18; ¼+; s; dau B724; no; Harlem, Blaine, Mont; no; none
1606 " Rosie C; f; 11 9-9-20; ¼+; s; dau B725; no; Harlem, Blaine, Mont; no; none
1607 " James; m; 9 9-1-22; ¼+; s; son B726; no; Harlem, Blaine, Mont; no; none
Dead " Matilda; f; 5 4-9-26; ¼+; s;   B727   (Died 8-3-28) Harlem, Blaine, Mont; no; none
Dead " Leonard; 1-24-28   (Died 3-22-29)

NE Douglas, Graham;   Head
1608 " Adelia (Gladue); f; 49; ¼+; m; wife B728; no; Dunseith, Rolette, ND; no; Id.349a, Al.H-038858

1609 Dressed in Stone; f; 106; F; wd; Head B729; no; Carlisle, Sask, Can; no; Id.16a, Al.G-272

1610 Dressed in Yellow; f; 75; F; wd; Head B730; no; Dunseith, Rolette, ND; yes; Id.46, Al.R-255

NE Dubois, Alex;   Head
1611 " Adeline (Thifault); f; 44; ¼+; m; wife B732; no; Dunseith, Rolette, ND; no; Id.354a, Al.W-38
1612 " Walter; m; 19 2-10-13; ¼+; s; son B733; no; Dunseith, Rolette, ND; no; Id.354b
1613 " Clinton; m; 17 10-19-14; ¼+; s; son B734; no; Dunseith, Rolette, ND; no; Id.354c
1614 " Melinda; f; 9 4-7-22; ¼+; s; dau B735; no; Dunseith, Rolette, ND; no; none

NE Dubois, Alexander;   Head
1615 " Mary (Peltier); f; 38; ¼+; m; wife B736; no; Fort Berthold; no; Id.355a, Al.G-425
1616 " Joseph; m; 16; ¼+; s; son B737; no; Fort Berthold; no; Id.355c
1617 " Mary E; f; 12 11-6-19; ¼+; s; dau B738; no; Fort Berthold; no; Id.355d

1618 Dubois, Alvina; f; 18; ¼+; s; Head A1994; yes; yes; Id.255, Al.MC-026508

Turtle Mountain Reservation
1932 Census Roll

Key: Number; Surname, Given; Sex; Age at Last Birthday, Birthdate (if given); Tribe (Chippewa, unless stated otherwise); Degree of Blood; Marital Status; Relationship to Head of Family; Last Year Census Number; At Jurisdiction Where Enrolled (Yes/No); Elsewhere - Post Office, County, State; Ward (Yes/No); Allotment [Al.], Annuity [An.] and/or Identification [Id.] Numbers

NE Dubois, Ben;   Head
1619   "   Mary (St Claire); f; 30; ¼+; m; wife B739; yes; yes; Id.935b, Al.H-030422
1620   "   Melvin; m; 8 5-23-23; ¼+; s; son; yes; yes; none
1621   "   Emilia; f; 6 10-8-25; ¼+; s; dau; yes; yes; none
1622   "   Benny J; m; 4 8-25-27; ¼+; s; son ----; yes; yes; none
1623   "   Alaxander[sic]; m; 2 9-4-29; ¼+; s; son ----; yes; yes; none
1624   "   Doreen C; f; 1 9-26-30; ¼+; s; dau ----; yes; yes; none

Ne[sic] Dubois, Michael;   Head
1625   "   Mary; f; 30; ¼+; m; wife B731; no; (Maiden name unknown) Dunseith, Rolette, ND; no; Id.353a, Al.M-29

NE Dubois, William;   Head
1626   "   Rosalie (Morin); f; 37; ¼+; m; wife B740; no; Dunseith, Rolette, ND; no; Id.352a, Al.G-589
1627   "   Clara; f; 19 2-22-13; ¼+; s; dau B741; no; Dunseith, Rolette, ND; yes; Id.352b, Al.H-024440
1628   "   Emile; m; 18 2-14-14; ¼+; s; son B742; no; Dunseith, Rolette, ND; no; Id.352c
1629   "   Lillian; f; 16 2-12-16; ¼+; s; dau B743; no; Dunseith, Rolette, ND; no; Id.352d
1630   "   Andrew; m; 14 5-12-17; ¼+; s; son B744; no; Dunseith, Rolette, ND; no; Id.352e
1631   "   Mabel; f; 12 6-2-19; ¼+; s; dau B745; no; Dunseith, Rolette, ND; no; Id.352f
1632   "   Helen; f; 10 8-10-21; ¼+; s; dau B746; no; Dunseith, Rolette, ND; no; Id.352g
1633   "   Florence; f; 5 2-21-27; ¼+; s; dau B747; no; Dunseith, Rolette, ND; no; Id.352h

1634 Ducept, Calixte; m; 48; ¼+; s; Head B748; no; Rolla, Rolette, ND; yes; Id.356, Al.GF-74

1635 Ducept, Josephine (St Arnaud); f; 28; ¼+; wd; Head A768; no; Nishu, McLean, ND; yes; Id.929b, Al.M-212
1636   "   Dora S; f; 9 11-3-22; ¼+; s; dau A769; no; Nishu, McLean, ND; yes; none
1637   "   Oscar H; m; 7 9-3-24; ¼+; s; son A770; no; Nishu, McLean, ND; yes; none
1638   "   Francis; m; 5 4-3-26; ¼+; s; don A771; no; Nishu, McLean, ND; yes; none
1639   "   Elmer J; m; 3 5-11-28; ¼+; s; son A772; no; Nishu, McLean, ND; yes; none
1640 " (Brien) Albert; m; 3/12 12-3-31; ¼+; s; son ----; no; Nishu, McLean, ND; yes; none

1641 Ducept, Marie; f; 44; ¼+; wd; Head A773; yes; yes; Id.358

Turtle Mountain Reservation
1932 Census Roll

Key: Number; Surname, Given; Sex; Age at Last Birthday, Birthdate (if given); Tribe (Chippewa, unless stated otherwise); Degree of Blood; Marital Status; Relationship to Head of Family, Last Year Census Number; At Jurisdiction Where Enrolled (Yes/No); Elsewhere - Post Office, County, State; Ward (Yes/No); Allotment [Al.], Annuity [An.] and/or Identification [Id.] Numbers

1642 Ducept, Pierre; m; 71; ¼+; m; Head A774; yes; yes; Id.359, Al.R110
1643 " Celina; f; 60; ¼+; m; wife A775; yes; (Maiden name not known) yes; Id.359a, AlH-12538
1644 " (Paul) Evelyn ; f; 14; ¼+; s; ad. dau A776; yes; yes; Id.811b

1645 Ducept, Pierre; m; 48; ¼+; s; Head B749; no; Rolla, Rolette, ND; no; Id.362, Al.G-07851

1646 Ducept, Robert; m; 27; ¼+; s; Head B750; no; Rolla, Rolette, ND; yes; Id.360c, Al.H-030460

1647 Duchain, Alex; m; 45; ¼+; m; Head B751; yes; no; Id.364, Al.M-401
NE   " Marie R (Faguant); wife
1648 " Pascal; m; 11 10-15-20; ¼+; s; son B752; yes; no; Id.364f
1649 " William; m; 9 9-19-22; ¼+; s; son B753; yes; no; Id.364e
1650 " Victoria; f; 6 6-20-25; ¼+; s; dau B754; yes; no; Id.none
1651 " Lillian; f; 3 9-6-28; ¼+; s; dau; yes; no; none

1652 Duchain, Laron; m; 73; ¼+; wd; Head B755; yes; no; Id.363, Al.G-07090
1653 " Charles; m; 28; ¼+; s; son B756; yes; yes; Id.363b, Al.M-397
1654 " Rose; f; 27; ¼+; as; dau B758; yes; yes; Id.363d, Al.G-07089

1655 Duchesneau, Albert; m; 24 8-4-07; ¼+; m; Head B762; no; Thorne, Rolette, ND; no; Id.365f
NE   " Mildred (Lahey); wife

NE   Duchesneau, Moses; Head
1656 " Julienne (Nicholas); f; 49 1-5-83; ¼+; m; wife B759; no; Dunseith, Rolette, ND; no; Id.365a, Al.M-249
1657 " Adolph; m; 25 6-29-06; ¼+; s; son B761; no; Spooner, Washburn, Wis; no; Id.365e
1658 " Joseph; m; 24 2-12-08; ¼+; s; son B763; no; Dunseith, Rolette, ND; no; Id.365g
1659 " Lionel; m; 22 9-2-09; ¼+; s; son B764; no; Dunseith, Rolette, ND; no; Id.365h
1660 " Rosilda; f; 20 11-4-11; ¼+; s; dau B765; no; Dunseith, Rolette, ND; no; Id.365i
1661 " Antoine; m; 18 6-2-13; ¼+; s; son B766; no; Dunseith, Rolette, ND; no; Id.365j
1662 " Alida; f; 17 7-6-14; ¼+; s; dau B767; no; Dunseith, Rolette, ND; no; Id.365k
1663 " Alexander; m; 16 11-6-15; ¼+; s; son B768; no; Dunseith, Rolette, ND; no; Id.365l

Turtle Mountain Reservation
1932 Census Roll

Key: Number; Surname, Given; Sex; Age at Last Birthday, Birthdate (if given); Tribe (Chippewa, unless stated otherwise); Degree of Blood; Marital Status; Relationship to Head of Family; Last Year Census Number; At Jurisdiction Where Enrolled (Yes/No); Elsewhere - Post Office, County, State; Ward (Yes/No); Allotment [Al.], Annuity [An.] and/or Identification [Id.] Numbers

1664 Duchesneau(cont), Angeline; f; 14 4-17-17; ¼+; s; dau B769; no; Dunseith, Rolette, ND; no; Id.365m

1665 " Theodore; m; 12 10-1-19; ¼+; s; son B770; no; Dunseith, Rolette, ND; no; Id.365n

1666 " Germain; m; 12 2-23-20; ¼+; s; son B771; no; Dunseith, Rolette, ND; no; Id.365o

1667 " Hector; m; 11 10-16-22; ¼+; s; son B772; no; Dunseith, Rolette, ND; no; Id.365p

1668 " Leonard; m; 6 9-40-25; ¼+; s; son B773; no; Dunseith, Rolette, ND; no; Id.365q

1669 " Raoul; m; 6 2-2-26; ¼+; s; son B774; no; Dunseith, Rolette, ND; no; Id.365r

NE Dufane, Frank;   Head
1670 " Rosalie (Grant); f; 25; ¼+; m; wife B775; no; Devils Lake, Ramsey, ND; yes; Id.454cl Al.G-0249

1671 Dumont, Alexander; m; 35; ¼+; m; Head B776; no; Unknown, Canada; no; Id.367b, Al.G-0441
NE " Mary Alice (Langer);   wife
1672 " Albert; m; 9; ¼+; s; son B777; no; Unknown, Canada; no; none
1673 " Francis; m; 8; ¼+; s; son B778; no; Unknown, Canada; no; none

NE Dumont, Bazil;   wd; Head
1674 " Alice; f; 26; ¼+; s; dau B779; no; Roy, Sheridan, Mont; yes; Id.367f, Al.G-0443
1675 " Edmond; m; 23; ¼+; s; son B780; no; Roy, Sheridan, Mont; no; Id.367g

1676 Dumont, Joseph; m; 48; ¼+; m; Head B781; no; Roy, Sheridan, Mont; no; Id.366, Al.G-0438
1677 " Virginia (Daignault); f; 56; ¼+; m; wife B782; no; Roy, Sheridan, Mont; no; Id.366a, Al.G-037051
1678 " Frank; m; 23; ¼+; s; son B783; no; Roy, Sheridan, Mont; no; Id.366c
1679 " Ernest; m; 22; ¼+; s; son B784; no; Roy, Sheridan, Mont; yes; Id.366b, Al.H-012527
1680 " Marie; f; 20; ¼+; s; dau B785; no; Roy, Sheridan, Mont; no; Id.366d
1681 " Cecelia; f; 19; ¼+; s; dau B786; no; Roy, Sheridan, Mont; no; Id.366e

NE Dunphey, Daniel;   Head
1682 " Lucy (Latrace); f; 36; ¼+; m; wife B787; no; Model Farm, Sask, Canada; no; Id.l369a, Al.G-0302
1683 " Ella R; f; 18; ¼+; s; dau B788; no; Model Farm, Sask, Canada; no; none
1684 " Joseph; m; 15 3-23-17; ¼+; s; son B789; no; Model Farm, Sask, Canada; no; none

Turtle Mountain Reservation
1932 Census Roll

Key: Number; Surname, Given; Sex; Age at Last Birthday, Birthdate (if given); Tribe (Chippewa, unless stated otherwise); Degree of Blood; Marital Status; Relationship to Head of Family, Last Year Census Number; At Jurisdiction Where Enrolled (Yes/No); Elsewhere - Post Office, County, State; Ward (Yes/No); Allotment [Al.], Annuity [An.] and/or Identification [Id.] Numbers

1685 Dunphey(cont), Edward; m; 13 1-26-19; ¼+; s; son B790; no; Model Farm, Sask, Canada; no; none

NE Dussome, Frank;   Head
1686   "   Rosanna (Delorme); f; 25; ¼+; m; wife B791; no; Unknown; yes; Id.332b, Al.H-012530

NE Ekman, Thomas;   Head
1687   "   Mary (Hayes); f; 38; ¼+; m; wife B792; no; St.Paul, Ramsey, Minn; no; Id.370a, Al.G-019364
1688   "   John; m; 21; ¼+; s; son B793; no; Goodrich, Sheridan, ND; Id.370b
1689   "   Augusta; f; 17; ¼+; s; dau B795; yes; no; Id.370d
Dead   "   Victor;   B794   (Died in 1915)
1690   "   Lizzie; f; 10 12-26-21; ¼+; s; dau B796; no; St.Paul, Ramsey, Minn

NE Eller, Herman;   Head
1691   "   Laura (Azure); f; 30; ¼+; m; wife B797; no; Dunseith, Rolette, ND; yes; Id.120d, Al.G-563
1692   "   Gladys; f; 2 4-27-29; ¼+; s; dau B798; no; Dunseith, Rolette, ND; yes; none
1693   "   Geraldine; f; 1 3-9-31; ¼+; s; dau B799; no; Dunseith, Rolette, ND; yes; none

NE Ellis, Lee;   Head
1694   "   Ernestine; f; 44; ¼+; m; wife B800; no; Unknown; no; Id.371a, Al.M-43
1695   "   Marie E; f; 19; ¼+; s; dau B801; no; Unknown; no; none

1484 Enno, Alexander; m; 42; ¼+; m; Head A777; yes; no; Id.378, Al.G-06039
1696   "   Rachel (Morin); f; 34; ¼+; m; wife A778; yes; no; Id.378a, Al.M-200
1697   "   George; m; 14 6-26-17; ¼+; s; son A779; yes; no; Id.378b
1698   "   Samuel R; m; 13 9-16-18; ¼+; s; son A780; yes; no; Id.378c
1699   "   Rosina; f; 11 5-31-20; ¼+; s; dau A781; yes; no; none
1700   "   Laura; f; 8 5-20-23; ¼+; s; dau A782; yes; no; none
1701   "   Francis; m; 5 11-26-26; ¼+; s; son A783; yes; no; none
Died   "   Louis;   A784   (Died 2-7-32)

1702 Enno, Baptiste; m; 63; ¼+; m; Head A785; yes; yes; Id.379, Al.R-114
1703   "   Mary (Azure); f; 60; ¼+; m; wife A786; yes; yes; Id.379a, Al.GF-116
1704   "   Rose; f; 19 9-1-12; ¼+; s; dau A787; yes; yes; Id.379d, Al.H-012539

1705 Enno, Louis; m; 61; ¼+; m; Head A788; yes; no; Id.372, Al.R-115
NE   "   Sarah (Morin);   wife
1706   "   Benjamin; m; 23; ¼+; s; son A789; yes; yes; Id.372e, Al.H-012540
1707   "   Albany; m; 14 4-2-17; ¼+; s; grandson A790; yes; yes; none

Turtle Mountain Reservation
1932 Census Roll

Key: Number; Surname, Given; Sex; Age at Last Birthday, Birthdate (if given); Tribe (Chippewa, unless stated otherwise); Degree of Blood; Marital Status; Relationship to Head of Family, Last Year Census Number; At Jurisdiction Where Enrolled (Yes/No); Elsewhere - Post Office, County, State; Ward (Yes/No); Allotment [Al.], Annuity [An.] and/or Identification [Id.] Numbers

1708 Enno, Louis; m; 39 7-6-92; ¼+; m; Head A791; yes; no; Id.381a, Al.GF-123
NE " Marion (Houle); wife
1709 " Rosilda; f; 13 2-17-19; ¼+; s; dau A792; yes; no; Id.381b
1710 " Eugenia; f; 10 5-18-21; ¼+; s; dau A793; yes; no; Id.381c
1711 " Sidney; m; 5 11-19-26; ¼+; s; son A794; yes; no; none
1712 " Gladys C; f; 4/12 11-11-31; ¼+; s; dau; yes; no; none

1713 Enno, Mary C (McKay); f; 63; ¼+; wd; Head A795; yes; yes; Id.376a, Al.G-06056
1714 " Alfred; m; 30; ¼+; s; son A796; yes; yes; Id.376b, Al.G-06053
1715 " Pierre; m; 27; ¼+; s; son A797; yes; yes; Id.376c, Al.G-06055
1716 " Francois; m; 23; ¼+; s; son A798; yes; yes; Id.3764e
1717 " Robert; m; 15 3-25-17; ¼+; s; grand-son A799; yes; yes; Id. 376f

1718 Enno, Norman; m; 37; ¼+; s; Head A800; yes; no; Id.380, Al.GF-119

NE Equall, Raymond; Head
1719 " Mary Ida (Premeau); f; 31; ¼+; m; wife B802; no; Hardin, Big Horn, Mont; yes; Id.880b, Al.M-170
1720 " Raymond; m; 3 10-25-28; ¼+; s; son B803; no; Hardin, Big Horn, Mont; yes; none

NE Erickson, August; Head
1721 " Adelphine (Marion); f; 26 10-13-05; ¼+; m; wife B1703; no; Grenora, Williams, ND; yes; Id.693e, Al.G-018552
(The children of this couple are listed as whites)

NE Everling, Nick; Head
1722 " Mary P (Poitra); f; 40; ¼+; m; wife A801; no; Unknown, Mont; no; Id.382a, Al.G-163
1723 " Elizabeth; f; 19; ¼+; s; dau A802; yes; yes; Id.382b, Al.H-024677
1724 " Wm Charley; m; 17 4-10-14; ¼+; s; son A803; yes; no; Id.382c
1725 " Louis; m; 16 2-10-16; ¼+; s; son A804; yes; no; Id.382d
1726 " Rose; f; 13 11-4-18; ¼+; s; dau A805; yes; no; Id.382e
1727 " August; m; 9 10-2-22; ¼+; s; son A806; yes; no; Id.382g

1728 Faguant, Louis J; m; 28; ¼+; m; Head B804; no; Dunseith, Rolette, ND; no; Id.383d, Al.none
1729 " Rose (Amyott); f; 23; ¼+; m; wife B805; no; Dunseith, Rolette, ND; no; Id.96f
1730 " Irene S; f; 3 7-26-28; ¼+; s; dau B806; no; Dunseith, Rolette, ND; no; none
1731 " Emma Rose; f; 2 3-30-30; ¼+; s; dau B807; no; Dunseith, Rolette, ND; no; none
1732 " Sylvia; f; 3/12 12-18-31; ¼+; s; dau; no; Dunseith, Rolette, ND; no; none

Turtle Mountain Reservation
1932 Census Roll

Key: Number; Surname, Given; Sex; Age at Last Birthday, Birthdate (if given); Tribe (Chippewa, unless stated otherwise); Degree of Blood; Marital Status; Relationship to Head of Family, Last Year Census Number; At Jurisdiction Where Enrolled (Yes/No); Elsewhere - Post Office, County, State; Ward (Yes/No); Allotment [Al.], Annuity [An.] and/or Identification [Id.] Numbers

1733 Faguant, Victor; m; 45; ¼+; m; Head B808; no; Dunseith, Rolette, ND; no; Id.384, Al.H-038857
NE   "   Mary (Godon);   wife
1734   "   Joseph; m; 22; ¼+; s; son B809; no; Dunseith, Rolette, ND; no; Id.384b
1735   "   Adolphus; m; 16 5-5-15; ¼+; s; son B810; no; Dunseith, Rolette, ND; no; Id.384d
1736   "   Frank; m; 13; ¼+; s; son B811; no; Dunseith, Rolette, ND; no; none
        Octavia; f; 12 3-7-20; ¼+; s; dau B812; no; Dunseith, Rolette, ND; no; none

1737 Faguant, William; m; 80; ¼+; m; Head B813; no; Dunseith, Rolette, ND; yes; Id.383, Al.DL-01725
1738   "   Julia (Lafontain); f; 64; ¼+; m; wife B814; no; Dunseith, Rolette, ND; yes; Id.383a, Al.H-030278
1739   "   Ezear; m; 33; ¼+; s; son B815; no; Dunseith, Rolette, ND; yes; Id.383b, Al.H-030397
1740   "   Joseph; m; 22; ¼+; s; son B816; no; Dunseith, Rolette, ND; yes; none

NE Falcon, Albert;   Head
1741   "   Rosina (Vandal); f; 23; ¼+; m; wife B820; no; Trenton, Williams, ND; yes; Id.978e, Al.H-012616
1742   "   George P; m; 6 3-15-26; ¼+; s; son; no; Trenton, Williams, ND; yes; none
1743   "   Louis A; m; 3 2-16-28; ¼+; s; son; no; Trenton, Williams, ND; yes; none

NE Falcon, Alfred;   Head
1744   "   Mary L (Vandal.Morin); f; ¼+; m; wife B821; no; Trenton, Williams, ND; no; Id.756a, Al.G-0245
1745   "   (Morin) Frank; m; 14 6-15-17; ¼+; s; step son B822; no; Trenton, Williams, ND; no; none
NE   "   Fred; 13 5-15-18; son
1746   "   Anna; f; 11 8-29-20; ¼+; s; dau B823; no; Trenton, Williams, ND; no; none
1747   "   James J; m; 8 6-1-23; ¼+; s; son B824; no; Trenton, Williams, ND; no; none
1748   "   Willis; m; 6 12-18-25; ¼+; s; son B825; no; Trenton, Williams, ND; no; none
1749   "   Walter; m; 3 9-8-28; ¼+; s; son B826; no; Trenton, Williams, ND; no; none
1750   "   Gladys J; f; 2 11-22-29; ¼+; s; dau B827; no; Trenton, Williams, ND; no; none
1751   "   Marie M; f; 5/12 10-25-31; ¼+; s; dau; no; Trenton, Williams, ND; no; none

1752 Falcon, Elie; m; 61; ¼+; wd; Head A807; yes; yes; Id.385, Al.R-116
1753   "   Joseph; m; 23; ¼+; s; son A808; yes; yes; Id.385d, Al.H-010520
1754   "   Jean B; m; 20; ¼+; s; son A809; yes; yes; Id.385e
1755   "   Mary V; f; 11 4-12-20; ¼+; s; dau A810; yes; yes; none
1756   "   Anna A; f; 10 9-13-22; ¼+; s; dau A811; yes; yes; none
1757   "   Irene G; f; 7 1-27-25; ¼+; s; dau A812; yes; yes; none

1758 Falcon, Flora; f; 18; ¼+; s; Head B962; no; Trenton, Williams, ND; no; Id.387

Turtle Mountain Reservation
1932 Census Roll

Key: Number; Surname, Given; Sex; Age at Last Birthday, Birthdate (if given); Tribe (Chippewa, unless stated otherwise); Degree of Blood; Marital Status; Relationship to Head of Family, Last Year Census Number; At Jurisdiction Where Enrolled (Yes/No); Elsewhere - Post Office, County, State; Ward (Yes/No); Allotment [Al.], Annuity [An.] and/or Identification [Id.] Numbers

NE Falcon, Frank;   Head
1759 " Mary V (Morin); f; 30; ¼+; m; wife A813; yes; yes; Id.755c, Al.M-197
1760 " John; m; 10 10-10-21; ¼+; s; son A814; yes; yes; none
1761 " Robert; m; 9 10-17-22; ¼+; s; son A815; yes; yes; none
1762 " Cecelia; f; 7 5-1-24; ¼+; s; dau A817; yes; yes; none
1763 " Ella; f; 5 3-12-27; ¼+; s; dau A818; yes; yes; none
1764 " Theresa; f; 3 1-30-29; ¼+; s; dau A819; yes; yes; none
1765 " Edwin; m; 1 3-8-31; ¼+; s; son A820; yes; yes; none
No such child PATRICK;   A816

NE Falcon, Peter;   Head
1766 " Josephine (Turcotte); f; 37; ¼+; m; wife B828; no; Trenton, Williams, ND; no; Id.388a, Al.M-143
1767 " Cecelia A; f; 15 8-27-16; ¼+; s; dau B829; no; Trenton, Williams, ND; no; none
1768 " Alvin F; m; 12 11-26-19; ¼+; s; son B830; no; Trenton, Williams, ND; no; none
1769 " Jane E; f; 19 4-9-22; ¼+; s; dau B831; no; Trenton, Williams, ND; no; none
1770 " Florence L; f; 7 10-5-24; ¼+; s; dau B832; no; Trenton, Williams, ND; no; none
1771 " Marion J; f; 4 4-20-27; ¼+; s; dau B833; no; Trenton, Williams, ND; no; none
1772 " Peter V; m; 2 8-11-29; ¼+; s; son ----; no; Trenton, Williams, ND; no; none

NE Falcon, Raphael;   Head
1773 " Virginia (Bonneau); f; 40; ¼+; m; wife B834; no; Trenton, Williams, ND; no; Id.386a, Al.G08422
1774 " Mary Emma; f; 19 2-10-13; ¼+; s; dau B835; no; Trenton, Williams, ND; yes; Id.386b, Al.H024573
1775 " Oliver D; m; 17 4-22-14; ¼+; s; son B836; no; Trenton, Williams, ND; no; Id.386c
1776 " Mary A; f; 16 10-18-15; ¼+; s; dau B837; no; Trenton, Williams, ND; no; Id.386d
1777 " Annie; f; 14 6-26-17; ¼+; s; dau B838; no; Trenton, Williams, ND; no; Id.386e
1778 " Rose E; f; 12 10-17-19; ¼+; s; dau B839; no; Trenton, Williams, ND; no; Id.386f
1779 " Victoria; f; 10 12-29-21; ¼+; s; dau B890; no; Trenton, Williams, ND; no; Id.386g
1780 " Joseph A; m; 8 3-15-24; ¼+; s; son B841; no; Trenton, Williams, ND; no; Id.386h
1781 " John R; m; 6 1-23-26; ¼+; s; son B842; no; Trenton, Williams, ND; no; Id.386i
Died " Eugene   (Born 1-23-28 & died 5-21-29)
1782 " Lillian; f; 1 7-12-30; ¼+; s; dau; Trenton, Williams, ND; no; none

Turtle Mountain Reservation
1932 Census Roll

Key: Number; Surname, Given; Sex; Age at Last Birthday, Birthdate (if given); Tribe (Chippewa, unless stated otherwise); Degree of Blood; Marital Status; Relationship to Head of Family, Last Year Census Number; At Jurisdiction Where Enrolled (Yes/No); Elsewhere - Post Office, County, State; Ward (Yes/No); Allotment [Al.], Annuity [An.] and/or Identification [Id.] Numbers

NE   Falk, Elmer;   Head
1783   "   Agnes (Brien); f; 20 5-30-11; ¼+; m; wife B426; no; Reserve, Sheridan, Mont; no; Id.201c
1784   "   Theodore; m; 6/12 9-12-31; ¼+; s; son; no; Reserve, Sheridan, Mont; no; none

NE   Farclough, Robert H;   Head
1785   "   Eliza (Latrace); f; 29; ¼+; m; wife B843; no; Boggy Creek, Manitoba, Cana; yes; Id.621b, Al.G-0299

NE   Fassett, Harry;   Head
1786   "   Rachel (Frederick); f; 24; ¼+; m; wife A821; no; Thorne, Rolette, ND; yes; Id.398f, Al.G-247
1787   "   James; m; 2 7-23-29; ¼+; s; son A822; no; Thorne, Rolette, ND; yes; none
1788   "   Donald R; m; 11/12 4-26-31; ¼+; s; son; no; Thorne, Rolette, ND; yes; none

1789   Favill, Gertrude; f; 20; ¼+; s; Head A2020; yes; Id.10[?]6b, Al.H-024577

NE   Farris, Albert;   Head
21   "   Veronica (McCloud); wife   (Divorced wife. #21 on this census); no; Id.389a
1790   "   Edward; m; 19; ¼+; s; son A823; yes; no; Id.389b   (Mother of these children)
1791   "   Roy; m; 16 7-23-15; ¼+; s; son A824; yes; no; Id.389c
1792   "   Samuel; m; 14 7-3-17; ¼+; s; son A825; yes; no; Id.389d

1793   Fiddler, Joseph; m; 44; ¼+; wd; Head B844; no; Rolla, Rolette, ND; no; Id.391, Al.H-03220
1794   "   Joseph R; m; 19; ¼+; s; son B845; no; Rolla, Rolette, ND; no; none

1795   Fiddler, Moses; m; 46; ¼+; m; Head B846; no; Rolla, Rolette, ND; no; Id.390, Al.G07834
1796   "   Florestine (Azure); f; 34; ¼+; m; wife B847; no; Rolla, Rolette, ND; no Id.111b, Al.GF-20
1797   "   John; m; 12; ¼+; s; son B848; no; Rolla, Rolette, ND; no; none
1798   "   Mary Agnes; f; 10 12-15-21; ¼+; s; dau B849; no; Rolla, Rolette, ND; no; none
1799   "   Cecelia M; f; 8 12-15-24; ¼+; s; dau B850; no; Rolla, Rolette, ND; no; none
1800   "   Francis; m; 6 5-12-25; ¼+; s; son B851; no; Rolla, Rolette, ND; no; none
1801   "   Joseph; m; 4 1-18-28; ¼+; s; son A852; no; Rolla, Rolette, ND; no; none
1802   "   Unnamed; f; 2; ¼+; s; dau A853; no; Rolla, Rolette, ND; no; none

NE   Flowers, A N;   Head
1803   "   Marie R (Daignault); f; 54; ¼+; m; wife B854; no; Sequim, Clallam, Wash; no; Id.392a, Al.H-031171
1804   "   Elmer; m; 23; ¼+; s; son B855; no; Sequim, Clallam, Wash; no; Id.392b
1805   "   William; m; 20; ¼+; s; son B857; no; Sequim, Clallam, Wash; no; Id.392c
1806   "   Anna; f; 18; ¼+; s; dau B858; no; Sequim, Clallam, Wash; no; Id.392e

Turtle Mountain Reservation
1932 Census Roll

Key: Number; Surname, Given; Sex; Age at Last Birthday, Birthdate (if given); Tribe (Chippewa, unless stated otherwise); Degree of Blood; Marital Status; Relationship to Head of Family; Last Year Census Number; At Jurisdiction Where Enrolled (Yes/No); Elsewhere - Post Office, County, State; Ward (Yes/No); Allotment [Al.], Annuity [An.] and/or Identification [Id.] Numbers

1807 Flowers(cont), Cecelia; f; 10-8-13-21; ¼+; s; dau; no; Sequim, Clallam, Wash; no; Id.392f

1808 Flying Nice; m; 59; F; wd; Head B859; no; Dunseith, Rolette, ND; yes; Id.15, Al.R-169
1809 " George; m; 21; F; s; son B860; no; Dunseith, Rolette, ND; yes; Id.15b, Al.H-024562
1810 " Mary; f; 13; F; s; dau B861; no; Dunseith, Rolette, ND; yes; none

1811 Foggy Cloud; m; 74; F; m; Head B862; no; Ft.Totten; yes; Id.60, Al.R-314
NE " Mayawia; wife

NE Folster, Fred;   Head
1812 " Mary Louise (Dionne); f; 33; ¼+; m; wife A826; no; Rolla, Rolette, ND; no; Id.394a, Al.M-200
1813 " Victoria; f; 16; ¼+; s; dau A827; no; Rolla, Rolette, ND; no; none
1814 " Alfred; m; 15; ¼+; s; son A828; no; Rolla, Rolette, ND; no; none
1815 " Ralph; m; 11 4-14-20; ¼+; s; son A829; no; Rolla, Rolette, ND; no; none
1816 " Irene; f; 10; ¼+; s; dau A830; no; Rolla, Rolette, ND; no; none
1817 " Russell; m; 9; ¼+; s; son A831; no; Rolla, Rolette, ND; no; none
1818 " Grace; f; 6 1-20-26; ¼+; s; dau A832; no; Rolla, Rolette, ND; no; none

NE Folster, Gabriel;   Head
1819 " Mary St Ann (Azure); f; 27; ¼+; m; wife B863; no; Rolla, Rolette, ND; yes; Id.132b, Al.G-016469
1820 " Larry; m; 7 4-13-24; ¼+; s; son B864; no; Rolla, Rolette, ND; yes; none
1821 " Mary E; f; 6 5-30-25; ¼+; s; dau B865; no; Rolla, Rolette, ND; yes; none
1822 " Cecile A; f; 5 3-19-27; ¼+; s; dau B866; no; Rolla, Rolette, ND; yes; none
1823 " Joseph; m; 2 6-28-29; ¼+; s; son B867; no; Rolla, Rolette, ND; yes; none
1824 " Margaret; f; 7/12 9-21-31; ¼+; s; dau; no; Rolla, Rolette, ND; yes; none

NE Foughty, Farel;   Head
1825 " Adeline (Poitra); f; 35; ¼+; m; wife B868; no; Rolette, Rolette, ND; no; Id.842b, Al.G-08129
1826 " Walter; m; 14 11-20-17; ¼+; s; son A1199; yes;   (Lived with Daniel Lafontain); no; none
1827 " Edna; f; 10 7-17-21; ¼+; s; dau B870; no; Rolette, Rolette, ND; no; none
1828 " Evelyn; f; 10 7-17-21; ¼+; s; dau B869; no; Rolette, Rolette, ND; no; none

1829 Fournier, Louis; m; 33; ¼+; s; Head B871; no; Rolette, Rolette, ND; yes; Id.395b, Al.G-011722
1830 " Alexander; m; 23; ¼+; s; bro B872; no; Rolette, Rolette, ND; yes; Id.395d, Al.G-011719
1831 " Evelyn; f; 17; ¼+; s; sis B873; no; Rolette, Rolette, ND; yes; none

Turtle Mountain Reservation
1932 Census Roll

Key: Number; Surname, Given; Sex; Age at Last Birthday, Birthdate (if given); Tribe (Chippewa, unless stated otherwise); Degree of Blood; Marital Status; Relationship to Head of Family, Last Year Census Number; At Jurisdiction Where Enrolled (Yes/No); Elsewhere - Post Office, County, State; Ward (Yes/No); Allotment [Al.], Annuity [An.] and/or Identification [Id.] Numbers

NE Franks, Harry;   Head
1832   "   Marie (Decouteau); f; 30; ¼+; m; wife B874; no; Denbigh, McHenry, ND; yes; Id.293c, Al.G137

NE Frasier, R W;   Head
1833   "   Rosalie (Gladue); f; 48; ¼+; m; wife B875; no; Plentywood, Sheridan, Mont; no; Id.709b, Al.GF44
1834   "   Walton; m; 29; ¼+; s; son B876; no; Plentywood, Sheridan, Mont; no; Id.396b, Al.G20
1835   "   Fred; m; 27; ¼+; s; son B877; no; Plentywood, Sheridan, Mont; yes; Id.396c, Al.G19
1836   "   Caroline; f; 24; ¼+; s; dau B878; no; Plentywood, Sheridan, Mont; yes; Id.396d, Al.H030757
1837   "   Emma; f; 21; ¼+; s; dau B879; no; Plentywood, Sheridan, Mont; yes; Id.396e, Al.H024581
1838   "   Nellie; f; 19; ¼+; s; dau B880; no; Plentywood, Sheridan, Mont; yes; Id.396f, Al.H204580

1839 Frederick, Andrew; m; 40; ¼+; m; Head A833; no; Devils Lake, Ramsey, ND; no; Id.401, Al.G-08243
1840   "   Caroline (Grant); f; 34; ¼+; m; wife A834; no; Devils Lake, Ramsey, ND; yes; Id.401a, Al.H-031055
1841   "   Wm Lawrence; m; 17; ¼+; s; son A835; no; Devils Lake, Ramsey, ND; yes; Id.401b
1842   "   Florence; f; 15 3-18-17; ¼+; s; dau A836; no; Devils Lake, Ramsey, ND; yes; Id.401c
1843   "   Genevieve; f; 10 8-23-21; ¼+; s; dau A837; no; Devils Lake, Ramsey, ND; yes; Id.401d
1844   "   Irene; f; 7 11-15-24; ¼+; s; dau A838; no; Devils Lake, Ramsey, ND; yes; Id.401e
1845   "   Gloria; f; 4 4-1-27; ¼+; s; dau A839; no; Devils Lake, Ramsey, ND; yes; Id.401f
1846   "   Roderick; m; 2 5-8-29; ¼+; s; dau A840; no; Devils Lake, Ramsey, ND; yes; Id.401g

1847 Frederick, Christine; f; 42; ¼+; s; Head A841; yes; no; Id.402, Al.G-01826

1848 Frederick, Henry; m; 33; ¼+; m; Head A842; yes; no; Id.399a, Al.G-08153
1849   "   Virginia (Belgarde); f; 27; ¼+; m; wife A843; yes; yes; Id.165d, Al.G-274
1850   "   George; m; 7 12-6-24; ¼+; s; son A844; yes; yes; none
1851   "   Frank; m; 5 4-23-26; ¼+; s; son A845; yes; yes; none
1852   "   Rose; f; 3 6-11-28; ¼+; s; dau A846; yes; yes; none

Turtle Mountain Reservation
1932 Census Roll

Key: Number; Surname, Given; Sex; Age at Last Birthday, Birthdate (if given); Tribe (Chippewa, unless stated otherwise); Degree of Blood; Marital Status; Relationship to Head of Family, Last Year Census Number; At Jurisdiction Where Enrolled (Yes/No); Elsewhere - Post Office, County, State; Ward (Yes/No); Allotment [Al.], Annuity [An.] and/or Identification [Id.] Numbers

1853 Frederick, John; m; 29; ¼+; m; Head A847; yes; yes; Id.399c, Al.G-08152
NE " Susie (Lafrance); wife
1854 " William; m; 3 12-19-28; ¼+; s; son A848; yes; yes; none

1855 Frederick, Joseph, Jr; m; 55; ¼+; wd; Head A849; yes; no; Id.398, Al.R-120
1856 " Louis; m; 22; ¼+; s; son A850; yes; no; none
1857 " Mary Rosina; f; 19; ¼+; s; dau A851; yes; no; none
1858 " Robert; m; 13 4-23-18; ¼+; s; son A852; yes; no; none

1859 Frederick, Joseph; m; 30; ¼+; m; Head A853; yes; yes; Id.398c, Al.M-352
1860 " Agnes (Paul); f; 34; ¼+; m; wife A854; yes; yes; Id.809b, Al.H-030459

1861 Frederick, Louis; m; 34; ¼+; m; Head A855; yes; no; Id.398b, Al.M-351
1862 " Clara (Perronteau); f; 29; ¼+; m; wife A856; yes; yes; Id.832c, Al.G-0410
1863 " Mabel Rose; f; 6 7-20-25; ¼+; s; dau A857; yes; yes; none

1864 Frederick, Robert; m; 36; ¼+; m; Head A858; yes; no; Id.400; Al.G-08155
1865 " Clemence (Houle); f; 24; ¼+; m; wife A859; yes; yes; Id.497a, Al.G-016646
1866 " Nora; f; 5 12-16-26; ¼+; s; dau A860; yes; yes; none

1867 Frederick, Sarah; m[sic]; 86; ¼+; wd; Head A861; yes; yes; Id.397b, Al.G-08311

1868 Frederick, William; m; 63; ¼+; m; Head A862; yes; no; Id.399, Al.R-121
1869 " Susan (Turcotte); f; 63; ¼+; m; wife A863; yes; no; Id.399a, Al.G-01825
1870 " Alexander; m; 27; ¼+; s; son A864; yes; yes; Id.399d, Al.G-08154
1871 " George B; m; 24; ¼+; s; son A865; yes; yes; Id.399e, Al.G-08344
1872 " Patrice; m; 21 8-10-11; ¼+; s; son A866; yes; no; Id.399f, none
1873 " Ernest; m; 19; ¼+; s; son A867; yes; no; Id.399g

NE Frederkison[sic], P; Head
1874 " Emma (Martell); f; 34; ¼+; m; wife B881; no; Poplar, Roosevelt, Mont; no; Id.709b, Al.GF-44
1875 " Wanita; f; 4 7-21-27; ¼+; s; dau -----; no; Poplar, Roosevelt, Mont; no; none

NE French, Tait; Head
1876 " Rose (Hayden); f; 19 10-9-12; ¼+; m; wife -----; no; Dominion City, Roseau Res, Can; yes; Id.469e, Al.none

1877 Gardner, George; m; 34; ¼+; m; Head B882; no; Address unknown; no; Id.404, Al.H024586
NE " Mary; wife

Turtle Mountain Reservation
1932 Census Roll

Key: Number; Surname, Given; Sex; Age at Last Birthday, Birthdate (if given); Tribe (Chippewa, unless stated otherwise); Degree of Blood; Marital Status; Relationship to Head of Family, Last Year Census Number; At Jurisdiction Where Enrolled (Yes/No); Elsewhere - Post Office, County, State; Ward (Yes/No); Allotment [Al.], Annuity [An.] and/or Identification [Id.] Numbers

1878 Gardner(cont), Annie; f; 22; ¼+; s; dau B883; no; Address unknown; yes; Id.404b, Al.G-16119
1879 " George; m; 20; ¼+; s; son B884; no; Address unknown; yes; Id.404c, Al.H024586
1880 " Myrtle; f; 18; ¼+; s; dau B885; no; Address unknown; no; Id.404d

1881 Gardner, William; m; 49; ¼+; s; Head B886; no; Chicago, Cook, Ill; no; Id.403, Al.G037046

NE Gauthier, Lucien;   Head
1882 " Vitalline (Grant); f; 35; ¼+; m; wife B887; no; Willow City, Bottineau, ND; no; Id.459, Al.M24
1883 " Dorothy; f; 9 9-5-22; ¼+; s; dau B888; no; Willow City, Bottineau, ND; no; Id.459a
1884 " Ernest; m; 7 6-20-24; ¼+; s; son B889; no; Willow City, Bottineau, ND; no; none
1885 " Gerald; m; 5 5-20-26; ¼+; s; son B890; no; Willow City, Bottineau, ND; no; none
1886 " Leo; m; 4 2-28-28; ¼+; s; son B891; no; Willow City, Bottineau, ND; no; none
1887 " Joseph; m; 2 8-28-29; ¼+; s; son -----; no; Willow City, Bottineau, ND; no; none
1888 " Marie; 1 10-24-30; ¼+; s; dau ----; no; Willow City, Bottineau, ND; no; none

NE Gillis, John;   Head
1889 " Lucy (Turcott); f; 28; ¼+; m; wife B892; no; Dunseith, Rolette, ND; no; Id.259c, Al.H24
1890 " Frank; m; 8 5-4-23; ¼+; s; son B893; no; Dunseith, Rolette, ND; no; none
1891 " Lucy; f; 7 8-27-24; ¼+; s; dau B894; no; Dunseith, Rolette, ND; no; none
1892 " Charles; m; 5 3-8-26; ¼+; s; son B895; no; Dunseith, Rolette, ND; no; none
1893 " Mildred; f; 3 11-27-28; ¼+; s; dau B896; no; Dunseith, Rolette, ND; no; none
1894 " Mary; f; 3 3-26-30; ¼+; s; dau B897; no; Dunseith, Rolette, ND; no; none
1895 " David Eugene; m; 1 2-27-31; ¼+; s; son -----; no; Dunseith, Rolette, ND; no; none

NE Girard, Gus;   Head
1896 " Mary L (Morin); f; 30; ¼+; m; wife B898; no; Madoc, Daniels, Mont; yes; Id.758c, Al.M166
1897 " Donald; m; 5 4-3-26; ¼+; s; son ----; no; Madoc, Daniels, Mont; no; none
1898 " Raymond; m; 3 7-6-28; ¼+; s; son ----; no; Madoc, Daniels, Mont; no; none
1899 " Howard; ; 1 5-19-30; ¼+; s; son ----; no; Madoc, Daniels, Mont; no; none

Turtle Mountain Reservation
1932 Census Roll

Key: Number; Surname, Given; Sex; Age at Last Birthday, Birthdate (if given); Tribe (Chippewa, unless stated otherwise); Degree of Blood; Marital Status; Relationship to Head of Family, Last Year Census Number; At Jurisdiction Where Enrolled (Yes/No); Elsewhere - Post Office, County, State; Ward (Yes/No); Allotment [Al.], Annuity [An.] and/or Identification [Id.] Numbers

1900 Girard(cont), Harold; m; 1/12 2-28-32; ¼+; s; son -----; no; Madoc, Daniels, Mont; no; none

1901 Gladue, Andrew; m; 36; ¼+; s; Head B899; no; Froid, Roosevelt, Mont; no; Id.405, Al.G016087

1902 Gladue, Bruno; m; 48; ¼+; m; Head B900; no; Dagmar, Sheridan, Mont; no; Id.410, Al.G07095

1903 " Mary L (Marion); f; 25; ¼+; m; wife B901; no; Dagmar, Sheridan, Mont; no; Id.693f, Al.G470

1904 " Charles E; m; 4/12 11-12-31; ¼+; s; son -----; no; Dagmar, Sheridan, Mont; no; Id.none

Dead Gladue, Charles; m; B902 (Died Oct. 14, 1928)

Dead Gladue, Claude; Head B903 (Died May 26, 1930)
NE " Adelaide (Dubois); wife Boissevain, Manitoba, Canada; yes; Id.408d, Al.G53k

1905 " Elizabeth; f; 24; ¼+; s; dau B904; no; Boissevain, Manitoba, Canada; yes; Id.408d, Al.G014941

1906 " Marie; f; 21; ¼+; s; dau B905; no; Boissevain, Manitoba, Canada; yes; Id.408g, Al.H024585

1907 " Arthur; m; 19; ¼+; s; son B906; no; Boissevain, Manitoba, Canada; yes; Id.408g, Al.H024885

1908 " Leocadiz; m; 18; ¼+; s; son B907; no; Boissevain, Manitoba, Canada; no; Id.408h

1909 " Alexander; m; 15 5-5-16; ¼+; s; son B908; no; Boissevain, Manitoba, Canada; no; Id.408i

1910 " Florence; f; 12 1-2-20; ¼+; s; son B909; no; Boissevain, Manitoba, Canada; no; Id.408j

1911 Gladue, Frank; m; 46; ¼+; m; Head B910; no; Belcourt, Rolette, ND; no; Id.418, Al.GF80

1912 " Mary R (Davis); f; 41; ¼+; m; wife B911; no; Belcourt, Rolette, ND; no; Id.418a, Al.G189

1913 " Rosina; f; 19 3-29-13; ¼+; f; dau B912; no; Belcourt, Rolette, ND; yes; Id.418b, Al.H024587

1914 " Joseph; m; 17 6-9-14; ¼+; s; son B913; no; Belcourt, Rolette, ND; no; Id.418c

1915 " Mary; f; 16 10-17-15; ¼+; s; dau B914; no; Belcourt, Rolette, ND; no; Id.418d

1916 " Alice; f; 14 12-17-19; ¼+; s; dau N915[sic]; no; Belcourt, Rolette, ND; no; Id.418e

Turtle Mountain Reservation
1932 Census Roll

Key: Number; Surname, Given; Sex; Age at Last Birthday, Birthdate (if given); Tribe (Chippewa, unless stated otherwise); Degree of Blood; Marital Status; Relationship to Head of Family, Last Year Census Number; At Jurisdiction Where Enrolled (Yes/No); Elsewhere - Post Office, County, State; Ward (Yes/No); Allotment [Al.], Annuity [An.] and/or Identification [Id.] Numbers

1917 Gladue(cont), George; m; 11 5-31-20; ¼+; s; son B916; no; Belcourt, Rolette, ND; no; Id.418f
1918 " Frank; m; 10 10-3-21; ¼+; s; son B917; no; Belcourt, Rolette, ND; no; Id.418g
1919 " Lyman; m; 9 2-12-23; ¼+; s; son B918; no; Belcourt, Rolette, ND; no; Id.418h
1920 " Carris R; m; 5 2-9-27; ¼+; s; son B919; no; Belcourt, Rolette, ND; no; Id.418i
1921 " Arthur C; m; 1 6-11-30; ¼+; s; son B920; no; Belcourt, Rolette, ND; no; Id.418j
1922 " John G; m; 6 5-5-25; ¼+; s; son -----; no; Belcourt, Rolette, ND; no; Id.418k

1923 Gladue, Isabel; f; 42; ¼+; s; Head B921; no; Rolla, Rolette, ND; no; Id.419a, Al.F08169

1924 Gladue, Israel; m; 42; ¼+; s; Head B922; no; Rolette, Rolette, ND; no; Id.406, Al.M399

1925 Gladue, Joseph; m; 49; ¼+; m; Head B923; no; no; Id.420, Al.G-0816 8
1926 " Mary (Poitra); f; 38; ¼+; m; wife B924; no; McLaughlin, Corson, SD; no; Id.420a, Al.G-603
1927 " Flora; f; 17 5-6-14; ¼+; s; dau B925; no; McLaughlin, Corson, SD; no; Id.420b
1928 " James; m; 16 10-7-15; ¼+; s; son B926; no; McLaughlin, Corson, SD; no; none
1929 " Hazel Jane; f; 13 10-12-18; ¼+; s; dau B927; no; McLaughlin, Corson, SD; no; none
1930 " Pat; m; 12 2-9-20; ¼+; s; son B928; no; McLaughlin, Corson, SD; no; none
1931 " Frank; m; 9 10-23-22; ¼+; s; son B929; no; McLaughlin, Corson, SD; no; none
1932 " Mabel Rose; f; 7 12-1-24; ¼+; s; dau; no; McLaughlin, Corson, SD; no; none
1933 " Richard; m; 4 12-19-28; ¼+; s; son; no; McLaughlin, Corson, SD; no; none

Dead Gladue, Julia;   A868   (Died 7-18-31)

1934 Gladue, Louis; m; 45; ¼+; s; Head B930; no; Dagmar, Sheridan, Mont; no; Id.407, Al.G-05137

NE Gladue, Pauline (Dubois);   Head   Cando, Towner, ND
1935 " Irene; f; 24; ¼+; s; dau B931; no; Cando, Towner, ND; no; Id.409b
1936 " Agnes; f; 21; ¼+; s; dau B932; no; Cando, Towner, ND; no; Id.409c, Al.G-016709
1937 " Elma; f; 20; ¼+; s; dau B933; no; Cando, Towner, ND; no; Id.409d
1938 " Bernice; f; 17 12-12-14; ¼+; s; dau B934; no; Cando, Towner, ND; no; none

Turtle Mountain Reservation
1932 Census Roll

Key: Number; Surname, Given; Sex; Age at Last Birthday, Birthdate (if given); Tribe (Chippewa, unless stated otherwise); Degree of Blood; Marital Status; Relationship to Head of Family; Last Year Census Number; At Jurisdiction Where Enrolled (Yes/No); Elsewhere - Post Office, County, State; Ward (Yes/No); Allotment [Al.], Annuity [An.] and/or Identification [Id.] Numbers

1939 Gladue(cont), Edna; f; 14 12-5-17; ¼+; s; dau B935; no; Cando, Towner, ND; no; none
1940   "   Raymond; m; 13 1-13-19; ¼+; s; son B936; no; Cando, Towner, ND; no; none
1941   "   Clarence; m; 10-8-3-21; ¼+; s; son B937; no; Cando, Towner, ND; no; none

NE Gladue, Phillip; m;   Head
1942   "   Rosalie (Gourneau); f; 36; ¼+; m; wife B938; no; St.John, Rolette, ND; no; Id.423, Al.M-363
1943   "   Thelma; f; 15 1-2-17; ¼+; s; dau B939; no; St.John, Rolette, ND; no; none
1944   "   Ina; f; 13 8-9-18; ¼+; s; dau B940; no; St.John, Rolette, ND; no; none
1945   "   Carl; m; 11 8-18-20; ¼+; s; son B941; no; St.John, Rolette, ND; no; none
1946   "   Carol R; f; 8; ¼+; s; dau; no; St.John, Rolette, ND; no; none

NE Gladue, Raphael;   Head
1947   "   Elizabeth (Poitra); f; 54; ¼+; m; wife B942; no; Rolette, Rolette, ND; no; Id.422a, Al.G-012606
1948   "   Joseph; m; 18; ¼+; s; son B943; no; Rolette, Rolette, ND; no; Id.422b
1949   "   Laura E; f; 12 4-25-19; ¼+; s; dau; no; Rolette, Rolette, ND; no; none

1950 Gladue, Rose Ann (Lafloe); f; 42; ¼+; wd; Head A869; yes; no; Id.412a, Al.G-08127
1951   "   Ethel; f; 18; ¼+; s; dau A870; yes; no; Id.412b
1952   "   Charles; m; 14; ¼+; s; son A871; yes; no; Id.412c
1953   "   Celia; f; 10 8-15-21; ¼+; s; dau A872; yes; no; Id.412d
1954   "   Michael; m; 8 8-4-23; ¼+; s; son A873; yes; no; Id.412e

1955 Gladue, William; m; 47; ¼+; m; Head B944; no; Froid, Roosevelt, Mont; no; Id.411, Al.G062
NE   "   Alice (Dubois);   wife
1956   "   William; m; 18 8-17-13; ¼+; s; son B945; no; Froid, Roosevelt, Mont; no; Id.411b
1957   "   Ruby; f; 17 1-14-15; ¼+; s; dau B946; no; Froid, Roosevelt, Mont; no; Id.411c
1958   "   Dora; f; 14 8-15-17; ¼+; s; dau B947; no; Froid, Roosevelt, Mont; no; Id.411d
1959   "   Lucille; f; 12 10-6-19; ¼+; s; dau B948; no; Froid, Roosevelt, Mont; no; Id.411e
1960   "   Rachel; f; 10 10-10-21; ¼+; s; dau B949; no; Froid, Roosevelt, Mont; no; Id.411f
1961   "   Leonard; m; 8 4-24-23; ¼+; s; son B950; no; Froid, Roosevelt, Mont; no; Id.411g
1962   "   Martha; f; 6 5-21-25; ¼+; s; dau B951; no; Froid, Roosevelt, Mont; no; Id.411h
1963   "   Hazel; f; 3 10-17-28; ¼+; s; dau ----; no; Froid, Roosevelt, Mont; no; Id.411i
1964   "   Harriet; f; 1 2-25-31; ¼+; s; dau B952; no; Froid, Roosevelt, Mont; no; Id.411j

1965 Godon, Edward; m; 19; ¼+; s; Head B953; no; Unknown; no; Id.425b

1966 Godon, Simeon; m; 52; ¼+; s; Head B955; no; Unknown; no; Id.426, Al.G-90

Turtle Mountain Reservation
1932 Census Roll

Key: Number; Surname, Given; Sex; Age at Last Birthday, Birthdate (if given); Tribe (Chippewa, unless stated otherwise); Degree of Blood; Marital Status; Relationship to Head of Family, Last Year Census Number; At Jurisdiction Where Enrolled (Yes/No); Elsewhere - Post Office, County, State; Ward (Yes/No); Allotment [Al.], Annuity [An.] and/or Identification [Id.] Numbers

NE Godon, William;   Head
1967   "   Florence (Amyott.Villeneuve); f; 27; ¼+; m; wife B956; no; Bottineau, Bottineau, ND; yes; Id.96d, Al.GF-183
1968   " (Villeneuve) Sarah; f; 9 3-20-23; ¼+; s; step dau B957; no; Bottineau, Bottineau, ND; yes; none
1969   "   Francis; m; 7 8-19-24; ¼+; s; son B958; no; Bottineau, Bottineau, ND; yes; none
1970   "   Alphonse; m; 4 9-29-27; ¼+; s; son; no; Bottineau, Bottineau, ND; yes; none
1971   "   Joseph; m; 2 6-4-29; ¼+; s; son; no; Bottineau, Bottineau, ND; yes; none
1972   "   Edward; m; 3/12 1-9-32; ¼+; s; son; no; Bottineau, Bottineau, ND; yes; none

NE Gossline, Joseph;   Head
1973   "   Elise (Morin.Lemay.Lavia); f; 69; ¼+; m; wife B959; no; Trenton, Williams, ND; yes; Id.427a, Al.M-131
1974   "   Alex; m; 23; ¼+; s; son B960; no; Trenton, Williams, ND; yes; Id.427c, Al.H-012543

1975 Gourneau, Albert G; m; 29; ¼+; m; Head A874; yes; yes; Id.432d, Al.M-238
1976   "   Florence (Frederick); f; ¼+; m; wife A875; yes; yes; Id.388e, Al.G-246

1977 Gourneau, Alex Emil; m; 29; ¼+; m; Head A878; yes; yes; Id.428c, Al.MC-02669
1978   "   Emily (Brunnell); f; ¼+; m; wife A354; yes; no; Id.215e

1979 Gourneau, Eliza (Charette); f; 71; ¼+; wd; Head A876; yes; yes; Id.428a, Al.R-40
1980   "   St Ann; f; 31; ¼+; s; dau A877; yes; yes; Id.428b, Al.MC-026695

1981 Gourneau, James; m; 30; ¼+; m; Head A881; yes; yes; Id.434c, Al.M-304
1982   "   Adaline (Morin); f; 27 10-12-04; ¼+; m; wife A895; yes; yes; Id.754d, Al.G-437
1983   "   Michael; m; 8 9-21-23; ¼+; s; son A896; yes; yes; none
1984   "   Henry; m; 6 4-23-25; ¼+; s; son A897; yes; yes; none
1986   "   Fred; m; 4 7-17-27; ¼+; s; son A898; yes; yes; none
1987   "   Mary Stella; f; 1 4-3-30; ¼+; s; dau; yes; yes; none
1988   "   Bernard; m; 1/12 3-9-32; ¼+; s; son; yes; yes; none

1989 Gourneau, John; m; 26; ¼+; m; Head A879; yes; yes; Id.428d, Al. none
1990   "   Rose Delima (Brunnell); f; 25; ¼+; m; wife A880; yes; yes; Id.215b, Al.W-25
1991 " (Papais) Elaine; f; 9; ¼+; s; step dau A362; yes; yes; none
1992   "   Mary Joan; f; 5/12 10-25-31; ¼+; s; dau; yes; (This child does not belong with this family – error) yes; none

1993 Gourneau, John; m; 38; ¼+; m; Head A899; yes; no; Id.435, Al.M302
1994   "   Florestine (Lavallie); f; 28; ¼+; m; wife A900; yes; no; Id.633b, Al.H012550
1995   "   Marie Lena; f; 8 5-5-23; ¼+; s; dau A901; yes; no; Id.435b
1996   "   Mary Rose; f; 2 4-16-29; ¼+; s; dau A902; yes; no; Id.435c

Turtle Mountain Reservation
1932 Census Roll

Key: Number; Surname, Given; Sex; Age at Last Birthday, Birthdate (if given); Tribe (Chippewa, unless stated otherwise); Degree of Blood; Marital Status; Relationship to Head of Family, Last Year Census Number; At Jurisdiction Where Enrolled (Yes/No); Elsewhere - Post Office, County, State; Ward (Yes/No); Allotment [Al.], Annuity [An.] and/or Identification [Id.] Numbers

1997 Gourneau(cont), Eloise; f; 1 3-27-31; ¼+; s; dau A903; yes; no; Id.435c[sic]

1998 Gourneau, John B; m; 34; ¼+; m; Head A904; yes; no; Id.429b, Al.G547
1999 " Sarah (Grandbois); f; 32; ¼+; m; wife A905; yes; yes; Id.437c, Al.M82
2000 " Earl; m; 9 4-17-22; ¼+; s; son A906; yes; yes; none
2001 " Ernest; m; 8 1-27-24; ¼+; s; son A907; yes; yes; none
2002 " Collin; m; 5 2-9-27; ¼+; s; son A908; yes; yes; none
2003 " Nora; f; 2 1-3-30; ¼+; s; dau A909; yes; yes; none
2004 " Mary Joan; f; 4/12 10-25-31; ¼+; s; dau -----; yes; yes; none

2005 Gourneau, Joseph; m; 80; ¼+; wd; Head A882; yes; yes; Id.430, Al.R127

2006 Gourneau, Joseph; m; 33; ¼+; wd; Head A883; yes; yes; Id.433b, Al.M365

2007 Gourneau, Joseph; m; 66; ¼+; m; Head A884; yes; yes; Id.429, Al.R126
2008 " Elise (McCloud); f; 57; ¼+; m; wife A885; yes; no; Id.429[sic]
2009 " Ben; m; 30; ¼+; s; son A886; yes; yes; Id.429b, Al.M289
2010 " Alexander; m; 25; ¼+; s; son A887; yes; yes; Id.429f, Al.G546
2011 " Justine; f; 23; ¼+; s; dau A888; yes; yes; Id.429g, Al.G08312
2012 " Flora; f; 20; 1;4; s; dau A889; yes; yes; Id.429h, Al. ---
2013 " Zilda; f; 18; ¼+; s; dau A890; yes; yes; Id.429i
2014 " Lawrence; m; 12 7-22-19; ¼+; s; son A891; yes; yes; Id.429j

2015 Gourneau, Leander; m; 34; ¼+; m; Head A892; yes; yes; Id.432b, Al.M286
2016 " Josephine (Jaste); f; 23; ¼+; m; wife A893; yes; yes; Id.432c, Al.H010418
2017 " Marie S; f; 2 9-21-29; ¼+; s; dau A894; yes; yes; none
2018 " Irene T; f; 11/12 2-21-31; ¼+; s; dau A----; yes; yes; none

2019 Gourneau, Leander; m; 69; ¼+; m; Head A910; yes; yes; Id.432, Al.R129
NE " Emerize (McCloud); f; wife
2020 " Louis; m; 25; ¼+; s; son A911; yes; yes; Id.432f, Al.G012
2021 " Ben; m; 22; ¼+; s; son A912; yes; yes; Id.432g, Al.G016087
2022 " Isadore; m; 18; ¼+; s; son A914; yes; yes; Id.432i

2023 Gourneau, Louis; m; 65; ¼+; m; Head A915; yes; yes; Id.433, Al.R130
2024 " Elise (Marion); f; 56; ¼+; m; wife A916; yes; no; Id.433a, Al.M366
2025 " Lucille; f; 17 4-21-14; ¼+; s; dau A917; yes; yes; Id.433f
2026 " Vivian; f; 14 9-1-17; ¼+; s; dau A918; yes; yes; Id.433g

2027 Gourneau, Patrice; m; 28; ¼+; m; Head A919; yes; yes; Id.429e, Al.M288
NE " Mary (LaFavor); wife
2028 " Charles J; m; 1 5-1-30; ¼+; s; son A920; yes; yes; none
2029 " Patrice K; m; 2/12 1-31-32; ¼+; s; son A----; yes; yes; none

Turtle Mountain Reservation
1932 Census Roll

Key: Number; Surname, Given; Sex; Age at Last Birthday, Birthdate (if given); Tribe (Chippewa, unless stated otherwise); Degree of Blood; Marital Status; Relationship to Head of Family, Last Year Census Number; At Jurisdiction Where Enrolled (Yes/No); Elsewhere - Post Office, County, State; Ward (Yes/No); Allotment [Al.], Annuity [An.] and/or Identification [Id.] Numbers

2030 Gourneau, Philip Joseph; m; 27; ¼+; m; Head ----; yes; yes; Id.434[?], Al.H012596
2031 " Rachel (Belgarde); f; 26; ¼+; m; wife ----; yes; yes; Id.168g, Al.G151
2032 " Mary E; f; 4 4-1-28; ¼+; s; dau ----; yes; yes; none
2033 " Viola May; f; 1 12-5-30; ¼+; s; dau ----; yes;
This family omitted from last years[sic] census by mistake

2034 Gourneau, Robert; m; 27; ¼+; m; Head A921; yes; yes; Id.432e, Al.M284
2035 " Delia (Allard); f; 25; ¼+; m; wife A922; yes; yes; Id.66b, Al.H-010484
2036 " Rosella; f; 1 9-1-30; ¼+; s; dau A923; yes; yes; none

2037 Gourneau, Wilfred; m; 26; ¼+; m; Head A924; yes; yes; Id.433d, Al.G-07915
2038 " Mary Eva (Lavallie); f; 18; ¼+; m; wife A925; yes; yes; Id.633f
Dead " Jane; f; 1-15-32 (Died 2-6-32)

2039 Gourneau, Wm Ernest; m; 20; ¼+; s; Head A1405; yes; [no information given]

NE Graham, Richard; Head
2040 " Mary Jane (Bercier); f; 26; ¼+; m; wife B963; no; Devils Lake, Ramsey, ND; yes; Id.195f, Al.G-0849

2041 Grandbois, Alexander; m; 47; ¼+; m; Head B964; no; Medicine Lake, Sheridan, Mont; no; Id.446, Al.G-469
NE " Florence (Myrick); wife
2042 " Fred; m; 22 1-7-10; ¼+; s; son B965; no; Medicine Lake, Sheridan, Mont; no; Id.446b
2043 " Louis; m; 20 12-6-11; ¼+; s; son B966; no; Medicine Lake, Sheridan, Mont; no; Id.446c
2044 " Mary Jane; f; 18 2-3-14; ¼+; s; dau B967; no; Medicine Lake, Sheridan, Mont; no; Id.446d
2045 " David; m; 16 1-7-16; ¼+; s; son B968; no; Medicine Lake, Sheridan, Mont; no; Id.446e
2046 " John; m; 13 11-8-18; ¼+; s; son B969; no; Medicine Lake, Sheridan, Mont; no; Id.446f
2047 " May Florence; f; 12 2-15-20; ¼+; s; dau B970; no; Medicine Lake, Sheridan, Mont; no; Id.446g
2048 " Dora H; f; 10 3-8-22; ¼+; s; dau B971; no; Medicine Lake, Sheridan, Mont; no; Id.446h
2049 " Evelyn S; f; 8 1-28-24; ¼+; s; dau B972; no; Medicine Lake, Sheridan, Mont; no; Id.446i
2050 " Viola G; f; 4 10-22-27; ¼+; s; dau; no; Medicine Lake, Sheridan, Mont; no; none
2051 " Henrietta; f; 3 1-22-29; ¼+; s; dau; no; Medicine Lake, Sheridan, Mont; no; none

Turtle Mountain Reservation
1932 Census Roll

Key: Number; Surname, Given; Sex; Age at Last Birthday, Birthdate (if given); Tribe (Chippewa, unless stated otherwise); Degree of Blood; Marital Status; Relationship to Head of Family, Last Year Census Number; At Jurisdiction Where Enrolled (Yes/No); Elsewhere - Post Office, County, State; Ward (Yes/No); Allotment [Al.], Annuity [An.] and/or Identification [Id.] Numbers

2052 Grandbois, Andrew; m; 38; ¼+; m; Head B973; no; Dagmar, Sheridan, Mont; yes; Id.443, Al.G-133
NE " Emma (Dionne); wife
2053 " May; f; 10 1-10-22; ¼+; s; dau B974; no; Dagmar, Sheridan, Mont; yes; Id.443a
2054 " Virginia; f; 8 6-6-23; ¼+; s; dau B975; no; Dagmar, Sheridan, Mont; yes; Id.443b
2055 " Delima; f; 6 12-23-25; ¼+; s; dau B976; no; Dagmar, Sheridan, Mont; yes; Id.443c
2056 " John; m; 5 7-23-26; ¼+; s; son B977; no; Dagmar, Sheridan, Mont; yes; Id.443d
2057 " Lucy; f; 5 12-7-27; ¼+; s; dau B978; no; Dagmar, Sheridan, Mont; yes; Id.443e
2058 " Geraldine; f; 1 6-22-30; ¼+; s; dau B979; no; Dagmar, Sheridan, Mont; yes; none

2059 Grandbois, David; m; 40; ¼+; m; Head A926; yes; no; Id.436, Al.R-133
2060 " Mary (Laverdure); f; 33; ¼+; m; wife A927; yes; no; Id.639, Al.G-144
2061 " Elise L; f; 14 12-26-17; ¼+; s; dau B928; yes; no; none
2062 " Anna; f; 12 7-23-19; ¼+; s; dau A929; yes; no; none
2063 " Amy Mary; f; 11 3-30-21; ¼+; s; dau A932; yes; no; none
2064 " Sara F; f; 9 9-21-22; ¼+; s; dau B932; yes; no; none
2065 " Eugene C; m; 7 5-30-24; ¼+; s; son A930; yes; no; none
2066 " Leo G; 6 2-28-26; ¼+; s; son A933; yes; no; none
2067 " Leona Mary; f; 3 6-14-28; ¼+; s; dau B934; yes; no; none
2068 " Cecelia M; f; 1 3-3-31; ¼+; s; dau B935; yes; no; none

NE Grandbois, Eliza (Morin); Head
2069 " Joseph; m; 25; ¼+; s; son B980; no; Medicine Lake, Sheridan, Mont; yes; Id.442e, Al.G-444
2070 " Robert; m; 18; ¼+; s; son B982; no; Medicine Lake, Sheridan, Mont; yes; Id.442h
2071 Grandbois, Ezear; m; 58; ¼+; m; Head B983; yes; no; Id.437, Al.R-134
2072 " Eliza (Lucier); f; 54; ¼+; m; wife B984; yes; no; Id.437a, Al.G-07325
2073 " Albert; m; 28; ¼+; s; son B985; yes; yes; Id.437c, Al.M-83
2074 " Isadore; m; 24; ¼+; s; son B986; yes; yes; Id.437g, Al.G-573
2075 " Frank; m; 20; ¼+; s; son B987; yes; no; Id.437h
2076 " Maria Alice; f; 18; ¼+; s; dau B988; yes; no; Id.437i
2077 " Ida Rose; f; 14 12-4-17; ¼+; s; dau B989; yes; no; Id.437j
2078 " Marie Gladys; f; 12 9-16-19; ¼+; s; dau B990; yes; no; Id.437k
2079 " Annie; f; 10; ¼+; s; dau -----; yes; no; none

Turtle Mountain Reservation
1932 Census Roll

Key: Number; Surname, Given; Sex; Age at Last Birthday, Birthdate (if given); Tribe (Chippewa, unless stated otherwise); Degree of Blood; Marital Status; Relationship to Head of Family, Last Year Census Number; At Jurisdiction Where Enrolled (Yes/No); Elsewhere - Post Office, County, State; Ward (Yes/No); Allotment [Al.], Annuity [An.] and/or Identification [Id.] Numbers

2080 Grandbois, Isadore; m; 83; ¼+; m; Head A936; yes; yes; Id.439, Al.R-135
553 " Louisa (Dejarlais.Belgarde); f; 71; ¼+; m; wife A206; yes; yes;
  Id.185a, Al.G-08299
554 " (Belgarde) Elie Wm; m; 32; ¼+; s; stepson A207; yes; yes; Id.185b, Al.G-08298

NE Grandbois, Joseph;   Head
2081 " M. Jane C (Morin); f; 33 3-24-99; ¼+; m; wife B991; no; East Grand
  Forks, Polk, Minn; no; Id.754b, Al.G-438
2082 " (Morin) Adele; f; 13 9-28-18; ¼+; s; step dau B992; no; East Grand Forks, Polk,
  Minn; no; none
2083 " Doris V; f; 7 1-11-24; ¼+; s; dau ----; no; East Grand Forks, Polk,
  Minn; no; none
2084 " Joseph E; m; 6 4-19-25; ¼+; s; son ----; no; East Grand Forks, Polk,
  Minn; no; none
2085 " Patrick E; m; 5 9-7-26; ¼+; s; son ----; no; East Grand Forks, Polk,
  Minn; no; none
2086 " David O; m; 4 10-28-27; ¼+; s; son B993; no; East Grand Forks, Polk,
  Minn; no; none
2087 " John M; m; 3 3-17-29; ¼+; s; son ----; no; East Grand Forks, Polk,
  Minn; no; none
2088 " Leona G; f; 1 4-24-30; ¼+; s; dau ----; no; East Grand Forks, Polk,
  Minn; no; none
2089 " Albert Leo; m; 10/12 5-19-31; ¼+; s; son ----; no; East Grand Forks,
  Polk, Minn; no; none

2090 Grandbois, Jos. Alfred; m; 34; ¼+; m; Head A937; no; East Grand Forks, Polk,
  Minn; no; Id.440, Al.G-452
2091 " Mary C (Gourneau); f; 40; ¼+; m; wir3 A938; no; East Grand Forks,
  Polk, Minn; no; Id.440a, Al.G-551
2092 " Rosalie M; f; 13 10-6-18; ¼+; s; dau A939; no; East Grand Forks, Polk,
  Minn; no; Id.440b
2093 " Francis; m; 10 12-9-21; ¼+; s; son A940; no; East Grand Forks, Polk,
  Minn; no; Id.440c
2094 " Shirley S; f; 1/12 2-9-32; ¼+; s; dau; no; East Grand Forks, Polk,
  Minn; no; none

NE Grandbois, Louis; m; ¼+;   Head
2095 " Peter S; m; 11; ¼+; s; son B994; no; Unknown; yes; Id.819h

2096 Grandbois, Michael; m; 45; ¼+; m; Head B995; no; Dagmar, Sheridan, Mont; no;
  Id.445, Al.G-026747
NE " Mary Ann (Brien);   wife
2097 " Robert; m; 21; ¼+; s; son B996; no; Dagmar, Sheridan, Mont; no; Id.445b

Turtle Mountain Reservation
1932 Census Roll

Key: Number; Surname, Given; Sex; Age at Last Birthday, Birthdate (if given); Tribe (Chippewa, unless stated otherwise); Degree of Blood; Marital Status; Relationship to Head of Family, Last Year Census Number; At Jurisdiction Where Enrolled (Yes/No); Elsewhere - Post Office, County, State; Ward (Yes/No); Allotment [Al.], Annuity [An.] and/or Identification [Id.] Numbers

2098 Grandbois(cont), Mitchell; m; 18 8-28-13; ¼+; s; son B997; no; Dagmar, Sheridan, Mont; no; Id.445c
2099 " Alice; f; 15 12-19-16; ¼+; s; dau B998; no; Dagmar, Sheridan, Mont; no; Id.445d
2100 " Marceline; f; 10; ¼+; s; dau B999; no; Dagmar, Sheridan, Mont; no; Id.445e
2101 " Eva; f; 7 4-22-24; ¼+; s; dau B1000; no; Dagmar, Sheridan, Mont; no; Id.445f
2102 " Phillip H; m; 2 7-24-29; ¼+; s; son B1001; no; Dagmar, Sheridan, Mont; no; none
2103 " Thomas; m; 1/12 3-9-32; ¼+; s; son; no; Dagmar, Sheridan, Mont; no; none

2104 Grandbois, Patrice #2; m; 44; ¼+; m; Head A941; yes; no; Id.441, Al.G-465
2105 " Margaret (Montriel); f; 42; ¼+; m; wife A942; yes; no; Id.441a, Al.W-0644
2106 " Mary S; f; 20; ¼+; s; dau A943; yes; no; Id.441c
2107 " Alma; f; 15 8-23-16; ¼+; s; dau A944; yes; no; Id.441d
2108 " Celina; f; 14 10-18-17; ¼+; s; dau A945; yes; no; Id.441e
2109 " Louise; f; 12 12-22-19; ¼+; s; dau A946; yes; no; Id.441f
Dead " Elmer; A947 (Died 12-15-20)
2110 " Stephen J; m; 9 2-17-23; ¼+; s; son A948; yes; no; none
2111 " Lillian; f; 7 4-18-24; ¼+; s; dau A949; yes; no; none
2112 " Gloria; f; 5 2-1-27; ¼+; s; dau A950; yes; no; none
2113 " Ernest; m; 2 6-2-29; ¼+; s; son A951; yes; no; none
2114 " Evelyn; f; 6/12 9-22-31; ¼+; s; dau; yes

2115 Grandbois, Paul; m; 70; ¼+; s; Head B1002; no; Unknown; no; Id.438, Al.H-024593

2116 Grant, Alfred; m; 30; ¼+; m; Head A980; yes; no; Id.457c, Al.M-23
NE " Ann (McArthur); wife
2117 " Vernon; m; 4 12-16-27; ¼+; s; son A981; yes; no; none

2118 Grant, Andrew; m; 31; ¼+; m; Head A952; yes; yes; Id.454c, Al.G-0253
2119 " Emma (Lafontain); f; 29; ¼+; m; wife A953; yes; yes; Id.550a, Al.G-290
2120 " Archie; m; 5 10-11-26; ¼+; s; son A954; yes; yes; none
2121 " Elnora; f; 4 12-4-27; ¼+; s; dau A955; yes; none
2122 " Andrew; m; 2 8-1-29; ¼+; s; son A956; yes; yes; none
2123 " Gladys; f; 1 12-10-30; ¼+; s; dau; yes; yes; none

2124 Grant, Charles; m; 52; ¼+; m; Head B1003; yes; no; Id.447, Al.R-136
2125 " Mary (Dumont); f; 50; ¼+; m; wife B1004; yes; no; Id.448a, Al.G-037049
2126 " Josephine; f; 29; ¼+; s; dau B1005; yes; yes; Id.447b, Al.G-03050
2127 " Adele; f; 21; ¼+; s; dau B1006; yes; no; Id.447d
2128 " Joschim; m; 19; ¼+; s; son B1007; yes; no; Id.447e
2129 " Lawrence B; m; 14 8-11-17; ¼+; s; son B1008; yes; no; Id.447f

Turtle Mountain Reservation
1932 Census Roll

Key: Number; Surname, Given; Sex; Age at Last Birthday, Birthdate (if given); Tribe (Chippewa, unless stated otherwise); Degree of Blood; Marital Status; Relationship to Head of Family, Last Year Census Number; At Jurisdiction Where Enrolled (Yes/No); Elsewhere - Post Office, County, State; Ward (Yes/No); Allotment [Al.], Annuity [An.] and/or Identification [Id.] Numbers

2130 Grant(cont), Dorris; f; 11; ¼+; s; dau B1009; yes; yes; Id.447g

2131 Grant, Frank; m; 34; ¼+; m; Head A957; no; Devils Lake, Ramsey, ND; yes; Id.454b, Al.G-0251
2132 " Virginia (Houle); f; 27; ¼+; m; wife A958; no; Devils Lake, Ramsey, ND; yes; Id.484b, Al.G-54
2133 " Stella V; f; 6 8-30-25; ¼+; s; dau A959; no; Devils Lake, Ramsey, ND; yes; none
2134 " Frank J; m; 2 6-26-29; ¼+; s; son A960; no; Devils Lake, Ramsey, ND; yes; none
2135 " Nettie H; f; 5/12 10-19-31; ¼+; s; dau; no; Devils Lake, Ramsey, ND; yes; none

Dead Grant, Gregory;   B1026   (Died 10-7-30)
2136 " St Ann (Dejarlais); f; 20; ¼+; wd; Head B651; no; Devils Lake, Ramsey, ND; no; Id.317d
2137 " Georgeline; f; 3 4-16-28; ¼+; s; dau; no; Devils Lake, Ramsey, ND; no; none

2138 Grant, James; m; 55; ¼+; m; Head B1010; no; Devils Lake, Ramsey, ND; no; Id.449, Al.R-139
2139 " Rosalie (Monette); f; 53; ¼+; m; wife B1011; no; Devils Lake, Ramsey, ND; no; Id.449e, Al.M-144
2140 " James; m; 27; ¼+; s; son B1012; no; Devils Lake, Ramsey, ND; yes; Id.449e, Al.G-0112
2141 " Mary Jane; f; 22; ¼+; s; dau B1014; no; Devils Lake, Ramsey, ND; no; Id.449f
2142 " Florestine; f; 20; ¼+; s; dau B1015; no; Devils Lake, Ramsey, ND; no; Id.449g
2143 " John; m; 14 5-18-17; ¼+; s; son B1016; no; Devils Lake, Ramsey, ND; no; none
2144 " Lawrence; m; 10; ¼+; s; son B1017; no; Devils Lake, Ramsey, ND; no; none

2145 Grant, John B; m; 71; ¼+; m; Head A961; yes; yes; Id.450, Al.R-140
2146 " Henrietta (Turcotte.Houle); f; 63; ¼+; m; wife A962; yes; yes; Id.486a, Al.G-194
2147 " (Houle) Cecelia; f; 11 5-25-20; ¼+; s; step dau A1049; yes; yes; none

2148 Grant, Joseph #1; m; 50; ¼+; m; Head A963; yes; yes; Id.453, Al.R-142
NE " Virginia (Bercier);   wife
2149 " Michael; m; 21 2-25-11; ¼+; s; son A964; yes; yes; Id.453d
2150 " Lester I; m; 19; ¼+; s; son A965; yes; yes; Id.453e
2151 " Irene; f; 15; ¼+; s; dau A966; yes; yes; Id.453f
2152 " Amelia; f; 14; ¼+; s; dau A967; yes; yes; Id.453g
2153 " Olive; f; 11 7-12-20; ¼+; s; dau A968; yes; yes; Id.453h
Dead " George H;   A969   (Died 9-25-31)
2154 " Peter; m; 6 11-25-25; ¼+; s; son A970; yes; yes; Id.453j

Turtle Mountain Reservation
1932 Census Roll

Key: Number; Surname, Given; Sex; Age at Last Birthday, Birthdate (if given); Tribe (Chippewa, unless stated otherwise); Degree of Blood; Marital Status; Relationship to Head of Family, Last Year Census Number; At Jurisdiction Where Enrolled (Yes/No); Elsewhere - Post Office, County, State; Ward (Yes/No); Allotment [Al.], Annuity [An.] and/or Identification [Id.] Numbers

2155   Grant, Joseph P; m; 39; ¼+; m; Head B1018; no; Devils Lake, Ramsey, ND; yes; Id.455, Al.G-0254
2156   "   Judith (Lafontain); f; 39; ¼+; m; wife B1019; no; Devils Lake; no; Id.455a, Al.G-286
Dead   "   Alfred;   B1020   (Died in 1918)
2157   "   Pierre; m; 16 6-20-15; ¼+; s; son B1021; no; Devils Lake, Ramsey, ND; yes; Id.455c
2158   "   Rosina; f; 15 9-27-16; ¼+; s; dau B1022; no; Devils Lake, Ramsey, ND; yes; Id.455d
2159   "   Delphine; f; 15 3-21-17; ¼+; s; dau B1023; no; Devils Lake, Ramsey, ND; yes; Id.455e
Dead   "   Louis;   B1024   (Died in 1926)
2160   "   Gloria; f; 5 9-30-26; ¼+; s; dau ----; no; Devils Lake, Ramsey, ND; yes; none
2161   "   Peter L; m; 3 2-5-29; ¼+; s; son ----; no; Devils Lake, Ramsey, ND; yes; none
2162   "   Clarence; m; 1 9-23-30; ¼+; s; son ----; no; Devils Lake, Ramsey, ND; yes; none

2163   Grant, Louis; m; 41; ¼+; m; Head A971; yes; no; Id.451, Al.M-242
2164   "   Mary Jane (Delorme); f; 35; ¼+; m; wife A972; yes; yes; Id.328b, Al.G-08093
      "   John; m; 13 4-29-18; ¼+; s; son; yes; (Adopted by Wm. Laverdure)
          Patrick; m; 13 4-29-18; ¼+; s; yes; (Adopted by Wm. Laverdure)
2165   "   Margaret m; f; 12 5-30-19; ¼+; s; dau A973; yes; yes; Id.451d
2166   "   Alma; f; 11 2-15-21; ¼+; s; dau A974; yes; yes; Id.451e
2167   "   Russell; m; 8 1-28-23; ¼+; s; son A975; yes; yes; Id.451e[sic]
2168   "   Marland; m; 4 4-18-27; ¼+; s; son A976; yes; yes; Id.451f
2169   "   Leona; f; 3 5-18-28; ¼+; s; dau; yes; yes; none
2170   "   Claude U; m; 1 4-4-30; ¼+; s; son A977; yes; yes; Id.451g

2171   Grant, Rose (Trothier); f; 61; ¼+; wd; Head B1025; no; Devils Lake, Ramsey, ND; no; Id.454a, Al.G-0247
2172   "   Lawrence; m; 23; ¼+; s; son B1027; no; Devils Lake, Ramsey, ND; Id.454f
2173   "   Frederick; m; 21; ¼+; s; son B1028; no; ND; no; Id.454g

2174   Grant, William; m; 60; ¼+; m; Head A978; yes; no; Id.457, Al.R-144
2175   "   Mary P (Monette); f; 54; ¼+; m; wife A979; yes; no; Id.457a, Al. M-22
2176   "   Ernestine; f; 22; ¼+; s; dau A983; yes; no; Id.457f
2177   "   Cuthbert; m; 19; ¼+; s; son A984; yes; no; Id.457g
2178   "   Romeo; m; 16 11-28-15; s; son A985; yes; no; Id.457h
2179   "   Antoinette; f; 13 4-10-18; ¼+; s; dau A986; yes; no; Id.457i
2180   "   Mabel; f; 8 1-26-23; ¼+; s; dau A987; yes; no; Id.457j

2181   Grant, William; m; 33; ¼+; m; Head A988; yes; yes; Id.457b, Al.M-25
2182   "   Alice (Langer); f; 24; ¼+; m; wife A989; yes; yes; Id.611e, Al.G-019
2183   "   Vincent; m; 2 1-25-30; ¼+; s; son A990; yes; yes; none
2184   "   Richard; m; 6/12 9-16-31; ¼+; s; son; yes; yes; none

Turtle Mountain Reservation
1932 Census Roll

Key: Number; Surname, Given; Sex; Age at Last Birthday, Birthdate (if given); Tribe (Chippewa, unless stated otherwise); Degree of Blood; Marital Status; Relationship to Head of Family, Last Year Census Number; At Jurisdiction Where Enrolled (Yes/No); Elsewhere - Post Office, County, State; Ward (Yes/No); Allotment [Al.], Annuity [An.] and/or Identification [Id.] Numbers

2185 Grant, William #2; m; 61; ¼+; m; Head B1029; no; Devils Lake, Ramsey, ND; yes; Id.460, Al.R-145
2186 " Josephine (Dejarlais); f; 57; ¼+; m; wife B1030; no; Devils Lake, Ramsey, ND; no; Id.460a, Al.G-139
2187 " Rachel; f; 22; ¼+; s; dau B1031; no; Devils Lake, Ramsey, ND; yes; Id.460d
2188 " Angeline; f; 20; ¼+; s; dau B1032; no; Devils Lake, Ramsey, ND; yes; Id.460e
2189 " Delphine; f; 18; ¼+; s; dau B1033; no; Devils Lake, Ramsey, ND; yes; Id.450f
792 " Madeline;   dau   (Adopted by Gregory Brien)
2190 " Benjamin; m; 12 5-7-19; ¼+; s; son B1034; no; Devils Lake, Ramsey, ND; yes; Id.450g

NE Graveline, Joe;   Head
2191 " Marie (Azure); f; 73; ¼+; m; wife B1035; no; Bainville, Sheridan, Mont; yes; Id.111a, Al.G-0153

2192 Great Walker, Joseph; m; 25; F; m; Head A991; yes; yes; Id.32b, Al.G0320
2193 " Emma (Kakenowash); f; 17; F; m; wife A992; yes; yes; Id.11e
2194 " Jane; f; 5/12 11-18-31; F; s; dau; yes; yes; none

NE Griffin, Martin;   Head
2195 " Marie (Thomas); f; 491 1/4; m; wife B1036; no; Sidney, Richland, Mont; no; Id.958, Al.G-037
2196 " Martin R; m; 15 8-26-16; ¼+; s; son B1037; no; Sidney, Richland, Mont; no; Id.958b
2197 " William H; m; 14 11-30-17; ¼+; s; son B1038; no; Sidney, Richland, Mont; no; Id.958c
2198 " Margaret V; f; 12 7-28-19; ¼+; s; dau B1039; no; Sidney, Richland, Mont; no; Id.958d
2199 " Thomas S; m; 10 7-19-21; ¼+; s; son B1040; no; Sidney, Richland, Mont; no; Id.958e
2200 " James V; m; 9 10-9-22; ¼+; s; son B1041; no; Sidney, Richland, Mont; no; Id.958f
2201 " John H; m; 6 7-15-25; ¼+; s; son B1041; no; Sidney, Richland, Mont; no; Id.958g
2202 " David C; m; 3 2-21-29; ¼+; s; son; no; Sidney, Richland, Mont; no; Id.958h

2203 Growing Feather, Kakenowash; m; 22; F; m; Head B1043; no; Dunseith, Rolette, ND; yes; Id.11d, Al.G-011717
2204 " Virginia (Iron Bear); f; 21; F; m; wife B1044; no; Dunseith, Rolette, ND; yes; Id.50d, Al.G-015893

Turtle Mountain Reservation
1932 Census Roll

Key: Number; Surname, Given; Sex; Age at Last Birthday, Birthdate (if given); Tribe (Chippewa, unless stated otherwise); Degree of Blood; Marital Status; Relationship to Head of Family, Last Year Census Number; At Jurisdiction Where Enrolled (Yes/No); Elsewhere - Post Office, County, State; Ward (Yes/No); Allotment [Al.], Annuity [An.] and/or Identification [Id.] Numbers

NE	Guineau, Joseph;		Head
2205	"	Adeline (Amyott.St.Claire); f; 56; ¼+; m; wife B1045; no; Dunseith, Rolette, ND; yes; Id.1040, Al.H-039206	
2206	"	Roderick; m; 14 10-25-17; ¼+; s; son B1046; no; Dunseith, Rolette, ND; yes; none	

2207 Gunderson, Genevieve (Decoteau); f; 47; ¼+; wd; Head B1047; no; Palermo, Mountrail, ND; no; Id.462a, Al.M-385
DEAD " Mary Jane; B1051 (Died 4-26-30)
2208 " William; m; 13 6-25-18; ¼+; s; son B1052; no; Palermo, Mountrail, ND; no; Id.462h
DEAD " Wilburn; B1053; (Died 8-17-29)
2209 " Ella Ione; f; 9 1-15-23; ¼+; s; dau B1054; no; Palermo, Mountrail, ND; yes; Id.462j

2210 Gunderson, Peter; m; 31; ¼+; m; Head B1048; no; Palermo, Mountrail, ND; yes; Id.462d, Al.M-384
NE " Bridget (Bergie); wife

2211 Gunderson, Walter; m; 23; ¼+; m; Head B1050; no; St.Paul, Ramsey, Minn; no; Id.462f
NE " Blanche M (Hintz); wife
2212 " Eugene S; m; 7/12 8-27-31; ¼+; s; son; no; St.Paul, Ramsey, Minn; no; none

NE Gunville, Antoine; Head
2213 " Emma (Azure); f; 39; ¼+; m; wife B1055; no; Dunseith, Rolette, ND; no; Id.463a, Al.G-07109
2214 " Matilda E; f; 19; ¼+; s; dau B1056; no; Dunseith, Rolette, ND; no; Id.463b
2215 " Jewel S; m; 16 9-11-15; ¼+; s; dau B1057; no; Dunseith, Rolette, ND; no; Id.463c
2216 " John; m; 14 1-21-18; ¼+; s; son B1058; no; Dunseith, Rolette, ND; no; Id.463d
2217 " Mary; f; 12 2-21-20; ¼+; s; dau B1059; no; Dunseith, Rolette, ND; no; Id.463e
2218 " Evelyn I; f; 8 1-28-24; ¼+; s; dau -----; no; Dunseith, Rolette, ND; no; none
2219 " Frances E; f; 5 2-23-27; ¼+; s; dau -----; no; Dunseith, Rolette, ND; no; none
2220 " Emil; m; 5/12 9-3-31; ¼+; s; son ------; no; Dunseith, Rolette, ND; no; none

NE Gunville, John; Head
2221 " St Ann, (Bottineau); f; 36; ¼+; m; wife; B1060; no; Dunseith, Rolette, ND; no; Id.464a, Al.GF-195
2222 " Rose; f; 18 12-3-13; ¼+; s; dau B1061; no; Dunseith, Rolette, ND; no; Id.464b

Turtle Mountain Reservation
1932 Census Roll

Key: Number; Surname, Given; Sex; Age at Last Birthday, Birthdate (if given); Tribe (Chippewa, unless stated otherwise); Degree of Blood; Marital Status; Relationship to Head of Family, Last Year Census Number; At Jurisdiction Where Enrolled (Yes/No); Elsewhere - Post Office, County, State; Ward (Yes/No); Allotment [Al.], Annuity [An.] and/or Identification [Id.] Numbers

2223 Gunville(cont), Fred; m; 17 12-14-14; ¼+; s; son B1062; no; Dunseith, Rolette, ND; no; Id.464c
2224 " James; m; 16 2-20-16; ¼+; s; son B1063; no; Dunseith, Rolette, ND; no; Id.464d
2225 " Amelai[sic]; f; 14 11-15-17; ¼+; s; dau B1065; no; Dunseith, Rolette, ND; no; Id.464e
2226 " Celina; f; 12 10-6-19; ¼+; s; dau B1065; no; Dunseith, Rolette, ND; no; Id.464f
Dead " Eliza; B1066 (Died 6-11-24)
2227 " Vincent; m; 6 8-17-25; ¼+; s; son B1067; no; Dunseith, Rolette, ND; no; none
2228 " Eugenia; f; 4 3-13-28; ¼+; s; dau ------; no; Dunseith, Rolette, ND; no; none

NE Hagen, Henry; Head
2229 " Eliza (Belgarde); f; 35; ¼+; m; wife B1068; no; Comertown, Sheridan, Mont; yes; Id.465a, Al.M-109
2230 " St Ann; f; 15; ¼+; s; dau B1069; no; Comertown, Sheridan, Mont; yes; Id.465b
2231 " Joseph; m; 13; ¼+; s; son B1070; no; Comertown, Sheridan, Mont; yes; Id.465c
2232 " John O; m; 10 10-18-21; ¼+; s; son B1071; no; Comertown, Sheridan, Mont; yes; Id.465d

2233 Hamley, Leonard; m; 49; ¼+; m; Head A993; yes; yes; Id.466, Al.G-450
2234 " Jospehine[sic] (Azure); f; 41; ¼+; m; wife A994; yes; no; Id.466a, Al.GF-17
2235 " Joseph; m; 16 11-[?]-15; ¼+; s; son A996; yes; yes; Id.466d
2236 " Leonard P; m; 14 6-4-17; ¼+; s; son A995; yes; yes; Id.466b
2237 " Rosalie S; f; 12 4-15-19; ¼+; s; dau A997; yes; yes; Id.466c
2238 " Celia; f; 11 2-4-21; ¼+; s; dau A998; yes; yes; Id.446e
2239 " Bernard; m; 9 7-1-22; ¼+; s; son A999; yes; yes; Id.446f
2240 " Leo; m; 7 5-2-24; ¼+; s; son A1000; yes; yes; Id.446g
2241 " Clarence; m; 6; ¼+; s; son A1001; yes; yes; Id.446h
2242 " Louis; m; 3 9-27-28; ¼+; s; son A1002; yes; yes; Id.446i
Dead Sylvia; f; 3-12-32 (Died 3-14-32)

2243 Hamley, Patrick; m; 45; ¼+; m; Head B1072; no; Havasupai; no; Id.467, Al.GF-151
NE " Maizie (McClintock); wife
2244 " Ellen J; f; 15; ¼+; s; dau B1073; no; Havasupai; no; Id.467b
2245 " Edna P; f; 0 10-4-23; ¼+; s; dau -----; no; Havasupai; no; Id.467c

NE Hardy, Charles; Head
2246 " Flora (Nanapush); f; 19; F; m; wife A1003; no; Ponemah, Beltrami, Minn; yes; Id.21c, Al.H-024464

Turtle Mountain Reservation
1932 Census Roll

Key: Number; Surname, Given; Sex; Age at Last Birthday, Birthdate (if given); Tribe (Chippewa, unless stated otherwise); Degree of Blood; Marital Status; Relationship to Head of Family, Last Year Census Number; At Jurisdiction Where Enrolled (Yes/No); Elsewhere - Post Office, County, State; Ward (Yes/No); Allotment [Al.], Annuity [An.] and/or Identification [Id.] Numbers

NE   Harris, Paul;   Head
2247   "   Rebecca (Hamley); f; 47; ¼+; s; wife B1074; no; Chief River Falls, Pennington, Minn; yes; Id.468a, Al.G-419
2248   "   Elizabeth; f; 22 4-26-09; ¼+; s; dau B1075; no; Chief River Falls, Pennington, Minn; yes; Id.468b, Al.G-011394
2249   "   Leonard; m; 20 10-19-11; ¼+; s; son B1076; no; Chief River Falls, Pennington, Minn; yes; Id.468c
2250   "   Patrick; m; 18 1-13-14; ¼+; s; son B1077; no; Chief River Falls, Pennington, Minn; yes; Id.468d
2251   "   Eleanor; f; 16 4-13-15; ¼+; s; dau B1078; no; Chief River Falls, Pennington, Minn; yes; Id.468e

NE   Hauge, Joseph;   Head
2252   "   St Ann (Grant); f; 24; ¼+; m; wife A1004; no; Walhalla, Pembina, ND; yes; Id453b, Al.H-010507
2253   "   Duane J. P; m; 8/12 7-18-31; ¼+; s; son ----; no; Walhalla, Pembina, ND; yes; none

NE   Hayden, Alexander;   Head
2254   "   (Long Nose); f; 53; F; m; wife B1079; no; Dominion City, Roseau Res, Can; yes; Id.469a, Al.G-348
2255   "   Samuel; m; 30; ¼+; s; son B1080; no; Dominion City, Roseau Res, Can; Id.469b, Al.G-337
2256   "   Joseph; m; 23; ¼+; s; son B1081; no; Dominion City, Roseau Res, Can; yes; none
2257   "   Gabriel; m; 12 5-5-19; ¼+; s; son ----; no; Dominion City, Roseau Res, Can; yes; none
2258   "   John; m; 8 9-15-23; ¼+; s; son ------; no; Dominion City, Roseau Res, Can; yes; none

2259   Hayes, John, Jr; m; 35; ¼+; s; Head B1082; no; Unknown; yes; Id.470b, Al.GF-146
2260   "   Robert; m; 21; ¼+; s; bro B1083; no; Canton (Asylum), Lincoln, SD; no; Id.470c
2261   "   Zilda; f; 18; ¼+; s; sis B1084; no; Bismarck, Burleigh, ND; no; Id.470d

2262   Henry, Charles; m; 31; ¼+; m; Head B1090; no; Great Falls, Cascade, Mont; yes; Id.471c, Al.M-227
2263   "   Angelique (Gourneau.Lillie); f; 41; ¼+; m; wife B1091; no; Great Falls, Cascade, Mont; no; Id.670a, Al.M-364

2264   Henry, Eugene; m; 33; ¼+; m; Head B1095; no; Dunseith, Rolette, ND; no; Id.473c, Al.G-0271
Dead   "   Philomeme;   B1096;   (Died 11-11-24)

Turtle Mountain Reservation
1932 Census Roll

Key: Number; Surname, Given; Sex; Age at Last Birthday, Birthdate (if given); Tribe (Chippewa, unless stated otherwise); Degree of Blood; Marital Status; Relationship to Head of Family, Last Year Census Number; At Jurisdiction Where Enrolled (Yes/No); Elsewhere - Post Office, County, State; Ward (Yes/No); Allotment [Al.], Annuity [An.] and/or Identification [Id.] Numbers

2265 Henry(cont), Veronica (Jerome); f; 20 4-13-11; ¼+; wife B1201; no; Dunseith, Rolette, ND; no; Id.513c

2266 Henry, Frederick; m; 36; ¼+; m; Head B1097; no; Thorne, Rolette, ND; no; Id.474, Al.G0272
NE   "   Malvina (Patenaud);   wife
2267 "   Clifford; m; 9; ¼+; s; son B1098; no; Thorne, Rolette, ND; no; none

NE   Henry, John B; m;   Head
2268 "   Mary (Poitra); f; 40; ¼+; m; wife A1005; yes; yes; Id.1041a, Al.G173
2269 "   Emma; f; 14 2-17-18; ¼+; s; dau A1006; yes; yes; Id.1041b
2270 "   Rosina; f; 9 9-26-22; ¼+; s; dau A1007; yes; yes; none
2271 "   Marie; f; 5 7-12-26; ¼+; s; dau A1008; yes; yes; none
2272 "   Florence; f; 3 10-14-28; ¼+; s; dau A1009; yes; yes; none
2273 "   Theodore; m; 1 1-16-31; ¼+; s; son -------; yes; yes; none

NE   Henry, Joe;   Head
2274 "   Eliza (Iron Bear); f; 26; ¼+; m; wife B1094; no; Dunseith, Rolette, ND; yes; Id.50b, Al.G305
2275 "   Flora; f; 9 1-30-23; ¼+; s; dau -----; no; Dunseith, Rolette, ND; no; none
2276 "   Cecilia; f; 6 11-25-25; ¼+; s; dau -----; no; Dunseith, Rolette, ND; no; none
2277 "   John; m; 4 12-28-27; ¼+; s; son -----; no; Dunseith, Rolette, ND; no; none
2278 "   James; m; 3 2-28-29; ¼+; s; son -----; no; Dunseith, Rolette, ND; no; none
2279 "   Henry; m; 7/12 8-30-31; ¼+; s; dau -----; no; Dunseith, Rolette, ND; no; none

NE   Henry, Prosper;   Head
2280 "   Mary Roe (Poitra); f; 20 1-27-12; ¼+; m; wife B2116; no; Boggy Creek, Manitoba, Can; yes; Id.868b, Al.H-025392
2281 "   Georgeline; f; 2 12-17-29; ¼+; s; dau -----; no; Boggy Creek, Manitoba, Can; yes; none

2282 Henry, Wm Joseph; m; 17 2-[?]-15; ¼+; s; Head B1099; no; Unknown; yes; Id.882b

NE   Henry, Xavier;   Head
2283 "   Mary Jane (Jolibois); f; 56; ¼+; m; wife B1100; no; Thorne, Rolette, ND; no; Id.473a, Al.G-0267
2284 "   Edward; m; 34; ¼+; s; son B1101; no; Thorne, Rolette, ND; no; Id.473b, Al.G-0265
2285 "   Phillip; m; 32; ¼+; s; son B1102; no; Thorne, Rolette, ND; yes; Id.473d, Al.G-0270
2286 "   Martin; m; 30; ¼+; s; son B1103; no; Thorne, Rolette, ND; yes; Id.473e, Al.G-0269

Turtle Mountain Reservation
1932 Census Roll

Key: Number; Surname, Given; Sex; Age at Last Birthday, Birthdate (if given); Tribe (Chippewa, unless stated otherwise); Degree of Blood; Marital Status; Relationship to Head of Family, Last Year Census Number; At Jurisdiction Where Enrolled (Yes/No); Elsewhere - Post Office, County, State; Ward (Yes/No); Allotment [Al.], Annuity [An.] and/or Identification [Id.] Numbers

2287 Henry(cont), Peter; m; 27; ¼+; s; son B1104; no; Thorne, Rolette, ND; yes; Id.473g, Al.G-0268
2288 " Gladys M; f; 19; ¼+; s; dau B1105; no; Thorne, Rolette, ND; yes; Id.473l, Al.H-024661
2289 " May; f; 13 5-13-18; ¼+; s; dau B1106; no; Thorne, Rolette, ND; no; Id.473m

2290 Herman, Alexander; m; 66; ¼+; m; Head B1107; no; Ft.Totten, Benson, ND; no; Id.475, Al.R-148
2291 " Mary (Belgarde.Montour); f; 49; ¼+; m; wife B1108; no; Ft.Totten, Benson, ND; no; Id.475a, Al.G-261
2292 " William; m; 23; ¼+; s; son B1109; no; Ft.Totten, Benson, ND; no; Id.475b, Al.G-015950
2293 " Ernest; m; 18; ¼+; s; son B1111; no; Ft.Totten, Benson, ND; no; Id.475e, none
2294 " Alfred; m; 15 1-121-17; ¼+; s; son B1112; no; Ft.Totten, Benson, ND; no; Id.475f
2295 " Roy; m; 12 5-19-19; ¼+; s; son B1113; no; Ft.Totten, Benson, ND; no; Id.475g
2296 " Florence; f; 10 6-17-21; ¼+; s; dau B1114; no; Ft.Totten, Benson, ND; no; Id.475h
2297 " Elizabeth; f; 8 12-23-23; ¼+; s; dau B1115; no; Ft.Totten, Benson, ND; no; Id.475i

2298 Herman, Charles; m; 31; ¼+; m; Head B1116; no; Devils Lake, Ramsey, ND; yes; Id.477b, Al.G-217
2299 " Grace (Charbonneau); f; 23; ¼+; m; wife B1117; no; Devils Lake, Ramsey, ND; no; Id.235b
Died " Inez; B1118 (Died 5-24-17)
2300 " Violet M; f; 4 3-17-28; ¼+; s; dau B1119; no; Devils Lake, Ramsey, ND; yes; none

2301 Herman, Ernest; m; 26; ¼+; s; Head B1120; yes; yes; Id.476b, Al.G-01325
2302 " Wilfred; m; 24; ¼+; s; bro B1121; no; Elbowoods, McLean, ND; yes; Id.476c, Al.G-016327
2303 " Joseph; m; 22; ¼+; s; bro B1122; yes; yes; Id.476d, Al.G-016327
2304 " Louis; m; 20; ¼+; s; bro B1123; yes; no; Id.476e
2305 " Rosina; f; 18; ¼+; s; sis B1124; yes; no; Id.476f
2306 " Madeline; f; 16; ¼+; s; sis B1125; yes; no; Id.476g

2307 Herman, Henry; m; 76; ¼+; m; Head B1126; no; Devils Lake, Ramsey, ND; no; Id.477, Al.DL-35
2308 " Cecelia (Lafrombois); f; 64; ¼+; m; wife B1127; no; Devils Lake, Ramsey, ND; no; Id.477, Al.G-214

Turtle Mountain Reservation
1932 Census Roll

Key: Number; Surname, Given; Sex; Age at Last Birthday, Birthdate (if given); Tribe (Chippewa, unless stated otherwise); Degree of Blood; Marital Status; Relationship to Head of Family, Last Year Census Number; At Jurisdiction Where Enrolled (Yes/No); Elsewhere - Post Office, County, State; Ward (Yes/No); Allotment [Al.], Annuity [An.] and/or Identification [Id.] Numbers

2309 Herman, Herman; m; 37; ¼+; s; Head B1129; no; Devils Lake, Ramsey, ND; no; Id.478, Al.G-213
NE Hill, Ernest;   Head
2310 " Mary (Olfert); f; 23; ¼+; m; wife B1130; no; Walhalla, Pembina, ND; yes; Id.781b, Al.H-012599
2311 " Harvey L; m; 4 12-30-27; ¼+; s; son ------; no; Walhalla, Pembina, ND; yes; none

NE Hintz, Clarence;   Head
2312 " Rachel (Gunderson); f; 25; ¼+; m; wife B1131; no; Palermo, Mountrail, ND; yes; Id.462e, Al.G-6

2313 Holm, Florestine (Brien.Anderson); f; 35; ¼+; wd; Head B1132; no; Lidgerwood, Richland, ND; yes; Id.981, Al.G-08263
2314 " (Anderson), Ray L; m; 13 5-31-18; ¼+; s; son B1133; no; Lidgerwood, Richland, ND; yes; none
2315 " (Anderson), James; m; 11 4-14-20; ¼+; s; son B1134; no; Lidgerwood, Richland, ND; yes; none
2316 " (Anderson), May Rhoda; f; 10 ¼+; s; dau B1135; no; Lidgerwood, Richland, ND; yes; none
2317 " Ernest J; m; 6; ¼+; s; son B1136; no; Lidgerwood, Richland, ND; yes; none

2318 Houle, Albert; m; 32; ¼+; m; Head B1137; no; Rolla, Rolette, ND; no; Id.491c, Al.M-10
2319 Houle, Clemance (Azure); f; 35; ¼+; m; wife B1138; no; Rolla, Rolette, ND; no; Id.113b, Al.G-08161
2320 " Arthur A; m; 11 1-15-21; ¼+; s; son B1139; no; Rolla, Rolette, ND; no; none
2321 " Joseph; m; 7 6-21-24; ¼+; s; son B1140; no; Rolla, Rolette, ND; no; none
DEAD " Barbara;   B1141   (Died 9-7-31)

2322 Houle, Baptiste; m; 60; ¼+; m; Head A1010; no; Devils Lake, Ramsey, ND; yes; Id.484, Al.R-151
2323 " Virginia (Lafontain); f; 46; ¼+; m; wife A1011; no; Devils Lake, Ramsey, ND; no; Id.484a, Al.G-06060
2324 " Rosina; f; 23 2-4-09; ¼+; m; dau A1012; no; (Separated from husband) Sidney, Richland, Mont; yes; id.484c
2325 " Edna; f; 19 9-17-12; ¼+; s; dau A1013; no; Devils Lake, Ramsey, ND; yes; Id.484e
2326 " Daniel; m; 18 2-28-14; ¼+; s; son A1014; no; Devils Lake, Ramsey, ND; yes; Id.484f
2327 " Benedict; m; 16 1-3-16; ¼+; s; son A1015; no; Devils Lake, Ramsey, ND; yes; Id.484g
2328 " Agnes J; f; 14 2-26-18; ¼+; s; dau; no; Devils Lake, Ramsey, ND; yes; Id.484h
DEAD " Josephine;   A1016; no   (Died 2-16-23)

Turtle Mountain Reservation
1932 Census Roll

Key: Number; Surname, Given; Sex; Age at Last Birthday, Birthdate (if given); Tribe (Chippewa, unless stated otherwise); Degree of Blood; Marital Status; Relationship to Head of Family, Last Year Census Number; At Jurisdiction Where Enrolled (Yes/No); Elsewhere - Post Office, County, State; Ward (Yes/No); Allotment [Al.], Annuity [An.] and/or Identification [Id.] Numbers

2329 Houle(cont), Lillian; f; 10 11-17-21; ¼+; s; dau A1017; no; Devils Lake, Ramsey, ND; yes; Id.484k
2330 " Irene; f; 9 6-25-23; ¼+; s; dau A1018; no; Devils Lake, Ramsey, ND; yes; Id.484l
2331 " Ethel; f; 6 6-9-25; ¼+; s; dau A1019; no; Devils Lake, Ramsey, ND; yes; yes; Id.484m
2332 " Stella; f; 4 7-22-27; ¼+; s; dau A1120; no; Devils Lake, Ramsey, ND; yes; Id.484n

2333 Houle, Baptiste; m; 44; ¼+; m; Head B1142; no; Culbertson, Roosevelt, Mont; no; Id.496, Al.GF-114
2334 " Emily (Caplette); f; 36; ¼+; m; wife B1143; no; Edmonds, Snohomish, Wash; no; Id.496a, Al.G-327
2335 " Dominick; m; 15 4-26-16; ¼+; s; son B1144; no; Chemawa, Marion, Ore; (This couple are[sic] separated)   no; none

2336 Houle, Bernard; m; 75; ¼+; wd; Head A1021; yes; yes; Id.485, Al.R-152

2337 Houle, Cuthbert; m; 62; ¼+; m; Head A1022; yes; yes; Id.489, Al.R-155
NE " Mary (Peltier); wife
2338 " Chresolings; m; 29; ¼+; s; son A1023; yes; yes; Id.489c, Al.G-011724
2339 " William; m; 24; ¼+; s; son A1024; yes; yes; Id.489d, Al.G-011725
2340 " Delia; f; 21; ¼+; s; dau A1025; yes; yes; Id.489e, Al.H-012545
2341 " Napoleon; m; 20; ¼+; s; son A1026; yes; yes; Id.489f
2342 " Louis; m; 16 10-30-15; ¼+; s; son A1027; yes; yes; Id.489h
2343 " Anna; f; 14; ¼+; s; dau A1028; yes; yes; Id.489i
2344 " Joseph; 11 6-8-20; ¼+; s; son A1029; yes; yes; Id.489j
2345 " Ernest; m; 10 12-23-21; ¼+; s; son A1030; yes; yes; Id.489k

2346 Houle, Edward; m; 41 9-15-91; ¼+; m; Head B1145; no; Rolla, Rolette, ND; no; Id.492, Al.M-5
2347 " Mary (Azure); f; 39 6-10-93; ¼+; m; wife B1146; no; Rolla, Rolette, ND; no; Id.492a, Al.G-08165
2348 " Joseph; m; 18 8-9-13; ¼+; s; son B1147; no; Rolla, Rolette, ND; no; Id.492b
2349 " Agnes; f; 14 3-27-18; ¼+; s; dau B1148; no; Rolla, Rolette, ND; no; Id.492bc
2350 " Ernest; m; 11 7-31-20; ¼+; s; son B1149; no; Rolla, Rolette, ND; no; Id.492d
2351 " Arthur; m; 9 10-28-22; ¼+; s; son B1150; no; Rolla, Rolette, ND; no; Id.492e
2352 " George; m; 5 4-7-26; ¼+; s; son B1151; no; Rolla, Rolette, ND; no; Id.492f
2353 " Joseph; m; 1 8-4-30; ¼+; s; son B1152; no; Rolla, Rolette, ND; no; none

2354 Houle, Frederick; m; 48; ¼+; wd; Head B1153; no; Dunseith, Rolette, ND; yes; Id.483, Al.G-04533
2355 " Daniel; m; 12 9-10-19; ¼+; s; son B1154; no; Dunseith, Rolette, ND; yes; Id.483b

Turtle Mountain Reservation
1932 Census Roll

Key: Number; Surname, Given; Sex; Age at Last Birthday, Birthdate (if given); Tribe (Chippewa, unless stated otherwise); Degree of Blood; Marital Status; Relationship to Head of Family, Last Year Census Number; At Jurisdiction Where Enrolled (Yes/No); Elsewhere - Post Office, County, State; Ward (Yes/No); Allotment [Al.], Annuity [An.] and/or Identification [Id.] Numbers

2356 Houle(cont), Jerome; m; 11 1-14-21; ¼+; s; son B1155; no; Dunseith, Rolette, ND; yes; Id.483c

2357 Houle, Hyacinth; m; 36; ¼+; m; Head A1031; yes; yes; Id.490, Al.G-011717
2358 " Mary Rose (Wilkie); f; 31 3-9-01; ¼+; m; wife; A1032; yes; yes; Id.490a, Al.M-95
2359 " Beulah; f; 14 9-19-17; ¼+; s; dau A1033; yes; yes; Id.490b
2360 " Victoria; f; 12 7-9-19; ¼+; s; dau A1034; yes; yes; Id.490c
2361 " Peter; m; 9 5-27-22; ¼+; s; son A1035; yes; yes; Id.490d
2362 " Rita; f; 5 12-3-26; ¼+; s; dau A1036; yes; yes; none
2363 " Nora; f; 5 12-3-26; ¼+; s; dau A1037; yes; yes; none
DEAD " George; A1038 (Died 6-18-30)

2364 Houle, John; m; 38; ¼+; m; Head A1039; yes; yes; Id.487, Al.G-196
NE " Mary (Flamand); wife
2365 " Della; f; 13 11-29-18; ¼+; s; dau A1040; yes; yes; Id.487a
2366 " Alvina M; f; 10/12 5-3-31; ¼+; s; dau; yes; yes; none

2367 Houle, John; m; 42; ¼+; s; Head B1156; no; Bottineau, Bottineau, ND; no; Id.488, Al.H-038900

2368 Houle, John; m; 76; ¼+; wd; Head B1157; no; Dunseith, Rolette, ND; yes; Id.488, Al.R-154
Dead " Cinya; B1158 (Died 1-17-32)

2369 Houle, Joseph; m; 73; ¼+; m; Head B1159; no; Unknown; no; Id.491, Al.R-156
2370 " Sarah (Langer); f; 68; ¼+; m; wife B1160; no; Unknown; no; Id.491a, Al.M-6

2371 Houle, Joseph; m; 29; ¼+; m; Head A1042; yes; yes; Id.999b, Al.M-341
2371 " Mary (Belgarde); f; 29; ¼+; wife; A1043; yes; yes; Id.158b, Al.M-114

NE Houle, Joseph; Head
2373 " Virginia (Lavallie); f; 48; ¼+; m; wife A1041; yes; no; Id.494a, Al.MC-026555

2374 Houle, Louis; m; 52; ¼+; m; Head A1044; yes; no; Id.497, Al.G-08316
2375 " Margaret (Pepin); f; 57; ¼+; m; wife A1045; yes; yes; Id.497a, Al.R-269

2376 Houle, Louise (Denomie); f; 65 (7-10-66); ¼+; wd; Head B1161; no; Brockton, Roosevelt, Mont; no; Id.485a, Al.G-05739
2377 " Frederick; m; 28 2-14-04; ¼+; s; son B1162; no; Brockton, Roosevelt, Mont; yes; Id.485c, Al.GF-113

2378 Houle, Napoleon; m; 52; ¼+; m; Head B1163; no; Bottineau, Bottineau, ND; no; Id.482, Al.G-27
NE " Mary (Bruce); wife

Turtle Mountain Reservation
1932 Census Roll

Key: Number; Surname, Given; Sex; Age at Last Birthday, Birthdate (if given); Tribe (Chippewa, unless stated otherwise); Degree of Blood; Marital Status; Relationship to Head of Family, Last Year Census Number; At Jurisdiction Where Enrolled (Yes/No); Elsewhere - Post Office, County, State; Ward (Yes/No); Allotment [Al.], Annuity [An.] and/or Identification [Id.] Numbers

2379 Houle(cont), John; m; 21 11-1-10; ¼+; s; B1164; no; Bottineau, Bottineau, ND; yes; Id.482b, Al.H-012544

2380 " Alvina; f; 19 12-16-13; ¼+; s; dau B1165; no; Bottineau, Bottineau, ND; no; Id.482c

2381 " Edward; m; 15 7-12-16; ¼+; s; son B1166; no; Bottineau, Bottineau, ND; no; Id.482d

2382 " Agnes; f; 12 9-16-19; ¼+; s; dau B1167; no; Bottineau, Bottineau, ND; no; Id.482e

2383 " Ernest Paul; m; 10 2-6-22; ¼+; s; son B1168; no; Bottineau, Bottineau, ND; no; Id.482f

2384 " Ida; f; 7 7-19-24; ¼+; s; dau B1169; no; Bottineau, Bottineau, ND; no; Id.482g

2385 " Francis; m; 6 2-20-26; ¼+; s; son B1170; no; Bottineau, Bottineau, ND; no; Id.482h

2386 " John S; m; 2 12-23-29; ¼+; s; son B1171; no; Bottineau, Bottineau, ND; no; Id.482i

2387 " James H; m; 6/12 9-19-31; ¼+; s; son; no; Bottineau, Bottineau, ND; no; Id.482j

2388 Houle, Phillip; m; 35; ¼+; m; Head B1172; no; Unknown, Canada; no; Id.479, Al.M-342

NE " Eliza (Peltier.Azure); wife
2389 " (Azure) Eliza V; f; 18; ¼+; s; step dau B1173; no; Unknown, Canada; no; none

2390 " (Azure) Ernest; m; 14 9-15-17; ¼+; s; stepson B1174; no; Unknown, Canada; no; none

2391 " (Azure) Cecil A; m; 12 12-20-19 ; ¼+; s; stepson B1175; no; Unknown, Canada; no; none

2392 Houle, Trefle; m; 32; ¼+; s; Head A1046; no; Grafton, Walsh, ND; yes; Id.486b, Al.G-192

2393 " Isadore; m; 30; ¼+; s; bro A1047; no; Grafton, Walsh, ND; yes; Id.486c, Al.G-446

2394 " Maxim; m; 27; ¼+; s; bro A1048; yes; yes; Id.486d, Al.G-191

NE Hubbell, Elbert; Head
2395 " Clarice (Grant); f; 25; ¼+; m; wife A982; yes; yes; Id.457e, Al.G-0111

NE Ingalls, Bert; Head
2396 " Amelia (Laverdure); f; 24; ¼+; m; wife B1176; no; Devils Lake, Ramsey, ND; yes; Id.647d, Al.G-07891

2397 " George; m; 3 22-22-29; ¼+; s; son; no; Devils Lake, Ramsey, ND; yes; none

Turtle Mountain Reservation
1932 Census Roll

Key: Number; Surname, Given; Sex; Age at Last Birthday, Birthdate (if given); Tribe (Chippewa, unless stated otherwise); Degree of Blood; Marital Status; Relationship to Head of Family, Last Year Census Number; At Jurisdiction Where Enrolled (Yes/No); Elsewhere - Post Office, County, State; Ward (Yes/No); Allotment [Al.], Annuity [An.] and/or Identification [Id.] Numbers

2398 Iron Bear, Mrs (Always Day); f; 49; F; wd; Head B1177; no; Dunseith, Rolette, ND; yes; Id.50a, Al.G-336
2399 " Mabel Lucy; f; 12 8-13-19; F; s; dau B1178; no; Dunseith, Rolette, ND; yes; Id.50g
2400 " Flora; f; 10 7-24-21; F; s; dau B1179; no; Dunseith, Rolette, ND; yes; Id.50h
2401 " Jane; f; 7; F; s; dau B1180; no; Dunseith, Rolette, ND; yes; Id.50i
2402 " Andrew; m; 5; F; s; son B1181; no; Dunseith, Rolette, ND; yes; Id.50j

NE Irving, Thomas; Head B_{434}
2403 " Marion (Godon); f; 28; ¼+; m; wife B954; no; (Counted twice 1931) Phoenix, Ariz; no; Id.424b
2404 " Thomas, Jr; m; 1 3-3-31; ¼+; s; son -----; no; Phoenix, Maricopa, Ariz; no; none

NE Jacoby, Charles H; Head
2405 " Alphonsine (Bonneau); f; 25 11-4-06; ¼+; m; wife B374; no; Madon[sic], Daniels, Mont; yes; Id.1177b, Al.G-08419

1985 Jacqmarct, Marceline; f; 34; ¼+; s; Head B1182; no; Fargo, Cass, ND; no; Id.499b, Al.M-396

2406 Jacqmarct, Peter; m; 31 8-7-00; ¼+; m; Head B1183^{A757}; no; (Counted twice 1931) Ft.Totten, Benson, ND; no; Id.499c, Al.M-398
2407 " Mary (Trothier); f; 27 4-28-04; ¼+; m; wife B1184; no; Ft.Totten, Benson, ND; yes; Id.933b, Al.G-158
2408 " Peter J; m; 6 1-3-26; ¼+; s; son B1185; no; Ft.Totten, Benson, ND; yes; none
2409 " Marchette; f; 2 11-24-29; ¼+; s; dau ----; no; Ft.Totten, Benson, ND; yes; none

NE Jaste, Ezear; wd; Head
2410 " Alexander; m; 18 ¼+; s; son 1051; yes; yes; Id.500g, Al. none
2411 " Mary A; f; 15 5-23-16; ¼+; s; dau A1052; yes; yes; Id.500h
2412 " Frank; m; 13 7-28-18; ¼+; s; dau A1053; yes; yes; Id.500i
2413 " Elmer Peter; m; 6; ¼+; s; son A1054; yes; yes; Id.500j

2414 Jaste, John Louis; m; 25; ¼+; m; Head A1050; yes; yes; Id.500e, Al.H-01421
2415 " Alice B (Morin); f; 23; ¼+; m; wife A1658; yes; no; Id.762b

2416 Jaste, Natalie (Jerome); f; 19; ¼+; wd; Head A1055; yes; yes; Id.521h, Al.G-016075

Turtle Mountain Reservation
1932 Census Roll

Key: Number; Surname, Given; Sex; Age at Last Birthday, Birthdate (if given); Tribe (Chippewa, unless stated otherwise); Degree of Blood; Marital Status; Relationship to Head of Family, Last Year Census Number; At Jurisdiction Where Enrolled (Yes/No); Elsewhere - Post Office, County, State; Ward (Yes/No); Allotment [Al.], Annuity [An.] and/or Identification [Id.] Numbers

NE	Jeannott[sic], David;	Head
2417	"	Marie Edna (Grandbois); f; 30; ¼+; m; wife A1056; yes; yes; Id.437d, Al.M-80
2418	"	Joseph; m; 9; ¼+; s; son A1057; yes; yes; none
2419	"	Mary Martine; f; 6; ¼+; s; dau A1058; yes; yes; none
2420	"	Leo; m; 4; ¼+; s; son A1059; yes; yes; none
2421	"	Mary Rita; f; 1 4-13-30; ¼+; s; dau A1060; yes; yes; none

2422 Jeannott[sic], Ernest; m; 34; ¼+; m; Head A1061; yes; yes; Id.503b, Al.M-76
2423 " Clara (Schindler); f; 27; ¼+; m; wife A1062; yes; yes; yes; Id.915, Al.G-0190
2424 " Theresa M; f; 8 10-15-23; ¼+; s; dau A1063; yes; yes; none
2425 " Leona; f; 6 12-25-25; ¼+; s; dau A1064; yes; yes; none
2426 " Nora; f; 3 3-9-29; ¼+; s; dau A1065; yes; yes; none
2427 " Ernest R; m; 1 2-1-31; ¼+; s; son A1066; yes; yes; none

2428 Jeannotte, Frederick; m; 70; ¼+; wd; Head B1186; no; Rolla, Rolette, ND; no; Id.501, Al.R-159

NE	Jeannotte, George;	Head
2429	"	Eliza (Aiken); m[sic]; 32; ¼+; m; wife B1187; no; St.John, Rolette, ND; no; Id.62b, Al.G-496
2430	"	Josephine; f; 9 1-7-23; ¼+; s; dau B1188; no; St.John, Rolette, ND; no; none
2431	"	Hubert; m; 7 4-2-24; ¼+; s; son B1189; no; St.John, Rolette, ND; no; none
2432	"	Mary Mae; f; 5 5-3-26; ¼+; s; dau ------; no; St.John, Rolette, ND; no; none
2433	"	Olive B; f; 3 9-16-28; ¼+; s; dau ------; no; St.John, Rolette, ND; no; none
2434	"	Elmer Wm; m; 1 7-22-30; ¼+; s; son ------; no; St.John, Rolette, ND; no; none

2435 Jeannotte, John; m; 59 11-30-72; ¼+; m; Head A1067; yes; no; Id.503, Al.R160
2436 " St Ann (Vivier); f; 46 4-8-86; ¼+; m; wife A1068; yes; yes; Id.503a, Al.G-036585
Dead " Josephine; A1069 (Died 6-24-1918)
2437 " Rebecca; f; 23; ¼+; s; dau A1085; yes; yes; Id.503e, Al.L-034149
2438 " Peter; m; 21; ¼+; s; son A1086; yes; yes; Id.503f, Al.H-024663
2439 " George; m; 16 7-27-15; ¼+; s; son A1087; yes; yes; Id.503g, Al.H-030867
2440 " Alex; m; 14; ¼+; s; son A1089; yes; yes; Id.503h
2441 " Antoine; m; 12 12-17-19; ¼+; s; son A1088; yes; yes; Id.503i
2442 " Blanche; f; 10; ¼+; s; dau A1090; yes; yes; Id.503j

Turtle Mountain Reservation
1932 Census Roll

Key: Number; Surname, Given; Sex; Age at Last Birthday, Birthdate (if given); Tribe (Chippewa, unless stated otherwise); Degree of Blood; Marital Status; Relationship to Head of Family, Last Year Census Number; At Jurisdiction Where Enrolled (Yes/No); Elsewhere - Post Office, County, State; Ward (Yes/No); Allotment [Al.], Annuity [An.] and/or Identification [Id.] Numbers

2443	Jeannotte, Joseph A; m; 31 9-19-00; ¼+; m; Head A1091; yes; yes; Id.503c, Al.M-11
2444	"	Ernestine (Langer); f; 30; ¼+; m; wife A1092; yes; yes; Id.611b, Al.G-0404
2445	"	Joe A, Jr; m; 7 5-2-24; ¼+; s; son A1093; yes; yes; none
2446	"	Irene M; f; 5-8-2-26; ¼+; s; dau A1094; yes; yes; none
2447	"	Henry; m; 3 12-25-28; ¼+; s; son ------; yes; yes; none
2448	"	Helen Doris; f; 1 3-23-31; ¼+; s; dau A1095; yes; yes; none

2449 Jeannotte, Leon; m; 27; ¼+; m; Head A1096; yes; yes; Id.507b, Al.G-07858
NE " Mary (Laroque); wife
2450 " Robert; m; 3 6-5-28; ¼+; s; son A1097; yes; yes; none
2451 " Joseph; m; 2 2-4-30; ¼+; s; son A1098; yes; yes; none
2452 " Simon S; m; 4-12 11-28-31; ¼+; s; son ------; yes; yes; none

2453 Jeannotte, Louise; f; 85; ¼+; wd; Head A1070; yes; no; Id.508a, Al.R-161

2454 Jeannotte, Patrice; m; 48 4-17-83; ¼+; m; Head A1071; yes; yes; Id.507, Al.R-162
2455 " Mary Jane (Houle); f; 44 11-4-87; ¼+; m; wife A1072; yes; Id.507a, Al.G-07839
2456 " Cecil; m; 21 8-1-10; ¼+; s; son A1073; yes; no; Id.507d, Al.G-031166
2457 " John B; m; 19 12-1-12; ¼+; s; son A1074; yes; yes; Id.507e, Al.H-024764
2458 " Marcil; m; 17 3-31-15; ¼+; s; son A1075; yes; yes; Id.507f
2459 " Lawrence; m; 15 5-27-16; ¼+; s; son A1076; yes; yes; Id.507g
2460 " Raymond; m; 12 5-9-19; ¼+; s; son A1077; yes; yes; Id.507g
2461 " Louis; m; 8 5-22-23; ¼+; s; son A1078; yes; yes; Id.507h
2462 " Louise G; f; 6 7-29-25; ¼+; s; dau A1079; yes; yes; Id.507i

2463 Jeannotte, Raphael; m; 52; ¼+; m; Head A1080; yes; yes; Id.509, Al.G-07836
2464 " Philomeme (Houle); f; 42; ¼+; m; wife A1081; yes; no; Id.509b, Al.M-7
2465 " James; m; 21; ¼+; s; son A1082; yes; yes; Id.509c
2466 " Mary A; f; 19; ¼+; s; dau A1083; yes; yes; Id.509d
2467 " Francis; m; 15 2-28-17; ¼+; s; son A1084; yes; yes; Id.509e
2468 " Arthur; m; 13 10-5-18; ¼+; s; son A1099; yes; yes; Id.509f
2469 " Veronica; f; 8 5-3-23; ¼+; s; dau A1100; yes; yes; Id.509g
2470 " Leo; m; 4 1-7-28; ¼+; s; son A1101; yes; yes; Id.509h

2471 Jerome, Alexander; m; 32 2-3-00; ¼+; m; Head B1191; yes; yes; Id.510b, Al.G-539
NE " Ellen (Mareau); wife
2472 " Marcil; m; 6 6-24-25; ¼+; s; son B1192; yes; yes; none
2473 " Irene; f; 4 2-6-28; ¼+; s; dau B1193; yes; yes; none
2474 " Alex L; m; 2 9-17-29; ¼+; s; son -----; yes; yes; none
2475 " Felicite M; f; 3/12 1-29-32; ¼+; s; dau -----; yes; yes; none

2476 Jerome, Alexander; m; 65; ¼+; m; Head B1194; yes; no; Id.510, Al.R-163
NE " Mary Louise (Morin); wife

Turtle Mountain Reservation
1932 Census Roll

Key: Number; Surname, Given; Sex; Age at Last Birthday, Birthdate (if given); Tribe (Chippewa, unless stated otherwise); Degree of Blood; Marital Status; Relationship to Head of Family, Last Year Census Number; At Jurisdiction Where Enrolled (Yes/No); Elsewhere - Post Office, County, State; Ward (Yes/No); Allotment [Al.], Annuity [An.] and/or Identification [Id.] Numbers

2477	Jerome(cont), Wallace; m; 28 1-19-04; ¼+; s; son B1195; yes; yes; Id.510c, Al.G-537
2478	"	Dominick; m; 20 5-2-11; ¼+; s; son B1196; yes; yes; Id.510e
2479	"	Barbara; f; 17 12-4-14; ¼+; s; dau B1197; yes; yes; Id.510g
2480	"	Annie; f; 10 11-15-21; ¼+; s; dau B1198; yes; yes; Id.510h
2481	Jerome, Daniel; m; 63; ¼+; wd; Head A1102; yes; yes; Id.514, Al.M-013488
2482	"	Romeo; m; 12 3-28-20; ¼+; s; son A1103; yes; yes; Id.514b
Dead	"	Daniel E; A1104 (Died 10-23-21)
2483	Jerome, Edmond; m; 52 7-23-79; ¼+; m; Head B1199; no; Rolette, Rolette, ND; yes; Id.513, Al.M-010084
2484	"	Mary Jane (Vivier); f; 40 11-19-91; ¼+; m; wife B1200; no; Rolette, Rolette, ND; no; Id.513a, Al.M-154
2485	"	Marceline; f; 18 1-14-14; ¼+; s; dau B1202; no; Rolette, Rolette, ND; yes; Id.513c
2486	"	May; f; 16 5-18-15; ¼+; s; dau B1203; no; Rolette, Rolette, ND; yes; Id.513d
2487	"	Elise; f; 16 2-25-16; ¼+; s; dau B1204; no; Rolette, Rolette, ND; yes; Id.513f
2488	"	Mary; f; 12 9-25-19; ¼+; s; dau B1205; no; Rolette, Rolette, ND; yes; Id.513g
2489	"	George; m; 11 7-27-20; ¼+; s; son B1206; no; Rolette, Rolette, ND; yes; Id.513h
2490	"	Alice; f; 8 4-3-23; ¼+; s; son[sic] B1207; no; Rolette, Rolette, ND; none
2491	"	Franklin; m; 7 12-26-24; ¼+; s; son B1208; no; Rolette, Rolette, ND; yes; none
2492	"	Marie; f; 6 12-21-25; ¼+; s; dau B1209; no; Rolette, Rolette, ND; none
2493	"	Ernestine; f; 4 9-20-27; ¼+; s; dau B1210; no; Rolette, Rolette, ND; yes; none
2494	"	Alma; f; 1 9-12-30; ¼+; s; dau B1211; no; Rolette, Rolette, ND; yes; none
2495	Jerome, Ferdinand; m; 44 7-5-87; ¼+; m; Head A1105; yes; no; Id.511, Al.G-535
2496	"	Emily (Lafrombois); f; 27 3-19-05; ¼+; m; wife A1106; yes; yes; Id.575d, Al.none
2497	"	Cecelia; f; 6 5-6-25; ¼+; s; dau A1107; yes; yes; none
DEAD	"	Eva; A1108 (Died 8-31-28) yes; none
2498	"	Joseph; m; 4 3-7-28; ¼+; s; son -----; yes; yes; none
2499	"	Alfred; m; ¼+; s; son A1109; yes; yes; none
2500	"	Julia Rose; f; 4/12 11-7-31; ¼+; s; dau ----; yes; yes; none
2501	Jerome, Frederick; m; 56; ¼+; wd; Head A1110; yes; yes; Id.512, Al.G-534
2502	Jerome, John Albert; m; 39; ¼+; m; Head B1212; no; Unknown; no; Id.520b, Al.M-89
NE	"	Myrtle (Watrous); wife
2503	"	Joan; f; 10; ¼+; s; dau B1213; no; Unknown; no; none

Turtle Mountain Reservation
1932 Census Roll

Key: Number; Surname, Given; Sex; Age at Last Birthday, Birthdate (if given); Tribe (Chippewa, unless stated otherwise); Degree of Blood; Marital Status; Relationship to Head of Family, Last Year Census Number; At Jurisdiction Where Enrolled (Yes/No); Elsewhere - Post Office, County, State; Ward (Yes/No); Allotment [Al.], Annuity [An.] and/or Identification [Id.] Numbers

2504 Jerome, Joseph; m; 40; ¼+; m; Head B1214; no; Crookston, Polk, Minn; no; Id.520c, Al.M-87
NE " Mary (Kaplin); wife
2505 " John; m; 14 5-8-17; ¼+; s; son B1215; no; Crookston, Polk, Minn; no; none

Died Jerome, Louis; A1111 (Died 7-9-31)

Died Jerome, Martin; B1216 (Died 1-25-32)

2506 Jerome, Patrick; m; 36; ¼+; m; Head B1217; no; Malta, Phillips, Mont; no; Id.516, Al.G-395
NE " Christine (Navavre); wife
2507 " Eugene M; m; 8 10-23-23; ¼+; s; son B1218; no; Malta, Phillips, Mont; no; none
2508 " Roger J; m; 7 10-20-24; ¼+; s; son B1219; no; Malta, Phillips, Mont; no; none

NE Jerome, Roger; Head
2509 " Sarah Jane (Grant); f; 56; ¼+; m; wife A1112; yes; no; Id.521, Al.M-110

NE Jetty, Fred; Head
2510 " Angelique (Morin); f; 33; ¼+; m; wife B1221; no; Devils Lake, Ramsey, ND; yes; Id.745b, Al.G-590
B1222 (No such child)
(All his children are enrolled at Fort Totten) B1223 (No such child)

NE Jetty, Maxime[sic]; Head
2511 " Rosine (Morin); f; 39; ¼+; m; wife B1220; no; Tokio, Benson, ND; no; Id.522e, Al.G-588
2512 " Rebecca; f; 4 3-27-28; ¼+; s; adpt dau; no; (Former name Edna Pearl Dubois) Tokio, Benson, ND; no; none

NE Johns, Frank; Head
2513 " Annie Mary (Rossknecht); f; 21 5-13-10; ¼+; m; wife B2240; no; Hendley, Furnas, Neb; no; Id.900d
2514 " Herbert F; m; 1 3-13-31; ¼+; s; son -----; no; Hendley, Furnas, Neb; no; none

NE Johnson, A M; Head
2515 " Celina (Renville.Gossline); f; 29; ¼+; m; wife B1644; no; St.Paul, Ramsey, Minn; yes; Id.888b, Al.M-114
2516 " (Gossline) Emile F; m; 11; ¼+; s; stepson B1645; no; St.Paul, Ramsey, Minn; yes; none
2517 " (Lippy) Stanley; m; 9; ¼+; s; stepson ------; no; St.Paul, Ramsey, Minn; yes; none

Turtle Mountain Reservation
1932 Census Roll

Key: Number; Surname, Given; Sex; Age at Last Birthday, Birthdate (if given); Tribe (Chippewa, unless stated otherwise); Degree of Blood; Marital Status; Relationship to Head of Family, Last Year Census Number; At Jurisdiction Where Enrolled (Yes/No); Elsewhere - Post Office, County, State; Ward (Yes/No); Allotment [Al.], Annuity [An.] and/or Identification [Id.] Numbers

NE	Johnson, Frank;	Head
2518	"	Mary (Lafontain); f; 34; ¼+; m; wife B1226; no; Breckenridge, Wilkin, Minn; no; Id.554b, Al.GF-229
2519	"	Phyllis; f; 6 8-5-25; ¼+; s; dau B1227; no; Breckenridge, Wilkin, Minn; no; none
2520	"	Bruce; m; 5 11-4-26; ¼+; s; son B1228; no; Breckenridge, Wilkin, Minn; no; none
2521	"	Lucille; f; 4 5-2-28; ¼+; s; dau B1229; no; Breckenridge, Wilkin, Minn; no; none

NE	Johnson, John Joseph;	Head
2522	"	Emily; f; 49; ¼+; m; wife B1230; no; (Maiden name not known) Unknown; yes; Id.523a, Al.H-024678
2523	"	Miles; m; 22 7-12-19; ¼+; s; son B1231; no; Unknown; yes; Id.523b
2524	"	Hubert; m; 21 10-10-10; ¼+; s; son B1232; no; Unknown; yes; Id.523c
2525	"	Norma; f; 19 4-8-12; ¼+; s; dau B1233; no; Unknown; yes; Id.523d
2526	"	Cathryn; f; 17 6-8-14; ¼+; s; dau B25; no; Unknown; yes; Id.523e

NE	Johnson, John;	Head	(This couple are[sic] separated)
2527	"	Evelyn (Standing); f; 23 1-2-09; F; m; wife B2364; no; Dunseith, Rolette, ND; yes; Id.53c, Al.G-011715	

NE	Johnson, Norman;	Head
2528	"	Nice Girl; f; 35; F; m; wife B1234; no; Dunseith, Rolette, ND; yes; Id.59a, Al.G-01890
NE	"	Cecelia; dau (Enrolled at White Earth)

NE	Johnson, Ole;	Head
2529	"	Emma (Demontigny); f; 28; ¼+; m; wife B1235; no; Plentywood, Sheridan, Mont; yes; Id.341d, Al.G-08355
2530	"	Andrew; m; 2 3-27-30; ¼+; s; son -----; no; Plentywood, Sheridan, Mont; yes; none
2531	"	Ruth; f; 7/12 5-14-31; ¼+; s; dau -----; no; Plentywood, Sheridan, Mont; yes; none

NE	Johnson, Orvil;	Head
2532	"	Matilda (Dionne); f; 25; ¼+; m; wife B1236; no; Plentywood, Sheridan, Mont; yes; Id.343b, Al.H-08998
2533	"	Mercedine; f; 4-24-27; ¼+; s; dau ----; no; Plentywood, Sheridan, Mont; yes; none
2534	"	Verna; f; 7/12 7-21-31; ¼+; s; dau -----; no; Plentywood, Sheridan, Mont; yes; none

Turtle Mountain Reservation
1932 Census Roll

Key: Number; Surname, Given; Sex; Age at Last Birthday, Birthdate (if given); Tribe (Chippewa, unless stated otherwise); Degree of Blood; Marital Status; Relationship to Head of Family, Last Year Census Number; At Jurisdiction Where Enrolled (Yes/No); Elsewhere - Post Office, County, State; Ward (Yes/No); Allotment [Al.], Annuity [An.] and/or Identification [Id.] Numbers

2535 Jolibois, Albert; m; 46 5-21-85; ¼+; m; Head B1238; no; Thorne, Rolette, ND; no; Id.525, Al.G-553
NE   "   Marion (Robert);   wife
2536 "   Naomi; f; 17 6-5-14; ¼+; s; dau B1239; no; Thorne, Rolette, ND; no; Id.525b
2537 "   Myrtle; f; 16 3-2-16; ¼+; s; dau B1240; no; Thorne, Rolette, ND; no; Id.525c
2538 "   Amos; m; 13 6-28-18; ¼+; s; son B1241; no; Thorne, Rolette, ND; no; Id.525d
2539 "   Franklin; m; 12 12-18-19; ¼+; s; son B1242; no; Thorne, Rolette, ND; no; Id.525e
2540 "   Delia M C; f; 9 4-2-22; ¼+; s ; dau B1243; no; Thorne, Rolette, ND; no; Id.525f
2541 "   Lawrence; m; 6 7-21-25; ¼+; s; son ------; no; Thorne, Rolette, ND; no; none
2542 "   Leroy; m; 4 7-6-27; ¼+; s; son ------; no; Thorne, Rolette, ND; no; none
2543 "   Violet; f; 3 8-15-28; ¼+; s; dau ------; no; Thorne, Rolette, ND; no; none
2544 "   Leslie; m; 1 2-24-31; ¼+; s; son -------; no; Thorne, Rolette, ND; no; none

2545 Jolibois, Marie; f; 58; ¼+; s; Head B1244; no; Rolette, Rolette, ND; no; Id.525, Al.G-552

2546 Jollie, David; m; 39; ¼+; m; Head A1113; yes; no; Id.529, Al.G-019252
2547 "   Philomeme (Warren); f; 30; ¼+; m; wife A1114; yes; yes; Id.1002d, Al.G-386
2548 "   George; m; 9 8-6-22; ¼+; s; son A1115; yes; yes; none
2549 "   Doris; f; 5 1-24-27; ¼+; s; dau A1116; yes; yes; none
2550 "   David; m; 2 11-8-29; ¼+; s; son A1117; yes; yes; none

2551 Jollie, George; m; 49; ¼+; m; Head B1245; yes; yes; Id.531, Al.G-044247

NE Jollie, James;   Head
2552 "   Marie (Belgarde); f; 75; ¼+; m; wife A1118; yes; yes; Id.527a, Al.R-166
2553 "   Edward; m; 25; ¼+; s; son A1119; yes; yes; Id.527e, Al.G-56

2554 Jollie, James; m; 47; ¼+; s; Head B1246; yes; no; Id.533, Al.M-329

2555 Jollie, Robert; m; 29; ¼+; m; Head A1120; yes; yes; Id.527d, Al.M-328
NE   "   Virginia (Lafrance);   wife

2556 Jollie, William; m; 51; ¼+; m; Head B1247; no; Great Falls, Cascade, Mont; no; Id.532, Al.M-356
NE   "   Louise (Barton);   wife
2557 "   Gordon; m; 22; ¼+; s; son B1248; no; Great Falls, Cascade, Mont; no; Id.532b

Turtle Mountain Reservation
1932 Census Roll

Key: Number; Surname, Given; Sex; Age at Last Birthday, Birthdate (if given); Tribe (Chippewa, unless stated otherwise); Degree of Blood; Marital Status; Relationship to Head of Family, Last Year Census Number; At Jurisdiction Where Enrolled (Yes/No); Elsewhere - Post Office, County, State; Ward (Yes/No); Allotment [Al.], Annuity [An.] and/or Identification [Id.] Numbers

NE Jones, Frank;   Head
2558   "   Cecelia (Belgarde); f; 21; ¼+; m; wife A183; yes; yes; Id.167g

NE Jones, Neal;   Head
2559   "   Wilhelmina (Turcotte); f; 40; ¼+; m; wife B1249; no; Coquille, Coos, Ore; no; Id.534a, Al.W-03545
2560   "   Claude; m; 18 3-6-14; ¼+; s; son B1250; no; Coquille, Coos, Ore; no; Id.534b
2561   "   Lorin; m; 15 1-9-17; ¼+; s; son B1251; no; Coquille, Coos, Ore; no; none
2562   "   Clinton; m; 13 4-28-18; ¼+; s; son B1252; no; Coquille, Coos, Ore; no; none
2563   "   Donald; m; 11 1-19-21; ¼+; s; son B1253; no; Coquille, Coos, Ore; no; none
2564   "   Shirley; f; 6 3-30-26; ¼+; s; dau B1254; no; Coquille, Coos, Ore; no; none

2565 Jones, Sarah (Montriel); f; 37; ¼+; wd; Head B1781; no; Milwaukee, Milwaukee, Wis; no; Id.738a, Al.W-0640
2566   "   Charles; m; 18 12-10-13; ¼+; s; son B1782; no; Milwaukee, Milwaukee, Wis; no; Id.738b, Al.H-024439

2567 Jordan, Christine (Brunnell); f; 33; ¼+; wd; Head A1121; yes; yes; Id.844a, Al.M-377

NE Joyce, William;   Head
2568   "   Florence (Gunderson.Regan); f; 34; ¼+; m; wife B2194; no; St.Paul, Ramsey, Minn; no; Id.462b, Al.M-383

NE Justice, Frank;   Head
2569   "   Elise (Marion.Johnson); f; 39; ¼+; m; wife B1224; no; Grenora, Williams, ND; no; Id.695, Al.DL-01724
2570 " (Johnson) Marion; f; 12 11-23-19; ¼+; s; step dau B1225; no; Grenora, Williams ND; no; none
2571 " (Johnson) Melvin; m; 10 1-13-22; ¼+; s; stepson ----; no; Grenora, Williams, ND; no; none
2572   "   Vernon R; m; 2 7-4-29; ¼+; s; son -----; no; Grenora, Williams, ND; no; none
2573   "   Dolores M; f; 10/12 5-7-31; ¼+; s; dau ------; no; Grenora, Williams, ND; no; none

2574 Kanick; m; 70; F; wd; Head B1255; yes; yes; Id.12, Al.R-171

NE Kannas, William;   Head
2575   "   Mary (Lambert.Mock); f; ¼+; m; wife B1778; no; Cando, Towner, ND; Id.597, Al.M-118
2576 " (Mock) Wm Elmer; m; 16 3-26-16; ¼+; s; stepson B1779; no; Cando, Towner, ND; no; none
2577   "   Carl; m; 9 4-26-22; ¼+; s; son -----; no; Cando, Towner, ND; no; none

Turtle Mountain Reservation
1932 Census Roll

Key: Number; Surname, Given; Sex; Age at Last Birthday, Birthdate (if given); Tribe (Chippewa, unless stated otherwise); Degree of Blood; Marital Status; Relationship to Head of Family, Last Year Census Number; At Jurisdiction Where Enrolled (Yes/No); Elsewhere - Post Office, County, State; Ward (Yes/No); Allotment [Al.], Annuity [An.] and/or Identification [Id.] Numbers

NE Kaufman, Edward;   Head
2578   "   Josephine (Lafontain); f; 22 4-16-09; ¼+; m; wife B1256; no;
                      Culbertson, Roosevelt, Mont; yes; Id.551c, Al.G-07900
2579   "   Leroy; m; 2 4-2-29; ¼+; s; son -----; no; Culbertson, Roosevelt, Mont;
                                                                                     yes; none
2580   "   Edward; m; 3/12 12-17-31; ¼+; s; son ------; no; Culbertson, Roosevelt,
                                                                                  Mont; yes; none
NE Kellett, Reginald;   Head
2581   "   Helen (Martell); f; 27; ¼+; m; wife B1257; no; Wolf Point, Roosevelt,
                                                                       Mont; yes; Id.709d, Al.G-07830
2582   "   Rosina; f; 8 8-11-23; ¼+; s; dau B1258; no; Wolf Point, Roosevelt,
                                                                              Mont; yes; none
2583   "   Mary; f; 6; ¼+; s; dau ------; no; Wolf Point, Roosevelt, Mont; yes; none

2584 Keplin, Alexander; m; 44; ¼+; m; Head A1122; yes; no; Id.537, Al.G-0577
2585   "   (Morin) Beatrice; f; 38; ¼+; m; wife A1123; yes; no; Id.537a, Al.GF-111
2586   "   Margaret; f; 19; ¼+; s; dau A1124; yes; yes; Id.537b, Al.H-024665
2587   "   Irene; f; 11 10-15-20; ¼+; s; dau A1125; yes; no; Id.537c
2588 " (Brien) Alex Wm; m; 1 6-8-30; ¼+; s; adpt son A1126; yes; no; none

2589 Keplin, John B; m; 30; ¼+; m; Head A1129; yes; yes; Id.535d, Al.G-0510
NE   "   Eleanor (Allard);   wife

2590 Keplin, Joseph; m; 76; ¼+; m; Head A1127; yes; no; Id.535, Al.R-176
2591   "   Margaret (McCloud); f; 63; ¼+; m; wife A1128; yes; no; Id.535a, Al.G-522
2592   "   Alice; f; 26; ¼+; s; dau A1130; yes; yes; Id.535e. Al.G-0512
2593   "   Alfred; m; 24; ¼+; s; son A1131; yes; yes; Id.535f, Al.G-0514
2594   "   Justine; f; 19; ¼+; s; dau A1132; yes; no; Id.535g
2595   "   John Louis; m; 11 5-10-20; ¼+; s; son A1134; yes; no; none

2596 Keplin, Joseph; m; 37; ¼+; m; Head A1133; yes; no; Id.536, Al.G-0516
NE   "   Agnes (Jerome);   wife
2597   "   Helen; f; 9 7-24-22; ¼+; s; dau A1135; yes; no; Id.536c
2598   "   Earl; m; 7 5-10-24; ¼+; s; son A1136; yes; no; Id.536d
2599   "   Sylvester; m; 4 12-27-27; ¼+; s; son A1137; yes; no; Id.536e
2600   "   Wm Joseph; m; 3/12 12-4-31; ¼+; s; son ------; yes; no; Id.536f

NE Keplin, Joseph R;   Head
2601   "   Rose (Enno Lafontain); f; 34; ¼+; m; wife A1241; yes; no; Id.272d
2602 " (Lafontain) Mary E; f; 2 11-18-29; ¼+; s; step dau A1242; yes; no; none

NE Killen, Gust[sic];   Head
2603   "   Veronica (Ducept.Renault); f; 42; ¼+; m; wife B1260; no; Rolette, Rolette,
                                                                       ND; no; Id.884a, Al.G-038632

Turtle Mountain Reservation
1932 Census Roll

Key: Number; Surname, Given; Sex; Age at Last Birthday, Birthdate (if given); Tribe (Chippewa, unless stated otherwise); Degree of Blood; Marital Status; Relationship to Head of Family, Last Year Census Number; At Jurisdiction Where Enrolled (Yes/No); Elsewhere - Post Office, County, State; Ward (Yes/No); Allotment [Al.], Annuity [An.] and/or Identification [Id.] Numbers

2604 Killen(cont), Elmer; m; 8 1-18-24; ¼+; s; son B1264; no; Rolette, Rolette, ND; no; none
2605 " Geo Olaf; m; 6 10-29-25; ¼+; s; son ----; no; Rolette, Rolette, ND; no; none
2606 " Howard; m; 5 12-14-26; ¼+; s; son -----; no; Rolette, Rolette, ND; no; none

NE Kingen, William;   Head
2607 " Virginia (Wilkie.Azure); f; 48; ¼+; m; wife B148; no; Devils Lake, Ramsey, ND; no; Id.115a, Al.G-0195

NE Kinney, Archie;   Head
2608 " Henrietta (Davis); f; 38; ¼+; m; wife A1138; yes; no; Id.275, Al.GF-71
2609 " Mary Ann; f; 11 7-31-20; ¼+; s; dau A1139; yes; no; Id.275b
2610 " Laura; f; 8 2-23-24; ¼+; s; dau A1140; yes; no; Id.275c
2611 " Rema; m; 3 10-3-28; ¼+; s; son A1141; yes; no; Id.275d
2612 " Francis; m; 1 9-7-30; ¼+; s; son A1142; yes; no; none

NE Knutson, Alvin;   Head
2613 " Emma (Grant); f; 23; ¼+; m; wife B1013; no; Devils Lake, Ramsey, ND; yes; Id.449e, Al.G-0182
2614 " Marcheta; f; 2 3-3-30; ¼+; s; dau ----; no; Devils Lake, Ramsey, ND; yes; none
2615 " Gerald; m; 4/12 11-7-31; ¼+; s; son -----; no; Devils Lake, Ramsey, ND; yes; none

NE Kohauke, Edd;   Head
2616 " Mary E (Delorme); f; 21 1-12-11; ¼+; m; wife B668; no; Canada; yes; Id.331d, Al.G-026816

2617 Laducer, Albert; m; 29; ¼+; m; Head A1143; yes; Id.544b, Al.N0175
2618 " Anna (Gourneau); f; 25; ¼+; m; wife A1144; yes; yes; Id.433e, Al.L-034155
2619 " Eugene; m; 6 5-17-25; ¼+; s; son A1145; yes; yes; none
2620 " Mary Sylvia; f; 1/12 3-6-32; ¼+; s; dau -----; yes; yes; none

2621 Laducer, Alexander; m; 46; ¼+; m; Head A1146; yes; no; Id.542, Al.M-173
2622 " Veronic[sic] (Azure); f; 51; ¼+; m; wife A1147; yes; no; Id.542a, Al.G-232
2623 " Antoine; m; 22; ¼+; s; son A1148; yes; yes; Id.542b, Al.H-012564
2624 " Mary; f; 20; ¼+; s; dau A1149; yes; no; Id.542c

2625 Laducer, Cuthbert; m; 59; ¼+; wd; Head A1150; yes; no; Id.539, Al.R-179
2626 " Edward; m; 22; ¼+; s; son A1151; yes; yes; Id.539d, Al.H012565
2627 " Eliza; f; 18; ¼+; s; dau A1152; yes; yes; Id.539e
2628 " John; m; 12 3-11-20; ¼+; s; son A1153; yes; yes; none

2629 Laducer, Francois; m; 42; ¼+; m; Head A1154; yes; no; Id.541, Al.M-174
2630 " Josephine (Morin); f; 21; ¼+; m; wife A1155; yes; yes; Id.755e, Al.H-012583

Turtle Mountain Reservation
1932 Census Roll

Key: Number; Surname, Given; Sex; Age at Last Birthday, Birthdate (if given); Tribe (Chippewa, unless stated otherwise); Degree of Blood; Marital Status; Relationship to Head of Family, Last Year Census Number; At Jurisdiction Where Enrolled (Yes/No); Elsewhere - Post Office, County, State; Ward (Yes/No); Allotment [Al.], Annuity [An.] and/or Identification [Id.] Numbers

2631 Laducer(cont), Joseph; m; 20; ¼+; s; son A1156; yes; no; Id.541b
2632   "   Edward; m; 18; ¼+; s; son A1157; yes; no; Id.541c
2633   "   Moses; m; 16; ¼+; s; son A1158; yes; no; none
2634   "   Rosie; f; 15; ¼+; s; dau A1159; yes; no; none
2635   "   Marie; f; 13; ¼+; s; dau A1160; yes; no; none
2636   "   John; m; 12; ¼+; s; son A1161; yes; no; none
2637   "   Dominic; m; 9 11-28-22; ¼+; s; son A1162; yes; no; none
Dead   "   Julius;   A1163   (Died 9-5-25)
Dead   "   Marie;   A1164   (Died 9-6-25)

2638 Laducer, James J; m; 36; ¼+; m; Head A1165; yes; no; Id.540, Al.M-344
2639   "   Clemence (Lenoir); f; 34; ¼+; m; wife A1166; yes; yes; Id.540a, Al.G-322
2640   "   (Belgarde) Agnes; f; 14 5-15-17; ¼+; s; step dau A1167; yes; (Counted twice 1931) yes; none
2641   "   John; m; 12 3-12-20; ¼+; s; son A1168; yes; yes; none
2642   "   Freda; f; 9 4-15-22; ¼+; s; dau A1169; yes; yes; none
2643   "   Francois; m; 7 4-19-24; ¼+; s; son A1170; yes; yes; none
2644   "   Louis; m; 5 12-4-26; ¼+; s; son A1171; yes; yes; none
2645   "   David; m; 2 7-19-29; ¼+; s; son A1172; yes; yes; none

2646 Laducer, John; m; 31 7-18-02; ¼+; m; Head A1173; yes; yes; Id.539b, Al.M-292
2647   "   Delima (Allery); f; 24 1-1-08; ¼+; m; wife A1174; yes; yes; Id.72c, Al.G-310
2648   "   Louise; f; 4 3-16-28; ¼+; s; dau A 175; yes; yes; none
2649   "   Joseph; m; 1 12-27-30; ¼+; s; son A----; yes; yes; none

2650 Laducer, Jos Max; m; 27; ¼+; m; Head A1176; yes; yes; Id.544c, Al.G-488
2651   "   Emily (Parisien); f; 27; ¼+; m; wife A1177; yes; yes; Id.798d, Al.H-012625
2652   "   Peter; m; 3 11-26-28; ¼+; s; son 1178; yes; yes; none
2653   "   Joseph; m; 2 10-22-29; ¼+; s; son A1179; yes; yes; none
2654   "   Alfred; m; 1 10-28-30; ¼+; s; son A1180; yes; yes; none

2655 Laducer, Lloyd B; m; ¼+; s; Head B1265; no; Unknown; yes; Id.538b, Al.H-03071

2656 Lafloe, Robert; m; 39 8-20-92; ¼+; m; Head A1181; yes; no; Id.545, Al.G-08126
2657   "   Rosalie (Davis); f; 28 10-4-03; ¼+; m; wife A1182; yes; yes; Id.545a, Al.G-188
2658   "   Evelyn; f; 11 8-19-20; ¼+; s; dau A1183; yes; Id.545b
2659   "   Louis; m; 10 12-6-21; ¼+; s; son A1184; yes; yes; Id.545c
2660   "   Cuthbert; m; 8 10-28-23; ¼+; s; son A1185; yes; yes; Id.545d
2661   "   Marie Angela; f; 5 3-11-27; ¼+; s; dau A1186; yes; (Counted twice last census) yes; Id.545e
2662   "   Helen Jane; f; 4/12 11-21-31; ¼+; s; dau A----; yes; yes; none

Turtle Mountain Reservation
1932 Census Roll

Key: Number; Surname, Given; Sex; Age at Last Birthday, Birthdate (if given); Tribe (Chippewa, unless stated otherwise); Degree of Blood; Marital Status; Relationship to Head of Family, Last Year Census Number; At Jurisdiction Where Enrolled (Yes/No); Elsewhere - Post Office, County, State; Ward (Yes/No); Allotment [Al.], Annuity [An.] and/or Identification [Id.] Numbers

2663 Lafontain, Adele (Amyott); f; 54; ¼+; wd; Head B1266; no; Roy, Fergus, Mont; no; Id.550a, Al.M-06921
2664 " Anna Jane; f; 23; ¼+; s; dau B1267; no; Roy, Fergus, Mont; no; Id.550f
2665 " Mary Cecelia; f; 20; ¼+; s; dau B1268; no; Roy, Fergus, Mont; no; Id.550h
2666 " Emily; f; 16 5-27-15; ¼+; s; dau B11269; no; Roy, Fergus, Mont; no; Id.550i
2667 " Victoris[sic]; f; 14 12-17-17; ¼+; s; dau B1270; no; Roy, Fergus, Mont; no; Id.550j
2668 " Florestine; f; 8 2-25-24; ¼+; s; dau B1271; no; Roy, Fergus, Mont; no; Id.550k

2669 Lafontain, Ambrose; m; 53; ¼+; m; Head A1188; yes; no; Id.552, Al.G-05258
NE " St Ann (Peltier); wife
DEAD " George; A1189 (Died Nov. 1917)
2670 " Emma Rose; f; 16 9-18-15; ¼+; s; dau A1190; yes; no; Id.552c
2671 " Josephine; f; 14 1-4-18; ¼+; s; dau A1191; yes; no; Id.552d
2672 " Albert P; m; 10 8-2-21; ¼+; s; son A1192; yes; no; Id.552e
2673 " Steven S; m; 9 10-15-22; ¼+; s; son A1193; yes; no; Id.552f
2674 " Alex C; m; 7 10-15-24; ¼+; s; son A1194; yes; no; Id.552g
2675 " Fred; m; 4 4-4-27; ¼+; s; son A1195; yes; no; Id.552h
2676 " William; m; 2 11-8-29; ¼+; s; son A1196; yes; no; Id.552i

2677 Lafontain, Anthony; m; 27 3-23-05; ¼+; m; Head B1277; no; Roy, Fergus, Mont; yes; Id.548f, Al.L-0877
NE " Lucille (Purdy); wife
2678 " Lawrence R; m; 5 6-28-26; ¼+; s; son ----; no; Roy, Fergus, Mont; yes; none
2679 " Billy; m; 4 1-29-28; ¼+; s; son ------; no; Roy, Fergus, Mont; yes; none
2680 " Beryl Faye; f; 1 8-30-30; ¼+; s; dau ----; no; Roy, Fergus, Mont; yes; none

2681 Lafontain, Daniel; m; 38; ¼+; m; Head A1197; yes; no; Id.563, Al.M-279
2682 " Elizabeth (Wilkie); f; 33; ¼+; m; wife A1198; yes; yes; Id.563a, Al.G-032691
1826 " (Foughty) Walter; A1199 (Lives with this couple)

2683 Lafontain, Edward; m; 25 1-26-07; ¼+; m; Head B1278; no; Roy, Fergus, Mont; yes; Id.548g, Al.L-0876
NE " Zilda (Plummer); wife
2684 " Norma; f; 2 8-14-29; ¼+; s; dau ----; no; Roy, Fergus, Mont; yes; none
2685 " Gladys; f; 9/11 6-9-31; ¼+; s; dau -----; no; Roy, Fergus, Mont; yes; none

2686 Lafontain, Ezear; m; 61; ¼+; m; Head B1273; no; Roy, Fergus, Mont; no; Id.548, Al.L-1
NE " Marie; wife (Maiden name unknown)
2687 " Collin; m; 35 7-31-96; ¼+; s; son B1272; no; Roy, Fergus, Mont; no; Id.549, Al.L-4
2688 " John; m; 30 2-10-02; ¼+; s; son B1175; no; Roy, Fergus, Mont; yes; Id.548d, Al.L-5

Turtle Mountain Reservation
1932 Census Roll

Key: Number; Surname, Given; Sex; Age at Last Birthday, Birthdate (if given); Tribe (Chippewa, unless stated otherwise); Degree of Blood; Marital Status; Relationship to Head of Family, Last Year Census Number; At Jurisdiction Where Enrolled (Yes/No); Elsewhere - Post Office, County, State; Ward (Yes/No); Allotment [Al.], Annuity [An.] and/or Identification [Id.] Numbers

2689 Lafontain(cont), Albert; m; 19 12-28-12; ¼+; s; son B1279; no; Roy, Fergus, Mont; yes; Id.548b, Al.I-015346
2690 " Francis; m; 16 7-2-15; ¼+; s; son B1281; no; Roy, Fergus, Mont; no; Id.548j
2691 " Joseph; m; 16 7-2-15; ¼+; s; son B1282; no; Roy, Fergus, Mont; no; Id.548k
2692 " Elizabeth; 15 1-2-17; ¼+; s; dau B1283; no; Roy, Fergus, Mont; no; Id.none
2693 " Dorothy; f; 13 2-18-19; ¼+; s; dau B1284; no; Roy, Fergus, Mont; no; none
2694 " James; m; 10 7-15-21; ¼+; s; son B1285; no; Roy, Fergus, Mont; no; none

NE Lafontain, Gaspard; Head
2695 " Mary (San Grait); f; 48; ¼+; m; wife A1200; yes; no; Id.562a, Al.H-038901

2696 Lafontain, John; m; ¼+; m; Head; yes; (This family left off of last census by mistake); no; Id.555, Al.G-232
NE " Philomeme (Short); wife
2697 " Loria; m; 14 7-21-17; ¼+; s; son; yes; no; none
2698 " Frank; m; 12 5-28-19; ¼+; s; son; yes; no; none
2699 " David; m; 10 4-14-21; ¼+; s; son; yes; no; none
2700 " Josephine; f; 8 3-15-24; ¼+; s; dau; yes; no; none
2701 " William; m; 6 4-28-25; ¼+; s; son; yes; no; none
2702 " George; m; 4 4-17-27; ¼+; s; son; yes; no; none
2703 " Mary Jane; f; 2 8-24-29; ¼+; s; dau; yes; no; none
2704 " Flora; f; 5/12 10-25-31; ¼+; s; dau; yes; no; none

2705 Lafontain, Joseph; m; 51; ¼+; m; Head A1201; yes; no; Id.556, Al.G-492
NE " Lizzie (Short); wife
2706 " Joseph; m; 21 9-28-10; ¼+; s; son A1202; yes; no; Id.556b
2707 " Alexander; m; 20 2-13-12; ¼+; s; son A1203; yes; no; Id.556c
2708 " Louis; m; 17 6-26-14; ¼+; s; son A1204; yes; no; Id.556d
2709 " Fred; m; 15 10-13-16; ¼+; s; son A1205; yes; no; Id.556e
2710 " Gabriel; m; 13 11-6-18; ¼+; s; son A1206; yes; no; Id.556f
2711 " Robert; m; 11 12-12-20; ¼+; s; son A1207; yes; no; Id.556g
2712 " Peter; m; 9 3-1-23; ¼+; s; son A1208; yes; no; Id.556h
2713 " Ernest Ed; m; 7 9-21-24; ¼+; s; son A----; yes; no; Id.556i
2714 " Cecilia; f; 5 9-24-26; ¼+; s; dau A-----; yes; no; Id.556j
2715 " Alice; f; 3 11-25-28; ¼+; s; dau A1209; yes; no; Id.556k

2716 Lafountain, Joseph (Tom); m; 21 9-28-10; ¼+; m; Head B1289; no; Havre, Hill, Mont; no; Id.551b
NE " Lillian (Kaufman); wife
2717 " Betty; f; 1 11-28-30; ¼+; s; dau -----; no; Havre, Hill, Mont; no; none
2718 " Doris; f; 5/12 9-28-31; ¼+; s; dau -----; no; Havre, Hill, Mont; no; none

Turtle Mountain Reservation
1932 Census Roll

Key: Number; Surname, Given; Sex; Age at Last Birthday, Birthdate (if given); Tribe (Chippewa, unless stated otherwise); Degree of Blood; Marital Status; Relationship to Head of Family, Last Year Census Number; At Jurisdiction Where Enrolled (Yes/No); Elsewhere - Post Office, County, State; Ward (Yes/No); Allotment [Al.], Annuity [An.] and/or Identification [Id.] Numbers

2719 Lafountain, Joseph; m; 52; ¼+; m; Head B1286; no; Culbertson, Roosevelt, Mont; no; Id.551, Al.G07901
2720 " Adeline (St Pierre); f; 46; ¼+; m; wife B1287; no; Culbertson, Roosevelt, Mont; no; Id.551a
2721 " Adele; f; 24; ¼+; s; dau B1288; no; Culbertson, Roosevelt, Mont; no; Id.551b
2722 " Mary; f; 20; ¼+; s; dau B1290; no; Culbertson, Roosevelt, Mont; no; Id.551c
2723 " Marie; f; 17; ¼+; s; dau B1291; no; Culbertson, Roosevelt, Mont; no; Id.551d
2724 " George; m; 15; ¼+; s; son B1292; no; Culbertson, Roosevelt, Mont; no; Id.551e
2725 " Martin; m; 13; ¼+; s; son B1293; no; Culbertson, Roosevelt, Mont; no; Id.551f
2726 " Clara; f; 9; ¼+; s; dau B1294; no; Culbertson, Roosevelt, Mont; no; Id.551g
2727 " Alex; m; 7 8-12-24; ¼+; s; son B1295; no; Culbertson, Roosevelt, Mont; no; Id.551h
2728 " Dailey; m; 5 9-13-26; ¼+; s; son B1296; no; Culbertson, Roosevelt, Mont; no; Id.551i
2729 " Arthur; m; 3 4-28-28; ¼+; s; son B1297; no; Culbertson, Roosevelt, Mont; no; Id.551j

2730 Lafountain, Josephine; f; 80; ¼+; wd; Head A1210; yes; no; Id.554a, Al.GF-231

2731 Lafontain, Louis; m; 57; ¼+; m; Head A1211; yes; no; Id.553, Al.L-8
2732 " Julianne (Poitra); f; 42; 5-18-90; ¼+; m; wife A1212; yes; no; Id.553a, Al.H-012658
2733 " Maxim; m; 21 1-16-11; ¼+; s; son A1213; yes; no; Id.553c
2734 " Joseph; m; 19 12-17-12; ¼+; s; son A1214; yes; no; Id.553d
2735 " Lucinda; f; 16 6-23-15; ¼+; s; dau A1215; yes; no; Id.553e
2736 " Alex N; m; 15 3-24-17; ¼+; s; son A1216; yes; no; Id.553f
2737 " Louis; m; 13 12-9-18; ¼+; s; son A1217; yes; no; Id.553g
2738 " Albert; m; 11 11-8-20; ¼+; s; son A1218; yes; no; Id.553h
2739 " Dora; f; 5 8-31-26; ¼+; s; dau A1219; yes; no; Id.553i

2740 Lafontain, Louis; m; 90; ¼+; m; Head A1220; yes; yes; Id.561, Al.R-182
2741 " Emily (Larat.Dejarlais); f; 80; ¼+; m wife A1221; yes; no; Id.561a, Al.M-314

NE Lafontain, Louise;   Head
2742 " Alex; m; 8 7-21-23; ¼+; s; son -----; no; Roy, Fergus, Mont; yes; Id.548c
2743 " Alfred; m; 7 2-25-25; ¼+; s; son -----; no; Roy, Fergus, Mont; yes; none
2744 " Lorraine; f; 2 4-17-29; ¼+; s; dau ------; no; Roy, Fergus, Mont; yes; none

Turtle Mountain Reservation
1932 Census Roll

Key: Number; Surname, Given; Sex; Age at Last Birthday, Birthdate (if given); Tribe (Chippewa, unless stated otherwise); Degree of Blood; Marital Status; Relationship to Head of Family, Last Year Census Number; At Jurisdiction Where Enrolled (Yes/No); Elsewhere - Post Office, County, State; Ward (Yes/No); Allotment [Al.], Annuity [An.] and/or Identification [Id.] Numbers

2745 Lafontain, Louis St.P; m; 34; ¼+; m; Head A1222; yes; no; Id.550b, Al.M-318
NE   "   Emma (Guyon);   wife
2746   "   Philbert; m; 14; ¼+; s; son A1223; yes; no; none
2747   "   Alice; f; 13; ¼+; s; dau A1224; yes; no; none
2748   "   Steve; m; 10 2-5-22; ¼+; s; son A1225; yes; no; none
2749   "   Joe; m; 8 2-19-24; ¼+; s; son A1226; yes; no; none

2750 Lafontain, Malain (Parisien); f; 55 12-15-76; 1/4; wd; Head A1227; yes; no; Id.557, Al.G-06048
2751   "   Joseph; m; 20 1-26-12; ¼+; s; son A1228; yes; no; Id.557c

NE Lafontain, Michael; m;   Head
2752   "   Mary B (Allery); f; 22; ¼+; m; wife A50; yes; yes; Id.80b, Al.G-012603
2753   "   James Ed; m; 3/12 1-23-32; ¼+; s; son -----; yes; yes; none

2754 Lafontain, Moses; m; 40; ¼+; m; Head A1229; yes; no; Id.559, Al.G-292
2755   "   Rosalie (Belgarde); f; 24; ¼+; m; wife A1230; yes; yes; Id.190d, Al.G-468
2756   "   Joseph; m; 19; ¼+; s; son A1231; yes; no; Id.559b
2757   "   Sylvia; f; 14 7-17-17; ¼+; s; dau A1232; yes; no; Id.559c
2758   "   Louis; m; 12 4-10-19; ¼+; s; son A1233; yes; no; Id.559d
2759   "   Marie; f; ¼+; s; dau A1234; yes; no; Id.559e

2760 Lafontain, Pierre Albert; m; 27 11-8-04; ¼+; m; Head A1243; yes; yes; Id.448d, Al.G-294
2761   "   Alvina (Nadeau); f; 26 5-17-05; ¼+; m; wife A1244; yes; yes; Id.771d, Al.G-04508
2762   "   Eliza A; f; 3 5-29-28; ¼+; s; dau A1245; yes; yes; none
2763   "   Rose Alice; f; 2 1-1-30; ¼+; s/ dau A1246; yes; yes; none
2764   "   Nora Stella; f; 4/12 11-22-31; ¼+; s; dau -----; yes; yes; none

2765 Lafontain, Pierre Arthur; m; 41; ¼+; m; Head B1298; no; Devils Lake, Ramsey, ND; no; Id.560, Al.G-293
2766   "   Virginia (Grant); f; 36; ¼+; m; wife B1299; no; Devils Lake, Ramsey, ND; no; Id.560b
2767   "   Andrew; m; 16 2-3-16; ¼+; s; son B1300; no; Devils Lake, Ramsey, ND; no; Id.560c
2768   "   Mary L; f; 13 4-10-18; ¼+; s; dau B1301; no; Devils Lake, Ramsey, ND; no; Id.560d
2769   "   Annie; f; 11 8-6-20; ¼+; s; dau B1302; no; Devils Lake, Ramsey, ND; no; Id.560e
2770   "   Rose; f; 9 1-17-22; ¼+; s; dau B1303; no; Devils Lake, Ramsey, ND; no; Id.560f
2771   "   Patrick; m; 7 3-12-25; ¼+; s; son B1304; no; Devils Lake, Ramsey, ND; no; Id.560g

Turtle Mountain Reservation
1932 Census Roll

Key: Number; Surname, Given; Sex; Age at Last Birthday, Birthdate (if given); Tribe (Chippewa, unless stated otherwise); Degree of Blood; Marital Status; Relationship to Head of Family, Last Year Census Number; At Jurisdiction Where Enrolled (Yes/No); Elsewhere - Post Office, County, State; Ward (Yes/No); Allotment [Al.], Annuity [An.] and/or Identification [Id.] Numbers

2772 Lafontain(cont), Hazel; f; 4 9-1-27; ¼+; s; dau B1305; no; Devils Lake, Ramsey, ND; no; Id.560h

2773 Lafontain, Pierre V; m; 64 1-25-68; ¼+; m; Head A1235; yes; no; Id.558, Al.R185
2774   "   Isabel (Delonais); f; 53 7-4-78; ¼+; m; wife A1236; yes; yes; Id.558a, Al.H012568
2775   "   Mary Isabel; f; 21 5-9-10; ¼+; s; dau A1237; yes; yes; Id.558f, Al.H012567
2776   "   Cecilia; f; 20 1-26-12; ¼+; s; dau A1238; yes; yes; Id.558g, Al.H012669
2777   "   Ernestine; f; 15 3-26-17; ¼+; s; dau A1239; yes; no; Id.558h
No such child   "   Edna   A1240   (To correct error in last year's census)

2778 Lafournais, James; m; 32; ¼+; m; Head B1315; yes; yes; Id.564[?], Al.M47
2779   "   Ernestine (Vivier); m; 20; ¼+; m; wife A2101; yes; yes; Id.992g

2780 Lafournais, Jerome; m; 48; ¼+; wd; Head B1306; no; Bottineau, Bottineau, ND; yes; Id.569, Al.G08326
2781   "   Josephine; f; 26; ¼+; s; dau B1307; no; Bottineau, Bottineau, ND; no; Id.569b
Dead   "   Lillian; f;   B1308   (Died 5-30-28)
2782   "   Rose S; f; 23; ¼+; s; dau B1309; no; Bottineau, Bottineau, ND; yes; Id.569d, Al. [blank]
2783   "   Mabel; f; 19; ¼+; s; dau B1310; no; Bottineau, Bottineau, ND; yes; Id.569e
2784   "   Joseph; m; 15 10-16-16; ¼+; s; son B1311; no; Bottineau, Bottineau, ND; yes; Id.569f
2785   "   Louis; m; 13 9-13-18; ¼+; s; son B1312; no; Bottineau, Bottineau, ND; yes; Id.569g

2786 Lafournais, Joseph; m; 70; ¼+; m; Head B1313; no; Boggy Creek, Manitoba, Can; no; Id.564
2787   "   Margaret; f; 70; ¼+; m; wife B1314; no; Boggy Creek, Manitoba, Can; no; Id.564a
2788   "   Christine; f; 30; ¼+; s; dau B1315; no; Boggy Creek, Manitoba, Can; no; Id.564c

2789 Lafournais, Joseph; m; 55; ¼+; s; Head B1317; no; Address unknown; no; Id.568, Al.H010489

2790 Lafournais, Moses; m; 48; ¼+; m; Head B1318; no; Medicine Lake, Sheridan, Mont; no; Id.565, Al.M50
NE   "   Josephine (Patnaud); wife

Turtle Mountain Reservation
1932 Census Roll

Key: Number; Surname, Given; Sex; Age at Last Birthday, Birthdate (if given); Tribe (Chippewa, unless stated otherwise); Degree of Blood; Marital Status; Relationship to Head of Family, Last Year Census Number; At Jurisdiction Where Enrolled (Yes/No); Elsewhere - Post Office, County, State; Ward (Yes/No); Allotment [Al.], Annuity [An.] and/or Identification [Id.] Numbers

2791 Lafournais(cont), Mary B; f; 20; ¼+; s; dau B1319; no; Medicine Lake, Sheridan, Mont; no; Id.565b
2792 " Alex; m; 16 5-4-15; ¼+; s; son B1320; no; Medicine Lake, Sheridan, Mont; no; Id.565c
2793 " Clara; f; 14 4-24-17; ¼+; s; dau B1321; no; Medicine Lake, Sheridan, Mont; no; Id.565d
2794 " Josephine; f; 13 1-10-19; ¼+; s; dau B1322; no; Medicine Lake, Sheridan, Mont; no; Id565f
2795 " Joe S; m; 10 5-1-21; ¼+; s; son B1323; no; Medicine Lake, Sheridan, Mont; no; Id565g
2796 " Dave; m; 8 5-10-23; ¼+; s; son B1324; no; Medicine Lake, Sheridan, Mont; no; Id565h

2797 Lafournais, Patrick; m; 68; ¼+; wd; Head A1247; yes; yes; Id.566, Al.R187

2798 Lafournais, Pierre; m; 35; ¼+; m; Head B1325; no; Boggy Creek, Manitoba, Can; no; Id.564b, Al.M46
2799 " Clara (Lavallie); f; 30; ¼+; m; wife B1326; no; Boggy Creek, Manitoba, Can; yes; Id.633c, Al.H012557
2800 " Joe; m; 12 2-6-20; ¼+; s; son B1327; no; Boggy Creek, Manitoba, Can; no; none
2801 " Peter; m; 9 6-3-22; ¼+; s; son B1328; no; Boggy Creek, Manitoba, Can; no; none
2802 " Earl; m; 8 3-10-24; ¼+; s; son B1329; no; Boggy Creek, Manitoba, Can; no; none
2803 " Verna; f; 5 6-12-26; ¼+; s; dau -----; no; Boggy Creek, Manitoba, Can; no; none
2804 " Bertha; f; 3 6-28-28; ¼+; s; dau -----; no; Boggy Creek, Manitoba, Can; no; none
2805 " Gilbert; m; 1 4-16-30; ¼+; s; son -----; no; Boggy Creek, Manitoba, Can; no; none

NE Lafrance, Canute; Head
2806 " Mary (Lacerte); f; 47; ¼+; m; wife B1330; no; Regina, Sask, Can; no; Id.570a

NE Lafrance, Canute; Head
Dead " Justine (Lattergrass); wife B1331 (Died 9-14-31)
2807 " Charles; m; 16 11-1-15; ¼+; s; son B1332; no; Rolla, Rolette, ND; yes; Id.572b, Al.H031154
2808 " Mary; f; 15 1-15-17; ¼+; s; dau B1333; no; Rolla, Rolette, ND; no; Id.572c
2809 " Bertha; f; 11 2-16-21; ¼+; s; dau B1334; no; Rolla, Rolette, ND; no; Id.572d

Turtle Mountain Reservation
1932 Census Roll

Key: Number; Surname, Given; Sex; Age at Last Birthday, Birthdate (if given); Tribe (Chippewa, unless stated otherwise); Degree of Blood; Marital Status; Relationship to Head of Family, Last Year Census Number; At Jurisdiction Where Enrolled (Yes/No); Elsewhere - Post Office, County, State; Ward (Yes/No); Allotment [Al.], Annuity [An.] and/or Identification [Id.] Numbers

2810 Lafrance(cont), John B; m; 8 1-19-23; ¼+; s; son ----; no; Rolla, Rolette, ND; no; Id.572e
2811 " Ella M; f; 7 3-2-25; ¼+; s; dau ----; no; Rolla, Rolette, ND; no; Id.572d
2812 " Morris; m; 4 6-3-27; ¼+; s; son ----; no; Rolla, Rolette, ND; no; Id.572g
2813 " William; m; 2 1-19-30; 1/4 s; son ----; no; Rolla, Rolette, ND; no; Id.572h
Dead " Theresa; 7-3-31 (Died 10-19-31)

NE Lafrance, Charles; Head
2814 " Clara (Sayer); f; 39; ¼+; m; wife B1335; no; Medicine Lake, Sheridan, Mont; no; Id.573a
2815 " (Sayer) Francis; m; 15; ¼+; s; ad. son B1336; no; Medicine Lake, Sheridan, Mont; no; Id.none

NE Lafrance, Louis; Head B2653
2816 " Evelyn (Schindler); f; 21; ¼+; m; wife B2510; yes; (Counted twice last year) yes; Id.913, Al.----

2817 Lafrance, Veronica (Toupin.Frederick); f; 50; ¼+; wd; Head B1337; no; Devils Lake, Ramsey, ND; no; Id.571a, Al.G-016078
2818 " Joe; m; 27; ¼+; s; son B1338; no; Devils Lake, Ramsey, ND; no; Id.571b
2819 " Dora; f; 22; ¼+; s; dau B1339; no; Devils Lake, Ramsey, ND; no; Id.571d
2820 " Marie; f; 20; ¼+; s; dau B1340; no; Devils Lake, Ramsey, ND; no; Id.571e
2821 " Ernest; m; 19; ¼+; s; son B1341; no; Devils Lake, Ramsey, ND; no; Id.571f
2822 " Annie; f; 14; ¼+; s; dau B1342; no; Devils Lake, Ramsey, ND; no; Id.571g

NE Lafraniere, Elie; Head
2823 " Rosalie (Brien); m[sic]; 48; ¼+; m; wife B1343; no; Hardin, Big Horn, Mont; no; Id.574a, Al.G-08264
2824 " Lillian; f; 20 7-8-11; ¼+; s; dau B1343; no; Hardin, Big Horn, Mont; no; Id.574b
2825 " Martin; m; 19 8-21-12; ¼+; s; son B1345; no; Hardin, Big Horn, Mont; no; Id.574c
2826 " Mary Ann; f; 18 11-21-13; ¼+; s; dau B1346; no; Hardin, Big Horn, Mont; no; Id.574d
2827 " Jerome; m; 15 5-2-16; ¼+; s; son B1347; no; Hardin, Big Horn, Mont; no; Id.574e
2828 " Emma; f; 14 10-23-17; ¼+; s; dau B1348; no; Hardin, Big Horn, Mont; no; Id.574f
2829 " Ernest S; m; 12 10-7-19; ¼+; s; son B1349; no; Hardin, Big Horn, Mont; no; Id.574g
2830 " Elizabeth; f; 10 7-26-21; ¼+; s; dau B1350; no; Hardin, Big Horn, Mont; no; Id.574h
2831 " Francis; m; 9 1-20-23; ¼+; s; son B1351; no; Hardin, Big Horn, Mont; no; Id.574i

Turtle Mountain Reservation
1932 Census Roll

Key: Number; Surname, Given; Sex; Age at Last Birthday, Birthdate (if given); Tribe (Chippewa, unless stated otherwise); Degree of Blood; Marital Status; Relationship to Head of Family, Last Year Census Number; At Jurisdiction Where Enrolled (Yes/No); Elsewhere - Post Office, County, State; Ward (Yes/No); Allotment [Al.], Annuity [An.] and/or Identification [Id.] Numbers

2832 Lafraniere(cont), Irene; f; 6 4-5-25; ¼+; s; dau B1352; no; Hardin, Big Horn, Mont; no; Id.574j
2833 " Leslie; m; 5 1-27-27; ¼+; s; son B1353; no; Hardin, Big Horn, Mont; no; Id.574k
2834 " Lyda; f; 5 1-27-27; ¼+; s; dau B1354; no; Hardin, Big Horn, Mont; no; Id.574l
2835 " Lawrence; m; 2 5-21-29; ¼+; s; son ------; no; Hardin, Big Horn, Mont; no; Id.574m
2836 " Vivian; f; 3/12 1-1-32; ¼+; s; dau -----; no; Hardin, Big Horn, Mont; no; Id.574n
2837 " Violet; f; 3/12 1-1-32; ¼+; s; dau -----; no; Hardin, Big Horn, Mont; no; Id.574o

2838 Lafrombois, Albert; m; 37; ¼+; s; Head B1355; yes; no; Id.589, Al.G201

2839 Lafrombois, Alfred; m; 35; ¼+; m; Head A1267; no; Poplar, Roosevelt, Mont; no; Id.585b, Al.G08184
NE " Katherine (Lethridge); f; wife
2840 " Lorraine; f; 1 12-16-30; ¼+; s; dau -----; no; Poplar, Roosevelt, Mont; no; none

NE Lafrombois, Annie; Head
2841 " John B; m; 4; ¼+; s; son B1356; no; Devils Lake, Ramsey, ND; no; Id.592i

NE Lafrombois, Dean; m; Head
2842 " Mary (Latraill); f; 31; ¼+; m; wife B1357; no; Great Falls, Cascade, Mont; no; Id.701b, Al.H030662
2843 " Louise; f; 13 6-17-18; ¼+; s; dau ----; no; Great Falls, Cascade, Mont; no; none
2844 " Clara; f; 10 4-10-21; ¼+; s; dau -----; no; Great Falls, Cascade, Mont; no; none
2845 " Irene; f; 8 7-16-23; ¼+; s; dau -----; no; Great Falls, Cascade, Mont; no; none

2846 Lafrombois, Elie; m; 37; ¼+; s; Head A1248; yes; yes; Id.587, Al.GF209

2847 Lafrombois, Elizabeth; f; 40; ¼+; s; Head A1249; yes; no; Id.588, Al.G036584

2848 Lafrombois, Gabriel; m; 65; ¼+; wd; Head A1250; yes; no; Id.575, Al.R190
2849 " Martin; m; 36; ¼+; s; son A1251; yes; yes; Id.575a, Al.G0415
2850 " Paulina; f; 19; ¼+; s; dau A1252; yes; yes; Id.575d

Turtle Mountain Reservation
1932 Census Roll

Key: Number; Surname, Given; Sex; Age at Last Birthday, Birthdate (if given); Tribe (Chippewa, unless stated otherwise); Degree of Blood; Marital Status; Relationship to Head of Family, Last Year Census Number; At Jurisdiction Where Enrolled (Yes/No); Elsewhere - Post Office, County, State; Ward (Yes/No); Allotment [Al.], Annuity [An.] and/or Identification [Id.] Numbers

2851 Lafrombois, Jerome; m; 41; ¼+; m; Head A1253; yes; no; Id.590, Al.G198
2852 " Julia (Vallie); f; 38; ¼+; m; wife A1254; yes; yes; Id.976, Al.GF221
2853 " Evelyn; f; 13 8-19-18; ¼+; s; dau A1255; yes; no; Id.590b
2854 " Cecile; f; 11 7-11-20; ¼+; s; dau A1256; yes; no; Id.590c
2855 " Frank; m; 9 4-22-22; ¼+; s; son A1257; yes; no; Id.590d
2856 " Patricia; f; 6 3-11-26; ¼+; s; dau A1258; yes; no; Id.590e
2857 " Julia; f; 4 11-27-27; ¼+; s; dau A1259; yes; no; Id.590f

2858 Lafrombois, John; m; 43; ¼+; m; Head B1358; no; Bottineau, Bottineau, ND; no; Id.580, Al.G037080
NE " Sadie (Holland); wife
2859 " Elizabeth; f; 9 6-8-22; ¼+; s; dau B1359; no; Bottineau, Bottineau, ND; no; none
2860 " Clifford; m; 10 5-20-21; ¼+; s; son B1360; no; Bottineau, Bottineau, ND; no; none
2861 " Clarence; m; 8 12-24-23; ¼+; s; son B1361; no; Bottineau, Bottineau, ND; no; none
2862 " Joseph; m; 3 10-4-28; ¼+; s; son B1362; no; Bottineau, Bottineau, ND; no; none
2863 " Marie; f; 1 7-27-30; ¼+; s; dau -----; no; Bottineau, Bottineau, ND; no; none

2864 Lafrombois, Joseph; m; 75 4-12-56; ¼+; m; Head A1260; yes; no; Id.579, Al.R192
2865 " Isabel (Trothier); f; 70 3-6-62; ¼+; m; wife A1261; yes; no; Id.579a, Al.G036580
2866 " Celina; f; 33 12-3-98; ¼+; s; dau A1262; yes; yes; Id.579b, Al.G036578
2867 " Joseph; m; 28 7-18-03; ¼+; s; son A1263; yes; yes; Id.579c, Al.H030470
2868 " Louis; m; 27 1-3-05; ¼+; s; son A1264; yes; yes; Id.579d, Al.G036579

2869 Lafrombois, Joseph #2; m; 67; ¼+; m; Head A1265; yes; no; Id.585, Al.R191
2870 " Rose (Perronteau); f; 59; ¼+; m; wife A1266; yes; no; Id.585a, Al.G08185
2871 " Florestine; f; 26; ¼+; s; dau A1268; yes; yes; Id.585c, Al.G08238
2872 " Sarah; f; 23; ¼+; s; dau A1269; yes; yes; 585h, Al.G08237
2873 " Geraldine; f; 5/12 10-6-31; ¼+; s; g-dau -----; yes; yes; none
2874 " Elvina; f; 21; ¼+; s; dau A1270; yes; yes; Id.585i, Al.H012566
2875 " Alexander; m; 19; ¼+; s; son A1271; yes; no; [Id.]585j
2876 " Mary; f; 17 5-31-15; ¼+; s; dau A1272; yes; no; Id.585k

2877 Lafrombois, Louis; m; 27; ¼+; m; Head A1274; yes; yes; Id.586c, Al.GF207
2878 " Delia (Davis); f; 34; ¼+; m; wife A1275; yes; yes; Id.274b, Al.GF72

Turtle Mountain Reservation
1932 Census Roll

Key: Number; Surname, Given; Sex; Age at Last Birthday, Birthdate (if given); Tribe (Chippewa, unless stated otherwise); Degree of Blood; Marital Status; Relationship to Head of Family, Last Year Census Number; At Jurisdiction Where Enrolled (Yes/No); Elsewhere - Post Office, County, State; Ward (Yes/No); Allotment [Al.], Annuity [An.] and/or Identification [Id.] Numbers

2879 Lafrombois(cont), Romeo; m; 4 11-4-27; ¼+; s; son A1276; yes; yes; none
2880 " Delima; f; 3 11-1-28; ¼+; s; dau A1277; yes; yes; none
2881 " James Leo; m; 1 7-25-30; ¼+; s; son A1279; yes; yes; none

2882 Lafrombois, Louis; m; 38; ¼+; m; Head B1363; no; Pisek, Walsh, ND; no; Id.576, Al.G0416
2883 " Lillian (Decouteau); f; 23; ¼+; m; wife A587; no; Pisek, Walsh, ND; yes; Id.295b
2884 " Irene; f; 12; ¼+; s; dau B1365; no; Pisek, Walsh, ND; no; Id.576d
2885 " Gabriel; m; 13; ¼+; s; son B1364; no; Pisek, Walsh, ND; no; Id576c
2886 " Roger; m; 8 12-14-23; ¼+; s; son N1366[sic]; no; Pisek, Walsh, ND; no; Id576e
2887 " John; m; 5 9-20-26; ¼+; s; son -----; no; Pisek, Walsh, ND; no; Id576f

2888 Lafrombois, Margaret (Vallie); f; 78; ¼+; wd; Head A1280; yes; no; Id.588a, Al.G016474

2889 Lafrombois, Mathais[sic]; m; ¼+; m; Head A1281; yes; no; Id.586, Al.R-194
NE " Marie (Bercier); wife
2890 " St.Pierre; m; 25; ¼+; s; son A1282; yes; no; Id.586d

2891 Lafrombois, Napoleon; m; 51; ¼+; m; Head B1367; no; Bottineau, Bottineau, ND; no; Id.581, Al.H-024072
2892 " Edna (Bradford); f; 19; ¼+; m; wife B1368; no; Bottineau, Bottineau, ND; no; Id.1188d

2893 Lafrombois, Pascal; m; 37; ¼+; s; Head B1369; no; Unknown; no; Id.582, Al.GF-215

2894 Lafrombois, Patrice; m; 31 6-30-00; ¼+; m; Head A1283; yes; yes; Id.585d, Al.G08182
2895 " Mary (Allery); f; 27 2-16-05; ¼+; m; wife A1284; yes; yes; Id.72b, Al.G335
2896 " Irene; f; 9 2-8-23; ¼+; s; dau A1285; yes; yes; Id.1198c
2897 " Ernest; m; 5 10-15-26; ¼+; s; son A1286; yes; yes; Id.1198d
2898 " Patrice; m; 2 1-13-30; ¼+; s; son A1287; yes; yes; Id.1198e

2899 Lafrombois, Patrick; m; 61; ¼+; m; Head B1370; no; Devils Lake, Ramsey, ND; no; Id.592, Al.R195
2900 " Virginia (Plante); f; 62; ¼+; m; wife B1371; no; Devils Lake, Ramsey, ND; no; Id.592a, Al.G71
2901 " Theodore; m; 26; ¼+; s; son B1373; no; Devils Lake, Ramsey, ND; yes; Id.592e, Al.G08113
2902 " Emma; f; 24; ¼+; s; dau B1374; no; Devils Lake, Ramsey, ND; yes; Id.593f, Al.G08114

Turtle Mountain Reservation
1932 Census Roll

Key: Number; Surname, Given; Sex; Age at Last Birthday, Birthdate (if given); Tribe (Chippewa, unless stated otherwise); Degree of Blood; Marital Status; Relationship to Head of Family, Last Year Census Number; At Jurisdiction Where Enrolled (Yes/No); Elsewhere - Post Office, County, State; Ward (Yes/No); Allotment [Al.], Annuity [An.] and/or Identification [Id.] Numbers

2903 Lafrombois(cont), Alexander; m; 23; ¼+; s; son B1375; no; Devils Lake, Ramsey, ND; yes; Id.592g, Al.G-08253

2904 Lafrombois, Riel; m; 34; ¼+; m; Head A1288; yes; no; Id.586b, Al.GF208
2905 " Mary Rose (Bruce); f; 54; ¼+; m; wife A1289; yes; yes; Id.209a, Al.R55
2906 " Edna Anna; f; 10; ¼+; s; dau A1290; yes; yes; none
2907 " (Bruce) Alexander; m; 15; ¼+; s; s-son B481; yes; no; none

2908 Lafrombois, Theresa; f; 36; ¼+; s; Head A1291; yes; yes; Id.577, Al.H030431
2909 " Stanley; m; 13; ¼+; s; son A1292; yes; no; none
2910 " Margaret; f; 11; ¼+; s; dau A1293; yes; Counted twice last year. no; none
2911 " June; f; 3; ¼+; s; dau A1294; yes; no; none

2912 Lagasse, Emma M; f; 28; ¼+; s; Head B1377; no; Address unknown; yes; Id.570b, Al.G0295

NE Lagimodiere, Ben; m;   Head
2913 " Adele (Grandbois); f; 26; ¼+; m; wife A1295; yes; yes; Id.437f, Al.G07324
2914 " Lillian; f; 16 12-8-15; ¼+; s; dau A1296; yes; no; none
2915 " Leo; m; 14 7-20-17; ¼+; s; son A1297; yes; no; none
2916 " Alvina; f; 4 4-17-27; ¼+; s; dau A1298; yes; no; none

2917 Lagimodiere, Joseph; m; 67; ¼+; m; Head B1378; no; Medicine Lake, Sheridan, Mont; no; Id.593
2918 " Eliza (Ducept); f; 61; ¼+; m; wife B1379; no; Medicine Lake, Sheridan, Mont; no; Id.593a
NE " Lillian;   B1380 (Counted last yr. error)
NE " Joseph;   B1381 do

2919 Lagimodiere, Leonidas; m; 37; ¼+; m; Head B1382; no; Address unknown; no; Id.594, GF79
NE " Dina;   wife (Maiden name not given on roll book)
2920 " Mary Helen; f; 8 3-16-24; ¼+; s; dau B1383; no; Address unknown; no; none
2921 " May F; f; 6 4-27-25; ¼+; s; dau B1384; no; Address unknown; no; none
2922 " Marian; f; 4 7-21-27; ¼+; s; dau B1385; no; Address unknown; no; none
2923 " Leonard; m; 2 7-4-29; ¼+; s; son B1386; no; Address unknown

Turtle Mountain Reservation
1932 Census Roll

Key: Number; Surname, Given; Sex; Age at Last Birthday, Birthdate (if given); Tribe (Chippewa, unless stated otherwise); Degree of Blood; Marital Status; Relationship to Head of Family, Last Year Census Number; At Jurisdiction Where Enrolled (Yes/No); Elsewhere - Post Office, County, State; Ward (Yes/No); Allotment [Al.], Annuity [An.] and/or Identification [Id.] Numbers

2924 Lambert, Alphonse; m; 29; ¼+; m; Head B1387; no; Dunseith, Rolette, ND; yes; Id.596c, Al.M119

2925 " Josephine (Alberts); f; 27; ¼+; m; wife B1388; no; Dunseith, Rolette, ND; yes; Id.64c, Al.DL47

2926 " Mary Joyce; f; 2 9-6-29; ¼+; s; dau B1389; no; Dunseith, Rolette, ND; yes; none

2927 Lambert, Francois; m; 51 7-3-82; ¼+; m; Head B1390; no; Dunseith, Rolette, ND; yes; Id.600, Al.G01493

NE " Rose Lena; wife (Maiden name not given on roll book)

2928 " Clarence; m; 19 12-22-12; ¼+; s; son B1391; no; Dunseith, Rolette, ND; no; Id.600a

2930 " Frank; m; 16 4-29-15; ¼+; s; son B1392; no; Dunseith, Rolette, ND; no; Id.600b

2931 " Rose Emily; f; 13 8-20-19; ¼+; s; dau B1393; no; Dunseith, Rolette, ND; no; Id.600c

2932 " May; f; 10 5-7-21; ¼+; s; dau B1394; no; Dunseith, Rolette, ND; no; Id.600d

2933 " Delbert; m; 6 2-11-26p ¼+; s; son B1395; no; Dunseith, Rolette, ND; no; Id.600f

2934 Lambert, Israel; m; 54; ¼+; m; Head B1396; no; Rolla, Rolette, ND; no; Id.603d

NE " Emma (Boyer); wife

2935 " Beatrice; f; 23 1-1-09; ¼+; s; dau B1397; no; Rolla, Rolette, ND; no; Id.603e

2936 " Stephen; m; 20 12-26-11; ¼+; s; son B1398; no; Rolla, Rolette, ND; no; Id.603f

2937 " Rose; f; 16 4-25-15; ¼+; s; dau B1399; no; Rolla, Rolette, ND; no; Id.603g

2938 " Willard; m; 12 8-4-19; ¼+; s; son B1400; no; Rolla, Rolette, ND; no; Id.603h

2939 " Vincent; m; 10 4-26-21; ¼+; s; son B1401; no; Rolla, Rolette, ND; no; Id.603i

2940 " Lorene Doris; f; 4 11-19-27; ¼+; s; dau B1402; no; Rolla, Rolette, ND; no; Id.603j

2941 Lambert, Joseph; m; 49; ¼+; s; Head B1403; no; Rolla, Rolette, ND; no; Id.602, Al.H024622

2942 Lambert, Lyman; m; 26; ¼+; m; Head B1404; no; Rolla, Rolette, ND; yes; Id.603c, Al.G613

2943 " Angeline (Warren); f; 22; ¼+; m; wife B1405; no; Rolla, Rolette, ND; yes; Id.1002g, Al.G015278

2944 " Augustine; m; 2 8-21-29; ¼+; s; son B1406; no; Rolla, Rolette, ND; yes; Id.none

Turtle Mountain Reservation
1932 Census Roll

Key: Number; Surname, Given; Sex; Age at Last Birthday, Birthdate (if given); Tribe (Chippewa, unless stated otherwise); Degree of Blood; Marital Status; Relationship to Head of Family, Last Year Census Number; At Jurisdiction Where Enrolled (Yes/No); Elsewhere - Post Office, County, State; Ward (Yes/No); Allotment [Al.], Annuity [An.] and/or Identification [Id.] Numbers

2945 Lambert, Peter; m; 54; ¼+; s; Head B1407; no; Dunseith, Rolette, ND; no; Id.599, Al.H039388

2946 Lambert, Philomene; f; 78; ¼+; wd; Head B1408; no; Dunseith, Rolette, ND; yes; Id.596a, Al.M121

2947 Lambert, William; m; 44; ¼+; s; Head B1409; no; Dunseith, Rolette, ND; no; Id.598, Al.M120

2948 Landry, John Louis; m; 34; ¼+; m; Head A1301; no; Dunseith, Rolette, ND; yes; Id.606b
NE " [Blank] (Monette); wife
2949 " John; m; 8 5-28-23; ¼+; s; son -----; no; Dunseith, Rolette, ND; yes; Id.none
2950 " Nora; f; 6 12-6-25; ¼+; s; dau -----; no; Dunseith, Rolette, ND; yes; none
2951 " Louis; m; 4 11-28-27; ¼+; s; son -----; no; Dunseith, Rolette, ND; yes; none

2952 Landry, John; m; 36; ¼+; m; Head B1410; no; Rolla, Rolette, ND; no; Id.605, Al.GF179
NE " Clara (Monette-Vandal); f; wife
2953 " William; m; 9 8-9-22; ¼+; s; son B1411; no; Rolla, Rolette, ND; no; Id.605b
2954 " Cecilia; f; 7 7-14-24; ¼+; s; dau B1412; no; Rolla, Rolette, ND; no; none
2955 " Aurelia; f; 4 10-12-27; ¼+; s; dau B1413; no; Rolla, Rolette, ND; no; none
2956 " Juanita; f; 1 4-10-30; ¼+; s; dau B1414; no; Rolla, Rolette, ND; no; none

2957 Landry, Maxim; m; 77; ¼+; m; Head A1299; yes; yes; Id.606, Al.GF175
2958 " Margaret (Peltier); f; 68; ¼+; m; wife A1300; yes; yes; Id.606a, Al.R196
2959 " George; m; 32; ¼+; s; son A1302; yes; yes; Id.606c, Al.GF180
2960 " Alfred; m; 24; ¼+; s; son A1303; yes; yes; Id.606e, Al.H010515
2961 " (Gourneau) John Victor; m; 9 5-28-22; ¼+; s; gr-son A1304; yes; yes; none

2962 Landry, Norbert; m; 46; ¼+; m; Head A1305; yes; no; Id.607, Al.GF176
2963 " Seraphine (Brien); f; 42; ¼+; m; wife A1306; yes; no; Id.607a, Al.G542
2964 " Gabriel; m; 19 3-21-13; ¼+; s; son A1307; yes; no; Id.607b
2965 " Joseph; m; 16 11-2-15; ¼+; s; son A1308; yes; no; Id.607c
2966 " Max; m; 13 8-2-18; ¼+; s; son A1309; yes; no; Id.607d
2967 " Lloyd; m; 9 10-10-11; ¼+; s; son A1310; yes; no; Id.607e
2968 " Alexander; m; 7 11-10-24; ¼+; s; son A1311; yes; no; Id.607f
2969 " Alvina; f; 5 2-19-27; ¼+; s; dau A1312; yes; no; Id.607g
2970 " Florence; f; 7-7-30; ¼+; s; dau A1313; yes; no; Id.607h
2971 " Nora Jennie; f; 1/12 2-2-32; ¼+; s; dau -----; yes; no; Id.607i

NE Lang, Fred; Head
2972 " Emma (Smith); f; 30; ¼+; m; wife B1415; no; Tokio, Benson, ND; yes; Id.927c, Al.G036599
2973 " Gilbert; m; 13 6-4-19; ¼+; s; son B1416; no; Tokio, Benson, ND; no; none

Turtle Mountain Reservation
1932 Census Roll

Key: Number; Surname, Given; Sex; Age at Last Birthday, Birthdate (if given); Tribe (Chippewa, unless stated otherwise); Degree of Blood; Marital Status; Relationship to Head of Family, Last Year Census Number; At Jurisdiction Where Enrolled (Yes/No); Elsewhere - Post Office, County, State; Ward (Yes/No); Allotment [Al.], Annuity [An.] and/or Identification [Id.] Numbers

2974 Lang(cont), Gladys; f; 11 11-23-20; ¼+; s; dau B1417; no; Tokio, Benson, ND; no; none
2975 " Dorothy; f; 7 4-13-24; ¼+; s; dau B1418; no; Tokio, Benson, ND; no; none
2976 " Irving; m; 6 12-10-25; ¼+; s; son ------; no; (Omitted from last census) Tokio, Benson, ND; no; none
2977 " Kathleen; f; 4 11-9-27; ¼+; s; dau B1419; no; Tokio, Benson, ND; no; none
2978 " Edna; f; 2 7-17-29; ¼+; s; dau ------; no; Tokio, Benson, ND; no; none
2979 " Marvin; m; 8/12 7-18-31; ¼+; s; son ------; no; Tokio, Benson, ND; no; none

NE Langan, Alex;   Head
2980 " Josephine (Enno); f; 30; ¼+; m; wife B1420; no; San Clara, Manitoba, Can; yes; Id.379, Al.GF-117
DEAD " Joseph;   B1421 (Died 1-20-22)
2981 " Helen C; f; 8 7-17-23; ¼+; s; dau B1422; no; San Clara, Manitoba, Can; yes; none
2982 " Celeste; f; 6 9-20-25; ¼+; s; dau ----; no; San Clara, Manitoba, Can; yes; none
2983 " Alvina M; f; 4 7-7-27; ¼+; s; dau ----; no; San Clara, Manitoba, Can; yes; none

NE Langan, Ed;   Head
2984 " Louise (Lafontain); f; 30; ¼+; m; wife B1423; no; Boggy Creek, Manitoba, Can; yes; Id.550c, Al.GF-173
2985 " Joseph; m; 10 4-23-21; ¼+; s; son B1424; no; Boggy Creek, Manitoba, Can; yes; none
2986 " Jane; f; 9 11-23-22; ¼+; s; dau B1425; no; Boggy Creek, Manitoba, Can; yes; none
2987 " Clara; f; 6 4-15-25; ¼+; s; dau B1426; no; Boggy Creek, Manitoba, Can; yes; none
2988 " Alice; f; 5 3-1-27; ¼+; s; dau -----; no; Boggy Creek, Manitoba, Can; yes; none
2989 " Cecelia; f; 1 5-10-30; ¼+; s; dau ------; no; Boggy Creek, Manitoba, Can; yes; none
2990 " Emile; m; 5/12 9-23-31; ¼+; s; son -----; no; Boggy Creek, Manitoba, Can; yes; none

NE Langan, Eugene;   wd; Head
2991 " Marie; f; 14 11-28-17; ¼+; s; dau B1427; no; Birtch[sic],River, Manitoba, Can; no; Id.730b
2992 " Virginia; f; 11 9-26-20; ¼+; s; dau B1428; no; Birtch[sic],River, Manitoba, Can; no; Id.730c

NE Langer, Alex;   Head
2993 " Rose (Belgarde); f; 18; ¼+; m; wife A237; no; Wolf Point, Roosevelt, Mont; no; Id.187c

Turtle Mountain Reservation
1932 Census Roll

Key: Number; Surname, Given; Sex; Age at Last Birthday, Birthdate (if given); Tribe (Chippewa, unless stated otherwise); Degree of Blood; Marital Status; Relationship to Head of Family, Last Year Census Number; At Jurisdiction Where Enrolled (Yes/No); Elsewhere - Post Office, County, State; Ward (Yes/No); Allotment [Al.], Annuity [An.] and/or Identification [Id.] Numbers

2994 Langer, Francois; m; 43; ¼+; m; Head A1314; yes; no; Id.609, Al.GF-169
2995 " St Ann (Decoteau); f; 38; ¼+; m; wife A1315; yes; no; Id.609a, Al.G-08133
2996 " Ernestine; f; 15 8-15-16; ¼+; s; dau A1316; yes; no; Id.609b
2997 " Patrick; m; 8 2-13-24; ¼+; s; son A1317; yes; no; Id.609c
2998 " George; m; 5 2-19-27; ¼+; s; son A1318; yes; no; Id.

2999 Langer, Frank; m; 63; ¼+; m; Head A1319; yes; yes; Id.608, Al.R-197
3000 " Caroline (Perronteau); f; 54; ¼+; m; wife A1320; yes; yes; Id.608a, Al.GF-172
3001 " Robert; m; 21; ¼+; s; son A1323; yes; yes; Id.608e, Al.H-010451
3002 " Ambrose; m; 19; ¼+; s; son A1324; yes; yes; Id.608g
3003 " Lillina[sic]; f; 16; ¼+; s; dau A1325; yes; yes; Id.698[sic]h
3004 " Ida Rose; f; 14; ¼+; s; dau A1326; yes; yes; Id.609[sic]i

3005 Langer, John B; m; 54; ¼+; m; Head A1327; yes; yes; Id.611, Al.DL-03644
3006 " Sarah (Morin); f; 51; ¼+; m; wife A1327; yes; yes; Id.611a, Al.G-0423
3007 " Alfred; m; 27 6-15-04; ¼+; wd; son A1329; yes; yes; Id.611c, Al.G-0405
3008 " John; m; 25 4-23-06; ¼+; s; son A1330; yes; yes; Id.611d, Al.G-017
3009 " Grace; f; 20 3-11-12; ¼+; s; dau A1331; yes; yes; Id.611f
3010 " Dora; f; 17 5-19-14; ¼+; s; dau A1332; yes; yes; Id.611g
3011 " Ernest J; m; 15 9-6-16; ¼+; s; son A1333; yes; yes; Id.611h
3012 " Annie; f; 13 12-1-18; ¼+; s; dau A1334; yes; yes; Id.611i
3013 " Raymond; m; 11 12-4-20; ¼+; s; son A1335; yes; yes; Id.611j
3014 " George; m; 10 2-16-22; ¼+; s; son A1336; yes; yes; Id.611k
3015 " Mary V; f; 4 5-8-27; ¼+; s; dau A1337; yes; yes; Id.611l

3016 Langer, Joseph; m; 37; ¼+; m; Head B1429; no; Ft.Totten, Benson, ND; no; Id.610, Al.G-168
NE " Gertrude (Pago);   wife
3017 " Joseph; m; 6 3-1-26; ¼+; s; son A1430; no; Ft.Totten, Benson, ND; no; none
3018 " Donald; m; 4 12-4-27; ¼+; s; son A1431; no; Ft.Totten, Benson, ND; no; none

3019 Langer, Louis; m; 46; ¼+; m; Head B1432; no; St.John, Rolette, ND; no; Id.614, Al.G-0293
NE " Amelia (Thibert);   wife
3020 " Joseph; m; 22; ¼+; s; son N1433; no; St.John, Rolette, ND; no; Id.614c
3021 " Peter; m; 21; ¼+; s; son B1434; no; St.John, Rolette, ND; no; Id.614d
3022 " Wilbert; m; 18; ¼+; s; son B1435; no; St.John, Rolette, ND; no; Id.614e
3023 " Hilda; f; 13 5-17-18; ¼+; s; dau B1436; no; St.John, Rolette, ND; no; Id.614f
3024 " Alex; m; 11 3-20-21; ¼+; s; son B1437; no; St.John, Rolette, ND; no; Id.614h
3025 " Luella; f; 8 10-20-23; ¼+; s; dau B1438; no; St.John, Rolette, ND; no; Id.614i
3026 " Verlin; m; 6 11-7-25; ¼+; s; son B1439; no; St.John, Rolette, ND; no; Id.none
3027 " Viola M; f; 4 5-26-28; ¼+; s; dau B1440; no; St.John, Rolette, ND; no; none

Turtle Mountain Reservation
1932 Census Roll

Key: Number; Surname, Given; Sex; Age at Last Birthday, Birthdate (if given); Tribe (Chippewa, unless stated otherwise); Degree of Blood; Marital Status; Relationship to Head of Family, Last Year Census Number; At Jurisdiction Where Enrolled (Yes/No); Elsewhere - Post Office, County, State; Ward (Yes/No); Allotment [Al.], Annuity [An.] and/or Identification [Id.] Numbers

3028 Langer, Simeon; m; 24; ¼+; m; Head A1322; no; Minneapolis, Hennepin, Minn; yes; Id.608d, Al.H010451
NE " Geraldine; wife
3029 " James Earl; m; 10/12 5-29-31; ¼+; s; son ------; no; Minneapolis, Hennepin, Minn; yes; none

3030 Laquette, Riel; m; 46; ¼+; s; Head B1441; no; Address unknown; yes; Id.615, Al.G016067

NE Laroque, Alex; Head
3031 " Mary Jane (Brien); f; 26 11-17-04; ¼+; m; wife B437; no; Medicine Lake, Sheridan, Mont; yes; Id.1191f
3032 " Loretta; f; 2 2-23-30; ¼+; s; dau -----; no; Medicine Lake, Sheridan, Mont; no; none

NE Laroque, David; Head
3033 " St Ann (Aiken); f; ¼+; m; wife B1442; no; St.John, Rolette, ND; yes; Id.62b, Al.G-08287
3034 " Harvey; m; 6 10-15-25; 1/4; s; son B1443; no; St.John, Rolette, ND; yes; none
3035 " Emma; f; 4 11-27-27; ¼+; s; dau B1444; no; St.John, Rolette, ND; yes; none
2929 " Joseph; m; 2 7-16-29; ¼+; s; son B1445; no; St.John, Rolette, ND; yes; none
3036 " Eugene; m; 3/12 1-10-32; ¼+; s; son ----; no; St.John, Rolette, ND; yes; none

NE Laroque, Fred; Head
3037 " Emily (Grandbois); f; 36; ¼+; m; wife B1446; no; Ft.Peck; no; Id.617a, Al.G-434
3038 " Andrew; m; 15 6-2-16; ¼+; s; son B1447; no; Ft.Peck; no; none
3039 " Fred Edward; m; 14 10-14-17; ¼+; s; son B1448; no; Ft.Peck; no; none
3040 " Nora May; f; 13 4-17-18; ¼+; s; dau B1449; no; Ft.Peck; no; none
3041 " Mary Jane; f; 11 6-25-20; ¼+; s; dau B1450; no; Ft.Peck; no; none
3042 " Oliver; m; 10; ¼+; s; son -----; no; Ft.Peck; no; none

NE Laroque, George; Head
3043 " St Ann (Beauchman); f; 30; ¼+; m; wife B208; no; Medicine Lake, Sheridan, Mont; yes; Id.157b, Al.GF-26
3044 " Lawrence Wn[sic]; m; 6 8-10-25; ¼+; s; son -------; no; Medicine Lake, Sheridan, Mont; yes; none
3045 " Margaret; f; 3 3-22-28; ¼+; s; dau ------; no; Medicine Lake, Sheridan, Mont; yes; none

Turtle Mountain Reservation
1932 Census Roll

Key: Number; Surname, Given; Sex; Age at Last Birthday, Birthdate (if given); Tribe (Chippewa, unless stated otherwise); Degree of Blood; Marital Status; Relationship to Head of Family, Last Year Census Number; At Jurisdiction Where Enrolled (Yes/No); Elsewhere - Post Office, County, State; Ward (Yes/No); Allotment [Al.], Annuity [An.] and/or Identification [Id.] Numbers

NE	Laroque, Patrice;		Head
3046	"	Mary (Enno); f; 40; ¼+; m; wife B1451; no; Dunseith, Rolette, ND; no; Id.616a, Al.G-06034	
1717	" (Enno) Robert;	step son B1452 A799 (#1717 on this census) Dunseith, Rolette, ND; no; Id.616b	
3047	"	Alexander; m; 13 7-29-18; ¼+; s; son B1453; no; Dunseith, Rolette, ND; no; Id.616c	
3048	"	Isadore; m; 12 3-11-20; ¼+; s; son B1454; no; Dunseith, Rolette, ND; no; Id.616d	
3049	"	Stella; f; 10 3-31-22; ¼+; s; dau B1455; no; Dunseith, Rolette, ND; no; Id.616e	
3050	"	Charley; m; 5 10-28-26; ¼+; s; son B1456; no; Dunseith, Rolette, ND; no; Id.616f	
3051	"	James; m; 4 4-19-27; ¼+; s; son B1457; no; Dunseith, Rolette, ND; no; Id.616g	
3052	"	Floyd; m; 3 8-28-28; ¼+; s; son B1458; no; Dunseith, Rolette, ND; no; Id.616h	
NE	Laroque, Peter;		Head
3053	"	Mary (Grandbois); f; 34; ¼+; m; wife B1459; no; Trenton, Williams, ND; no; Id.442b, Al.G-441	
3054	"	Peter; m; 12 10-14-19; ¼+; s; son B1460; no; Trenton, Williams, ND; no; Id.442c	
3055	"	Mary Jane; f; 11 2-26-21; ¼+; s; dau B1461; no; Trenton, Williams, ND; no; Id.442d	
3056	"	Julius; m; 8 7-21-23; ¼+; s; son B1452; no; Trenton, Williams, ND; no; Id.442e	
3057	"	George; m; 6 2-19-26; ¼+; s; son -----; no; Trenton, Williams, ND; no; none	
3058	"	Milton; m; 2 1-7-30; ¼+; s; son ----; no; Trenton, Williams, ND; no; none	
NE	Laroque, Peter;		Head
3059	"	Florestine (Azure); f; 35; ¼+; m; wife B1463; no; Froid, Roosevelt, Mont no; Id.99, Al.M-92	
3060	" (Sayers) Jean; m; 11 3-12-21; ¼+; s; step dau B1464; no; (Mary Florence Sayers now known as Jean Laroque) Froid, Roosevelt, Mont; no; none		
NE	Laroque, Vida E;		Head
3061	"	Olivine (Morin); f; 35 4-9-96; ¼+; m; wife B1871; no; Flaxville, Daniels, Mont; no; Id.759, Al.M-167	
3062	"	Ernest; m; 9 7-26-22; ¼+; s; son -----; no; Flaxville, Daniels, Mont; no; none	
3063	"	Ferdinand; m; 1 2-2-31; ¼+; s; son ----; no; Flaxville, Daniels, Mont; no; none	

Turtle Mountain Reservation
1932 Census Roll

Key: Number; Surname, Given; Sex; Age at Last Birthday, Birthdate (if given); Tribe (Chippewa, unless stated otherwise); Degree of Blood; Marital Status; Relationship to Head of Family, Last Year Census Number; At Jurisdiction Where Enrolled (Yes/No); Elsewhere - Post Office, County, State; Ward (Yes/No); Allotment [Al.], Annuity [An.] and/or Identification [Id.] Numbers

NE Laroque, Vital;   Head
3064   "   Marie (St Germain); f; 42; ¼+; m; wife B1465; no; Trenton, Williams, ND; no; Id.618a, Al.M-257
3065   "   Ernest; m; 20 2-28-12; ¼+; s; son B1467; no; Trenton, Williams, ND; no; Id.618c
3066   "   John; m; 18 10-25; 13; ¼+; s; son B1468; no; Trenton, Williams, ND; no; Id.618d
3067   "   Oliver; m; 16 4-2-15; ¼+; ; son B1469; no; Trenton, Williams, ND; no; Id.618e
Dead   "   Stella;   B1470   (Died in 1920)
3068   "   Julis[sic]; f; 13 12-23-18; ¼+; s; dau B1471; no; Trenton, Williams, ND; no; Id.618g
3069   "   Eldora; f; 6 11-20-25; ¼+; s; dau B1472; no; Trenton, Williams, ND; no; Id.618h
3070   "   Rose Veda; m; 4 5-8-27; ¼+; s; dau ----; no; Trenton, Williams, ND; no; Id.618i

NE Laroque, William;   Head
3071   "   Rosine (Boyer); f; 28; ¼+; m; wife B1473; no; Trenton, Williams, ND; no; Id.1185e, Al.G-18

3072 Larsen, Mary E; f; 20; ¼+; s; Head B961; no; Trenton, Williams, ND; no; Id.636

NE Larson, N J;   Head
3073   "   Mary Ann (Baker); f; 30; ¼+; m; wife B1474; no; Ft.Totten, Benson, ND; yes; Id.144b, Al.M-374
3074   "   Geo Thomas; m; 9 4-6-22; ¼+; s; son B1475; no; Ft.Totten, Benson, ND; yes; none
3075   "   Floyd R; m; 7 7-15-24; ¼+; s; son B1476; no; Ft.Totten, Benson, ND; yes; none
3076   "   Edward; m; 5 10-25-26; ¼+; s; son -----; no; Ft.Totten, Benson, ND; yes; none
3077   "   Melvin H; m; 4 3-3-28; ¼+; s; son B1477; no; Ft.Totten, Benson, ND; yes; none
3078   "   Larrian; m; 1 6-19-30; ¼+; s; son -----; no; Ft.Totten, Benson, ND; yes; none

NE Larson, Olaf;   Head
3079   "   Alvina (Thomas.Bercier); f; 25; ¼+; m; wife B328; no; Devils Lake, Ramsey, ND; y6es; Id.954b, Al.G-400
3080 " (Bercier) Raymond; m; 7 9-24-24; ¼+; s; stepson -----; no; (Omitted last census) Devils Lake, Ramsey, ND; yes; none
3081 " (Bercier) June; f; 3 6-8-28; ¼+; s; step dau B329; no;   Devils Lake, Ramsey, ND; yes; none

Turtle Mountain Reservation
1932 Census Roll

Key: Number; Surname, Given; Sex; Age at Last Birthday, Birthdate (if given); Tribe (Chippewa, unless stated otherwise); Degree of Blood; Marital Status; Relationship to Head of Family, Last Year Census Number; At Jurisdiction Where Enrolled (Yes/No); Elsewhere - Post Office, County, State; Ward (Yes/No); Allotment [Al.], Annuity [An.] and/or Identification [Id.] Numbers

NE	Lasota, Dan;		Head
Dead	"	Josephine (Montriel);	B1478 (Died 2-28-31)
3082	"	Francis R; m; 13 5-13-18; ¼+; s; son B1479; no; Devils Lake, Ramsey, ND; no; Id.739a
3083	"	Louise A; f; 12 1-18-20; ¼+; s; dau B1480; no; Devils Lake, Ramsey, ND; no; Id.739d

3084 Laterregrass, J B, Jr; m; 58; ¼+; m; Head A1340; yes; yes; Id.620, Al.R-200
NE   "   Sarah (Dionne);   wife
3085   "   Rosina; f; 33; ¼+; s; dau A1341; yes; yes; Id.620b, Al.H-038922
3086   "   Leona; f; 8 ¼+; s; grand dau A1342; yes; yes; none

3087 Laterregrass, John; m; 31; ¼+; m; Head A1343; yes; yes; Id.620c, Al.H-038920
3088   "   Clemence (Belgarde); f; 29; ¼+; m; wife A1344; yes; yes; Id.170c, Al.M404
3089   "   Mary Viola; f; 8 2-21-24; ¼+; s; dau A1345; yes; yes; none
3090   "   Louis P; m; 6 3-17-26; ¼+; s; son A1346; yes; yes; none
3091   "   Ernest E; m; 2 1-25-30; ¼+; s; son A1347; yes; yes; none
3092   "   Robert D; m; 1/12 2-8-32; ¼+; s; son ------; yes; yes; none

3093 Laterregrass, Mary; f; 79; ¼+; wd; Head A1348; yes; no; Id.619a, Al.G-0477

NE Latrace, George;   Head
3094   "   Lissett (McDonald); f; 60; ¼+; m; wife B1482; no; Boggy Creek, Manitoba, Can; no; Id.621a, Al.R-301
3095   "   Frank; m; 27; ¼+; s; son B1483; no; Boggy Creek, Manitoba, Can; yes; Id.621d, Al.G-303
3096   "   Ira; m; 25; ¼+; s; son B1484; no; Boggy Creek, Manitoba, Can; yes; Id.621e, Al.G-301
3097   "   John; m; 23; ¼+; s; son B1485; no; Boggy Creek, Manitoba, Can; no; Id.621f
3098   "   Mary K; f; 21; ¼+; s; dau B1486; no; Boggy Creek, Manitoba, Can; no; Id.621g

3099 Latrace, George; m; 39; ¼+; m; Head B1487; no; Canada; yes; Id.622, Al.G-0304
NE   "   Lillie (Saunders);   wife
3100   "   Emma L; f; 12 10-20-19; ¼+; s; dau B1488; no; Canada; yes; Id.622b
3101   "   Mabel E; f; 11 3-11-21; ¼+; s; dau B1489; no; Canada; yes; Id.622c
3102   "   Ferdinand; m; 7 8-14-24; ¼+; s; son B1490; no; Canada; yes; Id.622e
3103   "   June G; f; 6; ¼+; s; dau B1491; no; Canada; yes; Id.622f

3104 Latraille, Alexander; m; 84; ¼+; m; Head A1338; yes; no; Id.623, Al.R-202
3105   "   Clemence (Parisien); f; 76 ¼+; m; wife A1339; yes; no; Id.623a, Al.G-8338

3106 Latraille, Frederick; m; 44; ¼+; s; Head B1501; no; Helena, Clark, Mont; no; none

Turtle Mountain Reservation
1932 Census Roll

Key: Number; Surname, Given; Sex; Age at Last Birthday, Birthdate (if given); Tribe (Chippewa, unless stated otherwise); Degree of Blood; Marital Status; Relationship to Head of Family, Last Year Census Number; At Jurisdiction Where Enrolled (Yes/No); Elsewhere - Post Office, County, State; Ward (Yes/No); Allotment [Al.], Annuity [An.] and/or Identification [Id.] Numbers

3107 Latraille, Joseph; m; 50; ¼+; s; Head B1492; no; Unknown; no; Id.628

3108 Latraille, Louis N; m; 36; ¼+; s; Head B1502; no; Unknown; no; Id.625, Al.H-012562

3109 Latraille, Margaret; f; 53; ¼+; s; Head B1503; no; Unknown; no; Id.627, Al.DL-36

3110 Latraille, Napoleon; m; 77; ¼+; wd; Head B15041 no; Minot, Ward, ND; no; Id.624, Al.DL-14

3111 " Frank; m; 30; ¼+; s; son B1505; no; Minot, Ward, ND; no; Id.624b, Al.H-012556

3112 Latraille, Patrice; m; 48; ¼+; m; Head B1493; no; Devils Lake, Ramsey, ND; no; Id.629, Al.G-134

3113 " Elizabeth (Herman); f; 39; ¼+; m; wife B1494; no; Devils Lake, Ramsey, ND; no; Id.629a, Al.G-215

3114 " Albert; m; 19; ¼+; s; son B1495; no; Devils Lake, Ramsey, ND; no; Id.629b

3115 " Clemence; f; 16 12-22-15; ¼+; s; dau B1496; no; Devils Lake, Ramsey, ND; no; Id.629d

Dead " Mary Rose; B1497 (Died in 1921)

3116 " Sylvia; f; 9 9-11-22; ¼+; s; dau B1498; no; Devils Lake, Ramsey, ND; no; Id.629e3117

3117 " Patrice; m; 6 9-15-25; ¼+; s; son B1499; no; Devils Lake, Ramsey, ND; no; none

3118 " Dorothy; f; 4 10-30-27; ¼+; s; dau B1500; no; Devils Lake, Ramsey, ND; no; none

3119 " Elsie Mae; f; 2 5-7-29; ¼+; s; dau -----; no; Devils Lake, Ramsey, ND; no; none

NE Lavallie, Albert; Head
3120 " Mary Edna (Grant); f; 27; ¼+; m; wife B1506; no; Dunseith, Rolette, ND; no; Id.447e

3121 " Dorothy; f; 10 5-23-21; ¼+; s; dau B1507; no; Dunseith, Rolette, ND; no; none

3122 Lavallie, Alfred; m; 26; ¼+; m; Head B1508; no; Dunseith, Rolette, ND; yes; Id.631d, Al.G-0343

3123 " Mary (Amyott); f; 25; ¼+; m; wife B1509; no; Dunseith, Rolette, ND; yes; Id.96c, Al.H-024484

3124 " Mary; f; 4 2-25-28; ¼+; s; dau B1510; no; Dunseith, Rolette, ND; yes; none

3125 " Marguerite; f; 2 2-20-30; ¼+; s; dau B1511; no; Dunseith, Rolette, ND; yes; none

3126 " Alfred; m; 3/12 12-10-31; ¼+; s; son -----; no; Dunseith, Rolette, ND; yes; none

Turtle Mountain Reservation
1932 Census Roll

Key: Number; Surname, Given; Sex; Age at Last Birthday, Birthdate (if given); Tribe (Chippewa, unless stated otherwise); Degree of Blood; Marital Status; Relationship to Head of Family, Last Year Census Number; At Jurisdiction Where Enrolled (Yes/No); Elsewhere - Post Office, County, State; Ward (Yes/No); Allotment [Al.], Annuity [An.] and/or Identification [Id.] Numbers

3127 Lavallie, Antoine; m; 57; ¼+; m; Head A1349; yes; no; Id.630, Al.G-591
3128   "   Mary Louise (Morin); f; 54; ¼+; m; wife A1350; yes; no; Id.630a, Al.G-592
3129   "   Joseph T; m; 28; ¼+; s; son A1351; yes; yes; Id.630c, Al.G-451
3130   "   Philomeme; f; 26; ¼+; s; dau 1352; yes; yes; Id.630d, Al.G-466
3131   "   Noel; m; 22; ¼+; s; son A1354; yes; yes; Id.630f, Al.G-09218
3132   "   Simeon; m; 19; ¼+; s; son A1355; yes; no; Id.630g
3133   "   Wm John; m; 15 4-6-16; ¼+; s; son A1356; yes; no; Id.630h
3134   "   Mary Zilda; f; 13 4-1-18; ¼+; s; dau A1357; yes; no; Id.630i
3135   "   Edward; m; 11 8-6-20; ¼+; s; son A1358; yes; no; Id.630j
3136   "   Lillian; f; 9 8-3-22; ¼+; s; dau A1359; yes; no; Id.630k

3137 Lavallie, Antoine, Jr; m; 31; ¼+; m; Head A1360; yes; yes; Id.630b, Al.G-597
3138   "   Eliza (Houle); f; 20; ¼+; m; wife A1361; yes; yes; Id.485c
3139   "   Ernest; m; 4 2-5-28; ¼+; s; son A1362; yes; yes; none
3140   "   Antoine; m; 2 12-29-29; ¼+; s; son A1363; yes; yes; none

3141 Lavallie, Francois; m; 61; ¼+; m; Head A1364; yes; yes; Id.631, Al.R-203
3142   "   Eliza (Houle); f; 58; ¼+; m; wife A1365; yes; no; Id.631a, Al.G-0339
3143   "   John L; m; 20; ¼+; s; son A1366; yes; yes; Id.631f
3144   "   Alexander; m; 17; ¼+; s; son A1367; yes; none
3145   "   Helen; f; 15; ¼+; s; dau A1368; yes; yes; none

NE Lavallie, Jerome;   Head
3146   "   Mary Jane (Morin); f; 51; ¼+; m; wife A1369; yes; yes; Id.633a, Al.R-204
3147   "   Zachary; m; 23 7-20-08; ¼+; s; son A1370; yes; yes; Id.633d, Al.H-012552
3148   "   Jerome; m; 20 6-3-11; ¼+; s; son A1371; yes; yes; Id.633e, Al.H-013049
3149   "   Norman Toby; m; 15 3-27-17; ¼+; s; son A1372; yes; yes; Id.633g
3150   "   Archie; m; 13 1-23-19; ¼+; s; son A1373; yes; yes; Id.633h
3151   "   Mary; f; 6 5-26-25; ¼+; s; dau A1374; yes; yes; Id.633i
3152   "   Fred; m; 6 5-26-25; ¼+; s; son -----; yes; yes; Id.633j

3153 Lavallie, John B; m; 40; ¼+; m; Head A1375; yes; no; Id.635, Al.G-455
3154   "   Louise A (Morin); f; 35; ¼+; m; wife A1376; yes; no; Id.635a, Al.M-198
3155   "   Mary St Ann; f; 17 2-17-15; ¼+; s; dau A1377; yes; no; Id.635b
3156   "   Phillip John; m; 16 1-26-16; ¼+; s; son A1378; yes; no; Id.635c
3157   "   Francis; m; 14 5-1-17; ¼+; s; son A1379; yes; no; Id.635d
3158   "   Louis John; m; 13 10-18-18; ¼+; s; son A1380; yes; no; Id.635e
3159   "   Emil; m; 11 11-27-20; ¼+; s; son A1381; A1400 yes; (Duplication last census)
                  (Error last year in writing Emma) no; Id.635f
3160   "   Louise M; f; 8 4-27-23; ¼+; s; dau A1382; yes; no; Id.635h
3161   "   Alexander; m; 7 3-26-25; ¼+; s; son A1383; yes; no; Id.635i
3162   "   Virginia; f; 4 9-21-27; ¼+; s; dau A1384; yes; no; Id.635j

Turtle Mountain Reservation
1932 Census Roll

Key: Number; Surname, Given; Sex; Age at Last Birthday, Birthdate (if given); Tribe (Chippewa, unless stated otherwise); Degree of Blood; Marital Status; Relationship to Head of Family, Last Year Census Number; At Jurisdiction Where Enrolled (Yes/No); Elsewhere - Post Office, County, State; Ward (Yes/No); Allotment [Al.], Annuity [An.] and/or Identification [Id.] Numbers

NE   Laverdure, Albert;   Head
3163   "   Mary Louise (Allery); f; 37; ¼+; m; wife B1512; no; Dunseith, Rolette, ND; yes; Id.77e, Al.GF-189
3164   "   Eileen; f; 10 10-24-21; ¼+; s; dau B1513; no; Dunseith, Rolette, ND; yes; none
3165   "   Alice; f; 8 10-10-23; ¼+; s; dau B1514; no; Dunseith, Rolette, ND; yes; none
3166   "   Virginia; f; 6 7-24-25; ¼+; s; dau B1515; no; Dunseith, Rolette, ND; yes; none
3167   "   Albert; m; 5 7-26-27; ¼+; s; son A1516; no; Dunseith, Rolette, ND; yes; none

3168   Laverdure, Alfred; m; 38; ¼+; m; Head A1385; yes; no; Id.638, Al.G-145
3169   "   Mary Louise (Bercier); f; 29; ¼+; m; wife A1386; yes; yes; Id.169f, Al.W-08661
3170   "   Frances; f 1/12 3-3-32; ¼+; s; dau ------; yes; yes; none

NE   Laverdure, Arthur;   Head
3171   "   St Ann (Brunnell.Omar.Chambers); f; 37; ¼+; m; wife A1387; yes; yes; Id.782a, Al.G-8179

3172   Laverdure, David Joseph; m; 31; ¼+; m; Head A1391; yes; yes; Id.637a, Al.G-147
3173   "   Angeline M (Thomas); f; 28; ¼+; m; wife A1392; yes; yes; Id.980b, Al.GF-161
3174   "   Marion; f; 7 8-25-24; ¼+; s; dau A1393; yes; yes; none
3175   "   Grace; f; 6 3-2-26; ¼+; s; dau A1394; yes; yes; none
3176   "   Rita; f; 2 8-11-29; ¼+; s; dau A1395; yes; yes; none
3177   "   Leo David; m; 4/12 11-26-31; ¼+; s; son ------; yes; yes; none

NE   Laverdure, Dona;   Head
3178   "   Josette (Allery); f; 36; ¼+; m; wife B1517; no; Dunseith, Rolette, ND; no; Id.77b, Al.GF-187
3179   "   Ernest; m; 10 8-12-21; ¼+; m[sic]; son -----; no; Dunseith, Rolette, ND; no; none
3180   "   Marie; f; 8 6-4-23; ¼+; s; dau -----; no; Dunseith, Rolette, ND; no; none
3181   "   Yvonne Eva; f; 5 4-30-26; ¼+; s; dau B1518; no; Dunseith, Rolette, ND; no; none
3182   "   Mary Anne; f; 4 11-25-27; ¼+; s; dau B1519; no; Dunseith, Rolette, ND; no; none
3183   "   Cecelia; f; 1 6-16-30; ¼+; s; dau -----; no; Dunseith, Rolette, ND; no; none

3184   Laverdure, Elise (Lafrombois); f; 67; ¼+; wd; Head A1396; yes; no; Id.637a, Al.G-143

Turtle Mountain Reservation
1932 Census Roll

Key: Number; Surname, Given; Sex; Age at Last Birthday, Birthdate (if given); Tribe (Chippewa, unless stated otherwise); Degree of Blood; Marital Status; Relationship to Head of Family, Last Year Census Number; At Jurisdiction Where Enrolled (Yes/No); Elsewhere - Post Office, County, State; Ward (Yes/No); Allotment [Al.], Annuity [An.] and/or Identification [Id.] Numbers

3185 Laverdure, Fred; m; 32; ¼+; m; Head B1520; no; Ft.Totten, Benson, ND; yes; Id.643b, Al.G-0331
3186 " Mary Rose (Malaterre); f; 20; ¼+; m; wife A1475; no; Ft.Totten, Benson, ND; yes; Id.684b, Al.H-024637

3187 Laverdure, Horace; m; 31; ¼+; m; Head B1521; no; Comertown, Sheridan, Mont; yes; Id.644c, Al.M-268
NE " Eliza (King); wife
3188 " Irene; f; 7 2-1-24; ¼+; s; dau B1522; no; Comertown, Sheridan, Mont; yes; none
3189 " Morris; m; 5 12-28-26; ¼+; s; son B1523; no; Comertown, Sheridan, Mont; yes; none
3190 " Nora June; f; 1 6-11-30; ¼+; s; dau -----; no; Comertown, Sheridan, Mont; yes; none
3192 " Josephine; f; 4/12 11-6-31; ¼+; s; dau ------; no; Comertown, Sheridan, Mont; yes; none

3193 Laverdure, Isadore; m; 55; ¼+; m; Head A1398; yes; yes; Id.640, Al.R-209
3194 " Frances (Lavallie); f; 54; ¼+; m; wife A1399; yes; no; Id.640a, Al.G-039

NE Laverdure, Jerry; Head
3195 " Rosalie (Vivier); f; 37; ¼+; m; wife B1524; yes; no; Id.648a, Al.M-153
3196 " Anna; f; 17 7-26-14; ¼+; s; dau B1525; yes; no; none
3197 " Eva; f; 15 4-25-16; ¼+; s; dau B1526; yes; no; Id.648b
3198 " Wilfred; m; 13 7-29-18; ¼+; s; son B1527; yes; no; Id.648c
3199 " Ernest; m; 12 11-25-19; ¼+; s; son B1528; yes; no; Id.648d
3200 " William; m; 8 9-10-23; ¼+; s; son B1530; yes; no; Id.648e
3201 " Ludger; m; 5 5-25-26; ¼+; s; son -----; yes; no; none
3202 " James; m; 3 6-10-28; ¼+; s; son ------; yes; no; none
3203 " Edward; m; 1 1-27-31; ¼+; s; son -----; yes; no; none
5523 " Joseph; m; 10 11-5-21; ¼+; s; son B1529; yes; no; none

3204 Laverdure, John Wm; m; 29; ¼+; m; Head A1397; yes; yes; Id.637c, Al.G-148
3205 " Delima M (Delonais); f; 28; ¼+; m; wife A654; yes; yes; Id.319c, Al.G-49
3206 " Zelma J; f; 1/12 2-12-32; ¼+; s; dau -----; yes; yes; none

3207 Laverdure, Napoleon; m; 54; ¼+; m; Head B1531; no; Devils Lake, Ramsey, ND; no; Id.642, Al.R-211
NE " Mary (Premeau); wife
3208 " Elmira; f; 28 5-21-03; ¼+; s; dau B1532; no; Devils Lake, Ramsey, ND; yes; Id.642b, Al.G-031
3209 " Mary Louise; f; 22 8-9-09; ¼+; s; dau B1533; no; Devils Lake, Ramsey, ND; no; Id.642d

Turtle Mountain Reservation
1932 Census Roll

Key: Number; Surname, Given; Sex; Age at Last Birthday, Birthdate (if given); Tribe (Chippewa, unless stated otherwise); Degree of Blood; Marital Status; Relationship to Head of Family, Last Year Census Number; At Jurisdiction Where Enrolled (Yes/No); Elsewhere - Post Office, County, State; Ward (Yes/No); Allotment [Al.], Annuity [An.] and/or Identification [Id.] Numbers

3210 Laverdure(cont), Emile; m; 20 8-9-11; ¼+; s; son B1534; no; Devils Lake, Ramsey, ND; no; Id.642e
3211 " Mary Olivina; f; 18 9-21-13; ¼+; s; dau B1535; no; Devils Lake, Ramsey, ND; no; Id.642f
3212 " Frank; m; 16 8-21-15; ¼+; s; son B1536; no; Devils Lake, Ramsey, ND; no; Id.642g
3213 " Eva; f; 13 9-23-18; ¼+; s; dau B1537; no; Devils Lake, Ramsey, ND; no; Id.642h
3214 " Marie; f; 11 10-14-20; ¼+; s; dau B1538; no; Devils Lake, Ramsey, ND; no; Id.642i
3215 " Margaret; f; 10-1-9-22; ¼+; s; dau B1539; no; Devils Lake, Ramsey, ND; no; Id.642j
3216 " Andrew; m; 6 4-25-25; ¼+; s; son B1540; no; Devils Lake, Ramsey, ND; no; Id.642k

3217 Laverdure, Pierre; m; 69; ¼+; m; Head B1541; no; Dooley, Sheridan, Mont; no; Id.644, Al.R-207
NE " Eliza (Premeau); wife
3218 " John; m; 23; ¼+; s; son B1542; no; Dooley, Sheridan, Mont; no; Id.644g
3219 " Alex; m; 19; ¼+; s; son B1543; no; Dooley, Sheridan, Mont; no; Id.644i
3220 " George; m; 16 1-25-16; ¼+; s; son B1544; no; Dooley, Sheridan, Mont; no; Id.644j
3221 " Gladys; f; 14 2-3-18; ¼+; s; dau B1545; no; Dooley, Sheridan, Mont; no; Id.644k

3222 Laverdure, Raphael; m; 26 5-2-05; ¼+; m; Head B1546; no; Devils Lake, Rolette, ND; yes; Id.642e, Al.G-032
NE " Esther (Miller); wife
3223 " Ralph Gerald; m; 1 4-28-30; ¼+; s; son ----; no; Devils Lake, Rolette, ND; yes; none

3224 Laverdure, Stanilaus; m; 57; ¼+; m; Head B1547; no; Cando, Towner, ND; no; Id.647, Al.R-212
3225 " Rosina (Lizotte); f; 47; ¼+; m; wife B1548; no; Cando, Towner, ND; no; Id.647a, Al.Geeee-07889
3226 " Joseph M; m; 34; ¼+; s; son B1549; no; Cando, Towner, ND; no; Id.647b, Al.G-0332
3227 " Anna; f; 23; ¼+; s; dau B1550; no; Cando, Towner, ND; no; Id.647g
3228 " Emile; m; 19; ¼+; s; son B1552; no; Cando, Towner, ND; no; Id.647h
3229 " Mary Celina; f; 14 10-9-17; ¼+; s; dau B1553; no; Cando, Towner, ND; no; Id.647i
3230 " Christine; f; 14 3-5-18; ¼+; s; dau B1554; no; Cando, Towner, ND; no; Id.647j
3231 " Fred; m; 12 2-10-20; ¼+; s; son -----; no; Cando, Towner, ND; no; none

Turtle Mountain Reservation
1932 Census Roll

Key: Number; Surname, Given; Sex; Age at Last Birthday, Birthdate (if given); Tribe (Chippewa, unless stated otherwise); Degree of Blood; Marital Status; Relationship to Head of Family, Last Year Census Number; At Jurisdiction Where Enrolled (Yes/No); Elsewhere - Post Office, County, State; Ward (Yes/No); Allotment [Al.], Annuity [An.] and/or Identification [Id.] Numbers

3232 Laverdure(cont), Alvina; f; 10-3-27-22; ¼+; s; dau -----; no; Cando, Towner, ND; no; none
3233 " Francis; m; 7 10-7-24; ¼+; s; son -----; no; Cando, Towner, ND; no; none
3234 " Helen; f; 6 11-25-25; ¼+; s; dau -----; no; Cando, Towner, ND; no; none

3235 Laverdure, William; m; 64; ¼+; m; Head A1401; yes; no; Id.645, Al.R-213
3236 " Rose (Vandal.Gourneau); f; 54; ¼+; m; wife A1402; yes; no; Id.434a, Al.M-303
3237 " (Grant) Patrick; m; 13 3-29-18; ¼+; s; adpt son A1404; yes; no; Id.451b
3238 " (Grant) John; m; 13;4-2918; ¼+; s; adpt son A1403; yes; no; Id.451c
3239 " (Gourneau) Ernest; m; 20; ¼+; s; stepson A1405; yes; no; Id.434g

3240 Laverdure, William Ernest; m; 36; ¼+; m; Head A1406; yes; no; Id.646, Al.G-020
3241 " Rosina (Belgarde); f; 28; ¼+; m; wife A1407; yes; no; Id.165c, Al.M-263
3242 " Lillian; f; 6 1-24-26; ¼+; s; dau; yes; no; none
3243 " Eva; f; 2 4-15-29; ¼+; s; dau A1410; yes; no; none
3244 " Leocadia; m; 11/12 4-20-31; ¼+; s; son A1411; yes; no; none
DEAD " Marie; A1409 (Died 1-25-28)
No such child ERNEST A1408

3245 Lavia, Joseph; m; 49; ¼+; m; Head B1555; no; Dagmar, Sheridan, Mont; no; Id.649, Al.M-135
3246 " Emma (Grandbois); f; 40; ¼+; m; wife B1556; no; Dagmar, Sheridan, Mont; no; Id.649a, Al.G-433
3247 " Mary Jane; f; 16 9-8-15; ¼+; s; dau B1557; no; Dagmar, Sheridan, Mont; no; Id.649b
3248 " Helen; f; 14 7-28-17; ¼+; s; dau B1558; no; Dagmar, Sheridan, Mont; no; Id.649c
3249 " Joseph F; m; 12 9-18-19; ¼+; s; son ------; no; Dagmar, Sheridan, Mont; no; none
3250 " Lydia S; f; 10-12-13-211 1/4; s; dau B1559; no; Dagmar, Sheridan, Mont; no; Id.649d
3251 " Edward B; m; 7 7-28-24; ¼+; s; son ------; no; Dagmar, Sheridan, Mont; no; none
3252 " Katherine; f; 5 11-29-26; ¼+; s; dau -------; no; Dagmar, Sheridan, Mont; no; none

3253 Lavia, Louis; m; 42; ¼+; m; Head B1560; no; Culbertson, Roosevelt, Mont; yes; Id.450, Al.M-127
NE " Mary (Bauer); wife
3254 " Peter J; m; 19 8-7-12; ¼+; s; son B1561; no; Culbertson, Roosevelt, Mont; yes; Id.650b
3255 " Patrick; m; 17 8-2-14; ¼+; s; son B1562; no; Culbertson, Roosevelt, Mont; yes; Id.650c

Turtle Mountain Reservation
1932 Census Roll

Key: Number; Surname, Given; Sex; Age at Last Birthday, Birthdate (if given); Tribe (Chippewa, unless stated otherwise); Degree of Blood; Marital Status; Relationship to Head of Family, Last Year Census Number; At Jurisdiction Where Enrolled (Yes/No); Elsewhere - Post Office, County, State; Ward (Yes/No); Allotment [Al.], Annuity [An.] and/or Identification [Id.] Numbers

3256 Lavia(cont), Louise; f; 15 5-14-16; ¼+; s; dau B1563; no; Culbertson, Roosevelt, Mont; yes; Id.650d
3257 " Louis; m; 13 5-3-18; ¼+; s; son B1564; no; Culbertson, Roosevelt, Mont; yes; Id.650e
3258 " Mary Rose; f;1 1 9-20-20; ¼+; s; dau B1565; no; Culbertson, Roosevelt, Mont; yes; Id.650f
3259 " Alvina; f; 9 1-23-23; ¼+; s; dau B1566; no; Culbertson, Roosevelt, Mont; yes; Id.650g

NE Laviolette, Jacob;   Head
3260 " Julia (Aiken); f; 50; ¼+; m; wife B1568; no; St.John, Rolette, ND; no; Id.652, Al.G-07845
3261 " Joseph; m; 23 9-2-08; ¼+; s; son B1569; no; St.John, Rolette, ND; yes; Id.652b, Al.G-07846
3262 " Delbert; m; 11 3-4-21; ¼+; s; son B1570; no; St.John, Rolette, ND; no; none
3263 " Martin; m; 8 4-23-23; ¼+; s; son -----; no; St.John, Rolette, ND; no; none

3264 Lebrun, Alfred; m; 35; ¼+; m; Head A1412; yes; yes; Id.653b, Al.M-233
3265 " Margaret (Gourneau); f; 32; ¼+; m; wife A1413; yes; yes; Id.429c, Al.G-549
3266 " Elizabeth; f; 3 11-6-28; ¼+; s; dau A1414; yes; yes; none

3267 Lebrun, Mary Louise (Marion); f; 66; ¼+; wd; Head B1571; no; Rolla, Rolette, ND; yes; Id.653a, Al.M-115
3268 " Eudora; f; 36; ¼+; s; dau B1570; no; Rolla, Rolette, ND; yes; Id.654, Al.M-231

3269 Lecompt, Ernest; m; 30 11-27-02; ¼+; m; Head B1572; no; Bainville, Sheridan, Mont; yes; Id.655e, Al.G-559
3270 " Theresa; f; 31; ¼+; m; wife B1573; no; Bainville, Sheridan, Mont; yes; Id.876c, Al.G-07897
3271 " Laverne; f; 10 3-4-22; ¼+; s; dau ----; no; Bainville, Sheridan, Mont; yes; none
3272 " Willard; m; 8 5-25-23; ¼+; s; son -----; no; Bainville, Sheridan, Mont; yes; none
3273 " Corma; f; 7 1-12-25; ¼+; s; dau ------; no; Bainville, Sheridan, Mont; yes; none
3274 " Blanche; f; 6 2-4-26; ¼+; s; dau ------; no; Bainville, Sheridan, Mont; yes; none
3275 " Gladys; f; 4 9-7-27; ¼+; s; dau -----; no; Bainville, Sheridan, Mont; yes; none
3276 " Eugene; m; 3 1-9-29; ¼+; s; son ------; no; Bainville, Sheridan, Mont; yes; none

Turtle Mountain Reservation
1932 Census Roll

Key: Number; Surname, Given; Sex; Age at Last Birthday, Birthdate (if given); Tribe (Chippewa, unless stated otherwise); Degree of Blood; Marital Status; Relationship to Head of Family, Last Year Census Number; At Jurisdiction Where Enrolled (Yes/No); Elsewhere - Post Office, County, State; Ward (Yes/No); Allotment [Al.], Annuity [An.] and/or Identification [Id.] Numbers

3277 Lecompt(cont), Garley; m; 1 5-4-30; ¼+; s; son ------; no; Bainville, Sheridan, Mont; yes; none

NE Lecompt, Joseph;   wd; Head
3278 " Antoinette; f; 28 6-10-03; ¼+; s; dau B1575; no; Froid, Roosevelt, Mont; yes; Id.655c, Al.G-557
3279 " Henriette; f; 22 7-20-09; ¼+; s; dau B1577; no; Froid, Roosevelt, Mont; yes; Id.655f, Al.H-013021
3280 " Albert; m; 19 10-23-12; ¼+; s; son B1578; no; Froid, Roosevelt, Mont; yes; Id.655g
3281 " Victoria M; f; 18 9-27-13; ¼+; s; dau B1579; no; Froid, Roosevelt, Mont; yes; Id.655h
3282 " Josephine; f; 17 9-15-14; ¼+; s; dau B1580; no; Froid, Roosevelt, Mont; yes; Id.655i
3283 " Ione; f; 16 11-20-15; ¼+; s; dau B1581; no; Froid, Roosevelt, Mont; yes; Id.655j
3284 " Earl; m; 14 10-27-17; ¼+; s; son B1582; no; Froid, Roosevelt, Mont; yes; Id.655k

3285 Ledeaux, Antoine; m; 62; ¼+; m; Head A1415; yes; yes; Id.657, Al.R-214
NE " Julia;   wife (Maiden name not given on roll book)

3286 Ledeaux, Damian; m; 43; ¼+; m; Head A1417; yes; yes; Id.658, Al.G129
NE " Zilda (Swain); f;   wife
3287 " Alice; f; 16; ¼+; s; dau A1418; yes; yes; none
3288 " Amelia; f; 8 4-15-23; ¼+; s; dau A1419; yes; yes; none
3289 " Gertrude; f; 6; ¼+; s; dau A1420; yes; yes; none
3290 " Rosila; f; 4 ¼+; s; dau A1421; yes; yes; none
3291 " Marie L; f; 11/12 4-29-31; ¼+; s; dau A1422; yes; yes; none

3292 Ledeaux, Joseph; m; 55; ¼+; s; Head A1423; yes; yes; Id.656, Al.G016440

NE Leduc, Louis;   Head
3293 " Lillian (Trothier); f; 21 5-17-10; ¼+; m; wife B2535; no; Devils Lake, Ramsey, ND; yes; Id.963e, Al.H010514

3293[sic] Lefort, Francis; m; 25; ¼+; m; Head B1583; yes; yes; Id.659c, Al.G-08251
3294 " Jane (Laducer); f; 23; ¼+; m; wife B1584; yes; no; Id.538c
3295 " Betty Lou; f; 1 2-23-31; ¼+; s; dau B1585; yes; yes; none

NE Lefort, Jules;   Head
3296 " Elizabeth (Fredrick); f; 53; ¼+; m; wife B1586; no; St.Paul, Ramsey, Minn; no; Id.659a, Al.G-019132

Turtle Mountain Reservation
1932 Census Roll

Key: Number; Surname, Given; Sex; Age at Last Birthday, Birthdate (if given); Tribe (Chippewa, unless stated otherwise); Degree of Blood; Marital Status; Relationship to Head of Family, Last Year Census Number; At Jurisdiction Where Enrolled (Yes/No); Elsewhere - Post Office, County, State; Ward (Yes/No); Allotment [Al.], Annuity [An.] and/or Identification [Id.] Numbers

3297 Lefort(cont), Joseph; m; 30; ¼+; s; son B1587; no; St.Paul, Ramsey, Minn; yes;
Id.659b, Al.G-08131
3298 " Veronica; f; 22; ¼+; s; dau B1588; no; St.Paul, Ramsey, Minn; yes;
Id.659d, Al.H-012554
3299 " John; m; 19; ¼+; s; son B1589; no; St.Paul, Ramsey, Minn; yes; Id.659e,
Al.H-024632
3300 " Roy; m; 15 10-15-16; ¼+; s; son B1590; no; St.Paul, Ramsey, Minn; no;
Id.659f
3301 " Martha; f; 13 10-21-18; ¼+; s; dau B1591; no; St.Paul, Ramsey, Minn; no;
Id.659g
3302 " Jimmie; m; 10; ¼+; s; son B1592; no; St.Paul, Ramsey, Minn; no; none

NE Lefort, Louis; Head
3303 " Agnes (Azure); f; 24; ¼+; m; wife B1593; yes; yes; Id.124d, Al.H-012500
3304 " Joseph; m; 7; ¼+; s; son B1594; yes; yes; none
Dead " Emery; B1595 (Died 1927)
3305 " Dora; f; 5; ¼+; s; dau B1596; yes; yes; none
3306 " Mary Agnes; f; 1 5-7-30; ¼+; s; dau B1597; yes; yes; none

3307 Lefort, Wilfred; m; 36; ¼+; s; Head B1598; no; St.Paul, Ramsey, Minn; no;
Id.660, Al.G-248

NE Left Hand, George; Head
3308 " Mary Jane (Poitra); f; 33; ¼+; m; wife B1599; no; Kenel, Corson, SD;
no; Id.841c, Al.GF-61
3309 " Ambrose; m; 11 10-18-20; ¼+; s; son -----; no; Kenel, Corson, SD; no;
none
3310 " Mary Esther; f; 9 4-5-22; ¼+; s; dau ------; no; Kenel, Corson, SD; no;
none
3311 " Alberta M; f; 7 4-19-24; ¼+; s; dau ------; no; Kenel, Corson, SD; no;
none
3312 " Elaine C; f; 3 10-29-28; ¼+; s; dau -------; no; Kenel, Corson, SD; no;
none
3313 " Elsie Mae; f; 1 2-7-31; ¼+; s; dau ------; no; Kenel, Corson, SD; no;
none

3314 Lemay, Frederick; m; 32; ¼+; m; Head B1605; no; Bainville, Roosevelt[sic],
Mont[sic]; yes; Id.662, Al.M-129
NE " Lyda (Bauer); wife
3315 " Catherine; f; 9 4-13-22; ¼+; s; dau B1657; no; Bainville, Roosevelt[sic],
Mont[sic]; yes; none
3316 " Dora; f; 8 1-27-24; ¼+; s; dau -------; no; Bainville, Roosevelt[sic], Mont[sic];
yes; none

Turtle Mountain Reservation
1932 Census Roll

Key: Number; Surname, Given; Sex; Age at Last Birthday, Birthdate (if given); Tribe (Chippewa, unless stated otherwise); Degree of Blood; Marital Status; Relationship to Head of Family, Last Year Census Number; At Jurisdiction Where Enrolled (Yes/No); Elsewhere - Post Office, County, State; Ward (Yes/No); Allotment [Al.], Annuity [An.] and/or Identification [Id.] Numbers

3317 Lemay(cont), Madeline; f; 5 5-31-26; ¼+; s; dau ------; no; Bainville, Roosevelt[sic], Mont[sic]; yes; none
3318 " Napoleon; m; 4 1-1-28; ¼+; s; son ------; no; Bainville, Roosevelt[sic], Mont[sic]; yes; none
3319 " Leona; f; 1 8-8-30; ¼+; s; dau -----; no; Bainville, Roosevelt[sic], Mont[sic]; yes; none

3320 Lemay, Mary M; f; 18; ¼+; s; Head B1601; no; Trenton, Williams, ND; no; Id.661b
3321 " Alexander; m; 16; ¼+; s; bro B1602; no; Trenton, Williams, ND; no; Id.661c
Dead " Gilbert; B1603 (Died 1-1-27)

NE Lemere, Edward; Head
3322 " Mary (Allery.Fanning); f; 36; ¼+; m; wife ----; no; Whitewater, Phillips, Mont; yes; I.81b, Al.G-09278
3323 " (Fanning) John Lee; m; 14 1-21-18; ¼+; s; son -----; no; Whitewater, Phillips, Mont; yes; none
3324 " Ray; m; 10; ¼+; s; son -----; no; Whitewater, Phillips, Mont; yes; none

3325 Lenoir, Louis; m; 71; ¼+; m; Head A1424; yes; yes; Id.666, Al.R-216
NE " Mary Emily (Poitra); wife
3326 " Michael; m; 26 12-22-05; ¼+; s; son A1425; yes; yes; Id.666c, Al.G-319
3327 " Robert; m; 21 2-20-11; ¼+; s; son A1426; yes; yes; Id.666e
3328 " Bernard; m; 19 1-15-13; ¼+; s; son A1427; yes; yes; Id.666f
3329 " Mary Eva; f; 15 5-18-16; ¼+; s; dau A1428; yes; yes; Id.666g
3330 " Francois; m; 13 6-25-18; ¼+; s; son A1429; yes; yes; Id.none
Dead " Madeline; A1430 (Died in 1920)
3331 " Gregory; m; 8 3-27-24; ¼+; s; son A1431; yes; yes; Id.none

3332 Lenoir, Michael; m; 62; ¼+; m; Head B1605; no; Minnewauken[sic], Benson, ND; yes; Id.667, Al.DL-15
NE " Florestine (Fournier); wife
3333 " Antoine; m; 20; ¼+; s; son B1606; no; Minnewauken[sic], Benson, ND; yes; Id.667b
3334 " Rose; f; 18; ¼+; s; dau B1607; no; Minnewauken[sic], Benson, ND; yes; Id.667c

3335 Lenoir, St Pierre; m; 38; ¼+; m; Head B1608; no; Minnewauken[sic], Benson, ND; no; Id.665, Al.G-515
NE " Victoria (Dubois); wife
Dead " Donald; B1609 (Died in 1922)
3336 " Danville; m; 9 8-15-22; ¼+; s; son ----; no; Minnewauken[sic], Benson, ND; no; Id.665d
3337 " Ernest; m; 7 11-1-24; ¼+; s; son B1610; no; Minnewauken[sic], Benson, ND no; none

Turtle Mountain Reservation
1932 Census Roll

Key: Number; Surname, Given; Sex; Age at Last Birthday, Birthdate (if given); Tribe (Chippewa, unless stated otherwise); Degree of Blood; Marital Status; Relationship to Head of Family; Last Year Census Number; At Jurisdiction Where Enrolled (Yes/No); Elsewhere - Post Office, County, State; Ward (Yes/No); Allotment [Al.], Annuity [An.] and/or Identification [Id.] Numbers

3338 Lenoir(cont), Florence; f; 6 11-25-25; ¼+; s; dau B1911; no; Minnewauken[sic], Benson, ND; no; none
3339 " Dorothy; f; 4 2-2-28; ¼+; s; dau ------; no; Minnewauken[sic], Benson, ND; no; Id.665f
3340 " Joan; f; 3/12 12-14-31; ¼+; s; dau ------; no; Minnewauken[sic], Benson, ND; no; none
3341 " Jean; f; 3/12 12-14-32; ¼+; s; dau ------; no; Minnewauken[sic], Benson, ND no; none

3342 Lenoir, William; m; 38; ¼+; m; Head B1612; no; Minnewauken[sic], Benson, ND; yes; Id.664, Al.G-510
NE " Ella Olga (Michels); wife
3343 " John B; m; 11 12-5-20; ¼+; s; son B1613; no; Minnewauken[sic], Benson, ND; yes; none
3344 " Edith Mae; f; 9 3-10-23; ¼+; s; dau -------; no; Minnewauken[sic], Benson, ND; yes; none

NE Lequir, Louis; Head
3345 " Emily (Henry); f; 33; ¼+; m; wife B1614; no; Mahnomen, Mahnomen, Minn; no; Id.471b, Al.M-228

3346 L'Esperance, Alexander; m; 30; ¼+; m; Head A1432; yes; yes; Id.669c, Al.G-037070
3347 " Agnes (Falcon); f; 26; ¼+; m; wife A1433; yes; yes; Id.385c, Al.G-093
3348 " Theresa; f; 3 11-3-28; ¼+; s; dau A1434; yes; yes; none
3349 " Alexander; m; 5/12 10-3-31; ¼+; s; son -------; yes; yes; none

NE L'Esperance, Arthur; Head
3350 " Jane (Fagnant.Peltier); f; ¼+; m; wife B1615; no; San Haven, Rolette, ND; yes; Id.383c, Al.H-030277
3351 " (Peltier) Delia; f; 12 4-6-19; ¼+; s; step dau B1616; no; San Haven, Rolette, ND yes; none
3352 " (Peltier) Emma; f; 10 6-13-21; ¼+; s; step dau B1617; no; San Haven, Rolette, ND; yes; none

3353 L'Esperance, Francois; m; 32; ¼+; m; Head B1618; no; Ft.Totten, Benson, ND; yes; Id.669b, Al.G-028634
3354 " Evalina (Lenoir-Kress); f; 29; ¼+; m; wife B1619; no; Ft.Totten, Benson, ND; yes; Id.669c, Al.G-514
3355 " (Kress) Genevieve; f; 11 3-15-21; ¼+; s; step dau B1621; no; Ft.Totten, Benson ND; yes; none
3356 " (Kress) Marian; f; 8 6-11-23; ¼+; s; step dau B1622; no; Ft.Totten, Benson, ND yes; none
3357 " (Kress) Wm John; m; 6; ¼+; s; stepson ----; no; Ft.Totten, Benson, ND; yes; none

Turtle Mountain Reservation
1932 Census Roll

Key: Number; Surname, Given; Sex; Age at Last Birthday, Birthdate (if given); Tribe (Chippewa, unless stated otherwise); Degree of Blood; Marital Status; Relationship to Head of Family, Last Year Census Number; At Jurisdiction Where Enrolled (Yes/No); Elsewhere - Post Office, County, State; Ward (Yes/No); Allotment [Al.], Annuity [An.] and/or Identification [Id.] Numbers

3358 L'Esperance(cont), Evelyn; f; 1 10-10-30; ¼+; s; dau -----; no; Ft.Totten, Benson, ND; yes; none
Dead   "   Arthur;   B1620   (Died 1929)

                                  A1435
3359 L'Esperance, Frederick; m; 27; ¼+; s; Head B1623; no; (Counted twice last year)
       Rolla, Rolette, ND; no; Id.669d, Al.G-037072

NE Lillie, Charles;   Head
3360   "   Gloria (Gourneau); f; 31; ¼+; m; wife A1436; yes; yes; Id.433a, Al.M-368
3361   "   Mary Clara; f; 12 3-8-20; ¼+; s; dau A1437; yes; yes; none
3362   "   Irene; f; 6 3-18-26; ¼+; s; dau ------; yes; yes; none
Dead   "   Beatrice;   A1438   (Died 11-5-26)
3363   "   Charles; m; 2 8-5-29; ¼+; s; son A1439; yes; yes; none

NE Lillie, James;   Head
3364   "   Rose (Wilkie); f; 49; ¼+; m; wife B1624; no; St.John, Rolette, ND; no;
                                                       Id.671a, Al.G-036566
3365   "   Mary Edna; f; 14 8-23-17; ¼+; s; dau B1625; no; St.John, Rolette,
                                             ND; no; Id.671b
3366   "   Robert; m; 10 5-6-21; ¼+; s; son B1626; no; St.John, Rolette, ND; no;
                                                       Id.671d
Dead   "   Victoria;   B1627   (Died 7-5-31)

NE Lillie, Norman;   Head
3367   "   Alice (Azure); f; 231 ¼+; m; wife B1628; no; Nishu, McLean, ND; yes;
                                                       Id.132c, Al.G-016488
3368   "   Joseph; m; 5 7-25-26; ¼+; s; son -----; no; Nishu, McLean, ND; yes; none
3369   "   Rose; f; 2 12-27-29; ¼+; s; dau -----; no; Nishu, McLean, ND; yes; none
Dead   "   Mary   B1629   (Died 1-8-26)

NE Lind, Andrew;   Head
3370   "   Anna (Delonais); f; 35; ¼+; m; wife A1440; yes; yes; Id.319d, Al.G-48
3371   "   John Harry; m; 3 3-1-29; ¼+; s; son -----; yes; yes; none
3372   "   Bernard; m; 1 11-19-30; ¼+; s; son ------; yes; yes; none

NE Lindgren, Axel;   Head
3373   "   Virginia (Marion); f; 23; ¼+; m; wife B1642; no; Fargo, Cass, ND; yes;
                                                        Id.669c
3374   "   Ramona; f; 2 1-1-30; ¼+; dau B1643; no; Fargo, Cass, ND; yes; none
3375   "   Merville; m; 1 2-27-31; ¼+; s; son ------; no; Fargo, Cass, ND; yes; none

3376 Little Boy, Isadore; m; 35; F; m; Head B1630; yes; yes; Id.59, Al.G-014911
NE   "   Mary (Lefort.Hayes) wife
3377   "   Shanny; m; 13 2-21-19; F; s; son B1631; yes; yes; none

Turtle Mountain Reservation
1932 Census Roll

Key: Number; Surname, Given; Sex; Age at Last Birthday, Birthdate (if given); Tribe (Chippewa, unless stated otherwise); Degree of Blood; Marital Status; Relationship to Head of Family, Last Year Census Number; At Jurisdiction Where Enrolled (Yes/No); Elsewhere - Post Office, County, State; Ward (Yes/No); Allotment [Al.], Annuity [An.] and/or Identification [Id.] Numbers

3378 Little Boy(cont), Louis; 8 5-20-23; ¼+; s; son B1632; yes; yes; none
3379 " Patrick; m; 6 9-5-25; ¼+; s; son B1633; yes; yes; none
3380 " Mary Eva; f; 2 7-31-29; ¼+; s; dau B1634; yes; yes; none

3381 Little Boy, Jack; m; 60; F; m; Head B1635; no; Dunseith, Rolette, ND; yes; Id.42, Al.DL-28
3382 " Shining Light; f; 63; F; m; wife B1636; no; Dunseith, Rolette, ND; yes; Id.42a, Al.G-01903

3383 Little Elk, Foolish Boy; m; 76; F; wd; Head B1637; no; Dunseith, Rolette, ND; yes; Id.25, Al.DL-34
Dead " Striped Cloud; B1638 (Died 11-15-26)

3384 Little Rising Sun; m; 38; F; s; Head B1639; no; Dunseith, Rolette, ND; yes; Id.55b, Al.G-332

3385 Little Shell, Jane; f; 14 10-6-17; ¼+; s; Head B1640; no; Dunseith, Rolette, ND; yes; Id.26b

3386 Little Shell, Pierre; m; 32; F; s; Head B1641; no; Dunseith, Rolette, ND; yes; Id.12c, Al.G-014927

NE Livermort, Frank; Head
3387 " Victoria (Wilkie); f; 34; ¼+; m; wife B1646; no; Denver, Denver, Col; no; Id.1018b, Al.G-98
3388 " Myrtle; f; 12; ¼+; s; dau B1647; no; Denver, Denver, Col; no; none
3389 " Lawrence; m; 9 4-3-22; ¼+; s; son B1648; no; Denver, Denver, Col; no; none
3390 " Lorraine; f; 6; ¼+; s; dau B1649; no; Denver, Denver, Col; no; none

3391 Lizotte, Alfred; m; 24 1-3-08; ¼+; m; Head B1652; no; Brockton, Roosevelt, Mont; yes; Id.673c, Al.G-08159
NE " Marie; wife

NE Lizotte, Ernest; m; Head
3392 " Rosina (Morin); f; 35; ¼+; m; wife B1908; no; Dagmar, Sheridan, Mont; yes; Id.750b, Al.G-04840
3393 " Ernest, Jr; m; 3/12 12-21-31; ¼+; s; son -----; no; Dagmar, Sheridan, Mont; yes; none

3394 Lizotte, Joseph; m; 54; ¼+; wd; Head B1650; no; Great Falls, Cascade, Mont; no; Id.673, Al.G-08180
3395 " Michael; m; 26 3-18-06; ¼+; s; son B1651; no; Great Falls, Cascade, Mont; no; Id.673b

Turtle Mountain Reservation
1932 Census Roll

Key: Number; Surname, Given; Sex; Age at Last Birthday, Birthdate (if given); Tribe (Chippewa, unless stated otherwise); Degree of Blood; Marital Status; Relationship to Head of Family, Last Year Census Number; At Jurisdiction Where Enrolled (Yes/No); Elsewhere - Post Office, County, State; Ward (Yes/No); Allotment [Al.], Annuity [An.] and/or Identification [Id.] Numbers

3396 Lizotte(cont), Rose Edna; f; 16 9-17-15; ¼+; s; dau B1653; no; Great Falls, Cascade, Mont; no; Id.673f
Dead " Virginia; B1654 (Died 4-28-21)
3397 " John; m; 10 4-29-21; ¼+; s; son B1655; no; Great Falls, Cascade, Mont; no; Id.673h
Dead " Doris; B1656 (Died in 1927)
Dead " Mary Jean; B1657 (Died in 1928)

3398 Lizotte, Patrick; m; 39; ¼+; s; Head B1658; no; Williston, William, ND; no; Id.674, Al.M-326

3399 Lizotte, Stephen; m; 52; ¼+; m; Head A1441; yes; yes; Id.675, Al.R-218
3400 " Adele (Lefort); f; 48; ¼+; m; wife A1442; yes; no; Id.675a, Al.G-270
3401 " Josephine; f; 26 1-6-06; ¼+; s; dau A1443; yes; yes; Id.675c, Al.G-271
3402 " Elie; m; 21 8-8-10; ¼+; s; son A1444; yes; yes; Id.675d, Al.H-010534
3403 " Michael; m; 20 9-24-11; ¼+; s; son A1445; yes; yes; Id.675e, Al.H-024631
3404 " Oscar; m; 16 11-5-15; ¼+; s; son A1446; yes; yes; Id.675f
3405 " Amy Emma; f; 15 3-7-17; ¼+; s; dau A1447; yes; yes; Id.675g
3406 " Lillian; f; 9 6-17-22; ¼+; s; dau A1448; yes; yes; Id.675h
3407 " George Leo; m; 7 11-8-24; ¼+; s; son A1449; yes; yes; Id.675i

3408 Lockwood, Emily (Rolette); f; 62; ¼+; wd; Head B1659; no; Bismarck, Burleigh, ND; no; Id.676a, Al.RC-21771
3409 " James; m; 30 1-18-02; ¼+; s; son B1661; no; Los Angeles, Los Angeles, Cal; yes; Id.676c, Al.RC-21772
3410 " Reletta; f; 25 7-16-06; ¼+; s; dau B1662; no; Oakland, Alameda; Cal; yes; Id.676d, Al.RC-21770
3411 " Theodore; m; 21 12-31-10; ¼+; s; son B1663; no; Oakland, Alameda; Cal; yes; Id.676e, Al.R-012859

3412 Lockwood, Joseph; m; 33 11-26-98; ¼+; m; Head B1660; no; Washington, DC; yes; Id.676b, Al.RC-21774
NE " Marie; wife

3413 Lone Thunder, Phillip; m; 44; F; m; Head B1664; no; Unknown; no; Id.4, Al.MC-36434
NE " Mamie (Williams); wife
3414 " Four Claws; m; 22; F; s; son B1665; no; Unknown; no; Id.4b

NE Lonick, John; Head
3415 " Lillie (Decoteau); f; 23; 12-17-08; ¼+; m; wife B1666; no; Devils Lake, Ramsey, ND; yes; Id.278g, Al.H-024538
3416 " Lorraine; f; 6 11-1-25; ¼+; s; dau ------; no; Devils Lake, Ramsey, ND; yes; none

Turtle Mountain Reservation
1932 Census Roll

Key: Number; Surname, Given; Sex; Age at Last Birthday, Birthdate (if given); Tribe (Chippewa, unless stated otherwise); Degree of Blood; Marital Status; Relationship to Head of Family, Last Year Census Number; At Jurisdiction Where Enrolled (Yes/No); Elsewhere - Post Office, County, State; Ward (Yes/No); Allotment [Al.], Annuity [An.] and/or Identification [Id.] Numbers

3417 Lonick(cont), John, Jr; m; 4 8-27-27; ¼+; s; son ------; no; Devils Lake, Ramsey, ND; yes; none
3418 " Joseph R; m; 3/12 11-15-31; ¼+; s; son ------; no; Devils Lake, Ramsey, ND; yes; none
3419 Lucier, Alexander; m; 92; ¼+; wd; Head A1450; yes; no; Id.677, Al.R-220

3420 Lucier, Robert; m; 51; ¼+; m; Head A1451; yes; no; Id.678, Al.G-01859
3421 " Mary (Wilkie); f; 41; ¼+; m; wife A1452; yes; no; Id.678a, Al.G-88
3422 " John B; m; 21; ¼+; s; son A1453; yes; no; Id.678b
3423 " Frank; m; 19; ¼+; s; son A1454; yes; yes; Id.678c, Al.H-0246[?]5
3424 " Rosanna; f; 14 12-17-17; ¼+; s; dau A1455; yes; no; Id.678d

NE Lunak, Alfred; Head
3425 " Victoria (Azure); f; 27; ¼+; m; wife B1667; no; Devils Lake, Ramsey, ND; yes; Id.101d, Al.H-010432
3426 " Alfred E; m; 7 1-15-25; ¼+; s; son B1668; no; Devils Lake, Ramsey, ND; yes; none
3427 " Vernon; m; 4 4-28-29; 1/4; s; son ------; no; Devils Lake, Ramsey, ND; yes; none
3428 " Richard; m; 1/12 3-26-32; ¼+; s; son ------; no; Devils Lake, Ramsey, ND; yes; none

3429 Machipeness[sic], Thomas; m; 44; F; m; Head B1669; no; Dunseith, Rolette, ND; yes; Id.19, Al.G370
3430 " Pearl (Little Boy); f; 38; F; m; wife B1670; no; Dunseith, Rolette, ND; yes; Id19a, Al.G036661
3431 " Alice; f; 14; F; s; dau B1671; no; Dunseith, Rolette, ND; yes; none
3432 " Joe; m; 14; F; s; son B1672; no; Dunseith, Rolette, ND; yes; Id.19d
3433 " Alexander; m; 12 5-29-19; F; s; son B1673; no; Dunseith, Rolette, ND; yes; Id.19e
3434 " Rose; f; 10 7-21-21; F; s; dau B1674; no; Dunseith, Rolette, ND; yes; Id.19f
3435 " Elmer; m; 2 7-2-29; F; s; son B1675; no; Dunseith, Rolette, ND; yes; Id.19g

NE Maggs; Head
3436 " Eliza (McDonald); f; 52; ¼+; m; wife B1676; no; Address unknown; no; Id.679a, Al.G038293

3437 Makes It Rain, John; m; 40; F; m; Head B1677; no; Dunseith, Rolette, ND; yes; Id.24, Al.G-01894
3438 " Sunday; f; 35; F; m; wife B1678; no; Dunseith, Rolette, ND; yes; Id.24a, Al.G-01889

Turtle Mountain Reservation
1932 Census Roll

Key: Number; Surname, Given; Sex; Age at Last Birthday, Birthdate (if given); Tribe (Chippewa, unless stated otherwise); Degree of Blood; Marital Status; Relationship to Head of Family, Last Year Census Number; At Jurisdiction Where Enrolled (Yes/No); Elsewhere - Post Office, County, State; Ward (Yes/No); Allotment [Al.], Annuity [An.] and/or Identification [Id.] Numbers

3439 Makes It Rain(cont), George; m; 17 10-10-14; F; s; son B1679; no; Dunseith, Rolette, ND; yes; Id.24b
3440 " Frank; m; 14 5-2-17; F; s; son B1680; no; Dunseith, Rolette, ND; yes; Id.24c
    Peter;   B1681 (Same as Frank)
3441 " James; m; 11 9-29-20; F; s; son B1682; no; Dunseith, Rolette, ND; yes; Id.24d
3442 " Eliza; f; 10 1-6-22; F; s; dau B1683; no; Dunseith, Rolette, ND; yes; Id.24e
3443 " Gladys; f; 6 6-30-25; F; s; dau -----; no; Dunseith, Rolette, ND; yes; Id.24f

3444 Malaterre, Edward; m; 48; ¼+; m; Head A1456; yes; no; Id.683, Al.G-593
3445 " Marie (Davis); f; 43; ¼+; m; wife A1457; yes; no; Id.683a, Al.G-599
3446 " Paul; m; 21; ¼+; s; son A1458; yes; no; Id.683b
3447 " Martin E; m; 18 ¼+; s; son A1459; yes; no; Id.683c
3448 " Louisa; f; 15 1-16-17; ¼+; s; dau A1460; yes; no; Id.683d
3449 " Amy Emma; f; 13 4-8-18; ¼+; s; dau A1461; yes; no; Id.683e
3450 " Ernest; m; 11 10-5-20; ¼+; s; son A1462; yes; no; Id.683f
3451 " John; m; 8 6-16-23; ¼+; s; son A1463; yes; no; Id.683g
3452 " Eli; m; 7; ¼+; s; son A1464; yes; no; Id.683h
3453 " Emil; m; 4; ¼+; s; son A1465; yes; no; Id.683i

3454 Malaterre, John; m; 42; ¼+; wd; Head A1466; yes; no; Id.682, Al.G-594
3455 " Victoria; f; 15 11-19-16; ¼+; s; dau A1467; yes; no; Id.682b
3456 " Melvin; m; 11 6-7-20; ¼+; s; son A1468; yes; no; Id.682c
3457 " Mary; f; 9 2-7-23; ¼+; s; dau A1469; yes; no; Id.682d
3458 " Stella; f; 4 8-23-27; ¼+; s; dau A1470; yes; no; Id.682e

3459 Malaterre, John Louis; m; 35; ¼+; m; Head A1471; yes; no; Id.630b, Al.M-281
3460 " Alice (Henry); f; 20; ¼+; m; wife A1472; yes; yes; Id.473j, Al.H-0224662
3461 " Dorothy; f; 9/12 6-25-31; ¼+; s; dau ------; yes; yes; none

3462 Malaterre, Joseph; m; 50; ¼+; m; Head A1473; yes; no; Id.684, Al.G-477
3463 " Adeline (Wallett); f; 61; ¼+; m; wife A1474; yes; no; Id.684e, Al.M-147
3464 " Cyprian; m; 11 12-3-20; ¼+; s; son A1476; yes; no; Id.684d
3465 " Clifford; m; 9 12-25-22; ¼+; s; son A1477; yes; no; Id.684f

3466 Malaterre, Louis; m; 65; ¼+; m; Head A1478; yes; yes; Id.680, Al.R-233
3467 " Cecile (Gourneau); f; 61; ¼+; m; wife A1479; yes; no; Id.680a, Al.G-0198
3468 " Annie; f; 27; ¼+; s; dau 1480; yes; yes; Id.680f, Al.G-0196
3469 " Clemence; f; 22; ¼+; s; dau A1481; yes; yes; Id.680g
3470 " Eva; f; 17; ¼+; s; dau A1482; yes; yes; Id.680h

Turtle Mountain Reservation
1932 Census Roll

Key: Number; Surname, Given; Sex; Age at Last Birthday, Birthdate (if given); Tribe (Chippewa, unless stated otherwise); Degree of Blood; Marital Status; Relationship to Head of Family, Last Year Census Number; At Jurisdiction Where Enrolled (Yes/No); Elsewhere - Post Office, County, State; Ward (Yes/No); Allotment [Al.], Annuity [An.] and/or Identification [Id.] Numbers

3471 Malaterre, Napoleon; m; 49; ¼+; m; Head A1483; yes; no; Id.685, Al.G-010519
3472 " Justine (Delorme); f; 41; ¼+; m; wife A1484; yes; no; Id.685a, Al.G-127
3473 " Marie; f; 17 11-30-14; ¼+; s; dau A1485; yes; no; Id.685b
3474 " Pierre; m; 16 1-12-16; ¼+; s; son A1486; yes; no; Id.685c
3475 " Leroy; m; 12 11-7-19; ¼+; s; son A1487; yes; no; Id.685d
3476 " Marie S; f; 10 10-23-21; ¼+; s; dau A1488; yes; no; Id.685e
3477 " Blanche; f; 8 12-19-23; ¼+; s; dau A1489; yes; no; Id.685f

3478 Malaterre, Phillip; m; 53; ¼+; m; Head A1490; yes; no; Id.686, Al.R-224
3479 " Elizabeth (Delorme); f; 51; ¼+; m; wife A1491; yes; no; Id.686a, Al.G-07885
3480 " Martin; m; 28 2-15-04; ¼+; s; son A1492; yes; yes; Id.686b, Al.G-07886
3481 " Francois; m; 24 10-12-07; ¼+; s; son A1493; yes; yes; Id.686c, Al.H-012586

3482 Malaterre, Rebecca; f; 75; ¼+; wd; Head A1494; yes; no; Id.687a, Al.G-0298

3483 Malaterre, Riel; m; 34; ¼+; m; Head A1495; yes; yes; Id.681b, Al.G-595
3484 " Margaret (St.Arnaud.Ducept); f; 38; ¼+; m; wife A1496; yes; no; Id.361a, Al.M-214
3485 " (Ducept) Marguerite; f; 17 9-6-16; ¼+; s; step dau A1497; yes; yes; Id.361c
3486 " (Ducept) Alphonse; m; 12 2-22-20; ¼+; s; stepson A1498; yes; yes; Id.361d
3487 " (Ducept) Joseph; m; 10 9-23-22; ¼+; s; stepson A1499; yes; yes; Id.361d
3488 " Fred; m; 6 1-11-26; ¼+; s; son A1500; yes; yes; none
3489 " Irene; f; 5 2-6-27; ¼+; s; dau A1501; yes; yes; none
3490 " Mary L; f; 2 7-21-29; ¼+; s; dau A1502; yes; yes; none
3491 " Vernon; m; 5/12 10-3-31; ¼+; s; son ------; yes; yes; none

3492 Man of the Sky, Howard; m; 33; F; m; Head B1684; no; Dunseith, Rolette, ND; yes; Id.10b, Al.G-378
NE " Dora (Pring); wife
3493 " Louisa; f; 12; ¼+; s; dau B1685; no; Dunseith, Rolette, ND; yes; none

NE Manson, Danis; Head
3494 " Marie (Dejarlais); f; 32; ¼+; m; wife B1686; no; Rolla, Rolette, ND; no; Id.310b, Al.M-19
3495 " Spiro; m; 13; ¼+; s; son B1687; no; Rolla, Rolette, ND; no; none
3496 " Edward; m; 12 1-4-20; ¼+; s; son B1688; no; Rolla, Rolette, ND; no; none
3497 " Georgiana; f; 10 2-21-22; ¼+; s; dau B1689; no; Rolla, Rolette, ND; no; none
3498 " John; m; 7 6-18-24; ¼+; s; son B1690; no; Rolla, Rolette, ND; no; none
3499 " James; m; 5 8-9-26; ¼+; s; son ------; no; Rolla, Rolette, ND; no; none
3500 " William; m; 3 10-24-28; ¼+; s; son -----; no; Rolla, Rolette, ND; no; none

NE Manson, Spero; Head
3501 " Florestine (Martin); f; 34; ¼+; m; wife B1691; no; Antler, Bottineau, ND; yes; Id.712b, Al.M-12

Turtle Mountain Reservation
1932 Census Roll

Key: Number; Surname, Given; Sex; Age at Last Birthday, Birthdate (if given); Tribe (Chippewa, unless stated otherwise); Degree of Blood; Marital Status; Relationship to Head of Family, Last Year Census Number; At Jurisdiction Where Enrolled (Yes/No); Elsewhere - Post Office, County, State; Ward (Yes/No); Allotment [Al.], Annuity [An.] and/or Identification [Id.] Numbers

3502 Manson(cont), George; m; 14 3-21-18; ¼+; s; son B1692; no; Antler, Bottineau, ND; yes; none
3503 " Frank; m; 14 3-21-18; ¼+; s; son B1692; no; Antler, Bottineau, ND; yes; none
3504 " John; m; 12 6-27-19; ¼+; s; son B1694; no; Antler, Bottineau, ND; yes; none
3405 " Peter; m; 10 6-23-21; ¼+; s; son B1695; no; Antler, Bottineau, ND; yes; none
3406 " Spero, Jr; m; 8 2-1-24; ¼+; s; son ------; no; Antler, Bottineau, ND; yes; none
3507 " Grace; f; 5 6-9-26; ¼+; s; dau -----; no; Antler, Bottineau, ND; yes; none
3508 " Theresa; f; 4 6-17-27; ¼+; ; dau -----; no; Antler, Bottineau, ND; yes; none
3509 " Mary; f; 2 10-29-29; ¼+; s; dau -----; no; Antler, Bottineau, ND; yes; none

3510 Marcellais, Peter P; m; 27; ¼+; m; Head A1503; yes; yes; Id.689b, Al.G-353
3511 " Angelique (Frederick); f; 28; ¼+; m; wife A1504; yes; yes; Id.398d, Al.M-323
3512 " Joseph; m; 7 12-17-24; ¼+; s; son A1505; yes; yes; none
3513 " Charles; m; 6 2-20-26; ¼+; s; son A1506; yes; yes; none
3514 " Clarence; m; 3 8-1-28; ¼+; s; son A1507; yes; yes; none
3515 " Peter; m; 2 7-12-29; ¼+; s; son A1508; yes; yes; none
3516 " Dolores; f; 5/12 9-5-31; ¼+; s; dau ----; yes; yes; none

NE Marcil, Charles; Head
3517 " Elgina; f; 34; ¼+; m; wife A1510; no; Fonda, Rolette, ND; no; Id.732a, Al.GF-110
3518 " Alexander; m; 14 4-9-17; ¼+; s; son A1511; no; Fonda, Rolette, ND; no; Id.732c
3519 " Alfred; m; 13 3-23-19; ¼+; s; son A1512; no; Fonda, Rolette, ND; no; Id.732c
3520 " Alcide; m; 10 1-30-22; ¼+; s; son A1513; no; Fonda, Rolette, ND; no; Id.732c
3521 " Lillian M; f; 7 8-2-24; ¼+; s; dau A1514; no; Fonda, Rolette, ND; no; Id.732c
3522 " Antoine; m; 3 12-17-28; ¼+; s; son A1515; no; Fonda, Rolette, ND; no; Id.732c

3523 Marion, Albert Ed; m; 27; ¼+; m; Head B1696; no; Grenora, Williams, ND; yes; Id.693d, Al.M-160
3524 " Victoria (Gladue); f; 22; ¼+; m; wife B1697; no; Grenora, Williams, ND; yes; Id.410d, Al.G-016084
3525 " Donald E; m; 1 10-25-30; ¼+; s; son B1698; no; Grenora, Williams, ND; yes; none

3526 Marion, Elie J; m; 50; ¼+; m; Head A1516; yes; no; Id.699, Al.GF-236
3527 " Louise (Azure); f; 43; ¼+; m; wife A1517; yes; no; Id.699a, Al.GF-16

Turtle Mountain Reservation
1932 Census Roll

Key: Number; Surname, Given; Sex; Age at Last Birthday, Birthdate (if given); Tribe (Chippewa, unless stated otherwise); Degree of Blood; Marital Status; Relationship to Head of Family, Last Year Census Number; At Jurisdiction Where Enrolled (Yes/No); Elsewhere - Post Office, County, State; Ward (Yes/No); Allotment [Al.], Annuity [An.] and/or Identification [Id.] Numbers

3528 Marion(cont), Elise; f; 16 7-6-15; ¼+; s; dau A1519; yes; no; Id.699e
3529 " Francis; m; 14 11-11-17; ¼+; s; son A1520; yes; no; Id.699f
3530 " Marie; f; 12 2-23-20; ¼+; s; dau A1521; yes; no; Id.699g
3531 " Maxim; m; 9 11-19-22; ¼+; s; son A1522; yes; no; Id.699h
3532 " Irene; f; 7 3-26-25; ¼+; s; dau -----; yes; no; Id.699i

3533 Marion, Elise; m[sic]; 89; ¼+; wd; Head A1523; yes; yes; Id.698a, Al.G-05578

3534 Marion, Herman; m; 23; ¼+; m; Head A1524; yes; yes; Id.692b, Al.H-030393
3535 " Georgiana; f; 24; ¼+; m; wife A1525; yes; yes; Id.924e, Al.G-012931
3536 " Narcissa; f; 1 6-21-30; ¼+; s; dau A1526; yes; yes; none
3537 " Reginald; m; 3/12 1-2-32; ¼+; s; son -----; yes; yes; none

3538 Marion, John B; m; 40 5-16-91; ¼+; m; Head ----; no; (Left out last year, error)
 Dagmar, Sheridan, Mont; no; Id.696, Al.M-158
NE " Muriel (Sheffert); wife
3539 " Joyce; f; 5 7-3-26; ¼+; s; dau ------; no; Dagmar, Sheridan, Mont; no; none
3540 " Shirley; f; 1 7-9-30; ¼+; s; dau -----; no; Dagmar, Sheridan, Mont; no; none

3541 Marion, Joseph; m; 70; ¼+; m; Head B1699; no; Grenora, Williams, ND; no;
 Id.693, Al.M-192
3542 " Justine (Grant); f; 67; ¼+; m; wife B1700; no; Grenora, Williams, ND; no;
 Id.693a, Al.DL-1

3543 Marion, Julius; m; 35; 4-7-96; ¼+; m; Head B1704; no; Medford, Jackson, Ore;
 no; Id.694, Al.M-159
3544 " Mary Jane (Grandbois); f; 34; ¼+; m; wife B1705; no; Medford, Jackson,
 Ore; no; Id.437b, Al.M-81

3545 Marion, Louis; m; 62; ¼+; m; Head A1527; yes; no; Id.692, Al.R-227
NE " Philomeme (Demontigny); wife
3546 " Norman; m; 20 4-23-11; ¼+; s; son A1528; yes; yes; Id.692c, Al.H-030394
3547 " St.Ann; f; 18 8-23-13; ¼+; s; dau A1529; yes; no; Id.692d
3548 " Raymond; m; 12 8-6-19; ¼+; s; son A1530; yes; no; Id.692c
3549 " Bernadette; f; 10 11-7-21; ¼+; s; dau A1531; yes; no; Id.692d[sic]
3550 " Beatrice; f; 5 9-5-26; ¼+; s; dau A1533; yes; no; Id.692g
DEAD " Martha; A1532 (Died in 1925)

3551 Marion, Maxim; m; 68; ¼+; m; Head A1534; yes; yes; Id.691, Al.R-229
NE " Virginia (Morin); wife

NE Marion, Norman; Head
3552 " Helen (Marion); f; 12-16-98; ¼+; m; wife B1701; no; Central Point,
 Jackson, Ore; no; Id.692b

Turtle Mountain Reservation
1932 Census Roll

Key: Number; Surname, Given; Sex; Age at Last Birthday, Birthdate (if given); Tribe (Chippewa, unless stated otherwise); Degree of Blood; Marital Status; Relationship to Head of Family, Last Year Census Number; At Jurisdiction Where Enrolled (Yes/No); Elsewhere - Post Office, County, State; Ward (Yes/No); Allotment [Al.], Annuity [An.] and/or Identification [Id.] Numbers

3553 Marion(cont), Norma Lee; f; 7 10-9-24; ¼+; m; dau -----; no; Central Point, Jackson, Ore; no; none

3554 Marion, Phillip; m; 29 12-29-02; ¼+; m; Head B1702; no; Trenton, Williams, ND; no; Id.693b
NE " Margaret (Kent); wife
3555 " Marjorie; f; 7 3-16-25; ¼+; s; dau ------; no; Trenton, Williams, ND; no; none
3556 " Phillip; m; 4 4-10-27; ¼+; s; son ------; no; Trenton, Williams, ND; no; none
3557 " Charles; m; 3 5-11-28; ¼+; s; son ------; no; Trenton, Williams, ND; no; none
3558 " George; m; 2 7-6-29; ¼+; s; son -----; no; Trenton, Williams, ND; no; none

3559 Marion, Roderick; m; 60; ¼+; m; Head B1706; no; Great Falls, Cascade, Mont; yes; Id.700, Al.GF-235
NE " Mamie B (Pigg)
3560 " Allene B; f; 24; ¼+; s; dau B1707; no; Great Falls, Cascade, Mont; yes; Id.700b, Al.H-012593
3561 " Merrill; m; 23; ¼+; s; son B1708; no; Great Falls, Cascade, Mont; yes; Id.700c, Al.H-012594

3562 Marion, Roger; m; 44; ¼+; m; Head B1709; no; Zahl, Williams, ND; no; Id.697, Al.M-156
NE " Annie (Wolgast); wife
3563 " George; m; 17 3-26-14; ¼+; s; son B1710; no; Zahl, Williams, ND; no; none
3564 " Rosalie; f; 15 11-21-16; ¼+; s; dau -----; no; Zahl, Williams, ND; no; none
3565 " Melvin; m; 9 9-14-22; ¼+; s; son -----; no; Zahl, Williams, ND; no; none
3566 " Arline; f; 7 9-16-24; ¼+; s; dau -----; no; Zahl, Williams, ND; no; none
3567 " Christine; f; 6 5-3-25; ¼+; s; dau ------; no; Zahl, Williams, ND; no; none

3568 Martell, Charles; m; 41; ¼+; m; Head B1711; no; Medicine Lake, Sheridan, Mont; no; Id.711, Al.GF-39
NE " Sophia (Lambert); wife
3569 " Arthur; m; 19; ¼+; s; son B1712; no; Medicine Lake, Sheridan, Mont; no; Id.711b

3570 Martell, Eli Jerome; m; 50; ¼+; m; Head B1713; no; Medicine Lake, Sheridan, Mont; no; Id.705, Al.GF-241
NE " Elizabeth (Scott); wife

3571 Martell, Francis; m; 47 5-30-84; ¼+; m; Head A1535; yes; No; Id.707, Al.G-07807
3572 " Rosalie (Lizotte); f; 42 5-3-89; ¼+; m; wife A1536; yes; no; Id.707a, Al.M-32
3573 " Joseph; m; 22 11-22-09; ¼+; s; son A1537; yes; no; Id.707c

Turtle Mountain Reservation
1932 Census Roll

Key: Number; Surname, Given; Sex; Age at Last Birthday, Birthdate (if given); Tribe (Chippewa, unless stated otherwise); Degree of Blood; Marital Status; Relationship to Head of Family, Last Year Census Number; At Jurisdiction Where Enrolled (Yes/No); Elsewhere - Post Office, County, State; Ward (Yes/No); Allotment [Al.], Annuity [An.] and/or Identification [Id.] Numbers

3574 Martell(cont), Fred; m; 21 4-7-10; ¼+; s; son A1538; yes; no; Id.707d
3575 " Eliza; f; 20 1-12-12; ¼+; s; dau A1539; yes; yes; Id.707e, Al.H-030388
3576 " George; 17 7-10-14; ¼+; s; son A1540; yes; no; Id.707f
3577 " Mary L; f; 16 2-23-16; ¼+; s; dau A1541; yes; no; Id.707g
3578 " Gregory; m; 11 8-8-20; ¼+; s; son A1542; yes; no; none
3579 " Dora; f; 9 10-15-22; ¼+; s; dau A1543; yes; no; none
3580 " Ernest; m; 7 9-13-24; ¼+; s; son A1544; yes; no; none
3581 " Norman; m; 5 6-2-27; ¼+; s; son A1545; yes; no; none
3582 " Collin; m; 2 4-2-29; ¼+; s; son A1546; yes; no; none
3583 " Evelyn; f; 5-12 10-13-31; ¼+; s; dau ------; yes; no; none

3584 Martell, Hormidas; m; 42; ¼+; m; Head B1714; no; Havre, Hill, Mont; no; Id.702, Al.H012591
NE " Mary; wife
3585 " Mary Marg; f; 10 8-12-21; ¼+; s; dau B1715; no; Havre, Hill, Mont; no; none
3586 " Peter; m; 7 4-18-24; ¼+; s; son B1716; no; Havre, Hill, Mont; no; none
3587 " Jess; m; 4 6-18-27; ¼+; s; son -----; no; Havre, Hill, Mont; no; none
3588 " Mary Louise; f; 1 3-16-31; ¼+; s; dau ------; no; Havre, Hill, Mont; no; none

3589 Martell, John B; m; 24 5-10-07; ¼+; m; Head A1547; yes; yes; Id.707b, Al.G-07808
3590 " Mary Celina (Langer); f; 20; ¼+; m; wife A1548; yes; yes; Id.608f
3591 " Roland L; m; 8 12 7-18-31; ¼+; s; son ------; yes; yes; none

3592 Martell, Joseph; m; 63; ¼+; wd; Head B1717; no; Medicine Lake, Sheridan, Mont; no; Id.706
3593 " Alfred; m; 36; ¼+; s; son B1718; no; Medicine Lake, Sheridan, Mont; Id.708, Al.M-2

2594 Martell, Marie Rose; f; 66; ¼+; wd; Head B1719; no; Fort Peck; no; Id.709a, Al.GF-37

2595 Martell, Madeline; f; 76; ¼+; wd; Head B1720; no; Beulah, Mercer, ND; no; Id.701a, Al.H-012592

2596 Martell, Maxim; m; 47; ¼+; m; Head B1721; no; Beulah, Mercer, ND; no; Id.703, Al.H-012592[sic]
NE " Agnes (McLaughlin); wife
3597 " Carroll; m; 20; ¼+; s; son B1722; no; Beulah, Mercer, ND; yes; Al.H-024639
3598 " Lucille; f; 16 4-15-15; ¼+; s; dau B1724; no; Beulah, Mercer, ND; no; Id.703d
3599 " Dorothy; f; 15 1-7-17; ¼+; s; dau B1725; no; Beulah, Mercer, ND; no; Id.703e
3600 " Leo; m; 13 7-17-18; ¼+; s; son B1726; no; Beulah, Mercer, ND; no; Id.703f
3601 " Maxim; m; 12 11-9-19; ¼+; s; son B1727; no; Beulah, Mercer, ND; no; Id.703g

Turtle Mountain Reservation
1932 Census Roll

Key: Number; Surname, Given; Sex; Age at Last Birthday, Birthdate (if given); Tribe (Chippewa, unless stated otherwise); Degree of Blood; Marital Status; Relationship to Head of Family, Last Year Census Number; At Jurisdiction Where Enrolled (Yes/No); Elsewhere - Post Office, County, State; Ward (Yes/No); Allotment [Al.], Annuity [An.] and/or Identification [Id.] Numbers

3602 Martell, Michael; m; 36; ¼+; m; Head B1728; no; Poplar, Roosevelt, Mont; no; Id.710, Al.GF-45
NE " Laura (Lambert); wife
3603 " Alda; f; 14 2-17-18; ¼+; s; dau B1729; no; Poplar, Roosevelt, Mont; no; Id.710b
3604 " Patrick; m; 11 6-23-20; ¼+; s; son B1730; no; Poplar, Roosevelt, Mont; no; Id.710c
3605 " Rosina; f; 9 8-13-22; ¼+; s; dau B1731; no; Poplar, Roosevelt, Mont no; Id.710d
3606 " Clarence; m; 7 7-14-24; ¼+; s; son B1732; no; Poplar, Roosevelt, Mont, no; Id.710e
3607 " Della; f; 5 3-18-27; ¼+; s; dau B1733; no; Poplar, Roosevelt, Mont; no; Id.710f

3608 Martell, Thomas; m; 29; ¼+; m; Head B1734; no; Poplar, Roosevelt, Mont; no; Id.709c, Al.GF-43
3609 " Anna (Grandbois); f; 28; ¼+; m; wife B1735; no; Poplar, Roosevelt, Mont; yes; Id.442d, Al.G-442
3610 " Thomas; m; 7 3-4-25; ¼+; s; son B1736; no; Poplar, Roosevelt, Mont; yes; none
3611 " Charles; m; 5 9-17-26; ¼+; s; son B1737; no; Poplar, Roosevelt, Mont; yes none
3612 " John; m; 3 10-4-28; ¼+; s; son -----; no; Poplar, Roosevelt, Mont; yes; none

NE Martin, Alex; Head
3613 " Mary Rosina (Gladue); f; 24; ¼+; m; wife B1738; no; Trenton, Williams, ND; yes; Id.410, Al.G-07093
3614 " Mary Rose; f; 2 10-3-29; ¼+; s; dau B1739; no; Trenton, Williams, ND; yes; none

3615 Martin, Alexander; m; 31; ¼+; m; Head A1549; yes; yes; Id.714b, Al.G-576
NE " Minnie (Halliday); wife
3616 " Winifred; f; 7 1-7-25; ¼+; s; dau A1550; yes; yes; none
3617 " Gladys; f; 5 11-18-26; ¼+; s; dau A1551; yes; yes; none
3618 " Rose Anna; f; 2 11-19-29; ¼+; s; dau A1552; yes; yes; none

NE Martin, John; Head
3619 " Mary Jane (Premeau); f; 22; ¼+; m; wife B1740; no; Cando, Towner, ND; no; Id.881e
3620 " Shirley Mae; f; 1 9-1-30; ¼+; s; dau B1741; no; Cando, Towner, ND; no; none

Turtle Mountain Reservation
1932 Census Roll

Key: Number; Surname, Given; Sex; Age at Last Birthday, Birthdate (if given); Tribe (Chippewa, unless stated otherwise); Degree of Blood; Marital Status; Relationship to Head of Family, Last Year Census Number; At Jurisdiction Where Enrolled (Yes/No); Elsewhere - Post Office, County, State; Ward (Yes/No); Allotment [Al.], Annuity [An.] and/or Identification [Id.] Numbers

3621 Martin, Joseph; m; 63; ¼+; m; Head A1553; yes; no; Id.712, Al.W-10
3622   "   Mary; f; 59; ¼+; m; wife A1554; yes; (No maiden name given on roll book) no; Id.712a, Al.W-8
3623   "   Henry; n; 25; ¼+; s; son A1555; yes; yes; Id.712c, Al.W-03249

3624 Martin, Mary (Wilkie); f; 50; ¼+; wd; Head A1556; yes; yes; Id.714a, Al.R-232
3625   "   Elise; f; 25; ¼+; s; dau A1557; yes; yes; Id.714d, Al.G-577
3626   "   Delima; f; 22; ¼+; s; dau A1558; yes; yes; Id.714e
3637   "   Edna; f; 18; ¼+; s; dau A1561; yes; yes; Id.714f
3628   "   Florence; f; 16 2-27-16; ¼+; s; dau A1560; yes; yes; Id.714h
3629   "   Alice; f; 14; ¼+; s; dau A1561; yes; yes; Id.714g

NE Martin, Moses;   Head
3630   "   Virginia (Bercier); f; 33; ¼+; m; wife A1562; no; Devils Lake, Ramsey, ND; yes; Id.1169c, Al.M-58
3631   "   Laverne J; m; 9 7-14-22; ¼+; s; son A1563; no; (Error in stating a dau. on last census) Devils Lake, Ramsey, ND; yes; none
3632   "   Irene Agnes; f; 7 8-20-24; ¼+; s; dau A1564; no; Devils Lake, Ramsey, ND; yes; none
3633   "   Walter P; m; 5 12-12-26; ¼+; s; son A1565; no; Devils Lake, Ramsey, ND; yes; none
3634   "   Louis Moses; m; 3 6-17-28; ¼+; s; son ------; no; Devils Lake, Ramsey, ND; yes; none
3635   "   Alice Regina; f; 1 11-6-30; ¼+; s; dau ------; no; Devils Lake, Ramsey, ND; yes; none

3191 Martin, Patrice; m; 41; ¼+; m; Head A1566; yes; no; Id.713, Al.W-11
3636   "   Josephine; f; 41; ¼+; m; wife A1567; yes; no; Id.713a, Al.GF-7
3637   "   Edward; m; 16 10-8-15; ¼+; s; son A1568; yes; no; Id.713b
3638   "   Roy; m; 14 9-9-17; ¼+; s; son A1569; yes; no; Id.713c
3639   "   Lloyd; m; 12 7-22-19; ¼+; s; son A1570; yes; no; Id.713d
3640   "   Peter; m; 8 12-29-23; ¼+; s; son A1571; yes; no; Id.713f
3641   "   George; m; 5 5-9-26; ¼+; s; son A1572; yes; no; Id.713g

3642 Mason, Joseph; m; 40; ¼+; s; Head B1742; no; Minnewauken[sic], Benson, ND; no; Id.715, Al.MC-45

NE Mathias, Clifford;   Head
3643   "   Mary St.Ann (Baston); f; 29; ¼+; m; wife B1743; no; Bainville, Sheridan, Mont; yes; Id.149c, Al.W-09734
3644   "   George C; m; 6 1-14-25; ¼+; s; son -----; no; Bainville, Sheridan, Mont; yes; none
3645   "   Gerald N; m; 3 8-4-28; ¼+; s; son ------; no; Bainville, Sheridan, Mont; yes; none

Turtle Mountain Reservation
1932 Census Roll

Key: Number; Surname, Given; Sex; Age at Last Birthday, Birthdate (if given); Tribe (Chippewa, unless stated otherwise); Degree of Blood; Marital Status; Relationship to Head of Family, Last Year Census Number; At Jurisdiction Where Enrolled (Yes/No); Elsewhere - Post Office, County, State; Ward (Yes/No); Allotment [Al.], Annuity [An.] and/or Identification [Id.] Numbers

3646 Mathias(cont), James R; m; 2 11-25-29; ¼+; s; son B1744; no; Bainville, Sheridan, Mont; yes; none

3647 McCloud, Charles; m; 30; ¼+; m; Head A1573; yes; yes; Id.719d, Al.GF-147
3648 " Mary (Jeannotte); f; 24; ¼+; m; wife A1574; yes; yes; Id.507c, Al.G-07837
3649 " Charles; m; 3 2-1-29; ¼+; s; son A1575; yes; yes; none
3650 " Therese[sic]; f; 1 6-3-30; ¼+; s; dau A1576; yes; yes; none

3651 McCloud, Ezear Martin; m; 31; ¼+; m; Head A1577; yes; yes; Id.719c, Al.G-043
3652 " Flora (Bruce); f; 22; ¼+; m; wife A1578; yes; yes; Id.209g, Al.H-012508

3653 McCloud, Louis; m; 42; ¼+; s; Head A1580; yes; no; Id.720, Al.G-011

3654 McCloud, Margaret (Lafournais); f; 71; ¼+; wd; Head A1581; yes; yes; Id.716a, Al.R-233
3655 " Joseph; m; 39; ¼+; s; son B1746; yes; no; Id.718, Al.GF-87
3656 " St.Fidella; m; 35; ¼+; s; son A1582; yes; no; Id.716b, Al.GF-85

3657 McCloud, Margaret (Morin.Enno); f; 77; ¼+; wd; Head ----; yes; (Left off of last census, error) no; Id.721a, Al.R-247

3658 McCloud, Marie (Vallie); f; 65; ¼+; wd; Head B-1579; yes; no; Id.719a, Al.G-05

3659 McCloud, Mary; f; 46; ¼+; wd; Head B1747; no; Bottineau, Bottineau, ND; no; Id.722a, Al.H-031152
3660 " Alex; m; 22 4-15-09; ¼+; s; son B1749; no; Bottineau, Bottineau, ND; no; Id.722c
3661 " Norman; m; 21 2-9-11; ¼+; s; son B1750; yes; Bottineau, Bottineau, ND; no; Id.722d, Al.H-012580
3662 " Ernestine; f; 18 9-11-13; ¼+; s; dau B1751; no; Bottineau, Bottineau, ND; no; Id.722e
3663 " Paul; m; 16 2-12-16; ¼+; s; son B1752; no; Bottineau, Bottineau, ND; no; Id.722f
3664 " Patty; f; 13 1-8-19; ¼+; s; dau B1753; no; Bottineau, Bottineau, ND; no; Id.722g

Dead McCoy, Josphine[sic];   B1754   (Died 4-12-31)

3665 McGillis, Fred; m; 42; ¼+; s; Head B1755; no; St.John, Rolette, ND; no; Id.727, Al.H-013039

3666 McGillis, John; m; 45; ¼+; m; Head B1756; no; St.John, Rolette, ND; no; Id.725, Al.H-024642
NE   " Louise (Slater); wife

Turtle Mountain Reservation
1932 Census Roll

Key: Number; Surname, Given; Sex; Age at Last Birthday, Birthdate (if given); Tribe (Chippewa, unless stated otherwise); Degree of Blood; Marital Status; Relationship to Head of Family, Last Year Census Number; At Jurisdiction Where Enrolled (Yes/No); Elsewhere - Post Office, County, State; Ward (Yes/No); Allotment [Al.], Annuity [An.] and/or Identification [Id.] Numbers

3667 McGillis(cont), Frank; m; 8 5-14-23; ¼+; s; son B1757; no; St.John, Rolette, ND; no; none

NE   McGillis, Peter;   Head
3668   "   Mary Rose (Davis); f; 48; ¼+; m; wife B1758; no; Russell, Manitoba, Canada; no; Id.723a, Al.H-013040
3669   "   Robert; m; 22 6-29-09; ¼+; s; son B1760; no; Russell, Manitoba, Canada; no; Id.,723e

3670 McGillis, Solomon; m; 44; ¼+; s; Head B1762; no; St.John, Rolette, ND; no; Id.728, Al.H-013037

3671 McGillis, Starr; m; 81; ¼+; m; Head B1761; no; St.John, Rolette, ND; no; Id.726, Al.I.H.E.
NE   "   Eliza (Baston);   wife

3672 McGillis, William E; m; 28; ¼+; m; Head B1759; no; Russell, Manitoba, Canada; yes; Id.723c, Al.H-013042
NE   "   Flora (McKenzie);   wife
3673   "   Annie; f; 3 7-26-28; ¼+; s; dau ------; no; East Bay, Manitoba, Canada; yes; none

NE   McGillis, William;   Head
3674   "   Justine (Richard); f; 51; ¼+; m; wife B1763; no; St.John, Rolette, ND; yes; Id.724a, Al.H-010440
3675   "   Rose; f; 24; ¼+; s; dau B1764; no; St.John, Rolette, ND; yes; Id.724c, Al.H-010439
3676   "   Mary Louise; f; 23; ¼+; s; dau B1765; no; St.John, Rolette, ND; yes; Id.724d, Al.H-010437
3677   "   M Eleanor; f; 19; ¼+; s; dau B1766; no; St.John, Rolette, ND; no; Id.724e
3678   "   John; m; 15 10-1-16; ¼+; s; son B1767; no; St.John, Rolette, ND; no; Id.724g
3679   "   Joseph; m; 12; ¼+; s; son B1768; no; St.John, Rolette, ND; no; Id.724i
3680   "   Elizabeth; f; 11; ¼+; s; dau B1769; no; St.John, Rolette, ND; no; Id.724j
3681   "   Phyllis; f; 4 3-3-28; ¼+; s; grand dau B1770; no; (Dau. of Rose) St.John, Rolette, ND; no; Id.724k
3682   "   Marion; f; 1 3-12-31; ¼+; s; grand dau ----; no; (Dau. of Eleanor) St.John, Rolette, ND; no; none

NE   McKay, Joseph;   Head
3683   "   Adele (Morin); f; 57; ¼+; m; wife B1771; no; Unknown; no; Id.729, Al.R-236

3684 McKay, Joseph F; m; 34; ¼+; m; Head B1772; no; Unknown; no; Id.729b, Al.G-104
3685   "   Elvina (Dumont); f; 28; ¼+; m; wife B1773; no; Unknown; yes; Id.367e, Al.G-437

Turtle Mountain Reservation
1932 Census Roll

Key: Number; Surname, Given; Sex; Age at Last Birthday, Birthdate (if given); Tribe (Chippewa, unless stated otherwise); Degree of Blood; Marital Status; Relationship to Head of Family, Last Year Census Number; At Jurisdiction Where Enrolled (Yes/No); Elsewhere - Post Office, County, State; Ward (Yes/No); Allotment [Al.], Annuity [An.] and/or Identification [Id.] Numbers

NE	McLester, Richard;	Head
3686	"	Clemence (Paul); f;42; ¼+; m; wife B1774; no; Cando, Towner, ND; yes; Id.731e, Al.G-037059
3687	"	Malcolm; m; 17 6-8-14; ¼+; s; son B1775; no; Cando, Towner, ND; yes; Id.731b
3688	"	Richard; m; 2 11-27-29; ¼+; s; son -----; no; Cando, Towner, ND; yes; none
NE	McVay, Raymond;	Head
3689	"	Elvina (Brunnell); f; 23; ¼+; m; wife A1583; yes; yes; Id.215c, Al.H-10450
3690	"	Raymond R; m; 2 1-28-30; ¼+; s; son A1584; yes; yes; none
3691	"	Betty Jane; f; 1/12 2-1-32; ¼+; s; dau -----; yes; yes; none
NE	Meccas, Alex;	Head
3692	"	Pauline; f; 38; F; m; wife B1745; no; yes; Id.22a, Al.G-328
3693	Mekwam, Frank; m; 52; F; wd; Head A1585; yes; yes; Id.5, Al.R-4	
3694	"	Mary; f; 20 9-15-11; F; s; dau A1586; yes; yes; Id.5b, Al.H-024468
3695	"	Delia; f; 14 10-28-17; F; s; dau A1587; yes; yes; Id.5d
3696	Mekwam, John; f[sic]; 44; F; m; Head A1588; yes; yes; Id.40, Al.H-037747	
3697	"	Nancy; f; 35; F; m; wife A1589; yes; yes; Id.40a, Al.G-333
3698	"	Peter; m; 18 6-1-13; F; s; son A1590; yes; yes; Id.40b, Al.H-024465
3699	"	Fred Frank; m; 16 6-27-15; F; s; son A1591; yes; yes; Id.40c
3700	"	Clemence; f; 13 11-28-18; F; s; dau A1592; yes; yes; Id.40d
3701	"	Marie; f; 11 2-14-21; F; s; dau B1593; yes; yes; Id.40e
3702	"	Johnson; m; 9 8-13-22; F; s; son B1594; yes; yes; Id.40f
3703	"	Mary; f; 7 11-5-24; F; s; dau B1595; yes; yes; Id.40g
3704	"	Agnes Rose; f; 5 6-15-27; F; s; dau B1596; yes; yes; Id.40h
3705	"	Irene; f; 2 7-15-29; F; s; dau B1597; yes; yes; Id.40i
3706	"	Lucy; f; 4/12 10-12-31; F; s; dau -----; yes; yes; Id.40j
3707	Mekwam, Joseph; m; 49; F; m; Head A1598; yes; yes; Id.31, Al.G334	
3708	"	Maggie (Standing Across); f; 48; F; wife A1599; yes; yes; Id.31e, Al.G-11737
3709	"	Charles; m; 25 3-6-07; F; s; son A1500; yes; yes; Id.31b, Al.H031157
Dead	"	Francis; son A1501 (Died in 1922)
3710	"	George; m; 3 6-28-28; F; s; son A1502; yes; yes; Id.31f
Dead	"	Louise; A1503 (Died 5-15-28)
3711	"	Christopher; m; 1 12-25-30; F; s; son ------; yes; yes; none
NE	Melville, Edward;	Head A626
3712	"	Rhoda (Cannery); f; 19; ¼+; m; wife B503; no; (counted twice last year) Bannerman, Manitoba, Can; no; Id.221b

Turtle Mountain Reservation
1932 Census Roll

Key: Number; Surname, Given; Sex; Age at Last Birthday, Birthdate (if given); Tribe (Chippewa, unless stated otherwise); Degree of Blood; Marital Status; Relationship to Head of Family, Last Year Census Number; At Jurisdiction Where Enrolled (Yes/No); Elsewhere - Post Office, County, State; Ward (Yes/No); Allotment [Al.], Annuity [An.] and/or Identification [Id.] Numbers

NE Matzenberg, Chris;   Head
3713   "   Rosina (Lafrombois); f; 35; ¼+; m; wife B1372; no; Vancouver, Clark, Wash; no; Id.592a, Al.G-08110
3714   "   Constance; f; 9 4-9-22; ¼+; s; dau ------; no; Vancouver, Clark, Wash no; none
3715   "   Louise; f; 5 5-9-26; ¼+; s; dau ------; no; Vancouver, Clark, Wash; no; none

NE Michaels, Roy;   Head
3716   "   Ernestine (Hays.Patnaud); f; 32; ¼+; m; wife B1988; no; Devils Lake, Ramsey, ND; no; Id.805a, Al.GF-150

NE Milligan, Russell;   Head
3717   "   Ernestine (Wilkie); f; 26; ¼+; m; wife B1776; no; Plentywood, Sheridan, Mont; yes; Id.1018d, Al.G-08377

NE Minne, Harry;   Head
3718   "   Rosalie (Gladue); f; 30; ¼+; m; wife B1777; no; Mt.Side, Manitoba, Canada; yes; Id.408b, Al.G-532
3719   "   Edmond; m; 7 11-2-24; ¼+; s; son -------; no; Mt.Side, Manitoba, Canada; yes; none
3720   "   Emily; f; 6 3-27-25; ¼+; s; dau -----; no; Mt.Side, Manitoba, Canada; yes; none
3721   "   Dora; f; 9/12 6-6-31; ¼+; s; dau -----; no; Mt.Side, Manitoba, Canada; yes; none

3722 Mirage; m; 73; F; m; Head A1604; yes; yes; Id.18, Al.R-170
3723   "   Cloud Woman; f; 86; F; m; wife A1605; yes; yes; Id.18a, Al.G-01902

NE Mitchell, Harry;   Head
3724   "   Nancy (Delorme); f; 36; ¼+; m; wife A673; no; Minot, Ward, ND; no; Id.329, Al.MC-026786

3725 Monette, John; m; 52; ¼+; s; Head B1780; yes; no; Id.733, Al.W-0813

NE Monette, Joseph;   Head
3726   "   Caroline (Gladue); f; 40; ¼+; m; wife A1606; yes; yes; Id.734a, Al.H-041096
3727   "   George; m; 17 5-29-14; ¼+; s; son A1607; yes; yes; Id.734b
3728   "   Frank; m; 16 3-21-16; ¼+; s; son A1608; yes; yes; Id.734c
3729   "   Fred; m; 13 9-14-18; ¼+; s; son A1609; yes; yes; Id.734d
3730   "   Walter; m; 11 5-22-20; ¼+; s; son A1610; yes; yes; Id.734e
3731   "   Elmer; m; 9 3-5-23; ¼+; s; son A1611; yes; yes; Id.734f
3732   "   Stella; f; 6 6-19-25; ¼+; s; dau A1612; yes; yes; Id.734g
3733   "   Raymond; m; 4 3-8-28; ¼+; s; son A1613; yes; yes; Id.734h

Turtle Mountain Reservation
1932 Census Roll

Key: Number; Surname, Given; Sex; Age at Last Birthday, Birthdate (if given); Tribe (Chippewa, unless stated otherwise); Degree of Blood; Marital Status; Relationship to Head of Family, Last Year Census Number; At Jurisdiction Where Enrolled (Yes/No); Elsewhere - Post Office, County, State; Ward (Yes/No); Allotment [Al.], Annuity [An.] and/or Identification [Id.] Numbers

3734 Monette(cont), Resia Mae; f; 10/12 5-3-31; 1/4l s; dau -----; yes; yes; Id.734i

3735 Monette, Virginia; f; 20; ¼+; s; Head A1934; no; Devils Lake, Ramsey, ND; yes; Id.735b, Al.H-024643
3736 " Josie; f; 16 10-12-14; ¼+; s; sis A1935; yes; yes; Id.735c
3737 " Alice; f; 15; ¼+; s; sis A   936; yes; yes; Id.735d
3738 " (Kelland) Joseph H; m; 1 6-17-30; ¼+; s; son A1908; no; (Illeg) Devils Lake, Ramsey, ND; yes; Id.735e

NE Montour, Pascal;   Head
3739 " Mary Rose (Gourneau); f; 32; ¼+; m; wife A1614; yes; yes; Id.1055, Al.M-301

3740 Montour, Pauline (Laverdure); f; 43; ¼+; wd; Head A1615; yes; no; Id.735a, Al.M-07873
3741 " Louise; f; 20; ¼+; s; dau A1616; yes; yes; Id.736c, Al.H-024644

3742 Montriel, Francois; m; 63; ¼+; wd; Head A1617; yes; yes; Id.739, Al.R-341
Dead " Adele;   A1618   (Died 6-17-31)
3743 " Martin; m; 35; ¼+; s; son A1619; yes; yes; Id.739b, Al.W-0648
3744 " Joseph m; 28; ¼+; s; son A1620; yes; yes; Id.739e. Al.W-0642
3745 " Cecelia; f; 22; ¼+; s; dau A1621; yes; yes; Id.739f, Al.none

3746 Montriel, John; m; 39; ¼+; s; Head A1622; yes; no; Id.740, Al.W-0645

3747 Montriel, Severe; m; 41; ¼+; m; Head B1783; yes; no; Id.741, Al.W-0643
3748 " Emerize (Peltier); f; 41; ¼+; m; wife B1784; yes; no; Id.741a, Al.M-91
3749 " Agnes May; f; 14 2-5-18; ¼+; s; dau B1785; yes; no; Id.741b
3750 " Lena Bertha; f; 11 4-7-20; ¼+; s; dau B1786; yes; no; Id.741c
3751 " Raymond; m; 4 5-20-27; ¼+; s; son B1788; yes; no; Id.741d

NE Moore, Lynn C;   Head
3752 " Mary Elma (Demarais); f; 28; ¼+; m; wife B1789; no; Central City, Linn, Iowa; yes; Id.333; Al.LEM-017839
3753 " Rachel; m; 10 1-14-22; ¼+; s; dau B1790; no; Central City, Linn, Iowa; yes; none
3754 " Calvin Carl; m; 8 1-9-24; ¼+; s; son B1792; no; Central City, Linn, Iowa; yes; none
3755 " John L; m; 4 5-8-27; ¼+; s; son B1791; no; Central City, Linn, Iowa; yes; none
3756 " Sarah J; f; 2 8-21-29; ¼+; s; dau B1----; no; Central City, Linn, Iowa; yes; none

Turtle Mountain Reservation
1932 Census Roll
Key: Number; Surname, Given; Sex; Age at Last Birthday, Birthdate (if given); Tribe (Chippewa, unless stated otherwise); Degree of Blood; Marital Status; Relationship to Head of Family, Last Year Census Number; At Jurisdiction Where Enrolled (Yes/No); Elsewhere - Post Office, County, State; Ward (Yes/No); Allotment [Al.], Annuity [An.] and/or Identification [Id.] Numbers

Dead Morin, Abraham;   Head   (Not enrolled)(Died July 1931)
Dead   "   Josette;   A1623   (Died Oct. 1931)
3757   "   James; m; 18; ¼+; s; ad. son A1624; no; Address unknown; no; none

3758 Morin, Albert; m; 26; ¼+; m; Head 1625; yes; yes; Id.755d, Al.G08143
3759   "   Adeline (Decouteau); f; 24; ¼+; m; wife A1626; yes; yes; Id.296d
3760   "   Elizabeth; f; 9/12 6-14-31; ¼+; s; dau A-----; yes; yes; none

3761 Morin, Albert; m; 45; ¼+; m; Head B1794; no; Wolf Point, Roosevelt, Mont; no; Id.765
3762   "   Marie (Desjarlais); f; 30; ¼+; m; wife B1795; no; Wolf Point, Roosevelt, Mont; no; Id.318b, Al.H-10498
Dead   "   Lawrence;   son B1796   (Died 3-28-20)
3763   "   Margaret; f; 11 1-5-21; ¼+; s; son[sic] B1797; no; Wolf Point, Roosevelt, Mont; no; none
3764   "   May; f; 9 5-21-22; ¼+; s; dau B1798; no; Wolf Point, Roosevelt, Mont; no; none
3765   "   Matilda; f; 5 2-23-27; ¼+; s; da B1799; no; Wolf Point, Roosevelt, Mont; no; none
3766   "   Elizabeth; f; 2; ¼+; s; dau B1800; no; Wolf Point, Roosevelt, Mont; no; none

NE Morin, Alexander;   Head
3767   "   Elizabeth (Belgarde); f; 53; ¼+; m; wife B1801; no; Trenton, Williams, ND no; Id.753a, Al.W19
3769   "   Albert; m; 31; ¼+; s; son B1802; no; Trenton, Williams, ND; yes; Id.753b, Al.W17
3770   "   Emma; f; 20; ¼+; s; dau B1803; no; Trenton, Williams, ND; yes; Id.753f, Al.H044675
3771   "   Elizabeth; f; 18; ¼+; s; dau B1804; no; Trenton, Williams, ND; no; Id.753g
3772   "   Mary F; f; 9 5-21-22; ¼+; s; dau B1805; no; Trenton, Williams, ND; no; Id.753h
3773   "   Agnes; f; 8 1-8-24; ¼+; s; dau B1806; no; Trenton, Williams, ND; no; Id.753i

NE Morin, Alex;
3774   "   Eliza (Azure.Morin); f; 38; ¼+; m; wife B1839; no; Dunseith, Rolette, ND; no; Id.746a, Al.G569
3775   "   Frank; m; 15 2-9-17; ¼+; s; son B1840 [B1881]; no; (Counted twice last census) Dunseith, Rolette, ND; no; Id.746b
Dead   "   Annie;   B1841   (Died 8-24-31)
3778   "   Marian; f; 7 6-11-24; ¼+; s; s*dau B1842; no; Dunseith, Rolette, ND; no; Id.746c
3777   "   Evelyn; f; 4 4-9-27; ¼+; s; s-dau B1843; no; Dunseith, Rolette, ND; no; Id.746d

Turtle Mountain Reservation
1932 Census Roll

Key: Number; Surname, Given; Sex; Age at Last Birthday, Birthdate (if given); Tribe (Chippewa, unless stated otherwise); Degree of Blood; Marital Status; Relationship to Head of Family, Last Year Census Number; At Jurisdiction Where Enrolled (Yes/No); Elsewhere - Post Office, County, State; Ward (Yes/No); Allotment [Al.], Annuity [An.] and/or Identification [Id.] Numbers

3778 Morin(cont), Raymond; m; 11/12 4-12-31; ¼+; s; son -----; no; Dunseith, Rolette, ND; no; none

3779 Morin, Alexander; m; 62; ¼+; m; Head B1807; no; Trenton, Williams, ND; no; Id.743, Al.G04670

3780 " Philomene (Demontigny); f; 48; ¼+; m; wife B1808; no; Trenton, Williams, ND; no; Id.743a, Al.G04669

3781 " Martha; f; 8 12-14-23; ¼+; s; dau B1809; no; Trenton, Williams, ND; no; Id.743b

3782 Morin, Alfred; m; 57; ¼+; m; Head B1810; no; Medicine Lake, Sheridan, Mont; no; Id.744, Al.R242

NE " Rosalie (Lafrance); wife

3783 " Andrew; m; 29; ¼+; s; son B1811; no; Medicine Lake, Sheridan, Mont; yes; Id.744c, Al.M196

3784 " Minnie A; f; 15 10-9-16; ¼+; s; ad-dau ----; no; Medicine Lake, Sheridan, Mont; no; none

3785 " Lillian; f; 14 1-15-18; ¼+; s; ad-dau ----; no; Medicine Lake, Sheridan, Mont; no; none

3786 Morin, Alfred; m; 30; ¼+; m; Head B1812; no; Medicine Lake, Sheridan, Mont; yes; Id.744b, Al.M17

NE " Hilda; wife

3787 " James; m; 7 2-2-25; ¼+; s; son B1813; no; Medicine Lake, Sheridan, Mont; no; none

3788 " George; m; 6 3-7-26; ¼+; s; son B1814; no; Medicine Lake, Sheridan, Mont no; none

3789 " Eugene; m; 4 4-26-27; ¼+; s; son B1815; no; Medicine Lake, Sheridan, Mont; no; none

3790 " Thomas Ed; m; 2 5-18-29; ¼+; s; son B----; no; Medicine Lake, Sheridan, Mont; no; none

3791 Morin, Andrew; m; 63 11-20-68; ¼+; wd; Head B1816; no; Dunseith, Rolette, ND; no; Id.745, Al.DL-56

3792 " John; m; 30 6-4-01; ¼+; s; son B1817; no; Dunseith, Rolette, ND; yes; Id.745c, Al.G-584

3793 " William; m; 27 1-20-05; ¼+; s; so B1818; no; Dunseith, Rolette, ND; yes; Id.745e, Al.G-583

3794 " Frank; m; 24 4-8-07; ¼+; s; son B1819; no; Dunseith, Rolette, ND; yes; Id.745f, Al.G-587

Turtle Mountain Reservation
1932 Census Roll

Key: Number; Surname, Given; Sex; Age at Last Birthday, Birthdate (if given); Tribe (Chippewa, unless stated otherwise); Degree of Blood; Marital Status; Relationship to Head of Family, Last Year Census Number; At Jurisdiction Where Enrolled (Yes/No); Elsewhere - Post Office, County, State; Ward (Yes/No); Allotment [Al.], Annuity [An.] and/or Identification [Id.] Numbers

3795 Morin, Andrew; Andrew; m; 86; ¼+; m; Head B1820; no; Medicine Lake, Sheridan, Mont; no; I.d747, Al.R-243
3796 " Adelaide (Grandbois); f; 86; ¼+; m; wife B1821; no; Medicine Lake, Sheridan, Mont; no; Id.747a, Al.M-192

3797 Morin, Angela; f; 23; ¼+; s; Head B1824; no; Medicine Lake, Sheridan, Mont; yes Id.748c, Al.G-07322
3798 " Christine; f; 21; ¼+; s; sis B1825; no; Medicine Lake, Sheridan, Mont; yes; Id.748d
3799 " Charles; m; 19; ¼+; s; bro B1826; no; Medicine Lake, Sheridan, Mont; yes; Id.748e, Al.H-024645
3800 " Florence; f; 17; ¼+; s; sis B1827; no; Medicine Lake, Sheridan, Mont; yes; Id.748f
3801 " Clara; f; 15 2-11-17; ¼+; s; sis B1828; no; Medicine Lake, Sheridan, Mont; yes; Id.748g
3802 " Louis; m; 12 4-13-19; ¼+; s; bro B1829; no; Medicine Lake, Sheridan, Mont; yes; Id.748h
3803 " Evelyn; f; 11 9-5-20; ¼+; s; sis B1830; no; Medicine Lake, Sheridan, Mont; yes; Id.748i

NE Morin, A P; Head
3804 " Marie (Beauchman.Morin); f; 60; ¼+; m; wife B1865; no; Wolf Point, Roosevelt, Mont; no; Id.761a, Al.GF-12
3805 " Arthur; m; 17 3-27-15; ¼+; s ------; no; Wolf Point, Roosevelt, Mont; no; none
3806 " Leonard; m; 14 9-15-17; ¼+; s; son ------; no; Wolf Point, Roosevelt, Mont; no; none
3807 " Gabriel; m; 12 1-22-20; ¼+; s; son ------; no; Wolf Point, Roosevelt, Mont; no; none

3808 Morin, Arthur; m; 25; ¼+; m; Head B1823; no; Medicine Lake, Sheridan, Mont; yes; Id.748b, Al.G-48
NE " Beatrice (Harrison); wife
(The four children of this couple are enrolled at Elbowoods, ND)

3809 Morin, Bruno; m; 28 6-3-03; ¼+; m; Head B1831; no; Dunseith, Rolette, ND; yes; Id.745d, Al.G-586
3810 " Ida May (Poitra); f; 21; ¼+; m; wife B1832; no; Dunseith, Rolette, ND; yes; Id.872f, Al.G-016072
3811 " Francis P; m; 1 1-2-31; ¼+; s; son B1833; no; Dunseith, Rolette, ND; yes; none
3812 " Rose Delores; f; 3/12 12-7-31; ¼+; s; dau ------; no; Dunseith, Rolette, ND; yes; none

Turtle Mountain Reservation
1932 Census Roll

Key: Number; Surname, Given; Sex; Age at Last Birthday, Birthdate (if given); Tribe (Chippewa, unless stated otherwise); Degree of Blood; Marital Status; Relationship to Head of Family, Last Year Census Number; At Jurisdiction Where Enrolled (Yes/No); Elsewhere - Post Office, County, State; Ward (Yes/No); Allotment [Al.], Annuity [An.] and/or Identification [Id.] Numbers

3813 Morin, David; m; 26 6-2-05; ¼+; m; Head B1836; no; Medicine Lake, Sheridan, Mont;; yes; Id.758c, Al.G-01074
3814 " Mary (Laterregrass); f; 25; ¼+; m; wife B1837; no; Medicine Lake, Sheridan, Mont; yes; Id.620e

3815 Morin, David; m; 29; ¼+; m; Head B1834; no; Trenton, Williams, ND; yes; Id.753c, Al.W-18
NE " Emma (Allard); wife
3816 " Julia E; f; 3 9-23-28; ¼+; s; dau -----; no; Trenton, Williams, ND; yes; none
3817 " Dorothy; f; 1 4-19-30; ¼+; s; dau B1835; no; Trenton, Williams, ND; yes; none

3818 Morin, Edward; m; 54; ¼+; s; Head B1838; no; Wolf Point, Roosevelt, Mont; no; Id.768, Al.W-4

3819 Morin, Frederick; m; 27; ¼+; m; Head A1627; yes; yes; Id.770b, Al.G-014362
3820 " Anna (Perronteau); f; 19; ¼+; m; wife A1628; yes; yes; Id.832g, Al.H-024450
3821 " Joseph; m; 1 5-18-30; ¼+; s; son A1629; yes; yes; none

NE Morin, Frederick;   Head
3822 " Rose (Lavallie); f; 53; ¼+; m; wife B1847; no; Dunseith, Rolette, ND; no; Id.493a, Al.MC-26554
3823 " Joseph; m; 25; ¼+; s; son B1848; no; Dunseith, Rolette, ND; no; Id.770c, Al.G-07856
3824 " Roderick; m; 14; ¼+; s; son B1849; no; Dunseith, Rolette, ND; no; none
3825 " Edward; m; 12; ¼+; s; son B1850; no; Dunseith, Rolette, ND; no; none
3826 " Mary Ann; f; 10 10-6-21; ¼+; s; dau B1851; no; Dunseith, Rolette, ND; no; none

3828 Morin, Frederick; m; 48; ¼+; m; Head B1844; no; Dunseith, Rolette, ND; no; Id.766, Al.G-0154
NE " Eva (St.Arnaud); wife
3829 " Robert; m; 20; ¼+; s; son B1845; no; Dunseith, Rolette, ND; yes; Id.766b, Al.H-024647
3830 " Mae; f; 19; ¼+; s; dau B1846; no; Dunseith, Rolette, ND; no; Id.766c

NE Morin, Frederick;   Head
3831 " Laura (Decoteau.Amyotte); f; 34; ¼+; m; wife A1630; yes; yes; Id.93a, Al.GF-93
3832 " Delia; f; 24; ¼+; s; dau A1631; yes; yes; Id.751d, Al.G-04577
3833 " Anastasia; f; 22; ¼+; s; dau A1632; yes; yes; Id.751e, Al.H-012582
3834 " St.Pierre; m; 20; ¼+; s; son A1633; yes; yes; Id.751f
3835 " Mary Jane; f; 18; ¼+; s; dau A1634; yes; yes; none
3836 " (Amyotte) Alexandria; f; 15; ¼+; s; step dau A1640; yes; Id.93b
3837 " Alex; f[sic]; 13; ¼+; s; son A1635; yes; yes; none

Turtle Mountain Reservation
1932 Census Roll

Key: Number; Surname, Given; Sex; Age at Last Birthday, Birthdate (if given); Tribe (Chippewa, unless stated otherwise); Degree of Blood; Marital Status; Relationship to Head of Family, Last Year Census Number; At Jurisdiction Where Enrolled (Yes/No); Elsewhere - Post Office, County, State; Ward (Yes/No); Allotment [Al.], Annuity [An.] and/or Identification [Id.] Numbers

3838 Morin(cont), Antoine; m; 10 3-12-22; ¼+; s; son A1636; yes; yes; none
3839 " Joseph; m; 6 12-18-25; ¼+; s; son A1637; yes; yes; none
3840 " Irene; f; 3 ¼+; s; dau A1638; yes; yes; none
3841 " Gilbert; m; 1 8-3-30; ¼+; s; son A1639; yes; yes; none

3842 Morin, Isadore; m; 62; ¼+; m; Head A1641; yes; yes; Id.755, Al.R-246
3843 " Matilda (Jaste); f; 57; ¼+; m; wife A1642; yes; no; Id.755a, Al.M-204
3844 " Frank L; m; 16 10-20-15; ¼+; s; son A1643; yes; yes; Id.755f
3845 " Lillian; f; 13 3-23-19; ¼+; s; dau A1644; yes; yes; Id.755g

3846 Morin, John; m; 31 10-2-00; ¼+; m; Head B1866; no; Trenton, Williams, ND; yes; Id.761b, Al.GF-14
3847 " Rebecca (Laroque); f; 21 5-15-10; ¼+; m; wife B1466; no; Trenton, Williams, ND; no; Id.618b
3848 " Vivian; f; 5 5-4-26; ¼+; s; dau -------; no; Trenton, Williams, ND; yes; none
3849 " Kathleen; f; 3 6-17-29; ¼+; s; dau ------; no; Trenton, Williams, ND; yes; none
3850 " Rebecca; f; 9/12 6-15-31; ¼+; s; dau ------; no; Trenton, Williams, ND; yes; none

3851 Morin, Joseph; m; 37 11-4-94; ¼+; m; Head B1861; no; Medicine Lake, Sheridan, Mont; no; Id.757, Al.M-165
NE " Isabelle (Baney); wife
3852 " Doris; f; 10 4-10-11; ¼+; s; dau B1862; no; Medicine Lake, Sheridan, Mont no; Id.757b
3853 " Marguerite; f; 10 1-26-22; ¼+; s; dau B1863; no; Medicine Lake, Sheridan, Mont; no; Id.757c
3854 " Willis; m; 8 2-2-24; ¼+; s; son B1864; no; Medicine Lake, Sheridan, Mont; no; Id.757d
3855 " Willard M; m; 1 9-7-30; ¼+; s; son -------; no; Medicine Lake, Sheridan, Mont; no; Id.757e

3856 Morin, Joseph; m; 44; ¼+; wd; Head B1853; no; Medicine Lake, Sheridan, Mont; no; Id.742, Al.G-04702
3857 " Mary S; f; 22; ¼+; s; dau B1854; no; Medicine Lake, Sheridan, Mont; no; Id.742b
3858 " Ellis T; m; 20; ¼+; s; son B1855; no; Medicine Lake, Sheridan, Mont; no; Id.742c
3859 " Ida; f; 18; ¼+; s; dau B1856; no; Medicine Lake, Sheridan, Mont; no; Id.742d
3860 " Louise; f; 16; ¼+; s; dau B1857; no; Medicine Lake, Sheridan, Mont; no; Id.742e
3861 " Phillip; m; 14; ¼+; s; son B1858; no; Medicine Lake, Sheridan, Mont; no; Id.742f
3862 " Clarence; m; 12; ¼+; s; son B1859; no; Medicine Lake, Sheridan, Mont; no; Id.742g

Turtle Mountain Reservation
1932 Census Roll

Key: Number; Surname, Given; Sex; Age at Last Birthday, Birthdate (if given); Tribe (Chippewa, unless stated otherwise); Degree of Blood; Marital Status; Relationship to Head of Family, Last Year Census Number; At Jurisdiction Where Enrolled (Yes/No); Elsewhere - Post Office, County, State; Ward (Yes/No); Allotment [Al.], Annuity [An.] and/or Identification [Id.] Numbers

3863 Morin(cont), Cecile; f; 9 ¼+; s; dau B1860; no; Medicine Lake, Sheridan, Mont; no; Id.742h
3864 " Charles; m; 8 ¼+; s; son --------; no; Medicine Lake, Sheridan, Mont; no; Id.742i

5520 Morin, Joseph; m; 27; ¼+; m; Head B1822; no; Dunseith, Rolette, ND; no; Id.747b, Al.G-0236
NE " Vitaline (Jeannotte); wife
5521 " Mary M; f; 4-9-31; ¼+; s; dau ------; no; Dunseith, Rolette, ND; no; none

NE Morin, Mary (Lafrance); Head
3865 " Isabel; f; 24 12-26-07; ¼+; s; dau B1867; no; Flaxville, Daniels, Mont; yes; Id.758f, Al.G-03
3866 " Robert; m; 22 11-5-09; ¼+; s; son B1868; no; Medicine Lake, Sheridan, Mont; yes; Id.758g, Al.G-011328
3867 " Agnes; f; 19 1-24-13; ¼+; s; dau B1869; no; Flaxville, Daniels, Mont; yes; Id.758h, Al.H-024567
3868 " Alice; f; 16 6-29-15; ¼+; s; dau B1870; no; Flaxville, Daniels, Mont; yes; Id.758i, Al.G-036324

3869 Morin, Moses; m; 26 4-14-05; ¼+; m; Head B1872; no; Medicine Lake, Sheridan, Mont; yes; Id.758d, Al.M-163
3870 " Margaret (Sayer); f; 30; ¼+; m; wife B1873; no; Medicine Lake, Sheridan, Mont; yes; Id.909b, Al.G-0176
3871 " Richard; m; 4 4-24-27; ¼+; s; son -----; no; Medicine Lake, Sheridan, Mont; yes; none
3872 " Francis; m; 3 11-11-28; ¼+; s; son ------; no; Medicine Lake, Sheridan, Mont; yes; none

3873 Morin, Patrice; m; 47; ¼+; m; Head B1874; no; St.Louis, Mo; yes; Id.749, Al.M-194
NE " Ellen (Weekly); wife
3874 " Ramona; f; 20 ¼+; s; dau B1875; no; St.Louis, Mo; yes; Id.749b

NE Morin, Patrick; Head
3875 " Isabella (Laverdure); f; 51; ¼+; m; wife A1645; yes; no; Id.754a, Al.M-245
3876 " Alexander; m; 30 8-28-01; ¼+; s; son A1646; yes; yes; Id.754c, Al.G-439
3877 " Joseph; m; 20 3-6-12; ¼+; s; son A1648; yes; yes; Id.754f, Al.H-024676
3878 " Frederick; m; 15 5-8-16; ¼+; s; son A1649; yes; yes; Id.754g
3879 " Ernest; m; 13 10-15-18; ¼+; s; son A1650; yes; yes; none
3880 " Eugene; m; 9 1-9-23; ¼+; s; son A1651; yes; yes; none

3881 Morin, Peter; m; 98; ¼+; wd; Head B1876; yes; no; Id.764, Al.G-04587

Turtle Mountain Reservation
1932 Census Roll

Key: Number; Surname, Given; Sex; Age at Last Birthday, Birthdate (if given); Tribe (Chippewa, unless stated otherwise); Degree of Blood; Marital Status; Relationship to Head of Family, Last Year Census Number; At Jurisdiction Where Enrolled (Yes/No); Elsewhere - Post Office, County, State; Ward (Yes/No); Allotment [Al.], Annuity [An.] and/or Identification [Id.] Numbers

3882 Morin, Pierre; m; 53; ¼+; wd; Head B1877; no; Dunseith, Rolette, ND; no; Id.763, Al.R-248
3883 " Moses; m; 22 2-4-10; ¼+; s; son B1878; no; Dunseith, Rolette, ND; no; Id.763b
3884 " Mary Eva; f; 20 6-26-11; ¼+; s; dau B1879; no; Dunseith, Rolette, ND; yes; Id.763c, Al.H-013050
3885 " Emil; m; 19 1-30-13; ¼+; s; son B1880; no; Dunseith, Rolette, ND; yes; Id.763d, Al.H-0246489
3886 " Richard; m; 14 1-18-18; ¼+; s; son B1882; no; Dunseith, Rolette, ND; no; Id.763e
3887 " Roman C; m; 12 6-14-19; ¼+; s; son B1883; no; Dunseith, Rolette, ND; no; Id.763g

3888 Morin, Pierre; m; 53; ¼+; m ; Head A1652; yes; no; Id.767, Al.G-0161
NE " Georgiana;   wife   (Maiden name not given on roll book)
3889 " Victoria; f; 11 7-29-20; ¼+; s; dau A1653; yes; no; none
3890 " Mary Alice; f; 9 5-15-22; ¼+; s; dau A1654l yes; no; none
3891 " Moses; m; 7 7-15-24; ¼+; s; son A1655; yes; no; none

NE Morin, Roger;   Head
3892 " Theresa (Morin); f; 36 8-20-95; ¼+; m; wife B1884; no; Trenton, Williams, ND; no; Id.760, Al.GF-13
3893 " Cecelia; f; 16 12-21-15; ¼+; s; dau B1885; no; Trenton, Williams, ND; no; none
3894 " Agnes; f; 14 7-29-17; ¼+; s; dau B1886; no; Trenton, Williams, ND; no; none
3895 " Roger; m; 11 6-18-20; ¼+; s; son B1887; no; Trenton, Williams, ND; no; none
3896 " Charles; m; 10 2-10-22; ¼+; s; son B1888; no; Trenton, Williams, ND; no; none
3897 " Reuben; m; 8 1-24-24; ¼+; s; son ------; no; Trenton, Williams, ND; no; none
3898 " Sylvester; m; 6 1-14-26; ¼+; s; son ----; no; Trenton, Williams, ND; no; none
3899 " Alfred; m; 2 6-18-29; ¼+; s; son ------; no; Trenton, Williams, ND; no; none
3900 " Bernard; m; 1 6-9-30; ¼+; s; son ------; no; Trenton, Williams, ND; no; none

NE Morin, Solomon;   Head
3901 " Mary (Delorme); f; 30; ¼+; m; wife B1889; no; Ft.Totten, Benson, ND; no; Id.321b
3902 " Eugene; m; 16; ¼+; s; son B1890; no; Ft.Totten, Benson, ND; no; Id.769b
3903 " Roger; m; 13 9-26-18; ¼+; s; son B1891; no; Ft.Totten, Benson, ND; no; none
3904 " Gloria; f; 10 10-12-21; ¼+; s; dau B1892; no; Ft.Totten, Benson, ND; no; Id.769c
3905 " Harlan; m; 9 6-5-23; ¼+; s; son B1893; no; Ft.Totten, Benson, ND; no; Id.769d
3906 " Herbert; m; 6; 5-26-25; ¼+; s; son B1894; no; Ft.Totten, Benson, ND; no; Id.769e
3907 " Florence; f; 5 ¼+; s; dau B1895; no; Ft.Totten, Benson, ND; no; Id.769f

Turtle Mountain Reservation
1932 Census Roll

Key: Number; Surname, Given; Sex; Age at Last Birthday, Birthdate (if given); Tribe (Chippewa, unless stated otherwise); Degree of Blood; Marital Status; Relationship to Head of Family, Last Year Census Number; At Jurisdiction Where Enrolled (Yes/No); Elsewhere - Post Office, County, State; Ward (Yes/No); Allotment [Al.], Annuity [An.] and/or Identification [Id.] Numbers

3908 Morin(cont), David; m; 11/12 5-13-31; ¼+; s; son ------; no; Ft.Totten, Benson, ND; no; none

NE Morin, Theodore; Head
3909 " Mary; f; 45; ¼+; m; wife B1896; no; Devils Lake, Ramsey, ND; no; Id.752a, Al.G-08009
3910 " Louis; m; 19 3-26-13; ¼+; s; son B1898; no; Devils Lake, Ramsey, ND; yes; Id.752d, Al.H-024674
3911 " John; m; 17 ¼+; s; son B1899; no; Devils Lake, Ramsey, ND; no; Id.752e
3912 " Evelyn; f; 16 1-14-16; ¼+; s; dau B1900; no; Devils Lake, Ramsey, ND; no Id.752f
3913 " Archie; m; 14 11-13-17; ¼+; s; son B1901; no; Devils Lake, Ramsey, ND; no; Id.752g
3914 " Robert; m; 12 9-14-19; ¼+; s; son B1902; no; Devils Lake, Ramsey, ND; no; Id.752h
3915 " George; m; 10 10-2-21; ¼+; s; son B1903; no; Devils Lake, Ramsey, ND; no; Id.752i
3916 " Sylvester; m; 9 4-12-23; ¼+; s; son B1904; no; Devils Lake, Ramsey, ND; no; Id.752j
3917 " Theodore; m; 5 10-23-26; ¼+; s; son B1905; no; Devils Lake, Ramsey, ND; no; Id.752k
3918 " Joseph; m; 3 9-24-29; ¼+; s; son -----; no; Devils Lake, Ramsey, ND; no; none
3919 " James; m; 1 11-22-30; ¼+; s; son -----; no; Devils Lake, Ramsey, ND; no; none

3920 Morin, Tobey; m; 54; ¼+; m; Head A1656; yes; no; Id.762, Al.R-249
3921 " Sarah (Keplin); f; 46; ¼+; m; wife A1657; yes; no; Id.762a, Al.G-111
3922 " Peter; m; 21; ¼+; s; son A1659; yes; no; Id.762c
3923 " Mary E; f; 17 6-7-14; ¼+; s; dau A1660; yes; no; Id.762d
3924 " Ida Rose; f; 15 1-19-17; ¼+; s; dau A1661; yes; no; Id.762e
3925 " Dora; f; 7 10-25-24; ¼+; s; dau A1662; yes; no; Id.762f

3926 Morin, William; m; 27; ¼+; m; Head B1906; no; Medicine Lake, Sheridan, Mont; yes; Id.753d, Al.W-16
NE " Mary Jane (Allard); wife

NE Morin, William; Head
3927 " Anestesia (Gladue); f; 79; ¼+; m; wife B1907; no; Dagmar, Sheridan, Mont yes; Id.750a, Al.G-0114
3928 " John; m; 36; ¼+; s; son B1852; no; Dagmar, Sheridan, Mont; yes; Idl601, Al.G-04843
3929 " Sarah; f; 33; ¼+; s; dau B1909; no; Dagmar, Sheridan, Mont; yes; Id.750c, Al.G-04841

Turtle Mountain Reservation
1932 Census Roll

Key: Number; Surname, Given; Sex; Age at Last Birthday, Birthdate (if given); Tribe (Chippewa, unless stated otherwise); Degree of Blood; Marital Status; Relationship to Head of Family, Last Year Census Number; At Jurisdiction Where Enrolled (Yes/No); Elsewhere - Post Office, County, State; Ward (Yes/No) Allotment [Al.], Annuity [An.] and/or Identification [Id.] Numbers

3930 Morin, William; m; 20; ¼+; m; Head B1910; no; Devils Lake, Ramsey, ND; yes; Id.752c, Al.H-024646
3931 " Domethilde (Bercier); f; 25; ¼+; m; wife B1911; no; Devils Lake, Ramsey, ND; yes; Id.1169g, Al.H-010465
3932 " Dale Louis; m; 1 1-12-31; ¼+; s; son; no; Devils Lake, Ramsey, ND; yes; none

NE Murphy, John;   Head
3933 " Mary (Houle); f; 28; ¼+; m; wife B1912; yes; yes; Id.485a, Al.G-0810
3934 " Lawrence; m; 6 2-29-26; ¼+; s; son -----; yes; yes; none
3946 " John; m; 4 5-9-27; ¼+; s; son ------; yes; yes; none
3936 " Marie; f; 2 4-27-29; ¼+; s; dau ------; yes; yes; none

3937 Nadeau, Ambrose; m; 32; ¼+; m; Head B1913; yes; no; Id.771b, Al.M-272
3938 " Flora (Vivier); f; 25; ¼+; m; wife B1914; yes; no; Id.990f, Al.G-016061
3939 " Louis; m; 4 8-6-27; ¼+; s; son -----; yes; no; none
3940 " Elmer; m; 3 2-3-29; ¼+; s; son ------; yes; no; none
3941 " George P; m; 11/12 4-18-31; ¼+; s; son ------; yes; no; none

3942 Nadeau, Joseph; m; 71; ¼+; m; Head A1663; yes; no; Id.771, Al.R-250
3943 " Susan (Larat); f; 60; ¼+; m; wife A1664; yes; no; Id.771a, Al.M-275
3944 " Patrick; m; 25; ¼+; s; son A1665; yes; yes; Id.771c, Al.G-040509
3945 " Ernest; m; 17; ¼+; s; son A1666; yes; no; Id.771d

3946 Nadeau, Pierre; m; 39; ¼+; m; Head A1667; yes; no; Id.772, Al.M-277
3947 " Josephine (Lafontain); f; 34; ¼+; m; wife A1668; yes; yes; Id.772b, Al.G-288
Dead " Francois;   A1669   (Died 12-28-16)
3948 " Bruno; m; 14 12-2-17; ¼+; s; son A1670; yes; yes; Id.772c
3949 " Emily; f; 12 3-22-20; ¼+; s; dau A1671; yes; yes; Id.772d
Dead " Alexander;   A1672l yes;   (Died 4-24-25)
3950 " David Albert; m; 6 10-8-25; ¼+; s; son A1673; yes; yes; Id.772f
3951 " Dominick F; m; 3 8-30-28; ¼+; s; son A1674; yes; yes; Id.772g
3952 " Clement; m; 5/12 10-20-31; ¼+; s; son ------; yes; yes; none

3953 Nanapush, George; m; 32; F; m; Head B1915; no; Dunseith, Rolette, ND; yes; Id.21b, Al.G-011735
3954 " Maggie (Great Walker); f; 29; F; m; wife B1916; no; Dunseith, Rolette, ND; yes; Id.32c, Al.G-011738
3955 " Jack; m; 10; F; s; son B1917; no; Dunseith, Rolette, ND; yes; none
3956 " Edith; f; 8 10-30-23; F; s; dau B1918; no; Dunseith, Rolette, ND; yes; none
3957 " George; m; 7 F; s; son B1919; no; Dunseith, Rolette, ND; yes; none
3958 " Irene; f; 3 12-19-28; F; s; dau B1920; no; Dunseith, Rolette, ND; yes; none

Turtle Mountain Reservation
1932 Census Roll

Key: Number; Surname, Given; Sex; Age at Last Birthday, Birthdate (if given); Tribe (Chippewa, unless stated otherwise); Degree of Blood; Marital Status; Relationship to Head of Family, Last Year Census Number; At Jurisdiction Where Enrolled (Yes/No); Elsewhere - Post Office, County, State; Ward (Yes/No); Allotment [Al.], Annuity [An.] and/or Identification [Id.] Numbers

3959 Nanapush, Old; m; 65; F; wd; Head B1085; no; Dunseith, Rolette, ND; yes; Id.21, Al.G-011734
3960   "   Lucy Marie; f; 18; F; s; dau B1087; no; Dunseith, Rolette, ND; yes; Id.21d
DEAD   "   Clarice;   B1088   (Died in 1928)
3961   "   Fred; m; 9 12-9-23; F; s; son B1089; no; Dunseith, Rolette, ND; yes; Id.21f

NE Nanoff, Lazar;   Head
3962   "   Elizabeth (Decoteau); f; 25; ¼+; m; wife B1921; no; Unknown; yes; Id.297b, Al.G-023431
3963   "   Evan; m; 7 5-22-24; ¼+; s; son B1922; no; Unknown; yes; none

3964 Nelson, Marie (Jeannotte); f; 39; ¼+; wd; Head -----; no; Minneapolis, Hennepin, Minn; no; Id.773a, Al.M-221
3965   "   Edna; f; 17; ¼+; s; dau B1923; no; Minneapolis, Hennepin, Minn; no; Id.773b
3966   "   Clarence; m; 15 6-22-16; ¼+; s; son B1924; no; Minneapolis, Hennepin, Minn; no; Id.773c
3967   "   Ida Lavon; f; 12 12-21-19; ¼+; s; dau B1925; no; Minneapolis, Hennepin, Minn; no; Id.773d

NE Nelson, Roy H;   Head
3968   "   Celina (Poitra); f; 27; ¼+; m; wife B1926; no; Froid, Sheridan, Mont; yes; Id.876e, Al.G-08145
3969   "   Lorraine; f; 9 1-9-23; ¼+; s; dau ------; no; Froid, Sheridan, Mont; yes; none
3970   "   Jesa Royla; f; 3 1-3-29; ¼+; s; dau ------; no; Froid, Sheridan, Mont; yes; none

3971 Nepine, Fred; m; 28; F; m; Head B1927; no; Dunseith, Rolette, ND; yes; Id.35b, Al.G-331
3972   "   Rosina (Iron Bear); f; 23; F; m; wife B1928; no; Dunseith, Rolette, ND; yes; Id.50c, Al.G-011716
3973   "   Fred; m; 3 F; s; son B1929; no; Dunseith, Rolette, ND; yes; none

3974 Nepine, John; m; 50; F; m; Head B1933; no; Dunseith, Rolette, ND; yes; Id.35, Al.R-253
3975   "   Standing On All Fours; f; 46; F; m; wife B1931; no; Dunseith, Rolette, ND; yes; Id.11a, Al.G-364
3976   "   (Red Thunder) Tom; m; 14; F; s; stepson B1932; no; Dunseith, Rolette, ND; yes; none
3977   "   John; m; 11; ¼+; s; stepson B1933; no; Dunseith, Rolette, ND; yes; none
3978   "   Christine; f; 6; ¼+; s; step dau B1934; no; Dunseith, Rolette, ND; yes; none

3979 Nicholas, Alexander; m; 54; ¼+; m; Head A1675; yes; no; Id.774, Al.R254
3980   "   Rosalie (Montour); f; 34; ¼+; m; wife; A1676; yes; no; Id.774a, Al.G036588
3981   "   J E Joseph; m; 21; ¼+; s; son A1677; yes; yes; Id.774c, Al.H012598

Turtle Mountain Reservation
1932 Census Roll

Key: Number; Surname, Given; Sex; Age at Last Birthday, Birthdate (if given); Tribe (Chippewa, unless stated otherwise); Degree of Blood; Marital Status; Relationship to Head of Family, Last Year Census Number; At Jurisdiction Where Enrolled (Yes/No); Elsewhere - Post Office, County, State; Ward (Yes/No); Allotment [Al.], Annuity [An.] and/or Identification [Id.] Numbers

3982 Nicholas(cont), Mary S; f; 16; ¼+; s; dau A1678; yes; no; Id.774d
3983 " George S; m; 15; ¼+; s; dau A1679; yes; no; Id.774e
3984 " Delia; f; 13; ¼+; s; dau A1680; yes; no; Id.774f
3985 " Pascal; m; 10 9-10-21; ¼+; s; son A1681; yes; no; Id.774g
3986 " Louis; m; 7 6-1-24; ¼+; s; son A1682; yes; no; Id.774h
3987 " Claudia; f; 6; ¼+; s; dau A1683; yes; no; Id.774i
3988 " Alfred; m; 4; ¼+; s; son A1684; yes; no; Id.774j

NE Nicholas, Antoine; Head
Dead " Eliza (Villeneuve); B1935 (Died 1922)
3989 " Alfred; m; 32; ¼+; s; son B1936; no; Devils Lake, Ramsey, ND; yes; Id.776b, Al.M205

3990 Nicholas, Gideon; m; 37; ¼+; m; Head B1937; no; Devils Lake, Ramsey, ND; no; Id.777, Al.M207
3991 " Josephine (Villeneuve); f; 32; ¼+; m; wife B1938; no; Devils Lake, Ramsey, ND; yes; Id.777a, Al.G07861
3992 " Francis; m; 16 10-10-15; ¼+; s; son B1939; no; Devils Lake, Ramsey, ND; no; Id.777b
3993 " Gladys; f; 15 12-23-16; ¼+; s; dau B1940; no; Devils Lake, Ramsey, ND; no; Id.777c
3994 " Irwin; m; 13 3-13-18; ¼+; s; son B1941; no; Devils Lake, Ramsey, ND; no; Id.777d
3995 " Irene; f; 12 11-4-19; ¼+; s; dau B1942; no; Devils Lake, Ramsey, ND; no; Id.777e
3996 " Louis; m; 10 9-10-21; ¼+; s; son B1943; no; Devils Lake, Ramsey, ND; no; Id.777f
3997 " Robert; m; 5 6-23-26; ¼+; s; son B1944; no; Devils Lake, Ramsey, ND; no; Id.777g
3998 " Ralph; m; 4 1-20-28; ¼+; s; son B1945; no; Devils Lake, Ramsey, ND; no; Id.777h
3999 " Donald; m; 1 4-25-30; ¼+; s; son B1946; no; Devils Lake, Ramsey, ND; no; Id.777i

4000 Nicholas, Joseph; m; 31; ¼+; m; Head A1685; yes; yes; Id.774b, Al.W-0909
4001 " Matilda (Davis); f; 34; ¼+; m; wife A1686; yes; yes; Id.276b, Al.GF-073520
4002 " (Davis) Rose; f; 13 12-10-18; ¼+; s; niece A1687; yes; yes; none
4003 " Francis; m; 11/12 4-16-31; ¼+; s; son ------; yes; yes; none

4004 Nicholas, Joseph; m; 46; ¼+; wd; Head B1947; no; Devils Lake, Ramsey, ND; no; Id.780, Al.M-208
4005 " Joseph; m; 15; ¼+; s; son B1948; no; Devils Lake, Ramsey, ND; no; Id.780c

Turtle Mountain Reservation
1932 Census Roll

Key: Number; Surname, Given; Sex; Age at Last Birthday, Birthdate (if given); Tribe (Chippewa, unless stated otherwise); Degree of Blood; Marital Status; Relationship to Head of Family, Last Year Census Number; At Jurisdiction Where Enrolled (Yes/No); Elsewhere - Post Office, County, State; Ward (Yes/No); Allotment [Al.], Annuity [An.] and/or Identification [Id.] Numbers

4006 Nicholas, Michael; m; 42; ¼+; wd; Head A1689; yes; no; Id.779, Al.M-206
4007 " Michael; m; 17 1-19-15; ¼+; s; son A1690; yes; no; Id.779b
4008 " Marie E; f; 15 3-22-17; ¼+; s; dau A1691; yes; no; Id.779c

4009 Nicholas, Zaida (Jolibois); f; 48; ¼+; wd; Head B1949; no; Devils Lake, Ramsey, ND; no; Id.775a, Al.G-517
4010 " Albert; m; 20; ¼+; s; son B1950; no; Devils Lake, Ramsey, ND; yes; Id.775b, Al.H-024650

NE Norquay, James; Head
4011 " Flora (St.Claire); f; 18; ¼+; m; wife B1951; no; Dunseith, Rolette, ND; no; Id.934f
4012 " Ellen Mae; f; 1 11-25-30; ¼+; s; dau -----; no; Dunseith, Rolette, ND; no; none

NE Norquay, Ralph; Head
4013 " Annie (Iron Bear); f; 17; F; m; wife B1952; no; Dunseith, Rolette, ND; yes; Id.50f
4014 " Annabelle; f; 5/12 10-13-31; ¼+; s; dau ------; no; Dunseith, Rolette, ND; yes; none

NE Norwood, John; Head
4015 " Mary Ann (Wilkie); f; 25; ¼+; m; wife A2225; no; Bottineau, Bottineau, ND; yes; Id.1027e, Al.G-032692
4016 " May Blanch; f; 5; ¼+; s; dau -----; no; Bottineau, Bottineau, ND; yes; none
4017 " Roy; m; 3 ¼+; s; son ------; no; Bottineau, Bottineau, ND; yes; none

4018 Nwenapi, Fred; m; 40; F; m; Head B1953; no; Dunseith, Rolette, ND; yes; Id.33, Al.G-297
4019 " Minerva (Standing Chief); f; 33; F; m; wife B1954; no; Dunseith, Rolette, ND; yes; Id.33a, Al.G-01900
4020 " Mary; f; 17; F; s; dau B1955; no; Dunseith, Rolette, ND; yes; Id.33b
4021 " Lillie; f; 16 9-28-15; F; s; dau B1956; no; Dunseith, Rolette, ND; yes; none
4022 " Charles; m; 14 11-27-17; F; s; son -----; no; Dunseith, Rolette, ND; yes; none
4023 " Norman; m; 10 11-5-21; F; s; son ------; no; Dunseith, Rolette, ND; yes; none
4024 " Winifred; f; 6 11-8-25; F; dau ------; no; Dunseith, Rolette, ND; yes; none
4025 " Alex; m; 2 2-15-30; F; s; son B195-; no; Dunseith, Rolette, ND; yes; none

4026 Nwenapi, Fred; m; 24; F; m; Head B1959; no; Dunseith, Rolette, ND; yes; Id.44b, Al.G-368
4027 " Theresa (Skinner); f; 17 10-4-14; F; m; wife B2310; no; Dunseith, Rolette, ND; yes; Id.54c

Turtle Mountain Reservation
1932 Census Roll

Key: Number; Surname, Given; Sex; Age at Last Birthday, Birthdate (if given); Tribe (Chippewa, unless stated otherwise); Degree of Blood; Marital Status; Relationship to Head of Family, Last Year Census Number; At Jurisdiction Where Enrolled (Yes/No); Elsewhere - Post Office, County, State; Ward (Yes/No); Allotment [Al.], Annuity [An.] and/or Identification [Id.] Numbers

4028 Nwenapi, Oskine (Young); f; 61; F; wd; Head B1958; no; Dunseith, Rolette, ND; yes; Id.44a, Al.G-301
4029 " Alice; f; 18; F; s; dau B1960; no; Dunseith, Rolette, ND; yes; Id.44c
4030 Okemah, Windy Girl; f; 24; F; s; Head B1961; no; Dunseith, Rolette, ND; yes; Id.23b, Al.W-034157
4031 " Calling Around f; 21; F; s; sis B1962; no; Dunseith, Rolette, ND; yes; Id.23c, Al.G-017565

NE Olfert, Peter; Head
4032 " Celina (Lafrombois); f; 48; ¼+; m; wife B1963; no; Walhalla, Pembina, ND; no; Id.781a, Al.H-012600
4033 " James; m; 11 12-23-20; ¼+; s; son B1964; no; Walhalla, Pembina, ND; no; Id.781e, none
4034 " Evelyn; f; 10 3-5-22; ¼+; s; dau B1965; no; Walhalla, Pembina, ND; no; Id.781f

NE Olsen, Andy; Head
4035 " Clemence (Richard); f; 40; ¼+; m; wife B1966; no; Cando, Towner, ND; yes; Id.890a, Al.G-08416
4036 " Joyce; f; 9 12-21-22; ¼+; s; dau B1967; no; Cando, Towner, ND; yes; none
4037 " Olga May; f; 7 4-4-24; ¼+; s; dau B1968; no; Cando, Towner, ND; yes; none
4038 " Jeannette; f; 4 3-5-28; ¼+; s; dau ------; no; Cando, Towner, ND; yes; none
4039 " Elaine; f; 1 5-31-30; ¼+; s; dau ------; no; Cando, Towner, ND; yes; none
4040 " Clemence; f; 3/12 12-30-31; ¼+; s; dau -----; no; Cando, Towner, ND; yes; none

NE Olsen, Edward; Head
Dead " Virginia (McCloud); B1969 (Died 1-19-32) Id.717
4041 " Agnes May; f; 14 4-16-17; ¼+; s; dau B1970; no; Rolla, Rolette, ND; no; none
4042 " Clifford; m; 13 4-16-18; ¼+; s; son B1971; no; Rolla, Rolette, ND; no; none
4043 " Ella; f; 12 12-10-19; ¼+; s; dau B1972; no; Rolla, Rolette, ND; no; none
4044 " Victor; m; 10 11-17-21; ¼+; s; son B1973; no; Rolla, Rolette, ND; no; none
4045 " Lucille; f 4 9-22-27; ¼+; s; dau -----; no; Rolla, Rolette, ND; no; none
4046 " Virginia; f; 2 7-23-29; ¼+; s; dau -----; no; Rolla, Rolette, ND; no; none

NE Olsen, Olaf; Head
4047 " Rose (Lavallie); f; 24; ¼+; m; wife A1353; no; Coalridge, Sheridan, Mont; no; Id.630e
4048 " Morris; m; 9/12 6-22-31; ¼+; s; son -----; no; Coalridge, Sheridan, Mont; no; none

4049 Omar, Eli; m; 21; ¼+; s; Head A1388; yes; yes; Id.782b, Al.H-012601
4050 " Emma; f; 19; ¼+; s; sis A1389; yes; yes; Id.782c
4051 " Stella; f; 16; ¼+; s; sis A1390; yes; yes; Id.782d

Turtle Mountain Reservation
1932 Census Roll

Key: Number; Surname, Given; Sex; Age at Last Birthday, Birthdate (if given); Tribe (Chippewa, unless stated otherwise); Degree of Blood; Marital Status; Relationship to Head of Family, Last Year Census Number; At Jurisdiction Where Enrolled (Yes/No); Elsewhere - Post Office, County, State; Ward (Yes/No); Allotment [AL], Annuity [An.] and/or Identification [Id.] Numbers

4052 One Side, Pete; m; 33; ¼+; s; Head B1974; no; Dunseith, Rolette, ND; yes; Id.45b, Al.G-296

4053 Pacquin, Sampson; m; 54; ¼+; s; Head B1975; no; Address unknown; no; Id.783, Al.G0231g

4054 Page, Ezear; m; 59; ¼+; m; Head A1692; yes; no; Id.787, Al.G24422
4055 " Judith (Nadeau); f; 36; ¼+; m; wife A1693; yes; no; Id.787a, Al.M278
4056 " Solomon; m; 11 3-8-21; ¼+; s; son A1694; yes; no; Id.787b
4057 " Mary Ethel; f; 4 12-3-27; ¼+; s; dau A1695; yes; no; Id.787c

4058 Page, John B; m; 57; ¼+; m; Head A1696; yes; no; Id.784, Al.R256
4059 " Frances (Faguant); f; 40; ¼+; m; wife A1697; yes; yes; Id.784a, Al.G038631
4060 " Julia; f; 20 12-14-11; ¼+; s; dau A1698; yes; yes; Id.784b
4061 " Alice R; f; 14 3-4-18; ¼+; s; dau A1699; yes; yes; Id.784b
4062 " Sarah; m; 11 8-28-20; ¼+; s; dau A1700; yes; yes; Id.784c
4063 " William; m; 9 2-20-23; ¼+; s; son A1701; yes; yes; Id.784d
4064 " Leaneau; m; 6 8-7-25; ¼+; s; son A1702; yes; yes; Id.784e
4065 " Dophine; m; 5 3-24-27; ¼+; s; son A1703; yes; yes; Id.784f
4066 " Raymond; m; 2 9-14-29; ¼+; s; son A1704; yes; yes; Id.none
4067 " Frank; m; 1 3-18-31; ¼+; s; son -----; yes; yes; Id.784g
4068 " Thelma; f; 4/12 11-8-31; ¼+; s; gr-dau -----; yes; yes; none

4069 Parisien, Alexander; m; 34; ¼+; m; Head A1705; yes; no; Id.798d, Al.H012627
4070 " Beatrice (Poitra); d; 20; ¼+; m; wife A1706; yes; yes; Id.867a, Al.G175
4071 " (Poitra) M R Alvina; f; 14 6-18-18; ¼+; s; s-dau A1707; yes; no; Id.867b
4072 " (Poitra) Martin; m; 8 10-20-24; ¼+; s; s-dau[sic] A1708; yes; no; Id.867c
4073 " Elmer; m; 5 10-30-27; ¼+; s; son A1709; yes; no; Id.867d
4074 " Mary L; f; 2; 6-18-29; ¼+; s; dau A1710; yes; no; Id.867e

4075 Parisien, David; m; 68; ¼+; m; Head A1711; yes; no; Id.789, Al.R259
4076 " Josette (Page); f; 60; ¼+; m; wife A1712; yes; no; Id.789a
Dead " William C; ad-son A1713 (Died 12-1-30)
4077 " Mary D; f; 6 8-13-25; ¼+; s; ad-dau A1714; yes; no; none

4078 Parisien, David #2; m; 57; ¼+; m; Head A1715; yes; no; Id.791, Al.R258
4079 " Virginia (Gourneau); f; 43; ¼+; m; wife A1716; yes; no; Id.791a, Al.M274
4080 " Josephine; f; 30; ¼+; s; dau A1717; yes; yes; Id.791b, Al.H039037
4081 " Julia; f; 28; ¼+; s; dau A1718; yes; yes; Id.791c, Al.H039038
4082 " Bruno; m; 18; ¼+; s; son A1720; yes; yes; Id.791d, Al.H030478
4083 " Marie; f; 13 4-13-18; ¼+; s; dau A1721; yes; no; Id.791e
4084 " Francois; m; 7 7-21-24; ¼+; s; son A1722; yes; no; Id.791g

4085 Parisien, Edward; m; 50; ¼+; s; Head A1723; yes; yes; Id.796, Al.G121

Turtle Mountain Reservation
1932 Census Roll

Key: Number; Surname, Given; Sex; Age at Last Birthday, Birthdate (if given); Tribe (Chippewa, unless stated otherwise); Degree of Blood; Marital Status; Relationship to Head of Family, Last Year Census Number; At Jurisdiction Where Enrolled (Yes/No); Elsewhere - Post Office, County, State; Ward (Yes/No); Allotment [Al.], Annuity [An.] and/or Identification [Id.] Numbers

4086 Parisien, Henry; m; 53; ¼+; s; Head A1724; yes; yes; Id.794, Al.G016086

4087 Parisien, John; m; 41; ¼+; m; Head A1725; yes; no; Id.802, Al.H032211
4088   "   Mary Elise (McGillis); f; 31; ¼+; m; wife A1726; yes; no; Id.802a, Al.H010304
4089   "   Mary H; f; 13 11-8-18; ¼+; s; dau A1727; yes; no; Id.802b
4090   "   Lucy S; f; 12 11-7-19; ¼+; s; dau A1728; yes; no; Id.802c
4091   "   Norman J; m; 11 7-20-20; ¼+; s; son A1729; yes; no; Id.802d
4092   "   Martha; f; 10 8-6-21; ¼+; s; dau A1730; yes; no; Id.802e
4093   "   Laura; f; 8; ¼+; s; dau A1731; yes; no; Id.802f
4094   "   Irene; f; 6 7-21-25; ¼+; s; dau A1732; yes; no; Id.802g
4095   "   Verne; m; 5; ¼+; s; son A1733; yes; no; Id.802h
4096   "   Michael; m; 3 10-8-28; ¼+; s; son A1734; yes; no; Id.802i
xxxx   "   Charles;   A1735   (No such child Correction from last census)
4097   "   C. Arthur; m; 2 2-14-30; ¼+; s; son A1736; yes; no; Id.802k
5522   "   Alice; f; 3/12 12-7-31; ¼+; s; dau -----; no; Id.802l

4098 Parisien, John B; m; 29; ¼+; m; Head B1976; no; Dunseith, Rolette, ND; yes; Id.790, Al.G016079
NE   "   Melanie;   wife

4099 Parisien, Joseph; m; 47; ¼+; m; Head A1737; yes; no; Id.799, Al.H013050
4100   "   Virginia (Enno); f; 38; ¼+; m; wife A1738; yes; yes; Id.799a, Al.G06097
4101 " (Enno) August; m; 10 10-30-21; ¼+; s; stepson; yes; yes; Id.799b

4102 Parisien, Joseph; m; 48; ¼+; m; Head A1739; yes; no; Id.795, Al.G171
4103   "   Mary St.A (Enno); f; 36; ¼+; m; wife A1740; yes; no; Id.795a, Al?G4[sic]
4104   "   Fred; m; 15 6-10-16; ¼+; s; son A1741; yes; no; Id.795b
4105   "   Emma; f; 14 10-10-17; ¼+; s; dau A1742; yes; no; Id.795c
4106   "   John; m; 11 10-14-20; ¼+; s; son A1743; yes; no; Id.795d
4107   "   Agnes; f; 9 8-14-22; ¼+; s; dau A1744; yes; no; Id.795e
4108   "   Beatrice; f; 7 8-14-24; ¼+; s; dau A1745; yes; no; Id.795f
4109   "   Charlie; m; 6 10-3-25; ¼+; s; son A1746; yes; no; Id.795g
4110   "   Joan of A; f; 3 6-9-28; ¼+; s; dau A1747; yes; no; Id.795h
4111   "   Madeline; f; 2 12-7-29; ¼+; s; dau A1748; yes; no; Id.795i
4112   "   Ernest; m; 10/12 5-17-31; ¼+; s; son -----; yes; no; Id.795j

4113 Parisien, Julius; m; 36; ¼+; m; Head A1749; yes; no; Id.800, Al.H02623
4114   "   Flora (Poitra); f; 23; ¼+; m; wife A1750; yes; no; Id.872c, Al.G016070
4115   "   Phillip m; 3 4-19-28; ¼+; s; son A1751; yes; no; Id. none
4116   "   Oliver; m; 3 3-21-29; ¼+; s; son A1752; yes; no; none
4117   "   Julius; m; 1 3-6-31; ¼+; s; son A1753; yes; no; none

4118 Parisien, Justine; f; 63; ¼+; wd; Head A1754; yes; no; Id.798a, Al.H040624
4119   "   Fred; m; 32; ¼+; s; son A1755; yes; no; Id.798b, Al.H01262

Turtle Mountain Reservation
1932 Census Roll
Key: Number; Surname, Given; Sex; Age at Last Birthday, Birthdate (if given); Tribe (Chippewa, unless stated otherwise); Degree of Blood; Marital Status; Relationship to Head of Family, Last Year Census Number; At Jurisdiction Where Enrolled (Yes/No); Elsewhere - Post Office, County, State; Ward (Yes/No); Allotment [AL], Annuity [An.] and/or Identification [Id.] Numbers

4120 Parisien(cont), Madeline; f; 23; ¼+; s; dau A1756; yes; no; Id.798c, Al.--
4121   "   Peter; m; 22; ¼+; s; son A1757; yes; no; Id.798f
4122   "   Patrick; m; 19; ¼+; s; son A1758; yes; no; Id.798g

4123 Passing By; m; 67; F; m; Head B1977; no; Dunseith, Rolette, ND; yes; Id.17, Al.DL29
4124   "   Sitting On Four Legs; f; 55; F; m; wife B1978; no; Dunseith, Rolette, ND; yes; Id.17a, Al.G306

4125 Patnaud, Calixte; m; 33; ¼+; m; Head A1759; yes; no; Id.803b, Al.G0473
NE   "   Rosalie (Bercier);   wife A1760 (Error last years census)
4126   "   Mary; f; 9 7-24-22; ¼+; s; dau A1761; yes; no; none
4127   "   Sam; m; 6 10-11-25; ¼+; s; son A-----; yes; (Omitted from last census by error) no; none
4128   "   Agnes; f; 2 6-19-29; ¼+; s; dau A1762; yes; no; none
4129   "   Gertrude; f; 2/12 2-2-32; ¼+; s; dau ------; yes; no; none

4130 Patnaud, Gilbert; m; 36; ¼+; m; Head A1763; yes; yes; Id.804, Al.G0432
4131   "   Margaret; f; 32; ¼+; m; wife A1764; yes; yes; Id.804a, Al.H013034
4132   "   Louise; f; 12 7-7-19; ¼+; s; dau A1765; yes; yes; Id.804b
4133   "   Blanche; f; 11 11-18-20; ¼+; s; dau A1766; yes; yes; Id.804c
4134   "   Peter; m; 9 7-23-22; ¼+; s; son A1767; yes; yes; Id.804d
4135   "   Mary; f; 6 8-22-25; ¼+; s; dau A1768; yes; yes; Id.804e
4136   "   Ernest; m; 4 4-10-27; ¼+; s; son A1769; yes; yes; Id.804f
4137   "   Stanislaus; m; 2 5-20-29; ¼+; s; son A1770; yes; yes; Id.804g

NE Patnaud, Henry;   Head
4138   "   Domethilde; f; 45; ¼+; m; wife B1979; no; Boggy Creek, Manitoba, Can; no; Id.806a, Al.M51
4139   "   Marie; f; 24; ¼+; s; dau B1980; no; Boggy Creek, Manitoba, Can; yes; Id.805b, Al.H012608
4140   "   Pauline; f; 23; ¼+; s; dau B1981; no; Boggy Creek, Manitoba, Can; yes; Id.806c, Al.H012607
4141   "   Joseph; m; 21; ¼+; s; son B1982; no; Boggy Creek, Manitoba, Can; yes; Id.806d, Al.H24443
4142   "   Delia; f; 18; ¼+; s; dau B1983; no; Boggy Creek, Manitoba, Can; no; Id.806e
4143   "   Emma; f; 15 4-29-16; ¼+; s; dau B1984; no; Boggy Creek, Manitoba, Can; no; Id.806f
4144   "   David; m; 14 1-11-18; ¼+; s; son B1985; no; Boggy Creek, Manitoba, Can; no; Id.806g
4145   "   Ezear; m; 12 2-9-20; ¼+; s; son B1986; no; Boggy Creek, Manitoba, Can; no; Id.806h

Turtle Mountain Reservation
1932 Census Roll

Key: Number; Surname, Given; Sex; Age at Last Birthday, Birthdate (if given); Tribe (Chippewa, unless stated otherwise); Degree of Blood; Marital Status; Relationship to Head of Family, Last Year Census Number; At Jurisdiction Where Enrolled (Yes/No); Elsewhere - Post Office, County, State; Ward (Yes/No); Allotment [Al.], Annuity [An.] and/or Identification [Id.] Numbers

4146 Patnaud(cont), Harry; m; 8; ¼+; s; son B1987; no; Boggy Creek, Manitoba, Can; no; Id.806i

4147 Patnaud, John A; m; 26; ¼+; m; Head A1771; yes; yes; Id.803b, Al.G0475
4148 " Delia (Gladue); f; 25; ¼+; m; wife A1772; yes; yes; Id.410b, Al.G07093

NE Patnaud, Joseph; m;   Head
4149 " Stella (Delong); f; 17 6-24-14; ¼+; m; wife A665; no; St.John, Rolette, ND; no; Id.320c
4150 " Charles; m; 14; ¼+; s; son B1989; no; St.John, Rolette, ND; no; Id.805b
4151 " Veronica; f; 12; ¼+; s; dau B1990; no; St.John, Rolette, ND; no; Id.805c
4152 " Esther; f; 9; ¼+; s; dau B1991; no; St.John, Rolette, ND; no; Id.805d
4153 " Willie; m; 7; ¼+; s; son B1992; no; St.John, Rolette, ND; no; Id.805e
4154 " Francis; m; 2 11-13-29; ¼+; s; son B1993; no; St.John, Rolette, ND; no; Id.805f
4155 " James; m; 9/12 7-23-31; ¼+; s; son B----; no; St.John, Rolette, ND; no;
All children except James are from former wife   none

NE Patnaud, Louis;   Head
4156 " Agatha (Lenoir); f; 60; ¼+; m; wife B1994; no; St.John, Rolette, ND; no; Id.807a, Al.R263
4157 " Adam; m; 31; ¼+; s; son B1995; no; St.John, Rolette, ND; yes; Id.807b, Al.G352
4158 " Mary; f; 27; ¼+; s; dau B1996; no; St.John, Rolette, ND; yes; Id.807c, Al.G357
4159 " Francois; m; 25; ¼+; s; son B1997; no; St.John, Rolette, ND; yes; Id.807d Al.G358
4160 " Cuthbert; m; 23; ¼+; s; son B1998; no; St.John, Rolette, ND; no; Id.807e
4161 " Mary; f; 14 10-10-17; ¼+; s; dau B1999; no; St.John, Rolette, ND; no; Id.807f

NE Patnaud, Michael;   Head
4162 " Mary Jane (Sayer); f; 28; ¼+; m; wife B2000; no; Medicine Lake, Sheridan, Mont; yes; Id.909e, Al.G0715
4163 " Joseph; m; 23 1-19-30; ¼+; s; son ------; no; Medicine Lake, Sheridan, Mont; no; none
4164 " Marguerite; f; 6/12 9-12-31; ¼+; s; dau -----; no; Medicine Lake, Sheridan Mont; no; none

4165 Patnaud, Sampson; m; 57; ¼+; m; Head A1773; yes; yes; Id.803, Al.R264
4166 " Lasute (Jeannotte); f; 57; ¼+; m; wife A1774; yes; no; Id.803a, Al.H010427
4167 " Emile; m; 24; ¼+; s; son A1775; yes; yes; Id.803b, Al.H0104212
4168 " Ambrose; m; 24; ¼+; s; son A1776; yes; yes; Id.803f, Al.H010428
4169 " Emma; f; 19; ¼+; s; dau A1778; yes; yes; Id.803h, Al.H024441

Turtle Mountain Reservation
1932 Census Roll

Key: Number; Surname, Given; Sex; Age at Last Birthday, Birthdate (if given); Tribe (Chippewa, unless stated otherwise); Degree of Blood; Marital Status; Relationship to Head of Family, Last Year Census Number; At Jurisdiction Where Enrolled (Yes/No); Elsewhere - Post Office, County, State; Ward (Yes/No); Allotment [Al.], Annuity [An.] and/or Identification [Id.] Numbers

4170 Patnaud(cont), Alvina; f; 16; ¼+; s; dau A1779; yes; yes; Id.803i

4171 Paul, Alfred; m; 53; ¼+; m; Head B2001; no; St.John, Rolette, ND; no; Id.808, Al.G06693
NE " Clemence (Laroque); wife
4172 " Mary V; f; 28 5-6-03; ¼+; s; dau B2002; no; Palo Alto, Santa Clara, Cal; yes; Id.808c, Al.G06695
4173 " William; m; 26 10-27-05; ¼+; s; son B2003; no; San Francisco, San Francisco, Cal; no; Id.808d
4174 " Grace C; f; 13 9-16-18; ¼+; s; dau B2005; no; St.John, Rolette, ND; no; Id.808f
4175 " Mary M; f; 2 8-2-29; ¼+; s; ad-dau B2006; no; St.John, Rolette, ND; no; none

4176 Paul, Antoine; m; 72; ¼+; wd; Head B2007; no; St.John, Rolette, ND; yes; Id.809, Al.H030418

4177 Paul, Jacob; m; 45; ¼+; m; Head B2008; no; Minneapolis, Hennepin, Minn; no; Id.812, Al. H030420

4178 Paul, Jerome; m; 36; ¼+; s; Head B2009; no; St.Paul, Ramsey, Minn; no; Id.810, Al.H030420[sic]

NE Paul, John Louis; Head
4179 " Delia (McGillis); f; 25; ¼+; m; wife B2010; no; Boggy Creek, Manitoba, Can; yes; Id.723d, Al.H013013
4180 " Louise; f; 10 3-22-22; ¼+; s; dau B2011; no; Boggy Creek, Manitoba, Can; no; none
4181 " Mary; f; 8 9-8-23; ¼+; s; dau B2012; no; Boggy Creek, Manitoba, Can; no; none

4182 Paul, Joseph; m; 40; ¼+; wd; Head B2013; no; Address unknown; no; Id.811, Al.MC026538

4183 Paul, Joseph A; m; 22; ¼+; m; Head B2004; no; San Francisco (U.S. Navy); no; Id.808e
NE " Eva L (Scott); wife

NE Paulson, Lewis; Head
4184 " Mary L; f; 35; ¼+; m; wife B2014; no; Minneapolis, Hennepin, Minn; no; Id.501e

4185 Pays, Pierre; m; 59; ¼+; m; Head A1780; yes; no; Id.813, Al.G08139
NE " Marie (Ketchem); wife
4186 " Virginia; f; 28; ¼+; s; dau A1781; yes; yes; Id.813c, Al.G08138
4187 " Frank; m; 21; ¼+; s; son A1782; yes; yes; Id.813d, Al.H012694
4188 " Mary; f; 18; ¼+; s; dau A1783; yes; yes; Id.813f, Al.MC026543

Turtle Mountain Reservation
1932 Census Roll

Key: Number; Surname, Given; Sex; Age at Last Birthday, Birthdate (if given); Tribe (Chippewa, unless stated otherwise); Degree of Blood; Marital Status; Relationship to Head of Family, Last Year Census Number; At Jurisdiction Where Enrolled (Yes/No); Elsewhere - Post Office, County, State; Ward (Yes/No); Allotment [Al.], Annuity [An.] and/or Identification [Id.] Numbers

4189 Pays(cont), (Tipps) Dorothy; f; 4; ¼+; s; gr-dau A1784; yes; (Dau of #4186) no; none

NE   Peltier, Adolphus;   Head
4190   "   Caroline (Vallie); f; 49; ¼+; m; wife B2015; no; Address unknown; [blank]; Id.929a, Al.DL55
4191   "   Joseph; m; 32; 14; s; son B2016; no; Address unknown; yes; Id.828b, Al.G0195

4192 Peltier, Alexander; m; 41; ¼+; m; Head B2017; no; Address unknown (Canada); no; Id.815, Al.M294
NE   "   Mary A (Dubois); f;   wife
4193   "   Ernest; m; 12; ¼+; s; son B2018; no; Address unknown (Canada); no; Id.815a
4194   "   James; m; 11; ¼+; s; son B2019; no; Address unknown (Canada); no; Id.815b
4195   "   Octave; f; 10; ¼+; s; dau B2020; no; Address unknown (Canada); no; Id.815c
4196   "   Leon; m; 8; ¼+; s; son B2021; no; Address unknown (Canada); no; Id.815d

4197 Peltier, Alexander; m; 41; ¼+; m; Head A1785; yes; no; Id.822, Al.G0594
4198   "   Rosalie (Belgarde); f; 28; ¼+; m; wife A1786; yes; yes; Id.148c, Al.M112

4199 Peltier, Alfred; m; 44; ¼+; m; Head B2022; no; Minnewaukan, Benson, ND; no; Id.827
4200   "   Cecilia (Lenoir); f; 26; ¼+; m; wife B2023; no; Minnewaukan, Benson, ND yes; Id.667b, Al.G0314
4201   "   John Oliver; m; 7 6-16-24; ¼+; s; son B----; no; Minnewaukan, Benson, ND; no; none
4202   "   Mary Loria; f; 6 2-17-26; ¼+; s; dau -----; no; Minnewaukan, Benson, ND; no; none
4203   "   Joseph E; m; 3 6-14-28; ¼+; s; son -----; no; Minnewaukan, Benson, ND; no; none
4204   "   Mary Eva; f; 2 12-1-29; ¼+; s; dau B-----; no; Minnewaukan, Benson, ND; no; none
4205   "   Joseph G; m; 5/12 10-30-31; ¼+; s; son ------; no; Minnewaukan, Benson, ND; no; none

4206 Peltier, Angelique; f; 93; ¼+; wd; Head A1787; yes; yes; Id.814a, Al.R265
4207   "   Alexander; m; 34; ¼+; s; gr-son A1788; yes; no; Id.814b, Al.G07828

4208 Peltier, Bartholomew; m; 62; ¼+; m; Head A1789; yes; no; Id.818, Al.MC026747
4209   "   Mary Rose (Allery); f; 48; ¼+; m; wife A1790; yes; no; Id.351a, Al.G304

Turtle Mountain Reservation
1932 Census Roll

Key: Number; Surname, Given; Sex; Age at Last Birthday, Birthdate (if given); Tribe (Chippewa, unless stated otherwise); Degree of Blood; Marital Status; Relationship to Head of Family, Last Year Census Number; At Jurisdiction Where Enrolled (Yes/No); Elsewhere - Post Office, County, State; Ward (Yes/No); Allotment [Al.], Annuity [An.] and/or Identification [Id.] Numbers

4210	Peltier, Clement J; m; 48; ¼+; wd; Head B2024; no; Devils Lake, Ramsey, ND; no; Id.817, Al.H-28308	
4211	"	Fred; m; 24; ¼+; s; son B2025; no; Devils Lake, Ramsey, ND; no; Id.817b
4212	"	George; m; 22; ¼+; s; son B2026; no; Devils Lake, Ramsey, ND; no; Id.817c
4213	"	John; m; 20; ¼+; s; son B2027; no; Devils Lake, Ramsey, ND; no; Id.817d
4214	"	Joachim; m; 19; ¼+; s; son B2028; no; Devils Lake, Ramsey, ND; no; Id.817e
4215	"	Mary Rose; f; 16; ¼+; s; dau B2029; no; Devils Lake, Ramsey, ND; no; Id.817f
4216	"	Louis J; m; 13 4-11-18; ¼+; s; son B2030; no; Devils Lake, Ramsey, ND; no; Id.817g
4217	"	Rosina; f; 11; ¼+; s; dau B2031; no; Devils Lake, Ramsey, ND; no; Id.817h

4218 Peltier, Ellen; f; 68; ¼+; wd; Head B2032; no; Devils Lake, Ramsey, ND; no; Id.829a, Al.H010474
4219 " Joseph; m; 23; ¼+; s; son B2033; no; Devils Lake, Ramsey, ND; yes; Id.829b, Al.H010475

4220 Peltier, Francois; m; 56; ¼+; m; Head B2034; no; Bainville, Roosevelt, Mont; no; Id.d819, Al.H02445
NE " Virginia (Belanger); f; wife
4221 " Fred; m; 29; ¼+; s; son B2035; no; Bainville, Roosevelt, Mont; yes; Id.819e, Al.G-237
4222 " Adele; f; 25; ¼+; s; dau B2036; no; Bainville, Roosevelt, Mont; yes; Id.819f, Al.G-238
4223 " Riel; m; 22; ¼+; s; son B2037; no; Bainville, Roosevelt, Mont; yes; Id.819g
4224 " Frank; m; 20; ¼+; s; son B2038; no; Bainville, Roosevelt, Mont; yes; Id.819h, Al.H-024446

4225 Peltier, Isadore; m; 59; ¼+; m; head B2039; no; Ft.Berthold; no; Id.823, Al.R-266
4226 " Hattie (Schindler); f; 46; ¼+; m; wife B2040; no; Ft.Berthold; no; Id.823a, Al.G-426
4227 " St.Pierre; m; 24 6-22-07; ¼+; s; son B2041; no; Ft.Berthold; yes; Id.823b, Al.G-424
4228 " Prudent; m; 22 4-5-09; ¼+; s; son B2042; no; Ft.Berthold; yes; Id.823c, Al.H-020526
4229 " Fred; m; 12 5-23-19; ¼+; s; son B2043; no; Ft.Berthold; no; Id.823f
4230 " Daniel; m; 10 3-12-22; ¼+; s; son B2044; no; Ft.Berthold; no; Id.823g
4231 " Mary; f; 7 9-23-24; ¼+; s; dau B2045; no; Ft.Berthold; no; Id.823h
4232 " Louise; f; 4 7-27-27; ¼+; s; dau ------; no; Ft.Berthold; no; none
4233 " Gabriel; m; 6/12 9-16-31; ¼+; s; son ------; no; Ft.Berthold; no; none

Turtle Mountain Reservation
1932 Census Roll

Key: Number; Surname, Given; Sex; Age at Last Birthday, Birthdate (if given); Tribe (Chippewa, unless stated otherwise); Degree of Blood; Marital Status; Relationship to Head of Family, Last Year Census Number; At Jurisdiction Where Enrolled (Yes/No); Elsewhere - Post Office, County, State; Ward (Yes/No); Allotment [Al.], Annuity [An.] and/or Identification [Id.] Numbers

4234 Peltier, John B; m; 56; ¼+; s; Head B2046; no; Unknown, Canada; no; Id.824, Al.G-05629

NE Peltier, John B; wd; Head
4235 " Mary Ann; f; 13; ¼+; s; dau B2047; no; Dunseith, Rolette, ND; no. Id.830c, Al. none

4236 Peltier, Joseph; m; 54; ¼+; m; Head B2048; no; Bottineau, Bottineau, ND; no; Id.820, Al.H-010446
4237 " Adeline (Dauphinais); f; 52; ¼+; m; wife B2049; no; Bottineau, Bottineau, ND; no; Id.820a, Al.H-010445
xxxx " Rose; B2050 (Died 5-5-22)
4238 " Mary St.Ann; f; 10 12-29-11; ¼+; s; dau B2051; no; Bottineau, Bottineau, ND; yes; Id.820e, Al.H-024447
4239 " Joseph T; m; 17 11-1-¼+; ¼+; s; son B2052; no; Bottineau, Bottineau, ND; no; Id.820f
4240 " Phillip A; m; 15 12-22-16; ¼+; s; son B2053; no; Bottineau, Bottineau, ND; no; Id.820h
4241 " John Robert; m; 13 11-2-15; ¼+; s; son B2054; no; Bottineau, Bottineau, ND; no; Id.820i
4242 " Pierre; m; 9 4-9-22; ¼+; s; son B2055; no; Bottineau, Bottineau, ND; no; Id.820g

NE Peltier, Nazarie; Head
4243 " Mary Adeline (St.Pierre); f; 33; ¼+; m; wife B2056; no; Unknown; yes; Id.816a, Al.G-08109
4244 " Nora; f; 17; ¼+; s; dau B2057; no; Unknown; yes; Id.816b

4245 Peltier, Robert; m; 47; ¼+; m; Head A1792; yes; no; Id.826, Al.G-421
NE " Clemence (Azure); wife
4246 " Lloyd; m; 7; ¼+; s; son A1793; yes; no; none
4247 " Herman; m; 4 ¼+; s; son A1794; yes; no; none
4248 " Robert; m; 11/12 5-20-31; ¼+; s; son ----; yes; no; none

NE Peltier, William; Head
4249 " Mary Louise (Lenoir.Decoteau); f; 33; ¼+; m; wife B2058; no; Dunseith, Rolette, ND; yes; Id.668, Al.G-08033
4250 " (Decoteau) William; 12; ¼+; s; stepson B2059; no; Dunseith, Rolette, ND; yes; none
4251 " (Decoteau) Warren; m; 11; ¼+; s; stepson B2060; no; Dunseith, Rolette, ND; yes; none
4252 " (Decoteau) Mary Jane; f; 9 ¼+; s; step dau B2061; no; Dunseith, Rolette, ND; yes; none

Turtle Mountain Reservation
1932 Census Roll

Key: Number; Surname, Given; Sex; Age at Last Birthday, Birthdate (if given); Tribe (Chippewa, unless stated otherwise); Degree of Blood; Marital Status; Relationship to Head of Family, Last Year Census Number; At Jurisdiction Where Enrolled (Yes/No); Elsewhere - Post Office, County, State; Ward (Yes/No); Allotment [Al.], Annuity [An.] and/or Identification [Id.] Numbers

NE Pendergrast, Francis; Head
4253   "   Nora E (Rolette); f; 42; ¼+; m; wife B2067; no; Wenatchee, Chelan, Wash; no; Id.831a, Al.M-42
4254   "   Eleanor; f; 18; ¼+; s; dau B2068; no; Wenatchee, Chelan, Wash no; Id.831b

NE Perrine, William; Head
4255   "   Anna Jane (Rolette); f; 42; ¼+; m; wife B2069; no; Unknown; no; Id.833a, Al.H-010506

4256 Perronteau, Francis; m; 23; ¼+; m; Head A1795; yes; yes; Id.832f, Al.L-034142
4257   "   Anna (St.Arnaud); f; 21; ¼+; m; wife A1796; yes; no; Id.929c
4258   "   Cecile M; f; 1 10-3-30; ¼+; s; dau A1797; yes; yes; none
4259   "   Louise; f; 3/12 12-12-31; ¼+; s; dau -----; yes; yes; none

4260 Perronteau, Xavier; m; 56; ¼+; m; Head A1798; yes; yes; Id.832, Al.R-270
4261   "   Larose (LaPierre); f; 49; ¼+; m; wife A1799; yes; no; Id.832a, Al.G-0411
4262   "   John; m; 25; ¼+; s; son A1801; yes; yes; Id.832e, Al.G-0407
4263   "   Mary Louise; f; 17 11-1-14; ¼+; s; dau A1802; yes; yes; Id.832h
4264   "   Ernestine Ida; 14 1-2-18; ¼+; s; dau A1806/A1803; yes; (Ida and Ernestine same child) yes; Id.832i
4265   "   Victoria; f; 12 1-31-20; ¼+; s; dau A1804; yes; yes; Id.832j
4266   "   Rebecca; f; 10 2-27-22; ¼+; s; dau A1805; yes; yes; Id.832k
4267   "   Alexander; m; 8 3-15-24; ¼+; s; son A1807; yes; yes; Id.832l

NE Peterson, George John; Head
4268   "   Emily (Laverdure); f; 21; ¼+; m; wife B2062; no; Yelm, Thurston, Wash yes; Id.644h, Al.H-012553
4269   "   Dolores; f; 2 4-24-29; ¼+; s; dau B2063; no; Yelm, Thurston, Wash; yes; none
4270   "   Anna Pauline; f; 1 12-30-30; ¼+; s; dau B2064; no; Yelm, Thurston, Wash yes; none

NE Peterson, Peter; Head
4271   "   Lucy (Lenoir); f; 33; ¼+; m; wife B2065; no; Minnewauken[sic], Benson, ND; yes; Id.663b, Al.G-153
4272   "   Raymond; m; 6 5-15-25; ¼+; s; son B2066; no; Minnewauken[sic], Benson, ND; yes; none

NE Pflugardt, Carl; Head
4273   "   Nancy Rose (Fournier.Baker); f; 30; ¼+; m; wife B2070; no; Unknown; yes; Id.395c, Al.G-011721

Turtle Mountain Reservation
1932 Census Roll

Key: Number; Surname, Given; Sex; Age at Last Birthday, Birthdate (if given); Tribe (Chippewa, unless stated otherwise); Degree of Blood; Marital Status; Relationship to Head of Family, Last Year Census Number; At Jurisdiction Where Enrolled (Yes/No); Elsewhere - Post Office, County, State; Ward (Yes/No); Allotment [Al.], Annuity [An.] and/or Identification [Id.] Numbers

NE Pilon, Joseph;   Head
4274   "   Virginia (Amyotte); f; 50; ¼+; m; wife B2072; no; Unknown; no; Id.834a, Al.DL-8

NE Pippenger, Lee Oliver;   Head
4275   "   Flora (Lemay); f; 36; ¼+; m; wife B1600; no; Trenton, Williams, ND; yes; Id.661a, Al.M-128
4276   "   Levi O; m; 8 12-23-23; ¼+; s; son -----; no; Trenton, Williams, ND; yes; none
4277   "   Robert; m; 6 6-15-25; ¼+; s; son -----; no; Trenton, Williams, ND; yes; none
4278   "   David; m; 5 11-17-26; ¼+; s; son ------; no; Trenton, Williams, ND; yes; none
4279   "   Paul; m; 3 5-4-28; ¼+; s; son ------; no; Trenton, Williams, ND; yes; none
4280   "   Viola; f; 2 10-4-29; ¼+; s; dau ------; no; Trenton, Williams, ND; yes; none
4281   "   Albert; m; 1 7-29-30; ¼+; s; son ------; no; Trenton, Williams, ND; yes; none

4282 Plante, Alfred; m; 26; ¼+; m; Head B2074; no; St.Paul, Ramsey, Minn; yes; Id.840a, Al.G-67
NE   "   Lillian (Hager.Rothering); wife
4283   "   Alfred John; m; 2 4-10-29; ¼+; s; son ----; no; St.Paul, Ramsey, Minn; yes; none

4284 Plante, Daniel; m; 41; ¼+; m; Head B2076; no; Kalamazoo, Kalamazoo, Mich; no; Id.837, Al.G-64
NE   "   Harriet (Cox);   wife
4285   "   Daniel; m; 4 5-23-27; ¼+; s; son ------; no; Kalamazoo, Kalamazoo, Mich; no; none
4286   "   Francis; m; 2 7-22-29; ¼+; s; son ------; no; Kalamazoo, Kalamazoo, Mich; no; none
4287   "   Theresa M; f; 11/12 4-16-31; ¼+; s; dau ------; no; Kalamazoo, Kalamazoo, Mich; no; none

4288 Plante, Eugenie; f; 34; ¼+; s; Head B2072; no; Devils Lake, Ramsey, ND; no; Id.840b, Al.G-68
4289   "   Margaret; f; 25; ¼+; s; sis B2075; no; St.Paul, Ramsey, ND[sic]; yes; Id.840f, Al.G-70

NE Plante, Joseph;   Head
4290   "   Josephine (Azure); f; 51; ¼+; m; wife B2077; no; Cannonball, Sioux, ND; no; Id.835a, Al.R-272

Turtle Mountain Reservation
1932 Census Roll

Key: Number; Surname, Given; Sex; Age at Last Birthday, Birthdate (if given); Tribe (Chippewa, unless stated otherwise); Degree of Blood; Marital Status; Relationship to Head of Family, Last Year Census Number; At Jurisdiction Where Enrolled (Yes/No); Elsewhere - Post Office, County, State; Ward (Yes/No); Allotment [Al.], Annuity [An.] and/or Identification [Id.] Numbers

4291 Plante (cont), Norman; m; 27 12-29-04; ¼+; s; son B2078; no; Cannonball, Sioux, ND; yes; Id.835c, Al.G-07893
4292 " Louis; m; 24 6-16-07; ¼+; s; son B2079; no; Cannonball, Sioux, ND; yes; Id.835d, Al.G-07994
4293 " Joseph; m; 21 5-11-10; ¼+; s; son B2080; no; Cannonball, Sioux, ND; yes; Id.835e, Al.AH-020497

4294 Plante, Mary Ann (Dauphinais); f; 38; ¼+; wd; Head B2081; no; Devils Lake, Ramsey, ND; no; Id.778, Al.M-210
4295 " Louis; m; 10 9-10-21; ¼+; s; son B2082; no; Devils Lake, Ramsey, ND; no; Id.839c
4296 " Eugene; m; 9 2-17-23; ¼+; s; son B2083; no; Devils Lake, Ramsey, ND; no; Id.839d
4297 " Leo; m; 7 4-10-24; ¼+; s; son B2084; no; Devils Lake, Ramsey, ND; no; Id.839e
4298 " Alfred; m; 6 7-4-25; ¼+; s; son B2085; no; Devils Lake, Ramsey, ND; no; Id.839f
4299 " Albert; m; 4 11-9-27; ¼+; s; son B2086; no; Devils Lake, Ramsey, ND; no; Id.839g
4300 " Mary Angeline; f; 3 1-1-29; ¼+; s; dau B2087; no; Devils Lake, Ramsey, ND; no; Id.839h
4301 " George; m; 1 8-27-30; ¼+; s; son B2088; no; Devils Lake, Ramsey, ND; no; Id.839i

4302 Plante, Prudent; m; 31; ¼+; m; Head A1808; yes; yes; Id.835b, Al.G-07893
NE " Josephine (Short); wife
4303 " Henry; m; 8 1-26-24; ¼+; s; son A1809; yes; yes; none
4304 " Alice; f; 6 4-26-25; ¼+; s; dau A1810; yes; yes; none
4305 " Lola; f; 4 12-18-27; ¼+; s; dau A1811; yes; yes; none
4306 " Alfred; m; 2 10-4-29; ¼+; s; son A1812; yes; yes; none

4307 Plante, Simeon; m; 36; ¼+; s; Head B2089; no; St.Paul, Ramsey, Minn; no; Id.836, Al.G-08099

4308 Plante, William; m; 43; ¼+; s; Head A1813; yes; no; Id.838, Al.G-63

4309 Poitra, Albert; m; 35; ¼+; s; Head B2090; no; Kenel, Corson, SD; no; Id.819, Al.G165

4310 Poitra, Alfred; m; 60; ¼+; m; Head B2091; no; Devils Lake, Ramsey, ND; no; Id.841
4311 " Virginia (Gladue); f; 52; ¼+; m; wife B2092; no; Devils Lake, Ramsey, ND no; Id.841a
4312 " Albert; m; 34; ¼+; s; son B2093; no; Devils Lake, Ramsey, ND; no; Id.841b
4313 " George; m; 24; ¼+; s; son B2095; no; Devils Lake, Ramsey, ND; no; Id.841c

Turtle Mountain Reservation
1932 Census Roll

Key: Number; Surname, Given; Sex; Age at Last Birthday, Birthdate (if given); Tribe (Chippewa, unless stated otherwise); Degree of Blood; Marital Status; Relationship to Head of Family, Last Year Census Number; At Jurisdiction Where Enrolled (Yes/No); Elsewhere - Post Office, County, State; Ward (Yes/No); Allotment [Al.], Annuity [An.] and/or Identification [Id.] Numbers

4314 Poitra, Alfred; m; 40; ¼+; m; Head A1814; yes; no; Id.847, Al.G012608
4315 " Mary M (Parisien); f; 33; ¼+; m; wife A1815; yes; no; Id.847a, Al.H039003
4316 " Rose; f; 15 5-17-16; ¼+; s; dau A1816; yes; no; Id.847b
4317 " Alexander; m; 14 11-7-17; ¼+; s; son A1817; yes; no; Id.847c
4318 " Dominique; m; 8 2-6-24; ¼+; s; son A1818; yes; no; Id.847d
4319 " Fred Elmer; m; 6 12-26-25; ¼+; s; son A1819; yes; no; Id.847e
4320 " Oscar; m; 4 5-27-27; ¼+; s; son A----; yes; no; Id.847f
4321 " Clifford; m; 5/12 9-7-31; ¼+; s; son -----; yes; no; Id.847g

4322 Poitra, Charles; m; 65; ¼+; m; Head A1820; yes; no; Id.842, Al.DL13
4323 " Angelique (Lafloe); m; 77; ¼+; m; wife A1821; yes; yes; Id.842a, Al.R273

4324 Poitra, Charles; m; 68; ¼+; wd; Head A1822; yes; yes; Id.848, Al.R275
4325 " Francois; f[sic]; 27; ¼+; s; son A1823; yes; yes; Id.848f, Al.G130
4326 " Julius; m; 22; ¼+; s; son A1824; yes; yes; Id.848g, Al.H010531
4327 " Amanda; f; 21; ¼+; s; dau A1825; yes; yes; Id.848h, Al.H012602
4328 " Alice; f; 15; ¼+; s; dau A1826; yes; yes; Id.848i
4329 " Christine; f; 12; ¼+; s; dau A1927; yes; yes; Id.848j

4330 Poitra, Charles; m; 32; ¼+; wd; Head A1828; yes; yes; Id.859c, Al.M346
4331 " Frank; m; 7 4-9-24; ¼+; s; son A1829; yes; yes; none

4332 Poitra, Charles #4; m; 36; ¼+; m; Head A1830; yes; yes; Id.866, Al.G081
4333 " Beatrice (Davis); f; 30; ¼+; m; wife A1831; yes; yes; Id.866a, Al.GF104
4334 " John; m; 11 6-5-20; ¼+; s; son A1832; yes; yes; Id.866b
4335 " Melvin; m; 2 11-9-29; ¼+; s; son A1833; yes; yes; Id.866c
4336 " Mary Stella; f; 4/12 11-20-31; ¼+; s; dau -----; yes; yes; Id.866d

4337 Poitra, Charles S; m; 46; ¼+; m; Head B2096; no; Devils Lake, Ramsey, ND; no; Id.857, Al.M-15
NE " Adele (Langer); wife
4338 " Abbie Rose; f; 22 3-7-10; ¼+; s; dau B2097; no; Devils Lake, Ramsey, ND; no; Id.857b
4339 " Anthony m; 20 2-9-12; ¼+; s; son B2098; no; Devils Lake, Ramsey, ND; no; Id.857c
4340 " Louis; m; 16 1-1-16; ¼+; s; son B2099; no; Devils Lake, Ramsey, ND; no; Id.857d
3825 " Sandy; m; 11 8-11-20; ¼+; s; son B2100; no; Devils Lake, Ramsey, ND; no; none
4341 " Lillian; f; 2 10-8-29; ¼+; s; dau -----; no; Devils Lake, Ramsey, ND; no; none

4342 Poitra, Clement; m; 29; ¼+; m; Head A1834; yes; yes; Id.859d, Al.M-293
4343 " Margaret (Wilkie); f; 24; ¼+; m; wife A1835; yes; yes; Id.1005a, Al.H-012654

Turtle Mountain Reservation
1932 Census Roll

Key: Number; Surname, Given; Sex; Age at Last Birthday, Birthdate (if given); Tribe (Chippewa, unless stated otherwise); Degree of Blood; Marital Status; Relationship to Head of Family; Last Year Census Number; At Jurisdiction Where Enrolled (Yes/No); Elsewhere - Post Office, County, State; Ward (Yes/No); Allotment [Al.], Annuity [An.] and/or Identification [Id.] Numbers

4344 Poitra(cont), Rose; f; 7 1-13-25; ¼+; s; dau A1836; yes; yes; none
4345 " Phillip S; m; 5 7-26-26; ¼+; s; son A1837; yes; yes; none
4346 " Emil; m; 4 2-5-28; ¼+; s; son A1838; yes; yes; none
 " Ray Stephen born 4-29-31 and (Died 11-7-31)

4348 Poitra, Collin; m; 28; ¼+; m; Head B2101; no; Dunseith, Rolette, ND; yes; Idf.875, Al.G-01586
NE " Eva (Dionne); wife
4349 " John; m; 2 8-27-29; ¼+; s; son B2101; no; Dunseith, Rolette, ND; yes; none
4350 " Violet; f; 1 2-13-31; ¼+; s; dau B2103; no; Dunseith, Rolette, ND; yes; none

4351 Poitra, Cuthbert; m; 38; ¼+; m; Head A1839; yes; yes; Id.860, Al.M-348
4352 " Mary Ann (Bruce); f; 26; ¼+; m; wife A1840; yes; (Counted twice last census) yes; Id.209c
4353 " Wm Oliver; m; 3 7-16-28; ¼+; s; son A1841; yes; yes; none
Dead " Irene May; A1842 (Died 11-7-31)

4354 Poitra, Ernest; m; 24 12-31-07; ¼+; m; Head B2104; no; Dunseith, Rolette, ND; yes; Id.871g, Al.H-010457
4355 " Beatrice (Decoteau); f; 18 10-28-13; ¼+; m; wife B2105; no; Dunseith, Rolette, ND; yes; Id.298b
4356 " Louis Paul; m; 8/12 7-12-31; ¼+; s; son -----; no; Dunseith, Rolette, ND; yes; none

4357 Poitra, Francois; m; 27 6-22-04; ¼+; s; Head B2110; yes; yes; Id.865e, Al.G-083

4358 Poitra, Francois; m; 26 4-11-05; ¼+; m; Head B2106; no; Dunseith, Rolette, ND; yes; Id.871f, Al.H-010456
4359 " Mary Rose (Azure); f; 26; ¼+; m; wife B2107; no; Dunseith, Rolette, ND; yes; Id.120f, Al.G-013020
4360 " David; m; 7; ¼+; s; son B2111; no; Dunseith, Rolette, ND; yes; none
4361 " Clara; f; 6 4-4-25; ¼+; s; dau B2108; no; Dunseith, Rolette, ND; yes; Id.871g
4362 " Francis; f; 5 8-24-26; ¼+; s; son B2109; no; Dunseith, Rolette, ND; yes; none
4363 " Alfred R; m; 4 12-20-27; ¼+; s; son -----; no; Dunseith, Rolette, ND; yes; none
4364 " Arline Joe; m; 2 9-15-29; ¼+; s; son -----; no; Dunseith, Rolette, ND; yes; none
4365 " Mildred; f; 10/12 5-3-21; ¼+; s; dau -----; no; Dunseith, Rolette, ND; yes; none

4366 Poitra, Frank Z; m; 42; ¼+; m; Head B2166; no; Boggy Creek, Manitoba, Can; no; Id.875b, Al.G-016582
4367 " Florestine (McKay); f; 30; ¼+; m; wife B2112; no; Boggy Creek, Manitoba, Can; yes; Id.729c, Al.G-105
4368 " Agnes; f; 10 7-8-21; ¼+; s; dau -----; no; Boggy Creek, Manitoba, Can; yes; none

Turtle Mountain Reservation
1932 Census Roll

Key: Number; Surname, Given; Sex; Age at Last Birthday, Birthdate (if given); Tribe (Chippewa, unless stated otherwise); Degree of Blood; Marital Status; Relationship to Head of Family; Last Year Census Number; At Jurisdiction Where Enrolled (Yes/No); Elsewhere - Post Office, County, State; Ward (Yes/No); Allotment [Al.], Annuity [An.] and/or Identification [Id.] Numbers

4369 Poitra(cont), Bertha; f; 9 11-29-22; ¼+; s; dau -----; no; Boggy Creek, Manitoba, Can; yes; none
4370 " Ina; f; 7 5-21-24; ¼+; s; dau -----; no; Boggy Creek, Manitoba, Can; yes; none
4371 " Archie; m; 5 11-20-26; ¼+; s; son ------; no; Boggy Creek, Manitoba, Can; yes; none
4372 " Delma; f; 1 6-17-30; ¼+; s; dau ----; no; Boggy Creek, Manitoba, Can; yes; none

4373 Poitra, Hyacinth Isaac; m; 28 8-10-03; ¼+; m; Head B2130; no; Dunseith, Rolette, ND; yes; Id.871e, Al.H-010455
4374 " Martha (Smith); f; 21 6-13-10; ¼+; m; wife B2340; no; Dunseith, Rolette, ND; yes; Id.983c, Al.H-012633
4375 " Julius; m; 2 8-5-29; ¼+; s; dau[sic] -----; no; Dunseith, Rolette, ND; yes; none
4376 " Mary Verna; f; 3/12 12-21-31; ¼+; s; dau ------; no; Dunseith, Rolette, ND; yes; none

4377 Poitra, Israel; m; 33; ¼+; m; Head A1843; yes; no; Id.848b, Al.G-166
4378 " Justine (Parisien.Bonneau); f; 46; ¼+; m; wife A1844; yes; yes; Id.1176a, Al.G-120
4379 " Matilda M; f; 9 7-4-22; ¼+; s; dau A1845; yes; yes; none
4380 " Josephine; f; 6 10-8-25; ¼+; s; dau A1846; yes; yes; none
4381 " Louise; f; 4 5-27-27; ¼+; s; dau A1847; yes; yes; none
4382 " Joseph; m; 2 5-16-29; ¼+; s; son ------; yes; yes; none

4383 Poitra, John; m; 33; ¼+; m; Head B2113; no; Dunseith, Rolette, ND; no; Id.865b, Al.G-084
4384 " Virginia (Morin); f; 22 3-23-10; ¼+; m; wife A1647; no; Dunseith, Rolette, ND; yes; Id..754f, Al.H-024676
4385 " Corrine; f; 1/12 2-16-32; ¼+; s; dau ----; no; Dunseith, Rolette, ND; yes; none

4386 Poitra, John; m; 40; ¼+; m; Head A1848; yes; yes; Id.861, Al.M-359
4387 " Veronic[sic] (Malaterre); f; 40; ¼+; m; wife A1849; yes; no; Id.861a, Al.M-280
4388 " Marie C; f; 18 3-26-14; ¼+; s; dau A1850; yes; yes; Id.861b, Al.H-030298
4389 " Lena D; f; 16 6-26-15; ¼+; s; dau A1851; yes; yes; Id.861c, Al.H-030866
4390 " Justine; f; 14 4-6-17; ¼+; s; dau A1852; yes; yes; Id.861d
4391 " Lillian; f; 12 11-9-19; ¼+; s; dau A1853; yes; yes; Id.861e
4392 " Leona V; f; 3-24-23; ¼+; s; dau A1854; yes; yes; Id.861f
4393 " Ernest; m; 3 10-26-28; ¼+; s; son A1855; yes; yes; Id.861g

4394 Poitra, Joseph; m; 37; ¼+; m; Head 1856; yes; yes; Id.843, Al.G-08128
4395 " Virginia (Enno); f; 29; ¼+; m; wife A1857; yes; yes; Id.372b, Al.G-3
4396 " Louis; m; 11 12-6-20; ¼+; s; son A1858; yes; yes; Id.843b
4397 " Chester; m; 9 7-14-22; ¼+; s; son A1859; yes; yes; Id.843c
4398 " Frederick; m; 7 3-8-24; ¼+; s; son A1860; yes; yes; Id.843d
4399 " Floyd; m; 6 9-29-25; ¼+; s; son A1861; yes; yes; Id.843e

Turtle Mountain Reservation
1932 Census Roll

Key: Number; Surname, Given; Sex; Age at Last Birthday, Birthdate (if given); Tribe (Chippewa, unless stated otherwise); Degree of Blood; Marital Status; Relationship to Head of Family, Last Year Census Number; At Jurisdiction Where Enrolled (Yes/No); Elsewhere - Post Office, County, State; Ward (Yes/No); Allotment [Al.], Annuity [An.] and/or Identification [Id.] Numbers

4400 Poitra(cont), Orella Mary; f; 4 7-4-27; ¼+; s; dau A1862; yes; yes; none
4401 " Joseph N; m; 2 7-24-29; ¼+; s; son A1863; yes; yes; none

4402 Poitra, Joseph Geo; m; 50; ¼+; m; Head B2114; no; Boggy Creek, Manitoba, Can; no; Id.868, Al.G-044
4403 " Adele (Enno); f; 42 11-17-89; ¼+; m; wife B2115; no; Boggy Creek, Manitoba, Can; no; Id.868a, Al.G-06067
4404 " Joseph Geo; m; 18 6-15-13; ¼+; s; son B2117; no; Boggy Creek, Manitoba, Can; yes; Id.868c, Al.H-025395
4405 " Mary Laura; f; 15 9-10-16; ¼+; s; dau B2118; no; Boggy Creek, Manitoba, Can; no; Id.868d
4406 " Mary Jane; f; 14 12-5-17; ¼+; s; dau B2119; no; Boggy Creek, Manitoba, Can; no; Id.868e
4407 " David; m; 12 12-7-19; ¼+; s; son -----; no; Boggy Creek, Manitoba, Can; no; none
4408 " Mary Flora; f; 10 12-10-21; ¼+; s; dau B2120; no; Boggy Creek, Manitoba, Can; no; Id.868g
4409 " Alexander; m; 8 12-20-23; ¼+; s; son B2121; no; Boggy Creek, Manitoba, Can; no; Id.868h
4410 " Albertine; f; 4 8-18-27; ¼+; s; dau -----; no; Boggy Creek, Manitoba, Can; no; none
4411 " Ernestine; f; 2 12-15-29; ¼+; s; dau -----; no; Boggy Creek, Manitoba, Can; no; none

4412 Poitra, Joseph #3; m; 69; ¼+; m; Head B2122; no; Rolette, Rolette, ND; no; Id.869 Al.R-278
4413 " Larose (Delorme); f; 66; ¼+; m; wife B2123; no; Rolette, Rolette, ND; no; Id.869a, Al.G-131
4414 " Mary Rose; f; 33 9-10-98; ¼+; s; dau B2124; no; Rolette, Rolette, ND; yes; Id.869b, Al.M-337
4415 " Norman; m; 31 12-6-00; ¼+; s; son B2125; no; Rolette, Rolette, ND; yes; Id.869c, Al.M-3398
4416 " Julius; m; 28 7-21-03; ¼+; s; son B2126; no; Rolette, Rolette, ND; yes; Id.869d, Al.M-290
4417 " Albert; m; 26 3-30-06; ¼+; s; son B2127; no; Rolette, Rolette, ND; yes; Id.869e, Al.G-130

4418 Poitra, Joseph #2; m; 64; 14; m; Head B2128; no; Dunseith, Rolette, ND; yes; Id.871, Al.DL-1
4419 " Alphonsine (Belgarde); f; 60; ¼+; m; wife B2129; no; Dunseith, Rolette, ND; no; Id.871a, Al.H010461
4420 " Ray; m; 20 3-12-12; ¼+; s; son B2131; no; Dunseith, Rolette, ND; Id.871h, Al.H-030477½

Turtle Mountain Reservation
1932 Census Roll

Key: Number; Surname, Given; Sex; Age at Last Birthday, Birthdate (if given); Tribe (Chippewa, unless stated otherwise); Degree of Blood; Marital Status; Relationship to Head of Family, Last Year Census Number; At Jurisdiction Where Enrolled (Yes/No); Elsewhere - Post Office, County, State; Ward (Yes/No); Allotment [Al.], Annuity [An.] and/or Identification [Id.] Numbers

4421 Poitra, Joseph; m; 50; ¼+; m; Head B2132; no; Dunseith, Rolette, ND; no; Id.862, Al.G-037075
NE   "   Maggie (Lilley);   wife

4422 Poitra, Joseph A; m; 55; ¼+; s; Head A1864; yes; no; Id.852, Al.H-030293

4423 Poitra, Julius; m; 48; ¼+; s; Head A1865; yes; yes; Id.851
NE Poitra, Louis; m;   Head
4424   "   Isabel (Champagne); f; 45; ¼+; m; wife A1866; yes; no; Id.864a
4425   "   Josephine; f; 25; ¼+; s; dau A1867; yes; no; Id.864c

4426 Poitra, Louis; m; 35 4-16-96; ¼+; m; Head B2133; no; Dunseith, Rolette, ND; no; Id.871b, Al.H-010460
NE   "   Ruth (Demarais);   wife
4427   "   Irene; f; 10 7-3-21; ¼+; s; dau B2134; no; Dunseith, Rolette, ND; no; none
4428   "   Percy; m; 9 9-14-22; ¼+; s; son B3135; no; Dunseith, Rolette, ND; no; none
4429   "   Viola; f; 6 7-18-25; ¼+; s; dau -----; no; Dunseith, Rolette, ND; no; none
4430   "   Eleanor; f; 4 8-2-27; ¼+; s; dau ------; no; Dunseith, Rolette, ND; no; none
4431   "   Dorothy; f; 2 12-29-29; ¼+; s; dau ------; no; Dunseith, Rolette, ND; no; none

4432 Poitra, Marie (Breland); f; 79; ¼+; wd; Head A1868; yes; no; Id.846a, Al.G-012607

4433 Poitra, Mary (Grant); f; 69; ¼+; wd; Head A1869; yes; no; Id.859a, Al.M-358
4434   "   Mary Jane; f; 34; ¼+; s; dau A1870; yes; no; Id.859h, Al.M-349

4435 Poitra, Michael; m; 26 1-4-06; ¼+; m; Head A1871; yes; yes; Id.875d, Al.G-016588
4436   "   Josephine (Davis); f; 23; ¼+; m; wife A1872; yes; yes; Id.266g, Al.H-010499
4437   "   Ina; f; 4; ¼+; s; dau A1873; yes; yes; none
4438   "   Virginia; f; 2 12-29-29; ¼+; s; dau A1874; yes; yes; none
4439   "   James; m; 4/12 11-4-31; ¼+; s; son -----; yes; yes; none

NE Poitra, Moses;   Head
4440   "   Celina (Poitra); f; 45; ¼+; m; wife B2136; no; Rolette, Rolette, ND; no; Id.863a, Al.M-347
4441   "   Charles; m; 20 6-20-11; ¼+; s; son B2137; no; Rolette, Rolette, ND; yes; Id.863, Al.H-013055
4442   "   Mary Ida; f; 18 2-9-13; ¼+; s; dau B2138; no; Rolette, Rolette, ND; yes; Id.863c
4443   "   Eugene; m; 17 8-23-14; ¼+; s; son B2139; no; Rolette, Rolette, ND; yes; Id.863d
4444   "   Edward; m; 15 9-9-16; ¼+; s; son B2140; no; Rolette, Rolette, ND; yes; Id.863e
4445   "   Cecelia; f; 12 5-7-19; ¼+; s; dau B2141; no; Rolette, Rolette, ND; yes; none
4446   "   Fred; m; 10 9-7-21; ¼+; s; son B2142; no; Rolette, Rolette, ND; yes; none

Turtle Mountain Reservation
1932 Census Roll

Key: Number; Surname, Given; Sex; Age at Last Birthday, Birthdate (if given); Tribe (Chippewa, unless stated otherwise); Degree of Blood; Marital Status; Relationship to Head of Family, Last Year Census Number; At Jurisdiction Where Enrolled (Yes/No); Elsewhere - Post Office, County, State; Ward (Yes/No); Allotment [Al.], Annuity [An.] and/or Identification [Id.] Numbers

4447	Poitra, Napoleon; m; 32; ¼+; m; Head A1875; yes; no; Id.848c, Al.G-167	
4448	" Rachel (Dejarlais); f; 28; ¼+; m; wife A1876; yes; yes; Id.312c, Al.M-97	
4449	" Nora Lucy; f; 9 12-18-23; ¼+; s; dau A1877; yes; yes; none	
4450	" Josephine; f; 6 12-9-25; ¼+; s; dau A1878; yes; yes; none	
4451	" Raymond; m; 1 5-27-30; ¼+; s; son ------; yes; yes; none	

4452 Poitra, Napoleon; m; 62; ¼+; s; Head B2143; no; Rolette, Rolette, ND; no; Id.855, Al.W-39

4453 Poitra, Norbert; m; 44; ¼+; m; Head A1879; yes; no; Id.850, Al.G-012609
4454 " Blanche (Davis); f; 34; ¼+; m; wife A1880; yes; yes; Id.350a, Al.GF-129
4455 " Lawrence; m; 17 3-3-15; ¼+; s; son A1881; yes; yes; Id.850b
4456 " Blanche; f; 15 6-2-16; ¼+; s; dau A1882; yes; yes; Id.850c
4457 " Cecelia; f; 14 9-21-17; ¼+; s; dau A1883; yes; yes; Id.850d
4458 " Lucy; f; 13 10-24-18; ¼+; s; dau A1884; yes; yes; Id.850e
4459 " Peter G; m; 11 9-27-20; ¼+; s; son A1885; yes; yes; Id.850f
4460 " Fred Leon; m; 10 1-17-22; ¼+; s; son A1886; yes; yes; Id.850g
4461 " Christine; f; 9 3-28-23; ¼+; s; dau A1887; yes; yes; Id.850h
4462 " John Warren; m; 6 3-29-26; ¼+; s; son A1888; yes; yes; Id.850i
4463 " Rachel S; f; 3 12-19-28; ¼+; s; dau A1889; yes; yes; Id.850j
4464 " Raymond; m; 1 10-27-30; ¼+; s; son A1890; yes; yes; Id.850k

4465 Poitra, Norbert; m; 45; ¼+; s; Head B2144; no; Froid, Sheridan, Mont; no; Id.853, Al.G-160

NE Poitra, N J; Head
4466 " Amy Emma (Lecompt); f; 31 10-24-00; ¼+; m; wife B1574; no; Froid, Sheridan, Mont; yes; Id.655b, Al.G-556

4467 Poitra, Raphael; m; 30 7-20-01; ¼+; m; Head B2145; no; Dunseith, Rolette, ND; yes; Id.871d, Al.H-010459
NE " Alvina (Lagimodiere); wife
4468 " Eugene; m; 6 7-11-25; ¼+; s; son -----; no; Dunseith, Rolette, ND; yes; none
4469 " Charley; m; 5 3-2-27; ¼+; s; son ------; no; Dunseith, Rolette, ND; yes; none
4479 " Mae C; f; 1 5-13-30; ¼+; s; dau ------; no; Dunseith, Rolette, ND; yes; none

4471 Poitra, Robert; m; 27 9-7-05; ¼+; m; Head B2146; yes; no; Id.874b
NE " Eva (Lafrance); wife
4472 " Robert D; m; 4 3-23-28; ¼+; s; son B2147; yes; no; none
4473 " Marion G; f; 2 7-26-29; ¼+; s; dau B2148; yes; no; none
4474 " Theresa M; f; 2 7-26-29; ¼+; s; dau B2149; yes; no; none
4475 " Olympia; f; 4/12 11-5-31; ¼+; s; dau ------; yes; no; none

Turtle Mountain Reservation
1932 Census Roll

Key: Number; Surname, Given; Sex; Age at Last Birthday, Birthdate (if given); Tribe (Chippewa, unless stated otherwise); Degree of Blood; Marital Status; Relationship to Head of Family, Last Year Census Number; At Jurisdiction Where Enrolled (Yes/No); Elsewhere - Post Office, County, State; Ward (Yes/No); Allotment [Al.], Annuity [An.] and/or Identification [Id.] Numbers

4476 Poitra, Stanley G; m; 27; ¼+; m; Head B2094; no; Devils Lake, Ramsey, ND; yes; Id.841d, Al.G07829
4477 " Rosalie (Herman); f; 25; ¼+; m; wife B1128; no; Devils Lake, Ramsey, ND yes; Id.477d, Al.G216
4478 " Stanley M; m; 1 9-27-30; ¼+; s; son ------; no; Devils Lake, Ramsey, ND; yes; Id. none
4479 " Irene B; f; 2/12 1-31-32; ¼+; s; dau ------; no; Devils Lake, Ramsey, ND; yes; Id. none

4480 Poitra, Severe; m; 50l ¼+; m; Head A1891; yes; yes; Id.874, Al.R280
NE " Ellen (Peltier);─ wife
4481 " Minnie; f; 24 1-5-08; ¼+; s; dau A1892; yes; yes; Id.874c
4482 " Harry J; m; 21 12-11-10; ¼+; s; son A1893; yes; yes; Id.874d
4483 " Clarence; m; 18 3-3-14; ¼+; s; son A1894; yes; yes; Id.874e
4485 " Alberta; f; 16 1-1-16; ¼+; s; dau A1895; yes; yes; Id.874f
4486 " Martin T; m; 12 9-10-19; ¼+; s; son A1896; yes; yes; Id.874g
4487 " Emma; f; 10 7-8-21; ¼+; s; dau A1897; yes; yes; Id.874h
4488 " Roy F; m; 8 12-23-23; ¼+; s; son A1898; yes; yes; Id.874i
4489 " Elnora; f; 5 4-2-26; ¼+; s; dau A1899; yes; yes; Id.874j
4490 " Norine; f; 5 4-2-26; ¼+; s; dau A1900; yes; yes; Id.874k
4491 " Dorothy S; f; 8/12 7-26-31; ¼+; s; dau -----; yes; yes; Id.874l

NE Poitra, Vilena; Head
4492 " Cecil; m; 29 2-26-03; ¼+; s; son B2152; no; Detroit, Wayne, Mich; yes; Id.876d, Al.G08146
4493 " Jerome; m; 22 7-12-09; ¼+; s; son B2153; no; Froid, Sheridan, Mont; yes; Id.876f, Al.G07898
4494 " Sarah; f; 19 4-29-12; ¼+; s; dau B2154; no; Dagmar, Sheridan, Mont; no; Id.876g
4495 " Xavier; m; 18 3-22-14; ¼+; s; son B2155; no; Dagmar, Sheridan, Mont; no; Id.876h
4496 " James; m; 16 12-14-15; ¼+; s; son B2156; no; Dagmar, Sheridan, Mont; no; Id.876i
4497 " (Bohannon) Veronica; f; 1/12 2-16-32; ¼+; s; gr-dau ------; no; (Dau of #4494) Dagmar, Sheridan, Mont; no; none

4498 Poitra, William; m; 70; ¼+; m; Head A1901; yes; yes; Id.872, Al.R281
4499 " Alphonsine (Delorme); f; 59; ¼+; m; wife A1902; yes; no; Id.872a, Al.G177

NE Poitra, William; Head
4500 " Marie (Delorme); f; 48; ¼+; m; wife A1903; yes; no; Id.858, Al.G04
4501 " Justine; f; 20 7-24-11; ¼+; s; dau A1904; yes; yes; Id.858a, Al.H024679
4502 " Zaida; f; 17 4-26-14; ¼+; s; dau A1905; yes; yes; Id.858b, Al.H030296
4503 " Lillian; f; 15 4-5-16; ¼+; s; dau A1906; yes; no; Id.858c

Turtle Mountain Reservation
1932 Census Roll

Key: Number; Surname, Given; Sex; Age at Last Birthday, Birthdate (if given); Tribe (Chippewa, unless stated otherwise); Degree of Blood; Marital Status; Relationship to Head of Family, Last Year Census Number; At Jurisdiction Where Enrolled (Yes/No); Elsewhere - Post Office, County, State; Ward (Yes/No); Allotment [Al.], Annuity [An.] and/or Identification [Id.] Numbers

----- Poitra(cont), Alfred; A1907 (On roll last year by error)

4504 Poitra, Zachary; m; 62; ¼+; m; Head B2157; yes; yes; Id.875, Al.DL24575
4505 " Virginia (Morin); f; 40; ¼+; m; wife B2158; yes; no; Id.875a, Al.G016584
4506 " Norman; m; 24; 4-10-07; ¼+; s; son B2159; yes; yes; Id.875e, Al.G016585
4507 " Dominique; m; 23 11-3-08; ¼+; s; son B2160; yes; yes; Id.875f, Al.G016587
4508 " Mary; f; 22 1-28-10; ¼+; s; dau B2161; yes; yes; Id.875g, Al.G016589
4509 " Rose D; f; 18 11-30-13; ¼+; s; dau B2162; yes; yes; Id.875h, Al.H030449
4510 " Alda; f; 12 3-27-20; ¼+; s; dau B2163; yes; yes; Id.875i
4511 " Louis; m; 10 8-28-21; ¼+; s; son B2164; yes; yes; Id.875j
4512 " Wilmar D; m; 8 5-25-23; ¼+; s; son B2165; yes; yes; Id.875k

4513 Poitra, Zepherine; m; 43; ¼+; m; Head B2167; no; Froid, Sheridan, Mont; no; Id.878, Al.G609
4514 " Mary Ann (Parisien); f; 39; ¼+; m; wife B2168; no; Froid, Sheridan, Mont; no; Id.878a
4515 " Delima; f; 13 10-19-17; ¼+; s; dau B2169; no; Froid, Sheridan, Mont; no; Id.878c
4516 " Lillian; f; 12 7-2-19; ¼+; s; dau B2170; no; Froid, Sheridan, Mont; no; Id.878d
4517 " Caroline; f; 10 12-12-21; ¼+; s; dau B2171; no; Froid, Sheridan, Mont; no; Id.878e
4518 " Ida; f; 9 8-25-23; ¼+; s; dau B2172; no; Froid, Sheridan, Mont; no; Id.878f
4519 " Herman; m; 6 9-18-25; ¼+; s; son B2173; no; Froid, Sheridan, Mont; no; Id.878g
4520 " Albert; m; 4 9-18-27; ¼+; s; son B2174; no; Froid, Sheridan, Mont; no; Id.878h
4521 " Laura M; f; 2 10-8-29; ¼+; s; dau ------; no; Froid, Sheridan, Mont; no; Id.878i

NE Premeau, Alex; Head
4522 " Sarah (Lafontain); f; 49; ¼+; m; wife B2175; no; Cando, Towner, ND; no; Id.881a, R-283
4523 " Justine; f; 24 7-21-07; ¼+; s; dau B2176; no; Cando, Towner, ND; yes; Id.881c, Al.G494
4524 " John B; m; 23 9-21-08; ¼+; s; son B2177; no; Cando, Towner, ND; yes; Id.881d, Al.G-08341
4525 " Wm Morris; m; 16 9-15-15; ¼+; s; son B2178; no; Cando, Towner, ND; no; Id.881g
4526 " Ernest F; m; 15 9-9-16; ¼+; s; son B2179; no; Cando, Towner, ND; no; Id.881f
4527 " Amy Ruth; f; 14 2-12-18; ¼+; s; dau B2180; no; Cando, Towner, ND; no; Id.881h

Turtle Mountain Reservation
1932 Census Roll

Key: Number; Surname, Given; Sex; Age at Last Birthday, Birthdate (if given); Tribe (Chippewa, unless stated otherwise); Degree of Blood; Marital Status; Relationship to Head of Family, Last Year Census Number; At Jurisdiction Where Enrolled (Yes/No); Elsewhere - Post Office, County, State; Ward (Yes/No); Allotment [Al.], Annuity [An.] and/or Identification [Id.] Numbers

4528 Premeau(cont), Ernestine; f; 10 6-27-21; ¼+; s; dau B2181; no; Cando, Towner, ND; no; Id.881i
4529 " Frank S; m; 7 11-1-24; ¼+; s; son -----; no; Cando, Towner, ND; no; none
4530 " Esther M; f; 5 5-21-26; ¼+; s; dau -----; no; Cando, Towner, ND; no; none
4531 " (Poitra), Rita E; f; 2 4-27-29; ¼+; s; grand dau B2182; no; (Dau of Justine) Cando, Towner, ND; no; none

4532 Premeau, Arthur John; m; 30; ¼+; m; Head A1909; yes; yes; Id.880c, Al.M-160
NE " Mary (Lafrance); wife
4533 " Ida; f; 7 12-15-24; ¼+; s; dau A1910; yes; yes; none
4534 " Theresa V; f; 4 6-14-27; ¼+; s; dau A1911; yes; yes; none
4535 " Arthur R; m; 2 3-6-29; ¼+; s; son A1912; yes; yes; none
4536 " Joseph Wm; m; 1 12-24-30; ¼+; s; son; yes; yes; none

4537 Premeau, Joseph; m; 62; ¼+; m; Head A1913; yes; yes; Id.880, Al.R0282
NE " Ernestine (Dubois); wife
4538 " Aldina; f; 25; ¼+; s; dau A1914; yes; yes; Id.880d, Al.G-443
4539 " Andrew; m; 20; ¼+; s; son A1915; yes; yes; Id.880e
4540 " Leroy M; m; 16; ¼+; s; son A1917; yes; yes; Id.880g
4541 " Laura; f; 12 5-22-19; ¼+; s; dau A1918; yes; yes; Id.880h
4542 " Frances; f; 10 10-26-21; ¼+; s; dau A1919; yes; yes; Id.880i
4543 " Dolores; f; 3 12-12-28; ¼+; s; sau[sic] A1920; yes; yes; Id.880j

4544 Premeau, Pauline; f; 89; ¼+; wd; Head A1921; yes; no; Id.879a, Al.M-343

NE Purdy, George C; Head
4545 " Beatrice (Schindler); m; wife A1922; yes; yes; Id.916b, Al.G0188
4546 " Lorne W; m; 8 6-7-23; ¼+; s; son A1923; yes; yes; none
4547 " Elizabeth f; 6 6-12-25; ¼+; s; dau A1924; yes; yes; none
4548 " Clinton; m; 5 8-3-26; ¼+; s; son A1925; yes; yes; none
4549 " Clarence; m; 3 11-3-28; ¼+; s; son A1926; yes; yes; none

NE Purvis, John; Head
4550 " Florence (Crissler); f; 22 11-21-09; ¼+; m; wife B564; no; Scandinavia, Manitoba, Can; yes; Id.241f, Al.G-010491
4551 " Christine; f; 8/12 8-14-31; ¼+; s; dau ------; no; Scandinavia, Manitoba, Can; yes; none

NE Rakes, Edward; Head
4552 " Mary Rose (L'Esparance); f; 25; ¼+; m; wife B2183; no; (Counted twice last census) Devils Lake, Ramsey, ND; yes; Id.669e, Al.G-037071
4553 " Edward, Jr; m; 11/12 4-14-31; ¼+; s; son ------; no; Devils Lake, Ramsey, ND; yes; none

Turtle Mountain Reservation
1932 Census Roll

Key: Number; Surname, Given; Sex; Age at Last Birthday, Birthdate (if given); Tribe (Chippewa, unless stated otherwise); Degree of Blood; Marital Status; Relationship to Head of Family, Last Year Census Number; At Jurisdiction Where Enrolled (Yes/No); Elsewhere - Post Office, County, State; Ward (Yes/No); Allotment [Al.], Annuity [An.] and/or Identification [Id.] Numbers

NE Rerdon[sic], Cleo C;   Head
4554   "   Mary Rose (Laverdure); f; 21; ¼+; m; wife B1551; no; Cando, Towner, ND; no; ID.647f
4555   "   Cosette P; f; 3 2-6-29; ¼+; s; dau ------; no; Cando, Towner, ND; no; none

NE Reardon, James;   Head
4556   "   Agnes (Wilkie); f; 30; ¼+; m; wife B2184; yes; yes; Id.1018c, Al.G-08376
4557   "   Gertrude; f; 8 6-17-23; ¼+; s; dau B2185; yes; yes; none
4558   "   Gabriel; m; 7 3-21-25; ¼+; s; son B2186; yes; yes; none
4559   "   Louise; f; 4 4-13-27; ¼+; s; dau B2187; yes; yes; none
4560   "   James M; m; 3 12-25-28; ¼+; s; son -----; yes; yes; none
4561   "   Patrick; m; 9/12 6-12-31; ¼+; s; son B2188; yes; yes; none

4562 Reflection Man; John; m; 46; F; m; Head B2189; no; Dunseith, Rolette, ND; yes; Id.49, Al.R-304
4563   "   Ellen (Cree); f; 29; F; wife B2190; no; Dunseith, Rolette, ND; yes; Id.43c, Al.H-012576
4564   "   Kemeiosyik; m; 9 9-23-33; F; s; son B2191; no; Dunseith, Rolette, ND; yes; none
4565   "   Flying Away; f; 7 3-13-25; F; s; dau B2192; no; Dunseith, Rolette, ND; yes; none
4566   "   Blue Thunder; m; 6-28-29; F; s; son B2193; no; Dunseith, Rolette, ND; yes; none
4567   "   Mary; f; 4/12 11-27-31; F; s; dau ------; no; Dunseith, Rolette, ND; yes; none

NE Regan, Leonard;   Head
         Florence (Gunderson);   B2194   (Divorced from Regan. #2568 on this census)
4568   "   Ruth; f; 14 10-19-17; ¼+; s; dau ------; no; St.Paul, Ramsey, Minn; no; Id.462b, Al.M-383
4569   "   Genevieve; f; 12 10-9-19; ¼+; s; dau ----; no; St.Paul, Ramsey, Minn; no; none
4570   "   Dolores; f; 10 8-15-21; ¼+; s; dau -----; no; St.Paul, Ramsey, Minn; no; none

NE Regnier, John;   Head
4571   "   Emma (Latraille.Clark) f; 44; ¼+; m; wife B2195; no; Grenora, Williams, ND; no; Id.240a, Al.W-013071
4572 " (Clark) Evelyn; f; 20; ¼+; s; step dau B2196; no; Grenora, Williams, ND; no; Id.240b
4573 " (Clark) Laura Leona; f; 18; ¼+; s; step dau B2197; no; Grenora, Williams, ND; no; Id.240c
4574   "   Grace M; f; 16 2-15-16; ¼+; s; dau B2198; no; Grenora, Williams, ND; no; none
4575   "   Eva May; f; 14 10-17-17; ¼+; s; dau B2199; no; Grenora, Williams, ND; no; none

Turtle Mountain Reservation
1932 Census Roll

Key: Number; Surname, Given; Sex; Age at Last Birthday, Birthdate (if given); Tribe (Chippewa, unless stated otherwise); Degree of Blood; Marital Status; Relationship to Head of Family; Last Year Census Number; At Jurisdiction Where Enrolled (Yes/No); Elsewhere - Post Office, County, State; Ward (Yes/No); Allotment [Al.], Annuity [An.] and/or Identification [Id.] Numbers

4576 Regnier(cont), Bernice; f; 13 1-1-19; ¼+; s; dau B2200; no; Grenora, Williams, ND; no; none
4577 " Lawrence; m; 12 3-26-20; ¼+; s; son B2201; no; Grenora, Williams, ND; no; none

4578 Renault, Mary Rose; f; 9-6-13; ¼+; s; Head B1261; no; Rolette, Rolette, ND; no; Id.884b
4579 " Nora S; f; 15 5-5-16; ¼+; s; sis B1262; no; Rolette, Rolette, ND; no; Id.884c
4580 " Cordelia; f; 11 9-12-20; ¼+; s; sis B1263; no; Rolette, Rolette, ND; no; Id.884d

4581 Renault, Telesphore; m; 50; ¼+; m; Head A1928; yes; no; Id.885, Al.R-286
4582 " Emma (Vallie.Decoteau); f; 34; ¼+; m; wife A1929; yes; yes; Id.975b, Al.GF-224
4583 " John B; m; 25 6-23-06; ¼+; s; son A1930; yes; yes; Id.885b, Al.G616
4584 " Norman; m; 15 6-18-16; ¼+; s; son A1931; yes; yes; Id.885f
4585 " Albert; m; 12 5-20-19; ¼+; s; son A1932; yes; yes; Id.885h
4586 " Grant; m; 2 6-24-29; ¼+; s; son A1933; yes; yes; Id.885i
4587 " (Decoteau) St.Ann; f; 11 5-6-20; ¼+; s; step dau A1937; yes; yes; Id.293e
4588 " (Decoteau) Ruth; f; 10 3-18-22; ¼+; s; step dau A1938; yes; yes; Id.293f

4589 Renville, Elie; m; 29; ¼+; m; Head B2202; no; Buford, Williams, ND; yes; Id.886e, Al.M-225
4590 " Stella (Decoteau); f; 25; ¼+; m; wife B2203; no; Buford, Williams, ND; yes; Id.297d, Al.G-01417

4591 Renville, Josette; f; 72; ¼+; wd; Head B2204; no; Buford, Williams, ND; no; Id.886a, Al.M-126

4591 Renville, William; m; 32; ¼+; m; Head B2205; no; Buford, Williams, ND; yes; Id.886b, Al.M-124
NE " Caroline (Goosline); wife
4593 " Josephine; f; 9 9-16-22; ¼+; s; dau B2206; no; Buford, Williams, ND; yes; none
4594 " William; m; 8 12-9-23; ¼+; s; son B2207; no; Buford, Williams, ND; yes; none
4595 " Harry; m; 6 4-9-25; ¼+; s; son B2208; no; Buford, Williams, ND; yes; none
4596 " John; m; 4 11-4-27; ¼+; s; son B2209; no; Buford, Williams, ND; yes; none
4597 " Rose; f; 2 5-17-29; ¼+; s; dau ------; no; Buford, Williams, ND; yes; none
4598 " Virginia; f; 1 1-16-31; ¼+; s; dau ------; no; Buford, Williams, ND; yes; none

Turtle Mountain Reservation
1932 Census Roll

Key: Number; Surname, Given; Sex; Age at Last Birthday, Birthdate (if given); Tribe (Chippewa, unless stated otherwise); Degree of Blood; Marital Status; Relationship to Head of Family, Last Year Census Number; At Jurisdiction Where Enrolled (Yes/No); Elsewhere - Post Office, County, State; Ward (Yes/No); Allotment [Al.], Annuity [An.] and/or Identification [Id.] Numbers

4599 Richard, Hyacinth; m; 65; ¼+; m; Head B2210; no; St.John, Rolette, ND; no; Id.889, Al.G-08411
NE " Bebienne (Langer); wife
4600 " Alfred; m; 22; ¼+; s; son B2212; no; Canton, (Asylum) Lincoln, SD, yes Id.889f, Al.H-010444
4601 " (Nelson) Wayne; m; 9 5-26-22; ¼+; s; adpt son B2213; no; St.John, Rolette, ND; yes; Id.889g

4602 Riddle, Joschim; m; 30; ¼+; m; Head B2214; no; St.John, Rolette, ND; yes; Id.889c, Al.G-08413
NE " Mabel (Bergie); wife
4603 " Gladys; f; 4 4-1-27; ¼+; s; dau B2215; no; St.John, Rolette, ND; yes; none
4604 " Bernice; f; 3 3-22-28; ¼+; s; dau -----; no; St.John, Rolette, ND; yes; none
4605 " Willard; m; 2 1-10-29; ¼+; s; son B2216; no; St.John, Rolette, ND; yes; none
4606 " Francis; m; 7/12 8-16-31; ¼+; s; son -----; no; St.John, Rolette, ND; yes; none

NE Richwine, Harry; Head
4607 " St.Ann (Thomas); f; 35; ¼+; m; wife B2217; no; Medicine Lake, Sheridan. Mont; yes; Id.956b, Al.G-036
4608 " Margaret; f; 11 12-8-20; ¼+; s; dau B2218; no; Medicine Lake, Sheridan, Mont; yes; none
4609 " Leonard; m; 10 12-23-21; ¼+; s; son xxxxx; no; Medicine Lake, Sheridan, Mont; yes; none
4610 " Shirley; f; 1 9-23-30; ¼+; s; dau ------; no; Medicine Lake, Sheridan, Mont; yes; none

NE Riddle, Albert; Head
4611 " Rosine (Peltier.Henry); f; 34; ¼+; m; wife B2219; no; Yorkton, Sask, Can; yes; Id.1043a, Al.G-236
4612 " (Henry) Mary Jane; f; 19; ¼+; s; step dau B2220; no; Yorkton, Sask, Can; yes; Id.1043b
4613 " Alexander; m; 11 ¼+; s; son B2221; no; Yorkton, Sask, Can; yes; none

NE Ried, Wesley; Head
4614 " Anna (Gladue); f; 26; ¼+; m; wife B2222; no; Boissevain, Manitoba, Canada yes; Id.408a, Al.G530

NE Riendeau, Aledge; Head
4615 " Lillian (Duchesneau); f; 26 5-15-05; ¼+; m; wife B760; no; Thorne, Rolette, Rolette, ND; no; Id.365d
4616 " Serena; f; 6 9-4-25; ¼+; s; dau -----; no; Thorne, Rolette, ND; no; none
4617 " Alice Mae; f; 4 5-1-27; ¼+; s; dau ------; no; Thorne, Rolette, ND; no; none
4618 " Lucianna; f; 3 10-27-28; ¼+; s; dau ------; no; Thorne, Rolette, ND; no; none
4619 " Cecelia; f; 2 11-23-29; ¼+; s; dau ------; no; Thorne, Rolette, ND; no; none

Turtle Mountain Reservation
1932 Census Roll

Key: Number; Surname, Given; Sex; Age at Last Birthday, Birthdate (if given); Tribe (Chippewa, unless stated otherwise); Degree of Blood; Marital Status; Relationship to Head of Family, Last Year Census Number; At Jurisdiction Where Enrolled (Yes/No); Elsewhere - Post Office, County, State; Ward (Yes/No); Allotment [Al.], Annuity [An.] and/or Identification [Id.] Numbers

4620 Riendeau(cont), Adolph; m; 8/12 8-11-31; ¼+; s; son ------; no; Thorne, Rolette, ND; no; none

4621 Rising Sun, Little; m; 39; F; s; Head; no; Dunseith, Rolette, ND; yes; Id.55b, Al.G-332

4622 Rising Sun, Maynard; m; 21; F; Head B2223; no; Dunseith, Rolette, ND; yes; Id.51d, Al. none

NE Robert, Antonio; Head B2224 (Error in listing him last census)
4623 " Mary (Duchesneau); f; 30 1-29-02; ¼+; m; wife B2225; no; Thorne, Rolette, ND; yes; Id.365c, Al.M-247
4624 " Dolores; f; 7 8-22-24; ¼+; s; dau B2226; no; Thorne, Rolette, ND; yes; none
4625 " Edgar; m; 3 9-15-28; ¼+; s; son ------; no; Thorne, Rolette, ND; yes; none
4626 " Ophelia; f; 2 3-25-30; ¼+; s; dau ------; no; Thorne, Rolette, ND; yes; none

4627 Rolette, Alice; f; 40; ¼+; s; Head B2227; no; Willow City, Bottineau, ND; no; Id.898, Al.M-45

4628 Rolette, Ernest; m; 39; ¼+; s; Head B2228; no; Portland, Multnomah, Ore; no; Id.896, Al.M-233

Dead Rolette, Joseph; B2229 (Died 1-24-20)
NE " Lucinda (Frigon); Head
4629 " John; m; 33; ¼+; s; son B2230; no; Drumright, Creek Okla; yes; Id.894, Al.G-05576
4630 " Henry; m; 29; ¼+; s; son B2231; no; Drumright, Creek Okla; yes; Id.894c, Al.H-012631

4631 Rolette, Louis; m; 37; ¼+; s; Head B2232; no; Unknown; no; Id.895, Al.M-41

4632 Rolette, Martin; m; 50; ¼+; m; Head B2233; no; Tulsa, Tulsa, Okla; no; Id.892, Al.H-012629
NE " Emma (Daniels); wife

Dead Rolette, Martin; B2234 (Died in 1921)

NE Rondeau, A F; Head
4633 " Adele (Azure); f; 29; ¼+; m; wife B2235; no; Devils Lake, Ramsey, ND; no; Id.143, Al.M-295
4634 " Geneva; f; 6 1-10-26; ¼+; s; dau B2236; no; Devils Lake, Ramsey, ND; no; none
4635 " Muriel M; f; 4 7-6-27; ¼+; s; dau ------; no; Devils Lake, Ramsey, ND; no; none

Turtle Mountain Reservation
1932 Census Roll

Key: Number; Surname, Given; Sex; Age at Last Birthday, Birthdate (if given); Tribe (Chippewa, unless stated otherwise); Degree of Blood; Marital Status; Relationship to Head of Family, Last Year Census Number; At Jurisdiction Where Enrolled (Yes/No); Elsewhere - Post Office, County, State; Ward (Yes/No); Allotment [Al.], Annuity [An.] and/or Identification [Id.] Numbers

NE	Rossknecht, Gustave;	Head
4636	"	Mary Eliza (Marion); f; 46 5-12-85; ¼+; m; wife B2237; no; Hot Springs, Fall River, SD; no; Id.900a, Al.M-155
4637	"	Henry; m; 25 5-3-06; ¼+; s; son B2238; no; Hot Springs, Fall River, SD; Id.900b
4638	"	Mary Rose; f; 24 10-12-07; ¼+; s; dau B2239; no; Hot Springs, Fall River, SD; Id.900c
4639	"	Joseph; m; 20 3-31-12; ¼+; s; son B2241; no; Hot Springs, Fall River, SD; Id.900e
4640	"	Herman; m; 18 11-22-13; ¼+; s; son B2242; no; Hot Springs, Fall River, SD; Id.900f
4641	"	Lucy; f; 16 12-23-15; ¼+; s; dau B2243; no; Hot Springs, Fall River, SD; Id.900g
4642	"	Irene; f; 14 10-21-17; ¼+; s; dau B2244; no; Hot Springs, Fall River, SD; no; Id.900h
4643	"	Francis; m; 12 9-19-19; ¼+; s; son B2245; no; Hot Springs, Fall River, SD; no; Id.900i
4644	"	Alice; f; 10 10-1-21; ¼+; s; dau B2246; no; Hot Springs, Fall River, SD; no; Id.900j
4645	"	Gustave; m; 8 8-23-23; ¼+; ; son -----; no; Hot Springs, Fall River, SD; no; Id.900k
4646	"	Raymond; m; 6 12-26-25; ¼+; s; ------; no; Hot Springs, Fall River, SD; no; Id.900l
4647	"	Ralph; m; 4 1-11-29; ¼+; s; son ------; no; Hot Springs, Fall River, SD; no; Id.900m

4648	Roussin, Eustache; m; 72; ¼+; m; Head A1939; yes; yes; Id.901, Al.R-289	
4649	" Madeline (Champagne); f; 72; ¼+; m; wife A1940; yes; no; Id.901a, Al.M-391	

4650	Roussin, Louis Bruno; m; 37; ¼+; m; Head A1941; yes; no; Id.903, Al.M-392	
4651	" Clemence (Jerome); f; 25; ¼+; m; wife A1942; yes; yes; Id.521a, Al.G-393	
4652	" Louis, Jr; m; 3 3-5-29; ¼+; s; son A1943; yes; yes; none	
Dead	" Roger M;	A1944 (Died 1-20-31)

4653	Roussin, Pascal; m; 43; ¼+; m; Head A1945; yes; no; Id.902, Al.M-395	
4654	" Zoe (Morin); f; 38; ¼+; m; wife A1946; yes; no; Id.902a, Al.G-04842	
4655	" Louis; m; 16 8-31-15; ¼+; s; son A1947; yes; no; Id.902b	
4656	" Amelia; f; 12 11-18-19; ¼+; s; dau A1948; yes; no; Id.902c	
4657	" Evelyn; f; 10 9-4-21; ¼+; s; dau A1949; yes; no; Id.902d	
4658	" Edna; f; 8 7-18-23; ¼+; s; dau A1950; yes; no; Id.902e	
4659	" William; m; 6 8-18-25; ¼+; s; son A1951; yes; no; Id.902f	
4660	" John; m; 4 5-5-27; ¼+; s; son A1952; yes; no; Id.902g	
4661	" Leonard; m; 2 3-10-30; ¼+; s; son A1953; yes; no; none	
4662	" Charley; m; 5/12 10-4-31; ¼+; s; son -----; yes; no; none	

Turtle Mountain Reservation
1932 Census Roll

Key: Number; Surname, Given; Sex; Age at Last Birthday, Birthdate (if given); Tribe (Chippewa, unless stated otherwise); Degree of Blood; Marital Status; Relationship to Head of Family, Last Year Census Number; At Jurisdiction Where Enrolled (Yes/No); Elsewhere - Post Office, County, State; Ward (Yes/No); Allotment [Al.], Annuity [An.] and/or Identification [Id.] Numbers

NE Roy, Harry;   Head
4663 "   Mary Ann (Lambert); f; 28; ¼+; m; wife B2247; no; Rolette, Rolette, ND; yes; Id.603b, Al.DL-2
4664 "   Theodore; m; 4 12-8-27; ¼+; s; son B2248; no; Rolette, Rolette, ND; yes; none
4665 "   Delia Iris; f; 2 11-5-29; ¼+; s; dau -----; no; Rolette, Rolette, ND; yes; none
4666 "   Minerva; f; 5/12 10-21-31; ¼+; s; dau -----; no; Rolette, Rolette, ND; yes; none

NE Russell, James;   Head
4667 "   Mary Louise; f; 22; ¼+; m; wife B2624; no; Fargo, Cass, ND; yes; Id.988c, Al.G-02604
4668 "   James, Jr; m; 1 10-3-30; ¼+; s; son ------; no; Fargo, Cass, ND; yes; none

NE Ryan, W J;   Head
4669 "   Mary V (Morin); f; 22; ¼+; m; wife B1897; no; Devils Lake, Ramsey, ND; yes; Id.752b, Al.G-014954
4670 "   Wm Howard; m; 1 9-16-30; ¼+; s; son ------; no; Devils Lake, Ramsey, ND; yes; none
4671 "   Richard I; m; 1/12 3-1-32; ¼+; s; son ------; no; Devils Lake, Ramsey, ND; yes; none

NE St.Arnaud, Alcide;   Head
4672 "   Mary Jane (Belgarde.Caribou); f; 38; ¼+; m; wife A1995; no; Elbowoods, McLean, ND McLean, ND; no; Id.224a, Al.M-34
4673 "   Mary Louise; f; 16 11-20-15; ¼+; s; dau A1996; no; Elbowoods, McLean, ND; no; Id.933b
4674 "   Blanche; f; 14 9-17-17; ¼+; s; dau A1997; no; Elbowoods, McLean, ND; no; Id.933c
4675 "   Patrice; m; 12 11-9-19; ¼+; s; son A1998; no; Elbowoods, McLean, ND; no; Id.933c
4676 " (Caribou) Clemence; f; 3 5-14-28; ¼+; s; step dau A1999; no; Elbowoods, McLean, ND; no; none
4677 "   Raphael; m; 9/12 6-9-31; ¼+; s; son ----; no; Elbowoods, McLean, ND; no; none

4678 St.Arnaud, Alexander; m; 39; ¼+; m; Head B2366; no; Kansas City, Wyandotte, Kan; no; Id.931, Al.M-212
NE "   Sarah (Parkes);   wife
4679 "   Charles; m; 12; ¼+; s; son B2367; no; Kansas City, Wyandotte, Kan; no; Id.931b

4680 St.Arnaud, Alfred; m; 34; ¼+; m; Head A2000; yes; no; Id.930, Al.M-216
4681 "   Mary (Laverdure); f; 32; ¼+; m; wife A2001; yes; no; Id.930a, Al.G022
4682 "   Francis F; m; 9 10-8-22; ¼+; s; son A2002; yes; no; Id.930c
4683 "   Elmer; m; 5 7-17-26; ¼+; s; son A2003; yes; no; Id.930d

Turtle Mountain Reservation
1932 Census Roll

Key: Number; Surname, Given; Sex; Age at Last Birthday, Birthdate (if given); Tribe (Chippewa, unless stated otherwise); Degree of Blood; Marital Status; Relationship to Head of Family; Last Year Census Number; At Jurisdiction Where Enrolled (Yes/No); Elsewhere - Post Office, County, State; Ward (Yes/No); Allotment [Al.], Annuity [An.] and/or Identification [Id.] Numbers

4684 St.Arnaud(cont), Gloria; f; 1 9-23-30; ¼+; s; dau ------; yes; no; Id.930e

NE St.Arnaud, Fred; Head
4685 " Adelaide (Jerome); f; 51; ¼+; m; wife A2004; yes; yes; Id.932a, Al.G-037053
4686 " Delia; f; 30 9-25-01; ¼+; s; dau A2005; yes; yes; none

4687 St.Arnaud, John B; m; 66; ¼+; m; Head A2006; yes; yes; Id.929, Al.R-297
4688 " Julia (St.Arnaud); f; 61; ¼+; m; wife A2007; yes; no; Id.929a, Al.G-0130

4689 St.Claire, Emery; m; 35; ¼+; m; Head B2368; no; Ft.Totten, Benson, ND; no;
       Id.935c, Al.H-030429
4690 " Mary Alice (Villeneuve); f; 29; ¼+; m; wife A2369; no; Ft.Totten,
       Benson, ND; yes; Id.986d, Al.G-7859
4691 " Clenty; m; 10 12-25-21; ¼+; s; son A2370; no; Ft.Totten, Benson, ND;
       yes; none
4692 " Alvina; f; 8 6-30-23; ¼+; s; dau A2371; no; Ft.Totten, Benson, ND; yes;
       none
4693 " Lloyd; m; 5 6-21-26; ¼+; s; son A2372; no; Ft.Totten, Benson, ND; yes;
       none
4694 " Doris May; f; 4 2-13-28; ¼+; s; dau A2373; no; Ft.Totten, Benson, ND;
       yes; none

4695 St.Claire, John; m; 30; ¼+; m; Head A2374; no; Dunseith, Rolette, ND; yes;
       Id.935e, Al.H-030471
NE   " Victoria (Laroque); wife
4696 " Rosalie; f; 12; ¼+; s; dau A2375; no; Dunseith, Rolette, ND; yes; none
4697 " Catherine; f; 8 4-8-23; ¼+; s; dau A2394; no; (Counted twice) Dunseith,
       Rolette, ND; yes; none

4698 St.Claire, Louis; m; 38; ¼+; m; Head A2377; no; Dunseith, Rolette, ND; no;
       Id.945b, Al.H-030422
4699 " Mary Agnes (Villeneuve); f; 33; ¼+; m; wife A2378; no; Dunseith,
       Rolette, ND; yes; Id.986b, Al.G-07862
4700 " Carl; m; 13; ¼+; s; son A2380; no; Dunseith, Rolette, ND; yes; none
4701 " Wilmer; m; 12; ¼+; s; son A2379; no; Dunseith, Rolette, ND; yes; none
4702 " Laverne; m; 9; ¼+; s; son A2381; no; Dunseith, Rolette, ND; yes; none
4703 " Eugene; m; 8; ¼+; s; son A2382; no; Dunseith, Rolette, ND; yes; none
4704 " Marvin; m; 7/12 8-24-31; ¼+; s; son ------; no; Dunseith, Rolette, ND;
       yes; none

4705 St.Claire, Robert; m; 28; ¼+; m; Head A2383; no; Dunseith, Rolette, ND; yes;
       Id.934b, Al.H-030290
NE   " Alice (Norquay); wife

Turtle Mountain Reservation
1932 Census Roll

Key: Number; Surname, Given; Sex; Age at Last Birthday, Birthdate (if given); Tribe (Chippewa, unless stated otherwise); Degree of Blood; Marital Status; Relationship to Head of Family, Last Year Census Number; At Jurisdiction Where Enrolled (Yes/No); Elsewhere - Post Office, County, State; Ward (Yes/No); Allotment [Al.], Annuity [An.] and/or Identification [Id.] Numbers

4706 St.Claire(cont), Violet Mae; f; 7 9-6-24; ¼+; s; dau A2384; no; Dunseith, Rolette, ND; yes; none
4707 " Priscilla; f; 5 9-6-26; ¼+; s; dau; no; Dunseith, Rolette, ND; yes; none
4708 " Lucille A; f; 2 7-18-29; ¼+; s; dau A2385; no; Dunseith, Rolette, ND; yes; none

4709 St.Claire, William; m; 51; ¼+; m; Head B2386; no; Dunseith, Rolette, ND; no; Id.934, Al.H-020289
4710 " Veronica (Amyotte); f; 52; ¼+; m; wife B2387; no; Dunseith, Rolette, ND; no; Id.934a, Al.DL-04585
4711 " Walter; m; 24; ¼+; s; son B2388; no; Dunseith, Rolette, ND; no; Id.934c
4712 " Frank; m; 22; ¼+; s; son B2389; no; Dunseith, Rolette, ND; no; Id.934d
4713 " Louis; m; 20; ¼+; s; son B2390; no; Dunseith, Rolette, ND; no; Id.934e
4714 " Norman; m; 15 5-4-16; ¼+; s; son B2391; no; Dunseith, Rolette, ND; no; Id.934g
4715 " Rose Ann; f; 14 3-29-18; ¼+; s; dau B2392; no; Dunseith, Rolette, ND; no; Id.934h
4716 " Elva; f; 11 6-9-20; ¼+; s; dau B2393; no; Dunseith, Rolette, ND; no; Id.934j

NE St.Germaine, Alfred;   Head
4717 " Caroline (Grandbois); f; 30; ¼+; m; wife B2395; no; Highland Park, Wayne, Mich; yes; Id.442c, Al.G-08140
4718 " Alfred; m; 11; ¼+; s; son B2396; no; Highland Park, Wayne, Mich; yes; none
4719 " Raymond; m; 9; ¼+; s; son B2397; no; Highland Park, Wayne, Mich; yes; none

4720 St.Germaine, Francois; m; 69; ¼+; m; Head B2398; no; St.John, Rolette, ND; no; Id.936, Al.G-08388
4721 " Rosina (Vivier); f; 62; ¼+; m; wife A2399; no; St.John, Rolette, ND; no; Id.936a, Al.G-08389
4722 " Julien; m; 30; ¼+; s; son B2401; no; St.John, Rolette, ND; no; Id.,936d, Al.M-258
4723 " Delia; m[sic]; 24; ¼+; s; dau B2402; no; St.John, Rolette, ND; yes; Id.936g, Al.H-01304
4724 " Marguerite; f; 21; ¼+; s; dau B2403; no; St.John, Rolette, ND; yes; Id.936h, Al.H-013046
4725 " Ida Eliza; f; 18; ¼+; s; dau B2404; no; St.John, Rolette, ND; no; Id.936j

4726 St.Germaine, Joseph F; m; 32; ¼+; m; Head B2400; no; Cut Bank, Glacier, Mont; yes; Id.936c, Al.M-253
NE " Margaret (Giles);   wife

Turtle Mountain Reservation
1932 Census Roll

Key: Number; Surname, Given; Sex; Age at Last Birthday, Birthdate (if given); Tribe (Chippewa, unless stated otherwise); Degree of Blood; Marital Status; Relationship to Head of Family, Last Year Census Number; At Jurisdiction Where Enrolled (Yes/No); Elsewhere - Post Office, County, State; Ward (Yes/No); Allotment [Al.], Annuity [An.] and/or Identification [Id.] Numbers

4727 St.Germaine, Marcial; m; 34; ¼+; m; Head B2407; no; St.John, Rolette, ND; no; Id.936b, Al.M256
NE   "   Flora (Thibert);   wife   B2405
4738   "   Marie C; f; 11 4-20-20; ¼+; s; dau B2408; no; (Counted twice last yr) St.John, Rolette, ND; no; none
4739   "   Patrick M; m; 11 3-7-21; ¼+; s; son B2409; B2406 no; (Counted twice last yr) St.John, Rolette, ND; no; none
4730   "   Robert; m; 9 3-21-23; ¼+; s; son B2410; no; St.John, Rolette, ND; no; none
4731   "   Dolores; f; 6 4-15-25; ¼+; s; dau xxxxx; no; St.John, Rolette, ND; no; none
4732   "   John Finley; m; 5 9-1-26; ¼+; s; son ------; no; St.John, Rolette, ND; no; none
4733   "   Maynard; m; 3 12-5-28; ¼+; s; son ------; no; St.John, Rolette, ND; no; none

4734 St.Germaine, Phillip; m; 40; ¼+; s; Head B2412; no; Unknown; no; Id.938, Al.G-08390

4735 St.Germaine, Pierre; m; 27; ¼+; m; Head B2411; no; St.John, Rolette, ND; yes; Id.936e, Al.G-08391½
4736   "   Delia (Richard); f; 24; ¼+; m; wife B2211; no; St.John, Rolette, ND; yes; Id.889e, Al.G-08415

4737 St.Pierre, Alexander; m; 32; ¼+; m; Head B2413; no; Dunseith, Rolette, ND; yes; Id.941b, Al.G-112
NE   "   Virginia (Henry);   wife
4738   "   Florence; f; 7 7-31-24; 1/4; s; dau B2414; no; Dunseith, Rolette, ND; yes; none
4739   "   Celina; f; 6 8-14-25; ¼+; s; dau B2415; no; Dunseith, Rolette, ND; yes; none
4740   "   Rose; f; 5 12-28-26; ¼+; s; dau B2416; no; Dunseith, Rolette, ND; yes; none
4741   "   Seraphine; f; 4 3-12-28; ¼+; s; dau B2417; no; Dunseith, Rolette, ND; yes; none
4742   "   Mary; f; 1 12-5-30; ¼+; s; dau B2418; no; Dunseith, Rolette, ND; yes; none

4743 St.Pierre, Isabel (Houle); f; 54; ¼+; wd; Head B2419; no; Dunseith, Rolette, ND; no; Id.939a, Al.H-010537
4744   "   Alexander; m; 35; ¼+; s; son B2420; no; Dunseith, Rolette, ND; yes; 0Id.939b, Al.G-08108
4745   "   Mary; f; 24; ¼+; s; dau B2421; no; Dunseith, Rolette, ND; yes; Id.939c. Al.H-010536

Turtle Mountain Reservation
1932 Census Roll

Key: Number; Surname, Given; Sex; Age at Last Birthday, Birthdate (if given); Tribe (Chippewa, unless stated otherwise); Degree of Blood; Marital Status; Relationship to Head of Family, Last Year Census Number; At Jurisdiction Where Enrolled (Yes/No); Elsewhere - Post Office, County, State; Ward (Yes/No); Allotment [Al.], Annuity [An.] and/or Identification [Id.] Numbers

4746 St.Pierre(cont), Adele; f; 22; 1/4 s; dau B2422; no; Dunseith, Rolette, ND; yes; Id.939c, Al.G-016471
4747   "   Josephine; f; 18; ¼+; s; dau B2423; no; Dunseith, Rolette, ND; no; Id.939f
4748   "   Fred; m; 16; ¼+; s; son B2424; no; Dunseith, Rolette, ND; no; Id.939g
4749   "   Vivian; f; 12; ¼+; s; dau B2425; no; Dunseith, Rolette, ND; no; Id.939h
4750   "   Francis; m; 10; ¼+; s; son B2426; no; Dunseith, Rolette, ND; no; Id.939i

4751 St.Pierre, John B; m; 37; 14/ s; Head B2427; no; Unknown; no; Id.943, Al.G-505

4752 St.Pierre, Martin; m; 70; ¼+; m; Head B2428; no; Dunseith, Rolette, ND; no; Id.941, Al.H-0290
NE   "   Mary (Peltier);   wife
4753   "   Hyacinth; m; 24 2-10-08; ¼+; s; son B2429; no; Dunseith, Rolette, ND; no; Id.941e
4754   "   Riel; m; 22 3-3-10; ¼+; s; son B2430; no; Dunseith, Rolette, ND; no; Id.941f, Al.H-010524
4755   "   Sarah; f; 19 5-17-12; ¼+; s; dau B2431; no; Dunseith, Rolette, ND; no; Id.941g
4756   "   Josephine; f; 17 6-10-14; ¼+; s; dau B2432; no; Dunseith, Rolette, ND; no; Id.941h
4757   "   William; m; 11 7-31-20; ¼+; s; son B2433; no; Dunseith, Rolette, ND; Id.941i
4758   "   David; m; 10 7-12-21; ¼+; s; son B2434; no; Dunseith, Rolette, ND; no; Id.941j

4759 St.Pierre, Norbert; m; 76; ¼+; m; Head B2435; no; Dunseith, Rolette, ND; no; Id.942, Al.G-503
NE   "   Mary (Boyer.Allery);   wife
4760   "   Moses; m; 35; ¼+; s; son B2436; no; Dunseith, Rolette, ND; yes; Id.942b Al.G-506

NE Salmonson, Elmer;   Head
4761   "   Glenn; m; 7 1/4; s; son B2249; no; Roy, Fergus, Mont; no; Id.232f

NE Salo, Michael;   Head
4762   "   Margaret (Latraille.Turcotte); f; 39; ¼+; m; wife B2578; no; Minot, Ward, ND; no; Id.964a, Al.H-01256
4763   "   Grace; f; 10 8-10-21; ¼+; s; dau -----; no; Minot, Ward, ND; no; none
4764   "   Francis; m; 2 10-11-29; ¼+; s; son ------; no; Minot, Ward, ND; no; none
4765   "   Donald; m; 10/12 5-24-31; ¼+; s; son -----; no; Minot, Ward, ND; no; none

NE San Grait, Edward;   Head
4766   "   Adele (Laducer); f; 67; ¼+; m; wife A1954; yes; no; Id.904, Al.DL-5

Turtle Mountain Reservation
1932 Census Roll

Key: Number; Surname, Given; Sex; Age at Last Birthday, Birthdate (if given); Tribe (Chippewa, unless stated otherwise); Degree of Blood; Marital Status; Relationship to Head of Family, Last Year Census Number; At Jurisdiction Where Enrolled (Yes/No); Elsewhere - Post Office, County, State; Ward (Yes/No); Allotment [Al.], Annuity [An.] and/or Identification [Id.] Numbers

4767 San Grait, Celina; f; 46; ¼+; s; Head A1955; yes; no; Id.907, Al.G-036564

4768 San Grait, John B; m; 44; ¼+; m; Head A1956; yes; no; Id.906, Al.H-030427
4769   "   Adeline (Lafrombois); f; 29; ¼+; m; wife; A1957; yes; yes; Id.585c, Al.GF-211
4770   "   Marie; f; 8 7-12-23; ¼+; s; dau A1958; yes; yes; none
4771   "   Mary V; f; 6; ¼+; s; dau A1959; yes; yes; none
4772   "   Madeline; f; 4; ¼+; s; dau A1960; yes; yes; none
Dead   "   Joseph;   A1961   (Died 9-1-31)
4773   "   Casper; m; 3/12 12-25-31; ¼+; s; son -----; yes; yes; none

NE Sansaver, Roy;   Head
4774   "   Mary Agnes (Azure); f; 24; ¼+; m; wife A155; no; Mont; yes; Id.130c, Al.G-08284

4775 Sayer, Joseph; m; 66; ¼+; s; Head B2250; no; Medicine Lake, Sheridan, Mont; no; Id.909, Al.G-0706
NE   "   Charlotte (Patnaud); wife
4776   "   Charles; m; 20 5-28-11; ¼+; s; son B2252; no; Medicine Lake, Sheridan, Mont; no; Id.909f
4777   "   Phillip; m; 18 12-12-13; ¼+; s; son B2253; no; Medicine Lake, Sheridan, Mont; no; Id.909g

4778 Sayer, Joseph A; m; 40; ¼+; s; Head B2254; no; Medicine Lake; no; Id.911, Al.G-0710

4779 Sayer, Louis James; m; 42; ¼+; m; Head B2255; no; Medicine Lake, Sheridan, Mont; yes; Id.910, Al.G-0709
4780   "   Christine (Morin); f; 44; ¼+; m; wife B2256; no; Medicine Lake, Sheridan, Mont; no; Id.910a, Al.M-193
4781   "   Joseph Wm; m; 19 9-9-12; ¼+; s; son B2257; no; Medicine Lake, Sheridan, Mont; yes; Id.910b
4782   "   James Ed; m; 15 4-18-16; ¼+; s; son B2258; no; Medicine Lake, Sheridan, Mont; yes; Id.910c
4783   "   Rosalie; f; 14 3-2-18; ¼+; s; dau B2259; no; Medicine Lake, Sheridan, Mont; yes; Id.910d
4784   "   Annie; f; 12 2-3-20; ¼+; s; dau B2260; no; Medicine Lake, Sheridan, Mont; yes; Id.910e
4785   "   Ernest; m; 10 6-11-22; ¼+; s; son B2261; no; Medicine Lake, Sheridan, Mont; yes; Id.910f

4786 Sayer, Martin; m; 33 12-12-98; ¼+; m; Head B2251; no; Medicine Lake, Sheridan, Mont; no; Id.909, Al.G-07134
NE   "   Katie (Nygaard);   wife

Turtle Mountain Reservation
1932 Census Roll

Key: Number; Surname, Given; Sex; Age at Last Birthday, Birthdate (if given); Tribe (Chippewa, unless stated otherwise); Degree of Blood; Marital Status; Relationship to Head of Family, Last Year Census Number; At Jurisdiction Where Enrolled (Yes/No); Elsewhere - Post Office, County, State; Ward (Yes/No); Allotment [Al.], Annuity [An.] and/or Identification [Id.] Numbers

4787 Sayer(cont), Marshall; m; 9 6-9-22; ¼+; s; son -----; no; Medicine Lake, Sheridan, Mont; no; none

4788 " Clinton; m; 7 2-5-25; ¼+; s; son -----; no; Medicine Lake, Sheridan, Mont; no; none

4789 Sayer, Patrick; m; 42; ¼+; m; Head B2262; yes; no; Id.908, Al.G-0705
NE " Mary (St.Arnaud); Div wife (Divorced)
4790 " Moses; m; 15 7-6-16; ¼+; s; son B2263; no; Saint Pauls, Blaine, Mont; no; none

4791 Schindler, Frederick; m; 26; ¼+; s; Head B2264; no; Unknown, Canada; yes; Id.914; Al.G-0305

NE Schindler, William; Head
Dead " Rosalie; B2265 (Died 6-28-21)
4792 " Josephine; f; 19; ¼+; s; dau B2266; no; Wolf Point, Roosevelt, Mont; no; Id.912b
4793 " William; m; 17 1-14-15; ¼+; s; son B2267; no; Wolf Point, Roosevelt, Mont no; Id.912c
4794 " Lylah; f; 13 8-15-18; ¼+; s; dau ------; no; Wolf Point, Roosevelt, Mont; no; none
4795 " Joseph; m; 10 6-28-21; ¼+; s; son ------; no; Wolf Point, Roosevelt, Mont; no; none

4796 Schindler, William; m; 28; ¼+; m; Head A1962; yes; yes; Id.916a, Al.G-0191
4797 " Margaret (Martin); m[sic]; 27; ¼+; m; wife A1963; yes; yes; Id.714c, Al.G-576
4798 " Fred; m; 6 7-30-25; ¼+; s; son A1964; yes; yes; none
4799 " Ernestine; f; 5 10-3-26; ¼+; s; dau A1965; yes; yes; none
4800 " Francis; m; 3 5-10-28; ¼+; s; son A1966; yes; yes; none
4801 " Edna P; f; 1 5-17-30; ¼+; s; dau A1967; yes; yes; none
4347 " Elaine; f; 3/12 12-28-31; ¼+; s; dau -------; yes; yes; none

NE Schneider, Nick; Head
4801 " Mary E (Vivier); f; 21; ¼+; m; wife B2268; no; Fargo, Cass, ND; yes; Id.988f, Al.H-012649

NE Sedevik, Adam; Head
4802 " Vennery (Dionne); f; 23 9-4-08; ¼+; m; wife B2269; no; Plentywood, Sheridan, Mont; no; Id.343e
4804 " Darrell D; m; 9/12 6-8-31; ¼+; s; son -----; no; Plentywood, Sheridan, Mont; no; none

NE Sema, N E; Head
4805 " Florestine (Dauphinais); f; 32; ¼+; m; wife B2270; no; Red Wing, Goodhue, Minn; yes; Id.248, Al.GF-227

Turtle Mountain Reservation
1932 Census Roll

Key: Number; Surname, Given; Sex; Age at Last Birthday, Birthdate (if given); Tribe (Chippewa, unless stated otherwise); Degree of Blood; Marital Status; Relationship to Head of Family, Last Year Census Number; At Jurisdiction Where Enrolled (Yes/No); Elsewhere - Post Office, County, State; Ward (Yes/No); Allotment [Al.], Annuity [An.] and/or Identification [Id.] Numbers

NE Senecal, Horace;   wd; Head
4806 "   Bert Oliver; m; 18; ¼+; s; son B2271; no; Olga, Pembina, ND; yes;
                                                          Id.918b, Al.H-027716
4807 "   Mary; f; 15; ¼+; s; dau B2272; no; Olga, Pembina, ND; no; none
4808 "   Virginia; f; 8 9-1-23; ¼+; s; dau B2273; no; Olga, Pembina, ND; no; none

NE Senecal, Theodore;   Head
4809 "   Josephine (Rolette); f; 52; ¼+; m; wife B2274; no; Grenora, Williams,
                                                          ND; no; Id.917a, Al.G-84
4810 "   Lester; m; 22 1-22-10; ¼+; s; son B2275; no; Grenora, Williams, ND;
                                                          yes; Id.917b, Al.H-013018
4811 "   Elmer; m; 20; ¼+; s; son B2276; no; Grenora, Williams, ND; no; Id.917c

NE Shafer, J C;   Head
4812 "   Sarah (Morin); f; 30 5-9-01; ¼+; m; wife B2277; no; Flaxville, Daniels,
                                                          Mont; yes; Id.758b, Al.M-168
4813 "   Ilena; f; 5 10-28-26; ¼+; s; dau ------; no; Flaxville, Daniels, Mont; yes; none
4814 "   Leonard; m; 2 5-13-29; ¼+; s; son ------; no; Flaxville, Daniels, Mont; yes;
                                                          none

NE Shanks, Guy M;   Head
4815 "   Claudia (Turcotte); f; 32; ¼+; m; wife B2278; no; Parkdale, Hood River,
                                                          Ore; yes; Id.965c, Al.M-142
4816 "   Catherine; f; 12 11-17-19; ¼+; s; dau B2279; no; Parkdale, Hood River,
                                                          Ore; yes; none
4817 "   John; m; 10 2-9-22; ¼+; s; son B2280; no; Parkdale, Hood River, Ore;
                                                          yes; none
Dead "   Eldon;   B2281   (Died 8-5-30)
4818 "   Claudine M; f; 2 1-6-29; ¼+; s; dau B2282; no; Parkdale, Hood River,
                                                          Ore; yes; none

NE Shimming, Si S;   Head
4819 "   Eleanor (Landry); f; 27; ¼+; m; wife B2283; no; Columbus, Burke, ND
                                                          yes; Id.606d, Al.GF-181
4820 "   Dorothy M; f; 6 2-13-26; ¼+; s; dau B2284; no; Columbus, Burke, ND;
                                                          yes; none
4821 "   Frederick; m; 4 5-25-27; ¼+; s; son ------; no; Columbus, Burke, ND;
                                                          yes; none

NE Shireback, John L;   Head
4822 "   Blanche (Jollie); f; 37; ¼+; m; wife B2285; no; Wilton, Burley, ND; no;
                                                          Id.528, Al.G-58
4823 "   John Louis; m; 8 12-2-23; ¼+; s; son B2286; no; Wilton, Burley, ND;
                                                          no; none

Turtle Mountain Reservation
1932 Census Roll

Key: Number; Surname, Given; Sex; Age at Last Birthday, Birthdate (if given); Tribe (Chippewa, unless stated otherwise); Degree of Blood; Marital Status; Relationship to Head of Family, Last Year Census Number; At Jurisdiction Where Enrolled (Yes/No); Elsewhere - Post Office, County, State; Ward (Yes/No); Allotment [Al.], Annuity [An.] and/or Identification [Id.] Numbers

4824 Shireback(cont), Marie B; f; 6 8-25-25; ¼+; s; dau -----; no; Wilton, Burley, ND; no; none
4825 " Robert Paul; m; 5 3-11-27; ¼+; s; son ------; no; Wilton, Burley, ND; no; none
4826 " James Ed; m; 2 6-9-29; ¼+; s; son ------; no; Wilton, Burley, ND; no; none
4827 " Richard M; m; 10/12 5-31-31; ¼+; s; son ------; no; Wilton, Burley, ND; no; none

NE Short, John; Head
4828 " Delia (Allery); f; 39; ¼+; m; wife B2287; no; Malta, Phillips, Mont; no; Id.919a, Al.GF-134
4829 " John, Jr; m; 16 6-13-15; ¼+; s; son B2288; no; Malta, Phillips, Mont; no; Id.919c
4830 " Clarence; m; 14 4-22-17; ¼+; s; son B2289; no; Malta, Phillips, Mont; no; Id.919d
4832 " Howard; m; 12 10-10-19; ¼+; s; son -----; no; Malta, Phillips, Mont; no; none
4832 " Michael; m; 10-9-28-21; ¼+; s; son B2290; no; Malta, Phillips, Mont; no; Id.919d
4833 " Marian; f; 5 11-4-26; ¼+; s; dau B2291; no; Malta, Phillips, Mont; no; Id.919e
4834 " Vivian M; f; 2 8-1-29; ¼+; s; dau ------; no; Malta, Phillips, Mont; no; none

NE Short, Robert; Head
4835 " Josephine (Azure); f; 31; ¼+; m; wife A1968; yes; yes; Id.920a, Al.M-149
4836 " Julia B; f; 14 5-3-17; ¼+; s; dau A1969; yes; yes; Id.920b
4837 " Mary Jane; f; 13 12-21-18; ¼+; dau 1970; yes; yes; Id.920c
4838 " Alfred; m; 11 2-5-20; ¼+; s; son A1971; yes; yes; Id.920d
4839 " George; m; 10 12-13-22; ¼+; s; son A1972; yes; yes; Id.920e
4840 " Fabian; m; 6 2-15-26; ¼+; s; son A1973; yes; yes; Id.920f
4841 " Francis; m; 4 6-19-28; ¼+; s; son A1974; yes; yes; Id.920g
4842 " Evelyn; f; 1 1-7-31; ¼+; s; dau A1975; yes; yes; Id.920h

NE Shrimpshire, Abraham; Head
4843 " Justine M; f; 31; ¼+; m; wife B2292; no; Pocatello, Bannock, Ida; yes; Id.1167c, Al.M-15
4844 " Gladys; f; 4 1-11-28; ¼+; s; dau -----; no; Pocatello, Bannock, Ida; yes; none

NE Sinclair, Truman; Head
4845 " Marie (Jeanotte); f; 40; 14; m; wife B1190; no; Los Angeles, Los Angeles Cal; no; Id.505, Al.M-79

Turtle Mountain Reservation
1932 Census Roll

Key: Number; Surname, Given; Sex; Age at Last Birthday, Birthdate (if given); Tribe (Chippewa, unless stated otherwise); Degree of Blood; Marital Status; Relationship to Head of Family, Last Year Census Number; At Jurisdiction Where Enrolled (Yes/No); Elsewhere - Post Office, County, State; Ward (Yes/No); Allotment [Al.], Annuity [An.] and/or Identification [Id.] Numbers

NE Sindt, Martin;   Head
4846   "   Louise A (Laverdure); f; 34; ¼+; m; wife B2293; no; Bigfork, Flathead, Mont; yes; Id.664b, Al.M-269
4847   "   Louis M; m; 12 4-14-19; ¼+; s; son B2294; no; Bigfork, Flathead, Mont; yes; none
4848   "   Gordon M; m; 11 11-19-20; ¼+; s; son B2295; no; Bigfork, Flathead, Mont; yes; none
4849   "   Marjory D; f; 10 6-22-22; ¼+; s; dau B2296; no; Bigfork, Flathead, Mont; yes; none
4850   "   Vernon R; m; 7 5-23-24; ¼+; s; son B2297; no; Bigfork, Flathead, Mont; yes; none
4851   "   Wesley L; m; 5 7-27-26; ¼+; s; son B2298; no; Bigfork, Flathead, Mont; yes; none
4852   "   Gladys A; f; 2 7-15-29; ¼+; s; dau -----; no; Bigfork, Flathead, Mont; yes; none
4853   "   Grace; f 5-12 11-7-31; ¼+; s; dau ------; no; Bigfork, Flathead, Mont; yes; none

NE Skafel, C J;   Head
4854   "   Eva (Latrace); f; 28; ¼+; m; wife 2299; no; Boggy Creek, Manitoba, Can; yes; Id.621c, Al.G-0300

4855 Skinner, Always; m; 30; F; s; Head B2300; no; Dunseith, Rolette, ND; yes; Id.51b, Al.G-317
4856 Skinner, Joe; m; 36; F; m; Head B2301; no; Dunseith, Rolette, ND; yes; Id.41b, Al.D-01752
NE   "   Mary Rose (Peltier); wife
4857   "   Josephine; f; 13; 6-27-18; ¼+; s; dau B2302; no; Dunseith, Rolette, ND; yes; none
4858   "   Mary; f; 10 11-30-21; ¼+; s; dau B2303; no; Dunseith, Rolette, ND; yes; none
4859   "   Clifford; m; 9 5-15-22; ¼+; s; son B2304; no; Dunseith, Rolette, ND; yes; none
4860   "   Stanley; m; 7 ¼+; s; son B2305; no; Dunseith, Rolette, ND; yes; none
4861   "   Olive; f; 5; ¼+; s; dau B2306; no; Dunseith, Rolette, ND; yes; none

4862 Skinner, John; m; 29; F; m; Head B2307; no; Dunseith, Rolette, ND; yes; Id.51c, Al.D-01751
4863   "   Sky Blue; f; 23; F; m; wife B2308; no; Dunseith, Rolette, ND; yes; Id.8c
4864   "   Angeline; f; 6 2-4-26; F; s; dau ------; no; Dunseith, Rolette, ND; yes; none
4865   "   Flora; f; 3 4-19-28; F; s; dau -------; no; Dunseith, Rolette, ND; yes; none
4866   "   Mabel; f; 11/12 4-12-31; F; s; dau -----; no; Dunseith, Rolette, ND; yes; none

Turtle Mountain Reservation
1932 Census Roll

Key: Number; Surname, Given; Sex; Age at Last Birthday, Birthdate (if given); Tribe (Chippewa, unless stated otherwise); Degree of Blood; Marital Status; Relationship to Head of Family, Last Year Census Number; At Jurisdiction Where Enrolled (Yes/No); Elsewhere - Post Office, County, State; Ward (Yes/No); Allotment [Al.], Annuity [An.] and/or Identification [Id.] Numbers

4867 Skinner, Nachaiwe; m; 64; F; wd; Head B2315; no; Dunseith, Rolette, ND; yes; Id.41, Al.DL-24

4868 Skinner, William; m; 39; F; m; Head B2309; no; Dunseith, Rolette, ND; yes; Id.54 Al.D-01751
NE " Mary (Peltier); wife
4869 " Agnes; f; 13 9-2-18; ¼+; s; dau B2311; no; Dunseith, Rolette, ND; yes; Id.54d
4870 " Clara; f; 49 12-14-22; ¼+; s; dau B2312; no; Dunseith, Rolette, ND; yes; Id.54e
487 Skinner(cont), Moses; m; 8 12-15-23; ¼+; s; son B2313; no; Dunseith, Rolette, ND; yes; Id.54f
4872 " Amelia; f; 5 9-14-26; ¼+; s; dau B2314; no; Dunseith, Rolette, ND; yes; Id.54g

NE Slater, John; Head
4873 " Hannah M (McGillis); f; 26; ¼+; m; wife B2316; no; St.John, Rolette, ND; yes; Id.724b, Al.H-010438
4874 " Eleanor; f; 4 7-4-27; ¼+; s; dau B2317; no; St.John, Rolette, ND; yes; none
4875 " Albina; f; 3 10-17-28; ¼+; s; dau B2318; no; St.John, Rolette, ND; yes; none
4876 " Wm John; m; 2 9-6-29; ¼+; s; son -----; no; St.John, Rolette, ND; yes; none
4877 " Francis; m; 1 11-25-30; ¼+; s; son B2319; no; St.John, Rolette, ND; yes; none

NE Slater, Joseph; Head
4878 " Lucy (Decoteau.Jeannotte); f; 33; ¼+; m; wife B2320; no; Devils Lake, Ramsey, ND; yes; Id.278c, Al.M-307
4879 " Joseph; m; 26 9-18-05; ¼+; s; son B2321; no; Devils Lake, Ramsey, ND; yes; Id.921b, Al.H-013635
4880 " Alice; f; 21 11-12-10; ¼+; s; dau B2323; no; Devils Lake, Ramsey, ND; yes; Id.921d, Al.H-013638
4881 " Mary Rose; f; 18 4-13-13; ¼+; s; dau B2324; no; Devils Lake, Ramsey, ND; no; Id.921e
4882 " Ann Louise; f; 18 1-17-14; ¼+; s; dau B2325; no; Devils Lake, Ramsey, ND; no; Id.921f
4883 " Elizabeth; f; 16; ¼+; s; dau B2326; no; Devils Lake, Ramsey, ND; no; Id.921g
4884 " George; m; 13 2-22-19; ¼+; s; son B2327; no; Devils Lake, Ramsey, ND; no; Id.921h
4885 " (Jeannotte) Albert; m; 11 5-5-20; ¼+; s; stepson B2328; no; Devils Lake, Ramsey, ND; no; Id. none
4886 " Lucy; f; 8 11-15-23; ¼+; s; dau B2329; no; Devils Lake, Ramsey, ND; no; Id.921i

Turtle Mountain Reservation
1932 Census Roll

Key: Number; Surname, Given; Sex; Age at Last Birthday, Birthdate (if given); Tribe (Chippewa, unless stated otherwise); Degree of Blood; Marital Status; Relationship to Head of Family, Last Year Census Number; At Jurisdiction Where Enrolled (Yes/No); Elsewhere - Post Office, County, State; Ward (Yes/No); Allotment [Al.], Annuity [An.] and/or Identification [Id.] Numbers

4887 Small Mouth, James; m; 38; F; m; Head B2330; no; Dunseith, Rolette, ND; yes; Id.1, Al.G-016590
4888 " Repeats; f; 42; F; m; wife B2331; no; Dunseith, Rolette, ND; yes; Id.39a, Al.G381
4889 " Passing Cloud; m; 19; F; s; son B2332; no; Dunseith, Rolette, ND; yes; Id.39d, Al.H024698

NE Smigiel, Theodore;   Head
4890 " Mary Julia (Belgarde); f; 32 12-20-99; ¼+; m; wife B2443; no; Superior, Douglas, Wis; yes; Id.188b, Al.GF143
4891 " Chester; m; 10 6-23-21; ¼+; s; son -----; no; Superior, Douglas, Wis; no; none
4892 " Lorraine; f; 8 3-24-24; ¼+; s; dau ------; no; Superior, Douglas, Wis; no; none
4893 " Robert; m; 7 2-14-25; ¼+; s; son -----; no; Superior, Douglas, Wis; no; none
4894 " Betty; m[sic]; 4 12-22-27; ¼+; s; dau -----; no; Superior, Douglas, Wis; no; none
4895 " Carrie; f; 2 12-29-29; ¼+; s; dau -----; no; Superior, Douglas, Wis; no; none

4896 Smith, Alexander; m; 32; ¼+; m; Head B2333; yes; yes; Id.927b, Al.M-321
NE " Edna Pearl (Lang);   wife
4897 " Cecelia M; f; 10 5-8-21; ¼+; s; dau B2334; yes; yes; none
4898 " Howard; m; 8 4-8-23; ¼+; s; son B2335; yes; yes; none
4899 " Delia Jane; f; 6 11-20-25; ¼+; s; dau ------; yes; yes; none
4900 " Francis; m; 4 11-25-27; ¼+; s; son B2336; yes; yes; none
4901 " Winifred; f; 2 12-16-29; ¼+; s; dau -----; yes; yes; none

4902 Smith, Arthur; m; 47; ¼+; m; Head B2337; yes; no; Id.983, Al.G-08090
NE " Mary Jane (Morin);   wife B2338   (Error in listing her last year)
4903 " Alex; m; 23 12-27-08; ¼+; s; son B2339; yes; yes; Id.983b, Al.G-08260
4904 " Louis; m; 10 1-16-22; ¼+; s; son B2341; yes; no; Id.983d
4905 " Florestine; f; 5 6-21-26; ¼+; s; dau B2342; yes; no; Id.983e
4906 " Ruth Adel; f; 2 10-12-29; ¼+; s; dau ------; yes; no; none

4907 Smith, Arthur John; m; 26; ¼+; s; Head A1976; yes; yes; Id.924d, Al.G-278
4908 " Wallace; m; 22 ¼+; s; bro A1977; yes; yes; Id.924f, Al.H-012634
4909 " Frank; m; 15 3-16-17; ¼+; s; bro A1978; yes; yes; Id.924g

4910 Smith, Charles; m; 56; ¼+; m; Head B2343; no; Devils Lake, Ramsey, ND; yes; Id.922, Al.H-025398
4911 " Josette (Frederick); f; 46; ¼+; m; wife B2344; no; Devils Lake, Ramsey, ND; no; Id.922a, Al.W-35
4912 " Alfred; m; 22 3-17-10; ¼+; m[sic]; son; no; (Left out, error) Devils Lake, Ramsey, ND; yes; Id.922c, Al.H-012639

Turtle Mountain Reservation
1932 Census Roll

Key: Number; Surname, Given; Sex; Age at Last Birthday, Birthdate (if given); Tribe (Chippewa, unless stated otherwise); Degree of Blood; Marital Status; Relationship to Head of Family, Last Year Census Number; At Jurisdiction Where Enrolled (Yes/No); Elsewhere - Post Office, County, State; Ward (Yes/No); Allotment [Al.], Annuity [An.] and/or Identification [Id.] Numbers

4913 Smith(cont), Florestine; f; 17 12-30-14; ¼+; s; dau B2346; no; Devils Lake, Ramsey, ND; yes; Id.922d
4914 " Patrick; m; 15 3-8-17; ¼+; s; son B2347; no; Devils Lake, Ramsey, ND; yes; Id.922e
4915 " Clifford; m; 12 3-17-20; ¼+; s; son B2348; no; Devils Lake, Ramsey, ND; yes; Id.922f
4916 " Clarence; m; 5 3-10-27; ¼+; s; son ------; no; Devils Lake, Ramsey, ND; yes; none

NE Smith, John R;   Head
4917 " Adelia (Laverdure); f; 25; ¼+; m; wife B2349; no; Raymond, Sheridan, Mont; yes; Id.644f, Al.G-029
4918 " Cleo Marion; f; 6 3-28-26; ¼+; s; dau B2350; no; Raymond, Sheridan, Mont; yes; none
4919 " Barbara Mae; f; 3 5-17-28; ¼+; s; dau -------; no; Raymond, Sheridan, Mont yes; none

NE Smith, Jordan;   Head
4920 " Clarice (Brien); f; 30; ¼+; m; wife B2351; no; Dooley, Sheridan, Mont; yes; Id.1192b, Al.M-185
4921 " Roland; m; 8 ¼+; s; son B2352; no; Dooley, Sheridan, Mont; yes; none

4922 Smith, Louis; m; 41; ¼+; m; Head A1979; yes; no; Id.925, Al.G-13
4923 " Josephine (Belgarde); f; 35; ¼+; m; wife A1980; yes; no; Id.925a, Al.G-08300
4924 " Louis; m; 11 6-25-20; ¼+; s; son A1981; yes; no; Id.925c
4925 " Joseph; m; 8 6-24-23; ¼+; s; son A1982; yes; no; Id.925d
4926 " Michael; m; 4 10-4-27; ¼+; s; son A1983; yes; no; Id.925e
4927 " Arthur B; m; 9/12 5-11-31; ¼+; s; son ------; yes; no; Id.925f

                                                       A1984
4928 Smith, Pierre P; m; 27; ¼+; m; Head B2353; yes; (Counted twice last census); yes; Id.926b, Al.G-38
NE " Virginia (Dionne);   wife
4929 " Beverly Ann; f; 3/12 1-29-32; ¼+; s; dau -----; yes; yes; none

4930 Smith, Zachary; m; 59; ¼+; m; Head A1985; yes; no; Id.927, Al.R-297
4931 " Rosalie (Perronteau); f; 51; ¼+; m; wife A1986; yes; no; Id.927a, Al.W-34
4932 " Louis; m; 24; ¼+; s; son A1987; yes; no; Id.927e
4933 " Mary Edna; f; 20; ¼+; s; dau A1988; yes; no; Id.927f
4934 " William; m; 18; ¼+; s; son A1989; yes; no; Id.927g
4935 " Alphonse; m; 15 2-9-17; ¼+; s; son A1990; yes; no; Id.927h
4936 " Phoebe; f; 12 8-11-19; ¼+; s; dau A1991; yes; no; Id.927i
4937 " Madeline M; f; 9 6-28-22; ¼+; s; dau A1992; yes; no; Id.927j
4938 " Julienne; f; 8 12-13-23; ¼+; s; dau A1993; yes; no; Id.927k

Turtle Mountain Reservation
1932 Census Roll

Key: Number; Surname, Given; Sex; Age at Last Birthday, Birthdate (if given); Tribe (Chippewa, unless stated otherwise); Degree of Blood; Marital Status; Relationship to Head of Family, Last Year Census Number; At Jurisdiction Where Enrolled (Yes/No); Elsewhere - Post Office, County, State; Ward (Yes/No); Allotment [Al.], Annuity [An.] and/or Identification [Id.] Numbers

NE 4949	Snell, Albert; "	Christine (Delorme); f; 18 2-9-14; ¼+; m; wife B669; no; Ft. Belknap; no; Id.331e	Head

NE Southard, Edwin A;   Head
4940   "   Virginia (Rolette); f; 36; ¼+; m; wife B2354; no; Grenora, Williams, ND; no; Id.899, Al.M-234

NE Sprau, Charles H;   Head
4941   "   Rosalie (Laverdure); f; 33; ¼+; m; wife B2355; no; Unknown; no; Id.928a, Al.G-146
4942   "   Grace; f; 15 8-23-16; ¼+; s; dau B2356; no; Unknown; no; Id.928b
4943   "   Mary Louise; f; 11 7-1-20; ¼+; s; dau B2357; no; Unknown; no; Id.928c
4944   "   Ernest; m; 9 10-5-22; ¼+; s; son B2358; no; Unknown; no; Id.928d

NE Staley, David E;   Head
4945   "   Rosalie (Poitra); f; 36; ¼+; m; wife B2150; no; Froid, Sheridan, Mont; no; Id.877, Al.G-604
4946   "   Thelma; f; 12 2-28-20; ¼+; s; dau ------; no; Froid, Sheridan, Mont; no; none
4947   "   Dorothy; f; 10 4-1-21; ¼+; s; dau ------; no; Froid, Sheridan, Mont; no; none
4948   "   Jeannette; f; 8 2-10-24; ¼+; s; dau ------; no; Froid, Sheridan, Mont; no; none
4949   "   Jennie; f; 6 11-12-25; ¼+; s; dau ------; no; Froid, Sheridan, Mont; no; none
4950   "   David; m; 3 1-5-29; ¼+; s; son -----; no; Froid, Sheridan, Mont; no; none
4951   "   Richard A; m; 10/12 6-8-31; ¼+; s; son -----; no; Froid, Sheridan, Mont; no; none

4952 Standing, Thomas; m; 38; F; s; Head B2365; no; Dunseith, Rolette, ND; yes; Id.37, Al.G-307

4953 Standing Chief; m; 64; F; m; Head B2360; no; Dunseith, Rolette, ND; yes; Id.47, Al.G-01897
4954   "   She Knees; f; 76; F; m; wife B2361l no; Dunseith, Rolette, ND; yes; Id.28c, Al.G-371
4955   "   Smooth Face; m; 27; F; s; son B2362; no; Dunseith, Rolette, ND; yes; Id.47b, Al.G-01901
4956   "   (Faguant) Joseph; m; 22; F; adpt son B2363; no; Dunseith, Rolette, ND; yes; Id.28b

4957 Standing Cloud, Thomas; m; 51; F; s; Head B2359; no; Dunseith, Rolette, ND; yes; Id.56, Al.G-324

NE Stevenson, Melvin;   Head
4958   "   Lois; s; 8; ¼+; s; dau B2437; no; Dunseith, Rolette, ND; yes; Id.473h

Turtle Mountain Reservation
1932 Census Roll

Key: Number; Surname, Given; Sex; Age at Last Birthday, Birthdate (if given); Tribe (Chippewa, unless stated otherwise); Degree of Blood; Marital Status; Relationship to Head of Family, Last Year Census Number; At Jurisdiction Where Enrolled (Yes/No); Elsewhere - Post Office, County, State; Ward (Yes/No); Allotment [Al.], Annuity [An.] and/or Identification [Id.] Numbers

NE Steward, Charles;   Head
4959 "   Ernest C; m; 15 11-5-16; ¼+; s; son A2008; no; Webster, Ramsey, ND; no; Id.1038b
4960 "   Irene; f; 14 3-27-18; ¼+; s; dau A2009; no; Webster, Ramsey, ND; no; Id.1038c
4961 "   James M; m; 11 10-7-20; ¼+; s; son A2010; no; Webster, Ramsey, ND; no; Id.1038d
4962 "   Charles J; m; 9; ¼+; s; son A2011; no; Webster, Ramsey, ND; no; Id. none
4963 "   Flossie; f; 8; ¼+; s; dau A2012; no; Webster, Ramsey, ND; no; none

NE Stoen, Oliver;   Head
4964 "   Laura (Henry); f; 29; ¼+; m; wife B2438; no; Bismarck, Burleigh, ND; no; Id.473f, Al.G-0264
4965 "   Violette; f; 9 3-9-23; ¼+; s; dau -----; no; Bismarck, Burleigh, ND; no; none
4966 "   Joyce M; f; 7 7-23-24; ¼+; s; dau ------; no; Bismarck, Burleigh, ND; no; none

NE Stofiel, Oscar;   Head
4967 "   Emma (Lafontain); f; 28 4-13-03; ¼+; m; wife B1276; no; Lewiston, Nez Perce, Ida; yes; Id.548e, Al.L-3

NE Stofiel, Robert;   Head
4968 "   Mary Rose (Lafontain); f; 33 5-15-98; ¼+; m; wife B1274; no; Lewiston, Nez Perce, Ida; yes; Id.548b, Al.L-6
4969 "   Irene; f; 10 2-14-22; ¼+; s; dau ------; no; Lewiston, Nez Perce, Ida; yes; none
4970 "   John; m; 9 2-10-23; ¼+; s; son -----; no; Lewiston, Nez Perce, Ida; yes; none
4971 "   Marjory; f; 7 7-10-24; ¼+; s; dau ------; no; Lewiston, Nez Perce, Ida; yes; none
4972 "   Lilla; f; 6 11-21-25; ¼+; s; dau ------; no; Lewiston, Nez Perce, Ida; yes; none
4973 "   Elvin; m; 4 11-7-27; ¼+; s; son ------; no; Lewiston, Nez Perce, Ida; yes; none
4974 "   Violet; f; 3 2-12-29; ¼+; s; dau -----; no; Lewiston, Nez Perce, Ida; yes; none
4975 "   Maxine; f; 1 11-2-30; ¼+; s; dau ------; no; Lewiston, Nez Perce, Ida; yes; none
4976 "   Robert; m; 1/12 3-19-32; ¼+; s; son -----; no; Lewiston, Nez Perce, Ida; yes; none

4977 Stops The Day; f; 95; F; wd; Head B2439; no; Dunseith, Rolette, ND; yes; Id.52a, Al.G-308

Turtle Mountain Reservation
1932 Census Roll

Key: Number; Surname, Given; Sex; Age at Last Birthday, Birthdate (if given); Tribe (Chippewa, unless stated otherwise); Degree of Blood; Marital Status; Relationship to Head of Family, Last Year Census Number; At Jurisdiction Where Enrolled (Yes/No); Elsewhere - Post Office, County, State; Ward (Yes/No); Allotment [Al.], Annuity [An.] and/or Identification [Id.] Numbers

NE Strain, F S;   Head
4978   "   Mary E (Brunnell); f; 24; ¼+; m; wife B2440; no; yes; Id.217e, Al.H-010452

4979 Straussman, Mary Rose (Grant); f; 37; ¼+; wd; Head A2013; yes; no; Id.458, Al.M-21
4980   "   Cecelia; f; 9 2-19-23; ¼+; s; dau A2014; yes; no; Id.458a

NE Swain, Joseph;   Head
4981   "   Margaret (Allery.Favill); f; 45; ¼+; m; wife A2015; yes; yes; Id.945a, Al.G-03568
4982   "   Ida; f; 13 12-10-18; ¼+; s; dau A2016; yes; yes; Id.945b
4983   "   Joseph; m; 10 4-1-21; ¼+; s; son A2017; yes; yes; Id.945c
4984   "   Madeline; f; 7 3-5-24; ¼+; s; dau A1028; yes; yes; Id.945d
4985   "   Zelma; f; 3-17-26; ¼+; s; dau A2019; yes; yes; none

NE Swain, Patrice;   Head
4986   "   Agnes (Gourneau); f; 38; ¼+; m; wife A2021; yes; no; Id.944a, Al.M-367
4987   "   Fred; m; 20; ¼+; s; son A2022; yes; no; Id.944b
4988   "   Georgic; m; 18; ¼+; s; son A2023; yes; no; Id.944c
4989   "   Eliza; f; 14 6-11-17; ¼+; s; dau A2024; yes; no; Id.944d
4990   "   Roderick; m; 13 6-1-18; ¼+; s; son A2025; yes; no; Id.944e

4991 Swife, Charles; m; 43; F; m; Head B2441; yes; yes; Id.36, Al.G-346
4992   "   Hard Sky; f; 53; F; m; wife B2442; yes; yes; Id.36a, Al.G-411

NE Swoboda, James;   Head
4993   "   Flora (Bartlette); f; 42; ¼+; m; wife B2444; no; Bainville, Roosevelt,
                 Mont; no; Id.946a, Al.GF-143

4994 Taken Care Of, John; m; 70; F; m; Head B2445; yes; yes; Id.10, Al.R-174
4995   "   Mary; f; 66; F; m; wife B2446; yes; yes; Id.10a, Al.G-376
4996   "   Thomas; m; 20 11-1-11; F; s; son B2447; yes; yes; Id.10e, Al. none

NE Tetrault, Joseph;   Head
4997   "   Mary Jane (Grant); f; 23; ¼+; m; wife B2448; no; Rolette, Rolette, ND;
                 yes; Id.453e, Al.H-010508
4998   "   Cecelia; f; 3 7-27-28; ¼+; s; dau -----; no; Rolette, Rolette, ND; yes; none
4999   "   Dorothea; f; 2 10-16-29; ¼+; s; dau B2449; no; Rolette, Rolette, ND; yes;
                 none
5000   "   Benora; f; 7/12 7-12-31; ¼+; s; dau ------; no; Rolette, Rolette, ND; yes;
                 none

NE Tetrault, Stanislaus;   Head
5001   "   Mary P (Brunnell); f; 29; ¼+; m; wife A2026; yes; yes; Id.211c, Al.GF-156
5002   "   Ernest; m; 9 11-10-22; ¼+; s; son A2027; yes; yes; none
5003   "   Doris E; f; 7 6-16-24; ¼+; s; dau A2028; yes; yes; none

Turtle Mountain Reservation
1932 Census Roll

Key: Number; Surname, Given; Sex; Age at Last Birthday, Birthdate (if given); Tribe (Chippewa, unless stated otherwise); Degree of Blood; Marital Status; Relationship to Head of Family, Last Year Census Number; At Jurisdiction Where Enrolled (Yes/No); Elsewhere - Post Office, County, State; Ward (Yes/No); Allotment [Al.], Annuity [An.] and/or Identification [Id.] Numbers

5004 Tetrault(cont), Lucille B; f; 6 12-9-25; ¼+; s; dau A2029; yes; yes; none
5005 " Gilbert S; m; 4 8-11-27; ¼+; s; son A2030; yes; yes; none
5006 " Margaret; f; 1 2-9-31; ¼+; s; dau A2031; yes; yes; none

NE Thibert, Arthur;   Head
5007 " Florestine (Richard); f; 26; ¼+; m; wife B2450; no; St.John, Rolette, ND; yes; Id.889d, Al.G-08414
5008 " Arthur, Jr; m; 5 4-17-26; ¼+; s; son B2451; no; St.John, Rolette, ND; yes; none
5009 " Adolph; m; 4 7-19-27; ¼+; s; son B2452; no; St.John, Rolette, ND; yes; none
5010 " Wanelda; f; 3 9-19-28; ¼+; s; dau ------; no; St.John, Rolette, ND; yes; none
5011 " Dorothy; f; 2 10-30-29; ¼+; s; dau ------; no; St.John, Rolette, ND; yes; none

NE Thibert, Frank;   Head
5012 " Marie Rose (St.Germaine); f; 29; ¼+; m; wife B2453; no; St.John, Rolette, ND; yes; Id.936f, Al.G-08392
5013 " Vernon; m; 7 12-26-24; ¼+; s; son B2454; no; St.John, Rolette, ND; yes; none
5014 " Angeline M; f; 5 3-18-27; ¼+; s; dau ------; no; St.John, Rolette, ND; yes; none
5015 " Pauline; f; 3 7-15-28; ¼+; s; dau -----; no; St.John, Rolette, ND; yes; none

5016 Thifault, Clara; f; 22 3-19-10; ¼+; s; Head B2455; no; Dunseith, Rolette, ND; yes; Id.948bm Al.H-010488
5017 " Joseph; m; 19 5-18-12; ¼+; s; bro B2456; no; Dunseith, Rolette, ND; yes; Id.948c
5018 " William; m; 17 5-20-14; ¼+; s; bro B2457; no; Dunseith, Rolette, ND; yes; Id.948d
5019 " Agnes; f; 14 4-21-17; ¼+; s; sis B2458; no; Dunseith, Rolette, ND; yes; Id.948e
5020 " Evelyn; f; 11 9-5-20; ¼+; s; sis B2460; no; Dunseith, Rolette, ND; yes; Id.848h, none
Dead " Rose;   B2459   (Died 11-11-79)
   " Mildred;   B2461   (No such child)

5021 Thifault, Frank; m; 27; ¼+; m; Head B2462; no; Buford, Williams, ND; yes; Id.947c, Al.W-3
5022 " Mabel (Morin); f; 24; ¼+; m; wife B2463; no; Buford, Williams, ND; yes Id.753c, Al.G-013081
5023 " Cleobelle; f; 3 11-26-28; ¼+; s; dau ------; no; Buford, Williams, ND; yes; none

Turtle Mountain Reservation
1932 Census Roll

Key: Number; Surname, Given; Sex; Age at Last Birthday, Birthdate (if given); Tribe (Chippewa, unless stated otherwise); Degree of Blood; Marital Status; Relationship to Head of Family, Last Year Census Number; At Jurisdiction Where Enrolled (Yes/No); Elsewhere - Post Office, County, State; Ward (Yes/No); Allotment [Al.], Annuity [An.] and/or Identification [Id.] Numbers

5024 Thifault, Louis; m; 52; ¼+; m; Head B2464; no; Trenton, Williams, ND; no; Id.947, Al.M-29672

5025 " Mary (Renville); f; 50; ¼+; m; wife B2465; no; Trenton, Williams, ND; no; Id.947a, Al.M-11

5026 " St.Ann; f; 22; ¼+; s; dau B2466; no; Trenton, Williams, ND; no; Id.947e

5027 Thifault, Raphael; m; 42 3-21-90; ¼+; m; Head B2467; no; Dunseith, Rolette, ND; no; Id.949, Al.W-37

5028 " Julia (Poitra); f; 39 5-25-93; ¼+; m; wife B2468; no; Dunseith, Rolette, ND; no; Id.949a, Al.H-010453

5029 " Rose Lillian; f; 16 9-17-15; ¼+; s; dau B2469; no; Dunseith, Rolette ND; no; Id.949b

5030 " Betsey; f; 14 11-25-17; ¼+; s; dau B2470; no; Dunseith, Rolette, ND; no; Id.949c

5031 " Mabel; f; 12 3-16-20; ¼+; s; dau B2471; no; Dunseith, Rolette, ND; no; Id.949d

5032 " Alice; f; 9 6-7-22; ¼+; s; dau B2472; no; Dunseith, Rolette, ND; no; Id.949e

5033 " Raymond; m; 7 6-7-24; ¼+; s; son ------; no; Dunseith, Rolette, ND; no; Id.949f

5034 " Harry; m; 5 10-10-27; ¼+; s; son -----; no; Dunseith, Rolette, ND; no; Id.949g

5035 " Wallace; m; 1 9-10-30; ¼+; s; son ------; no; Dunseith, Rolette, ND; no; Id.949h

5036 Thomas, Alexander; m; 49; ¼+; m; Head ----; no; (Omitted last year) Malta, Phillips, Mont; no; Id.954, Al.G-409

NE " Louise (Premeau); wife; Devils Lake, Ramsey, ND

5037 " Adelphine; f; 17 1-15-15; ¼+; s; dau B2485; no; Devils Lake, Ramsey, ND; no; Id.954c

5038 " Alexander; m; 14 10-10-17; ¼+; s; son B2486; no; Devils Lake, Ramsey, ND; no; Id.954d

5039 " Louis; m; 13 4-31-18; ¼+; s; son B2487; no; Devils Lake, Ramsey, ND; no; Id.954e

5040 " Angeline M; f; 11 4-10-20; ¼+; s; dau B2488; no; Devils Lake, Ramsey, ND; no; Id.954f

5041 " Mary Louise; f; 10 4-25-21; ¼+; s; dau B2489; no; Devils Lake, Ramsey, ND; no; Id.954g

5042 " Alvin Henry; m; 9 6-4-22; ¼+; s; son B2490; no; Devils Lake, Ramsey, ND; no; Id.954h

5043 " Margaret; f; 7 10-16-24; ¼+; s; dau B2491; no; Devils Lake, Ramsey, ND no; Id.954i

5044 " Doris; f; 3 1-15-29; ¼+; s; dau xxxxx; no; Devils Lake, Ramsey, ND; no; Id.954j

Turtle Mountain Reservation
1932 Census Roll

Key: Number; Surname, Given; Sex; Age at Last Birthday, Birthdate (if given); Tribe (Chippewa, unless stated otherwise); Degree of Blood; Marital Status; Relationship to Head of Family, Last Year Census Number; At Jurisdiction Where Enrolled (Yes/No); Elsewhere - Post Office, County, State; Ward (Yes/No); Allotment [Al.], Annuity [An.] and/or Identification [Id.] Numbers

Dead   Thomas(cont), Allen;   B2492   (Died 1927)

5045   Thomas, Clement; m; 52; ¼+; m; Head B2473; no; Rolette, Rolette, ND; no; Id.950, Al.G-36589
5046   "   Mary (Poitra); f; 48; ¼+; m; wife B2474; no; Rolette, Rolette, ND; no; Id.950a, Al.G-036587
5047   "   Mary Helen; f; 21 12-23-10; ¼+; s; dau B2475; no; Rolette, Rolette, ND; yes; Id.950b, Al.G-016077
5048   "   Wm John; m; 19 5-23-12; ¼+; s; son B2476; no; Rolette, Rolette, ND; yes Id.950c, Al.H-024654
5049   "   Joseph L; m; 18 12-18-13; ¼+; s; son B2477; no; Rolette, Rolette, ND; yes; Id.950d, Al.H-024655
5050   "   Martin Roy; m; 16 11-13-15; ¼+; s; son B2478; no; Rolette, Rolette, ND; no; Id.950e
5051   "   Rosalie; f; 14 11-9-17; ¼+; s; dau B2479; no; Rolette, Rolette, ND; no; Id.950f
5052   "   Malvina; f; 12 3-12-20; ¼+; s; dau B2480; no; Rolette, Rolette, ND; no; Id.950g
5053   "   Edward; m; 9 10-28-22; ¼+; s; son B2481; no; Rolette, Rolette, ND; no; Id.950h
5054   "   Edmund; m; 9 10-28-22; ¼+; s; son B2482; no; Rolette, Rolette, ND; no; Id.950i
5055   "   May Albina; f; 6 5-20-25; ¼+; s; dau B2483; no; Rolette, Rolette, ND; no; Id.950j
5056   "   Ernest Allen; m; 3 2-20-28; ¼+; s; son B2484; no; Rolette, Rolette, ND; no; Id.950k

NE   Thomas, Frank;   Head
5057   "   Mary Rose (Dionne); f; 26; ¼+; m; wife A2032; yes; yes; Id.346c, Al.G-400
5058   "   Antoine; m; 11 3-4-21; ¼+; s; son A2033; yes; yes; none
5059   "   Nora; f; 9 12-23-23; ¼+; s; dau B2034; yes; yes; none
5060   "   Alex; m; 5 2-23-27; ¼+; s; son A2035; yes; yes; none
5061   "   Francis; m; 2 1-29-30; ¼+; s; son A2036; yes; yes; none

5062   Thomas, James; m; 38; ¼+; wd; Head A2037; yes; no; Id.953, Al.G-402
5063   "   William; m; 17; ¼+; s; son A2038; yes; no; Id.953b
5064   "   Rita; f; 16; ¼+; s; dau A2039; yes; no; Id.953c
5065   "   Mary Louise; f; 10 4-25-21; ¼+; s; dau A2040; yes; no; Id.953d

5066   Thomas, John; m; 54; ¼+; m; Head A2041; yes; yes; Id.951, Al.R-299
NE   "   Philomeme (Berthium); wife
5067   "   Nora St.Ann; f; 22; ¼+; s; dau A2042; yes; yes; Id.951c
5068   "   Clara Jane; f; 19; ¼+; s; dau A2043; yes; yes; Id.951d
5069   "   Albert Ed; m; 15 11-13-16; ¼+; s; son A2044; yes; yes; Id.951e

Turtle Mountain Reservation
1932 Census Roll

Key: Number; Surname, Given; Sex; Age at Last Birthday, Birthdate (if given); Tribe (Chippewa, unless stated otherwise); Degree of Blood; Marital Status; Relationship to Head of Family, Last Year Census Number; At Jurisdiction Where Enrolled (Yes/No); Elsewhere - Post Office, County, State; Ward (Yes/No); Allotment [Al.], Annuity [An.] and/or Identification [Id.] Numbers

5070 Thomas(cont), Leroy E; m; 9 2-25-23; ¼+; s; son A2045; yes; yes; Id.951f

5071 Thomas, Joseph; m; 85; ¼+; wd; Head A2046; yes; yes; Id.952, Al.R-300

5072 Thomas, Norman; m; 50; ¼+; m; Head B2493; no; Devils Lake, Ramsey, ND; no; Id.955, Al.G-7866
5073   "   Ellen (Nicholas); f; 39; ¼+; m; wife B2494; no; Devils Lake, Ramsey, ND; no; Id.955a, Al.H-026341

5074 Thomas, Patrice; m; 27; ¼+; m; Head A2047; no; Van Hook, Mountrail, ND; yes; Id.951b, Al.[?]-30
5075   "   Victoria (Belgarde); f; 20; ¼+; wife A2048; no; Van Hook, Mountrail, ND; yes; Id.184c, Al.H-016386

5076 Thomas, Thomas; m; 73; ¼+; m; Head A2049; yes; no; Id.956, Al.G-034
5077   "   Margaret (Herman); f; 66; ¼+; m; wife A2050; yes; no; Id.956a, Al.G-033

5078 Thomas, William; m; 46; ¼+; m; Head B2495; no; Devils Lake, Ramsey, ND; no; Id.957, Al.G-038
5079   "   Veronica (Godon); f; 48; ¼+; m; wife B2496; no; Devils Lake, Ramsey, ND; no; Id.957a, Al.H-08107
5080   "   William, Jr; m; 21 4-19-10; ¼+; s; son B2497; no; Devils Lake, Ramsey, ND; no; Id.957b
5081   "   Louis; m; 20; 6-4-11; ¼+; s; son B2498; no; Devils Lake, Ramsey, ND; yes; Id.957c, Al.H-013036
5082   "   Robert; m; 19 8-4-12; ¼+; s; son B2499; no; Devils Lake, Ramsey, ND; no; Id.957d
5083   "   Irene; f; 17 10-23-14; ¼+; s; dau B2500; no; Devils Lake, Ramsey, ND; no; Id.957e
5084   "   Joseph; m; 14 4-16-17; ¼+; s; son B2502; no; Devils Lake, Ramsey, ND; no; Id.957f
5085   "   Agnes; f; 13 8-7-18; ¼+; s; dau B2401; no; Devils Lake, Ramsey, ND; no; Id.957g

NE Thompson, William;   Head
5086   "   Florence (Peltier.Johnson); f; 27; ¼+; m; wife B2503; no; Bisbee, Towner, ND; yes; Id.818b, Al.MC-026746
5087 " (Johnson) Irene; f; 10 6-1-21; ¼+; s; step dau B2504; no; (Counted twice last yr) Bisbee, Towner, ND; yes; none

NE Thorne, James;   Head
5088   "   Emma (Dumont); f; 32; ¼+; m; wife B2505; no; Boggy Creek, Manitoba, Can; yes; Id.367c, Al.G-0441

Turtle Mountain Reservation
1932 Census Roll

Key: Number; Surname, Given; Sex; Age at Last Birthday, Birthdate (if given); Tribe (Chippewa, unless stated otherwise); Degree of Blood; Marital Status; Relationship to Head of Family, Last Year Census Number; At Jurisdiction Where Enrolled (Yes/No); Elsewhere - Post Office, County, State; Ward (Yes/No); Allotment [Al.], Annuity [An.] and/or Identification [Id.] Numbers

5089 Thomas(cont), Lillian; f; 11 12-2-20; ¼+; s; dau B2506; no; Boggy Creek, Manitoba, Can; yes; none
5090 " Florence; f; 10 9-22-22; ¼+; s; dau B2507; no; Boggy Creek, Manitoba, Can; yes; none
5091 " Rose; f; 8 3-14-24; ¼+; s; dau B2508; no; Boggy Creek, Manitoba, Can; yes; none
5092 " Joseph; m; 3 11-7-28; ¼+; s son ------; no; Boggy Creek, Manitoba, Can; yes; none
5093 " Bertha; f; 3/12 12-19-31; ¼+; s; dau -----; no; Boggy Creek, Manitoba, Can; yes; none

NE Thorpe, A W;   Head
5094 " Emma (Schindler); f; 43; ¼+; m; wife B2509; no; Unknown, Canada; no; Id.961a, Al.G-0187
5095 " Catherine; f; 18; ¼+; s; dau B2511; no; Unknown, Canada; no; Id.961b
5096 " Beatrice; f; 16 3-24-16; ¼+; s; dau B2512; no; Unknown, Canada; no; Id.961c
5097 " Arthur; m; 14 10-28-17; ¼+; s; son B2513; no; Unknown, Canada; no; Id.961d
5098 " Ethel; f; 12 7-23-19; ¼+; s; dau B2514; no; Unknown, Canada; no; Id.961e
5099 " Winifred; f; 10 7-28-21; ¼+; s; dau B2515; no; Unknown, Canada; no; Id.961f
5100 " Patrick; m; 8 4-19-23; ¼+; s; son b2516; no; Unknown, Canada; no; Id.961g

NE Tibbits, Ross N;   Head
5101 " Ruth (Jollie.Azure); f; 35; ¼+; m; wife B144; no; Wilton, McLean, ND; no; Id.537b, Al.G-57
5102 " Nora Yvonne; f; 2 7-22-29; ¼+; s; dau -----; no; Wilton, McLean, ND; no; none

NE Tinkay, Ray;   Head
5102[sic] " Rose (Laverdure); f; 27; ¼+; m; wife B2517; no; Plentywood, Sheridan, Mont; yes; Id.644e, Al.G-028
5103 " Laverne; m; 5 5-8-26; ¼+; s; son -----; no; Plentywood, Sheridan, Mont; yes; none
5104 " Violet May; f; 2 6-16-29; ¼+; s; dau -----; no; Plentywood, Sheridan, Mont yes; none
5105 " Rosella; f; 1 1-28-31; ¼+; s; dau ------; no; Plentywood, Sheridan, Mont; yes; none

NE Tobiness;   Head
5106 " Girl; f; 48; F; m; wife B2518; no; Dunseith, Rolette, ND; yes; Id.8a, Al.DL-33
5107 " Circling Thunder; m; 30; F; s; son B2519; no; Dunseith, Rolette, ND; yes; Id. 8b, Al.H-028305

Turtle Mountain Reservation
1932 Census Roll

Key: Number; Surname, Given; Sex; Age at Last Birthday, Birthdate (if given); Tribe (Chippewa, unless stated otherwise); Degree of Blood; Marital Status; Relationship to Head of Family, Last Year Census Number; At Jurisdiction Where Enrolled (Yes/No); Elsewhere - Post Office, County, State; Ward (Yes/No); Allotment [Al.], Annuity [An.] and/or Identification [Id.] Numbers

5108	Tobiness(cont), Hanging In The Air; m; 16; F; s; son B2520; no; Dunseith, Rolette, ND; yes; Id.8e
5109	"	Mary; f; 14; F; s; dau B2521; no; Dunseith, Rolette, ND; yes; Id.8f
5110	"	Lester; m; 12; F; s; son B2522; no; Dunseith, Rolette, ND; yes; Id.8g
5111	"	Roy; m; 9 F; s; son B2523; no; Dunseith, Rolette, ND; yes; none
5112	"	Iron Feather; m; 7 F; s; son B2524; no; Dunseith, Rolette, ND; yes; Id.8h

NE   Torgerson, Marvin O;   Head
5113   "   Mary (Belgarde); f; 24; ¼+; m; wife B309; no; Dagmar, Sheridan, Mont; no; Id.175c
5114   "   Glen Allen; m; 7/12 8-10-31; ¼+; s; son ------; no; Dagmar, Sheridan, Mont; no; none

NE   Travis, Elmer;   Head
5115   "   Mary Louise (Lafournais); f; 33; ¼+; m; wife B2525; no; Togo, Sask, Can; yes; Id.564d, Al.M-53

NE   Trester, Alex M;   Head
5116   "   Margaret (Demontigny); f; 23; ¼+; m; wife B2526; no; Rolla, Rolette, ND yes; Sid.341f, Al.G-08245
5117   "   Alexander; m; 9 6-9-22; ¼+; s; son B2527; no; Rolla, Rolette, ND; no; none

5118   Trothier, Joseph; m; 50; ¼+; wd; Head B2528; no; Devils Lake, Ramsey, ND; yes; Id.963, Al.R-303
5119   "   Patrice; m; 23 4-15-08; ¼+; s; son B2529; no; Devils Lake, Ramsey, ND; yes; Id.963d, Al.G-141
5120   "   John; m; 19 8-6-12; ¼+; s; son B2531; no; Devils Lake, Ramsey, ND; yes Id.963f

NE   Trothier, Joseph;   Head
5121   "   Laura (Belgarde); f; 34; ¼+; m; wife B2532; yes; no; Id.168b, Al.G-155
5122   "   Alexander; m; 10 11-15-21; ¼+; s; son B2533; yes; no; none
5123   "   Roy; m; 9 2-18-23; ¼+; s; son B2534; yes; no; none
5124   "   Mary; f; 6 1-7-26; ¼+; s; dau B2535; yes; no; none
5125   "   Eugene; m; 1 4-9-30; ¼+; s; son B2536; yes; no; none

NE   Trothier, Joseph;   Head
5126   "   Agnes (Donsey); f; 21 9-6-09; ¼+; m; wife B2537; no; Harlem, Blaine, Mont; yes; Id.347e, Al.G-017067
5127   "   Betty; f; 3 11-9-28; ¼+; s; dau B2538; no; Harlem, Blaine, Mont; yes; none

NE   Trothier, Martin;   Head
5128   "   Mary Rose (Belgarde); f; 26; ¼+; m; wife B2539; no; Devils Lake, Ramsey, ND; yes; Id.190c, Al.G-468

Turtle Mountain Reservation
1932 Census Roll

Key: Number; Surname, Given; Sex; Age at Last Birthday, Birthdate (if given); Tribe (Chippewa, unless stated otherwise); Degree of Blood; Marital Status; Relationship to Head of Family, Last Year Census Number; At Jurisdiction Where Enrolled (Yes/No); Elsewhere - Post Office, County, State; Ward (Yes/No); Allotment [Al.], Annuity [An.] and/or Identification [Id.] Numbers

5129 Trothier(cont), Marie Louise; f; 2 9-15-29; ¼+; s; dau B2540; no; Devils Lake, Ramsey, ND; yes; none

NE   Trothier, Maxim;   Head
5130   "   Mary Alice (Doney); f; 24 8-15-07; ¼+; m; wife B2541; no; Malta, Phillips, Mont; yes; Id.347b, Al.G-500
5131   "   Everett P; m; 6 3-11-26; ¼+; s; son B2542; no; Malta, Phillips, Mont; yes; none
5132   "   Maxine; f; 2 6-4-29; ¼+; s; dau B2543; no; Malta, Phillips, Mont; yes; none

NE   Trothier, Patrice;   Head A1777
5133   "   Mary (Patnaud); f; 20; ¼+; m; wife A2051; yes; (Counted twice last census) yes; Id.803g, Al.H-024442
5134   "   Sylvia; f; 4 ¼+; s; dau A2052; yes; yes; none
5135   "   Gerald; m; 6/12 9-16-31; ¼+; s; son ------; yes; yes; none

5136 Trothier, Raphael; m; 25 4-15-06; ¼+; m; Head B2544; no; Devils Lake, Ramsey, ND; yes; Id.963c, Al.G-159
5137   "   Marie Rose (Laducer); f; 19; ¼+; m; wife B2545; no; Devils Lake, Ramsey, ND; yes; Id.538d, Al.H-020544
5138   "   Wayne; m; 1 4-15-30; ¼+; s; son B2546; no; Devils Lake, Ramsey, ND; yes; none

5139 Turcotte, Antoine; m; 48; ¼+; m; Head B2547; no; Dunseith, Rolette, ND; no; Id.972. Al.MC-026652
NE   "   Adele (Peltier.Standing); wife
5140   "   Celine; f; 21 4-15-10; ¼+; s; dau B2548; no; Dunseith, Rolette, ND; no; Id.972b
5141   "   Mary; f; 16 7-31-15; ¼+; s; dau B2549; no; Dunseith, Rolette, ND; no; Id.972c
5142   "   Vitaline; f; 10 1-19-22; ¼+; s; dau B2550; no; Dunseith, Rolette, ND; no; Id.972e
5143   "   Albert; m; 8 2-23-24; ¼+; s; son B2551; no; Dunseith, Rolette, ND; no; Id.972d
5144   "   Alfred; m; 5 11-27-26; ¼+; s; son B2552; no; Dunseith, Rolette, ND; no; Id.972f
5145   "   Alvina; f; 3 2-8-29; ¼+; s; dau B2553; no; Dunseith, Rolette, ND; no; Id.972g
5146   "   Roselina; f; 1 3-17-31; ¼+; s; dau ------; no; Dunseith, Rolette, ND; no; Id.972h

Turtle Mountain Reservation
1932 Census Roll

Key: Number; Surname, Given; Sex; Age at Last Birthday, Birthdate (if given); Tribe (Chippewa, unless stated otherwise); Degree of Blood; Marital Status; Relationship to Head of Family, Last Year Census Number; At Jurisdiction Where Enrolled (Yes/No); Elsewhere - Post Office, County, State; Ward (Yes/No); Allotment [Al.], Annuity [An.] and/or Identification [Id.] Numbers

5147	Turcotte, Collin; m; 45; ¼+; m; Head B2554; no; Rolla, Rolette, ND; no; Id.969, Al.W-26	
5148	"	Christine (Jeannotte); f; 41; ¼+; m; wife B2555; no; Rolla, Rolette, ND; no; Id.969a, Al.M-222
5149	"	Larose; f; 20 5-8-11; ¼+; s; dau B2556; no; Rolla, Rolette, ND; no; Id.969b, Al.H-012642
5150	"	Fred; m; 19 8-27-12; ¼+; s; son B2557; no; Rolla, Rolette, ND; no; Id.969c
5151	"	Cecelia; f; 17 4-24-14; ¼+; s; dau B2558; no; Rolla, Rolette, ND; no; Id.969d
5152	"	Andrew; m; 15 3-14-17; ¼+; s; son B2559; no; Rolla, Rolette, ND; no; Id.969f
5153	"	William; m; 13 3-6-19; ¼+; s; son B2560; no; Rolla, Rolette, ND; no; Id.969e
5154	"	Edna Pearl; f; 11 3-7-21; ¼+; s; dau B2561; no; Rolla, Rolette, ND; no; Id.969g
5155	"	Alvina E; f; 9 11-7-22; ¼+; s; dau B2562l no; Rolla, Rolette, ND; no; Id.969i
5156	"	Lawrence; m; 8 10-3-23; ¼+; s; son B2563; no; Rolla, Rolette, ND; no; Id.969j
5157	"	Irene; f; 6 8-7-25; ¼+; s; dau B2564; no; Rolla, Rolette, ND; no; Id.969k
5158	"	Stanley; m; 5 11-8-26; ¼+; s; son B2565; no; Rolla, Rolette, ND; no; Id.969l
5159	"	Henry; m; 2 7-2-29; ¼+; s; son B2566; no; Rolla, Rolette, ND; no; Id.969m
5160	"	Rita; f; 11/12 4-2-31; ¼+; s; dau -----; no; Rolla, Rolette, ND; no; Id.969n

5161	Turcotte, Daniel; m; 41; ¼+; m; Head B2567; no; Trenton, Williams, ND; no; Id.966, Al.M-136	
NE	"	Clara (Burns); wife B2577
5162	"	Joseph; m; 10 3-20-22; ¼+; s; son B2568; no; (Counted twice last yr) Trenton, Williams, ND; no; Id.966b, none
5163	"	Edna; f; 8 2-12-24; ¼+; s; dau B2569; no; Trenton, Williams, ND; no; Id.966c
5164	"	Evelyn; f; 5 4-16-26; ¼+; s; dau ------; no; Trenton, Williams, ND; no; none
5165	"	Viola; f; 2 10-6-29; ¼+; s; dau -----; no; Trenton, Williams, ND; no; none
Dead	"	Michael; B2570 (Died 6-13-29)

5166	Turcotte, Daniel; m; 60; ¼+; m; Head B2571; no; Trenton, Williams, ND; no; Id.965, Al.M-141	
5167	"	Rosine (Dubois); f; 58; ¼+; m; wife B2572; no; Trenton, Williams, ND; no; Id.965a, Al.M-138
5168	"	Joseph; m; 28; ¼+; s; son B2573; no; Trenton, Williams, ND; no; Id.965d, Al.M-137
5169	"	Mary F; f; 21; ¼+; s; dau B2574; no; Trenton, Williams, ND; no; Id.965f

Turtle Mountain Reservation
1932 Census Roll

Key: Number; Surname, Given; Sex; Age at Last Birthday, Birthdate (if given); Tribe (Chippewa, unless stated otherwise); Degree of Blood; Marital Status; Relationship to Head of Family, Last Year Census Number; At Jurisdiction Where Enrolled (Yes/No); Elsewhere - Post Office, County, State; Ward (Yes/No); Allotment [Al.], Annuity [An.] and/or Identification [Id.] Numbers

5170 Turcotte(cont), James; m; 18; ¼+; s; son B2575; no; Trenton, Williams, ND; no; Id.965g
5172 " Clarence; m; 15 5-9-16; ¼+; s; son B2576; no; Trenton, Williams, ND; no; Id.965h

5173 Turcotte, John; m; 20 1-25-12; ¼+; s; Head B2579; no; Minot, Ward, ND; no; Id.964b
5174 " Elmer; m; 17 7-30-14; ¼+; s; bro B2580; no; Minot, Ward, ND; no; Id.964c
5175 " Louis; m; 13 8-25-18; ¼+; s; bro B ------; no; Minot, Ward, ND; no; none

5176 Turcotte, Margery (Decoteau); f; 78; ¼+; wd; Head A2053; yes; yes; Id.967, Al.R-302

5177 Turcotte, Pierre; m; 47; ¼+; m; Head A2054; yes; no; Id.970, Al.H-013094
5178 " Elise (Jaste); f; 30; ¼+; m; wife A2055; yes; yes; Id.500b, Al.H-010419
5179 " Ernest; m; 9 3-24-23; ¼+; s; son A2056; yes; yes; none
5180 " Georgeline; f; 6 8-4-25; ¼+; s; dau B2057; yes; yes; none
5181 " Louis P; m; 4 3-7-28; ¼+; s; son A2058; yes; yes; none
5182 " Vitaline; f; 1/12 2-3-32; ¼+; s; dau ------; yes; yes; none

5183 Turcotte, Robert; m; 25; ¼+; m; Head B2581; no; Trenton, Williams, ND; yes; Id.965e, Al.W-23
NE " Emma (Slater); wife
5184 " June Mary; f; 1 6-4-30; ¼+; s; dau A2582; no; Trenton, Williams, ND; yes; none

5185 Turcotte, William; m; 51; ¼+; m; Head A2059; yes; yes; Id.968, Al.W28
5186 " Mary Matilda; f; 33 1-29-99; ¼+; m; wife A2060; yes; yes; Id.968a, Al.G-08183

5187 Vallie, Abraham; m; 46; ¼+; s; Head B2583; no; Unknown; no; Id.974, Al.H-012648

5188 Vallie, Baptiste; m; 45; ¼+; m; Head A2061; yes; no; Id.977, Al.GF-0220
5189 " Mary Jane (Lafontain); f; 36; ¼+; m; wife A2062; yes; yes; Id.977a, Al.G-27
5190 " Francis; m; 14 7-10-17; ¼+; s; son A2063; yes; yes; Id.977b
5191 " Emil; m; 12 6-6-19; ¼+; s; son A2064; yes; yes; Id.977c
5192 " Eleanor; f; 11 11-6-20; ¼+; s; dau A2065; yes; yes; Id.977d
5193 " Joseph; m; 8 2-28-24; ¼+; s; son A2066; yes; yes; Id.977e
5194 " Mary Jane; f; 7; ¼+; s; dau A2067; yes; yes; Id.977f
5195 " Louis; m; 5 ¼+; s; son A2068; yes; yes; Id.977g
5196 " Helen; f; 3 3-4-29; ¼+; s; dau A2069; yes; yes; Id.977h
5197 " Cecelia; f; 1 3-17-31; ¼+; s; dau A2070; yes; yes; none

5198 Vallie, John B; m; 48; ¼+; s; Head B2584; no; Unknown; no; Id.973, Al.W-21

Turtle Mountain Reservation
1932 Census Roll

Key: Number; Surname, Given; Sex; Age at Last Birthday, Birthdate (if given); Tribe (Chippewa, unless stated otherwise); Degree of Blood; Marital Status; Relationship to Head of Family, Last Year Census Number; At Jurisdiction Where Enrolled (Yes/No); Elsewhere - Post Office, County, State; Ward (Yes/No); Allotment [Al.], Annuity [An.] and/or Identification [Id.] Numbers

Dead Vallie, Julia;   A2071   (Died 3-29-25)

5199 Vandal, Alfred; m; 23; ¼+; m; Head B2589; no; Trenton, Williams, ND; yes;
                                                                                    Id.987d, Al.H-012647
NE   "   Palma (Kringen);   wife

5200 Vandal, Edmund; m; 30; ¼+; m; Head B2585; no; Trenton, Williams, ND; yes;
                                                                                    Id.978c, Al.G-0240
NE   "   Ernestine (Laroque);   wife
5201   "   Edmund, Jr; m; 3 3-31-29; ¼+; s; son B2586; no; Trenton, Williams, ND;
                                                                                      yes; none
5202   "   Erma; f; 1 12-27-30; ¼+; s; dau -------; no; Trenton, Williams, ND; yes; none

5203 Vandal, Frank; m; 57; ¼+; m; Head B2587; yes; no; Id.978, Al.DL-17
5204   "   Georgiana (Houle); f; 21; ¼+; m; wife B2588; yes; yes; Id.486e, Al.G-016819
5205   "   Ernest; m; 21; ¼+; m; son B2590; yes; yes; Id.978f, Al.G-016635
5206   "   Catherine; f; 18; ¼+; s; dau B2591; yes; no; Id.978g
5207   "   Veronica; f; 16; ¼+; s; dau B2592; yes; no; Id.978h
5208   "   Madeline; f; 10; ¼+; s; dau B2593; yes; no; Id.978i
5209   "   Rose; f; 1/12 3-25-32; ¼+; s; dau ------; yes; yes; Id.978j

5210 Vandal, John B; m; 75; ¼+; m; Head A2078; yes; no; Id.979, Al.R-306
NE   "   Madeline (Grant);   wife

5211 Vandal, John; m; 47; ¼+; m; Head A2079; yes; no; Id.984, Al.GF-166
5212   "   Jane (Gourneau); f; 40; ¼+; m; wife A2080; yes; no; Id.984a, Al.G-07955
5213   "   Michael J; m; 18 12-30-13; ¼+; s; son A2081; yes; no; Id.984b
5214   "   Rita; f; 15 5-17-16; ¼+; s; dau A2082; yes; no; Id.984c
5215   "   Cecelia M; f; 12 9-29-19; ¼+; s; dau A2083; yes; no; Id.984d
5216   "   Esther; f; 4 10-27-27; ¼+; s; dau A2084; yes; no; Id.984e

NE Vandal, Joseph;   Head
5217   "   Josephine (Gladue); f; 38; ¼+; m; wife A2072; yes; yes; Id.416, Al.GF-82
5218   "   Luke; m; 12 11-7-19; ¼+; s; son A2073; yes; yes; Id.416b
5219   "   Leo; m; 11 1-6-21; ¼+; s; son A2074; yes; yes; Id.416c
5220   "   Lillie; f; 8 12-22-23; ¼+; s; dau A2075; yes; yes; Id.416d
5221   "   Albert; m; 7 2-22-25l ¼+; s; son A2076; yes; yes; Id.416e
5222   "   Marie; f; 5 8-11-26; ¼+; s; dau A2077; yes; yes; Id.416f

5223 Vandal, Joseph; m; 41; ¼+; m; Head B2594; no; Rolla, Rolette, ND; no; Id.981,
                                                                                      Al.GF-164
5224   "   Agatha (Lafontain); f; 36; ¼+; m; wife B2595; no; Rolla, Rolette, ND; no;
                                                                                 Id.081a[sic]; Al.GF-230
5225   "   Louis; m; 14 5-19-17; ¼+; s; son B2596; no; Rolla, Rolette, ND; no; Id.981e

Turtle Mountain Reservation
1932 Census Roll

Key: Number; Surname, Given; Sex; Age at Last Birthday, Birthdate (if given); Tribe (Chippewa, unless stated otherwise); Degree of Blood; Marital Status; Relationship to Head of Family, Last Year Census Number; At Jurisdiction Where Enrolled (Yes/No); Elsewhere - Post Office, County, State; Ward (Yes/No); Allotment [Al.], Annuity [An.] and/or Identification [Id.] Numbers

5226 Vandal(cont), Mary May; f; 12; ¼+; s; dau B2597; no; Rolla, Rolette, ND; no; Id.981b
5227 " Raymond; m; 10; ¼+; s; son B2598; no; Rolla, Rolette, ND; no; Id.981c
5228 " Lorene; f; 2 4-29-29; ¼+; s; dau B2599; no; Rolla, Rolette, ND; no; Id.981g

5229 Vandal, Margaret; f; 19; ¼+; s; Head B2600; no; Rolla, Rolette, ND; no; Id.982a
5230 " Josephine; f; 17 3-17-15; ¼+; s; sis B2601; no; Rolla, Rolette, ND; no; Id.982b
5231 " Mary Louise; f; 14 2-13-18; ¼+; s; sis B2602; no; Rolla, Rolette, ND; no; Id.982c
5232 " Petroline; f; 11 6-5-20; ¼+; s; sis B2603; no; Rolla, Rolette, ND; no; Id.982d

NE Vanoss, Antoine; Head
5233 " Mary Rose (Gladue); f; 40; ¼+; m; wife B2604; no; Ft.Totten, Benson, ND; yes; Id.985a, Al.H-010502
5234 " Leon; m; 17 9-13-14; ¼+; s; son B2605 no; Waubun, Mahnomen, Minn; yes; Id.985b
5235 " Laverne; f; 16 1-8-16; ¼+; s; dau B2606; no; Devils Lake, Ramsey, ND; yes; Id.985c
5236 " Francis; m; 15 3-20-17; ¼+; s; son B2607; no; Ft.Totten, Benson, ND; yes; Id.985d

NE Venne, Patrice; Head
5237 " Philomeme (Davis); f; 40; ¼+; m; wife B585; no; Sidney, Richland, Mont; no; Id.271, Al.GF-64
5238 " Elmer; m; 7 6-8-24; ¼+; s; son ------; no; Sidney, Richland, Mont; no; none
5239 " Laura; f; 4 8-30-27; ¼+; s; dau ------; no; Sidney, Richland, Mont; no; none

NE Villebrun, Paul; Head
5240 " Annie (Saice.Rolette); f; 77; ¼+; m; wife A2085; yes; no; Id.891a, Al.H-010504

5241 Villeneuve, Joseph; m; 25 7-11-06; ¼+; m; Head A2086; yes; yes; Id.985e, Al.G-07865
NE " Rachel (St.Claire); wife
5242 " Leona C; f; 1 8-27-30; ¼+; s; dau A2087; yes; yes; none

5243 Villeneuve, Pascal; m; 58; ¼+; m; Head A2088; yes; no; Id.986, Al.G-07864
5244 " Eliza (Parisien); f; 44; ¼+; m; wife A2089; yes; no; Id.986a, Al.G-019
5245 " Herman; m; 19 10-15-12; ¼+; s; son A2090; yes; no; Id.986f
5246 " Henry; m; 16 3-6-16; ¼+; s; son A2091; yes; no; Id.986g
5247 " Martin; m; 13 10-15-18; ¼+; s; son A2092; yes; no; Id.986h
5248 " Albert; m; 10 4-2-21; ¼+; s; son A2093; yes; no; Id.986i
5249 " Nora; f; 8 4-29-24; ¼+; s; dau A2094; yes; no; Id.986j
5250 " Emelia; f; 5 7-5-26; ¼+; s; dau A2095; yes; no; Id.986k
5251 " Evangeline; f; 3 9-26-28; ¼+; s; dau A2096; yes; no; Id.986l

Turtle Mountain Reservation
1932 Census Roll

Key: Number; Surname, Given; Sex; Age at Last Birthday, Birthdate (if given); Tribe (Chippewa, unless stated otherwise); Degree of Blood; Marital Status; Relationship to Head of Family, Last Year Census Number; At Jurisdiction Where Enrolled (Yes/No); Elsewhere - Post Office, County, State; Ward (Yes/No); Allotment [Al.], Annuity [An.] and/or Identification [Id.] Numbers

5252 Vivier, Ambrose; m; 77; ¼+; m; Head B2608; no; Rolla, Rolette, ND; no; Id.987, Al.R-307
5253 " Genevieve (Azure); f; 77; ¼+; m; wife B2609; no; Rolla, Rolette, ND; no; Id.987a, Al.G-036573

5254 Vivier, Charles; m; 38; ¼+; m; Head B2610; no; Dunseith, Rolette, ND; no; Id.991, Al.G-016064
5255 " Rosine; f; 32; ¼+; m; wife B2611; no; Dunseith, Rolette, ND; yes; Id.719b, Al.G-042
5256 " Francis P; m; 13 2-19-19; ¼+; s; son B2612; no; Dunseith, Rolette, ND; yes Id.991b
5257 " Patrice M; m; 11 11-25-20; ¼+; s; son B2613; no; Dunseith, Rolette, ND; yes; Id.991c
5258 " Louis Leo; m; 9 5-19-23; ¼+; s; son B2614; no; Dunseith, Rolette, ND; yes; Id.991d
5259 " Fred; m; 6 10-9-25; ¼+; a; son ----; no; Dunseith, Rolette, ND; yes; none
5260 " Leona V; f; 2 6-24-28; ¼+; s; dau B2615; no; Dunseith, Rolette, ND; yes; Id.991e
5261 " Archie; m; 10/12 4-16-31; ¼+; s; son ------; no; Dunseith, Rolette, ND; yes; none

NE Vivier, Elie
5262 " Virginie (Azure); f; 60; ¼+; m; Head B2616; no; Unknown, Canada; no; Id.990a, Al.R-310
5263 " Alexander; m; 34; ¼+; s; son B2617; no; Unknown, Canada; no; Id.990b, Al.G-016064
5264 " Francois; m; 30; ¼+; s; son B2618; no; Unknown, Canada; yes; Id.990d, Al.G-016069
5265 " Robert; m; 23; ¼+; s; son B2619; no; Unknown, Canada; yes; Id.990g, Al.G-016068

5266 Vivier, Israel; m; 31 12-15-02; ¼+; m; Head A2106; yes; yes; Id.989b, Al.D-01747
NE " Margaret (Gwinn); wife

NE Vivier, Joseph; Head
5267 " Rosine (Trothier); f; 46; ¼+; m; wife A2097; yes; yes; Id.992a, Al.G-037045
5268 " William; m; 28; ¼+; s; son A2098; yes; yes; Id.992b, Al.H-030439
5269 " Alfred; m; 26; ¼+; s; son A2099; yes; yes; Id.992d
5270 " Marvin; m; 23; ¼+; s; son A2100; yes; yes; Id.992f
5271 " Eugene; m; 18; ¼+; s; son A2101; yes; yes; Id.992h

5272 Vivier, Michael; m; 26 4-23-05; ¼+; m; Head A2103; yes; yes; Id.989c, Al.D-01749
5273 " Catherine (Bercier); f; 35; ¼+; m; wife A2104; yes; yes; Id.1167b, Al.M-14

Turtle Mountain Reservation
1932 Census Roll

Key: Number; Surname, Given; Sex; Age at Last Birthday, Birthdate (if given); Tribe (Chippewa, unless stated otherwise); Degree of Blood; Marital Status; Relationship to Head of Family, Last Year Census Number; At Jurisdiction Where Enrolled (Yes/No); Elsewhere - Post Office, County, State; Ward (Yes/No); Allotment [Al.], Annuity [An.] and/or Identification [Id.] Numbers

5274 Vivier, Napoleon; m; 50; ¼+; wd; Head A2105; yes; yes; Id.989, Al.R-308
5275 " Jacob; m; 24 9-13-07; ¼+; s; son A2107; yes; yes; Id.989d, Al.D-01748
5276 " Mary Jane; f; 20 3-28-12; ¼+; s; dau A2108; yes; yes; Id.989e
5277 " Seraphine; f; 17 9-6-14; ¼+; s; dau A2109; yes; yes; Id.989f
5278 " Eva; f; 15 12-20-16; ¼+; s; dau A2110; yes; yes; Id.989g
5279 " Ernest; m; 8 7-8-23; ¼+; s; son A2111; yes; yes; Id.989h
5280 " Napoleon; m; 5 4-8-26; ¼+; s; son A2112; yes; yes; Id.989i
5281 " Esther; f; 4 1-28-28; ¼+; s; dau A2113; yes; yes; Id.989j

5282 Vivier, Norman; m; 27; ¼+; m; Head B2620; no; Devils Lake, Ramsey, ND; yes; Id.988c, Al.G-471
NE " Zoe (Lafrance); wife
5283 " Stella Mae; f; 5 11-29-26; ¼+; s; dau ------; no; Devils Lake, Ramsey, ND; yes; none
5284 " Catherine; f; 2 5-19-29; ¼+; s; dau ------; no; Devils Lake, Ramsey, ND; yes; none
5285 " Vincent; m; 1 7-20-30; ¼+; s; son ------; no; Devils Lake, Ramsey, ND; yes; none

5286 Vivier, Phillip; m; 34; ¼+; m; Head A2114; yes; yes; Id.990c, Al.G-01
5287 " Marguerite (Nadeau); f; 30; ¼+; m; wife A2115; yes; yes; Id.771c, Al.M-273
5288 " Patrick; m; 5 9-7-26; ¼+; s; son A2116; yes; yes; none
5289 " Norbert; m; 3 9-2-28; ¼+; s; son A2117; yes; yes; none
5290 " Gladys; f; 6/12 9-8-31; ¼+; s; dau ------; yes; yes; none

5291 Vivier, St.Pierre; m; 32; ¼+; m; Head B2622; yes; yes; Id.988b, Al.M-152
NE " Yvonne (Laverdure); wife
5292 " Ernestine; f; 5 7-16-26; ¼+; s; dau ------; yes; yes; none
5293 " Isabel M; f; 3 6-10-28; ¼+; s; dau ------; yes; yes; none
5294 " Louis V; m; 2 12-3-29; ¼+; s; son ------; yes; yes; none
5295 " James S; m; 3-31-32; ¼+; s; son ------; yes; yes; none

5296 Vivier, Theresa (Herman); f; 61; ¼+; wd; Head B2621; yes; no; Id.988a, Al.M-151
5297 " Louis; m; 26; ¼+; s; son B2623; no; Bismarck (pen), Burleigh, ND; yes; Id.988d, Al.G-472

NE Waits, Lyle; Head
5298 " Martine (Lafontain); f; 18 10-20-13; ¼+; m; wife B1280; no; Roy, Fergus, Mont; no; Id.548i, Al. none

NE Walke, Richard; Head
5299 " Louise (Aiken); f; 25; ¼+; m; wife B2625; no; Cando, Towner, ND; yes; Id.62c, Al.G-498

Turtle Mountain Reservation
1932 Census Roll

Key: Number; Surname, Given; Sex; Age at Last Birthday, Birthdate (if given); Tribe (Chippewa, unless stated otherwise); Degree of Blood; Marital Status; Relationship to Head of Family, Last Year Census Number; At Jurisdiction Where Enrolled (Yes/No); Elsewhere - Post Office, County, State; Ward (Yes/No); Allotment [Al.], Annuity [An.] and/or Identification [Id.] Numbers

```
NE     Walking Elk;                             Head
5300      "      Florestine (Peltier); f; 33; ¼+; m; wife B2626; no; Forkston,
                                         Manitoba, Can; yes; Id.819c, Al.G-234

5301   Walking By Eights; m; 42; F; s; Head B2627; no; Unknown, Canada; yes; Id.38,
                                                                           Al.G-382

5302   Wallett, Gregory; m; 36; ¼+; m; Head A2118; yes; no; Id.995, Al.GF-9
5303      "      Mary (Charette); f; 23; ¼+; m; wife A2119; yes; no; Id.237c
5304      "      Henry; m; 4 5-1-27; ¼+; s; son A2120; yes; no; none

5305   Wallett, Isadore; m; 34; ¼+; m; Head A2121; yes; no; Id.1001, Al.M-73
5306      "      Ernestine (Delorme); f; 28; ¼+; m; wife A2122; yes; yes; Id.326b, Al.M-68
5307      "      Michael; m; 10 9-6-21; ¼+; s; son A2123; yes; yes; none
5308      "      Edna; f; 8 9-19-23; ¼+; s; dau A2124; yes; yes; none
5309      "      Emma; f; 6; ¼+; s; dau A2125; yes; yes; none
5310      "      Alvina; f; 4 ¼+; s; dau A2126; yes; yes; none
5311      "      Lillian; f; 3 3-3-29; ¼+; s; dau A2127; yes; yes; none

5312   Wallett, James; m; 38; ¼+; m; Head A2128; yes; no; Id.994b, Al.GF-10
5313      "      Mary Rose (Laducer); f; 27; ¼+; m; wife A2129; yes; yes; Id.539c, Al.G-75
5314      "      Cecelia; f; 3 12-5-28; ¼+; s; dau A2130; yes; yes; none
5315      "      Sarah; f; 5/12 10-19-31; ¼+; s; dau ------; yes; yes; none

5316   Wallett, John B; m; 41; ¼+; m; Head A2131; yes; no; Id.997, Al.G-08287
5317      "      Delia (L'Esperance); f; 34; ¼+; m; wife A2132; yes; yes; Id.997b, Al.G-037069
5318      "      Verna; f; 15 3-22-17; ¼+; s; dau A2133; yes; yes; Id.997c
5319      "      Agnes; f; 11 5-7-20; ¼+; s; dau A2134; yes; yes; Id.997d
5320      "      George; m; 8 2-14-24; ¼+; s; son A2135; yes; yes; Id.997e
5321      "      Patrick; m; 6 10-10-25; ¼+; s; son A2136; yes; yes; Id.997f
5322      "      Moses; m; 4 6-1-27; ¼+; s; son A2137; yes; yes; Id.997g
5323      "      John; m; 2 5-12-29; ¼+; s; son A2138; yes; yes; Id.997h
5324      "      David; m; 11/11 4-13-31; ¼+; s; son ----; yes; yes; Id.997i

5325   Wallett, Joseph; m; 45; ¼+; m; Head A2139; yes; no; Id.998, Al.GF-6
5326      "      Caroline (Martin); f; 39; ¼+; m; wife A2140; yes; no; Id.998a, Al.W-9
5327      "      Pierre; m; 22 8-8-09; ¼+; s; son A2141; yes; yes; Id.998b, Al.H-010525
5328      "      Florence; f; 17 8-14-14; ¼+; s; dau A2142; yes; no; Id.998d
5329      "      Elmer; m; 15 2-19-17; ¼+; s; son A2143; yes; no; Id.998e
5330      "      Martin; m; 11 2-14-21; ¼+; s; son A2144; yes; no; none
5331      "      Delima; f; 7 6-15-24; ¼+; s; dau A2145; yes; no; none
5332      "      Alex; m; 5 1-20-27; ¼+; s; son A2146; yes; yes; none
5333      "      Gertrude; f; 2 10-29-29; ¼+; s; dau A2147; yes; yes; none
```

Turtle Mountain Reservation
1932 Census Roll

Key: Number; Surname, Given; Sex; Age at Last Birthday, Birthdate (if given); Tribe (Chippewa, unless stated otherwise); Degree of Blood; Marital Status; Relationship to Head of Family, Last Year Census Number; At Jurisdiction Where Enrolled (Yes/No); Elsewhere - Post Office, County, State; Ward (Yes/No); Allotment [Al.], Annuity [An.] and/or Identification [Id.] Numbers

5334 Wallett, Marcial; m; 20; ¼+; s; Head B2628; no; Unknown; no; Id.993b

5335 Wallett, Margaret; f; 66; ¼+; wd; Head B2629; no; no; Id.1000a, Al.M-324

NE Wallett, Michael; Head
928 " Mary Clara (Azure); f; 26; ¼+; n; wife B2630; yes; yes; Id.124c, Al.G-08272

NE Wallett, Norman; Head
3768 " Catherine (Azure); f; 30; ¼+; m; wife A2148; yes; yes; Id.124b, Al.G-08276
4484 " David; m; 12 3-14-20; ¼+; s; son A2149; yes; yes; none

5171 Wallett, Seraphine; f; 38; ¼+; s; Head A2150; yes; yes; Id.996, Al.GF-8
5336 " Ruth; f; 7 2-14-25; ¼+; s; dau A2151; yes; yes; Id.996a

NE Walsh, Henry E; Head
5337 " Zilda (Grandbois); f; 43; ¼+; m; wife B2631; no; Dore, McKenzie, ND; no; Id.1039a, Al.G-432½
5338 " Mathew; m; 16 8-24-15; ¼+; s; son B2632; no; Dore, McKenzie, ND; no; Id.1039b
5339 " Amelia C; f; 15 3-3-17; ¼+; s; dau B2633; no; Dore, McKenzie, ND; no; Id.1039c
5340 " Patrick H; m; 11 10-20-20; ¼+; s; son B2634; no; Dore, McKenzie, ND; no Id.1039e
5341 " Michael J; m; 10 8-20-21; ¼+; s; son B2535; no; Dore, McKenzie, ND; no; Id.1039f
5342 " Andrew John; m; 7 4-12-24; ¼+; s; son B2636; no; Dore, McKenzie, ND; no; Id.1039g
5343 " Virginia; f; 3 4-5-28; ¼+; s; dau -----; no; Dore, McKenzie, ND; no; none

5344 Warren, Joseph; m; 35; ¼+; m; Head B2637; yes; no; Id.1002b, Al.G-384
5345 " Nora (Jollie); f; 32; ¼+; m; wife B2638; yes; yes; Id.527e, Al.M-327
5346 " Ruth M; f; 9 12-23-22; ¼+; s; dau B2639; yes; yes; none
5347 " Edward; m; 7 2-10-24; ¼+; s; son -----; yes; yes; none
5348 " William; m; 3 7-13-28; ¼+; s; son ------; yes; yes; none
5349 " Joseph; m; 1 4-1-30; ¼+; s; son ------; yes; yes; none

5350 Warren, Mary (Dionne.Thomas); f; 58; ¼+; wd; Head A2152; yes; yes; Id.1002a, Al.R-106
5351 " John B; m; 26; ¼+; s; son A2153; yes; yes; Id.1002e, Al.G-387
5352 " Cecelia; f; 17; ¼+; s; dau A2154; yes; yes; none

NE Weeks, W B; Head
5353 " Marie (Lafrombois); f; 28; 14; m; wife A2640; no; Forest Grove, Washington, Ore; yes; Id.592b, Al.G-08112

Turtle Mountain Reservation
1932 Census Roll

Key: Number; Surname, Given; Sex; Age at Last Birthday, Birthdate (if given); Tribe (Chippewa, unless stated otherwise); Degree of Blood; Marital Status; Relationship to Head of Family, Last Year Census Number; At Jurisdiction Where Enrolled (Yes/No); Elsewhere - Post Office, County, State; Ward (Yes/No); Allotment [Al.], Annuity [An.] and/or Identification [Id.] Numbers

5354 Weeks(cont), Leila Mae; f; 2 2-18-30; ¼+; s; dau ------; no; Forest Grove, Washington, Ore; yes; none

NE Welsh, Joseph;   Head
5355   "   Virginia (Wilkie); f; 32; ¼+; m; wife B2641; no; Fonda, Rolette, ND; yes; Id.1018c, Al.G-08375
5356   "   John Leo; m; 6 2-22-26; ¼+; s; son B2642; no; Fonda, Rolette, ND; yes; none

NE West, John S;   Head
5357   "   Margaret (Hayes); f; 41; ¼+; m; wife B2643; yes; no; Id.1004a, Al.GF-144
5358   "   Kenneth; m; 9 9-18-22; ¼+; s; son B2644; yes; no; none
5359   "   Fannie; f; 8 1-21-24; ¼+; s; dau B2645; yes; no; none
5360   "   Bernice; f; 6 4-6-25; ¼+; s; dau B2646; yes; no; none
5361   "   Levi; m; 4 9-7-27; ¼+; s; son B2647; yes; no; none

NE Westfall, Harold;   Head
5362   "   Mary Jane (Davis); f; 21; ¼+; m; wife A496; yes; yes; Id.277b, Al.H-02538
5363   "   Frank Ed; m; 1 10-28-30; ¼+; s; son ------; yes; yes; none
5364   "   Harold J; m; 1/12 2-3-32; ¼+; s; son -------; yes; yes; none

NE Westphall, Ernest;   Head
5365   "   Delia (Ducept); f; 23; ¼+; m; wife B2648; no; Poplar, Roosevelt, Mont; no; Id.360c

NE Wheeler, Carl;   Head
5366   "   Caroline (Henry); f; 21; ¼+; m; wife B1092; yes; yes; Id.471e, Al.H-024559
5367 " (Wilburn), Marian Edna; f; 1 9-4-30; ¼+; s; step dau B1093; yes; yes; none

NE Wheeler, Harold;   Head
5368   "   Adele (Jeannotte); f; 38; ¼+; m; wife B2649; yes; yes; Id.504, Al.M-75

5369 White Cloud; m; 31; F; s; Head B2650; no; Dunseith, Rolette, ND; yes; Id.57d, Al.G-01892

5370 White Stone; m; 51; F; m; Head B2651; no; Indian Springs, Manitoba, Can; yes; Id.58a, Al.G-03657
NE   "   Atawikijikowinin; wife
5371   "   John; m; 22; F; s; son B2652; no; Indian Springs, Manitoba, Can; yes; Id.58b, Al.H-030865
5372   "   Standing; f; 20; F; s; dau B2653; no; Indian Springs, Manitoba, Can; yes; Id.58c
5373   "   Louis; m; 18; F; s; son B2654; no; Indian Springs, Manitoba, Can; yes; Id.58d

Turtle Mountain Reservation
1932 Census Roll

Key: Number; Surname, Given; Sex; Age at Last Birthday, Birthdate (if given); Tribe (Chippewa, unless stated otherwise); Degree of Blood; Marital Status; Relationship to Head of Family, Last Year Census Number; At Jurisdiction Where Enrolled (Yes/No); Elsewhere - Post Office, County, State; Ward (Yes/No); Allotment [Al.], Annuity [An.] and/or Identification [Id.] Numbers

NE Wilcox, Harry;   Head
Dead   "   Cecelia (Langer);   B2655   (Died 11-26-28)
5374   "   Hollis; m; 5 11-8-26; ¼+; s; son B2656; no; St.John, Rolette, ND; no;
                                                                          Id.614b

5375 Wilkie, Albert; m; 73; ¼+; m; Head A2156; yes; yes; Id.1005, Al.R-316
5376   "   Josephine (Laverdure); f; 59; ¼+; m; wife A2157; yes; yes; Id.1005a, Al.G-019360
5377   "   Jerome; m; 26 9-14-05; ¼+; s; son A2158; yes; yes; Id.1005c, Al.G-86
5378   "   Robert; m; 19; ¼+; s; son A2159; yes; yes; Id. 1005f, Al.MC-26627
5379   "   Dorothy; f; 14 4-23-17; ¼+; s; dau A2160; yes; yes; Id.1005g

5380 Wilkie, Albert #2; m; 53; ¼+; m; Head A2161; yes; no; Id.1007, Al.R-317
NE   "   Elizabeth (Allard);   A2162   (Counted last year by mistake)
5381   "   Patrice; m; 20; ¼+; s; son A2163; yes; no; Id.1007e
5382   "   Veronica; f; 17; ¼+; s; dau A2164; yes; no; Id.1007f
5383   "   Richard; m; 15; ¼+; s; son A2165; yes; no; Id.1007g
5384   "   George; m; 12 2-5-20; ¼+; s; son A2166; yes; no; Id.1007h
5385   "   Michael; m; 9 2-5-23; ¼+; s; son A2167; yes; no; Id.1007i
5386   "   Elizabeth; f; 1 6-2-30; ¼+; s; dau A2168; yes; no; none

5387 Wilkie, Augustine; m; 82; ¼+; wd; Head A2169; yes; yes; Id.1015, Al.R-321

5388 Wilkie, Clara; f; 37; ¼+; s; Head B2658; no; St.Paul, Ramsey, Minn; no; Id.1006,
                                                                          Al.H-012655

5389 Wilkie, Eva (St.Arnaud); f; 42; ¼+; wd; Head B2659; no; Keams Canyon; no;
                                                                       Id.1022a, Al.M-213
5390   "   (St.Arnaud) Leona; f; 12 12-13-19; ¼+; s; adpt dau B2660; no; Keams Canyon;
                                                                             no; Id.931c

5391 Wilkie, Frederick; m; 35; ¼+; m; Head A2170; yes; no; Id.1014b, Al.M-91
5392   "   Rose (Vivier); f; 31; ¼+; m; wife A2171; yes; yes; Id.992, Al.H-030441
5393   "   May; f; 13; ¼+; s; dau A2172; yes; yes; none
5394   "   Evelyn; f; 11 2-14-21; ¼+; s; dau A2173; yes; yes; none
5395   "   Laureat; m; 9 8-29-22; ¼+; s; son A2174; yes; yes; none
5396   "   Dorothy; f; 7 7-30-24; ¼+; s; dau A2175; yes; yes; none
5397   "   Fred Louis; m; 5 7-1-26; ¼+; s; son A2176; yes; yes; none

5398 Wilkie, Gabriel; m; 67; ¼+; wd; Head A2177; yes; yes; Id.1018, Al.R-322
5399   "   Angeline; f; 20; ¼+; s; dau A2178; yes; yes; Id.1018f

5400 Wilkie, John A; m; 26; ¼+; m; Head A2179; yes; Id.1007a, Al.H-010483
5401   "   Virginia (Jerome); f; 19 1-11-13; ¼+; m; wife A2180; yes; no; Id.510f

Turtle Mountain Reservation
1932 Census Roll

Key: Number; Surname, Given; Sex; Age at Last Birthday, Birthdate (if given); Tribe (Chippewa, unless stated otherwise); Degree of Blood; Marital Status; Relationship to Head of Family, Last Year Census Number; At Jurisdiction Where Enrolled (Yes/No); Elsewhere - Post Office, County, State; Ward (Yes/No); Allotment [Al.], Annuity [An.] and/or Identification [Id.] Numbers

5402	Wilkie, John; m; 43; ¼+; m; Head A2181; yes; no; Id.1011, Al.M-100	
5403	"	Mary Jane (Belgarde); f; 42; ¼+; m; wife A2182; yes; no; Id.1011a. Al.H-038899
5404	"	Mary Agnes; f; 23; ¼+; s; dau A2183; yes; no; Id.1011b
5405	"	Ernest; m; 20; ¼+; s; son A2184; yes; no; Id.1011c
5406	"	Mabel; f; 18; ¼+; s; dau A2185; yes; no; Id.1011d
5407	"	Alice; f; 14 2-22-18; ¼+; s; dau A2186; yes; no; Id.1011f
5408	"	Cecile; f; 10 6-26-21; ¼+; s; dau A2187; yes; no; Id.1011g
5409	"	Wilbur; m; 8 8-13-23; ¼+; s; son A2188; yes; no; Id.1011h
5410	"	John; m; 6 8-9-25; ¼+; s; son A2189; yes; no; Id.1011i
5411	"	Martha; f; 3 8-1-28; ¼+; s; dau A2190; yes; no; Id.1011j
5412	"	Florestine; f; 1 6-2-30; ¼+; s; dau A2191; yes; no; Id.1011k
5413	Wilkie, John B; m; 56; ¼+; wd; Head A2192; yes; yes; Id.1026, Al.R-324	
5414	"	Alexander; m; 29 11-24-02; ¼+; s; son A2193; yes; yes; Id.1-26b, Al.M-370
5415	"	Louise Ann; f; 27 9-24-04; ¼+; s; dau A2194; yes; yes; Id.1026c, Al.M-371
5416	"	Julius; m; 21 10-12-10; ¼+; s; son A2195; yes; yes; Id.1026d
5417	"	Josephine; f; 17 2-11-15; ¼+; s; dau A2197; yes; (Sarah and Josephine one and the same) yes; none
5418	"	Francis; m; 13 7-12-16; ¼+; s; son A2198; yes; yes; Id.1026f
5419	Wilkie, Joseph; m; 37; ¼+; m; Head A2199; yes; no; Id.1016, Al.G-230	
5420	"	Georgiana (Dionne); f; 32; ¼+; m; wife A2200; yes; yes; Id.1016a, Al.M-297
5421	"	James Wm; m; 14 11-19-17; ¼+; s; son A2201; yes; yes; none
5422	"	Mary Irene; f; 10 4-14-21; ¼+; s; dau A2202; yes; yes; none
5423	"	Doris; f; 7 8-12-24; ¼+; s; dau A2203; yes; yes; none
5424	"	Patrick; m; 5 8-12-26; ¼+; s; son A2204; yes; yes; none
5425	"	Marie Clara; f; 2 8-8-29; ¼+; s; dau A2205; yes; yes; none
5426	"	Susan Marie; 3/12 1-29-32; ¼+; s; dau ------; yes; yes; none
5427	Wilkie, Joseph; m; 44; ¼+; m; Head A2206; yes; no; Id.1025, Al.M-382	
5438	"	Elise (Grandbois); f; 44; ¼+; m; wife A2207; yes; no; Id.1025a, Al.G-461
5439	"	Frank H; m; 21; ¼+; s; son A2208; yes; yes; Id.1025b, Al.G-016494
5430	"	John Ed; m; 18-9 3-10-13; ¼+; s; son A2209; yes; no; Id.1025c
5431	"	David; m; 17 8-1-14; ¼+; s; son A2210; yes; no; Id.1025d
5432	"	Mary Ann; f; 15 7-22-16; ¼+; s; dau A2211; yes; no; Id.1025e
5433	"	Edna Rose; f; 13 4-18-18; ¼+; s; dau A2212; yes; no; Id.1025f
5434	"	Charles; m; 11 7-22-20; ¼+; s; son A2213; yes; no; Id.1025h
5435	"	Fabian; m; 10; ¼+; s; son A2214; yes; no; Id.1025i
5436	"	Sara; f; 9 1-3-23; ¼+; s; dau A2215; yes; no; Id.1025j
5437	"	Mavis; f; 8; ¼+; s; dau A2216; yes; no; none
5438	"	Ezear; m; 6; ¼+; s; son A2217; yes; no; none
5439	"	Michael; m; 3; ¼+; s; son A2218; yes; no; none

Turtle Mountain Reservation
1932 Census Roll

Key: Number; Surname, Given; Sex; Age at Last Birthday, Birthdate (if given); Tribe (Chippewa, unless stated otherwise); Degree of Blood; Marital Status; Relationship to Head of Family, Last Year Census Number; At Jurisdiction Where Enrolled (Yes/No); Elsewhere - Post Office, County, State; Ward (Yes/No); Allotment [Al.], Annuity [An.] and/or Identification [Id.] Numbers

5440 Wilkie, Joseph; m; 29; ¼+; m; Head A2219; yes; yes; Id.1027b, Al.G-032688
5441 " Eliza (Peltier); f; 28; ¼+; m; wife A2220; yes; yes; Id.820b, Al.H-010444
5442 " Fabian; m; 9 6-1-22; ¼+; s; son A2221; yes; yes; none
5443 " Mary Cecelia; f; 7 7-1-24; ¼+; s; dau A2222; yes; yes; none
5444 " Lillian; f; 4; ¼+; s; dau A2223; yes; yes; none
5445 " Pauline; f; 2; ¼+; s; dau ------; yes; yes; none

5446 Wilkie, Joseph; m; 62; ¼+; m; Head A2224; yes; no; Id.1027, Al.R-235
NE " Jennie (Bruce); wife
5447 " Marie; f; 20; ¼+; s; dau A2226; yes; no; Id.1027e
5448 " Clemence; f; 16 12-19-14; ¼+; s; dau A2227; yes; no; Id.1027f
5449 " Fabian; m; 15 2-2-17; ¼+; s; son A2228; yes; no; none
5450 " Edna; f; 12 7-25-19; ¼+; s; dau A2228; yes; no; none
5451 " Blanche; f; 10 12-18-21; ¼+; s; dau A2230; yes; no; none

5452 Wilkie, Louis; m; 37; ¼+; m; Head A2231; yes; no; Id.1009, Al.M-103
5453 " Eliza (Decoteau); f; 34; ¼+; m; wife A2232; yes; no; Id.1009a, Al.M-305
5454 " Louis; m; 13 7-4-18; ¼+; s; son A2233; yes; no; Id.1009b
5455 " Marie Ann; f; 12 1-30-20; ¼+; s; dau A2234; yes; no; Id.1009c
5456 " Elmer; m; 10 2-17-22; ¼+; s; son A2235; yes; no; Id.1009d
5457 " Raymond; m; 7 6-12-24; ¼+; s; son A2236; yes; no; Id.1009e
5458 " Veronica; f; 6 8-30-25; ¼+; s; dau A2237; yes; no; Id.1009f
5459 " Patrick; m; 2 2-26-30; ¼+; s; son A2238; yes; no; Id.1009g
5460 " Pamela B; f; 11/12 4-29-31; ¼+; s; dau ------; yes; no; Id.1009h

5461 Wilkie, Louis; m; 35; ¼+; m; Head A2239; yes; no; Id.1005b, Al.G-85
5462 " St.Ann (Dauphinais); f; 30; ¼+; m; wife A2240; yes; yes; Id.250b, Al.H-012524
5463 " David; m; 10 3-30-22; ¼+; s; son A2241; yes; yes; none

5464 Wilkie, Michael; m; 38; ¼+; s; Head A2242; yes; no; Id.1019, Al.G-97

5465 Wilkie, Moses; m; 45; ¼+; m; Head B2661; no; Standing Rock; no; Id.1012, Al.M-105
NE " Bella (Demarais); wife
5466 " Rose Ann; f; 21 10-3-10; ¼+; s; dau B2662; no; Standing Rock; no; Id.1012b
5467 " Moses, Jr; m; 19 2-20-13; ¼+; s; son B2663; no; Standing Rock; no; Id.1012c
5468 " Annabelle; f; 16 7-26-17; ¼+; s; niece B2657; no; Standing Rock; no; Id.1012a
5469 " Esther; f; 11 4-16-20; ¼+; s; dau B2664; no; Standing Rock; no; Id.1012d
5470 " Charles A; m; 9 5-23-22; ¼+; s; son B2665; no; Standing Rock; no; Id.1012e
5471 " Lucille; f; 7 5-17-24; ¼+; s; dau ------; no; Standing Rock; no; Id.1012g
5472 " Eugene; m; 5 3-9-27; ¼+; s; son B2666; no; Standing Rock; no; Id.1012f

5473 Wilkie, Napoleon; m; 49; ¼+; m; Head B2667; no; St.John, Rolette, ND; no; Id.1013, Al.W-02930
NE " Clemence (Laviolette); wife

Turtle Mountain Reservation
1932 Census Roll

Key: Number; Surname, Given; Sex; Age at Last Birthday, Birthdate (if given); Tribe (Chippewa, unless stated otherwise); Degree of Blood; Marital Status; Relationship to Head of Family, Last Year Census Number; At Jurisdiction Where Enrolled (Yes/No); Elsewhere - Post Office, County, State; Ward (Yes/No); Allotment [Al.], Annuity [An.] and/or Identification [Id.] Numbers

5474 Wilkie(cont), Stephen; m; 12 2-1-20; ¼+; s; son B2668; no; St.John, Rolette, ND; no; Id.1013b, none
5475 " Leo; m; 11 2-19-21; ¼+; s; son B2669; no; St.John, Rolette, ND; no; Id.1013c
5476 " Leona; f; 8 12-6-23; ¼+; s; dau B2670; no; St.John, Rolette, ND; no; Id.1013d
5477 " Mary Ann; f; 6 2-12-26; ¼+; s; dau B2671; no; St.John, Rolette, ND; no; Id.1013e
5478 " Amelia; f; 11/12 4-26-31; ¼+; s; dau ------; no; St.John, Rolette, ND; no; Id.1013f

5479 Wilkie, Onesine; m; 76; ¼+; s; Head B2672; no; Unknown; no; Id.1029, Al.G-025

5480 Wilkie, Pierre; m; 40; ¼+; s; Head B2673; no; Unknown; no; Id.1020. Al.G-96

5481 Wilkie, Raphael; m; 42; ¼+; s; Head B2674; no; Hopkins, Hennepin, Minn; no; Id.1021, Al.G-95

5482 Wilkie, Sarah; f; 80; ¼+; wd; Head A2243; yes; no; Id.1023a, Al.M-380

5483 Wilkie, William; m; 41; ¼+; m; Head A2244; yes; no; Id.1024, Al.M-380
NE " Pauline (Allard); wife
5484 " John; m; 19 10-20-13; ¼+; s; son A2245; yes; no; Id.1024b
5485 " Lawrence; m; 9 9-29-22; ¼+; s; son A2246; yes; no; none
5486 " Bertha; f; 6 8-24-25; ¼+; s; dau A2247; yes; no; none
5487 " Leona; f; 5 10-26-26; ¼+; s; dau A2248; yes; no; none
5488 " Evelyn Marie; f; 2 12-21-29; ¼+; s; dau A2249; yes; no; none

NE Williams, Ray; Head
5489 " Mary Celina (Lizotte); f; 22; ¼+; m; wife B2675; no; Sidney, Richland, Mont; no; Id.673d
5490 " Robert R; m; 3 7-23-28; ¼+; s; son ------; no; Sidney, Richland, Mont; no; none
5491 " Gale Alta; m; 2 2-12-30; ¼+; s; son -----; no; Sidney, Richland, Mont; no; none

NE Wilson, Clifton; Head
5492 " Lena (Turcotte); f; 43; ¼+; m; wife B2676; no; Wichita, Sedgwick, Kan; yes; Id.1030a, Al.W-03546
5493 " Lucille; f; 21 4-11-10; ¼+; s; dau B2677; no; Wichita, Sedgwick, Kan; yes; Id.1030b, Al.G-016520
5494 " Clifton; m; 20 11-8-11; ¼+; s; son B2678; no; Wichita, Sedgwick, Kan; yes; Id.1030c

Turtle Mountain Reservation
1932 Census Roll

Key: Number; Surname, Given; Sex; Age at Last Birthday, Birthdate (if given); Tribe (Chippewa, unless stated otherwise); Degree of Blood; Marital Status; Relationship to Head of Family, Last Year Census Number; At Jurisdiction Where Enrolled (Yes/No); Elsewhere - Post Office, County, State; Ward (Yes/No); Allotment [Al.], Annuity [An.] and/or Identification [Id.] Numbers

5495 Wilson(cont), Charles; m; 19 11-16-13; ¼+; s; son B2679; no; Wichita, Sedgwick, Kan; yes; Id.1030d
5496 " Billy Lee; m; 11 2-19-21; ¼+; s; son ------; no; Wichita, Sedgwick, Kan; yes; Id.1030e

NE Wing, Willis R; Head
5497 " Elizabeth (Poitra); f; 34; ¼+; m; wife B2151; no; Seattle, King, Wash; no; Id.876b, Al.G-608

NE Winter, John; Head
5498 " Ernestine (Dejarlais); f; 39; ¼+; m; wife B2680; no; Unknown; no; Id.1031a, Al.M-177
5499 " Ursula; f; 19; ¼+; s; dau B2681; no; Unknown; no; Id.1031b
5500 " Frederick; m; 18; ¼+; s; son B2682; no; Unknown; no; Id.1031c

5501 Wong, Agnes (Grant); f; 26; ¼+; wd; Head B2683; no; Devils Lake, Ramsey, ND; yes; Id.460c, Al.G-140
5502 " Lucille; f; 7 8-6-24; ¼+; s; dau B2684; no; Devils Lake, Ramsey, ND; yes; none

NE Wong, Dick; Head
5503 " Delima (Langer); f; 26; ¼+; m; wife A1321; no; Devils Lake, Ramsey, ND; yes; Id.608c, Al.G-019243

NE Wong, Harry; Head
5504 " Louise (Brien); f; 27; ¼+; m; wife B2685; no; Devils Lake, Ramsey, ND; no; Id.197d, Al.G-0233
5505 " Harry, Jr; m; 8; ¼+; s; son B2686; no; Devils Lake, Ramsey, ND; no; none
5506 " Jennie; f; 6; ¼+; s; dau B2687; no; Devils Lake, Ramsey, ND; no; none
Dead " Herbert; B2688 (Died 2-

NE Young, J F; Head
5507 " Marie (Baston); f; 34; ¼+; m; wife B2689; no; Unknown; no; Id.1032, Al.M-387
5508 " Delma; f; 15; ¼+; s; dau B2690; no; Unknown; no; Id.1032b
5509 " Joseph; m; 13; ¼+; s; son B2691; no; Unknown; no; Id.1032c
5510 " Jeannette; f; 8; ¼+; s; dau ------; no; Unknown; no; Id.1032d

NE Zura, Alfred; Head
5511 " Elise (Poitra); f; 36; ¼+; m; wife B2692; yes; yes; Id.870a, Al.M-336
5512 " Kathleen; f; 12 4-11-19; ¼+; s; dau B2693; yes; yes; Id.870c
5513 " Annie; f; 10 11-13-21; ¼+; s; dau B2694; yes; yes; Id.870d
5514 " Irene; f; 8 10-31-23; ¼+; s; dau B2695; yes; yes; Id.870e
5515 " Frederick; m; 6 9-28-25; ¼+; s; son B2696; yes; yes; Id.870f

Turtle Mountain Reservation
1932 Census Roll

Key: Number; Surname, Given; Sex; Age at Last Birthday, Birthdate (if given); Tribe (Chippewa, unless stated otherwise); Degree of Blood; Marital Status; Relationship to Head of Family, Last Year Census Number; At Jurisdiction Where Enrolled (Yes/No); Elsewhere - Post Office, County, State; Ward (Yes/No); Allotment [Al.], Annuity [An.] and/or Identification [Id.] Numbers

5516   Zura(cont), Robert; m; 4 11-2-27; ¼+; s; son B2697; yes; yes; Id.870g
5517   "   Margaret; f; 2 10-21-29; ¼+; s; dau ------; yes; yes; Id.870h
5518   "   Leon; m; 3/12 12-20-31; ¼+; s; son -------; yes; yes; Id.870i

5519   Name is on page [36]
5520   Name is on page [162]
5521   Name is on page [162]
5522   Name is on page [172]
5523   Name is on page [133]

LIVE BIRTHS

Turtle Mountain Agency
North Dakota

July 1, 1924 – June 30, 1930
April 1, 1930 – March 31, 1932

Turtle Mountain Reservation
Live Births
Key: Census Roll Number; Surname, Given; Date of Birth (Year-Month-Day); Sex; Tribe (Chippewa unless stated otherwise); Ward (yes/no); Degree of Blood (Father- Mother- Child); At Jurisdiction Where Enrolled (Yes/No); (If no – Where – Post Office, State)

Births Occurring between the Dates of July 1, 1924 and June 30, 1925 to Parents Enrolled at Jurisdiction

1926- 191	Allard, Alfred Wilmar; 1925-April 19; male; yes; ¼+; ¼+; ¼+; yes;
1932	Allery, Nicholas; 1924-Dec 1; male; yes; ¼+; ¼+; ¼+; no; Dunseith, ND
1925- 297	Amyott, Norbert Francis; 1925-Feb 23; male; yes; ¼+; ¼+; ¼+; yes
	Azure, Andrew; 1924-Aug 30; male; no; ¼+; ¼+; ¼+; no; Rolla, ND
1930- 123	Azure, Peter; 1924-Dec 24; male; yes; ¼+; ¼+; ¼+; yes
1926- 385	Azure, St.Pierre; 1925-June 5; male; no; ¼+; ¼+; ¼+; no; Dunseith, ND
1926- 420	Azure, Edna; 1925-Feb 23; fem; no; ¼+; ¼+; ¼+; yes
1926- 471	Baker, George; 1924-Oct 28; male; no; ¼+; ¼+; ¼+; no; Fort Totten, ND
1926- 514	Beauchman, James Benedict; 1925-June 8; male; no; ¼+; ¼+; ¼+; no; Wolf Point, Mont
	Belgarde, Mary; 1924-Nov 18; fem; yes; ¼+; ¼+; ¼+; yes
1925- 562	Belgarde, Andrew; 1925-April 30; male; no; ¼+; ¼+; ¼+; yes
1927- 633	Belgarde, John; 1924-July 3; male;; no; ¼+; ¼+; ¼+; no; Elbowoods, ND
1930- 429	Bercier, Raymond; 1924-Sept 24; male; yes; ¼+; ¼+; ¼+; no; Devils Lake, ND
1926- 694½	Bercier, Charlie Walter; 1925-April 29; male; no; ¼+; ¼+; ¼+; yes
1925- 698	Bottineau, Napoleon; 1924-July 26; male; yes; ¼+; ¼+; ¼+; no; Dunseith, ND
1925- 706	Boyer, Marie Jeanne; 1924-Aug 1; fem; no; ¼+; ¼+; ¼+; yes
1932	Boyer, Stanley; 1924-July 7; male; yes; ¼+; ¼+; ¼+; yes; Montana
1932	Boyer, Mary Rose; 1924-July 11; fem; no; ¼+; ¼+; ¼+; no; Sidney, Mont
1926- 791½	Brien, Peter Wilfred; 1925-March 23; male; no; ¼+; ¼+; ¼+; no; Medicine Lake, Mont
1926- 830½	Briere, Albert David; 1925-Jan 17; male; no; ¼+; ¼+; ¼+; no; Unknown
xxxxxxxxx	Bruce, Mary Josephine; 1924-Sept 13; fem; yes; ¼+; ¼+; ¼+; yes
1926- 844½	Bruce, Cecile; 1924-Sept 5; fem; yes; ¼+; ¼+; ¼+; yes
1926- 859	Brunell[sic], Ellen Jane; 1925-March 11; fem; no; ¼+; ¼+; ¼+; yes
1925- 835	Brunnell, Paul Arthur; 1924-Sept 4; male; no; ¼+; ¼+; ¼+; yes
1932	Caldwell, Nina May; 1924-Sept 24; fem; yes; ¼+; ¼+; ¼+; no; Strool, SD
1932	Bell, Viola; 1924-July 18; fem; no; ¼+; ¼+; ¼+; no; Semans, Sask
1932	Constance, Lloyd Joseph; 1924-Aug 1; male; yes; W;¼+;¼+; no; Independence, Mo
1932	Caribou, Peggy; 1925-March 20; fem; yes; ¼+; ¼+; ¼+; no; Cando, ND
	Cree, Ernest; 1925-July 26; male; yes; F;1/4;¼+; no; Dunseith, ND
1926-1051	Davis, Stella; 1924-Aug 3; fem; yes; ¼+; ¼+; ¼+; yes
1926- 122	Davis, Romeo; 1925-Feb 25; male; yes; ¼+; ¼+; ¼+; yes
1925-1003	Davis, Ruth May; 1925-May 7; fem; yes; ¼+; ¼+; ¼+; yes
1925-1030	Davis, Mary Clemence; 1925-March 13; fem; no; ¼+; ¼+; ¼+; yes
1925-1049	Decoteau, Ambrose; 1924-Aug 11; male; no; ¼+; ¼+; ¼+; yes
1926-1120	Decoteau, John Fred; 1924-Aug 15; male; no; ¼+; ¼+; ¼+; yes
	Decoteau, Louis William; 1924-Oct 19; male; yes; ¼+; ¼+; ¼+; yes
1926-1158	Decoteau, Henry Eugene; 1924-July 9; male; no; ¼+; ¼+; ¼+; yes
1925-1144	Decoteau, Stanley; 1924-Sept 2; male; no; ¼+; ¼+; ¼+; yes
1932	Dejarlais, Russell Francis; 1925-Jan 29; male; no; ¼+; ¼+; ¼+; no; Buford, ND
1926-1225	Dejarlais, Gregory; 1924-Aug 18; male; yes; ¼+; ¼+; ¼+; yes
	Dejarlais, William John; 1924-Oct 8; male; yes; ¼+; ¼+; ¼+; yes
1927-1338	Delorme, Dolores; 1925-June 30; fem; no; ¼+; ¼+; ¼+; yes

Turtle Mountain Reservation
Live Births
Key: Census Roll Number; Surname, Given; Date of Birth (Year-Month-Day); Sex; Tribe (Chippewa unless stated otherwise); Ward (yes/no); Degree of Blood (Father- Mother- Child); At Jurisdiction Where Enrolled (Yes/No); (If no – Where – Post Office, State)

1932	Demarais, Josephine; 1924-July 7; fem; no; ¼+; ¼+; ¼+; yes
	Demarais, Albert; 1924-Nov 29; male; yes; F;¼+;¼+; no; Dunseith, ND
1925-1294	Demarais, Edward Leonard; 1925-Feb 19; male; no; ¼+; ¼+; ¼+; no; Malta, Mont
1930- 581	Demontigny, Hazel; 1924-Nov 3; fem; yes; ¼+; ¼+; ¼+; yes
1930- 573	Demontigny, Harry; 1924-July 28; male; no; ¼+; ¼+; ¼+; yes
1931- 738	Dionne, Frank; 1924-Oct 24; male; yes; ¼+; ¼+; ¼+; yes
1927-1471	Ducept, Henry Oscar; 1924-Sept 3; male; yes; ¼+; ¼+; ¼+; no; Nishu, ND
1932	Duchain, Victoria; 1925-June 10; fem; yes; ¼+; ¼+; ¼+; yes
1926-1491	Duchesneau, Leonard Omer; 1924-Sept 30; male; no; ¼+; ¼+; ¼+; no; Thorne, ND
1926-1476	Falcon, Irene Genevieve; 1925-Jan 27; fem; yes; ¼+; ¼+; ¼+; yes
1929-1661	Falcon, Florence; 1924-Oct 5; fem; no; ¼+; ¼+; ¼+; no; Trenton, ND
1928-1659	Fiddler, Francis; 1925-May 12; male; no; ¼+; ¼+; ¼+; no; Rolla, ND
1931- 865	Foster, May Evelyn; 1925-May 30; fem; yes; ¼+; ¼+; ¼+; no; Rolla, ND
1925-1552	Frederick, George Ambrose; 1924-Dec 6; male; yes; ¼+; ¼+; ¼+; yes
1926-1657	Frederick, Irene; 1924-Nov 15; fem; no; ¼+; ¼+; ¼+; yes
1927-1678	Gillis, Lucy Viola; 1924-August 27; fem; yes; ¼+; ¼+; ¼+; no; Dunseith, ND
1928-1763	Gladue, Martha; 1924-May 21; fem; no; ¼+; ¼+; ¼+; no; Froid, Mont
1927-4102	Gladue, Albert Oscar; 1925-Feb 22; male; yes; ¼+; ¼+; ¼+; yes
1932	Gladue, John Gilbert; 1924-May 5; male; yes; ¼+; ¼+; ¼+; yes
1930-1055	Godon, Francis; 1924-August 19; male; yes; ¼+; ¼+; ¼+; no; Bottineau, ND
1926-1772	Gourneau, Henry; 1925-April 23; male; yes; ¼+; ¼+; ¼+; yes
1932	Grandbois, Joseph Edward; 1925-April 19; male; no; ¼+;¼+;¼+; no; East Grand Forks, Minn
1932	Grant, Mary Cecelia; 1925-April 29; fem; yes; ¼+; ¼+; ¼+; yes;
1926-1881	Grant, Louis; 1924-July 26; male; no; ¼+; ¼+; ¼+; no; Devils Lake, ND
1927-2019	Houle, Ida Diana; 1924-July 19; fem; no; ¼+; ¼+; ¼+; no; Bottineau, ND
1926-2020	Houle, Ethel Mae; 1925-June 19; fem; yes; ¼+; ¼+; ¼+; no; Devils Lake, ND
1930-1291	Jerome, Marcil; 1925-June 24; male; yes; ¼+; ¼+; ¼+; yes
1926-2134	Jerome, Mary Cecelia; 1925-May 6; fem; no; ¼+; ¼+; ¼+; yes
1931-1208	Jerome, Franklin; 1924-Dec 26; male; yes; ¼+; ¼+; ¼+; no; Rolette, ND
1927-2164	Jerome, Roger Joseph; 1924-Oct 20; male; yes; ¼+; ¼+; ¼+; no; Madoc, Mont
1930- 991	Laducer, Eugene; 1925-May 17; male; yes; ¼+; ¼+; ¼+; yes
1932	Lafontain, Alfred; 1925-Jan 25; male; yes; ¼+; ¼+; ¼+; no; Roy, Mont
1927-2301	Lafontain, Alex; 1924-August 12; male; no; ¼+; ¼+; ¼+; no; Culbertson, Mont
1926-2283	Lafontain, Alex Chester; 1924-Oct 15; male; no; ¼+; ¼+; ¼+; yes
1932	Lafontain, William; 1925-April 28; male; no; ¼+; ¼+; ¼+; yes
1932	Lafontain, Ernest Edward; 1925-Sept 21; male; no; ¼+; ¼+; ¼+; no; Unknown
1925-2221	Lafontain, Patrick Clifford; 1925-March 13; male; no; ¼+; ¼+; ¼+; no; Devils Lake, ND
1932	Lafrance, Ella Marie; 1925-March 2; fem; no; ¼+; ¼+; ¼+; no; Rolla, ND
1927-2409	Lafraniere, Irene Marie; 1925-April 5; fem; no; ¼+; ¼+; ¼+; no; Hardin, Mont
1926-2443	Lagimodiere, May Florence; 1925-April 27; fem; no; ¼+;¼+;¼+; no; Medicine Lake, Mont
1930-1527	Landry, Cecelia; 1924-July 14; fem; no; ¼+; ¼+; ¼+; no; Rolla, ND
1927-2529	Langer, Clara; 1925-April 16; fem; yes; ¼+; ¼+; ¼+; no; Boggy Creek, Manitoba
1932	Larsen, Floyd; 1924-July 15; male; yes; W; ¼+; ¼+; no; Fort Totten, ND
1927-2608	Latrace, Frederick Nelson; 1924-August 19; male; yes; ¼+;¼+;¼+; no; Boggy Creek, Manitoba

Turtle Mountain Reservation
Live Births
Key: Census Roll Number; Surname, Given; Date of Birth (Year-Month-Day); Sex; Tribe (Chippewa unless stated otherwise); Ward (yes/no); Degree of Blood (Father- Mother- Child); At Jurisdiction Where Enrolled (Yes/No); (If no – Where – Post Office, State)

1925-2482	Lavallie, Mary; 1925-May 26; fem; no; ¼+; ¼+; ¼+; yes
1925-2481	Lavallie, Fred; 1925-Fred[sic]-26; male; no; ¼+; ¼+; ¼+; yes
1925-2493	Lavallie, Alexander; 1925-March 26; male; no; ¼+; ¼+; ¼+; yes
1925-2501	Laverdure, Annie Marian; 1924-August 25; fem; yes; ¼+; ¼+; ¼+; yes
1926-2637	Laverdure, Andrew R; 1925-April 25; male; no; ¼+; ¼+; ¼+; no; Devils Lake, ND
1932	Lavia, Edward Benedict; 1924-July 28; male; no; ¼+; ¼+; ¼+; no; Dagmar, Mont
1932	LeCompt, Corma; 1925-Jan 12; fem; yes; ¼+; ¼+; ¼+; no; Bainville, Mont
1931-1610	Lenoir, Ernest; 1924-Nov 1; male; no; ¼+; ¼+; ¼+; no; Minnewauken[sic], ND
1929-2971	Lizotte, George L; 1924-Nov 8; male; yes; ¼+; ¼+; ¼+; yes
1929-2985	Lonick, Alfred Eugene; 1925-Jan 15; male; yes; Negro; ¼+; ¼+; Devils Lake, ND
1929-3038	Manson, John Louis; 1925-June 18; male; no; W; ¼+; ¼+; no; Rolla, ND
1930-1301	Marcellais, Joseph Edward; 1924-Dec 17; male; yes; ¼+; ¼+; ¼+; yes
1926-2861	Marcil, Marie Lillian; 1024-July 2; fem; no; ¼+; ¼+; ¼+; no; Fonda, ND
1929-3078	Marion, Irene Agnes; 1925-Mch-26; fem; no; ¼+; ¼+; ¼+; yes
1926-2914	Martell, Ernest; 1924-Sept 13; male; no; ¼+; ¼+; ¼+; yes
1925-2789	Martell, Thomas Wm; 1925-Mch-4; male; no; ¼+; ¼+; ¼+; no; Poplar, Mont
1926-2927	Martell, Clarence; 1924-July 14; male; no; ¼+; ¼+; ¼+; no; Poplar, Mont
1926-2949	Martin, Irene Agnes; 1924-Aug 20; fem; yes; ¼+; ¼+; ¼+; yes
1926-2946	Martin, Winifred; 1925-Jan 7; fem; yes; ¼+; ¼+; ¼+; yes
1930-1366	Monette, Estella; 1924-June 19; fem; yes; ¼+; ¼+; ¼+; yes
1925-2892	Morin, James Leo; 1925-Feb 2; male; yes; ¼+; ¼+; ¼+; no; Medicine Lake, Mont
1926-3118	Morin, Dora Virginia; 1924-Oct 25; fem; no; ¼+; ¼+; ¼+; yes
1930-1406	Morin, Moses; 1924-July 15; male; no; ¼+; ¼+; ¼+; yes
1925-3005	Morin, John Herbert; 1925-May 26; male; no; 14; no; Fort Totten, ND
1930-1907	Mekwam, Mary; 1924-Nov 5; fem; yes; F; F; F; yes
1932	Makes It Rain, Gladys; 1925-June 30; fem; yes; F; F; F; no; Dunseith, ND
1926-3202	Parisien, Francois Martin; 1924-July 21; male; no; ¼+; ¼+; ¼+; yes
	Poitra, Joseph Martin; 1924-Oct 20; male; yes; ¼+; ¼+; ¼+; yes
1931-2045	Peltier, Mary Ann; 1924-Sept 23; fem; no; ¼+; ¼+; ¼+; no; Fort Berthold, ND
1932	Pippenger, Robert Brown; 1924-June 15; male; no; W; ¼+; ¼; no; Trenton, ND
1927-3463	Plante, Alice Rose; 1924-April 26; fem; yes; ¼+; ¼+; ¼+; yes
	Poitra, Rose; 1925-Jan 13; fem; yes; ¼+; ¼+; ¼+; yes
1925-3102	Poitra, Martin; 1924-Oct 20; male; yes; ¼+; ¼+; ¼+; yes
1926-3543	Premeau, Ida Jean; 1924-Dec 15; fem; yes; ¼+; ¼+; ¼+; yes
1926-3551	Purdy, Elizabeth J; 1925-June 12; fem; no; W; ¼+; ¼; yes
1925-3430	Reardon, Gabriel; 1925-March 21; male; yes; W; ¼+; ¼; yes
1926-3585	Renville, Harry Joseph; 1925-April 9; male; yes; ¼+; ¼+; ¼+; no; [Not given]
1932	St. Germain, Irene Dolores; 1925-April 15; fem; no; 14; no; St.John, ND
1932	Stoen, Joyce Marjory; 1924-July 23; fem; no; W; ¼+; ¼; no; Bismarck, ND
1932	Smigiel, Robert Joseph; 1925-Feb 14; male; no; W; ¼+; ¼; no; Superior, Wis
1926-3825	Thibert, Vernon Stephen; 1924-Dec 26; male; no; ¼+; ¼+; ¼+; no; St.John, ND
1927-3975	Thomas, Nora; 1925-Jan 5; male; no; ¼+; ¼+; ¼+; yes
1927-4063	Turcott, Irene; 1925-Feb 22; male; yes; ¼+; ¼+; ¼+; yes
1926-3984	Vandal, John Ernest; 1924-Oct 5; male; no; ¼+; ¼+; ¼+; no; Rolla, ND

Turtle Mountain Reservation
Live Births

Key: Census Roll Number; Surname, Given; Date of Birth (Year-Month-Day); Sex; Tribe (Chippewa unless stated otherwise); Ward (yes/no); Degree of Blood (Father- Mother- Child); At Jurisdiction Where Enrolled (Yes/No);
(If no – Where – Post Office, State)

1926-4049	Wallett, Ruth; 1925-Feb 14; fem; yes; ¼+; ¼+; ¼+; yes
1930-2786	West, Bernice; 1925-April 6; fem; no; W; ¼+; ¼; yes
1925-3943	Wilkie, Dorothy; 1924-July 30; no; ¼+; ¼+; ¼+; yes

Births Occurring between the Dates of July 1, 1925 and June 30, 1926 to Parents Enrolled at Jurisdiction

1926-2701	Alec, Frank; 1925; male; yes; W; ¼+; ¼; yes
1931- 35	Allard, Roy; 1925; male; no; ¼+; ¼+; ¼+; yes
1928- 207	Allard, Louis; 1925; male; no; ¼+; ¼+; ¼+; yes
1930- 24	Allery, Margaret; 1926-June 7; fem; yes; ¼+; ¼+; ¼+; yes;
1926- 299	Amyott, Raymond; 1925; male; yes; ¼+; ¼+; ¼+; no; Unknown
1932-	Azure, Roger Louis; 1926-June 30; male; no; ¼+; ¼+; ¼+; no; Rolla, ND
	Azure, Veronica; 1926-June 30; fem; no; ¼+; ¼+; ¼+; no; Rolla, ND
1926- 350	Azure, Mary Alice; 1926-March 3; fem; no; ¼+; ¼+; ¼+; no; Rolla, ND
	Azure, George; 1925-July 11; male; yes; ¼+; ¼+; ¼+; no; Boggy Creek, Manitoba
1932-	Baker, Marceline; 1926-Feb-3; fem; yes; ¼+; ¼+; ¼+; yes
1927- 485	Baston, Mary Rose; 1925-May 26; fem; yes; ¼+; ¼+; ¼+; no; Elbowoods, ND
1932-	Bauer, John Jr; 1926-March 8; male; no; W; ¼+; ¼; no; Homestead, Mont
1925- 500	Beauchman, Agnes Violet; 1925; fem; no; ¼+; ¼+; ¼+; no; Wolf Point, Mont
1926- 538	Belgarde, Ernestine; 1925-August-2; fem; yes; ¼+; ¼+; ¼+; no; Bainville, Mont
1926- 576	Belgarde, Louisa; 1925; fem; no; ¼+; ¼+; ¼+; no; Fort Totten, ND
1926- 612	Belgarde, Edward Martin; 1925-Aug 23; male; no; ¼+; ¼+; ¼+; no; Fort Berthold
1927- 648	Belgarde, Alfred; 1926-Jan 7; male; no; ¼+; ¼+; ¼+; no; Elbowoods, ND
1930- 306	Belgarde, Mabel; 1925; fem; no; ¼+; ¼+; ¼+; no; Elphinstone, Sask
1927- 648	Belgarde, Wm Clifford; 1926-April 4; male; yes; ¼+; ¼+; ¼+; yes
1930- 445	Bergier, Laurine Lucy; 1926-April 3; fem; no; ¼+; ¼+; ¼+; no; Montana
1926- 715	Blue, Elsie Stella; 1925-Oct 21; fem; yes; ¼+; ¼+; ¼+; yes
1932-	Bell, Fred; 1926-May 16; male; no; W; ¼+; ¼; no; Seamans[sic], Sask
1932-	Brinkman, Erma; 1926-Jan 14; fem; yes; W; ¼+; ¼; no; Dagmar, Mont
1926- 842½	Bruce, Ernest Norbert; 1925-Nov 15; male; yes; ¼+; ¼+; ¼+; yes
1930- 293	Champagne, Willard; 1925-Oct 30; male; yes; ¼+; ¼+; ¼+; yes
1926- 953	Champagne, Rita; 1925-Oct 9; fem; yes; ¼+; ¼+; ¼+; yes
1932-	Constance, Dean Richard; 1926-March 24; male; no; W; ¼+; ¼; no; Independence, Mo
1926-1007	Daignault, George Lester; 1925-Aug 8; male; no; ¼+; ¼+; ¼+; no; St.John, ND
1930- 521	Day, George; 1925-Nov 1; male; yes; F; F; F; yes
1926-1018½	Dauphinais, Josephine Delia; 1925-Oct 15; fem; yes; ¼+; ¼+; ¼+; yes
1927-1079	Davis, Benedict; 1925-Oct 10; male; no; ¼+; ¼+; ¼+; yes
1932-	Davis, Vinier James; 1925-Dec 16; male; no; ¼+; ¼+; ¼+; yes
1927-2053	Decoteau, Oliver John; 1926-June 12; male; yes; ¼+; ¼+; ¼+; yes
1926-1165½	Decoteau, Joseph Bruno; 1925-Sept 12; male; yes; ¼+; ¼+; ¼+; yes
1932-	Decoteau, George; 1926-May 7; male; yes; ¼+; ¼+; ¼+; yes
1926-1206	Dejarlais, Andrew Albert; 1925-Aug 2; male; yes; ¼+; ¼+; ¼+; no; Devils Lake, ND
1930- 526	Delonais, Mary Adele; 1925-July 11; fem; yes; ¼+; ¼+; ¼+; yes
1926-1303	Delong, Rose Delima; 1926-March 2; fem; no; ¼+; ¼+; ¼+; yes

Turtle Mountain Reservation
Live Births
Key: Census Roll Number; Surname, Given; Date of Birth (Year-Month-Day); Sex; Tribe (Chippewa unless stated otherwise); Ward (yes/no); Degree of Blood (Father- Mother- Child); At Jurisdiction Where Enrolled (Yes/No); (If no – Where – Post Office, State)

1926-1367	Demontigny, Lloyd; 1926-Jan 16; male; yes; ¼+; ¼+; ¼+; yes
1931- 739	Dionne, Blanche; 1926-April 25; fem; yes; ¼+; ¼+; ¼+; yes
1930- 604	Dionne, Julia; 1925-Aug 16; fem; no; ¼+; ¼+; ¼+; yes
1932	Dionne, Clarence; 1926-May 3; male; no; ¼+; ¼+; ¼+; yes
1925-1359	Doney, Matilda; 1926-April 9; fem; no; ¼+; ¼+; ¼+; no; Harlem, Mont
1929-1472	Ducept, Francis; 1926-April 3; male; yes; ¼+; ¼+; ¼+; no; Nishu, ND
1926-1491	Duchesneau, Leonard Omer; 1925-Sept 30; male; no; ¼+; ¼+; ¼+; no; Dunseith, ND
1926-1574	Falcon, John Raymond; 1926-Jan 23; male; no; ¼+; ¼+; ¼+; no; Trenton, ND
1931 825	Falcon, Willis Lawrence; 1925-Dec 18; male; no; ¼+; ¼+; ¼+; no; Trenton, ND
1932	Falcon, George Patrick; 1926-March 15; male; no; ¼+; ¼+; ¼+; no; Trenton, ND
1930 689	Foster, Grace; 1926-Jan 20; fem; no; ¼+; ¼+; ¼+; no; Rolla, ND
1925-1541	Frederick, Mary Rose; 1925-July 20; fem; no; ¼+; ¼+; ¼+; yes
1926-1649	Frederick, Frank; 1926-April 23; male; yes; ¼+; ¼+; ¼+; yes
1927-1679	Gillis, Charles Raymond; 1926-March 8; male; yes; ¼+; ¼+; ¼+; no; Dunseith, ND
1926-1776	Gourneau, Peter Henry; 1925-Oct 22; male; no; ¼+; ¼+; ¼+; yes
1926-1784	Grandbois, Leo Gilbert; 1926-Feb 28; male; no; ¼+; ¼+; ¼+; yes
1928-1891	Grandbois, Delima Louise; 1925-Dec 23; fem; yes; ¼+; ¼+; ¼+; no; Dagmar, Mont
1930- 821	Grant, Peter; 1925-Nov 25; male; yes; ¼+; ¼+; ¼+; yes
1925-1773	Grant, Viola Stella; 1925-July 30; fem; yes; ¼+; ¼+; ¼+; yes
1929-1993	Gauthier, Gerald Norbert; 1926-May 20; male; no; W; ¼+; ¼; no; Willow City, ND
1926-1909	Griffin, John Howard; 1926-July 15, male; no; W; ¼+; ¼; no; Sidney, Mont
1931-1067	Gunville, Vincent; 1925-Aug 27; male; no; W; ¼+; ¼; no; Dunseith, ND
1931-1267	Houle, Francis; 1926-Feb 20; male; no; ¼+; ¼+; ¼+; no; Bottineau, ND
1927-2075	Houle, George; 1926-April 7; male; no; ¼+; ¼+; ¼+; no; Rolla, ND
1929-2187	Jacqmarct, Peter J; 1926-Jan 3; male; no; ¼+; ¼+; ¼+; no; Fort Totten, ND
1926-2099	Jeanotte, Leona; 1925-Dec 25; fem; yes; ¼+; ¼+; ¼+; yes
1926-2114	Jeannott[sic], Louisa Genevieve; 1925-July 29; fem; no; ¼+; ¼+; ¼+; yes
1932	Jeannotte, Mary Mae; 1926-May 3; fem; no; ¼+; ¼+; ¼+; no; St.John, ND
1931-1209	Jerome, Marie; 1925-Dec 21; fem; yes; ¼+; ¼+; ¼+; no; Rolette, ND
1927-2184	Johnson, Phyllis Laura; 1925-Aug 5; fem; no; ¼+; ¼+; ¼+; no; Breckenridge, Minn
1932	Jolibois, Lawrence; 1925-July 21; male; no; ¼+; ¼+; ¼+; no; Rolette, ND
1929-2316	Jones, Shirley Ellen; 1926-March 30; fem; no; ¼+; ¼+; ¼+; no; Coquille, Ore
1932	Killen, George Olaf; 1925-Oct 29; male; no; W; ¼+; ¼; no; Rolette, ND
1931-1259	Kellett, Mary; 1925; fem; no; W; ¼+; ¼; no; Wolf Point, Mont
1927-2239	Laducer, Mary Clara; 1926-March 12; fem; no; ¼+; ¼+; ¼+; yes
	Laducer, Julius; 1925-July 20; male; no; ¼+; ¼+; ¼+; yes
	Laducer, Marie; 1925-July 20; fem; no; ¼+; ¼+; ¼+; yes
1926-2244	Lafloe, Frank; 1925-Nov 6; male; yes; ¼+; ¼+; ¼+; yes
1932	Lafontain, Lawrence Robert; 1926-June 28; male; no; ¼+; ¼+; ¼+; no; Roy, Mont
1930-1078	Lafrombois, Patricia Mary; 1926-March 17; fem; no; ¼+; ¼+; ¼+; yes
1926-2460	Lambert, Delbert Alfred; 1926-Feb 11; male; no; ¼+; ¼+; ¼+; no; Snowden, Mont
1932	Lang, Irving Eugene; 1925-Dec 10; male; yes; W; ¼+; ¼; no; Tokio, ND
1927-2548	Langer, Joseph Francis; 1926-March 1; male; no; ¼+; W; ¼; no; Fort Totten, ND
1931-1439	Langer, Verlin; 1925-Nov 7; male; no; ¼+; ¼+; ¼+; no; St.John, ND

Turtle Mountain Reservation
Live Births
Key: Census Roll Number; Surname, Given; Date of Birth (Year-Month-Day); Sex; Tribe (Chippewa unless stated otherwise); Ward (yes/no); Degree of Blood (Father- Mother- Child); At Jurisdiction Where Enrolled (Yes/No); (If no – Where – Post Office, State)

1932-	Laroque, Wm Lawrence; 1925-Aug 10; male; yes; ¼+; ¼+; ¼+; no; Medicine Lake, Mont
1927-2590	Laroque, Mary Jane Eldora; 1925-Nov 20; fem; no; ¼+; ¼+; ¼+; no; Trenton, ND
1932	Laroque, George; 1926-Feb 19; male; no; ¼+; ¼+; ¼+; no; Trenton, ND
1931-1443	Laroque, Harvey David; 1925-Oct 15; male; yes; ¼+; ¼+; ¼+; no; St.John, ND
1930-1168	Lattergrass, Louis P. Wayne; 1926-March 17; male; yes; ¼+; ¼+; ¼+; yes
1929-2752	Latrail, Patrice Jr; 1925; male; no; ¼+; ¼+; ¼+; no; Fort Totten, ND
1930-1914	Mekwam, George; 1925; male; yes; F; F; F; yes
1932	Morin, Vivian; 1926-May 4; fem; yes; ¼+; ¼+; ¼+; no; Trenton, ND
1927-3087	Morin, Geo Michael; 1926-March 7; male; yes; ¼+; ¼+; ¼+; no; Medicine Lake, Mont
1930-2043	Morin, Joseph; 1925; male; yes; ¼+; ¼+; ¼+; yes
1932	Morin, Sylvester; 1925-Jan 14; male; no; ¼+; ¼+; ¼+; no; Fort Totten
1932	Murphy, Lawrence; 1926-Feb 29; male; yes; W; ¼+; ¼; yes
1931-1673	Nadeau, David Albert; 1925-Oct 8; male; no; ¼+; ¼+; ¼+; yes
1929-3396	Nicholas, Robert Lee; 1926-June 23; male; yes; ¼+; ¼+; ¼+; yes
1926-3190	Page, Fillian Albany; 1925-Aug 7; male; yes; ¼+; ¼+; ¼+; no; Devils Lake, ND
1930-1466	Parisien (Lagimodiere), Mary Dorothy; 1925-Aug 13; fem; no; ¼+; ¼+; ¼+; yes
1930-1496	Parisien, Charlie; 1925; male; no; ¼+; ¼+; ¼+; yes
1927-3316	Parisien, Beulah; 1926-Feb 16; fem; no; ¼+; ¼+; ¼+; yes
1927-3324	Parisien, Irene Mae; 1925-July 31; fem; no; ¼+; ¼+; ¼+; yes
1932	Patnaud, Sam Eugene; 1925-Oct 25; male; no; ¼+; ¼+; ¼+; yes
1930-1513	Patnaud, Mary; 1925-Aug 22; fem; yes; ¼+; ¼+; ¼+; yes
1927-3348	Patnaud, Willie; 1925; male; yes; ¼+; ¼+; ¼+; yes
1926-3391	Poitra, Floyd; 1925-Sept 29; male; yes; ¼+; ¼+; ¼+; no; Ft.Totten, ND
1926-3398	Poitra, Fred Elmer; 1925-Dec 23; male; no; ¼+; ¼+; ¼+; no; St.John, ND
1925-3282	Poitra, Josephine; 1925-Oct 8; fem; no; ¼+; ¼+; ¼+; no; St.John, ND
1926-3413	Poitra, Josephine R; 1925-Dec 9; fem; yes; ¼+; ¼+; ¼+; yes
1927-3322	Poitra, John Warren; 1926-May 29; male; yes; ¼+; ¼+; ¼+; yes
1930-1204	Laverdure, Grace Lillian; 1926-March 2; fem; yes; ¼+; ¼+; ¼+; yes
1927-2671	Laverdure, Yvonne Eva; 1926-April 30; fem; yes; ¼+; ¼+; ¼+; no; Dunseith, ND
1930-1629	Laverdure, Virginia; 1925-July 24; fem; yes; ¼+; ¼+; ¼+; yes
1932	Laverdure, Lillian; 1926-Jan 24; fem; no; ¼+; ¼+; ¼+; yes
1932	Laverdure, Helen; 1924-Nov 25; fem; no; ¼+; ¼+; ¼+; no; Devils Lake, ND
1932	Laverdure, Ludger; 1926-May 25; male; no; ¼+; ¼+; ¼+; yes
1932	Lecompt, Blanche; 1926-Feb 4; fem; yes; ¼+; ¼+; ¼+; no; Bainville, Mont
1925-2594	Lefort, Joseph; 1925; male; yes; ¼+; ¼+; ¼+; no; St.Paul, Minn
1930	Lemay, Madeline; 1926-May 31; fem; yes; ¼+; W; ¼; no; Bainville, Mont
1931-1811	Lenoir, Florence; 1925-Nov 25; fem; no; ¼+; ¼+; ¼+; Minnewauken[sic], ND
1929-2943	Lillie, Irene Maggie; 1926-March 18; fem; yes; W; ¼+; ¼; yes
1927-2816	Livermont, Lorraine; 1925; fem; no; W; ¼+; ¼; no; Unknown
1926-2777	Lizotte, Mary Jane; 1926-April 8, fem; no; ¼+; ¼+; ¼+; no; Great Falls, Mont
1926- 173	Little Boy, Patrick; 1925-Sept 5; male; yes; F; ¼+; ¼+; yes
1926-2809	Malaterre, Fred; 1926-Jan 11; male; no; ¼+; ¼+; ¼+; yes
1926-2823	Malaterre, Felix Eli; 1925; male; no; ¼+; ¼+; ¼+; yes
1932	Manson, Grace; 1926-June 9; fem; yes; W; ¼+; ¼; no; Antler, ND

Turtle Mountain Reservation
Live Births
Key: Census Roll Number; Surname, Given; Date of Birth (Year-Month-Day); Sex; Tribe (Chippewa unless stated otherwise); Ward (yes/no); Degree of Blood (Father- Mother- Child); At Jurisdiction Where Enrolled (Yes/No); (If no – Where – Post Office, State)

1926-2857	Marcellais, Charles; 1926-Feb 20; male; no; ¼+; ¼+; ¼+; yes
1928-3079	Martin, George; 1926-May 9; male; no; ¼+; ¼+; ¼+; yes
1932	Mathais, Geo Clifford; 1926-Jan 14; male; yes; W; ¼+; ¼; no; Bainville, Mont
1932	Metzenberg, Louise Mae; 1926-May 9; fem; no; W; ¼+; ¼; no; Vancouver, Wash
1932	Minne, Emily Matilda; 1926-March 27; fem; yes; ¼+; ¼+; ¼+; no; Mountain Side, Manitoba
1927-3391	Poitra, David Lloyd; 1925; male; yes; ¼+; ¼+; ¼+; no; Unknown
	Poitra, Angela; 1925-Aug 5; fem; yes; ¼+; ¼+; ¼+; yes
	Poitra, Stella Mae; 1925; fem; yes; ¼+; ¼+; ¼+; yes
1930-2318	Poitra, Herman; 1925-Sept 18; male; no; ¼+; ¼+; ¼+; no; Froid, Mont
1927-3567	Poitra, Clara; 1925; fem; yes; ¼+; ¼+; ¼+; no; Dunseith, ND
1932	Poitra, Viola; 1925-July 18; fem; no; ¼+; ¼+; ¼+; Dunseith, ND
1927-3607	Poitra, Elnora; 1926-April 2; fem; no; ¼+; ¼+; ¼+; yes
1927-3608	Poitra, Norine; 1926-April 2; fem; no; ¼+; ¼+; ¼+; yes
1932	Reindeau, Serena; 1925-Sept 4; fem; yes; W; ¼+; ¼; no; Thorne, ND
1927-3708	Rondeau, Geneva Olive; 1926-Jan 10; fem; no; W; ¼+; ¼; no; Devils Lake, ND
1926-3623	Roussin, Wm Bruno; 1925-Aug 17; male; no; ¼+; ¼+; ¼+; yes
1928-3842	Salmonson, Glenn; 1925; male; no; W; ¼+; ¼; no; Roy, Mont
1926-3659	Schindler, Fred William; 1925-July 30; male; no; ¼+; ¼+; ¼+; yes
1932	Shireback, Mary Belgarde; 1925-August 25; fem; no; W; ¼+; ¼; no; Wilton, ND
1930-1704	Short, Fabian; 1925; male; yes; ¼+; ¼+; ¼+; yes
1932	Smith, Delia Jane; 1925-Nov 20; fem; no; ¼+; ¼+; ¼+; no; Tokio, ND
1932	Skinner, Angeline; 1926-Feb 14, fem; yes; F; F; F; yes
1930-2446	Skinner, Stanley; 1925; male; yes; F; ¼+; ¼+
1932	Staley, Jennie; 1925-Nov 13; fem; yes; no; W; ¼+; ¼+; no; Froid, Mont
1929-4089	St.Claire, Lloyd Edward; 1926-June 21; male; yes; ¼+; ¼+; ¼+; no; Dunseith, ND
1931-2415	St.Pierre, Celine; 1925-Aug 14; fem; yes; ¼+; ¼+; ¼+; no; Dunseith, ND
1930-1746	Swain, Zelma; 1926-March 17; fem; no; ¼+; ¼+; ¼+; yes
1931-2524	Tobiness, Iron Feather; 1925; male; yes; F; F; F; no; Dunseith, ND
1930-1756	Tetrault, Lucille Bernice; 1925-Dec 9; fem; yes; ¼+; ¼+; ¼+; yes
1928-4055	Thibert, Arthur Lawrence; 1926-April 17; male; yes; ¼+; ¼+; ¼+; no; St.John, ND
1927-3975	Thomas, Nora; 1925-Dec 23; fem; yes; ¼+; ¼+; ¼+; yes
1932	Tinkay, Laverne Leo; 1926-May 8; male; yes; W; ¼+; ¼; no; Plentywood, Mont
1927-4025	Trothier, Patrick Everett; 1926-March 11; male; yes; ¼+; ¼+; ¼+; no; Malta, Mont
1930-2678	Trothier, Mary; 1926-Jan 7; fem; yes; ¼+; ¼+; ¼+; yes
1932	Turcott, Evelyn Agnes; 1926-April 16; fem; no; ¼+; ¼+; ¼+; no; Trenton, ND
1927-4063	Turcott, Irene; 1925-Aug 7; fem; no; ¼+; ¼+; ¼+; no; Rolla, ND
1926-3946	Turcott, Georgeline Rita; 1925-Aug 4; fem; no; ¼+; ¼+; ¼+; yes
1926-3965	Vallie, Mary Jane 1925; fem; yes; ¼+; ¼+; ¼+; yes
1929-4368	Vivier, Napoleon; 1926-April 8, male; no; 14; yes
1932	Vivier, Fred; 1925-Oct 9; male; yes; ¼+; ¼+; ¼+; no; Dunseith, ND
1926-4055	Wallett, Patrick; 1925-Oct 10; male; yes; ¼+; ¼+; ¼+; yes
	Walsh, Mary Louise; 1925-Sept 25; fem; no; W; ¼+; ¼; no; Dove, ND
1930-2857	Wilkie, Veronica; 1925-Aug 30; fem; no; ¼+; ¼+; ¼+; yes
1926-4118	Wilkie, John Israel; 1925-Aug 9; male; no; 14; yes

Turtle Mountain Reservation
Live Births

Key: Census Roll Number; Surname, Given; Date of Birth (Year-Month-Day); Sex; Tribe (Chippewa unless stated otherwise); Ward (yes/no); Degree of Blood (Father- Mother- Child); At Jurisdiction Where Enrolled (Yes/No); (If no – Where – Post Office, State)

1928-4377	Wilkie, Mary Ann; 1926-Feb 12; fem; no; ¼+; ¼+; ¼+; no; St.John, ND
1930-1902	Wilkie, Doris; 1925; fem; yes; ¼+; ¼+; ¼+; yes
1926-4158	Wilkie, Bertha; 1925-Aug 14; fem; no; ¼+; ¼+; ¼+; yes

Births Occurring between the Dates of July 1, 1926 and June 30, 1927 to Parents Enrolled at Jurisdiction

1931- 14	Alick, Selma; 1926; fem; no; W; ¼+; ¼; no; Bonetrail, ND
1932	Allery, Gladys; 1926-Sept 26; fem; no; ¼+; ¼+; ¼+; yes
1932-	Allery, Willard Monteith; 1927-March 10; male; yes; ¼+; ¼+; ¼+; no; Tokio, ND
1928- 376	Anderson, Adeline Mae; 1926-Nov 26; fem; no; W; ¼+; ¼; no; Devils Lake, ND
1930- 112	Andriff, Lawrence Evan; 1926-August 24; male; no; W; ¼+; ¼; no; Dunseith, ND
1928- 316	Azure, Raymond Joseph; 1927-Jan 23; male; yes; ¼+; ¼+; ¼+; no; Devils Lake, ND
1928- 347	Azure, Rose; 1926-Dec 23; fem; no; ¼+; ¼+; ¼+; yes
1928- 375	Azure, Mabel; 1927-May 27; fem; no; ¼+; ¼+; ¼+; yes
1928- 418	Azure, Martin; 1926; male; yes; ¼+; ¼+; ¼+; yes
-	Baker, Louis; 1926-Oct 18; male; yes; ¼+; ¼+; ¼+; yes
1930- 232	Baker, Emma; 1926-Oct 6; fem; yes; ¼+; ¼+; ¼+; no; Dunseith, ND
1932-	Beauchman, Herman; 1926-July 18; male; yes; ¼+; ¼+; ¼+; no; Wolf Point, Mont
1927- 515	Beauchman, John Albert; 1926-July 8; male; yes; ¼+; ¼+; ¼+; no; Wolf Point, Mont
1927- 527	Beaudry, Rose Helen; 1927-May 18; fem; no; W; ¼+; ¼; no; Malta, Mont
1930- 91	Belgarde, Patrice; 1926; male; yes; ¼+; ¼+; ¼+; yes
	Belgarde, Irene Amelia; 1926; fem; yes; ¼+; ¼+; ¼+; no; Dunseith, ND
	Belgarde, Irene; 1927-May 31; fem; no; ¼+; ¼+; ¼+; no; Ft.Totten, ND
1930- 113	Belgarde, Ralph; 1928-March 30; male; yes; ¼+; ¼+; ¼+; no; Ft.Totten, ND
1929- 743	Blue, Marie Alice; 1927-May 29; fem; yes; ¼+; ¼+; ¼+; yes
1928- 753	Bottineau, Ruth; 1926-July 22; fem; yes; ¼+; ¼+; ¼+; no; Dunseith, ND
1930- 187	Boyer, Maggie; 1926-Dec 15; fem; yes; ¼+; ¼+; ¼+; yes
1930- 528	Brien, Frank Theodore; 1926-Aug 18; male; yes; ¼+; ¼+; ¼+; no; Medicine Lake, Mont
1932	Brien, Josephine; 1926; fem; no; ¼+; ¼+; ¼+; yes
1930- 534	Brien, Gloria Belle; 1926-Oct 3; fem; no; ¼+; ¼+; ¼+; no; Medicine Lake, Mont
	Bruce, Louis Albert; 1926-Nov 25; male; yes; ¼+; ¼+; ¼+; yes
1932	Brunnell, Martha; 1926-Aug 24; fem; no; ¼+; ¼+; ¼+; yes
1932- 277	Brunnell, Jessica; 1926; fem; yes; ¼+; ¼+; ¼+; no; Bottineau, ND
1932	Carmer, Lewis; 1926-Dec 20; male; no; W; ¼+; ¼; no; St.Paul, Minn
1928- 935	Champagne, Edna; 1926; fem; no; ¼+; ¼+; ¼+; yes
1928- 993	Champagne, Helen; 1927-Jan 8; fem; yes; ¼+; ¼+; ¼+; yes
1927-1016	Croteau, Leo; 1926; male; no; ¼+; ¼+; ¼+; yes
1928-1057	Dauphinais, Peter Elmer; 1927-Feb 10; male; yes; ¼+; ¼+; ¼+; yes
	Davis, Delima; 1927-May 13; fem; no; ¼+; ¼+; ¼+; yes
1927-1126	Decoteau, Frank Lawrence; 1926-Oct 1; male; no; ¼+; ¼+; ¼+; yes
1930- 471	Decoteau, Ernest; 1927-Jan 17; male; yes; ¼+; ¼+; ¼+; yes
1932	Decoteau, Walter; 1926; male; yes; ¼+; ¼+; ¼+; yes
1930- 427	Decoteau, Albert; 1927-Jan 24; male; yes; ¼+; ¼+; ¼+; yes

Turtle Mountain Reservation
Live Births
Key: Census Roll Number; Surname, Given; Date of Birth (Year-Month-Day); Sex; Tribe (Chippewa unless stated otherwise); Ward (yes/no); Degree of Blood (Father- Mother- Child); At Jurisdiction Where Enrolled (Yes/No); (If no – Where – Post Office, State)

1932	Dejarlais, Blanch Patricia; 1927-March 17; fem; no; ¼+; ¼+; ¼+; no; Buford, ND
1928-1296	Dejarlais, Flora; 1926-Aug 5; fem; yes; ¼+; ¼+; ¼+; yes
1926-1256	Dejarlais, Lucy Nora; 1926-Oct 4; fem; yes; ¼+; ¼+; ¼+; yes
1928-1301	Dejarlais, Marguerite; 1926-Aug 18; fem; yes; ¼+; ¼; ¼; yes
	Day, Joseph; 1926-July; male; yes; F; F; F; no; Dunseith, ND
1927-1333	Delorme, Peter Clifford; 1927-March 20; male; yes; ¼+; ¼+; ¼+; yes
1928-1423	Demontigny, James; 1927-April 1; male; yes; ¼+; ¼+; ¼+; yes
1930- 574	Demontigny, Wilfred; 1926-Aug 18; fem[sic]; no; ¼+; ¼+; ¼+; yes
1930- 605	Dionne, Mary; 1926-Nov 20; fem; no; ¼+;F; ¼; yes
1932	Doney, Martin Thomas; 1926; male; no; ¼+; ¼+; ¼+; no; Malta, Mont
1928-1491	Dubois, Florence; 1927-Feb 21; male; no; ¼+; ¼+; ¼+; no; Dunseith, ND
1928-1530	Duchain, Alex Martin; 1926-Oct; male; no; ¼+; ¼+; ¼+; yes
1926-1492	Duchesneau, Raoul; 1926-Nov 2; male; no; ¼+; ¼+; ¼+; no; Dunseith, ND
1930- 637	Enno, Louis; 1927-Feb 10; male; no; ¼+; ¼+; ¼+; yes
1930- 635	Enno, Sidney; 1926-Nov 19; male; no; ¼+; ¼+; ¼+; yes
1930- 676	Falcon, Ella; 1927-March 12; fem; yes; ¼+; ¼+; ¼+; yes
1929-1662	Falcon, Jeanette; 1927-April 20; fem; no; ¼+; ¼+; ¼+; no; Trenton, ND
1931- 866	Foster, Cecile Alice; 1927-Mach 19; fem; no; ¼+; ¼+; ¼+; no; Rolla, ND
1928-1714	Frederick, Nora; 1926-Dec 16; fem; no; ¼+; ¼+; ¼+; yes
1928-1721	Frederick, Gloria; 1927-April 1; fem; yes; ¼+; ¼+; ¼+; yes
1932	Gladue, Marie; 1926; fem; yes; ¼+; ¼+; ¼+; yes
1928-1781	Gladue, Caris Raymond; 1927-Feb 9; male; no; ¼+; ¼+; ¼+; yes
1930-1752	Gourneau, Collin; 1927-Feb 9; male; yes; ¼+; ¼+; ¼+; yes
1932	Grandbois, Patrick Roger; 1926-Sept 7; male; no; ¼+; ¼+; ¼+; no; East Grand Forks, Minn
1930- 801	Grandbois, Gloria; 1927-Feb 1; fem; no; ¼+; ¼+; ¼+; yes
1928-1892	Grandbois, John Lawrence; 1926-July 23; male; yes; ¼+; ¼+; ¼+; no; Dagmar, Mont
1930- 827	Grant, Marland; 1927-April 18; male; yes; ¼+; ¼+; ¼+; yes
1930- 805	Grant, Archie; 1926-Oct 11; male; yes; ¼+; ¼+; ¼+; yes
1932	Grant, Gloria Patricia; 1926-Sept 30; fem; no; ¼+; ¼+; ¼+; no; Devils Lake, ND
1932-	Gunville, France Elizabeth; 1927-Feb 27; fem; no; ¼+; ¼+; ¼+; no; Dunseith, ND
1927-1952	Hamley, Clarence; 1926; male; yes; ¼+; ¼+; ¼+;
1927-1986	Henry, Marie Louise; 1926-July 12; fem; yes; ¼+; ¼+; ¼+; yes
1927-2007	Herman, Inez Marie; 1927-March 24; fem; yes; ¼+; ¼+; ¼+; no; Devils Lake, ND
1927-2060	Houle, Rita; 1926-Dec 3; fem; yes; ¼+; ¼+; ¼+; yes
1927-2061	Houle, Nora;^{twins} 1926-Dec 3; fem; yes; ¼+; ¼+; ¼+; yes
1928-2158	Jast, Elmer Peter; 1926; male; yes; ¼+; ¼+; ¼+; yes
1927-2109	Jeannott, Irene Mildred; 1926-Aug 2; fem; yes; ¼+; ¼+; ¼+; yes
1926-2124	Jeannott, Mary Martine; 1926; fem; yes; ¼+; ¼+; ¼+; yes
1927-2164	Jerome, Joseph; 1927-March 7; male; yes; ¼+; ¼+; ¼+; yes
1927-2185	Johnson, Bruce; 1926-Nov 4; male; no; W; ¼+; ¼; no; Breckenridge, Minn
1932-	Johnson, Mercedine Ardith; 1927-April 24; fem; yes; W; ¼+; ¼; no; Plentywood, Mont
1932-	Killen, Howard Clarence; 1926-Dec 14; male; no; W; ¼+; ¼; no; Rolette, ND
1928-2311	Laducer, Louis; 1926-Dec 4; male; yes; ¼+; ¼+; ¼+; yes
1928-2332	Lafloe, Mary Angela; 1927-March 11; fem; yes; ¼+; ¼+; ¼+; yes

Turtle Mountain Reservation
Live Births
Key: Census Roll Number; Surname, Given; Date of Birth (Year-Month-Day); Sex; Tribe (Chippewa unless stated otherwise); Ward (yes/no); Degree of Blood (Father- Mother- Child); At Jurisdiction Where Enrolled (Yes/No); (If no – Where – Post Office, State)

1927-2302 Lafontain, Daily; 1926-Sept 13; male; yes; ¼+; ¼+; ¼+; no; Havre, Mont
1930-1036 Lafontain, Fred; 1927-April 4, male; no; ¼+; ¼+; ¼+; yes
1930-1051 Lafontain, Dora; 1926-August 31; fem; no; ¼+; ¼+; ¼+; yes
1932-   Lafontain, George; 1927-April 17; male; no; ¼+; ¼+; ¼+; yes
1932-   Lafontain, Cecelia; 1926-Sept 24; fem; no; ¼+; ¼+; ¼+; yes
1932-   Lafrance, Maurice; 1927-June 3; male; no; ¼+; ¼+; ¼+; no; Rolla, ND
1930-1106 Lafrombois, Ernest; 1926-Oct 15; male; yes; ¼+; ¼+; ¼+; yes
1928-2470 Lafraniere, Leslie; 1927-Jan 27; male; no; ¼+; ¼+; ¼+; no; Hardin, Mont
1928-2471 Lafraniere, Lyda; 1927-Jan 27; fem; no; ¼+; ¼+; ¼+; no; Hardin, Mont
           Lafraniere, Lyle; 1927-Jan 27; fem; no; ¼+; ¼+; ¼+; no; Hardin, Mont
1927-2482 Lagimodiere, Alma; 1927-Apr 17; fem; yes; ¼+; ¼+; ¼+; yes
1929-2641 Landry, Alvina; 1926-July 7; fem; no; ¼+; ¼+; ¼+; yes
1932-   Langan, Alice; 1927-March 1; fem; yes; ¼+; ¼+; ¼+; no; Boggy Creek, Manitoba
1930-1139 Langer, George Frank; 1927-Feb 19; male; no; ¼+; ¼+; ¼+; yes
1927-2567 Langer, Mary Virginia; 1927-May 8; fem; no; ¼+; ¼+; ¼+; yes
1928-2640 Laroque, Charley Steven; 1926-Oct 28; male; no; ¼+; ¼+; ¼+; no; Dunseith, ND
1932-   Laroque, Rose Veda; 1927-May 8; fem; no; ¼+; ¼+; ¼+; no; Trenton, ND
1932-   Larsen, Edward; 1926-Oct 25; male; yes; W; ¼+; ¼; no; Ft.Totten, ND
1927-2609 Latrace; Gwendolen; 1926; fem; yes; ¼+; ¼+; ¼+; no; Boggy Creek, Manitoba
1927-2706 Laverdure, Morris Herman; 1926-Dec 28; male; yes; ¼+; ¼+; ¼+; Comerton, Mont
1932-   Lavia, Catherine Marie; 1926-Nov 29; fem; no; ¼+; ¼+; ¼+; Dagmar, Mont
1928-2818 Lavia, Dora Katherine; 1927-June 23; fem; yes; ¼+; ¼+; ¼+; no; Culbertson, Mont
1930-1219 Ledeaux, Gertrude; 1926; fem; no; ¼+; ¼+; ¼+; yes
1932-   Lillie, Joseph; 1926-July 25; male; yes; ¼+; ¼+; ¼+; no; Nishu, ND
           Lillie, Victoria Mary; 1927-June 19; fem; no; ¼+; ¼+; ¼+; St.John, ND
1930-1297 Malaterre, Irene; 1927-Feb 6; fem; no; ¼+; ¼+; ¼+; yes
1932   Manson, James Joseph; 1926-Aug 9; male; no; W; ¼+; ¼; no; Rolla, ND
1930-1320 Marion, Beatrice; 1926-Sept 5; fem; yes; ¼+; ¼+; ¼+; yes
1927-3051 Martell, Norman; 1929-June 2; male; no; ¼+; ¼+; ¼+; yes
1926-2920 Martell, Charles P; 1926-Sept 17; male; yes; ¼+; ¼+; ¼+; no; Poplar, Mont
1928-3066 Martell, Della; 1927-Mar 18; fem; no; ¼+; ¼+; ¼+; no; Poplar, Mont
1932   Manson, Theresa G; 1927-June 17; fem; yes; W; ¼+; ¼; no; Antler, ND
1928-3091 Martin, Walter Patrick; 1926-Dec 12; male; yes; ¼+; ¼+; ¼+; yes
1929-3222 Moore, John Lindley; 1927-May 8; male; no; W; ¼+; ¼; no; Central City, Iowa
1930-1908 Mekwam, Agnes Rose; 1927-June 15; fem; yes; F; F; F; yes
1927-3088 Morin, Eugene; 1927-April 26; male; yes; ¼+; ¼+; ¼+; no; Medicine Lake, Mont
1928-3199 Morin, Evelyn; 1927-Apfil 9; fem; no; ¼+; ¼+; ¼+; no; Dunseith, ND
1925-2904 Morin, Rebecca Alvina; 1926; fem; no; ¼+; ¼+; ¼+; no; Dunseith, ND
1930-3044 Morin, Theodore, Jr; 1926-Oct 23; male; no; ¼+; ¼+; ¼+; no; Devils Lake, ND
1927-3190 Morin, Matilda Hannah; 1927-Feb 23; fem; yes; ¼+; ¼+; ¼+; no; Wolf Point, Mont
1927-3211 Murphy, John; 1927-May 29; male; no; W; ¼+; ¼; yes
           Nadeau, Rosella; 1927-Jan 12; fem; yes; ¼+; ¼+; ¼+; yes
           Nelson, Donald; 1926-Nov 19; male; yes; W; ¼+; ¼; no; Froid, Mont
1927-3246 Nicholas, Claudia; 1926; fem; no; ¼+; ¼+; ¼+; yes

Turtle Mountain Reservation
Live Births
Key: Census Roll Number; Surname, Given; Date of Birth (Year-Month-Day); Sex; Tribe (Chippewa unless stated otherwise); Ward (yes/no); Degree of Blood (Father- Mother- Child); At Jurisdiction Where Enrolled (Yes/No); (If no – Where – Post Office, State)

1931-1934	Nepine, Christine; 1926; fem; yes; F; F; F; no; Dunseith, ND
1929-3442	Page, Dophine; 1927-Mar 24; male; yes; ¼+; ¼+; ¼+; yes
1927-3326	Parisien, Verne S; 1926; male; no; ¼+; ¼+; ¼+; yes
1930-1514	Patnaud, Ernest; 1927-Apr 19; male; yes; ¼+; ¼+; ¼+; yes
1932	Pippenger, David Gregor[sic]; 1926-Nov 17; male; yes; W; ¼+; ¼; no; Trenton, ND
1932	Plante, Daniel Francis; 1927-May 23; male; no; ¼+; W; ¼; no; Kalamazoo, Mich
1930-1552	Plante, Alfred; 1926; male; no; ¼+; ¼+; ¼+; no; Devils Lake, ND
1932-	Poitra, Arthur Archie; 1926-Nov 20; male; yes; ¼+; ¼+; ¼+; no; Boggy Creek, Manitoba
1932-	Poitra, Oscar Clenoy; 1927-May 27; male; no; ¼+; ¼+; ¼+; no; St.John, ND
1927-3507	Poitra, Redempta Louise; 1927-May 27; fem; no; ¼+; ¼+; ¼+; yes
	Poitra, Wallace Lawrence; 1926-July 12; male; yes; ¼+; ¼+; ¼+; yes
1929-3719	Poitra, Phillip Albert; 1926-July 26; male; yes; ¼+; ¼+; ¼+; yes
1927-2412	Poitra, Francis Albert; 1926-Aug 24; male; yes; ¼+; ¼+; ¼+; no; Dunseith, ND
	Premeau, Olympia; 1926; fem; yes; ¼+; ¼+; ¼+; yes
1928-3753	Premeau, Theresa; 1927-June 14; fem; yes; ¼+; ¼+; ¼+; yes
1927-3654	Purdy, Clinton James; 1928-Aug 3; male; yes; W; ¼+; ¼; yes
1928-3777	Reardon, Louise Patricia; 1927-April 13; male[sic]; yes; W; ¼+; ¼; yes
1932-	Riendeau, Alice Mae; 1927-May 1; fem; yes; W; ¼+; ¼; no; Thorne, ND
1938-3801	Richard, Gladys Grace; 1927-April 1; fem; yes; ¼+; ¼+; ¼+; no; St.John, ND
1927-3631	San Grait, Mary V; 1926; fem; yes; ¼+; ¼+; ¼+; yes
1927-3763	Schindler, Ernestine E; 1926-Oct 3; male; yes; ¼+; ¼+; ¼+; yes
1932-	Shafer, Ilene Agnes; 1926-Oct 28; fem; no; W; ¼+; ¼; no; Flaxville, Mont
1932-	Shireback, Robert Paul; 1927-March 11; male; no; W; ¼+; ¼; no; Wilton, ND
1929-3994	Sindt, Wesley Leroy; 1926-Aug 27; male; yes; W; ¼+; ¼; no; Big Fork, Mont
1932	Smith; Clarence Louie; 1927-March 10; male; yes; ¼+; ¼+; ¼+; no; Devils Lake, ND
1927-3855	St.Arnaud, Elmer; 1926-July 17; male; no; ¼+; ¼+; ¼+; yes
1930-2455	Skinner, Amelia; 1926; fem; yes; F; F; F; no; Dunseith, ND
1932	St.Claire, Priscilla Rose; 1926-Sept 6; fem; yes; ¼+; ¼+; ¼+; no; Dunseith, ND
1927-3843	Smith; Mary Florestine; 1926; fem; no; ¼+; ¼+; ¼+; yes
1932-	St.Germain, John Findley; 1926-Sept 1; male; no; ¼+; ¼+; ¼+; no; St.John, ND
1931-2416	St.Pierre, Rose; 1926-Dec 28; fem; yes; ¼+; ¼+; ¼+; no; Dunseith, ND
1927-3995	Thomas, Allen Edward; 1926; male; no; ¼+; ¼+; ¼+; no; Devils Lake, ND
1930-2663	Thomas, Alex; 1927-Feb 23; male; yes; ¼+; ¼+; ¼+; yes
	Trothier, Doris; 1927-May 10; fem; no; ¼+; ¼+; ¼+; yes
1929-4277	Turcott, Stanley Roger; 1926-Nov 8; male; no; ¼+; ¼+; ¼+; no; Rolla, ND
1927-4073	Turcott, Alfred; 1926-Nov 27; male; no; ¼+; ¼+; ¼+; no; Dunseith, ND
1928-4219	Vandal, Marie Evelyn; 1926-Aug 11; fem; yes; ¼+; ¼+; ¼+; yes
1929-4246	Villeneuve, Emilia; 1926-Aug 5; fem; no; ¼+; ¼+; ¼+; yes
1932-	Vivier, Stella Mae; 1926-Nov 29; fem; yes; ¼+; ¼+; ¼+; yes
1930-1836	Vivier, Patrice Sylvester; 1926-Sept 7; male; yes; ¼+; ¼+; ¼+; yes
1929-4401	Wallett, Henry; 1927-May 1; male; no; ¼+; ¼+; ¼+; yes
1939-4410	Wallett, Moses; 1927-June 1; male; yes; ¼+; ¼+; ¼+; yes
1929-4309	Wallett, Alexander; 1927-Jan 20; male; no; ¼+; ¼+; ¼+; yes
1930-1845	Wallett, Emma; 1926; fem; no; ¼+; ¼+; ¼+; yes

Turtle Mountain Reservation
Live Births
Key: Census Roll Number; Surname, Given; Date of Birth (Year-Month-Day); Sex; Tribe (Chippewa unless stated otherwise); Ward (yes/no); Degree of Blood (Father- Mother- Child); At Jurisdiction Where Enrolled (Yes/No); (If no – Where – Post Office, State)

1932-	Wilcox, Hillie Harry; 1926-Nov 7; male; no; W; ¼+; ¼; no; St.John, ND
1927-4252	Wilkie, Eugene David; 1927-March 27; male; no; ¼+; ¼+; ¼+; no; Standing Rock
1929-4497	Wilkie, Fred Louis; 1926-July 19; male; yes; ¼+; ¼+; ¼+; yes
1930-2827	Wilkie, Patrick; 1926-Aug 12; male; yes; ¼+; ¼+; ¼+; yes
1931-2248	Wilkie, Leona; 1926-Oct 25; male[sic]; no; ¼+; ¼+; ¼+; yes
1928-4421	Wilkie, Elzear; 1926; male; no; ¼+; ¼+; ¼+; yes
1930-2856	Wong, Jennie; 1926; fem; yes; ¼+; ¼+; ¼+; no; Unknown

Births Occurring between the Dates of July 1, 1927 and June 30, 1928 to Parents Enrolled at Jurisdiction

1932-		Alberts, Emma; 1927-Dec 3; fem; yes; ¼+; ¼+; ¼+; no; Dunseith, ND
1931:	8	Alick, Raymond; 1928-June 1; male; no; ¼+; ¼+; ¼+; yes
1928-	187	Allard, Irene; 1927-Oct 18; fem; yes; ¼+; ¼+; ¼+; yes
		Allery, Vivian; 1927-July 16; fem; yes; ¼+; ¼+; ¼+; no; Dunseith, ND
1932-		Allery, Ida; 1928-June 29; male[sic]; no; ¼+; ¼+; ¼+; yes
1928-	317	Azure, Doris Mae; 1928-Feb 22; fem; yes; ¼+; ¼+; ¼+; no; Devils Lake, ND
1932-		Azure, Mildred Helen; 1928-Feb 23; fem; no; ¼+; ¼+; ¼+; no; Rolla, ND
1928-	419	Azure; Florence; 1928-March 6; fem; yes; ¼+; ¼+; ¼+; yes
1927-	431	Azure, Ernest; 1928-Jan 2; male; no; ¼+; ¼+; ¼+; no; Nishu, ND
1932-		Baker, Cecil Raphael; 1928-Feb 15; male; no; ¼+; ¼+; ¼+; yes
1930-	330	Belgrade, Angeline; 1928-June 28; fem; yes; ¼+; ¼+; ¼+; no; Dunseith, ND
1928-	608	Belgrade, Daniel James; 1928-March 26; male; yes; ¼+; ¼+; ¼+; yes
1927-	624	Bercier, Norman; 1927; male; yes; ¼+; ¼+; ¼+; yes
1928-	647	Belgarde, Mary Rose; 1927-Dec 22; fem; yes; ¼+; ¼+; ¼+; no; Nishu, ND
1927-	663	Bercier, Victoria; 1927; fem; no; ¼+; F; ¼; yes
1931-	329	Bercier, June; 1928-June 8; fem; no; ¼+; ¼+; ¼+; no; Devils Lake, ND
1932-		Boe, Wm Laverne; 1927-Dec 11; male; no; W; ¼+; ¼; no; Long Beach, Calif
		Boyer, May; 1928-May 27; fem; no; ¼+; ¼+; ¼+; yes
1932		Boyer, Corrine Jane; 1927-July 8; fem; yes; ¼+; ¼+; ¼+; no; Sidney, Mont
1930-	208	Brien, Adele; 1928-May 3; fem; no; ¼+; ¼+; ¼+; yes
1930-	216	Brien, John Verlin; 1928-June 8; male; yes; ¼+; ¼+; ¼+; yes
1932-		Brien, Susanna; 1927-August 27; fem; yes; ¼+; ¼+; ¼+; yes
1928-	879	Bruce, Edna; 1927-Dec 13; fem; yes; ¼+; ¼+; ¼+; yes
		Brunnell, Eva; 1928-Feb 22; fem; yes; ¼+; ¼+; ¼+; yes
1928-	911	Brunnell, Theresa Blanche; 1928-June 12; fem; yes; ¼+; ¼+; ¼+; yes
1930-	241	Brunnell, Beulah; 1927-Oct 12; fem; no; ¼+; ¼+; ¼+; yes
		Barsness[sic], Bernice Rosalie; 1928-Feb 14; fem; no; W; ¼+; ¼; no; Medicine Lake, Mont
1932-		Constance, Edward Clarence; 1927-Aug 23; male; no; W; ¼+; ¼; no; Independence, Mo
1928-1041		Croteau, Mary A; 1927; fem; yes; ¼+; ¼+; ¼+;
1928-	121	Crec[sic], Rosina; 1928-Feb 24; fem; yes; F; F; F; no; Dunseith, ND
1930-	695	Day, Mary; 1928-March 22; fem; yes; F; F; F; yes
1931-	522	Day, Evelyn; 1927-Dec 4; fem; yes; F; F; F; no; Dunseith, ND
1931-	487	Davis, Lillian; 1927; fem; yes; ¼+; ¼+; ¼+; yes
1932-		Davis, John Lloyd; 1928-June 11; male; yes; ¼+; ¼+; ¼+; yes

Turtle Mountain Reservation
Live Births
Key: Census Roll Number; Surname, Given; Date of Birth (Year-Month-Day); Sex; Tribe (Chippewa unless stated otherwise); Ward (yes/no); Degree of Blood (Father- Mother- Child); At Jurisdiction Where Enrolled (Yes/No); (If no – Where – Post Office, State)

1930- 360	Davis, Raymond; 1927-Dec 23; male; no; ¼+; ¼+; ¼+; yes
1928-1108	Davis, Elmer Fred; 1927-July 15; male; yes; ¼+; ¼+; ¼+; yes
1930- 391	Davis, Stella Justine; 1928-Jan 15; fem; no; ¼+; ¼+; ¼+; yes
1932-	Davis, Josephine; 1927-Oct 2; fem; no; ¼+; ¼+; ¼+; no; Reedy Creek, Manitoba
1927-1150	Decoteau, Louis Alfred; 1927-July 5; male; yes; ¼+; ¼+; ¼+; yes
1929-1209	Decoteau, Elmer; 1927-Dec 29; male; yes; ¼+; ¼+; ¼+; yes
1930- 456	Decoteau, Stella; 1927; fem; no; ¼+; ¼+; ¼+; yes
1929-1290	Dejarlais, Ernest Gabriel; 1928-May 16; male; no; ¼+; ¼+; ¼+; yes
1 [sic]	Dejarlais, Florestine; 1927-Oct 27; fem; yes; ¼+; ¼+; ¼+; yes
1930- 544	Delorme, Alma Frances; 1928-Feb 27; fem; no; ¼+; ¼+; ¼+; yes
1930- 710	Delorme, Gladys; 1927-Nov 23; fem; yes; ¼+; ¼+; ¼+; yes
1930- 564	Delorme, Madeline; 1927-Nov 2; fem; yes; ¼+; ¼+; ¼+; yes
1930- 593	Dionne, Mary Eva; 1927-July 11; fem; no; ¼+; ¼+; ¼+; yes
	Doney, Leonard; 1928-Jan 24; male; no; W; ¼+; ¼; no; Harlem, Mont
	Dubois, Martina; 1928-May 22; fem; no; ¼+; ¼+; ¼+; no; Fort Berthold
1928-1513	Ducept, Elmer Jean; 1928-May 11; male; yes; ¼+; ¼+; ¼+; no; Nishu, ND
1928-1610	Faine, Joseph Lloyd; 1928-Ar 23; male; no; W; ¼+; ¼; no; Kalispell, Mont
	Falcon, Eugene Albert; 1928-Jan 1; male; no; ¼+; ¼+; ¼+; no; Trenton, ND
1928-1660	Fiddler, Joseph Albert; 1928-Jan 1; male; no; ¼+; ¼+; ¼+; no; Rolla, ND
1930- 703	Frederick, Rose; 1928-June 11; fem; yes; ¼+; ¼+; ¼+; yes
1932-	Frederickson, Wanita; 1927-July 21; fem; no; ¼+; ¼+; ¼+; no; Poplar, Mont
1932-	Godon, Alphonse; 1927-Sept 29; male; no; ¼+; ¼+; ¼+; no; Bottineau, ND
1930- 746	Gourneau, Fred; 1927-July 17; male; yes; ¼+; ¼+; ¼+; yes
1930- 786	Grandbois, Mary Leona; 1928-June 14; fem; no; ¼+; ¼+; ¼+; yes
1932-1083	Grandbois, Lucy; 1927-Dec 7; fem; yes; ¼+; ¼+; ¼+; no; Dagmar, Mont
1932-	Grandbois, Viola Georgina; 1927-Oct 22; fem; no; ¼+; ¼+; ¼+; no; Medicine Lake, Mont
1932-	Grant, Leona; 1928-May 18; fem; no; ¼+; ¼+; ¼+; yes
1932-	Grant, Georgeline; 1928-April 16; fem; yes; ¼+; ¼+; ¼+; no; Devils Lake, ND
1930- 806	Grant, Nora Eleanor; 1927-Dec 4; fem; yes; ¼+; ¼+; ¼+; yes
1930- 831	Grant, Vernon; 1927-Dec 16; male; no; ¼+; W; ¼; yes
1929-1994	Gauthier, Leo Vincent; 1928-Feb 28; male; no; W; ¼+; ¼; no; Willow City, ND
1932-	Gunville, Eugenia; 1928-March 13; fem; no; ¼+; ¼+; ¼+; no; Dunseith, ND
1932-	Henry, John; 1927-Dec 28; male; yes; ¼+; F; ¼; no; Dunseith, ND
1932-	Hill, Harvey Louis; 1927-Dec 30; male; no; W; ¼+; ¼; no; Walhalla, ND
1929-2105	Herman, Violet; 1928-March 17; fem; yes; ¼+; ¼+; ¼+; no; Devils Lake, ND
1928-2096	Houle, Stella Annie; 1927-July 22; fem; no; ¼+; ¼+; ¼+; no; Devils Lake, ND
1930-1279	Iron Bear, Andrew; 1927; male; yes; F; F; F; yes
1930- 928	Jeannott, Robert; 1928-June 5; male; yes; ¼+; ¼+; ¼+; yes
1928-2203	Jeannott, Leo; 1928-Jan 7; male; no; ¼+; ¼+; ¼+; yes
1928-2211	Jerome, Irene; 1928-Feb 6; fem; no; ¼+; ¼+; ¼+; yes
1929-2252	Jerome, Joseph; 1928-March 7; male; yes; ¼+; ¼+; ¼+; yes
1931-1210	Jerome, Ernestine; 1927-Sept 20; fem; yes; ¼+; ¼+; ¼+; no; Rolette, ND
1928-1492	Jetty, (Dubois) Rebecca Pearl; 1928-March 27; fem; no; ¼+; ¼+; ¼+; no; Tokio, ND
1931-1229	Johnson, Lucille; 1928-May 2; fem; no; W; ¼+; ¼; no; Breckenridge, Minn

Turtle Mountain Reservation
Live Births
Key: Census Roll Number; Surname, Given; Date of Birth (Year-Month-Day); Sex; Tribe (Chippewa unless stated otherwise); Ward (yes/no); Degree of Blood (Father- Mother- Child); At Jurisdiction Where Enrolled (Yes/No); (If no – Where – Post Office, State)

1932-	Jollibois, Leroy; 1927-July 6; male; no; ¼+; ¼+; ¼+; no; Thorne, ND
1930- 984	Kaplin, Sylvester; 1927-Dec 4; male; no; ¼+; ¼+; ¼+; yes
1931-1175	Laducer, Louise; 1928-Mrch 15; fem; yes; ¼+; ¼+; ¼+; yes
1932-	Lafontain, Billy Melbaren; 1928-Jan 29; male; yes; ¼+; ¼+; ¼+; no; Roy, Mont
1932-	Lafontain, Arthur; 1928-April 28; male; yes; ¼+; ¼+; ¼+; no; Hevre[sic], Mont
1929-2543	Lafontain, Eliza Angeline; 1928-May 29; fem; yes; ¼+; ¼+; ¼+; yes
1931-1305	Lafontain, Hazel; 1927-Sept 1; male; no; ¼+; ¼+; ¼+; no; Devils Lake, ND
1928-2515	Lafrombois, Romeo; 1927-Nov 4; male; yes; ¼+; ¼+; ¼+; yes
1929-2584	Lafrombois, John B, Jr; 1927-Dec; male; yes; ¼+; ¼+; ¼+; no; Devils Lake, ND
1931-1385	Lagimodiere, Maryann; 1927-July 24; fem; no; ¼+; ¼+; ¼+; no; Medicine Lake, Mont
1928-2568	Lambert, Doris Lorene W; ¼+; ¼; 1927-Nov 19; fem; no; ¼+; ¼+; ¼+; no; Rolla, ND
1928-2572	Landry, Aurelia; 1927-Dec 10; fem; no; ¼+; ¼+; ¼+; no; Rolla, ND
1928-2590	Lang, Kathleen A; 1927-Nov 9; fem; yes; W; ¼+; ¼; no; Tokio, ND
1928-2613	Langer, Darrell; 1927-Dec 4; male; no; ¼+; ¼+; ¼+; no; Ft.Totten, ND
1931-1440	Langer, Viola Mae; 1928-May 26; fem; no; ¼+; ¼+; ¼+; no; St.John, ND
1932-	Laroque, Margaret; 1928-March 22; fem; no; ¼+; ¼+; ¼+; no; Medicine Lake, Mont
1929-2705	Laroque, Emma Louise; 1927-Nov 27; fem; yes; ¼+; ¼+; ¼+; no; St.John, ND
1928-2661	Larsen, Melvin; 1928-March 3; male; yes; W; ¼+; ¼; no; Ft.Totten, ND
1928-2692	Latrail, Dorothy Jane; 1928-Oct 30; fem; no; ¼+; ¼+; ¼+; no; Ft.Totten, ND
1928-2704	Lavallie, Ernest; 1928-Feb 5; male; yes; ¼+; ¼+; ¼+; yes
1930-1620	Lavallie, Mary Florestine; 1928-Feb 25; fem; yes; ¼+; ¼+; ¼+; no; Dunseith, ND
1927-2658	Lavallie, Virginia; 1927-Sept 21; fem; no; ¼+; ¼+; ¼+; yes
	Laverdure, Sarah Jane; 1927-Oct 21; fem; yes; ¼+; ¼+; ¼+; yes
1929-2806	Laverdure, Mary Ann; 1927-Nov 25; fem; yes; ¼+; ¼+; ¼+; no; Dunseith, ND
1930-1630	Laverdure, Albert; 1927-July 26; male; yes; ¼+; ¼+; ¼+; yes
	Laverdure, Marie Hilda; 1927-Dec 18; fem; yes; ¼+; ¼+; ¼+; yes
1932	Laverdure, James; 1928-June 10; male; no; ¼+; ¼+; ¼+; yes
1932	Lecompt, Gladys; 1927-Sept 7; male; yes; ¼+; ¼+; ¼+; no; Bainville, Mont
1932	Lemay, Napoleon Jacob; 1928-Jan 1; male; yes; ¼+; ¼+; ¼+; no; Bainville, Mont
1928-2868	Lenoir, Dorothy; 1928-March 2; fem; no; ¼+; ¼+; ¼+; no; Minnewauken[sic], ND
	Lillie, Francis; 1928-May 19; male; yes; ¼+; ¼+; ¼+; yes
1930-1268	Malaterre, Stella; 1927-Aug 22; fem; no; ¼+; ¼+; ¼+; yes
	Machipeness, George; 1928-Feb 22; male; yes; F; F; F; no; Dunseith, ND
1932-	Marion, Charles Edward; 1928-May 1; male; no; ¼+; W; ¼; no; Grenora, ND
1932-	Martin, Louis Moses; 1928-June 17; male; yes; ¼+; ¼+; ¼+; yes
1029-3196	Monette, Raymond; 1928-March 8; male; yes; ¼+; ¼+; ¼+; yes
1927-3205	Morin, Florence; 1927; fem; no; ¼+; ¼+; ¼+; no; Ft.Totten
1932-	Nadeau, Louis; 1927-August 6; male; yes; ¼+; ¼+; ¼+; yes
1931-1945	Nicholas, Ralph Edward; 1928-Jan 20; male; yes; ¼+; ¼+; ¼+; Devils Lake, ND
	Nwenapi, Hunting; 1928-Feb 28; male; yes; F; F; F; no; Dunseith, ND
1932-	Olsen, Lucille; 1927-Sept 22; fem; no; W; ¼+; ¼; no; Rolla, ND
1932	Olsen, Mary Jeannette; 1928-March 5, fem; yes; W; ¼+; ¼; no; Cando, ND
1929-3447	Page, Mary Ethel; 1927-Dec 3; fem; no; ¼+; ¼+; ¼+; yes
1930-1459	Parisien, Elmer John; 1927-Oct 30; male; yes; ¼+; ¼+; ¼+; yes

Turtle Mountain Reservation
Live Births
Key: Census Roll Number; Surname, Given; Date of Birth (Year-Month-Day); Sex; Tribe (Chippewa unless stated otherwise); Ward (yes/no); Degree of Blood (Father- Mother- Child); At Jurisdiction Where Enrolled (Yes/No); (If no – Where – Post Office, State)

1929-3487	Parisien, Phillip Jerome; 1928-April 19; male; yes; ¼+; ¼+; ¼+; yes
1932-	Peltier, Louise; 1927-July 27; fem; no; ¼+; ¼+; ¼+; no; Fort Berthold
1932-	Pippenger, Paul Eugene; 1928-May 4; male; yes; W; ¼+; ¼; no; Trenton, ND
1930-1551	Plante, Lola; 1927-Dec 18; fem; yes; ¼+; ¼+; ¼+; yes
1928-3571	Plante, Albert Edward; 1927-Nov 9; male; no; ¼+; ¼+; ¼+; no; Devils Lake, ND
1928-3591	Poitra, Mary Aurelia; 1927-July 4; fem; yes; ¼+; ¼+; ¼+; yes
1930-1572	Poitra, Emil; 1928-Feb 5; male; yes; ¼+; ¼+; ¼+; yes
1932	Poitra, Albertine; 1927-Aug 18; fem; no; ¼+; ¼+; ¼+; no; Boggy Creek, Manitoba
1932	Poitra, Alfred Raymond; 1927-Dec 20; male; yes; ¼+; ¼+; ¼+; no; Dunseith, ND
1932	Poitra, Eleanor; 1927-Aug 2; fem; no; ¼+; ¼+; ¼+; no; Dunseith, ND
1930-2319	Poitra, Albert; 1927-Dec 24; male; no; ¼+; ¼+; ¼+; no; Froid, Mont
1928-3795	Renville, John Francis; 1927-Nov 4; male; yes; ¼+; ¼+; ¼+; no; Buford, ND
1932	Richard; Bernice Marie; 1928-March 22; fem; no; ¼+; ¼+; ¼+; no; St.John, ND
1932	Rondeau, Muriel Marie; 1927-Aug 6; fem; yes; W; ¼+; ¼; no; Devils Lake, ND
1929-3832	Roy, Theodore Albert; 1927-Dec 8; male; no; W; ¼+; ¼; no; Rolette, ND
1927-3726	Roussin, John; 1927; male; no; ¼+; ¼+; ¼+; yes
1928-3878	Schindler, Adrine Frances; 1928-May 10; fem; yes; ¼+; ¼+; ¼+; yes
1929-4005	Slater, Eleanor; 1927-July 4; fem; yes; ¼+; ¼+; ¼+; no; St.John, ND
1932-	Skinner, Flora; 1928-April 19; fem; yes; F; F; F; no; Dunseith, ND
1930-2445	Skinner, Olive; 1927; fem; yes; F; F; F; no; Dunseith, ND
1932-	Smith, Barbara Mae; 1928-May 17; fem; yes; W; ¼+; ¼; no; Raymond, Mont
1930-1711	Smith, Michael; 1927; male; no; ¼+; ¼+; ¼+; yes
1929-4041	Smith, Francis Sylvester; 1927-Nov 25; male; yes; ¼+; ¼+; ¼+; yes
1929-4090	St.Claire, Doris May; 1918-Feb 13; fem; yes; ¼+; ¼+; ¼+; no; Ft.Totten, ND
1931-2417	St.Pierre, Seraphine; 1928-March 12; fem; yes; ¼+; ¼+; ¼+; no; Dunseith, ND
1932	Smigiel, Betty Jane; 1927-Dec 22; fem; yes; W; ¼+; ¼; no; Superior, Wis
1931-1757	Tetrault, Gilbert Wm; 1927-Aug 11; male; yes; ¼+; ¼+; ¼+; yes
1928-4056	Thibert, Adolph Peter; 1927-July 19; male; yes; ¼+; ¼+; ¼+; no; St.John, ND
1932-	Thifault, Harry; 1927-Oct 10; male; no; ¼+; ¼+; ¼+; no; Dunseith, ND
1931-2629	Thomas, Ernest Allen; 1928-Feb 20; male; no; ¼+; ¼+; ¼+; no; Rolette, ND
1929-4262	Turcott, Michael Richard; 1928-April 26; male; no; ¼+; ¼+; ¼+; no; Trenton, ND
1928-4179	Turcott, Flora; 1928-May 4; fem; no; ¼+; ¼+; ¼+; no; Rolla, ND
1928-4184	Turcott, Louis Patrick; 1928-March 17; male; no; ¼+; ¼+; ¼+; yes
1930-1787	Vallie, Louis; 1927; male; yes; ¼+; ¼+; ¼+; yes
1929-4336	Vandal, Esther Beulah; 1927-Oct 26; fem; no; ¼+; ¼+; ¼+; yes
1928-4264	Vivier, Esther; 1928-Jan 28; fem; yes; ¼+; ¼+; ¼+; yes
1929-4384	Vivier, Leona Vilma; 1928-June 24; fem; no; ¼+; ¼+; ¼+; no; Dunseith, ND
	Wallett, Francis; 1928-Feb 17; male; yes; ¼+; ¼+; ¼+; yes
1932-	Walsh, Virginia; 1928-April 5; fem; no; W; ¼+; ¼; no; Dove, ND
	Walsh, Arlene; 1928-Jan 20; fem; no; ¼+; ¼+; ¼+; no; Fonda, ND
	Wilkie, Morris; 1928-June 30; male; yes; ¼+; ¼+; ¼+; yes
1928-4334	Zura, Robert Norman; 1927-Nov 2; male; no; W; ¼+; ¼; no; Rolette, ND

Turtle Mountain Reservation
Additional Names
Key: Census, Census Roll Number; Surname, Given; Date of Birth (Year-Month-Day); Live Births; Still Births; Sex; Tribe (Chippewa unless stated otherwise); Ward (yes/no); Degree of Blood (Father- Mother- Child); At Jurisdiction Where Enrolled (Yes/No); (If no – Where – Post Office, State)

[Note: The key has changed slightly from previous Live Births pages]

Births Occurring between the Dates of **July 1, 1927** and **June 30, 1928** to Parents Enrolled at Jurisdiction

1928 #1407 Demarais, Patrick; 1927-Oct 31; yes; no; m; yes; ½;½;½; no; Malta, Mont
1928 #2267 Jollie, Doris; 1928-Jan 24; yes; no; f; yes; ½;½;½; yes
1928 #3117 McGillis, Phyllis Jean; 1928-Mch 27; yes; no; f; yes; ?;½;½; no; St.John, ND

(Children who were born alive and died before enrollment)

Died before en. Frederick, Marie; 1928-Feb 15; yes; no; f; yes; ½;½;½; yes
   do   Poitra, Irene Mabel; 1927-Dec 22; yes; no; f; yes; ½;½;½; yes

[Parents not enrolled]

Parents not enrolled Laviolette, Dovaline; 1928-Jan 27; yes; no; f; no; ½;½;½; yes
   do   Packineau, Warren; 1928-Jan 24; yes; no; m; no; ½;½;½; no; Nishu, ND
   do[sic]

Turtle Mountain Reservation

Live Births

Key: Census Roll Number; Surname, Given; Date of Birth (Year-Month-Day); Sex; Tribe (Chippewa unless stated otherwise); Ward (yes/no); Degree of Blood (Father- Mother- Child); At Jurisdiction Where Enrolled (Yes/No); (If no – Where – Post Office, State)

Births Occurring between the Dates of **July 1, 1928** and **June 30, 1929** to Parents Enrolled at Jurisdiction

1930-2093	Akenensi, Iron Thumder[sic]; 1928; fem; yes; F; F; F; no; Dunseith, ND
1931- 21	Allard, Florence Stella; 1929-June 18; fem; yes; ¼+; ¼+; ¼+; yes
1932	Allard, Patrice W; ¼+; ¼; 1928-Oct 12; male; yes; ¼+; ¼+; ¼+; yes
1930- 17	Allard, Elmer; 1928; male; no; ¼+; ¼+; ¼+; yes
1929- 221	Allery, Louise; 1928-Nov 3; male; yes; ¼+; ¼+; ¼+; yes
1930- 48	Allery, Georaline[sic]; 1929-Jan 9; fem; no; ¼+; ¼+; ¼+; no; Dunseith, ND
1932-	Allery, Clifford; 1929-March 7; male; yes; ¼+; ¼+; ¼+; no; Tokio, ND
1930- 86	Amyott, Leonard; 1928; male; yes; ¼+; ¼+; ¼+; no; Dunseith, ND
1931- 92	Anderson, John Henry; 1929-Jan 11; male; no; W; ¼+; ¼; no; Devils Lake, ND
1932-	Andriff, Dorothy; 1929-June 18; fem; no; W; ¼+; ¼; no; Dunseith, ND
1929- 315	Azure, Mary Rosalie; 1929-March 21; fem; yes; ¼+; ¼+; ¼+; yes
1931- 103	Azure, Ruby Mae; 1929-March 14; fem; yes; ¼+; ¼+; ¼+; no; Dunseith, ND
1930- 123	Azure, Peter Clifford; 1930-Feb 10; male; yes; ¼+; ¼+; ¼+; yes
1931- 79	Azure, Donald Louis; 1929-May 10; male; yes; ¼+; ¼+; ¼+; yes
1929- 522	Beauchman, Mary Jane; 1928-Sept 22; fem; no; ¼+; ¼+; ¼+; no; Wolf Point, Mont
1932-	Beaudry, Theresa; 1929-March 10; fem; no; ¼+; ¼+; ¼+; no; Malta, Mont
1929- 593	Belgarde, Donald Louis; 1928-Dec 22; male; yes; ¼+; ¼+; ¼+; no; Dunseith, ND
1930- 148	Bercier, Marion; 1928; fem; yes; ¼+; ¼+; ¼+; yes
1930- 307	Belgarde, Frank; 1928; male; no; ¼+; ¼+; ¼+; no; Elphinstone, Sask
1929- 672	Belgarde, Martha; 1928-Aug 12; fem; yes; ¼+; ¼+; ¼+; yes
1929- 680	Bercier, Angeline Marie; 1929-Jan 17; fem; no; ¼+; ¼+; ¼+; yes
1929- 722	Bercier, Jean Louis; 1929-March 16; male; yes; ¼+; ¼+; ¼+; yes
1929- 744	Blue; John Monte; 1929-Feb 8; male; yes; ¼+; ¼+; ¼+; yes
1930- 188	Boyer, Lloyd; 1928-Dec 30; male; yes; ¼+; ¼+; ¼+; yes
1932-	Brien, Alvina; 1929-Feb 4; fem; yes; ¼+; ¼+; ¼+; no; Dunseith, ND
1928- 912	Brunnell, Peter Raymond; 1929-Feb 12; male; yes; ¼+; ¼+; ¼+; yes
1929- 927	Brunnell, Edna Marie; 1928-Oct 29; fem; no; ¼+; ¼+; ¼+; yes
1929- 938	Brunnell, Louise Lucille; 1919-June 4; fem; yes; ¼+; ¼+; ¼+; no; Bottineau, ND
1932-	Bell, Lloyd; 1928-July 11; male; no; ¼+; ¼+; ¼+; no; Semans, Sask
1930- 246	Cook, John Fay; 1928-July 23; male; no; W; ¼+; ¼+; ¼+; yes
1929-1005	Champagne, Joseph Paul; 1928-Sept 5; male; yes; ¼+; ¼+; ¼+; yes
1932-	Counts, Mary Louise; 1928-Aug 25; fem; yes; ¼+; ¼+; ¼+; no; Dunseith, ND
1932-	Constance, Albert Arthur; 1929-May 12; male; no; W; ¼+; ¼; no; Independence, Mo
1929-1086	Davis, Gilbert Albert; 1929-April 17; male; no; ¼+; ¼+; ¼+; yes
1929-1143	Davis, Flora; 1928-Nov 2; fem; yes; ¼+; ¼+; ¼+; yes
1929-1155	Decoteau, John Wilfred; 1928-Aug 28; male; yes; ¼+; ¼+; ¼+; yes
1929-1158	Decoteau, Lorraine; 1928-Sept 13; fem; yes; ¼+; ¼+; ¼+; yes
	Decoteau, Joseph Patrice; 1929-Jan 13; male; no; ¼+; ¼+; ¼+; yes
1930- 407	Decoteau, Rita; 1928; fem; yes; ¼+; ¼+; ¼+; yes
1929-1200	Decoteau; Raphael; 1928-Dec 7; male; yes; ¼+; ¼+; ¼+; yes
1929-1238	Decoteau, No name; 1929-May 1; fem; yes; ¼+; ¼+; ¼+; no; Rosebud Agency, SD
1920- 484	Decoteau, Mabel Rose; 1928-July 1; fem; yes; ¼+; ¼+; ¼+; yes

Turtle Mountain Reservation
Live Births
Key: Census Roll Number; Surname, Given; Date of Birth (Year-Month-Day); Sex; Tribe (Chippewa unless stated otherwise); Ward (yes/no); Degree of Blood (Father- Mother- Child); At Jurisdiction Where Enrolled (Yes/No); (If no – Where – Post Office, State)

1929-1173	Decoteau, Paul Melvin; 1929-March 4; male; yes; ¼+; ¼+; ¼+; no; Devils Lake, ND
1929-1279	Dejarlais, Jacob Clifford; 1928; male[sic]; no; ¼+;¼+;¼+; no; Devils Lake, ND
1932-	Dejarlis[sic], Grace Margaret; 1929-Feb 2; fem; no; ¼+; ¼+; ¼+; no; Buford, ND
1929-1307	Dejarlais, Flora Marie; 1929-June 16; fem; yes; ¼+;¼+;¼+; yes
1929-1361	Delong, Leona; 1928-Dec 12; fem; no; ¼+;¼+;¼+; yes
1930- 558	Delorme, Eugene Edward; 1928-Aug 10; male; yes; ¼+;¼+;¼+; yes
1930- 565	Delorme, William; 1928-July 1; male; no; ¼+;¼+;¼+; yes
1932-	Demarais, Victoria; 1929-May 1; fem; no; ¼+;¼+;¼+; yes
1930- 589	Demontigny, John, Jr; 1929-Jan 1; male; yes; ¼+;¼+;¼+; no; Rolla, ND
1930- 595	Dionne, Marie Alice; 1928-Oct 4; fem; yes; ¼+;¼+;¼+; yes
1930- 617	Dionne, Benedict; 1928-Oct 7; male; yes; ¼+;¼+;¼+; yes
1929-1487	Dionne, Mary Delima; 1929-Feb 2; fem; yes; ¼+;¼+;¼+; yes
1932-	Dionne, Edward G; 1928-Sept 22; male; no; ¼+; ¼+; ¼+; no; Medicine Lake, Mont
1932-	Duchain, Lillian; 1928-Sept 6; fem; yes; ¼+;¼+;¼+; yes
1929-1588	Eller, Gladys Mae; 1929-April 27; fem; yes; ¼+;¼+;¼+; no; Dunseith, ND
	Enno, Francis; 1929-May 23; male; no; ¼+;¼+;¼+; yes
1929-1625	Faguant, Irene Stella; 1928-July 26; fem; yes; ¼+;¼+;¼+; no; Dunseith, ND
1930- 677	Falcon, Theresa; 1929-Jan 30; fem; yes; ¼+;¼+;¼+; yes
1932-	Falcon, Walter Ray; 1928-Sept 8; male; no; ¼+;¼+;¼+; no; Trenton, ND
1931- 867	Foster, Joseph; 1929-June 28; male; no; ¼+;¼+;¼+; no; Rolla, ND
1929-1738	Frederick, Roderick; 1929-May 8; male; yes; ¼+;¼+;¼+; yes
1929-1751	Gillis, Mary Ann; 1929-March 26; fem; yes; ¼+; ¼+; ¼+; no; Dunseith, ND
1932-	Gladue, Hazel; 1928-Oct 17; fem; no; ¼+;¼+;¼+; no; Froid, Mont
1932-	Godon, Joseph; 1929-June 4; male; yes; ¼+;¼+;¼+; no; Bottineau, ND
1930- 747	Gourneau, Mary Rose; 1929-April 16; fem; yes; ¼+;¼+;¼+; yes
1932-	Grandbois, John Michael; 1929-March 17; male; no; ¼+;¼+;¼+; no; East Grand Forks, Minn
1929-1900	Grandbois, Ernest; 1929-June 2; male; no; ¼+; ¼+; ¼+; yes
1932-	Grandbois, Henrietta Rose; 1929-Jan 22; fem; no; ¼+;¼+;¼+; no; Medicine Lake, Mont
1930- 811	Grant, Frank Julius; 1929-Mar 26; male; yes; ¼+;¼+;¼+; yes
1932-	Grant, Peter Lloyd; 1929-Feb 5; male; no; ¼+;¼+;¼+; no; Devils Lake, ND
1932-	Griffin, David Clinton; 1929-Feb 21; male; no; W; ¼+; ¼; no; Sidney, Mont
1929-2046	Hamley, Lewis; 1929-Sept 27; male; yes; ¼+;¼+;¼+; yes
1932-	Henry, James; 1929-Feb 28; male; yes; ¼+;F;¼+; no; Dunseith, ND
1929-2083	Henry, Florence; 1928-Oct 14; fem; yes; ¼+;¼+;¼+; yes
1932-	Ingalls, George; 1929-Feb 222[sic]; male; yes; W; ¼+; ¼; no; Devils Lake, ND
1932-	Jeannotte, Henry Lawrence; 1929-Dec 25; male; yes; ¼+;¼+;¼+; yes
1930- 915	Jeannotte, Nora S; 1929-Mar 3; fem; yes; ¼+;¼+;¼+; yes
1932	Jeannotte, Olive Bernice; 1928-Sept 16; fem; no; ¼+;¼+;¼+; no; St.John, ND
	Jerome, Charles Robert; 1928-Sept 28; male; no; ¼+;¼+;¼+; no; Malta, Mont
1932-	Jollibois, Violet; 1928-Aug 15; fem; no; ¼+;¼+;¼+; no; Thorne, ND
1932-	Kaufman, Lee Roy; 1929-April 2; male; no; ¼+;¼+;¼+; no; Havre, Mont
1929-2338	Kinney, Remy Cornelius; 1928-Oct 3; male; no; W; ¼+; ¼; no; Devils Lake, ND
1929-2371	Laducer, Peter; 1928-Nov 26; male; yes; ¼+; ¼+;¼+; yes
1932-	Lafontaine, Lorraine; 1929-April 17; fem; yes; ¼+; ¼+; ¼+; no; Roy, Mont

Turtle Mountain Reservation
Live Births
Key: Census Roll Number; Surname, Given; Date of Birth (Year-Month-Day); Sex; Tribe (Chippewa unless stated otherwise); Ward (yes/no); Degree of Blood (Father- Mother- Child); At Jurisdiction Where Enrolled (Yes/No); (If no – Where – Post Office, State)

1932-	Lafraniere, Lawrence; 1929-May 21; male; no; ¼+; ¼+; ¼+; no; Hardin, Mont
1930-1479	Lafrombois, Joseph; 1928-Oct 4; male; no; ¼+; ¼+; ¼+; no; Bottineau, ND
1929-2563	Lafrombois, Delima; 1928-Nov; fem; yes; ¼+; ¼+; ¼+; yes
1932-	Langan, Cecelia; 1929-May 10; fem; yes; ¼+; ¼+; ¼+; no; Boggy Creek, Manitoba
1930-1570	Laroque, Floyd; 1928-Aug 28; male; no; ¼+; ¼+; ¼+; no; Dunseith, ND
1929-2839	Laverdure, Eva Elizabeth; 1929-April 15; fem; yes; ¼+; ¼+; ¼+; yes
1929-2867	Lebrun, Elizabeth; 1928-Nov 6; fem; yes; ¼+; ¼+; ¼+; yes
1930-1220	Ledeaux, Rosilia; 1928; fem; no; ¼+; ¼+; ¼+; yes
1932-	Left Hand, Elaine Cecelia; 1928-Oct 29; male[sic]; no; F; ¼+; ¼+; no; Kenel, SD
1928-2853	Lefort, Dora Katherine; 1928; fem; no; ¼+; ¼+; ¼+; no; St.Paul, Minn
1929-2929	L'Esparance, Arthur; 1928-Nov 11; male; yes; ¼+; ¼+; ¼+; no; Ft.Totten, ND
1929-2932	L'Esparance, Agnes Theresa; 1928-Nov 3; fem; yes; ¼+; ¼+; ¼+; yes
	Lillie, Alma Blanch; 1928-July 2; fem; yes; ¼+; ¼+; ¼+; no; Nishu, ND
1932-	Lind, John Harry; 1929-March 1; male; yes; W; ¼+; ¼; yes
1929-2985	Lonick, Vernon Phillip; 1929-March 28; fem[sic]; no; Neg;¼+; ¼; no; Devils Lake, ND
1930-1263	Malaterre, Emil; 1928; male; no; ¼+; ¼+; ¼+; yes
1932-	Manson, William; 1928-Oct 24; male; no; W; ¼+; ¼; no; Rolla, ND
1930-1303	Marcellais, Clarence Jos; 1928-Aug 1; male; yes; ¼+; ¼+; ¼+; yes
1929-3049	Marcil, Antone Albert; 1928-Dec 17; male; no; ¼+; ¼+; ¼+; Fonda, ND
1931-1546	Martell, Collin Joseph; 1930-April 2; male; no; ¼+; ¼+; ¼+; yes
1932-	Martell, John Michael; 1928-Oct 4; male; yes; ¼+; ¼+; ¼+; no; Poplar, Mont
1932-	Mathias, Gerald Norman; 1928-Aug 4; male; yes; W; ¼+; ¼; no; Bainville, Mont
1930-1355	McCloud, Charles, Jr; 1929-Feb 7; male; yes; ¼+; ¼+; ¼+; yes
1932-	Morin, Kathleen; 1929-June 17; fem; yes; ¼+; ¼+; ¼+; no; Trenton, ND
1932-	Morin, Thomas Edward; 1929-May 18; male; yes;¼+;¼+;¼+; no; Medicine Lake, Mont
	Morin, Charles Christopher; 1929-Jan 1; male; no; ¼+; ¼+; ¼+; yes
1932	Morin, Alfred V; 1929-June 18; fem; no; ¼+; ¼+; ¼+; no; Trenton, ND
1932-	Murphy, Marie; 1929-May 27; fem; yes; W; ¼+; ¼; yes
1932-	Nadeau, Elmer; 1929-Feb 3; male; no; ¼+; ¼+; ¼+; yes
1930-1424	Nadeau, Fred Dominick; 1928-Aug 30; male; yes; ¼+; ¼+; ¼+; yes
1932-	Nelson, Royla Jeanne; 1929-Jan 3; fem; no; W; ¼+; ¼; no; Froid, Mont
1929-3413	Nicholas, Alfred; 1928; male; no; ¼+; ¼+; ¼+; yes
1932-	Olsen, Vierginia[sic] Norma; 1929-July 23; fem; no; W; ¼+; ¼; no; Rolla, ND
1929-3468	Parisien, Joan O'Arc[sic]; 1928; fem; no; ¼+; ¼+; ¼+; yes
1930-1460	Parisien, Mary Lillian; 1929-June 18; fem; yes; ¼+; ¼+; ¼+; yes
1930-1502	Parisien, Ralph Oliver; 1929-March 21; male; yes; ¼+; ¼+; ¼+; yes
1929-3497	Parisien, Michael George; 1928-Oct 8; male; no; ¼+; ¼+; ¼+; yes
1929-3508	Patnaud, Agnes Laverne; 1929-June 19; fem; yes; ¼+; ¼+; ¼+; yes
1930-1515	Patnaud, Stanilaus; 1929-May 20; male; yes; ¼+; ¼+; ¼+; yes
	Paul (Jeannott) Mary Madeline; 1929-August 2; fem; yes; ¼+;¼+;¼+; no; St.John, ND
1929-3623	Peterson, Dolores Elaine; 1929-April 24; fem; no; W; ¼+; ¼; no; Yelm, Wash
1929-3646	Plante, Mary Angeline; 1929-Jan 1; fem; yes; ¼+; ¼+; ¼+; no; Devils Lake, ND
1932-	Poitra, Joseph; 1929-May 16; male; no; ¼+; ¼+; ¼+; yes
1928-3625	Poitra, Rachel Sylvia; 1928-Dec 19; fem; yes; ¼+; ¼+; ¼+; yes

Turtle Mountain Reservation
Live Births

Key: Census Roll Number; Surname, Given; Date of Birth (Year-Month-Day); Sex; Tribe (Chippewa unless stated otherwise); Ward (yes/no); Degree of Blood (Father- Mother- Child); At Jurisdiction Where Enrolled (Yes/No); (If no – Where – Post Office, State)

1929-3732	Poitra, John Ernest; 1928-Oct 26; male; yes; ¼+; ¼+; ¼+; yes
	Poitra, David John; 1928-Nov 6; male; no; ¼+; ¼+; ¼+; no; Boggy Creek, Manitoba
1930-1608	Poitra, Ina; 1928; fem; yes; ¼+; ¼+; ¼+; yes
1929-3829	Premeau, Theresa Dolores; 1928-Dec 12; fem; yes; ¼+; ¼+; ¼+; yes
1929-3834	Premeau, Arthur Roger; 1929-March 6; male; yes; ¼+; ¼+; ¼+; yes
1929-3848	Purdy, Clarence Wm; 1928-Nov 3; male; no; W; ¼+; ¼; yes
1932-	Rardon[sic], Cosette Pauline; 1929-Feb 6; fem; yes; W; ¼+; ¼; no; Cando, ND
1932-	Reardon, James Michael; 1928-Dec 25; male; yes; W; ¼+; ¼; yes
1930-2337	Reflection Man, Blue Thunder; 1929-June 28; male; yes; F; F; F; no; Dunseith, ND
1929-3873	Renault, Grace; 1929-June 24; fem; no; ¼+; ¼+; ¼+; yes
1929-3874	Renault, Grant; 1929-June 24; male; no; ¼+; ¼+; ¼+; yes
1932-	Renville, Rose Myrtle; 1929-May 17; fem; yes; ¼+; ¼+; ¼+; no; Buford, ND
1932-	Riendeau, Luciana; 1928-Oct 27; fem; no; W; ¼+; ¼; no; Rolette, ND
1929-3889	Richard, Willard Hubert; 1929-Jan 10; male; yes; ¼+; ¼+; ¼+; no; St.John, ND
1932-	Robert, Edgar Norbert; 1929-Sept 15; male; no; ¼+; ¼+; ¼+; no; Thorne, ND
1932-	Rossknecht, Ralph; 1929-Jan 1; male; no; W; ¼+; ¼; no; Hot Springs, SD
1929-3930	Roussin, Louis Joseph; 1929-March 5; male; no; ¼+; ¼+; ¼+; yes
1928-3948	San Grait, Madeline; 1928; fem; yes; ¼+; ¼+; ¼+; yes
1932-	Shafer, Leonard Palmer; 1929-May 13; male; no; W; ¼+; ¼; no; Flaxville, Mont
1932-	Shireback, James Edward; 1929-June 9; male; no; W; ¼+; ¼; no; Wilton, ND
1931-2282	Shanks, Marie Lyda; 1929-Jan 6; fem; no; W; ¼+; ¼; no; Mt.Hood, Ore
1929-4006	Slater, Albina; 1928-Oct 17; fem; yes; ¼+; ¼+; ¼+; no; St.John, ND
1932-	Staley, David; 1929-Jan 5; male; no; W; ¼+; ¼; no; Froid, Mont
1932-	St.Germain, Maynard Sylvester; 1928-Dec 5; male; no; ¼+; ¼+; ¼+; no; St.John, ND
1932-	Tetrault, Cecelia; 1928-July 27; fem; yes; ¼+; ¼+; ¼+; yes
1932-	Thibert, Pauline Marcella; 1928-Aug 15; fem; yes; ¼+; ¼+; ¼+; no; St.John, ND
1932-	Thibert, Wanelda Jeannette; 1928-Sept 19; fem; yes; ¼+; ¼+; ¼+; no; St.John, ND
1932-	Tinkay, Violet Mar[sic]; 1929-June 16; fem; no; W; ¼+; ¼; no; Plentywood, Mont
1931-2683	Trothier, Maxine Rosella; 1929-June 4; fem; yes; ¼+; ¼+; ¼+; no; Phillip, Mont
1929-4242	Trothier, Sylvia; 1929-12/4; fem; yes; ¼+; ¼+; ¼+; yes
1932-	Trothier, Betty; 1928-Nov 9; fem; no; ¼+; ¼+; ¼+; no; Harlem, Mont
1930-2670	Turcott, Alvina; 1919-Feb 8; fem; no; ¼+; F; ¼; no; Dunseith, ND
1930-1788	Vallie, Helen; 192-March 4; fem; yes; ¼+; ¼+; ¼+; yes
1929-4310	Vandal, Edmund Francis; 1929-March 31; male; yes; ¼+; ¼+; ¼+; no; Trenton, ND
1929-4326	Vandal, Lorene; 1929-May 29; fem; no; ¼+; ¼+; ¼+; no; Rolla, ND
1932-	Vivier, Catherine Inez; 1929-May 19; fem; yes; ¼+; ¼+; ¼+; no; Devils Lake, ND
1930-1837	Vivier, Norbert; 1928-Sept 2; male; yes; ¼+; ¼+; ¼+; yes
1929-4399	Wallett, Cecelia Gladys; 1928-Dec 5; fem; no; ¼+; ¼+; ¼+; yes
1929-4411	Wallett, John Baptiste; 1928-May 12; male; yes; ¼+; ¼+; ¼+; yes
1930-1846	Wallett, Alvina; 1928; fem; no; ¼+; ¼+; ¼+; yes
1932-	Warren, Wm Belgarde; 1928-July 13; male; no; ¼+; ¼+; ¼+; yes
1931-2190	Wilkie, Martha; 1928-Aug; fem; no; ¼+; ¼+; ¼+; yes
	Wilkie, Name unknown; 1928-Nov 20; fem; no; ¼+; ¼+; ¼+; yes
1930-1922	Wilkie, Lillian; 1928; fem; yes; ¼+; ¼+; ¼+; yes

Turtle Mountain Reservation
Live Births
Key: Census Roll Number; Surname, Given; Date of Birth (Year-Month-Day); Sex; Tribe (Chippewa unless stated otherwise); Ward (yes/no); Degree of Blood (Father- Mother- Child); At Jurisdiction Where Enrolled (Yes/No); (If no – Where – Post Office, State)

1930-2859 ~~Wong~~ Wond, Herbert; 1928-Aug 10; male; no; Chin;¼+; ¼; no; Devils Lake, ND

Turtle Mountain Reservation
Additional Names

Key: Census, Census Roll Number; Surname, Given; Date of Birth (Year-Month-Day); Live Births; Still Births; Sex; Tribe (Chippewa unless stated otherwise); Ward (yes/no); Degree of Blood (Father- Mother- Child); At Jurisdiction Where Enrolled (Yes/No); (If no – Where – Post Office, State)

[Note: The key has changed slightly from previous Live Births pages]

<u>Births Occurring between the Dates of **July 1, 1928** and **June 30, 1929** to Parents Enrolled at Jurisdiction</u>

1929 #1722 Frederick, William; 1928-Dec 19; yes; no; m; yes; ½;½;½; yes
1932 #1623 Dubois, Alex; 1928-Sept 4; yes; no; m; yes; ½;½;½; no; Ft.Totten, ND
1929 #2440 Lafontain, Alice; 1928-Nov 25; yes; no; f; no; ½;½;½; yes
1929 #4351 Villeneuve, Evangeline; 1928-Sept 26; yes; no; f; no; ½;½;½; yes
1929 # 884 Bruce, Raymond; 1928-July 29; yes; no; m; yes; ½;½;½; yes
1929 # 350 Azure, James; 1929-May 26; yes; no; m; no; ½;½;½; yes
1929 # 590 Christenson or Belgarde, Ruth; 1929-May 9; yes; no; f; no; W; ¼+; ¼; no; Warwick, ND
1929 #4425 Wallett, Lillian; 1929-March 5; yes; no; f; yes; ½;½;½; yes
1929 #3620 Perronteau, Alex Peter; 1929-March 15; yes; no; m; yes; ½;½;½; yes

(Children who were born alive and died before enrollment)

Died before
enrollment   Keplin, Rose; 1928-Sept 22; yes; no; f; no; ½;½;½; yes
    do   Belgarde, Infant; 1929-Jan 9; yes; no; m; yes; ½;½;½; yes
    do   Azure, Ann; 1929-Mch 30; yes; no; f; yes; ½;½;½; no; Rolla, ND
    do   Azure, Mary; 1929-Mch 30; yes; no; f; yes; ½;½;½; no; Rolla, ND
    do   Belgarde, Mary Dorothy; 1928-Sept 22; yes; no; f; no; ½;½;½; yes

Turtle Mountain Reservation
Live Births
Key: Census Roll Number; Surname, Given; Date of Birth (Year-Month-Day); Sex; Tribe (Chippewa unless stated otherwise); Ward (yes/no); Degree of Blood (Father- Mother- Child); At Jurisdiction Where Enrolled (Yes/No); (If no – Where – Post Office, State)

Births Occurring between the Dates of **July 1, 1929** and **June 30, 1930** to Parents Enrolled at Jurisdiction

1930-	22	Allard, Rita; 1929-Aug 25; fem; no; ¼+; ¼+; ¼+; yes
1930-	5	Alex, Morris; 1929; male; yes; Syrian; ¼+; ¼; yes
1932-		Allard, Michael J; 1930-June 18; male; no; ¼+; ¼+; ¼+; yes
1932-		Allery, John; 1930-May 1; male; yes; ¼+; ¼+; ¼+; no; Dunseith, ND
1931-	23	Allery, Donald Fred; 1930; May 11; male; yes; ¼+; ¼+; ¼+; no; Dunseith, ND
1930-	73	Allery, Evelyn Dora; 1929-Nov 6; fem; no; ¼+; ¼+; ¼+; yes
1930-	105	Amyott, Mary Cecilia; 1929-Sept 2; fem; yes; ¼+; ¼+; ¼+; yes
1930-	50	Azure, Cecelia Doris; 1930-Feb 24; fem; yes; ¼+; ¼+; ¼+; yes
		Azure, Mary Lola; 1930-April 9; fem; yes; ¼+; ¼+; ¼+; yes
1931-	123	Azure, Clarence Richard; 1930-April 28; male; no; ¼+; ¼+; ¼+; no; Dunseith, ND
1931-	99	Azure, Fred, Jr; 1930-Feb 16; male; yes; ¼+; ¼+; ¼+; no; Globe, Ariz
1930-	558	Azure, Clifford Sylvester; 1930-March 9; male; no; ¼+; ¼+; ¼+; yes
1930-	84	Azure, Marie Louise; 1930-Feb 5; fem; yes; ¼+; ¼+; ¼+; yes
1930-	229	Babach, Peter; 1929-Oct 1; male; no; W; ¼+; ¼; no; [blank]
1932-		Baston, Robert; 1929-Aug 28; male; yes; ¼+; ¼+; ¼+; no; Elbowoods, ND
1932-		Bauer, Joseph; 1930-Feb 12; male; no; W; ¼+; ¼; no; Brocton, Mont
1932-		Beauchman, Marie Pearl; 1929-Oct 24; fem; yes; ¼+; ¼+; ¼+; no; Wolf Point, Mont
		Beaudry, Theresa Dorothy; 1930-June 2; male[sic]; no; ¼+; ¼+; ¼+; no; Poplar, Mont
1930-	401	Belgarde, Harold Elmer; 1929-Oct 12; male; no; ¼+; ¼+; ¼+; no; Omemee, ND
1931-	216	Belgarde, Maragret[sic] L; 1929-July Aug[sic] 1; fem; yes; ¼+; ¼+; ¼+; yes
1931	214	Belgarde, Alice; 1929-Oct 25; fem; yes; ¼+; ¼+; ¼+; yes
1931-	271	Belgarde, No name; 1930-March 5; male; yes; ¼+; ¼+; ¼+; no; Elbowoods, ND
1930-	373	Belgarde, Louis; 1929-Sept 4; male; yes; ¼+; ¼+; ¼+; no; Nishu, ND
1930-	156	Bercier, Agnes Vitaline; 1930-March 21; fem; no; ¼+; ¼+; ¼+; yes
1930-	420	Bercier, George; 1930-March 9; male; yes; ¼+; ¼+; ¼+; yes
1932-		Boe, Ralph Edwin; 1929-July 29; male; no; W; ¼+; ¼; no; Long Beach, Cal
1930-	192	Bradford, Stanley Emil; 1929-July 3; male; yes; ¼+; ¼+; ¼+; yes
1931-	314	Brien, Aloysius; 1930-June 30; male; yes; ¼+; ¼+; ¼+; yes
1930-	535	Brien, Albert Verne; 1929-July 10; male; no; ¼+; ¼+; ¼+; no; Trenton, ND
1930-	226	Brien, Wm Leo James; 1930-Jan 13; male; yes; ¼+; ¼+; ¼+; yes
1931-	369	Brunnell, Phillip Jerome; 1930-May 3; male; yes; ¼+; ¼+; ¼+; yes
1930-	286	Champagne, Frank; 1930-Jan 29; male; yes; ¼+; ¼+; ¼+; yes
1932-		Charette, Geo William; 1929-Oct 28; male; yes; ¼+; ¼+; ¼+; no; Medicine Lake, Mont
1932-		Counts, Lloyd; 1930-Jan 30; male; yes; ¼+; ¼+; ¼+; no; Dunseith, ND
1932-		Cotterell, Carl Raymond; 1930-Jan 10; male; no; W; ¼+; ¼; no; Kelispell[sic], Mont
1931-	465	Davis, Verna Cecelia; 1929-Sept 9; fem; yes; ¼+; ¼+; ¼+; yes
		Davis, Verlin Clifford; 1930-May 28; male; yes; ¼+; ¼+; ¼+; yes
1930-	392	Davis, Norbert; 1929-Sept 11; male; no; ¼+; ¼+; ¼+; yes
1930-	667	Davis, Leon Felix; 1929-Sept 11; male; no; ¼+; ¼+; ¼+; no; Sidney, Mont
1931-	477	Davis, Maggie Barbara; 1930-April 6; fem; yes; ¼+; ¼+; ¼+; yes
1930-	472	Decoteau, Cecelia; 1929-Ag 24; male[sic]; yes; ¼+; ¼+; ¼+; yes
1930-	447	Decoteau, Sylvester; 1929; male; yes; ¼+; ¼+; ¼+; yes

Turtle Mountain Reservation
Live Births
Key: Census Roll Number; Surname, Given; Date of Birth (Year-Month-Day); Sex; Tribe (Chippewa unless stated otherwise); Ward (yes/no); Degree of Blood (Father- Mother- Child); At Jurisdiction Where Enrolled (Yes/No); (If no – Where – Post Office, State)

1930- 428 Decoteau, Ethel Laverne; 1929-July 26; fem; yes; ¼+; ¼+; ¼+; no; St.John, ND
1930- 460 Decoteau, Lorraine C; 1930-May 10; fem; yes; ¼+; ¼+; ¼+; yes
1931- 624 Dejarlais, Antoine; 1930-April 9; male; yes; ¼+; ¼+; ¼+; yes
1930- 545 Delorme, Lucy Rhea; 1930-Feb 26; fem; no; ¼+; ¼+; ¼+; yes
1931- 697 Delorme, Genevieve; 1930-April 11; fem; yes; ¼+; ¼+; ¼+; yes
1930- 566 Delorme, Wendell John; 1930-March 21; male; no; ¼+; ¼+; ¼+; yes
1930- 784 Delorme, Calixite; 1929-Sept 26; male; yes; ¼+; ¼+; ¼+; yes
1930- 805 Demarais, Ernest Martin; 1929-Oct 24; male; yes; ¼+; ¼+; ¼+; no; Malta, Mont
1932-   Demarais, Victoria; 1929; fem; yes; ¼+; ¼+; ¼+; no; Boggy Creek, Manitoba
1930- 596 Dionne, Edward; 1929-Dec 5; male; yes; ¼+; ¼+; ¼+; yes
1930- 606 Dionne, Rosa; 1929-August 10; male; no; ¼+; ¼+; ¼+; yes
1931- 807 Faguant, Emma Rose; 1930-March 30; fem; yes; ¼+; ¼+; ¼+; no; Dunseith, ND
1931- 827 Falcon, Julia Gladys; 1929-Nov 22; fem; no; ¼+; ¼+; ¼+; no; Trenton, ND
1931- 823 Fassett (Frederick), James; 1929-July 23; male; yes; ¼+; ¼+; ¼+; no; Thorne, ND
1932-   Falcon, Peter Virgil; 1929-Aug 11; male; yes; ¼+; ¼+; ¼+; no; Trenton, ND
1931- 920 Gladue, Arthur C; 1930-June 30; male; no; ¼+; ¼+; ¼+; yes
1931- 920[sic] Gourneau, Charles Joe; 1930-May 1; male; yes; ¼+; ¼+; ¼+; yes
1930- 753 Gourneau, Nora Laura; 1930-Jan 3; fem; yes; ¼+; ¼+; ¼+; yes
1930- 766 Gourneau, Marie Stella; Sept 21-1930; fem; yes; ¼+; ¼+; ¼+; yes
1932-   Gourneau, Nora Stella; 1930-April 3; fem; yes; ¼+; ¼+; ¼+; yes
1932-   Grandbois, Leona Gertrude; 1930-April 24; fem; no; ¼+; ¼+; ¼+; no; East Grand Forks, Minn
1931- 979 Grandbois, Celie Geraldine; 1930-June 22; fem; yes; ¼+; ¼+; ¼+; no; Dagmar, Mont
1931-1001 Grandbois, Phillip Harrison; 1929-July 24; male; no; ¼+; ¼+; ¼+; no; Dagmar, Mont
1931- 977 Grant, Claude Ulysses; 1930-April 4; male; yes; ¼+; ¼+; ¼+; yes
1930- 907 Grant, Andrew Albert; 1929-August 1; male; yes; ¼+; ¼+; ¼+; yes
1930- 840 Grant, Wm Vincent; 1930-Jan 25; male; yes; ¼+; ¼+; ¼+; yes
1932   Gauthier, Jos Martin C; 1929-August 28; male; no; W; ¼+; ¼; no; Willow City, ND
              Herman, Florence; 1929-Aug 29; fem; yes; ¼+; ¼+; ¼+; no; Devils Lake, ND
1930-1268 Houle, Joseph Wilfred; 1929-Dec 23; male; no; ¼+; ¼+; ¼+; no; Bottineau, ND
1930- 885 Houle, George Joseph; 1930-March 18; male; yes; ¼+; ¼+; ¼+; yes
1932-   Jacqmarct, Marchetta; 1929-Nov 24; fem; yes; ¼+; ¼+; ¼+; no; Ft.Totten, ND
1931-1060 Jeannotte, Mary Rita; 1930-April 13; fem; yes; ¼+; ¼+; ¼+; yes
1932-   Jerome, Alex Lawrence; 1929-Sept 17; male; yes; ¼+; ¼+; ¼+; yes
1930- 957 Jerome, Alfred Daniel; 1930-Jan 13; male; yes; ¼+; ¼+; ¼+; yes
1932-   Johnson, Andy; 1930-March 27; male; no; W; ¼+; ¼; no; Plentywood, Mont
              Jollibois, Lucille; 1929-Aubust 25; fem; no; ¼+; ¼+; ¼+; no; Thorne, ND
1930p-968[sic] Jollie, David Wm Jos; 1929-Nov; male; yes; ¼+; ¼+; ¼+; yes
1932-   Justice, Vernon Richard; 1929-July 4; male; no; W; ¼+; ¼; no; Grenora, ND
1931-1126 Keplin (Brien), Alex William; 1930-June 8; male; yes; ¼+; ¼+; ¼+; yes
1932-   Keplin, Rose; 1929-Dec 2; fem; no; ¼+; ¼+; ¼+; yes
1932-   Knutson, Marchetta M; 1930-March 3; fem; no; W; ¼+; ¼; no; Rolette, ND
1930-1066 Lafontain, M/Ernestine[sic]; 1929-Nov 18; fem; yes; ¼+; ¼+; ¼+; yes
1930-1018 Laducer, David Joseph; 1929-July 19; male; yes; ¼+; ¼+; ¼+; yes
1930-1022 Laducer, Joseph Rogers; 1929-Oct 22; male; yes; ¼+; ¼+; ¼+; yes

Turtle Mountain Reservation
Live Births
Key: Census Roll Number; Surname, Given; Date of Birth (Year-Month-Day); Sex; Tribe (Chippewa unless stated otherwise); Ward (yes/no); Degree of Blood (Father- Mother- Child); At Jurisdiction Where Enrolled (Yes/No); (If no – Where – Post Office, State)

	Lafloe, Joseph Alfred; 1929-July 31; male; yes; ¼+; ¼+; ¼+; yes
1932-	Lafontain, Norma; 1929-Aug 14; fem; yes; ¼+; ¼+; ¼+; no; Roy, Mont
1930-1037	Lafontain, William Harry; 1929-Nov 8; male; no; ¼+; ¼+; ¼+; yes
1932-	Lafontain, Mary Jane; 1929-Aug 24; fem; no; ¼+; ¼+; ¼+; yes
1930-1070	Lafontain, Rose Alice; 1930-Jan 1; fem; yes; ¼+; ¼+; ¼+; yes
1932-	Lafontain, Gilbert; 1930-March 16; male; yes; ¼+; ¼+; ¼+; no; Boggy Creek, Manitoba
1932-	Lafrance, William; 1930-Jan 19; male; no; ¼+; ¼+; ¼+; yes
1930-1107	Lafrombois, Patrice, Jr; 1930-Jan 13; male; yes; ¼+; ¼+; ¼+; yes
1931-1386	Lagimodiere, Leonard; 1929-July 4; male; no; ¼+; ¼+; ¼+; no; Medicine Lake, Mont
1930-1504	Lambert, Mary Joyce; 1929-Sept 6; fem; yes; ¼+; ¼+; ¼+; no; Dunseith, ND
1931-1406	Lambert, Augustine; 1929-Aug 21; male; yes; ¼+; ¼+; ¼+; yes
1931-1414	Landry, Mary Juanita; 1930-April 10; fem; no; ¼+; ¼+; ¼+; no; Rolla, ND
1932-	Lang, Edna Marie; 1929-July 17; fem; yes; ¼+; ¼+; ¼+; no; Tokio, ND
1930-1133	Landry, Florence Jane; 1929-July 9; fem; no; ¼+; ¼+; ¼+; yes
1932-	Laroque, Loretta; 1920-Feb 23; fem; yes; ¼+; ¼+; ¼+; no; Medicine Lake, Mont
1832-	Laroque, Milton Vernon; 1930-Jan 7; male; no; ¼+; ¼+; ¼+; no; Trenton, ND
1930-1557	Laroque, Jos A Lawrence; 1929-July 16; male; yes; ¼+; ¼+; ¼+; no; St.John, ND
1932-	Laresen, Larrian; 1930-June 19; male; yes; W; ¼+; ¼; no; Devils Lake, ND
1930-1174	Lavallie, Antonia Sylvio; 1929-Dec 29; male; yes; ¼+; ¼+; ¼+; yes
1931-1511	Lavallie, Marguerite J; 1930-Feb 20; fem; yes; ¼+; ¼+; ¼+; no; Dunseith, ND
1930-1205	Laverdure, Rita Evelyn; 1929-Aug 19; fem; yes; ¼+; ¼+; ¼+; yes
1932-	Laverdure, No name; 1930-June 16; fem; no; ¼+; ¼+; ¼+; Dunseith, ND
1932-	Laverdure, Ralph Gerald; 1930-April 28; male; yes; ¼+; ¼+; ¼+; no; Devils Lake, ND
1932-	Laverdure, Nora June; 1930-June 11; fem; yes; ¼+; ¼+; ¼+; no; Dooley, Mont
1932-	Lecompt, Garley; 1930-May 4; male; no; ¼+; ¼+; ¼+; no; Bainville, Mont
1931-1597	Lefort, Mary Agnes; 1930-May 7; fem; no; ¼+; ¼+; ¼+; no; St.Paul, Minn
1932-	Lillie, Rose; 1929-Dec 27; fem; yes; ¼+; ¼+; ¼+; no; Nishu, ND
1930-1236	Lillie, Charles Stanley; 1929-Aug 5; male; yes; ¼+; ¼+; ¼+; yes
1930-1756	Lindgren, Ramona Marie; 1930-Jan 1; fem; yes; ¼+; ¼+; ¼+; no; Fargo, ND
1931-1624	Little Boy, Mary Eva; 1929-July 31; f; yes; F; F; F; yes
1930-1788	Machipeness, Elmer; 1929-July 22; m; yes; F; F; F; no; Dunseith, ND
1930-1909	Mekwam, Irene; 1929-July 15; f; yes; F; F; F; yes
1930-1304	Marcellais, Peter; 1929-July 29; m; yes; ¼+; ¼+; ¼+; yes
1931-1526	Marion, Narcissus Isabel; 1930-June 21; f; yes; ¼+; ¼+; ¼+; yes
1932-	Marion, George Henry; 1929-July 6; m; no; ¼+; ¼+; ¼+; no; Grenora, ND
1932-	Manson, Mary H; 1929-Oct 29; f; yes; W; ¼+; ¼; no; Antler, ND
1932-	Martin, Mary Rose; 1929-Oct 3; f; yes; ¼+; ¼+; ¼+; no; Dagmar, Mont
1930-1337	Martin, Rose Anne; 1929-Nov 19; f; yes; ¼+; ¼+; ¼+; yes
1931-1774	Mathias, James Raymond; 1929-Nov 25; m; yes; W; ¼+; ¼; no; Bainville, Mont
1931-1576	McCloud, Therese; 1930-June 3; f; yes; ¼+; ¼+; ¼+; yes
	McCloud, Vivian Virginia; 1929-Nov 24; f; yes; ¼+; ¼+; ¼+; yes
1932-1584	McVay, Raymond R; 1930-Jan 28; m; yes; ¼+; ¼+; ¼+; yes
1931-1908	Monette, Jos Howard; 1930-June 17; m; yes; W; ¼+; ¼; no; [blank]
1932-	Moore, Sarah Jean; 1929-Aug 21; f; yes; W; ¼+; ¼; no; Central City, Iowa

Turtle Mountain Reservation
Live Births

Key: Census Roll Number; Surname, Given; Date of Birth (Year-Month-Day); Sex; Tribe (Chippewa unless stated otherwise); Ward (yes/no); Degree of Blood (Father- Mother- Child); At Jurisdiction Where Enrolled (Yes/No); (If no – Where – Post Office, State)

	Morin, Frank Joseph; 1929-Aug 14; m; yes; ¼+; ¼+; ¼+; no; Dunseith, ND
1930-1390	Morin, Irene; 1929; f; yes; ¼+; ¼+; ¼+; yes
1932-	Morin, Joseph; 1929-Sept 13; m; no; ¼+; ¼+; ¼+; no; Devils Lake, ND
1931-1835	Morin, Dorothy Mae; 1930-April 19; f; yes; ¼+; ¼+; ¼+; no; Fortuna, ND
	Morin, Rose; 1930-Jan 3; f; yes; ¼+; ¼+; ¼+; yes
1932-	Morin, Bernard; 1930-June 9; m; no; ¼+; ¼+; ¼+; no; Trenton, ND
1931-1629	Morin, Joseph; 1930-May 18; m; yes; ¼+; ¼+; ¼+; yes
1931-1946	Nicholas, Donald Edgar; 1930-April 25; m; yes; ¼+; ¼+; ¼+; yes[sic]; Devils Lake, ND
1931-1957	Nwenapi, Alex; 1930-Feb 15; m; yes; F; F; F; no; Dunseith, ND
1932	Olsen, Elaine Frances; 1930-May 31; f; no; W; ¼+; ¼; no; Cando, ND
1930-1455	Page, Raymond; 1929-Sept 14; m; yes; ¼+; ¼+; ¼+; yes
1930-1498	Parisien, Mary Madeline; 1929-Dec 7; f; no; ¼+; ¼+; ¼+; yes
1931-1736	Parisien, Charles Arthur; 1930-Feb 14; m; yes; ¼+; ¼+; ¼+; yes
1931-1993	Patnaud, Francis; 1929-Nov 13; m; yes; ¼+; ¼+; ¼+; no; Devils Lake, ND
1932-	Patnaud, Joseph B; 1930-Jan 30; m; yes; ¼+; ¼+; ¼+; no; Medicine Lake, Mont
1930-2147	Paul, Mary Madeline; 1929-Aug 2; f; yes; ¼+; ¼+; ¼+; no; St.John, ND
1932-	Pippenger, Viola Phoebe; 1929-Oct 4; f; no; W; ¼+; ¼; no; Trenton, ND
1930-1552	Plante, Alfred; 1929-Oct 4; m; yes; ¼+; ¼+; ¼+; yes
1932-	Plante, Francis James; 1929-July 22; m; yes; ¼+; W; ¼; no; Kalamazoo, Mich
1932-	Poitra, Delima; 1930-June 17; f; yes; ¼+; ¼+; ¼+; no; Boggy Creek, Mani
1930-1597	Poitra, Joseph Norman; 1929-July 17; m; yes; ¼+; ¼+; ¼+; yes
1932-	Poitra, Raymond; 1930-May 27; m; yes; ¼+; ¼+; ¼+; yes
1932-	Poitra, Lillian; 1929-Oct 8; f; no; ¼+; ¼+; ¼+; no; Devils Lake, ND
19[sic]	Poitra, Stella; 1930-March 16; f; yes; ¼+; ¼+; ¼+; yes
1930-1567	Poitra, Melvin Francis; 1929-Nov 9; m; yes; ¼+; ¼+; ¼+; yes
1932-	Poitra, Ernestine; 1929-Dec 15; f; no; ¼+; ¼+; ¼+; no; Boggy Creek, Mani
1932-	Poitra, Julius Maxim; 1929-Aug 5; m; yes; ¼+; ¼+; ¼+; no; Dunseith, ND
1932-	Poitra, Arline Jos; 1929-Sept 15; m; yes; ¼+; ¼+; ¼+; no; Dunseith, ND
1932-	Poitra, Dorothy; 1929-Dec 29; f; no; ¼+; ¼+; ¼+; no; Dunseith, ND
1930-2293	Poitra, Marion; 1929-July 26; f; yes; ¼+; ¼+; ¼+; yes
1930-2294	Poitra, Theresa; 1929-July 26; f; yes; ¼+; ¼+; ¼+; yes
1930-2250	Poitra, John Jos Clarence; 1929-Aug 27; m; yes; ¼+; ¼+; ¼+; no; Dunseith, ND
1932-	Poitra, Laura; 1929-Oct 8; f; no; ¼+; ¼+; ¼+; no; Froid, Mont
1930-2328	Premeau, No name; 1929; f; yes; ¼+; ¼+; ¼+; yes
1932-	Riendeau, Cecelia; 1929-Nov 23; f; no; W; ¼+; ¼; no; Thorne, ND
1932-	Robert, Ophelia; 1930-March 25; f; yes; ¼+; ¼+; ¼+; no; Thorne, ND
1932-	Roy, Mont Delia Iris Elaine; 1929-Nov 5; f; yes; W; ¼+; ¼; no; Rolette, ND
1930-1684	Roussin, Leonard; 1930-March 10; m; no; ¼+; ¼+; ¼+; yes
1932-	Salo, Francis Michael; 1929-Lct 11; m; no; ¼+; ¼+; ¼+; no; Minot, ND
1930-1693	San Grait, Joseph; 1929-Oct 20; m; yes; ¼+; ¼+; ¼+; yes
1931-1967	Schindler, Edna Patricia; 1930-May 17; f; yes; ¼+; ¼+; ¼+; yes
1932-	Short, Mary Vivian; 1929-Aug 1; f; no; ¼+; ¼+; ¼+; no; Malta, Mont
1930-1705	Short, Francis; 1929; m; yes; ¼+; ¼+; ¼+; yes
1932-	Sindt, Gladys Agnes; 1929-Aug 15; f; yes; W; ¼+; ¼; no; Big Fork, Mont

Turtle Mountain Reservation
Live Births
Key: Census Roll Number; Surname, Given; Date of Birth (Year-Month-Day); Sex; Tribe (Chippewa unless stated otherwise); Ward (yes/no); Degree of Blood (Father- Mother- Child); At Jurisdiction Where Enrolled (Yes/No); (If no – Where – Post Office, State)

1932-	Slater, William John; 1919-Sept 6; m; yes; ¼+; ¼+; ¼+; no; St.John, ND
1932-	Smith, Ruth Adele M; 1929-Oct 12; f; no; ¼+; ¼+; ¼+; yes
1932-	Mary Winifred; 1929-Dec 16; f; yes; ¼+; ¼+; ¼+; yes
	Smith, Cecelia May; 1930-Feb 1; f; yes; ¼+; ¼+; ¼+; yes
1931-2385	St.Clair, Lucille Alvina; 1929-July 18; f; yes; ¼+; ¼+; ¼+; no; Dunseith, ND
1932-	Smigiel, Carrie Joyce; 1929-Dec 29; f; no; W; ¼+; ¼; no; Superior, Wis
1930-2584	Tetrault, Dorothea Mae; 1929-Oct 16; f; yes; ¼+; ¼+; ¼+; no; Rolette, ND
1932-	Thibert, Dorothy Margaret; 1929-Oct 30; f; yes; no; St.John, ND
1931-2036	Thomas, Jero Francis; 1930-Jan 29; m; yes; ¼+; ¼+; ¼+; yes
1931-2546	Trothier, Wayne Sanford; 1930-April 15; m; yes; ¼+; ¼+; ¼+; no; Devils Lake, ND
1931-2536	Trothier, Eugene; 1930-April 9; m; no; ¼+; ¼+; ¼+; yes
1930-2680	Trothier, Mary Louise; 1929-Sept 15; f; yes; ¼+; ¼+; ¼+; no; Devils Lake, ND
1931-2582	Turcott, June Marvena; 1930-June 4; f; yes; ¼+; ¼+; ¼+; no; Trenton, ND
1932-	Turcott, Viola Margaret; 1929-Oct 6; f; no; ¼+; ¼+; ¼+; no; Trenton, ND
1930-2683	Turcott, Henry; 1929-July 2; m; no; ¼+; ¼+; ¼+; no; Rolla, ND
	Vandal, Lucille; 1929-Aug; f; yes; ¼+; ¼+; ¼+; yes
1932-	Warren, Joseph John; 1930-April 1; m; no; ¼+; ¼+; ¼+; yes
1932-	Weeks, Leila Mae; 1930-Feb 18; f; no; ¼+; ¼+; ¼+; no; Forest Grove, Ore
1931-2168	Wilkie, Elizabeth C; 1930-June 2; f; no; ¼+; ¼+; ¼+; yes
1931-2191	Wilkie, Florestine; 1930-June 2; f; no; ¼+; ¼+; ¼+; yes
1930-1904	Wilkie, Marie Clara; 1929-July 7; f; yes; ¼+; ¼+; ¼+; yes
1930-1938	Wilkie, Adeline M E; 1929-Dec 21; f; no; ¼+; ¼+; ¼+; yes
1931-2248	Wilkie, Patrick; 1930-Feb 26; m; no; ¼+; ¼+; ¼+; yes
1930-1917	Wilkie, Michael Stephen; 1929; m; no; ¼+; ¼+; ¼+; yes
NE	Yepson, Virginia Ann; 1930-May 30; f; no; W; ¼+; ¼; no; Rolla, ND
1932-	Zura, Margaret; 1929-Oct 21; f; no; W; ¼+; ¼; no; Rolette, ND

Turtle Mountain Reservation
Additional Names

Key: Census, Census Roll Number; Surname, Given; Date of Birth (Year-Month-Day); Live Births; Still Births; Sex; Tribe (Chippewa unless stated otherwise); Ward (yes/no); Degree of Blood (Father- Mother- Child); Turtle Mt ~~At~~ Jurisdiction ~~Where Enrolled~~ (Yes/No); (If no – Where – Post Office, State)

[Note: The key has changed slightly from previous Live Births pages]

Births Occurring between the Dates of **July 1, 1929** and **June 30, 1930** to Parents Enrolled at Jurisdiction

1930 #1298 Malaterre, Marie Louise; 1929-July 21; yes; no; f; yes; ½;½;½; yes
1930 #1867 Wallett, Gertrude; 1919-Oct 29; yes; no; f; no; ½;½;½; yes
1930 #1169 Lattergrass, Ernest Edward; 1930-Jan 25; yes; no; m; yes; ½;½;½; yes
1930 # 929 Jeannotte, Joseph; 1930-Feb 4; yes; no; m; yes; ½;½;½; yes

[Parents not enrolled]

Parents not enrolled Sager, Teda NE; 1930-May 2; yes; no; f; no; W; ½; ¼; yes
    do   St.Arnaud, Albert NE; 1929-Dec 14; yes; no; m; no; 1/16; 1/16; 1/16; no; Ft. Totten

Turtle Mountain Reservation
Live Births

Key: Census Roll Number; Surname, Given; Date of Birth (Year-Month-Day); Sex; Tribe (Chippewa unless stated otherwise); Ward (yes/no); Degree of Blood (Father- Mother- Child); At Jurisdiction Where Enrolled (Yes/No); (If no – Where – Post Office, State)

Births Occurring between the Dates of April 1, 1930 and March 31, 1931 to Parents Enrolled at Jurisdiction

1931-	23	Allard, Clarence S; 1931-Feb 3; m; yes; ¼+; ¼+; ¼+; yes
1932		Allard, Michael J; 1930-June 18; m; no; ¼+; ¼+; ¼+; yes
1932		Allery, John; 1930-May 1; m; yes; ¼+; ¼+; ¼+; no; Dunseith, ND
1931-	23[sic]	Allery, Donald Fred; 1930-May 11; m; yes; ¼+; ¼+; ¼+; no; Dunseith, ND
1932		Allery, Doris; 1930-Oct 29; f; no; ¼+; ¼+; ¼+; yes
1931-	65	Amudson, Dolores; 1930-Oct 18; f; no; W; ¼+; ¼; yes
1931-	93	Anderson, Irene Velma; 1930-Oct 2; f; yes; W; ¼+; ¼; no; Devils Lake, ND
1932-		Azure, Margaret Mary; 1931-Feb19; f; yes; ¼+; ¼+; ¼+; no; Devils Lake, ND
1931-	80	Azure, Mary Ann; 1930-July 7; f; yes; ¼+; ¼+; ¼+; yes
1931-	81	Azure, Marie Josephine; 1930-July 7; f; yes; ¼+; ¼+; ¼+; yes
1931-	141	Azure, Lazarus; 1930-Nov 8; m; yes; ¼+; ¼+; ¼+; yes
		Azure, Mary Lola; 1930-April 9; f; yes;; ¼+; ¼+; ¼+; yes
1931-	123	Azure, Clarence R; 1930-April 28; m; no; ¼+; ¼+; ¼+; no; Dunseith, ND
1932-		Beaudry, Teresa Dorothy; 1930-June 2; f; no; ¼+; ¼+; ¼+; no; Poplar, Mont
1931-	164	Baker, Helen Blanch; 1930-July 12; f; no; ¼+; ¼+; ¼+; yes
1932		Baker, Moses; 1930-Dec 17; m; yes; ¼+; ¼+; ¼+; no; Ft.Totten, ND
1932		Baker, Marie Elizabeth; 1930-June 25; f; yes; ¼+; ¼+; ¼+; no; Ft.Totten, ND
1931-	245	Belgarde, Collin; 1931-Feb 8; m; no; ¼+; ¼+; ¼+; no; Elphinstone, Sask
1932		Bottineau, Alice; 1930-Aug 6; f; yes; ¼+; ¼+; ¼+; no; Dunseith, ND
1932		Boyer, Selina; 1930-Nov 25; f; no; ¼+; ¼+; ¼+; no; Sidney, Mont
1931-	314	Brien, Aloysius; 1930-June 30; m; yes; ¼+; ¼+; ¼+; yes
1931-	369	Brunnell, Phillip Jerome; 1930-May 3; m; yes; ¼+; ¼+; ¼+; yes
1931-	418	Braugh, Donald D; 1931-Jan 11; m; no; W; ¼+; ¼; no; Unknown, Okla
1932		Brien, Mary Celina; 1930-Dec 11; f; yes; ¼+; ¼+; ¼+; no; Dunseith, ND
1932		Brien, Laureat Frank; 1931-Feb 18; m; no; ¼+; ¼+; ¼+; no; St.John, ND
1931-	323	Bruce, Lawrence M; 1930-Aug 7; m; yes; ¼+; ¼+; ¼+; yes
1930-	226	Bruce, William; 1930; m; yes; ¼+; ¼+; ¼+; yes
1932-		Brunnell, Theresa Flora; 1930-~~Dee~~ Nov 18; f; no; ¼+; ¼+; ¼+; yes
1932-		Brunnell, Bernealia; 1931-March 28; f; no; ¼+; ¼+; ¼+; yes
1931-	331	Brunnell, Corinne Marie; 1930-Aug 1; f; yes; ¼+; ¼+; ¼+; yes
1931-	486	Barsness, Gladys Cecelia; 1930-Oct 26; f; no; W; ¼+; ¼; no; Medicine Lake, Mont
1931-1126		Brien, Alex William; 1930-June 30; m; no; ¼+; ¼+; ¼+; yes
1931-	516	Cartwright, Irene Mae; 1931-March 10; f; no; W; ¼+; ¼; no; St.John, ND
1932-		Counts, Roy; 1931-Feb 28; m; yes; W; ¼+; ¼; no; Dunseith, ND
1932		Cree, Sounding Nice; 1930; f; yes; F; F; F; no; Dunseith, ND
1932		Cree, Jerome; 1930-Sept 24; m; yes; F; F; F; no; Dunseith, ND
1931-	477	Davis, Maggie Barbara; 1930-April 6; f; yes; ¼+; ¼+; ¼+; yes
1932		Davis, Jerome; 1931-March 24; m; no; ¼+; ¼+; ¼+; yes
1932		Davis, Lucy Catherine; 1930-Aug 25; f; no; ¼+; ¼+; ¼+; no; Reedy Creek, Manitoba
1931-	618	Decoteau, Mary Ann; 1931-March 14; f; yes; ¼+; ¼+; ¼+; yes
1930-	457	Decoteau, Charley; 1930- m; yes; ¼+; ¼+; ¼+; yes
1932		Decoteau, Lucy Laverne; 1930-Sept 14; f; yes; ¼+; ¼+; ¼+; yes

267

Turtle Mountain Reservation
Live Births
Key: Census Roll Number; Surname, Given; Date of Birth (Year-Month-Day); Sex; Tribe (Chippewa unless stated otherwise); Ward (yes/no); Degree of Blood (Father- Mother- Child); At Jurisdiction Where Enrolled (Yes/No); (If no – Where – Post Office, State)

1931- 460	Decoteau, Lorraine C; 1930-May 10; f; yes; ¼+; ¼+; ¼+; yes
1932-	Dejarlais, Alma Rose; 1930-July 19; f; no; ¼+; ¼+; ¼+; no; Trenton, ND
1932- 624	Dejarlais, Antoine; 1930-April 9; m; yes; ¼+; ¼+; ¼+; yes
1931- 697	Delorme, Genevieve; 1930-April 11; f; yes; ¼+; ¼+; ¼+; yes
	Davis, Verlin Clifford; 1930-May 28; m; yes; ¼+; ¼+; ¼+; yes
1932	Dionne, Theresa Mae; 1931-Feb 24; f; yes; ¼+; ¼+; ¼+; yes
1931- 716	Dionne, Dorothy; 1931-Feb 24; f; no; ¼+; ¼+; ¼+; no; Medicine Lake, Mont
1931- 799	Eller, Geraldine F; F; F; 1931-March 9; f; no; W; ¼+; ¼; no; Dunseith, ND
	Enno, Rose; 1930-August 31; f; no; ¼+; ¼+; ¼+; yes
1932	Falcon, Lillian Jane; 1930-July 12; f; no; ¼+; ¼+; ¼+; no; Trenton, ND
1931- 920	Gladue, Arthur C; 1930-June 30; m; no; ¼+; ¼+; ¼+; yes
1931- 920[sic]	Gourneau, Charles Joseph; 1930-May 1; m; yes; ¼+; ¼+; ¼+; yes
1932-	Gourneau, Nora Stella; 1930-April 3; f; yes; ¼+; ¼+; ¼+; yes
1932-	Grandbois, Leona Gertrude; 1930-April 24; f; no; ¼+; ¼+; ¼+; no; East Grand Forks, Minn
1931- 979	Grandbois, Celia Geraldine; 1930-June 22; f; yes; ¼+; ¼+; ¼+; no; Dagmar, Mont
1931- 977	Grant, Claude Ulysses; 1930-April 4; m; yes; ¼+; ¼+; ¼+; yes
1932	Gillis, David Eugene; 1931-Feb 27; m; yes; ¼+; ¼+; ¼+; no; Dunseith, ND
1931- 952	Gladue Harriet; 1931-Feb 25; f; no; ¼+; ¼+; ¼+; no; Froid, Mont
1932	Gourneau, Irene Teresa; 1931-Feb 21; f; yes; ¼+; ¼+; ¼+; yes
1932- 923	Gourneau, Rosella Alice; 1930-Sept 1; f; yes; ¼+; ¼+; ¼+; yes
1931- 903	Gourneau, Mary Eloise; 1931-March 17; f; no; ¼+; ¼+; ¼+; yes
1931- 935	Grandbois, Mary Cecelia; 1931-March 3; f; no; ¼+; ¼+; ¼+; yes
1932	Grant. Gladys; 1930-Dec 10; f; yes; ¼+; ¼+; ¼+; yes
1932	Grant, Clarence Richard; 1930-Sept 23; m; no; ¼+; ¼+; ¼+; no; Devils Lake, ND
1932	Gauthier, Marie Teresa; 1930-Oct 24; f; no; W; ¼+; ¼; no; Willow City, ND
1932	Henry, Theodore; 1931-Jan 16; m; yes; ¼+; ¼+; ¼+; yes
1931-1141	Houle, Barbara; 1930-Oct 15; f; no; ¼+; ¼+; ¼+; no; Rolla, ND
1931-1152	Houle, Jos Clarence; 1930-Aug 4; m; no; ¼+; ¼+; ¼+; no; Rolla, ND
1932	Irving, Thomas G, Jr; 1931-March 20; m; no; W; ¼+; ¼; no; Phoenix, Ariz
1931-1095	Jeannotte, Helen Doris; 1931-March 31; f; yes; ¼+; ¼+; ¼+; yes
1931-1066	Jeannotte, Ernest Richard; 1931-Feb 1; m; yes; ¼+; ¼+; ¼+; yes
1932	Jeannotte, Elmer William; 1930-July 22; m; no; ¼+; ¼+; ¼+; no; St.John, ND
1931-1211	Jerome, Alme[sic]; 1930-Sept 12; f; yes; ¼+; ¼+; ¼+; no; Rolette, ND
1932	Johnson, Vera Doris; 1930-July 31; f; no; ¼+; ¼+; ¼+; no; Plentywood, Mont
1932	Jolibois, Leslie; 1931-Feb 24; m; no; ¼+; ¼+; ¼+; no; Thorne, ND
1931-1142	Kinney, Francis; 1930-Sept 7; m; no; W; ¼+; ¼; yes
1931-1585	Lefort, Betty Lou; 1931-Feb 23; f; yes; ¼+; ¼+; ¼+; yes
1932	Laducer, Joseph; 1930-Dec 27; m; yes; ¼+; ¼+; ¼+; yes
1932	Laducer, Gertrude; 1931-March 6; f; yes; ¼+; ¼+; ¼+; yes
1931-1180	Laducer, Alfred Stanley; 1930-Oct 28; m; yes; ¼+; ¼+; ¼+; yes
1932	Lafontain, Beryl Faye; 1930-Aug 20; f; yes; ¼+; ¼+; ¼+; no; Roy, Mont
1932	Lafontain, Betty; 1930-Nov 28; f; no; ¼+; ¼+; ¼+; no; Havre, Mont
1932	Lafontain, Lorraine; 1930-Dec 16; f; yes; ¼+; ¼+; ¼+; no; Poplar, Mont
1932	Lafrombois, Marie; 1930-July 27; f; no; ¼+; ¼+; ¼+; no; Bottineau, ND

Turtle Mountain Reservation
Live Births
Key: Census Roll Number; Surname, Given; Date of Birth (Year-Month-Day); Sex; Tribe (Chippewa unless stated otherwise); Ward (yes/no); Degree of Blood (Father- Mother- Child); At Jurisdiction Where Enrolled (Yes/No); (If no – Where – Post Office, State)

1931-1279	Lafrombois, James Leo; 1930-July 25; m; yes; ¼+; ¼+; ¼+; yes
1932	Langer, Emil; 1930-Sept 23; m; yes; ¼+; ¼+; ¼+; no; Boggy Creek, Manitoba
1931-1060	Jeannotte, Mary Rita; 1930-April 13; f; yes; ¼+; ¼+; ¼+; yes
1932	Laverdure, Edward M Roy; 1931-Jan 27; m; no; ¼+; ¼+; ¼+; yes
1932	Left Hand, Elsie Mae; 1931-Feb 7; f; no; ¼+; ¼+; ¼+; no; Kanel[sic], ND
1932	Lemay, Leona Genevieve; 1930-Aug 8; f; yes; ¼+; ¼+; ¼+; no; Bainville, Mont
1932	L'Esparance, Evelyn; 1930-Oct 10; f; yes; ¼+; ¼+; ¼+; no; Ft.Totten, ND
1932	Lind, Bernard Marvin; 1930-Nov 19; m; no; W; ¼+; ¼+; yes;
1931-1414	Landry, Mary Juanita; 1930-April 10; f; no; ¼+; ¼+; ¼+; no; Rolla, ND
1932	Larsen, Larrian; 1930-Junw 19; m; yes; ¼+; ¼+; ¼+; no; Devils Lake, ND
1932	Laverdure, No name; 1930-June 16; f; no; ¼+; ¼+; ¼+; no; Dunseith, ND
1932	Laverdure, Ralph Gerald, 1930-April 28; m; yes; ¼+; ¼+; ¼+; Devils Lake, ND
1932	Laverdure, Nora June; 1930-June 11; f; yes; ¼+; ¼+; ¼+; no; Dooley, Mont
1932	Lecompt, Garley; 1930-May 4; m; no; ¼+; ¼+; ¼+; no; Bainville, Mont
1931-1597	Lefort, Mary Agnes; 1930-May 7; f; no; ¼+; ¼+; ¼+; no; St.Paul, Minn
1932	Marion, Donald Edward; 1930-Oct 25; m; yes; ¼+; ¼+; ¼+; no; Grenora, ND
1931-1741	Martin, Shirley Mae; 1930-Sept 1; f; yes; W; ¼+; ¼; no; Cando, ND
1931-1516	Marion, Narcissa; 1930-June 21; f; yes; ¼+; ¼+; ¼+; yes
1931-1576	McCloud, Therese; 1930-June 3; f; yes; ¼+; ¼+; ¼+; yes
1931-1908	Monette, Jos Howard; 1930-June 17; m; yes; ¼+; ¼+; ¼+; no; Unknown, ND
1932	Martin, Alice Regina; 1930-Nov 6; f; yes; ¼+; ¼+; ¼+; yes
~~Martin~~	McCloud, Joseph; 1930-Dec 14; m; yes; ¼+; ¼+; ¼+; yes
~~Martin~~	McCloud, Mary; 1930-Dec 14; f; yes; ¼+; ¼+; ¼+; yes
1932	McGillis, Mary Rosalie; 1931-March 12; f; yes; ¼+; ¼+; ¼+; no; St.John, ND
1932	Melwam, Christopher; 1930-Dec 25; m; yes; F; F; F; yes
1932	Morin, Bernard; 1930-June 9; m; no; ¼+; ¼+; ¼+; no; Trenton, ND
1931-1835	Morin, Dorothy Mae; 1930-April 19; f; yes; ¼+; ¼+; ¼+; no; Fortuna, ND
1931-1629	Morin, Joseph; 1930-May 18; m; yes; ¼+; ¼+; ¼+; yes
1931-1833	Morin, Francis Peter; 1931-Jan 2; m; yes; ¼+; ¼+; ¼+; no Dunseith, ND
1932	Morin, James; 1930-Nov 22; m; no; ¼+; ¼+; ¼+; no; Devils Lake, ND
1932	Morin, Dale Louis; 1931-Jan 12; m; yes; ¼+; ¼+; ¼+; no; Devils Lake, ND
1932	Morin, Willard Marlin; 1930-Sept 7; m; no; ¼+; ¼+; ¼+; no; Medicine Lake, Mont
1931-1946	Nicholas, Donald Edgar; 1930-April 25; m; yes; ¼+; ¼+; ¼+; yes
1932	Norquay, Ellen Mae; 1930-Nov 25; f; yes; ¼+; ¼+; ¼+; no; Dunseith, ND
Died	Nepine, White Thunder; 1930-Dec 17; f; yes; F; F; F; no; Dunseith, ND
19312	Page, Frank; 1931-March 18; m; yes; ¼+; ¼+; ¼+; yes
1931-1753	Parisien, Julius Melvin; 1931-March 6; m; yes; ¼+; ¼+; ¼+; yes
1931-1797	Perronteau, Marie Cecile; 1930-Oct 3; f; yes; ¼+; ¼+; ¼+; yes
1932	Peterson, Annie Pauline; 1930-Dec 30; f; no; W; ¼+; ¼; no; Yelm, Wash
1932	Pippenger, Albert Andrew; 1930-July 29; m; no; ¼+; ¼+; ¼+; no; Trenton, ND
1931-2088	Plante, George James; 1930-Aug 27; m; yes; ¼+; ¼+; ¼+; no; Devils Lake, ND
1932	Poitra, Stanley Michael; 1930-Sept 27; m; yes; ¼+; ¼+; ¼+; no; Devils Lake, ND
1931-1890	Poitra, Raymond Sylvester; 1930-Oct 27; m; yes; ¼+; ¼+; ¼+; yes
1931-1842	Poitra, Irene May; 1930-Aug 13; f; yes; ¼+; ¼+; ¼+; yes

Turtle Mountain Reservation
Live Births

Key: Census Roll Number; Surname, Given; Date of Birth (Year-Month-Day); Sex; Tribe (Chippewa unless stated otherwise); Ward (yes/no); Degree of Blood (Father- Mother- Child); At Jurisdiction Where Enrolled (Yes/No); (If no – Where – Post Office, State)

Died	Poitra, Rosella; 1930-Dec; f; yes; ¼+; ¼+; ¼+; no; Dunseith, ND
1932	Poitra, Delima; 1930-June 17; f; yes; ¼+; ¼+; ¼+; no; Boggy Creek, Manitoba
1932	Poitra, Raymond; 1930-May 27; m; yes; ¼+; ¼+; ¼+; yes
1931-2103	Poitra, Violet Nora; 1931-Feb 13; f; yes; ¼+; ¼+; ¼+; no; Dunseith, ND
1932	Premeau, Joseph William; 1930-Dec 24; m; yes; ¼+; ¼+; ¼+; yes
1932	Renville, Virginia June; 1931-Jan 16; f; yes; ¼+; ¼+; ¼+; no; Buford, ND
1932	Richwine, Shirley Ann; 1930-Sept 23; f; yes; W; ¼+; ¼; no; Medicine Lake, Mont
1932	Russell, James, Jr; 1930-Oct 3; m; no; W; ¼+; ¼; no; Fargo, ND
1931-1944	Roussin, Roger Raymond; 1930-Oct 4; m; no; ¼+; ¼+; ¼+; yes
1932	Ryan, Wm Howard; 1930-Sept 16; m; no; W; ¼+; ¼; no; Devils Lake, ND
1931-1975	Short, Evelyn; 1931-Jan 7; f; yes; ¼+; ¼+; ¼+; no; St.John, ND
1931-1967	Schindler, Edna Patricia; 1930-May 17; f; yes; ¼+; ¼+; ¼+; yes
1931-2319	Slater, Frances; 1930-Nov 25; m; yes; ¼+; ¼+; ¼+; no; St.John, ND
1932	Stofiel, Maxine; 1930-Nov 2; f; yes; W; ¼+; ¼; no; Roy, Mont
1932	St.Arnaud, Gloria; 1930-Sept 23; f; no; ¼+; ¼+; ¼+; yes
1931-2418	St.Pierre, Mary; 1930-Dec 5; f; yes; ¼+; ¼+; ¼+; no; Dunseith, ND
1931-2031	Tetrault, Margaret; 1931-Feb 9; f; yes; ¼+; ¼+; ¼+; yes
1932	Thifault, Wallace; 1930-Sept 16; m; no; ¼+; ¼+; ¼+; no; Dunseith, ND
1931-2546	Trothier, Wayne Sanford; 1930-April 15; m; yes; ¼+; ¼+; ¼+; no; Devils Lake, ND
1931-2536	Trothier, Eugene; 1930-April 9; m; yes; ¼+; ¼+; ¼+; yes
1931-2582	Turcott, June Marvena; 1930-June 4; f; yes; ¼+; ¼+; ¼+; no; Trenton, ND
1932	Tinkay, Rosella Evelyn; 1931-Jan 28; f; yes; W; ¼+; ¼; no; Plentywood, Mont
1932	Turcott, Rose Lena; 1931-March 17; f; no; ¼+; ¼+; ¼+; no; Dunseith, ND
1931-2070	Vallie, Cecelia; 1931-March 17; f; yes; ¼+; ¼+; ¼+; yes
1932	Vandal, Erma D; 1930-Dec 27; f; yes; ¼+; ¼+; ¼+; no; Trenton, ND
1931-2087	Villeneuve, Leona Christine; 1930-Aug 27; f; yes; ¼+; ¼+; ¼+; yes
1932	Vivier, Vincent; 1930-July 20; m; yes; ¼+; ¼+; ¼+; no; Devils Lake, ND
1932	Warren, Joseph John; 1930-April 1; m; no; ¼+; ¼+; ¼+; yes
1932	Westfall, Frank Edward; 1930-Oct 28; m; yes; W; ¼+; ¼; yes
1932	Wilburn, Mary Edna; 1930-Sept 4; f; yes; W; ¼+; ¼; yes
1931-2168	Wilkie, Elizabeth; 1930-June 2; f; no; ¼+; ¼+; ¼+; yes
1931-2191	Wilkie, Florestine; 1930-June 2; f; no; ¼+; ¼+; ¼+; yes

Turtle Mountain Reservation
Additional Names

Key: Census, Census Roll Number; Surname, Given; Date of Birth (Year-Month-Day); Live Births; Still Births; Sex; Tribe (Chippewa unless stated otherwise); Ward (yes/no); Degree of Blood (Father- Mother- Child); Turtle Mt At Jurisdiction ~~Where Enrolled~~ (Yes/No); (If no – Where – Post Office, State)

[Note: The key has changed slightly from previous Live Births pages]

<u>Births Occurring between the Dates of **April 1, 1930** and **March 31, 1931** to Parents Enrolled at Jurisdiction</u>

1931 #1639 Morin, Gilbert; 1930-Aug 12; yes; no; m; yes; ½;½;½; yes

1932 #2840 Lafrombois, Kate; 1930-Dec 16; yes; no; f; no; ½;½;½; no; Poplar, Mont

1931 #1736 Parisien, Charley; 1931-Feb 14; yes; no; m; no; ½;½;½; yes

1931   820 Falcon, Edwin Lincoln; 1931-Mch 8; yes; no; m; yes; ½;½;½; yes

Turtle Mountain Reservation
Live Births

Key: Census Roll Number; Surname, Given; Date of Birth (Year-Month-Day); Sex; Tribe (Chippewa unless stated otherwise); Ward (yes/no); Degree of Blood (Father- Mother- Child); At Jurisdiction Where Enrolled (Yes/No); (If no – Where – Post Office, State)

Births Occurring between the Dates of **April 1, 1931 and March 31, 1932** to Parents Enrolled at jurisdiction

24	Alick, Ramona; 1931-April 1; f; no; ¼; ¼; ¼; no; Bonetrail, ND	
Died before enrollment	Aiken, Raymond; 1931-Aug 11; m; no; ¼; ¼; ¼; no; Rolla, ND	
55	Allard, Sylvester; 1931-Dec 21; m; yes; ¼; ¼; ¼; yes	
103	Allery, Dorothy; 1931-July 3; f; yes; ¼; ¼; ¼; yes	
64	Allery, Fred Joseph; 1931-Oct 18; m; yes; ¼; ¼; ¼; no; Dunseith, ND	
339	Azure, John Joseph; 1931-Sept 21; m; yes; ¼; ¼; ¼; yes	
194	Azure, Rose Marie; 1931-April 6; f; no; ¼; ¼; ¼; yes	
187	Azure, Raymond; 1931-Dec 3; m; yes; ¼; ¼; ¼; yes	
353	Azure, Fred Sylvester; 1931- June 8; m; yes; ¼; ¼; ¼; yes	
251	Azure, Frances; 1931-Sept 7; f; yes; ¼; ¼; ¼; yes	
306	Azure, Florence Doris; 1931-Sept 9; f; no; ¼; ¼; ¼; yes	
389	Baston, Wilfred; 1931-Dec 13; m; yes; ¼; ¼; ¼; no; Elbowoods, ND	
431	Beauchman, Ramona; 1931-April 8; f; yes; ¼; ¼; ¼; no; Wolf Point, Mont	
485	Belgarde, Eugene; 1932-Mar 15; m; no; ¼; ¼; ¼; no; Fort Totten, ND	
468	Belgarde, Raymond R; 1931-May 10; m; yes; ¼; ¼; ¼; yes	
1931- 217	Belgarde, Stanley; 1931-Apriol 8; m; yes; ¼; ¼; ¼; yes	
2004	Belgarde, Ella; 1931-Nov 20; f; yes; ¼; ¼; ¼; yes	
500	Belgarde, John Sylvester; 1931-July 17; m; no; ¼; ¼; ¼; yes	
Died before enrollment	Belgarde, Dorothy; 19310April 22; f; yes; ¼; ¼; ¼; yes	
496	Belgarde, Jane Genevieve; 1931-Nov 7; f; yes; ¼; ¼; ¼; no; Dunseith, ND	
612	Bercier (Warren), Sylvester; 1931-May 13; m; yes; ¼; ¼; ¼; yes	
Died before enrollment	Blue, Carroll R; 1931-April 17; m; yes; ¼; ¼; ¼; yes	
704	Bouvier, Verna Ritha; 1931-Dec 28; f; no; ¼; ¼; ¼; no; San Clara, Manitoba	
733	Boyer, Gordon Louie; 1931-April 5; m; no; ¼; ¼; ¼; yes	
738	Boyer, Irene; 1931-Oct 10; f; yes; ¼; ¼; ¼; yes	
816	Brien, Gordon; 1931-Aug 31; m; yes; ¼; ¼; ¼; yes	
1640	Brien, Albert, Jr; 1831-Dec 3; m; no; ¼; ¼; ¼; no; Nishu, ND	
840	Briere (Adams), Tracey; 1932-Feb 2; m; yes; ¼; ¼; ¼; no; Chinook, Mont	
444	Bell, Robert James; 1931-June 14; m; no; ¼; ¼; ¼; no; Seamens[sic], Sask	
852	Bruce, Irene; 1931-Nov 30; f; yes; ¼; ¼; ¼; yes	
439	Beaudry, Victor Albert; 1932-March 30; m; no; ¼; ¼; ¼; no; Malta, Mont	
955	Cartnell, Marian Belle; 1931-Nov 5; f; yes; ¼; ¼; ¼; no; Sidney, Mont	
NE	Carrington, LeGrande A; 1932-Jan 30; m; no; ¼; ¼; ¼; no; St.John, ND	
1012	Charette, Peter Eugene; 1931-Aug 3; m; yes; ¼; ¼; ¼; no; Medicine Lake, Mont	
1043	Cotterell, Violet May; 1931-Nov 6; f; yes; ¼; ¼; ¼; no; Kalispell, Mont	
1078	Croteau, Mary Louise; 1931-May 14; f; yes; ¼; ¼; ¼; yes	

Turtle Mountain Reservation
Live Births
Key: Census Roll Number; Surname, Given; Date of Birth (Year-Month-Day); Sex; Tribe (Chippewa unless stated otherwise); Ward (yes/no); Degree of Blood (Father- Mother- Child); At Jurisdiction Where Enrolled (Yes/No); (If no – Where – Post Office, State)

1140 Davis, Dolores; 1931-Dec 12; f; yes; ¼; ¼; ¼; yes
1180 Davis, Mary Dolores; 1931-Sept 6; f; yes; ¼; ¼; ¼; yes
1116 Davis, Mary Joyce; 1931-Aug 26; f; yes; ¼; ¼; ¼; no; Sidney, Mont
1228 Decoteau, June Angela; 1932-Feb 17; f; no; ¼; ¼; ¼; yes
1290 Decoteau, Florus; 1932-March 21; f; yes; ¼; ¼; ¼; yes
1260 Decoteau, Jeannette C; 1931-Feb 5; f; yes; ¼; ¼; ¼; yes
1315 Decoteau, Charlie; 1931-May 17; m; yes; ¼; ¼; ¼; yes
1362 Dejarlais, Roman; 1931-Oct 30; m; yes; ¼; ¼; ¼; yes
1379 Dejarlais, Norabelle; 1931-April 25; f; yes; ¼; ¼; ¼; yes
1336 Dejarlais, Elise Rose; 1931-July 10; f; yes; ¼; ¼; ¼; no; St.John, ND
1431 Delong, Elizabeth; 1931-Oct 28; f; no; ¼; ¼; ¼; yes
1451 Delorme, Rita Marie; 1931-Nov 18; f; yes; ¼; ¼; ¼; yes
1480 Delorme, Beatrice Ann; 1932-Feb 16; f; no; ¼; ¼; ¼; yes
1495 Demarais, John; 1931-Aug 4; m; yes; ¼; ¼; ¼; yes
1489 Demarais, Eli; 1932-Jan 15; m; yes; ¼; ¼; ¼; no; Dunseith, ND
1553 Dionne, Francis R; 1931-April 25; m; yes; ¼; ¼; ¼; yes
1596 Dionne, Marguerite; 1931-May 23; f; yes; ¼; ¼; ¼; yes
1578 Dionne (Premeau), Dorothy Mae; 1931-May 26; f; yes; ¼; ¼; ¼; yes
1575 Dionne, Robert; 1931-Aug 18; m; no; ¼; ¼; ¼; yes
Died before enrollment Day, Mary; 1931-July 4; f; yes; F; F; F; no; Dunseith, ND
NE Doney (Berronteau), John Leslie; 1931-Feb 21; Illeg; m; no ¼; ¼; ¼; no; Malta, Mont

1712 Enno, Cecelia Gladys; 1931-Nov 11; f; no; ¼; ¼; ¼; yes

1784 Falk, Theodore; 1931-Sept 30; m; no; ¼; ¼; ¼; no; Reserve, ND[sic]
1751 Falcon, Marie Madonna; 1931- Oct 25; f; no; ¼; ¼; ¼; no; Trenton, ND
1788 Fassett, Donald Robert; 1931-Apr 26; m; yes; ¼; ¼; ¼; no; Thorne, ND
1824 Foster, Margaret; 1931-Sept 21; f; no; ¼; ¼; ¼; no; Rolla, ND
1732 Fagnant, Sylvia; 1931-Dec 18; f; yes; ¼; ¼; ¼; no; Dunseith, ND

1900 Girard, Harold Lloyd; 1932-Feb 28; m; yes; ¼; ¼; ¼; no; Madoc, Mont
1904 Gladue, Charles Ed; 1931-Nov 12; m; no; ¼; ¼; ¼; no; Dagmar, Mont
1972 Godon, Edward; 1932-Jan 9; m; yes; ¼; ¼; ¼; no; Bottineau, ND
2004 Gourneau, Mary Joan; 1931-Oct 25; f; yes; ¼; ¼; ¼; yes
2029 Gourneau, Kenneth Leo; 1932-Jan 31; m; yes; ¼; ¼; ¼; yes
Died before enrollment Gourneau, Jane; 1932-Jan 15; f; yes; ¼; ¼; ¼; yes
1988 Gourneau, Bernard; 1932-Mar 9; m; yes; ¼; ¼; ¼; yes
2089 Grandbois, Albert Leo; 1931-May 19; m; no; ¼; ¼; ¼; no; East Grand Forks, Minn
2094 Grandbois, Shirley Ann; 1932-Feb 9; f; no; ¼; ¼; ¼; yes
2114 Grandbois, Evelyn; 1931-Sept 22; f; no; ¼; ¼; ¼; yes
2135 Grant, Nettie Hilda; 1931-Oct 19; f; yes; ¼; ¼; ¼; yes
2184 Grant, Richard James; 1931-Sept 16; m; no; ¼; ¼; ¼; yes

Turtle Mountain Reservation
Live Births
Key: Census Roll Number; Surname, Given; Date of Birth (Year-Month-Day); Sex; Tribe (Chippewa unless stated otherwise); Ward (yes/no); Degree of Blood (Father- Mother- Child); At Jurisdiction Where Enrolled (Yes/No); (If no – Where – Post Office, State)

- 2194 Great Walker, Jane; 1931-Nov 16; f; yes; F; F; F; yes
- 2212 Gunderson, Walter Eugene; 1931-Aug 27; m; yes; ¼; W; ¼; no; St.Paul, Minn
- 2220 Gunville, Emile; 1931-Sept 3; m; no; ¼; ¼; ¼; no; Dunseith, ND
- 2103 Grandbois, Thomas; 1931-March 9; m; no; ¼; ¼; ¼; no; Dagmar, Mont

Died before enrollment   Hamley, Sylvia; 1932-March 12; f; yes; ¼; ¼; ¼; yes

- 2253 Hauge, Duane Joseph; 1931-July 18; m; yes; ¼; ¼; ¼; no; Walhalla, ND
- 2279 Henry, Lester; 1931-Aug 30; m; yes; ¼; F; ¼; no; Dunseith, ND
- 2281 Henry, Georgeline; 1931-June 17; f; yes; ¼; ¼; ¼; no; Boggy Creek, Manitoba
- 2387 Houle, James Howard; 1931-Sept 19; f[sic]; no; ¼; ¼; ¼; no; Bottineau, ND
- 2366 Houle, Mary Alvina; 1931-May 3; f; yes; ¼; ¼; ¼; yes

- 2452 Jeannotte, Walter Simon; 1931-~~Nov~~ Dec 28; m; yes; ¼; ¼; ¼; yes
- 2475 Jerome; Phyllis Felicite; 1931-Jan 29; f; no; ¼; ¼; ¼; yes
- 2500 Jerome, Julia Rose; 1931-Nov 7; f; no; ¼; ¼; ¼; yes
- 2531 Johnson, Ruth; 1931-June 14; f; no; ¼; ¼; ¼; no; Plentywood, Mont
- 2573 Justice, Dolores Mae; 1931-May 7; f; no; W; ¼; ¼; no; Grenora, ND

- 2580 Kaufman, Edward, Jr; 1931-Dec 17; m; no; W; ¼; ¼; no; Havre, Mont
- 2600 Keplin, Wm Joseph; 1931-Dec 4; m; no; ¼; ¼; ¼; yes
- 2615 Knutson, Gerald; 1931-Nov 7; m; no; W; ¼; ¼; no; Rolette, ND

- 2662 Lafloe, Helen Jane; 1931-Nov 21; f; yes; ¼; ¼; ¼; yes
- 2685 Lafontain, Gladys; 1931-June 9; f; yes; ¼; ¼; ¼; no; Roy, Mont
- 2753 Lafontain, James Edward; 1932-Jan 23; m; yes; ¼; ¼; ¼; yes
- 2704 Lafontain, Flora; 1931-Oct 25; f; no; ¼; ¼; ¼; yes
- 2718 Lafontain, Doris; 1931-Sept 28; f; yes; ¼; ¼; ¼; no; Havre, Mont

Died before enrollment   Lafontain, Roy; 1931-July 1; m; no; ¼; ¼; ¼; yes

- 2764 Lafontain, Nora Stella; 1931-Nov 22; f; yes; ¼; ¼; ¼; yes

Died before enrollment   Lafrance, Theresa; 1931-July 3; f; no; ¼; ¼; ¼; yes

- 2836 Lafraniere, Vivian Doris; 1932-Jan 1; twin; f; no; ¼; ¼; ¼; no; Hardin, Mont
- 2837 Lafraniere, Violet Rita; 1932-Jan 1 twin; f; no; ¼; ¼; ¼; no; Hardin, Mont
- 2863 Lafrombois, Geraldine; 1931-Oct 6; Illeg; f; yes; [?]; ¼; ¼; yes
- 2971 Landry, Nora Jennie; 1932-Feb 21; f; no; ¼; ¼; ¼; yes
- 2990 Langan, Emile; 1931-Sept 23; m; yes; ¼; ¼; ¼; no; Boggy Creek, Manitoba
- 2979 Lang, Martin Duane; 1931-July 18; m; no; ¼; ¼; ¼; no; Tokio, ND
- 3029 Langer, James Earl; 1931-May 29; m; yes; ¼; ¼; ¼; no; St.Paul, Minn
- 3036 Laroque, Eugene; 1932-Jan 10; m; yes; ¼; ¼; ¼; no; St.John, ND
- 3092 Lattergrass, Robert David; 1932-Feb 8; m; yes; ¼; ¼; ¼; yes
- 3126 Lavallie, Alfred; 1931-Dec 10; m; yes; ¼; ¼; ¼; yes
- 3177 Laverdure, Leo David; 1931-Nov 26; m; yes; ¼; ¼; ¼; yes

Turtle Mountain Reservation
Live Births
Key: Census Roll Number; Surname, Given; Date of Birth (Year-Month-Day); Sex; Tribe (Chippewa unless stated otherwise); Ward (yes/no); Degree of Blood (Father- Mother- Child); At Jurisdiction Where Enrolled (Yes/No); (If no – Where – Post Office, State)

3170	Laverdure, Frances; 1932-Mar 3; f; yes; ¼; ¼; ¼; yes
3192	Laverdure, Gertrude J; 1931-Nov 6; f; yes; ¼; ¼; ¼; no; Comertown, Mont
3244	Laverdure, Leocadia; 1931-April 20; f; yes; ¼; ¼; ¼; yes
3206	Laverdure, Jennie Bede; 1932-Feb 12; f; yes; ¼; ¼; ¼; yes
1931-1422	Ladeaux, Marie Louise; 1931-Apr 27; f; no; ¼; ¼; ¼; yes
3340	Lenoir, Joan; 1931-Dec 14; twin; f; no; ¼; ¼; ¼; no; Ft.Totten, ND
3341	Lenoir, Jean; 1931-Dec 14; twin; f; no; ¼; ¼; ¼; no; Ft.Totten, ND
3349	L'Esparance, Alexander; 1931-Oct 3; m; yes; ¼; ¼; ¼; yes
Died before enrollment	Lillie, Mary Victoria; 1931-July 5; f; yes; ¼; ¼; ¼; yes
3393	Lizotte, Ernest; 1931-Dec 14; m; no; ¼; ¼; ¼; no; Great Falls, Mont
3428	Lunak[sic], Richard Ronald; 1932-Mar 26; m; yes; ¼; ¼; ¼; no; Devils Lake, ND
2620	Laducer, Gertrude Sylvia; 1932-Mar 6; f; yes; ¼; ¼; ¼; yes
3418	Lonick, Joseph R; 1931-Nov 15; m; yes; ¼; ¼; ¼; no; Devils Lake, ND
3461	Malaterre, Dorothy; 1931-June 25; f; yes; ¼; ¼; ¼; yes
3491	Malaterre, Vernon; 1931-Oct 3; m; yes; ¼; ¼; ¼; yes
3516	Marcellais, Dolores; 1931-Sept 5; f; yes; ¼; ¼; ¼; yes
3537	Marion, Reginald; 1932-Jan 2; m; yes; ¼; ¼; ¼; yes
3583	Martell, Evelyn; 1931-Oct 13; f; no; ¼; ¼; ¼; yes
3591	Martell, Roland Lloyd 1931-July 18; m; yes; ¼; ¼; ¼; yes
Died before enrollment	McCloud, Patricia Jean; 1931-Sept 28; f; yes; ¼; ¼; ¼; yes
3721	Minne, Dora Elizabeth; 1931-June 6; f; yes; ¼; ¼; ¼; no; Mountain Side, Manitoba
3734	Monette, Resia Mae; 1931-May 3; f; yes; ¼; ¼; ¼; yes
3850	Morin, Rebecca; 1931-June 15; f; yes; ¼; ¼; ¼; no; Trenton, ND
3778	Morin, Raymond; 1931-April 12; m; no; ¼; ¼; ¼; no; Dunseith, ND
5521	Morin, Mary Margaret; 1931-April 9; f; yes; ¼; ¼; ¼; no; Dunseith, ND
3812	Morin, Rose Dolores; 1931-Dec 7; f; yes; ¼; ¼; ¼; yes
3760	Morin, Virginia E; 1931-June 14; f; yes; ¼; ¼; ¼; yes
3908	Morin, David Solomon; 1931-April 13; m; no; ¼; ¼; ¼; no; Fort Totten, ND
3691	McVay, Betty Jane; 1932-Feb 1; f; yes; ¼; ¼; ¼; yes
3706	Mekwam, Lucy; 1931-Oct 12; f; yes; F; F; F; no; Dunseith, ND
3941	Nadeau, Peter George; 1931-April 18; m; no; ¼; ¼; ¼; yes
3951	Nadeau, Clement; 1931-Oct 20; m; yes; ¼; ¼; ¼; yes
4003	Nicholas, Francis R; 1931-April 16; m; yes; ¼; ¼; ¼; yes
4014	Norquay, Annabelle; 1931-Oct 12; f; yes; ¼; F; ¼; no; Dunseith, ND
4048	Olson, Morris Edward; 1931-June 22; m; no; ¼; ¼; ¼; no; Coalridge, Mont
4040	Olson, Clemence; 1931-Dec 30; f; no; ¼; ¼; ¼; no; Cando, ND
4248	Peltier, Robert; 1931-May 20; m; no; ¼; ¼; ¼; yes[sic]; Coalridge, Mont
4551	Purvis, Christine; 1931-Aug 14; f; yes; W; ¼; ¼; no; Scandinavia, Manitoba
4497	Poitra, Veronica; 1932-Feb 26; f; no; ¼; ¼; ¼; no; Dagmar, Mont

Turtle Mountain Reservation
Live Births

Key: Census Roll Number; Surname, Given; Date of Birth (Year-Month-Day); Sex; Tribe (Chippewa unless stated otherwise); Ward (yes/no); Degree of Blood (Father- Mother- Child); At Jurisdiction Where Enrolled (Yes/No); (If no – Where – Post Office, State)

4553	Rakes, Edward, Jr; 1931-April 14; m; yes; W;¼; ¼; no; Devils Lake, ND
1931-2188	Rearden, Patricxk Dean; 1931-June 12; m; yes; W;¼; ¼; yes
4606	Richard; Francis Elmer; 1931-Aug 16; m; yes; ¼; ¼; ¼; no; St.John, ND
4666	Roy, Minerva; 1931-Oct 21; f; yes; W;¼; ¼; no; Rolette, ND
4567	Reflection Man, Mary; 1931-Nov 27; yes; F; F; F; yes
4662	Roussin, Charley Raymond; 1931-Oct 4; m; no; ¼; ¼; ¼; yes
4620	Riendeau, Adolph; 1931-Aug 11; m; yes; W;¼; ¼; no; Rolette, ND
4671	Ryan, Richard Lee; 1932- March 1; m; yes; ¼; ¼; ¼; no; Devils Lake, ND

4804	Sedevik, Darrell; 1931-June 4; m; no; W;¼; ¼; no; Plentywood, Mont
4866	Skinner, Mebel[sic]; 1931-April 12; f; yes; F; F; F; no; Dunseith, ND
4765	Salo, Donald Martin; 1931-May 27; m; no; ¼; ¼; ¼; no; Minot, ND
4773	San Grait, Casper; 1931-Dec 26; m; no; ¼; ¼; ¼; yes
4347	Schindler, Elaine M; 1931-Dec 28; f; yes; ¼; ¼; ¼; yes
4827	Shireback, Richard Mark; 1931-May 31; m; no; W;¼; ¼; no; Wilton, ND
4853	Sindt, Grace; 1931-Nov 17; f; yes; W;¼; ¼; no; Big Fork, Mont
4927	Smith, Arthur Ben; 1931-May 11; m; no; ¼; ¼; ¼; yes
4929	Smith, Beverly Ann; 1931-Jan 29; f; yes; ¼; ¼; ¼; yes
4951	Staley, Richard Abraham; 1931-June 8; m; no; ¼; ¼; ¼; no; Froid, Mont
4976	Stofiel, Robert; 1932-March 19; m; yes; W;¼; ¼; no; Roy, Mont
4677	St.Arnaud, Raphael; 1931-June 9; m; no; ¼; ¼; ¼; yes
4704	St.Claire, Marion; 1931-Aug 25; m; yes; ¼; ¼; ¼; no; Dunseith, ND

4068	Page, Delonais Thelma; 1931-Nov 18; Illeg; f; yes; [?]; ¼; ¼; yes
4112	Parisien, Ernest Melvin; 1931-May 17; m; no; ¼; ¼; ¼; yes
5522	Parisien, Alice; 1931-Dec 7; f; no; ¼; ¼; ¼; yes
4129	Patnaud, Gertrude E; 1932-Feb 2; f; no; ¼; ¼; ¼; yes
4155	Patnaud, James; 1931-July 23; m; yes; ¼; ¼; ¼; yes
4164	Patnaud, Marguerite; 1931-Sept 12; f; yes; ¼; ¼; ¼; no; Medicine Lake, Mont
4233	Peltier, Gabriel; 1931-Sept 26; m; no; ¼; ¼; ¼; no; Ft.Berthold, ND
4205	Peltier, Joseph Gilbert; 1931-Oct 30; m; no; ¼; ¼; ¼; no; Minnewauken[sic], ND
4259	Perronteau, Louise; 1931-Dec 12; f; yes; ¼; ¼; ¼; yes
4287	Plante, Mary Teresa; 1931-April 16; f; no; ¼; W; ¼; no; Kalamazoo, Mich
4479	Poitra, Irene Bernice; 1932-Jan 31; f; yes; ¼; ¼; ¼; no; Devils Lake, ND
4321	Poitra, Clifford J; 1931-Sept 7; m; yes; no; ¼; ¼; ¼; no; St.John, ND
Died before enrollment	Poitra, Ray Stephen; 1931-April 29; m; yes; ¼; ¼; ¼; yes
4336	Poitra, Mary Stella; 1931-Nov 20; f; yes; ¼; ¼; ¼; yes
4376	Poitra, Mary Verna; 1931-Dec 21; f; yes; ¼; ¼; ¼; no; Dunseith, ND
4365	Poitra, Mildred Marie; 1931-May 3; f; yes; ¼; ¼; ¼; no; Dunseith, ND
4356	Poitra, Louis Paul; 1931-July 12; m; yes; ¼; ¼; ¼; no; Dunseith, ND
4475	Poitra, Olympia B; 1931-Nov 5; f; yes; ¼; ¼; ¼; yes
4491	Poitra, Dorothy Ann; 1931-July 26; f; yes; ¼; ¼; ¼; yes
4439	Poitra, James; 1931-Nov 4; m; yes; ¼; ¼; ¼; yes

Turtle Mountain Reservation
Live Births
Key: Census Roll Number; Surname, Given; Date of Birth (Year-Month-Day); Sex; Tribe (Chippewa unless stated otherwise); Ward (yes/no); Degree of Blood (Father- Mother- Child); At Jurisdiction Where Enrolled (Yes/No); (If no – Where – Post Office, State)

4497 Poitra, Veronica V; 1931-Feb 16; f; yes; ¼; ¼; ¼; no; Froid, Mont
4385 Poitra, Mary Corinne; 1931-Feb 16; f; yes; ¼; ¼; ¼; no; Dunseith, ND

5000 Tetrault, Margaret B; 1931-July 12; f; no; ¼; ¼; ¼; no; Rolette, ND
5093 Thorne, Bertha Loma; 1931-Dec 19; f; yes; ¼; ¼; ¼; no; Boggy Creek, Manitoba
5114 Torgerson, Glenn Allen; 1931-Aug 10; m; yes; W; ¼; ¼; no; Dagmar, Mont
5135 Trothier, Gerald; 1931-Sept 16; m; yes; ¼; ¼; ¼; yes
5160 Turcott, Rita; 1931-April 2; f; no; ¼; ¼; ¼; no; Rolla, ND
5182 Turcott, Vitaline; 1932-Feb 3; f; no; ¼; ¼; ¼; yes

5209 Vandal, Rose; 1932-March 26; f; no; ¼; ¼; ¼; yes
5295 Vivier, James Stephen; 1932-March 31; m; yes; ¼; ¼; ¼; yes
5290 Vivier, Gladys; 1931-Sept 8; f; yes; ¼; ¼; ¼; yes
5261 Vivier, Archie C; 1931-April 16; m; yes; ¼; ¼; ¼; no; Dunseith, ND

5315 Wallett, Sarah; 1931-Oct 19; f; no; ¼; ¼; ¼; yes
5324 Wallett, David; 1931-April 13; m; yes; ¼; ¼; ¼; yes
5364 Westfall, Harold Joel; 1932-Feb 3; m; no; W; ¼; ¼; yes
5460 Wilkie, Pamelia[sic]; 1931-April 26; f; no; ¼; ¼; ¼; yes
5478 Wilkie, Amelia Alice; 1931-April 26; f; no; ¼; ¼; ¼; yes
5426 Wilkie, Susan Marie; 1932-Jan 29; f; yes; ¼; ¼; ¼; yes
5518 Zura, Leon; 1931-Dec 30; m; yes; ¼; ¼; ¼; yes

Turtle Mountain Reservation
Additional Names

Key: Census, Census Roll Number; Surname, Given; Date of Birth (Year-Month-Day); Live Births; Still Births; Sex; Tribe (Chippewa unless stated otherwise); Ward (yes/no); Degree of Blood (Father- Mother- Child); Turtle Mt At Jurisdiction Where Enrolled (Yes/No); (If no – Where – Post Office, State)

[Note: The key has changed slightly from previous Live Births pages]

Births Occurring between the Dates of **April 1, 1931** and **March 31, 1932** to Parents Enrolled at Jurisdiction

[Parents not enrolled]

Parents not enrolled Langan, Marie Annabelle; 1931-Aug 13; yes; no; f; no; ¼; ¼; ¼; no; St.John, ND
do Godon, Ruby Monica; 1931-Feb 29; yes; no; f; no; ½;½;½; no; Bottineau, ND
do Allard, Raymond; 1931-Dec 26; yes; no; m; no; ½;½;½; yes
do Kline, Benjamin Joseph; 1931-Feb 29; yes; no; m; no; ¼; ¼; ¼; no; Harlem, Mont

DEATHS

Exclusive of Stillbirths

July 1, 1924 – June 30, 1930
April 1, 1930 – March 31, 1932

Turtle Mountain Reservation
Deaths

Key: Year and Number Last Census Roll ; Surname, Given; Date of Birth (Year-Month-Day); Age at Death; Sex;
Tribe (Chippewa unless stated otherwise); Ward (Yes/No); Degree of Blood; Cause of Death (if given);
At Jurisdiction Where Enrolled (Yes/No); (If no – Where)

Deaths Occurring between the Dates of **July 1, 1924** and **June 30, 1925** of Indians Enrolled at Jurisdiction

1929	217	Allery, Clara J; 1925-April 15; 10m; f; ¼+; yes
xxxxxxxxx		Azure, Andrew; 1925-March 6; 7m; m; no; ¼+; no; Rolla
1924		Boyer, Andrew; 1924-Dec 13; 48y; m; no; ¼+; no; Culbertson, Mont
1925	700	Boyer, Abraham; 1924-June 14; 79y; m; no; ¼+; Diabetes; yes
xxxxxxxxx		Belgarde, Mary; 1924-Dec 17; 1m; f; yes; ¼+; yes
1925	521	Belgarde, Josephine; 1925-April 24; 16y; f; ¼+; Tuberculosis; yes
1929	868	Briere, Edna; 1925-June 2; 7y; f; yes; ¼+; no; White Mound, Sask
xxxxxxxxx		Bruce, Josephine; 1925-Jan 1; 3m; f; yes; ¼+; yes
1924		Caplette, Modeste; 1925-March 26; 58y; m; no; ¼+; Tuberculosis; yes
1926	925	Champagne, Mary Louise; 1924-July 20; 22y; f; yes; ¼+; Tuberculosis; no; Unknown
1924		Caplette, Ernest; 1925-May 26; 13y; m; no; ¼+; Tuberculosis; yes
1925	975	Davis, Mary (Azure); 1925-March 21; 61y; f; no; ¼+; Peritonitis; yes
xxxxxxxxx		Decoteau, Louis Wm; 1925-Jan 19; 3m; m; yes; ¼+; yes
No date of death given on roll book		Dejarlais, Wm John; m; yes; ¼+; yes
1924		Dejarlais, Andrew; 1925-March 21; 80y; m; yes; ¼+; Heart failure; yes
xxxxxxxxx		Demarais, Albert; 1925-Nov 30; 1d; m; yes; ¼+; no; Dunseith, ND
Never on the census		Duchesneau, Moses; 1924-July 2; 21y; m; no; ¼+; no; Dunseith, ND
1925	1509	Foi, Pierre; 1924-Dec 12; 95y; m; no; ¼+; Tuberculosis; yes
1924		Grant, Sylvester; 1923-July 3; 24y; m; no; ¼+; Tuberculosis; yes
1924		Grandbois, Clarice; 1924-April 4; 26y; f; no; ¼+; no; Dunseith, ND
xxxxxxxxx		Gunville, Emma; 1924-July 14; 2m; f; yes; ¼+; no; Bottineau, ND
xxxxxxxxx		Gunville, Lillian; 1924-July 26; 3y; f; yes; ¼+; no; Bottineau, ND
1925	963	Henry, Philomeme; 1924-Nov 11; 18y; f; no; ¼+; yes
1924		Laducer, Delima; 1924-Sept 16; 7y; f; no; ¼+; yes
1924		Lafontain, Mary Grant; 1925-April 9; 31y; f; yes; ¼+; yes
1926	2383	Lafrombois, Florestine; 1924-Nov 19; 25y; f; no; ¼+; Tuberculosis; no; Pisek, ND
xxxxxxxxx		Langer, Fabian; 1924-Dec 5; 4m; m; no; ¼+; yes
1926		Latrace, George; 1925-April 8; 3y; m; yes; ¼+; no; Sask
1926	2724	Lenoir, Joseph; 1925-May 24; 70y; m; yes; ¼+; no; Minnewauken[sic], ND
1926	2841	Malaterre, Emma; 1924-Nov 1; 1y; f; no; ¼+; yes
xxxxxxxxx		Morin, Christine; 1924-July 20; 3m; f; yes; ¼+; yes
1925	3006	Morin, Mary (Belgarde); 1925-June 12; 29y; f; yes; ¼+; Tuberculosis; yes
xxxxxxxxx		Nadeau, Alexander; 1925-April 25; 1y; m; yes; ¼+; yes
1929	3347	Nicholas, Claude; 1924-Oct 17; 43y; m; no; ¼+; yes
xxxxxxxxx		Peltier, Joseph; 1924; 1y; m; yes; ¼+; no; Devils Lake, ND
1924		Peltier, Paul; 1925-March 20; 80y; m; no; ¼+; Tuberculosis; yes
xxxxxxxxx		Pippenger, Violet; 1924-Oct 23; 3y; f; no; ¼+; no; Trenton, ND
1924		Poitra, Henry; 1925-April 3; 70y; m; no; ¼+; Pneumonia; yes
1925-3625		Salmonson, Florestine; 1925-Marh 4, 18y; f; yes; ¼+; no; Unknown
1927	3810	Smith, Israel; 1924-Nov 2- 63y; m; yes; ¼+; yes

Turtle Mountain Reservation
Deaths

Key: Year and Number Last Census Roll ; Surname, Given; Date of Birth (Year-Month-Day); Age at Death; Sex; Tribe (Chippewa unless stated otherwise); Ward (Yes/No); Degree of Blood; Cause of Death (if given); At Jurisdiction Where Enrolled (Yes/No); (If no – Where)

1924		Skinner, Puyat; 1923-August 11; 59y; m; yes; F; no; Dunseith, ND
1924		Thifault, Norbert; 1924-August 28; 3m; m; yes; ¼+; no; Dunseith, ND
1925	3757	Trester, Clara; 1924-July 25; 20y; f; no; ¼+; Burned to death; no; Rolla, ND
xxxxxxxxx		Trothier, William; 1925-March 4; 3m; m; yes; ¼+; yes
1924		Vallie, Julia; 1925-March 29; 68y; f; yes; ¼+; yes
1929	4406	Wilkie, Francis; 1925-Feb 2; 9m; m; no; ¼+; Pneumonia; yes

Deaths Occurring between the Dates of July 1, 1925 and June 30, 1926 of Indians Enrolled at Jurisdiction

1925	620	Belgarde, Marie Rosina; 1926-April 6; 2y; f; yes; ¼+; Tuberculosis; yes
1925	753	Brien, Mary Rose; 1926-May 10; 64y; f; no; ¼+; yes
1925	800	Bruce, Joseph Louis; 1926-April 6; 45y; m; no; ¼+; yes
1926	915	Caplette, Rosina; 1925-Aug; 23y; f; yes; ¼+; yes
1925	939	Crissler, Carey M, Jr; 1925-Dec 11; 15y; m; yes; ¼+; no; Scandinivia[sic], Man
Cannot locate on census		Charbonneau, Mary Rosina; 1926-April 9; 71y; f; no; ¼+; Gall stones; yes
1925	1089	Decoteau, John B; 1926-June 14; 83y; m; yes; ¼+; yes
1926	1368	Demontigny, Mary Jane; 1926-May 27; 35y; f; no; ¼+; yes
xxxxxxxxx		Davis, Mary Clemence; 1925-Juy 10; 3m; f; no; ¼+; yes
1925	1598	Gladue, Joseph; 1925-August 9; 77y; m; yes; ¼+; no; Unknown
1925	963	Henry, Philomeme; 1925-Dec 11; 19y; f; no; ¼+; Heart Trouble; no; Thorne, ND
1925	1972	Houle, Mary Ann; 1926-April 18; 15y; f; no; ¼+; Tuberculosis; yes
1926	2074	Houle, Napoleon; 1925-Dec 10; 40y; m; no; ¼+; yes
1025	1923	Houle, Charles; 1926-June 10; 71y; m; yes; ¼+; Tuberculosis; yes
xxxxxxxxx		Laducer, Julius; 1925-Sept 5; 2m; m; no; ¼+; yes
xxxxxxxxx		Laducer, Marie; 1925-Sept 6; 2m; f; no; ¼+; yes
1925	2118	Laducer (Poitra), Angelique; 1926-May 1; 36y; f; no; ¼+; no; Maryville, ND
1927	2267	Lafloe, Frank; 1926-Feb 16; 4m; m; yes; ¼+; yes
1925	2307	Lafrombois, Michael; 1925-Nov 16; 64y; m; no; ¼+; Nephritis, Chronic Intestinal; yes
1926	2626	Laverdure, Mary; 1926-June 16; 89y; f; yes; ¼+; Rheumatism, Old age; yes
1925	2541	Laverdure, Marcial; 1926-March 19; 20y; m; yes; ¼+; Typhoid fever; yes
xxxxxxxxx		Martin, Fred; 1925-Dec 29; 44y; m; NE; ¼+; Ulcer of the stomach; yes
1925	2481	McCloud, Peter; 1926-Feb 10; 76y; m; no; ¼+; Apoplexy; yes
1925	2895	Morin, Sarah; 1926-Jan 16; 56y; f; no; ¼+; Heart trouble; yes
1928	10	Makwam[sic], Alexander; 1926-April 3; 14y; m; yes; F; Tuberculosis; no; Dunseith, ND
xxxxxxxxx		Mekwam, Equazance; 1925-Aug 10; 4y; f; yes; F; no; Dunseith, ND
xxxxxxxxx		Peltier, Abraham; 1925-Nov 17; 64y; m; no; ¼+; yes
1925	3340	Poitra, Ernest; 1926-May 28; 3y; m; yes; ¼+; Tuberculosis; yes
1926	3472	Poitra, Francois; 1926-April 28; 2y; m; yes; ¼+; Congestion of the brain; yes
xxxxxxxxx		Poitra, Irene; 1925-Sept 23; 5m; f; yes; ¼+; no; Dunseith, ND
1926	3584	Renville, Joseph; 1926-June 16; 32y; m; no; ¼+; Tuberculosis; no; Buford, ND
xxxxxxxxx		Renville, Fred; 1926-May 27; 5m; m; yes; ¼+; Pneumonia; yes
xxxxxxxxx		Skinner, Mrs; 1925-Aug 18; 76y; f; yes; F; Tumor in abdomen; no; Dunseith, ND

Turtle Mountain Reservation
Deaths

Key: Year and Number Last Census Roll ; Surname, Given; Date of Birth (Year-Month-Day); Age at Death; Sex; Tribe (Chippewa unless stated otherwise); Ward (Yes/No); Degree of Blood; Cause of Death (if given); At Jurisdiction Where Enrolled (Yes/No); (If no – Where)

1915 3965 Wilkie, Mary Edna; 1925-July 13; 9y; f; no; ¼+; yes
1925 3852 Villeneuve, Alfred Louis; 1926-Feb 6; 11y; m; no; ¼+; yes

<u>Deaths Occurring between the Dates of **July 1, 1926** and **June 30, 1927** of Indians Enrolled at Jurisdiction</u>

1926   6 Anakonik, Offers the Pipe; 1927-June 6; 86y; f; yes; F; Old age; yes
1926 322 Azure, Jossett; 1927-Feb 11; 88y; f; yes; ¼+; Old age; yes
1926 524 Belgarde, Ida Rose; 1927-June 15; 23y; f; no; ¼+; no; Bainville, Mont
1927 603 Belgarde, Francois; 1927-March 29; 36y; m; no; ¼+; no; Unknown
1926 612 Belgarde, Edward M; 1926-Nov 17; 1y; m; no; ¼+; Meningitis; yes
1929 663 Belgarde, Robert; 1926-Aug 11; 22y; m; yes; ¼+; yes
1930 430 Bercier, Vernon; 1926-Nov 13; 6m; m; yes; ¼+; no; Devils Lake, ND
1927   Bruce, Louis Albert; 1927-March 9; 4m; m; yes; ¼+; yes
1927 869 Brunnell, Mary Louise; 1926-Nov 27; 28y; f; no; ¼+; Pulmonary Tuberculosis; yes
1927 1034 Dauphinais, Josephine; 1927-June 24; 2y; f; yes; ¼+; yes
xxxxxxxxx Decoteau, Patrice; 1927-Jan 17; 2m; m; yes; Pneumonia; no; Devils Lake, ND
1927 1248 Dejarlais, James; 1927-Feb 23; 56y; m; no; ¼+; yes
1926 1459 Duchain, Julia; 1926-Oct 6; 63y; f; yes; ¼+; Heart failure; yes
1930 1567 Dumont, Mary Rose; 1926-29; 63y; f; no; ¼+; no; Boggy Creek, Manitoba
1929 114 Day, Joseph; 1927-April 2; 8m; m; yes; F; no; Dunseith, ND
1929 1800 Gladue, Pierre; 1926; 84y; m; yes; ¼+; yes
1926 1745 Gourneau, Angelique; 1926-Sept 16; 65y; f; no; ¼+; yes
1926 1795 Grandbois, Sarah; 1926-Aug 24; 65y; f; no; ¼+; no; ¼+; Heart trouble; yes
1927 1862 Grant, Margaret; 1927-June 16; 63y; f; no; ¼+; Pneumonia; yes
1931 1024 Grant, Louis; 1926; 2y; m; yes; ¼+; no; Devils Lake, ND
1926 1951 Hayden, Mary St.Ann; 1926-July 2; 18y; f; yes; ¼+; Pleurisy; no; Dominion City, Man
1929 2057 Hayes, John; 1927-May 4; 61y; m; yes; ¼+; yes
1926 1959 Henry, William; 1926-July 7; 17y; m; no; ¼+; Tuberculosis; yes
1926 1961 Henry, Edna Lucille; 1927-April 12; 14y; f; no; ¼+; TB pulmonary; yes
xxxxxxxxx Herman, Inez M; 1927-May 24; 2m; f; yes; ¼+; no; Devils Lake, ND
1927 2161 Jerome, Mary L; 1927-April 22; 18y; f; yes; ¼+; no; Madoc, Mont
1928 2239 Laducer, Mary Clara; 1927-Jan 13; 1y; f; yes; ¼+; yes
1928 2332 Lafontain, St.Pierre; 1926-Dec 24; 53y; m; yes; ¼+; Pneumonia; yes
1927 2412 Lafranierre, Lyle; 1927-Jan 27; 0[sic]; m; no; ¼+; no; Hardin, Mont
1926 2378 Lafrombois, Cecile; 1926-Dec 4; 57y; f; no; ¼+; Gall stones; yes
1926 2503 Langer, Edward; 1927-April 22; 6y; m; yes; ¼+; yes
1929 2696 Laroque, Roy Joseph; 1926-Dec 17; 2y; m; no; ¼+; Pneumonia; yes
1926 2736 Lenoir, Elizabeth; 1926-Oct 30; 17y; f; yes; ¼+; yes
1931 1629 Lillie, Mary Madeline; 1926-July 8; 1y; f; yes; ¼+; no; St.John, ND
1931 1438 Lillie, Beatrice; 1926-Nov 5; 3y; f; yes; ¼+; yes
1926 2768 Lizotte, Mary; 1927-April; 44y; f; no; ¼+; no; Great Falls, Mont
1926 2917 Martell, John B; 1927-Feb 10; 20y; m; no; ¼+; Rupture of Hapatic[sic] vessels; no; Culbertson, Mont
xxxxxxxxx McCloud, Moses; 1926-Nov 3; m; no; ¼+; yes

283

Turtle Mountain Reservation
Deaths
Key: Year and Number Last Census Roll ; Surname, Given; Date of Birth (Year-Month-Day); Age at Death; Sex; Tribe (Chippewa unless stated otherwise); Ward (Yes/No); Degree of Blood; Cause of Death (if given); At Jurisdiction Where Enrolled (Yes/No); (If no – Where)

xxxxxxxxx Nwenapi, John; 1927-March 2; 10y; m; yes; F; Died suddenly; no; Dunseith, ND
xxxxxxxxx Poitra, Angela; 1926-July 2; 1y; f; yes; ¼+; Tuberculosis; yes
1926 3203 Parisien, Louis; 1926-Aug 2; 36y; m; no; ¼+; yes
1927 3563 Reardon, Abraham; 1927-May 24; 2y; m; yes; ¼+; yes
1926 3577 Renville, Octave; 1926-Dec; 71y; f; yes; ¼+; no; Buford, ND
1927 3767 Senecal, Mary Rose; 1927-March 1; 38y; f; no; ¼+; no; Grenora, ND
1925 3632 Stewart, Angeline; 1927-Feb 27; 23y; f; yes; ¼+; yes

Deaths Occurring between the Dates of July 1, 1927 and June 30, 1928 of Indians Enrolled at Jurisdiction

1929 194 Allard, Alice; 1927-Aug 6; 11y; f; yes; ¼+; Tubercular menenigitis[sic]; yes
1927 198 Allard, Justine; 1928-April 20; 34y; f; no; ¼+; yes
1931 11 Allard, Mary L; 1928-April 9; 16y; f; no; ¼+; Tuberculosis of the lungs; yes
1929 441 Azure, Dometilda; 1927-July 11; 51y; f; no; ¼+; Tuberculosis pulmonary; yes
xxxxxxxxx Baker, Louis; 1928-April 23; 2y; m; no; ¼+; no; Ft.Totten, ND
1929 662 Belgarde, Wm Clifford; 1927-Sept 18; 1y; m; no; ¼+; Measles; yes
1927 717 Blue, Albert; 1927-Dec 5; 52y; m; no; ¼+; Lobar pneumonia; yes
1928 999 Charbonneau, Josephine; 1928-March 24; 10y; f; n; ¼+; no; Ft.Totten, ND
1927 1190 Decoteau, Norbert; 1928-April 13; 82y; m; yes; ¼+; yes
1927 1235 Dejarlais, Mary Mae; 1928-April 20; 7y; f; no; ¼+; yes
xxxxxxxxx Dejarlais, Florestine; 1927-Oct 27; 0; f; yes; ¼+; yes
1931 696 Demarais, Delmer; 1927-Dec; 2m; m; yes; ¼+; no; Dunseith, ND
1931 704 Demo, Jerry; 1927-Oct 30; 3y; m; no; ¼+; no; Glasgow, Mont
1930 863 Duchain, Alex Martin; 1928-Jan 22; 2y; m; yes; ¼+; yes
1929 1606 Everling, Joseph; 1928-May 13; 7y; m; no; ¼+; yes
1927 1573 Falcon, Virginia; 1927-Nov 24; 44y; f; no; ¼+; Endocarditis; yes
xxxxxxxxx Frederick, Marie; 1927-Feb 17; 1d; f; yes; ¼+; Hernia abdominal viscera; yes
1926 31 Flying Eagle, Kakenowash; 1927; 66y; m; yes; F; no; Dunseith, ND
1927 1787 Gourneau, Peter Henry; 1928-April 25; 3y; m; yes; ¼+; yes
1927 1818 Grandbois, Patrice No[sic]; 1927-Augues 26; 64y; m; no; ¼+; Tubercular menenigitis[sic]; yes
1929 2076 Henry (St.Pierre), Alexandra; 1928-Jan; 30y; f; yes; ¼+; no; Dunseith, ND
1927 2160 Jerome, Clara; 1928-Mar 14; 21y; f; yes; ¼+; no; Madoc, Mont
1927 2165 Jerome, Roger; 1927-Dec 13; 81y; m; no; ¼+; no; Unknown
1929 37 Kanick, Mary St.Ann; 1927-July; 36y; f; yes; F; Pneumonia; yes
Reported dead in 1919. Error Laducer, Jerome; 1928-Mar 9; 43y; m; no; ¼+; Dropped dead; yes
1927 2382 Lafournais, Lillian; 1928-May 30; 21y; f; no; ¼+; lobar pneumonia; no; Lawrence, Kan
1931 1308 Landry, John Joseph; 1928-Feb 25; 9y; m; no; ¼+; yes
xxxxxxxxx Laverdure, Sarah Jane; 1928-Jan 18; 3m; f; yes; ¼+; yes
xxxxxxxxx Laverdure, Marie Hilda; 1928-Jan 25; 1m; f; yes; ¼+; yes
1927 2777 Lenoir, Leo; 1928-April 13; 18y; m; yes; ¼+; no; Minnewauken[sic], ND
xxxxxxxxx Lillie, Francis; 1928-May 21; 3d; m; no; ¼+; yes
1931 1656 Lizotte, Doris May; 1937; 3y; f; no; ¼+; no; Great Falls, Mont

Turtle Mountain Reservation
Deaths

Key: Year and Number Last Census Roll ; Surname, Given; Date of Birth (Year-Month-Day); Age at Death; Sex; Tribe (Chippewa unless stated otherwise); Ward (Yes/No); Degree of Blood; Cause of Death (if given); At Jurisdiction Where Enrolled (Yes/No); (If no – Where)

1931	1657	Lizotte, Mary Jean; 1927; 1y; f; no; ¼+; no; Great Falls, Mont
1927	2559	Langer, Adele; 1927-Dec 9; 19y; f; yes; ¼+; Pulmonary tuberculosis; yes
1929	56	Machipeness, George; 1928-May 16; 2m; m; yes; F; General Tuberculosis; no; Dunseith, ND
1928	3120	McGillis, Rosalie; 1928-Jan 1; 10y; f; yes; ¼+; no; St.John, ND
1928	3194	Morin, Antoine; 1927-Aug 16; 30y; m; no; ¼+; Tuberculosis; no; Dunseith, ND
1927	3184	Morin, Genevieve; 1927-Oct 3; 91y; f; yes; ¼+; Chronic interstitial nephritis; yes
xxxxxxxxx		Parisien, Dora May; 1927-Nov 3; 4y; f; yes; ¼+; Intestienal obstruction; yes
xxxxxxxxx		Parisien, Mary Emily; 1927-Dec 16; 3y; f; yes; ¼+; Drinking lye; yes
1927	136	Pewapacomawat, Iron Bear; 1927; 48y; m; yes; F; Chronic valvular heart trouble; no; Dunseith, ND
xxxxxxxxx		Poitra, Wallace; 1927-Sept 9; 1y; m; yes; ¼+; yes
1928	3645	Poitra, Josephine; 1927-Sept 7; 19y; f; yes; ¼+; Pulmonary tuberculosis; yes
1929	3478	Parisien, Stella May; 1928-Aug 30; 2y; f; yes; ¼+; yes
1927	3675	Renault, Benjamin; 1927-Nov 5; 16y; m; yes; ¼+; General tuberculosis; yes
1927	3705	Rolette, Jane; 1927-42y; f; no; ¼+; no; Unknown
1927	3914	St.Pierre, Marie; 1928-May 1; 102y; f; no; ¼+; Senility; yes
1928	4044	Swain, Marie Zelma; 1927; 7y; f; no; ¼+; yes
1927	1978	Stevenson (Henry), Mary Louise; 1928-April 17; 23y; f; yes; ¼+; Tuberculosis; no; Thorne, ND
1928	4176	Turcott, Josephine; 1927-Aug 27; 5y; f; no; ¼+; no; Rolla, ND
Cannot locate on any census		Wilkie; Mary Delia; 1928-March 9; 35y; f; no; ¼+; Broncho pneumonia; yes
1928		Wallett, Francis; 1928-Feb 17; 0; m; yes; ¼+; yes
xxxxxxxxx		Walsh, Mary Louise; 1927-2y; f; no; ¼+; no; Dove, ND
1928	4324	Warren, William; 1928-May 10; 56y; m; no; ¼+; Chronic interstitial nephritis; yes
xxxxxxxxx		Welsh, Arline; 1927-Jan 26; 5d; f; no; ¼+; Cerebral hemorrhage; yes

Deaths Occurring between the Dates of July 1, 1928 and June 30, 1929 of Indians Enrolled at Jurisdiction

1927	60	All Still, Just One Sound; 1928; 6; m; yes; F; yes
1929	329	Azure, Virginia; 1928; 6; f; no; ¼+; yes
1929		Azure, Mary; 1929-March 30; 1h; f; no; ¼+; no; Rolla, ND
1929		Azure, Ann; 1929-March 30; 1h; f; no; ¼+; no; Rolla, ND
1928	438	Azure, Flora; 1928-Aug 21; 17y; f; no; ¼+; Accidental drowning; yes
1928	439	Azure, Mary Louise; 1928-Aug 21; 13y; f; no; ¼+; Accidental drowning; yes
1928	376	Azure, Mary Emma; 1929-Feb 4; 11y; f; no; ¼+; Pulmonary TB; no; Rolla, ND
1928	465	Azure, Raymond; 1928-Oct 20; 12y; m; no; ¼+; General TB Osteomeylitis[sic]; yes
1928	548	Belgarde, Margaret; 1928-Nov 28; 14y; f; yes; ¼+; Pulmonary TB; yes
1928	578	Belgarde (Wilkie), Mary Flora; 1928-July 6; 27y; f; yes; ¼+; Pneumonia & chronic heart trouble; yes
xxxxxxxxx		Belgarde, Irene Amelia; 1928-Nov; 17; 2y; f; yes; ¼+; Paralysis; yes
1929		Belgarde, Infant son; 1929-Jan 11; 2d; m; yes; ¼+; Congenital heart lesion; yes
1929	748	Bonneau, Alexis; 1928-Oct 7; 46y; m; yes; ¼+; no; Madoc, Mont
	NE	Carbou, Pete; 1929-March 17; m; no; ¼+; yes
1928	997	Charbonneau, Marie; 1928; 14y; f; no; ¼+; yes

Turtle Mountain Reservation
Deaths

Key: Year and Number Last Census Roll ; Surname, Given; Date of Birth (Year-Month-Day); Age at Death; Sex; Tribe (Chippewa unless stated otherwise); Ward (Yes/No); Degree of Blood; Cause of Death (if given); At Jurisdiction Where Enrolled (Yes/No); (If no – Where)

1928   120   Cree, Ernest; 1929-Feb 24; 4y; m; yes; ¼+; no; Dunseith, ND
1931   551   Cree, Julia; 1929-Mayl 23y; f; yes; F; no; Dunseith, ND

1931   451   Davis, Delima; 1929-May 19; 2y; f; no; ¼+; yes
1931   450   Davis, Romeo; 1929-April 17; 4y; m; no; ¼+; yes
1928   1393   Demarais, William; 1929-March 21; 21y; m; yes; ¼+; Tubercular pernitonitis[sic]; no; Malta, Mont
1928   1227   Decoteau, Moses; 1929-May 3; 79y; m; yes; ¼+; Flu; yes
1929   Decoteau, Joseph; 1929-Feb 26; 1m; m; no; ¼+; yes
1931   727   Doney, Matilda; 1928-Aug 3; 2y; f; no; ¼+; no; Harlem, Mont
xxxxxxxxx   Doney, Leonard; 1929-March 22; 1y; m; no; ¼+; no; Harlem, Mont
1938   1500   Dubois, Marie Ann; 1928-July 31; 5y; f; no; ¼+; Pneumonia TB; yes
1929   Dubois, Martina; 1929-May 24; 1y; f; no; ¼+; no; Garrison, ND
1928   1508   Ducept, Jean; 1928-Dec 20; 27y; m; yes; ¼+; Tuberculosis; yes
1930   860   Duchain, Mary Rose; 1928-July 26; 21y; f; yes; ¼+; yes

xxxxxxxxx   Falcon, Eugene; 1929-May 21; 1y; m; yes; ¼+; no; Trenton, ND
1928   1676   Fournier, Norbert; 1929-Feb 23; 40y; m; yes; ¼+; yes

1931   902   Gladue, Charles, Jr; 1928-Oct 14; 59y; m; no; ¼+; no; Unknown
1928   1830   Gourneau, Julia; 1929-Jan 5; 23y; f; yes; ¼+; Pulmonary TB; yes
1928   1847   Gourneau, Natalie Rose; 1929-May 5; 30y; f; yes; ¼+; Pulmonary TB; yes
1929   Gourneau, George; 1929-Mar 18; 15m; m; yes; ¼+; yes
xxxxxxxxx   Gourneau, Cecelia; 1929-Nov 28; 10m; f; yes; ¼+; yes
1929   Grant, Mary Cecelia; 1928-Sept 9; 3y; f; yes; ¼+; yes
1928   1964   Grant (Brien), Emma; 1929-Feb 17; 23y; f; yes; ¼+; Pulmonary TB; yes

1928   2140   Jast, Adele; 1929-Mar 9; 41y; f; yes; ¼+; yes
1928   2161   Jeannott, Patrice; 1929-Feb 27; 31y; m; yes; ¼+; Pneumonia; no; Minneapolis, Minn
1931   1108   Jerome, Eva Marline; 1928-Aug 31; 2y; f; yes; ¼+; yes
xxxxxxxxx   Jerome, Charles; 1929-Apr9l 28; 6m; m; yes; ¼+; no; Madoc, Mont
1928   2224   Jerome (Enno), Beatrice; 1929-March 18; 22y; f; yes; ¼+; Pulmonary TB; yes

1929   Laducer, Ernest; 1929-May 2; 2y; m; yes; ¼+; yes
1929   2386   Lafontain, Isadore; 1928-Aug 26; 28y; m; yes; ¼+; Poinsoned[sic]; no; Roy, Mont
1929   2532   Lafrombois, Dean; 1928-July 6; 27y; m; yes; ¼+; yes
1931   1603   Lemay, Gilbert L; 1929-Jan 13; 11y; m; yes; ¼+; no; Trenton, ND
1928   2889   Lillie, Alma Blanch; 1929-June 2; 1y; f; yes; ¼+; yes
1928   2886   Linklater, Philomeme; 1929-March 23; 77y; f; yes; ¼+; Carcinoma uterus; no; Devils Lake, ND

1928   3122   McGillis, Eugene; 1928-Aug 3; 10y; m; yes; ¼+; no; St.John, ND
1928   3151   Montrail, Margaret; 1928-July 25; 87y; f; yes; ¼+; no; Unknown
1928   3198   Morin, Rebecca; 1928-Nov 23; 2y; f; yes; ¼+; Pulmonary TB; no; Dunseith, ND
1928   54   Machipeness, Night S; 1928-Oct 17; 3m; f; yes; F; Whooping cough; no; Dunseith, ND

Turtle Mountain Reservation
Deaths
Key: Year and Number Last Census Roll ; Surname, Given; Date of Birth (Year-Month-Day); Age at Death; Sex; Tribe (Chippewa unless stated otherwise); Ward (Yes/No); Degree of Blood; Cause of Death (if given); At Jurisdiction Where Enrolled (Yes/No); (If no – Where)

xxxxxxxxx Nadeau, Mary; 1928-Sept 10; 2y; f; yes; ¼+; yes
xxxxxxxxx Nadeau, Rosella; 1928-Oct 13; 1y; f; yes; ¼+; yes

1929 3595 Peltier, Mary Emma; 1928-Oct 9; 16y m[sic]; yes; ¼+; yes
1928 911 Peterson, Mary; 1928-Dec 19; 17y; f; yes; ¼+; Pulmonary TB; no; Rolette
1929 Poitra, Mabel Irene; 1928-Nov 5; 1y; f; yes; ¼+; yes
xxxxxxxxx Poitra, David John; 1929-June 3; 7m; m; no; ¼+; no; Boggy Creek, Manitoba
xxxxxxxxx Poitra, Josephine; 1929-June 4; 3y; f; no; ¼+; no; Boggy Creek, Manitoba

1928 3787 Renault, Eliza; 1928-July 28; 16y; f; no; ¼+; Pulmonary TB; yes
xxxxxxxxx Richwine, Lucille; 1928-Sept 6; 5y; f; no; ¼+; no; Medicien[sic] Lake, Mont

1928 4098 Thomas, Catherine; 1929-Jan 31; 87y; f; yes; ¼+; yes
xxxxxxxxx Trothier, Doris; 1929-Jan 31; 2y; f; yes; ¼+; yes
1931 2570 Turcotte, Michael; 1929-June 13; 1y; m; yes; ¼+; no; Trenton, ND
1928 4278 Turcotte, Flora; 1928-Aug 31; 3m; f; yes; ¼+; no; Rolla, ND

1931 2655 Wilcox, Cecelia; 1928-Nov 26; 21y; f; yes; ¼+; no; St.John, ND
xxxxxxxxx Wilkie, Morris; 1928-Aug 9; 2m; m; no; ¼+; yes
1929 Wilkie, Unknown; 1929-Jan 30; 1m; f; no; ¼+; yes

Deaths Occurring between the Dates of July 1, 1929 and June 30, 1930 of Indians Enrolled at Jurisdiction

1929 11 Assiness, Little Stone; 1929-Oct 23; 59; f; yes; F; no; Devils Lake, ND

1929 548 Belgarde, Louise V; 1930-April 4; 18; f; yes; ¼+; Tuberculosis; no; Bainville, Mont
2939 575 Belgarde, Louis; 1929-July 28; 72; m; yes; ¼+; yes
xxxxxxxxx Belgarde, Alice; 1930-April 14; 6m; f; yes; ¼+; yes
1931 305 Belgarde, Irene; 1930-Jan 18; 3; f; no; ¼+; no; Hamar, ND
xxxxxxxxx Bercier, Alfred; 1930-June; 6; m; no; ¼+; yes
xxxxxxxxx Brien, John; 1929-Nov 3; 8; m; no; ¼+; Lagrippe[sic]; yes

1929 992 Champagne, Louis; 1930-April 16; 64; m; yes; ¼+; yes
1929 1052 Croteau, Mary L; 1929-Dec 11; 2; f; no; ¼+; no; Rolla, ND
1929 118 Cree, Victor; 1930-Feb 24; 16; m; yes; F

1929 1071 Dauphinais, J B; 1929-Nov 24; 77; m; no; ¼+; yes
1929 1076 Davis, Alexander; 1929-Nov 19; 47; m; no; ¼+; yes
xxxxxxxxx Davis, No name; 1929-Feb 25; 1d; m; yes; ¼+; yes
1929 1304 Dejarlais, Paul; 1929-Oct 3; 31; m; no; ¼+; Pulmonary TB; yes

1929 1704 Frederick, Rosalie; 1929-July 16; 41; f; no; ¼+; Tuberculosis; yes

Turtle Mountain Reservation
Deaths

Key: Year and Number Last Census Roll ; Surname, Given; Date of Birth (Year-Month-Day); Age at Death; Sex; Tribe (Chippewa unless stated otherwise); Ward (Yes/No); Degree of Blood; Cause of Death (if given); At Jurisdiction Where Enrolled (Yes/No); (If no – Where)

1931   903   Gladue, Claude; 1930-May 26; 50; m; no; ¼+; no; Brandon, Mont
1931 1051 Gunderson, Mary Jane; 1930-April 26; 15; f; no; ¼+; no; Palermo, ND
1931 1053 Gunderson, Wilburn G; 1929-Aug 17; 10; m; no; ¼+; no; Palermo, ND

xxxxxxxxx Herman, Florence; 1929-Nov 29; 3m; f; yes; ¼+; no; Devils Lake, ND
xxxxxxxxx Houle, Geo Joseph; 1930-June 18; 3m; m; yes; ¼+; yes

1930   905   Jaste, Leroy; 1930-June 22; 27; m; yes; ¼+; Pulmonary TB; yes
xxxxxxxxx Jollibois, Lucille; 1930-Jan 7; 4m; f; no; ¼+; no; Thorne, ND

xxxxxxxxx Lafloe, Jos Alfred; 1929-Dec 24; 5m; m; yes; ¼+; yes
1929 2446 Lafontain, Horace E; 1929-Oct 1; 23; m; yes; ¼+; Appendicitis; no; Rolette
1929 2622 Landry, Napoleon; 1929; 61; m; yes; ¼+; no; Unknown
1929 2772 Lavallie, Francois; 1930-March 30; 20; m; yes; ¼+; Pulmonary TB; yes
1930 1198 Laverdure, David; 1930-May 5; 70; m; no; ¼+
1929 1209 Laverdure, Matilda; 1929-Sept 3; 61; f; no; ¼+; Meningitis; yes
1929 2956 Lizotte, Joseph; 1929-Nov 2; 16; m; no; ¼+; no; Great Falls, Mont

1929 2989 Malaterre, Julius; 1929-July 11; 21; m; yes; ¼+; yes
1929 2997 Malaterre, Genevieve; 1929-Aug 29; 35; f; no; ¼+; Blood poisoning; yes
1929 3029 Malaterre, Alexis; 1929-Oct 19; 66; m; yes; ¼+; Heart trouble; yes
xxxxxxxxx McCloud, Vivian; 1930-Feb 14; 2m; f; yes; ¼+; yes
xxxxxxxxx Morin, Frank J; 1929-Aug 29; 15d; m; yes; ¼+; yes
xxxxxxxxx Morin, Rose; 1930-Jan 5; 2d; f;   yes; ¼+; yes
1929   10 Mekwam, Alex; 1929-Nov 20; 15; m; yes; F; Pulmonary TB; no; Dunseith, ND

1929 3443 Page, Nancy; 1929-Oct 7; 88; f; yes; ¼+; Old age; yes
1929 3450 Parisien (Champagne), William; 1930-Feb 2; 25; m; yes; ¼+; Pulmonary TB; yes
1929 2060 Parisien (Hayes), Joseph; 1930-Feb 9; 13; m; yes; ¼+; Ran away from school and froze to death; yes
1929 3595 Peltier, Mary Emma; 1929-Aug 26; 13; f; no; ¼+; no; Dunseith, ND
1929 3743 Poitra, Mary Laura; 1929-Nov 13; 19; f; yes; ¼+; Pulmonary TB; yes

1929 3865 Renault, Elalie; 1929-Aug 8; 73; f; yes; ¼+; Pneumonia; yes
1929 3873 Renault, Grace; 1929-Dec 21; 6m; f; no; ¼+; yes

1929   47 Shining Cloud; 1930-Jan 30; 70; f; yes; F; no; Dunseith, ND
1930 2452 Skinner, Madeline; 1930-April; 10; f; yes; F; no; Dunseith, ND

xxxxxxxxx Vandal, Lucille; 1929-Dec 19; 4m; f; yes; ¼+; yes

1929 4396 Wallett, Melanie; 1929-Dec 10; 67; f; yes; ¼+; yes

Turtle Mountain Reservation
Deaths

Key: Year and Number Last Census Roll ; Surname, Given; Date of Birth (Year-Month-Day); Age at Death; Sex; Tribe (Chippewa unless stated otherwise); Ward (Yes/No); Degree of Blood; Cause of Death (if given); At Jurisdiction Where Enrolled (Yes/No); (If no – Where)

Deaths Occurring between the Dates of **April 1, 1930** and **March 31, 1931** of Indians Enrolled at Jurisdiction

1929 188 Allard, Mary Eva; 1930-Dec 1; 7; f; yes; ¼+; Diphtheria; yes
1931 23 Allery, Donald; 1931-Jan 25; 7m; m; yes; ¼+; yes
1930 32 Allery, Irene; 1931-Feb 20; 17; f; yes; ¼+; Tuberculosis; yes
1931 74 Azure, Mary Lola; 1930-Sept 28; 4m; f; yes; ¼+; yes
1931 143 Azure, James; 1930-Aug 24; 1; m; no; ¼+; yes
xxxxxxxxx Azure, Clifford; 1930-Sept 6; 5m; m; no; ¼+; Summer complaint; yes

xxxxxxxxx Baker, John Martin; 1930-Aug 23; 2; m; no; ¼+; no; Ft.Totten, ND
1929 548 Belgarde, Louise; 1930-April 4; 18; f; yes; ¼+; Tuberculosis; no; Bainville, Mont
xxxxxxxxx Belgarde, Alice; 1930-Apeil 14; 6m; f; yes; ¼+; yes
xxxxxxxxx Bercier, Alfred; 1930-June; 6; m; no; ¼+; yes
1930 167 Blue, John Monte; 1930-Aug 5; 1; m; yes; ¼+; Colitis; yes
1930 465 Bottineau, ND Julia; 1930-Nov 19; 31; f; yes; ¼+; Paralysis; yes
1930 177 Boyer, May; 1930-Nov 8; 2; f; no; ¼+; yes
1930 268 Brunnell, Eva; 1930-Sept 1; 2; f; yes; ¼+; Infection; yes
1931 485 Bursness, Bernice; 1930-Nov 3; 2; f; no; ¼+; yes

1929 992 Champagne, Louis; 1930-April 16; 54; m; yes; ¼+; yes

xxxxxxxxx Davis, Verlin; 1930-Sept 3; 3m; m; yes; ¼+; Cholera; yes
1930 414 Decoteau, St.Ann; 1930-Nov 5; 16; f; no; ¼+; Pulmonary TB; yes
1930 497 Dejarlais, Rachel; 1930-Nov 2; 74; f; no; ¼+; Old Age Senility; yes
1930 784 Delorme, Calixte; 1930-Sept 21; 1; m; yes; ¼+; yes

1930 638 Enno, Antoine, Jr; 1930-Sept 19; 71; m; yes; ¼+; Old age; yes
xxxxxxxxx Enno, Rose; 1931-March 7; 7m; f; no; ¼+; yes
1930 654 Enno, Lawrence; 1930-July 29; 7; m; no; ¼+; Pneumonia; yes
1930 656 Enno, Francis; 1930-Aug 7; 1; m; no; ¼+; Colitis; yes

1931 903 Gladue, Claude; 1930-May 26; 50; m; no; ¼+; no; Brandon, Mont
1930 734 Gourneau, Alexander; 1931-March 3; 64; m; no; ¼+; yes
1931 1051 Gunderson, Mary Jane; 1930-Spril 26; 15; f; no; ¼+; no; Palermo, ND

xxxxxxxxx Houle, Joseph Geo; 1930-June 18; 3m; m; yes; ¼+; yes

1930 905 Jast, Leroy; 1930-June 22; 27; m; yes; ¼+; Tuberculosis; yes
1930 1337 Jollibois, Marie; 1930-Aug 20; 75; f; no; ¼+; Old age; yes

1930 1432 Lafournais, Ernest; 1931-Jan 26; 17; m; no; ¼+
1930 1149 Langer, John B; 1930-Nov 20; 75; m; no; ¼+; Old age; yes
1931 1478 Lasota, Josephine; 1931-Feb 28; 30; f; yes; ¼+; no; Unknown
1930 1198 Laverdure, David; 1930-May 5; 70; m; no; ¼+; yes

Turtle Mountain Reservation
Deaths

Key: Year and Number Last Census Roll ; Surname, Given; Date of Birth (Year-Month-Day); Age at Death; Sex; Tribe (Chippewa unless stated otherwise); Ward (Yes/No); Degree of Blood; Cause of Death (if given); At Jurisdiction Where Enrolled (Yes/No); (If no – Where)

xxxxxxxxx McCloud, Joseph; 1930-Dec 14; 0; m; yes; ¼+; yes
xxxxxxxxx McCloud, Mary; 1930-Dec 14; 0; f; yes; ¼+; yes
xxxxxxxxx Morin, Charles C; 1930-Sept; 1; m; yes; ¼+; no; Dunseith, ND
1930 1784 Machipeness, Ida; 1931-March 31; 21; f; yes; F; no; Dunseith, ND

xxxxxxxxx Nepine, White Thunder; 1931-Feb 8; 3m; m; yes; F; no; Dunseith, ND

1930 1476 Parisien, Ezear; 1930-July 17; 92; m; yes; ¼+; yes
xxxxxxxxx Parisien, Roy; 1930-Aug 9; 3m; m; no; ¼+; Colitis; yes
1930 1569 Peltier, Mary; 1931-Feb 4; 41; f; yes; ¼+; Carcinoma of uterus; no; Devils Lake, ND
1930 1559 Poitra, J Alphonse; 1930-Oct 20; 17; m; yes; ¼+; Tuberculosis; yes
1930 1573 Poitra, Stella A; 1930-July 16; 4m; f; yes; ¼+; Pneumonia; yes
1930 1651 Premeau, Olympia; 1931-March 9; 5; f; yes; ¼+; Appendicitis; yes
1930 2224 Plante, Louis; 1931-March 9; 43; m; no; ¼; Heart attack; no; Devils Lake, ND

1930 1662 Renault, Regina; 1930-Dec 3; 21; f; yes; ¼+; Pulmonary Tuberculosis; yes
1930 2068 Red Thunder, Fred; 1930-Oct 15; 7; m; yes; F; Pulmonary Tuberculosis; no; Dunseith, ND

1931 1961 San Grait, Joseph; 1930-Sept 1; 11m; m; no; ¼+; yes
1930 1686 San Grait, Caroline; 1931-Feb 13; 87; f; yes; ¼+; yes
1930 1791 Smith, Julienne; 1931-Feb 14; 65; f; no; ¼+; Stroke paralysis; yes
1930 2555 St.Pierre, Francois; 1930-Aug 24; 63; m; no; ¼+; Pulmonary TB; yes
1930 1722 Smith, Cecelia Mae; 1931-March 25; 1; f; yes; ¼+; Pneumonia; yes
1930 2452 Skinner, Madeline; 1930-April; 10; f; yes; F; Tuberculosis; no; Dunseith, ND

1930 1789 Vallie, John; 1931-March 19; 80; m; yes; ¼+; yes
1930 2724 Vandal, Mary; 1930-May 24; 55; f; no; ¼+; Died after an operation; yes
1930 2740 Vandal, William; 1930-July 4; 30; m; yes; ¼+; yes
1930 1879 Wilkie, Emil; 1930-Aug 17; 20; m; yes; ¼+; Killed in auto accident; yes
1930 2802 Wilkie, Marie; 1930-July 14; 63; f; no; ¼+; yes
1930 2815 Wilkie, Josephine; 19300Sept; 54; f; no; ¼+; Blood Poisoning; yes

Deaths Occurring between the Dates of **April 1, 1931** and **March 31, 1932** of Indians Enrolled at Jurisdiction

1931 B 2 Aiken, Virginia; 1931-Oct 8; 56; f; no; ¼; no; Rolla, ND
Died before enrollment Aiken, Raymond; 1931-Nov 26; 3m m; yes; ¼; Pneumonia; no; Rolla, ND
1931 A 3 Alex, Frank; 1931-Nov 26; 6; m; yes; ¼; Tubercular meningitis; yes
1931 A37 Allard, Josephine; 1931; 72; f; no; ¼; yes
1931 B21 Allery, Fred; 1931-June 5; 23; m; yes; ¼; Lobar pneumonia; yew
1931 B18 Allery, Frank; 1931-Sept 25; 26; m; yes; ¼; Pulmonary TB; no; Whitewater, Mont
1931 A87 Azure, Francois; 1931-Dec 25; 75; m; no; ¼; yes
1931 A80 Azure, Mary Ann; 1931-Dec 3; 3m; f; yes; ¼; yes
1931 B23 Allery, Donald; 1931-Jan 25; 8m; m; yes; ¼; yes

Turtle Mountain Reservation
Deaths

Key: Year and Number Last Census Roll ; Surname, Given; Date of Birth (Year-Month-Day); Age at Death; Sex; Tribe (Chippewa unless stated otherwise); Ward (Yes/No); Degree of Blood; Cause of Death (if given); At Jurisdiction Where Enrolled (Yes/No); (If no – Where)

1931 A179	Belgarde, Gilbert; 1932-Feb 25; 63; m; yes; ¼; Syphilis myocarditis; yes
1931 B235	Belanger, Pete; 1931-April 9; 77; m; yes; F; no; Dunseith, ND
1931 A214	Belgarde, Dorothy; 1931-June 9; 2m; f; yes; ¼; yes
Died before enrollment	Blue; Carroll R; 1931-Oct 19; 6m; n[sic]; yes; ¼; Broncho pneumonia; yes
1931 A585	Blue (Decoteau), Marie Louise; 1931-Sept 24; 22; f; yes; ¼; Pulmonary Tuberculosis; yes
1931 A266	Bonneau, LaGlore; 1931-May 28; 76; m; yes; ¼; yes
1931 A288	Boyer, Julia; 1931-Nov 12; 83; f; no; ¼; yes
1931 A480	Bruce, Virginia; 1931-Nov 2; 18; f; yes; ¼; Pulmonary TB and syphilis; yes
1931 A346	Brunnell, Claudia; 1931-Dec 1; 55; f; no; ¼; Operation goitre[sic]; yes
1931 A514	Davis, Norbert F; 1931-Dec 31; 2; m; no; ¼; yes
NE	Decoteau, Fred; 1931-Dec 13; 43; m; yes; ¼; Broncho-pneumonia; yes
1931 A746	Dionne, Marie; 1931-Dec 26; 16; f; no; ¼; Pneumonia; yes
Died before enrollment	Day; Mary; 1932-Feb 15; 7m; f; yes; F; Pneumonia; no; Dunseith, ND
1931 A784	Enno, Louis; 1932-Feb 7; 5; m; no; ¼; Pyelo-nephritis; yes
Died before enrollment	Gourneau, Jane; 1932-Feb 6; 1m; f; yes; ¼; Diarrhea enteritis; yes
1931 A868	Gladue, Julia; 1931-July 20; 80; f; yes; ¼; Valvular heart disease; yes
1931 A969	Grant, Geo Harry; 1931-Sept 25; 7; m; yes; ¼; yes
Died before enrollment	Hamley, Sylvia; 1932-Mar 14; 2d; f; yes; ¼; Atelectasis congenital; yes
1931 B1158	Houle, Cinya; 1932-Jan 17; 69; f; no; ¼; Chronic myocardial degeneration; no; Canton Asylum, SD
Died before enrollment	Houle, Barbara; 1931-Sept 7; 11m; f; no; ¼; yes
1931 B1216	Jerome, Martin; 1932-Jan 25; 74; m; yes; ¼; no; Madoc, Mont
1931 A1111	Jerome, Louis; 1931-July 9; 32; m; yes; ¼; Lobar pneumonia; yes
Died before enrollment	Lafontain, Roy; 1932-Mar 14; 8m; m; no; ¼; Acute laryngitis streptococoous[sic] infection, yes
1931 B1331	Lafrance, Justine; 1931-Sept 14; 41; f; no; ¼; yes
Died before enrollment	Lafrance, Theresa; 1931-Oct 22; 3m; f; no; ¼; yes
Died before enrollment	Lafrombois, Nels; 1931-Aug 7; 1; m; yes; ¼; yes
1931 A1627	Lillie, Mary V; 1931-July 5; 0; f; no; ¼; yes

Turtle Mountain Reservation
Deaths

Key: Year and Number Last Census Roll ; Surname, Given; Date of Birth (Year-Month-Day); Age at Death; Sex; Tribe (Chippewa unless stated otherwise); Ward (Yes/No); Degree of Blood; Cause of Death (if given); At Jurisdiction Where Enrolled (Yes/No); (If no – Where)

Died before enrollment   McCloud, Patricia; 1931-Sept 28; 2hrs; f; yes; ¼; Atelectasis new born; yes

1931 B1754   McCoy, Josephine; 1931-April 11; 25; f; yes; ¼; Lobar pneumonia; no; Sidney, Mont

1931 A1618   Montriel, Adele; 1931-June 17; 62; f; no; ¼; no; Canton Asylum, SD

1931 B1623   Morin, Josette; 1931-Oct; 78; f; no; ¼; no; Dunseith, ND

1931 B1841   Morin, Anna; 1931-Aug 24; 14; f; yes; ¼; Pulmonary TB; no; Dunseith, ND

1931 B1969   Olson, Virginia; 1932-Jan 19; 36; f; no; ¼; no; Rolla, ND

Died before enrollment   Poitra, Stephen; 1931-Nov 7; 6m; m; yes; ¼; Pneumonia; yes

1931 A1842   Poitra, Irene; 1931-Nov 7; 1; f; yes; ¼; Rickets; yes

1931 A1944   Roussin, Roger; 1931-July 20; 9m; m; no; ¼; Rickets & inanition; yes

Index

[UNKNOWN], Mary Winifred 265
ADAMS, Tracey 38
AIKEN
   Eliza 103
   Julia 138
   Louise 226
   Raymond 272,290
   St Ann 128
   Virginia 290
AKENENSI, Iron Thumder 255
ALBERTS
   Emma 250
   Eva 3
   Josephine 124
   Justine 3
ALEC, Frank 242
ALEX
   Frank 290
   Morris 261
ALICK
   Ramona 272
   Raymond 250
   Selma 246
ALL STILL, Just One Sound 285
ALLARD
   Alfred Wilmar 239
   Alice 284
   Clarence S 267
   Delia 86
   Donald 289
   Eleanor 110
   Eliza 63
   Elizabeth 230
   Elmer 255
   Emma 163
   Florence Stella 255
   Irene 250,289
   Josephine 290
   Justine 284
   Louis 242
   Margaret 13
   Mary Eva 289
   Mary Jane 167
   Mary L 284
   Michael 267
   Michael J 261
   Patrice W 255
   Pauline 233

Raymond 278
Rita 261
Roy 242
Sylvester 272
ALLERY
   Alphonsine 38
   Caroline 64
   Cecelia 25
   Celia 47
   Clara J 281
   Clifford 255
   Delia 206
   Delima 112
   Donald 290
   Donald Fred 261,267
   Doris 267
   Dorothy 272
   Elizabeth 67,68
   Emma 15
   Evelyn Dora 261
   Flavis 51
   Frank 290
   Fred 290
   Fred Joseph 272
   Genevieve 49
   Georaline 255
   Gladys 246
   Harriet 61
   Ida 250
   John 261,267
   Josette 134
   Louis 255
   Louise 9
   Margaret 242
   Mary 122
   Mary B 116
   Mary Louise 134
   Mary Rose 178
   Nicholas 239
   Virginia 62
   Vivian 250
   Willard Monteith 246
ALLERY.FANNING, Mary 141
ALLERY.FAVILL, Margaret 213
ALWAYS DAY, Mrs 102
AMUDSON, Dolores 267
AMYOTT
   Julia 23

Index

Leonard 255
Mary 132
Mary Cecilia 261
Mary Rose 32
Norbert Francis 239
Raymond 242
Rose 73
AMYOTT.ST CLAIRE, Adeline 93
AMYOTT.VILLENEUVE, Florence
.... 84
AMYOTTE
   Adele 113
   Alexandria 163
   Veronica 200
   Virginia 182
ANAKONIK, Offer The Pipe 283
ANDERSON
   Adeline Mae 246
   Irene Velma 267
   James 98
   John Henry 255
   May Rhoda 98
   Ray L 98
ANDRIFF
   Dorothy 255
   Lawrence Evan 246
ASSINESS, Little Stone 287
AUER, John, Jr 242
AZURE
   Adele 196
   Agnes 140
   Alice 143
   Andrew 239,281
   Ann 260,285
   Annie 28
   Catherine 228
   Cecil A 101
   Clarence R 267
   Clarence Richard 261
   Clemance 98
   Clemence 180
   Clifford 289
   Clifford Sylvester 261
   Delia 64
   Dometilda 284
   Donald Louis 255
   Doris Mae 250
   Edna 239

Eliza V 101
Emma 93
Ernest 101,250
Flora 285
Florence 250
Florence Doris 272
Florestine 76,129
Frances 272
Francois 290
Fred Sylvester 272
Fred, Jr 261
Genevieve 225
George 242
Ida 48
James 260,289
John Joseph 272
Josephine 67,182,206
Jospehine 94
Jossett 283
Julia 65
Laura 72
Lazarus 267
Louise 149
Mabel 246
Margaret 20
Margaret Mary 267
Marie 92
Marie Josephine 267
Marie Louise 261
Martin 246
Mary 6,17,72,99,260,285
Mary Agnes 203
Mary Alice 242
Mary Ann 267,290
Mary Clara 228
Mary Emma 285
Mary Lola 261,267,289
Mary Louise 285
Mary Rosalie 255
Mary Rose 185
Mary St Ann 77
Mildred Helen 250
Octavie 27
Peter 239
Peter Clifford 255
Philomeme 55
Raymond 272,285
Raymond Joseph 246

Index

Roger Louis 242
Rose 246
Rose Marie 272
Ruby Mae 255
Sarah 29,33
St Pierre 239
Veronic 111
Veronica 242
Virginia 285
Virginie 225
AZURE.MORIN, Eliza 160
BABACH, Peter 261
BAILEY, Mary 45
BAKER
   Cecil Raphael 250
   Emma 246
   George 239
   Helen Blanch 267
   John Martin 289
   Josephine 34
   Louis 246,284
   Marceline 242
   Marie Elizabeth 267
   Mary Ann 130
   Moses 267
BANEY, Isabelle 164
BARSNESS
   Bernice Rosalie 250
   Gladys Cecelia 267
BARTLETTE, Flora 213
BARTON, Louise 108
BASTON
   Eliza 156
   Marie 234
   Mary Rose 242
   Mary St Ann 154
   Robert 261
   Wilfred 272
BAUER
   Joseph 261
   Mary 137
BAURT, Lyda 140
BEAUCHMAN
   Agnes Violet 242
   Herman 246
   James Benedict 239
   John Albert 246
   Marie Pearl 261

Mary Jane 255
Ramona 272
St Ann 128
BEAUCHMAN.MORIN, Marie ... 162
BEAUDRY
   Rose Helen 246
   Teresa Dorothy 267
   Theresa 255
   Theresa Dorothy 261
   Victor Albert 272
BELANGER
   Pete 291
   Virginia 179
BELGARD, Mary Rose 219
BELGARDE
   Agnes 112
   Alfred 242
   Alice 261,287,289
   Alphonsine 187
   Andrew 239
   Cecelia 109
   Celina 33
   Clara 63
   Clemence 131
   Collin 267
   Donald Louis 255
   Dorothy 272,291
   Edward M 283
   Edward Martin 242
   Elie Wm 88
   Eliza 94
   Elizabeth 160
   Ella 272
   Ernestine 242
   Eugene 272
   Eva 29
   Francois 283
   Frank 255
   Gilbert 291
   Harold Elmer 261
   Ida Rose 283
   Infant 260
   Infant son 285
   Irene 246,287
   Irene Amelia 246,285
   Jane Genevieve 272
   John 239
   John Sylvester 272

Index

Josephine 210,281
Laura 219
Louis 261,287
Louisa 242
Louise 289
Louise V 287
Mabel 242
Maragret L 261
Margaret 285
Marie 108
Marie Rosina 282
Martha 255
Mary 9,100,219,239,281
Mary Dorothy 260
Mary Jane 13,35,231
Mary Julia 209
Mary Rose 61
No Name 261
Patrice 246
Rachel 42,86
Ralph 246
Raymond R 272
Robert 283
Rosalie 7,116,178
Rose 8,126
Rosina 54,137
Ruth 260
St Ann 60
Stanley 272
Victoria 29,217
Virginia 78
Wm Clifford 242,284
BELGARDE (WILKIE), Mary Flora.
.... 285
BELGARDE.CARIBOU, Mary Jane
.... 198
BELGARDE.MONTOUR, Mary 97
BELGRADE
   Angeline 250
   Daniel James 250
   Mary Rose 250
BELL
   Fred 242
   Lloyd 255
   Robert James 272
   Viola 239
BERCIER
   Agnes Vitaline 261

Alfred 287,289
Angeline Marie 255
Catherine 15,225
Celia 57
Charlie Walter 239
Domethilde 168
Eugenia 16
Felicite 58
George 261
Jean Louis 255
June 130,250
Marie 122
Marion 255
Mary 61
Mary Jane 86
Mary Louise 134
Norman 250
Raymond 130,239
Rosalie 175
Vernon 283
Victoria 250
Virginia 43,90,154
BERCIER (WARREN), Sylvester 272
BERGIE
   Bridget 93
   Mabel 195
BERGIER, Laurine Lucy 242
BERTHIUM, Philomeme 216
BESON, Mary 43
BLEFF, Madeline R 57
BLUE
   Albert 284
   Carroll R 272,291
   Elsie Stella 242
   John Monte 255,289
   Marie Alice 246
   Mary L 55
BLUE (DECOTEAU), Marie Louise .
.... 291
BOE
   Ralph Edwin 261
   Wm Laverne 250
BOHANNON, Veronica 190
BONNAUP
   Catherine 48
   Daisy 8
BONNEAU
   Alexis 285

Index

Alphonsine 102
LaGlore 291
Mary Jane 66
Pauline 44
Virginia 75
BONNEAUP, Virginia...................30
BOTTINEAU
   Alice 267
   Julia 289
   Napoleon 239
   Ruth 246
   St Ann 93
BOUVIER
   Mary 45
   Verna Ritha 272
BOYER
   Abraham 281
   Andrew 281
   Corine Jane 250
   Emma 124
   Gordon Louie 272
   Irene 272
   Julia 291
   Lloyd 255
   Maggie 246
   Marie Jeanne 239
   Mary 43
   Mary Rose 239
   May 250,289
   Rosine 130
   Selina 267
   Stanley 239
BOYER.ALLERY, Mary 202
BRADFORD
   Edna 122
   Stanley Emil 261
BRADFORD.FAINE, Flora 47
BRAUGH, Donald D 267
BRELAND, Marie 188
BRIEN
   Adele 250
   Agnes 76
   Albert 69
   Albert Verne 261
   Albert, Jr 272
   Alex William 267
   Alex Wm 110
   Aloysius 261,267

Alvina 255
Clarice 210
Frank Theodore 246
Gloria Belle 246
Gordon 272
John 287
John Verlin 250
Josephine 246
Laureat Frank 267
Louise 234
Mary Ann 88
Mary Celina 267
Mary Jane 128
Mary Rose 282
Peter Wilfred 239
Rosalie 119
Seraphine 125
Susanna 250
Wm Leo James 261
BRIEN.ANDERSON, Florestine 98
BRIERE
   Albert David 239
   Edna 281
BRIERE (ADAMS), Tracey 272
BRINKMAN, Erma 242
BRUCE
   Alexander 123
   Cecile 239
   Edna 250
   Ernest Norbert 242
   Flora 155
   Irene 272
   Jennie 232
   Joseph Louis 282
   Josephine 281
   Lawrence M 267
   Louis Albert 246,283
   Mary 100
   Mary Ann 185
   Mary Josephine 239
   Mary Rose 123
   Raymond 260
   Virginia 291
   William 267
BRUNELL, Ellen Jane 239
BRUNNEL
   Julia 11
   Rose Delima 84

Index

BRUNNELL
  Bernealia 267
  Beulah 250
  Christine 109
  Claudia 291
  Corinne Marie 267
  Edna Marie 255
  Elvina 157
  Emily 84
  Eva 250,289
  Jessica 246
  Louise Lucille 255
  Martha 246
  Mary E 213
  Mary Louise 283
  Mary P 213
  Paul Arthur 239
  Peter Raymond 255
  Phillip Jerome 261,267
  Theresa Blanche 250
  Theresa Flora 267
BRUNNELL.OMAR.CHAMBERS,
  St Ann 134
BURNS, Clara 221
BURSNESS, Bernice 289
CALDWELL
  Jessie 43
  Nina May 239
CANNERY, Rhoda 157
CAPLETTE
  Emily 99
  Ernest 281
  Modeste 281
  Rosina 282
CARBOU, Pete 285
CARDINAL, Betsey 36
CARIBOU
  Clemence 198
  Peggy 239
CARMER, Lewis 246
CARRINGTON, LeGrande A 272
CARTNELL, Marian Belle 272
CARTWRIGHT, Irene Mae 267
CHAMPAGNE
  Edna 246
  Frank 261
  Helen 246
  Isabel 188

Joseph Paul 255
Larose 57
Louis 287,289
Madeline 197
Mary Louise 281
Rita 242
Rose 60
Theresa 34
Willard 242
CHARBONNEAU
  Grace 97
  Josephine 284
  Marie 285
  Mary Rosina 282
CHARETTE
  Catherine 22
  Eliza 84
  Geo William 261
  Margaret 59
  Mary 227
  Peter Eugene 272
CHRISTENSON
  No Name 26
  Ruth 260
CLARK
  Evelyn 193
  Laura Leona 193
CONSTANCE
  Albert Arthur 255
  Dean Richard 242
  Edward Clarence 250
  Lloyd Joseph 239
COOK
  John Fay 255
  John Faye 40
COTTERELL
  Carl Raymond 261
  Violet May 272
COUNTS
  Lloyd 261
  Mary Louise 255
  Roy 267
COX, Harriet 182
CREC, Rosina 250
CREE
  Ellen 193
  Ernest 239,286
  Jerome 267

Index

Julia..286
Sounding Nice........................267
Victor......................................287
CRISSLER
   Carey M, Jr 282
   Florence 192
CROTEAU
   Leo..246
   Mary A....................................250
   Mary L 287
   Mary Louise 272
DAIGNAULT
   George Lester..........................242
   Marie R 76
   Virginia.....................................71
DAIGNON, Josette......................... 6
DANIELS, Emma........................196
DAUPHINAIS
   Adeline....................................180
   Florestine 204
   J B 287
   Josephine.................................283
   Josephine Delia 242
   Marian.......................................56
   Mary Ann................................183
   Mary Jane..................................13
   Peter Elmer 246
   St Ann.....................................232
DAVIS
   Alexander................................287
   Alvina 51
   Beatrice 184
   Benedict 242
   Blanche 189
   Delia..121
   Delima..............................246,286
   Dolores....................................273
   Elise 43
   Elmer Fred 251
   Flora..255
   Gilbert Albert 255
   Henietta...................................111
   Jerome.....................................267
   John Lloyd 250
   Josephine..........................188,251
   Laura...33
   Leon Felix 261
   Lillian......................................250

Louise... 4
Lucy Catherine 267
Maggie Barbara 261,267
Marie 147
Mary 34
Mary (Azure)........................... 281
Mary Clemence 239,282
Mary Dolores.......................... 273
Mary Jane 229
Mary Joyce 273
Mary R...................................... 81
Mary Rose 156
Matilda 170
No Name 287
Norbert 261
Norbert F 291
Ohilomeme 224
Raymond 251
Romeo 239,286
Rosalie 112
Rose 170
Ruth May................................ 239
Stella 239
Stella Justine.......................... 251
Verlin...................................... 289
Verlin Clifford 261,268
Verna Cecelia 261
Vinier James.......................... 242
DAY
   Evelyn..................................... 250
   George 242
   Joseph 247,283
   Lucille...................................... 19
   Mary 250,273,291
DECOTEAU
   Agnes....................................... 12
   Albert..................................... 246
   Ambrose 239
   Beatrice.................................. 185
   Caroline 15
   Cecelia 261
   Charley 267
   Charlie 273
   Eliza....................................... 232
   Elizabeth................................ 169
   Elmer 251
   Eme rse..................................... 8
   Ernest..................................... 246

Ethel Laverne 262
Florus 273
Frank Lawrence 246
Fred 291
Genevieve 93
George 242
Henry Eugene 239
Ida Rose 62
Jeannette C 273
John B 282
John Fred 239
John Wilfred 255
Joseph 286
Joseph Bruno 242
Joseph Patrice 255
Josephine 10,50
June Angela 273
Lillie 145
Lorraine 255
Lorraine C 262,268
Louis Alfred 251
Louis William 239
Louis Wm 281
Lucy Laverne 267
Mabel Rose 255
Madeline 14
Margery 222
Mary Ann 267
Mary Jane 180
Moses 286
No Name 255
Norbert 284
Oliver John 242
Patrice 283
Paul Melvin 256
Raphael 255
Rita 255
Ruth 194
St Ann 127,194,289
Stanley 239
Stella 194,251
Sylvester 261
Victoria 32
Walter 246
Warren 180
William 180
DECOTEAU.AMYOTTE, Laura .163
DECOTEAU.JEANNOTTE, Lucy 208
DECOUTEAU
  Adeline 160
  Eliza 50
  Lillian 122
  Marie 78
DEJARLAIS
  Alma Rose 268
  Andrew 281
  Andrew Albert 242
  Antoine 262,268
  Blanch Patricia 247
  Elise Rose 273
  Eliza 17
  Ellen 16
  Ernest Gabriel 251
  Ernestine 234
  Flora 247
  Flora Marie 256
  Florence 21
  Florestine 251,284
  Gregory 239
  Jacob Clifford 256
  James 283
  Josephine 18,92
  Lucy Nora 247
  Marguerite 247
  Marie 148
  Mary 37
  Mary Eliza 15
  Mary Mae 284
  Norabelle 273
  Paul 287
  Rachel 189,289
  Russellfrancis 239
  St Ann 90
  William John 239
  Wm John 281
DEJARLAIS.BELGARDE, Louisa
  88
DEJARLIS, Grace Margaret 256
DELONAIS
  Anna 143
  Delima M 135
  Isabel 117
  Mary Adele 242
DELONG
  Elizabeth 273

Index

Leona 256
Rose Delima 242
Stella 176
DELORME
   Alphonsine 190
   Beatrice Ann 273
   Betsey 40
   Calixite 262
   Calixte 289
   Christine 211
   Dolores 239
   Eliza 11
   Elizabeth 148
   Ernestine 227
   Eugene Edward 256
   Genevieve 262,268
   Justine 148
   Larose 187
   Lucy Rhea 262
   Madeline 251
   Marie 190
   Mary 166
   Mary E 111
   Mary Jane 91
   Nancy 158
   Ogila 6
   Peter Clifford 247
   Rita Marie 273
   Rosanna 72
   Virginia 21,52
   Wendell John 262
   William 256
DEMARAIS
   Albert 240,281
   Bella 232
   Delmer 284
   Edward Leonard 240
   Eli 273
   Ernest Martin 262
   John 273
   Josephine 240
   Mary Elma 159
   Patrick 254
   Ruth 188
   Victoria 256,262
   Virginia 31
   William 286
DEMO, Jerry 284

DEMONT, Josephine 17
DEMONTIGNY
   Ella 35
   Emma 107
   Harry 240
   Hazel 240
   James 247
   John, Jr 256
   Lloyd 243
   Margaret 219
   Mary Jane 282
   Mary M 29
   Philomeme 150
   Philomene 161
   Wilfred 247
DENOMIE, Louise 100
DESJARLAIS
   Harriet 43
   Marie 160
DIONNE
   Benedict 256
   Blanche 243
   Clarence 243
   Dorothy 268
   Edward 262
   Edward G 256
   Emma 87
   Eva 185
   Francis R 273
   Frank 240
   Georgiana 231
   Julia 243
   Marguerite 273
   Marie 291
   Marie Alice 256
   Mary 247
   Mary Delima 256
   Mary Eva 251
   Mary Louise 77
   Mary Rose 216
   Matilda 107
   Robert 273
   Rosa 262
   Sarah 131
   Theresa Mae 268
   Vennery 204
   Virginia 210
DIONNE (PREMEAU), Dorothy Mae

Index

....273
DIONNE.THOMAS, Mary 228
DONEY
   Leonard 251,286
   Louise 38
   Martin Thomas..........................247
   Mary Alice 220
   Matilda........................243,286
DONEY (BERRONTEAU), John Leslie
....273
DONSEY, Agnes 219
DUBBIS, Virginia..........................11
DUBOIS
   Adelaide 81
   Alex..260
   Alice...83
   Edna Pearl..............................106
   Ernestine 192
   Florence 247
   Marie Ann 286
   Martina........................251,286
   Mary A 178
   Pauline 82
   Rosina 12
   Rosine 221
   Syphrine 18
   Victoria 141
DUBOIUS, Adeline 14
DUCEPT
   Alphonse 148
   Delia.......................................229
   Eliza.......................................123
   Elmer Jean.............................251
   Francis...................................243
   Henry Oscar 240
   Jean 286
   Joserph 148
   Marguerite..............................148
   Rosalie 39
DUCEPT.RENAULT, Veronica ...110
DUCHAIN
   Alex Martin.....................247,284
   Julia..283
   Lillian.....................................256
   Marie..55
   Mary Rose..............................286
   Victoria 240
DUCHESNEAU

   Leonard Omer................. 240,243
   Lillian 195
   Mary 196
   Moses 281
   Raoul 247
DUMONT
   Elvina 156
   Emma 217
   Mary 89
   Mary Rose 283
   Rosanna 33
DUNCHAIN, Virginia................... 27
ELLER
   Geraldine 268
   Gladys Mae............................ 256
ENNO
   Adele 187
   Antoine, Jr 289
   August 174
   Cecelia Gladys........................ 273
   Clemence 23
   Francis 256,289
   Josephine 126
   Lawrence 289
   Louis............................... 247,291
   Mary 129
   Mary St A 174
   Robert 129
   Rose................................ 268,289
   Sidney.................................... 247
   Virginia...................... 10,174,186
ENNO LAFONTAIN, Rose 110
EVERLING, Joseph 284
FAGNANT
   Mary L..................................... 63
   Sarah....................................... 31
   Sylvia..................................... 273
FAGNANT.PELTIER, Jane 142
FAGUANT
   Emma Rose............................ 262
   Frances 173
   Irene Stella............................. 256
   Joseph 211
   Marie R.................................... 70
FAINE
   Ella 47
   Irene.. 47
   Joseph 47

Index

Joseph Lloyd 251
FALCON
   Agnes 142
   Edwin Lincoln 271
   Ella 247
   Emma 17
   Eugene 286
   Eugene Albert 251
   Florence 240
   Frezene 5
   George Patrick 243
   Irene Genevieve 240
   Jeanette 247
   John Raymond 243
   Julia Gladys 262
   Lillian Jane 268
   Marie Madonna 273
   Peter Virgil 262
   Theresa 256
   Virginia 284
   Walter Ray 256
   Willis Lawrence 243
FALK, Theodore 273
FANNING, John Lee 141
FASSETT, Donald Robert 273
FASSETT (FREDERICK), James .....
   262
FIDDLER
   Francis 240
   Joseph Albert 251
FLAMAND, Mary 100
FLEFORT, Adele 145
FLETTE
   Christine 51
   Louise 52
FLOWERS, Rachel 19
FLYING EAGLE, Kakenowash ... 284
FOI, Pierre 281
FOSTER
   Cecile Alice 247
   Grace 243
   Joseph 256
   Margaret 273
   May Evelyn 240
FOUGHTY, Walter 113
FOURNIER
   Florestine 141
   Norbert 286

FOURNIER.BAKER, Nancy Rose 181
FREDERICK
   Angelique 149
   Florence 84
   Frank 243
   George Ambrose 240
   Gloria 247
   Irene 240
   Josette 17, 209
   Margaret 56
   Marie 254, 284
   Mary Rose 243
   Nora 247
   Rachel 76
   Roderick 256
   Rosalie 287
   Rose 251
   William 260
FREDERICKSON, Wanita 251
FREDRICK, Elizabeth 139
FRIGON, Lucinda 196
GARDNER.GODON, Lucy 36
GAUTHIER
   Gerald Norbert 243
   Jos Martin C 262
   Leo Vincent 251
   Marie Teresa 268
GERALLY, Clara 11
GILES, Margaret 200
GILLIS
   Charles Raymond 243
   David Eugene 268
   Lucy Viola 240
   Mary Ann 256
GIRARD, Harold Lloyd 273
GLADUE
   Adelia 68
   Albert Oscar 240
   Anestesia 167
   Anna 195
   Arthur C 262, 268
   Caris Raymond 247
   Caroline 158
   Charles Ed 273
   Charles, Jr 286
   Claude 288, 289
   Cleophile 61
   Delia 176

Index

Harriet 268
Hazel 256
John Gilbert 240
Joseph 282
Josephine 223
Julia 291
Marie 247
Martha 240
Mary 51,57
Mary Rose 224
Mary Rosina 153
Pierre 283
Rosalie 78,158
Victoria 149
Virginia 183
GODON
    Alphonse 251
    Edward 273
    Francis 240
    Joseph 256
    Marion 102
    Mary 74
    Ruby Monica 278
    Veronica 217
GOOSELINE, Mary Rose 37
GOOSLINE, Caroline 194
GOSSLINE, Emile F 106
GOURNEAU
    Agnes 213
    Alexander 289
    Angelique 283
    Anna 111
    Bernard 273
    Cecelia 286
    Cecile 147
    Charles Joe 262
    Charles Joseph 268
    Collin 247
    Elizabeth 50
    Ernest 137
    Fred 251
    George 286
    Gloria 143
    Henry 240
    Irene Teresa 268
    Jane 223,273,291
    John Victor 125
    Julia 286
    Kenneth Leo 273
    Margaret 138
    Marie 58
    Marie Stella 262
    Mary C 88
    Mary Eloise 268
    Mary Joan 273
    Mary Rose 159,256
    Mary V 25
    Natalie Rose 286
    Nora Laura 262
    Nora Stella 262,268
    Peter Henry 243,284
    Rosalie 83
    Rosella Alice 268
    Sarah Jane 22
    Virginia 173
GOURNEAU.LILLIE, Angelique .. 95
GRANDBOIA
    Lucy 251
    Mary Leona 251
    Viola Georgina 251
GRANDBOIS
    Adelaide 162
    Adele 123
    Agnes 5
    Albert Leo 273
    Anna 153
    Caroline 200
    Celia Geraldine 268
    Celie Geraldine 262
    Clarice 281
    Delima Louise 243
    Elise 231
    Eliza 30
    Emily 128
    Emma 137
    Ernest 256
    Evelyn 273
    Gloria 247
    Henrietta Rose 256
    John Lawrence 247
    John Michael 256
    Joseph Edward 240
    Leo Gilbert 243
    Leona Gertrude 262,268
    Marie Edna 103
    Mary 129

Index

Mary Cecelia 268
Mary Jane 150
Mary R 66
Patrice No 284
Patrick Roger 247
Phillip Harrison 262
Rosalie 39
Sarah 85,283
Shirley Ann 273
Thoms 274
Zilda 228
GRANT
   Agnes 234
   Alice 40
   Andrew Albert 262
   Archie 247
   Caroline 78
   Clarence Richard 268
   Clarice 101
   Claud Ulysses 262
   Claude Ulysses 268
   Emma 111
   Frank Julius 256
   Geo Harry 291
   Georgeline 251
   Gladys 268
   Gloria Patricia 247
   John 137
   Julia 62
   Justine 150
   Leona 251
   Louis 240,283
   Louise 41
   Madeline 36,223
   Margaret 35,283
   Marland 247
   Mary 188
   Mary Cecelia 240,286
   Mary Edna 132
   Mary Jane 213
   Mary Rose 213
   Nettie Hilda 273
   Nora Eleanor 251
   Patrick 137
   Peter 243
   Peter Lloyd 256
   Richard James 273
   Rosalie 71

Sarah Jane 106
St Ann 95
Sylvester 281
Vernon 251
Viola Stella 243
Virginia 116
Vitalline 80
Wm Vincent 262
GRANT (BRIEN), Emma 286
GREAT WALKER
   Jane 274
   Maggie 168
GREEN FEATHER, Rose 3
GRIFFIN
   David Clinton 256
   John Howard 243
GUNDERSON
   Florence 193
   Mary Jane 288,289
   Nora 42
   Rachel 98
   Walter Eugene 274
   Wilburn G 288
GUNDERSON.REGAN, Florence
   109
GUNVILLE
   Emile 274
   Emma 281
   Eugenia 251
   France Elizabeth 247
   Lillian 281
   Rose 24
   Vincent 243
GUYON, Emma 116
GWINN, Margaret 225
HAGER.ROTHERING, Lillian 182
HALLIDAY
   Dorothy 65
   Minnie 153
HAMLEY
   Clarence 247
   Lewis 256
   Rebecca 95
   Sylvia 274,291
HARRISON
   Beatrice 162
   Margaret 58
HAUGE, Duane Joseph 274

Index

HAYDEN
  Mary St Ann.............................283
  Rose 79
HAYES
  John..283
  Margaret....................................229
  Mary..72
  Sallie...181
HAYS.PATNAUD, Ernestine.......158
HENRY
  Alice..147
  Caroline....................................229
  Edna Lucille.............................283
  Emily...142
  Florence...................................256
  Georgeline...............................274
  James..256
  John..251
  Laura..212
  Lester.......................................274
  Marie Louise............................247
  Mary Jane................................195
  Philomeme........................281,282
  Theodore.................................268
  Virginia....................................201
  William.....................................283
HENRY (ST PIERRE), Alexandra
 284
HERMAN
  Elizabeth..................................132
  Florence............................262,288
  Inex Marie...............................247
  Inez M.....................................283
  Louise 9
  Margaret..................................217
  Rosalie....................................190
  Theresa...................................226
  Violet.......................................251
HILL, Harvey Louis.....................251
HINTZ, Blanche M........................93
HOFF, Daniel................................. 8
HOLLAND, Sadie.......................121
HOULE
  Barbara.............................268,291
  Cecelia......................................90
  Charles....................................282
  Cinya.......................................291
  Clemence..................................79

Earnestine.................................. 14
Eliza.................................... 19,133
Elizabeth.................................... 31
Ethel Mae................................. 240
Francis..................................... 243
Geo Joseph.............................. 288
George...................................... 243
George Joseph......................... 262
Georgiana................................ 223
Ida Diana................................. 240
Isabel....................................... 201
James Howard......................... 274
Jos Clarence............................ 268
Joseph Geo.............................. 289
Joseph Wilfred........................ 262
Justine....................................... 19
Marion....................................... 73
Mary... 168
Mary Alvina............................ 274
Mary Ann................................ 282
Mary Jane................................ 104
Mary Rose................................. 12
Napoleon................................. 282
Nora... 247
Philomeme............................... 104
Rita.. 247
Stella Annie............................. 251
Virginia...................................... 90
INGALLS, George....................... 256
IRON BEAR
  Andrew.................................... 251
  Annie....................................... 171
  Eliza.. 96
  Rosina..................................... 169
  Virginia..................................... 92
IRVING, Thomas G, Jr................. 268
JACQKARCT, Marchetta............ 262
JACQMARCT, Peter J................. 243
JACQMARET, Louis..................... 17
JAST
  Adele....................................... 286
  Elmer Peter............................. 247
  Leroy....................................... 289
JASTE
  Delia.. 67
  Elise... 222
  Jane... 62
  Josephine.................................. 85

Index

Leroy 288
Matilda 164
JEANNOTT
   Irene Mildred 247
   Leo 251
   Louisa Genevieve 243
   Mary Martine 247
   Patrice 286
   Robert 251
JEANNOTTE
   Adele 229
   Albert 208
   Christine 221
   Elmer William 268
   Ernest Richard 268
   Helen Doris 268
   Henry Lawrence 256
   Joseph 266
   Lasute 176
   Marie 169
   Mary 155
   Mary Mae 243
   Mary Rita 262,269
   Nora S 256
   Olive Bernice 256
   Vitaline 165
   Walter Simon 274
JEANOTTE
   Leona 243
   Marie 206
JEROME
   Adelaide 199
   Agnes 110
   Alex Lawrence 262
   Alfred Daniel 262
   Alme 268
   Beatrice 16
   Charles 286
   Charles Robert 256
   Clara 284
   Clemence 197
   Emily 31
   Ernestine 251
   Eva Marline 286
   Franklin 240
   Irene 251
   Joseph 247,251
   Julia Rose 274

Louis 291
Marcil 240
Marguerite 10
Marie 243
Martin 291
Mary Cecelia 240
Mary L 283
Natalie 102
Phyllis Felicite 274
Roger 284
Roger Joseph 240
Veronica 96
Virginia 48,230
JEROME (ENNO), Beatrice 286
JETTY (DUBOIS), Rebecca Pearl .....
.... 251
JOHNSON
   Andy 262
   Bruce 247
   Irene 217
   Lucille 251
   Marion 109
   Melvin 109
   Mercedine Ardith 247
   Phyllis Laura 243
   Ruth 274
   Vera Doris 268
JOLIBOIS
   Lawrence 243
   Leslie 268
   Mary Jane 96
   Zaida 171
JOLLIBOIS
   Leroy 252
   Lucille 262,288
   Marie 289
   Violet 256
JOLLIE
   Blanche 205
   David Wm Jos 262
   Doris 254
   Margaret 62
   Nora 228
JOLLIE.AZURE, Ruth 218
JONES, Shirley Ellen 243
JUSTICE
   Dolores Mae 274
   Vernon Richard 262

Index

KAKENOWASH, Emma 92
KANICK
    Mary St Ann 284
    May Julia 67
KAPLIN
    Mary 106
    Sylvester 252
KAUFMAN
    Edward, Jr 274
    Lee Roy 256
    Lillian 114
KELLAND, Joseph H 159
KELLETT, Mary 243
KENT, Margaret 151
KEPLIN
    Cecelie 4
    Mary Jane 52
    Rose 260,262
    Sarah 167
    Wm Joseph 274
KEPLIN (BRIEN), Alex William .262
KETCHEM, Marie 177
KILLEN
    George Olaf 243
    Howard Clarence 247
KING, Eliza 135
KINNEY
    Francis 268
    Remy Cornelius 256
KLINE, Benjamin Joseph 278
KNUTSON
    Gerald 274
    Marchetta M 262
KRESS
    Genevieve 142
    Marian 142
    Wm John 142
KRINGEN, Palma 223
LACERTE
    Mary 118
    Rose 42
LADEAUX, Marie Louise 275
LADUCER
    Adele 202
    Alfred Stanley 268
    David Joseph 262
    Delima 281
    Ernest 286

Eugene 240
Gertrude 268
Gertrude Sylvia 275
Jane 139
Jerome 284
Joseph 268
Joseph Rogers 262
Julius 243,282
Louis 247
Louise 252
Marie 243,282
Marie Rose 220
Mary Clara 243,283
Mary Rose 227
Peter 256
LADUCER (POITRA), Angelique .....
    282
LAFAVOR, Mary 85
LAFLOE
    Angelique 184
    Frank 243,282
    Helen Jane 274
    Jos Alfred 288
    Joseph Alfred 263
    Mary Angela 247
    Rose Ann 83
LAFONTAIN
    Agatha 223
    Alex 240
    Alex Chester 240
    Alfred 240
    Alice 260
    Arthur 252
    Beryl Faye 268
    Betty 268
    Billy Melbaren 252
    Cecelia 248
    Clarice 12
    Daily 248
    Dora 248
    Doris 274
    Eliza Angeline 252
    Emma 89,212
    Ernest Edward 240
    Flora 274
    Fred 248
    George 248
    Gilbert 263

Index

Gladys 274
Hazel 252
Horace E 288
Isadore 286
James Edward 274
Josephine 110,168
Judith 91
Julia 74
Lawrence Robert 243
Lorraine 256,268
Louise 126
M Ernestine 262
Martine 226
Mary 107
Mary Ann 56
Mary E 110
Mary Grant 281
Mary Jane 222,263
Mary Rose 54,212
Nora Stella 274
Norma 263
Patrick Clifford 240
Philomeme 26
Rose 10
Rose Alice 263
Rose Delia 12
Roy 274,291
Sarah 191
St Pierre 283
Virginia 98
William 240
William Harry 263
LAFONTAIN.CHAMPAGNE,
  Philomene 64
LAFOUNTAIN
  Celina 30
  Mary 8
  Mary J 8
LAFOURNAIS
  Eliza 48
  Emily 32
  Ernest 289
  Justine 28
  Lillian 284
  Margaret 155
  Marie R 29
  Mary Louise 219
LAFRANCE

Ella Marie 240
Eva 189
Justine 291
Mary 165,192
Maurice 248
Rosalie 161
Susie 79
Theresa 274,291
Virginia 108
William 263
Zoe 226
LAFRANIERE
  Irene Marie 240
  Lawrence 257
  Leslie 248
  Lyda 248
  Lyle 248
  Violet Rita 274
  Vivian Doris 274
LAFRANIERRE, Lyle 283
LAFRENIERE, Alvina M 20
LAFROMBOIS
  Adeline 203
  Angeline 43
  Cecelia 97
  Cecile 283
  Celina 172
  Dean 286
  Delima 257
  Elise 28,134
  Eliza 61
  Emily 105
  Ernest 248
  Florestine 281
  Geraldine 274
  James Leo 269
  John B, Jr 252
  Joseph 257
  Kate 271
  Madeline 62
  Marie 228,268
  Michael 282
  Nels 291
  Patrice, Jr 263
  Patricia Mary 243
  Romeo 252
  Rose 37
  Rosina 158

Index

LAFURNAIS, Ernestine 5
LAGIMODIERE
   Alma 248
   Alvina 189
   Delia 10
   Leonard 263
   Maryann 252
   May Florence 240
   St Ann 46
LAHEY, Mildred 70
LAMBERT
   Augustine 263
   Delbert Alfred 243
   Doris Lorene 252
   Laura 24,153
   Mary Ann 198
   Mary Joyce 263
   Rose 46
   Sophia 151
LAMBERT.MOCK, Mary 109
LANDRY
   Alvina 248
   Aurelia 252
   Cecelia 240
   Eleanor 205
   Florence Jane 263
   John Joseph 284
   Mary Juanita 263,269
   Napoleon 288
   Nora Jennie 274
LANG
   Edna Marie 263
   Edna Pearl 209
   Irving Eugene 243
   Kathleen A 252
LANGAN
   Alice 248
   Cecelia 257
   Emile 274
   Marie Annabelle 278
   Rosella 23
LANGER
   Adele 184,285
   Alice 91
   Bebienne 195
   Cecelia 230
   Clara 240
   Darrell 252

   Delima 234
   Edward 283
   Emil 269
   Ernestine 104
   Fabian 281
   George Frank 248
   James Earl 274
   John B 289
   Joseph Francis 243
   Mary Alice 71
   Mary B 7
   Mary Celina 152
   Mary Virginia 248
   Philomeme 53
   Rosalie 28
   Rosina 56
   Sarah 100
   Verlin 243
   Viola Mae 252
LAPIERRE, Larose 181
LAQSOTA, Stella 13
LARAT, Susan 168
LARAT.DEJARLAIS, Emily 115
LAROQUE
   Charley Steven 248
   Clemence 177
   Emma Louise 252
   Ernestine 223
   Eugene 274
   Floyd 257
   George 244
   Harvey David 244
   Jean 129
   Jos A Lawrence 263
   Loretta 263
   Margaret 252
   Mary 104
   Mary Jane Eldora 244
   Milton Vernon 263
   Rebecca 164
   Rose Veda 248
   Roy Joseph 283
   Victoria 8,21,199
   Wm Lawrence 244
LARSEN
   Edward 248
   Floyd 240
   Larrian 263,269

Index

Melvin.................................252
LASOTA, Josephine.................289
LATERREGRASS, Mary............163
LATRACE
   Eliza..................................76
   Eva....................................207
   Frederick Nelson...............240
   George..............................281
   Gwendolen.......................248
   Lucy...................................71
LATRAIL
   Dorothy Jane....................252
   Mary...................................43
   Patricel Jr.........................244
LATRAILL, Mary.......................120
LATRAILLE, Ellen......................45
LATRAILLE.CLARK, Emma......193
LATRAILLE.TURCOTTE, Margaret
....202
LATTERGRASS
   Agnes.................................38
   Eliza...................................24
   Ernest Edward..................266
   Justine..............................118
   Louis P Wayne.................244
   Robert David....................274
LAVALLIE
   Alexander.........................241
   Alfred...............................274
   Antonia Sylvio..................263
   Clara..............................9,118
   Emerize..............................50
   Ernest...............................252
   Florestine...........................84
   Frances............................135
   Fred..................................241
   Margaret.............................54
   Marguerite J.....................263
   Mary.................................241
   Mary Eva...........................86
   Mary Florestine................252
   Mary T...............................27
   Rose...........................163,172
   Virginia......................100,252
LAVBERDURE, Emily................181
LAVERDURE
   Adele..................................49
   Adelia...............................210

   Agnes.................................42
   Albert...............................252
   Amelia..............................101
   Andrew R.........................241
   Annie Marian....................241
   Catherine............................13
   David..........................288,289
   Edward M Roy.................269
   Elsie.....................................4
   Eva Elizabeth...................257
   Frances............................275
   Gertrude J.......................275
   Grace Lillian....................244
   Helen...............................244
   Isabella............................165
   James...............................252
   Jennie Bede.....................275
   Josephine.........................230
   Leo David........................274
   Leocadia..........................275
   Lillian...............................244
   Louise A..........................207
   Ludger.............................244
   Marcial............................282
   Margaret............................51
   Marie Hilda................252,284
   Mary..................19,87,198,282
   Mary Ann........................252
   Mary Rose.......................193
   Matilda............................288
   Morris Herman................248
   No Name....................263,269
   Nora June...................263,269
   Pauline............................159
   Ralph Gerald..............263,269
   Rita Evelyn......................263
   Rosalie.............................211
   Rose................................218
   Sarah Jane.................252,284
   Virginia............................244
   Yvonne............................226
   Yvonne Eva.....................244
LAVIA
   Catherine Marie...............248
   Dora Katherine................248
   Edward Benedict.............241
   Elise...................................37
LAVILLE, Francois....................288

Index

LAVILLIE, Marie 3
LAVIOLETTE
    Clemence 232
    Dovaline 254
LEBRUN
    Elizabeth 257
    Lillian 48
LECLAIRE, Delia 3
LECOMPT
    Amy Emma 189
    Blanche 244
    Corma 241
    Garley 263,269
    Gladys 252
    Lucille 47
LEDEAUX
    Gertrude 248
    Rosilia 257
LEFORT
    Betty Lou 268
    Dora Katherine 257
    Joseph 244
    Mary Agnes 263,269
LEFORT.HAYES, Mary 143
LEFT HAND
    Elaine Cecelia 257
    Elsie Mae 269
LEMAY
    Flora 182
    Gilbert L 286
    Leona Genevieve 269
    Madeline 244
    Napoleon Jacob 252
LEMERE, Josephine 6
LEMIRE, Mary 6
LENGER, Pauline 24
LENOIR
    Adele 22
    Agatha 176
    Cecilia 178
    Clemence 112
    Dorothy 252
    Elizabeth 283
    Emily 181
    Ernest 241
    Florence 244
    Jean 275
    Joan 275
    Joseph 281
    Leo 284
    Lucy 181
    Margaret 5
LENOIR.DECOTEAU, Mary Louise 180
LENOIR-KRESS, Evalina 142
L'ESPARANCE
    Agnes Theresa 257
    Alexander 275
    Arthur 257
    Evelyn 269
    Mary Rose 192
L'ESPERANCE, Delia 227
LETHRIDGE, Katherine 120
LILLEY, Maggie 188
LILLIE
    Alma Blanch 257,286
    Beatrice 283
    Charles Stanley 263
    Francis 252,284
    Irene Maggie 244
    Joseph 248
    Mary Madeline 283
    Mary V 291
    Mary Victoria 275
    Rose 263
    Victoria Mary 248
LIND
    Bernard Marvin 269
    John Harry 257
LINDGREN, Ramona Marie 263
LINKLATER, Philomeme 286
LIPPY, Stanley 106
LITTLE BOY
    Mary Eva 263
    Patrick 244
    Pearl 146
LITTLE GIRL, Laura 52
LITTLE SHELL III, Chief v
LIVERMONT, Lorraine 244
LIZOTTE
    Doris May 284
    Ernest 275
    George L 241
    Joseph 288
    Mary 283
    Mary Celina 233

Index

Mary Jane 244
Mary Jean 285
Rosalie 66,151
Rosina 136
LOHNES, Sarah Jane.....................16
LONG NOSE 95
LONICK
   Alfred Eugene 241
   Joseph R 275
   Vernon Phillip 257
LUCIER
   Eliza 87
   Mary 12
LUNWK, Richard Ronald............275
MACHIPENESS
   Elmer 263
   George 252,285
   Ida 290
   Night S 286
MAKES IT RAIN, Gladys 241
MALATERRE
   Alexis 288
   Amy 35
   Cecila M 53
   Dorothy 275
   Emil 257
   Emma 281
   Felix Eli 244
   Fred 244
   Genevieve 288
   Irene 248
   Julius 288
   Marie Louise 266
   Mary 135
   Mary E 50
   Stella 252
   Vernon 275
   Veronic 186
MALWAM, Alexander 282
MANSON
   Grace 244
   James Joseph 248
   John Louis 241
   Mary H 263
   Theresa G 248
   William 257
MARCELLAIS
   Charles 245

Clarence Jos 257
Dolores 275
Joseph Edward 241
Mary 13
Peter 263
MARCIL
   Antone Albert 257
   Marie Lillian 241
MAREAU, Ellen 104
MARION
   Adelphine 73
   Beatrice 13,248
   Charles Edward 252
   Donald Edward 269
   Elise 85
   George Henry 263
   Helen 150
   Irene Agnes 241
   Maria 66
   Mary Eliza 197
   Mary L 81
   Mary Louise 138
   Narcissa 269
   Narcissus Isabel 263
   Reginald 275
   Virginia 143
MARION.JOHNSON, Elise 109
MARSDEN, Raymond 8
MARTELL
   Charles P 248
   Clarence 241
   Collin Joseph 257
   Della 248
   Emma 79
   Ernest 241
   Evelyn 275
   Helen 110
   Irene 42
   John B 283
   John Michael 257
   Norman 248
   Roland Lloyd 275
   Thomas Wm 241
MARTIN
   Alice Regina 269
   Caroline 227
   Elise 10
   Elizabeth 26

Index

Florestine 148
Fred 282
George 245
Irene Agnes 241
Jessie 60
Louis Moses 252
Margaret 204
Mary 49
Mary Rose 263
Rose Anne 263
Shirley Mae 269
Ursula 58
Walter Patrick 248
Winifred 241
MATHAIS, Geo Clifford 245
MATHIAS
   Gerald Norman 257
   James Raymond 263
MCARTHUR, Ann 89
MCCLINTOCK, Maizie 94
MCCLOUD, Veronica 4
MCCLOUD
   Charles, Jr 257
   Elise 28,85
   Emerize 85
   Helen 47
   Joseph 269,290
   Margaret 110
   Mary 269,290
   Moses 283
   Patricia 292
   Patricia Jean 275
   Peter 282
   Therese 263,269
   Veronica 76
   Virginia 172
   Vivian 288
   Vivian Virginia 263
MCCOY, Josephine 292
MCDONALD
   Eliza 146
   Lissett 131
MCDONALD.SCHINDLER, Elise 58
MCGILLIS
   Delia 177
   Eugene 286
   Hannah M 208
   Marceline 12

Mary Elise 174
Mary Rosalie 269
Phyllis Jean 254
Rosalie 285
Rose 37
MCKAY
   Florestine 185
   Mary C 73
MCKENZIE, Flora 156
MCLAUGHLIN, Agnes 152
MCVAY
   Betty Jane 275
   Raymond R 263
MEKWAM
   Agnes Rose 248
   Alex 288
   Equazance 282
   George 244
   Irene 263
   Lucy 275
   Mary 241
MELWAM, Christopher 269
METZENBERG, Louis Mae 245
MICHELS, Ella Olga 142
MILLER, Esther 136
MINNE
   Dora Elizabeth 275
   Emily Matilda 245
MOCK, Wm Elmer 109
MONETTE
   [Blank] 125
   Emma 62
   Estella 241
   Jos Howard 263,269
   Mary P 91
   Raymond 252
   Resia Mae 275
   Rosalie 90
MONETTE-VANDAL, Clara 125
MONTOUR
   Marceline 17
   Rosalie 169
MONTRAIL, Margaret 286
MONTRIEL
   Adele 292
   Albert 37
   Josephine 131
   Margaret 89

Index

Mary 9
Sarah 109
MOORE
  John Lindley 248
  Sarah Jean 263
MORIN
  Adaline 84
  Adele 88,156
  Alfred V 257
  Alice B 102
  Angelique 106
  Anna 292
  Antoine 285
  Beatrice 110
  Bernard 264,269
  Charles C 290
  Charles Christopher 257
  Christine 203,281
  Dale Louis 269
  David Solomon 275
  Delia 46
  Dora Virginia 241
  Dorothy Mae 264,269
  Eliza 87
  Eugene 248
  Evelyn 248
  Florence 252
  Francis Peter 269
  Frank 74
  Frank J 288
  Frank Joseph 264
  Genevieve 285
  Geo Michael 244
  Gilbert 271
  Irene 264
  James 269
  James Leo 241
  John Herbert 241
  Joseph 244,264,269
  Josephine 111
  Josette 292
  Kathleen 257
  Louise A 133
  M Jane C 88
  Mabel 214
  Maggie 53
  Mary 45
  Mary (Belgarde) 281
  Mary Jane 133,209
  Mary L 80
  Mary Louise 104,133
  Mary Margaret 275
  Mary V 75,198
  Matilda Hannah 248
  Moses 241
  Olivine 129
  Rachel 72
  Raymond 275
  Rebecca 275,286
  Rebecca Alvina 248
  Rosalie 22,69
  Rosalind 41
  Rose 264,288
  Rose Dolores 275
  Rosina 144
  Rosine 106
  Sarah 72,127,205,282
  St Ann 39
  Sylvester 244
  Theodore, Jr 248
  Theresa 166
  Thomas Edward 257
  Victoria 27
  Virginia 150,186,191
  Virginia E 275
  Vivian 244
  Willard Marlin 269
  Zoe 197
MORIN HARRISON, Sarah 36
MORIN.ENNO, Margaret 155
MORIN.LAFRANCE, Adeline 36
MORIN.LEMAY.LAVIA, Elise 84
MURPHY
  John 248
  Lawrence 244
  Marie 257
MYRICK, Florence 86
NADEAU
  Alexander 281
  Alvina 116
  Clement 275
  David Albert 244
  Elmer 257
  Flora 33
  Fred Dominick 257
  Judith 173

Index

Louis 252
Marguerite 226
Marie 6
Mary 287
Peter George 275
Rosella 248,287
NANAPUSH, Flora 94
NAVAVRE, Christine 106
NEIL, Dorothy 39
NELSON
   Donald 248
   Royla Jeanne 257
   Wayne 195
NEPINE
   Christine 249
   White Thunder 269,290
NEWNAPI, John 284
NICHOLAS
   Alfred 257
   Claude 281
   Claudia 248
   Donald Edgar 264,269
   Ellen 217
   Francis R 275
   Julienne 70
   Ralph Edward 252
   Robert Lee 244
NOLIN, Sarah 52
NORQUAY
   Alice 199
   Annabelle 275
   Ellen Mae 269
NWENAPI
   Alex 264
   Hunting 252
NYGAARD, Katie 203
OADOTTE, Celina 26
OLFERT, Mary 98
OLSEN
   Elaine Frances 264
   Lucille 252
   Mary Jeannette 252
   Virginia Norma 257
OLSON
   Clemence 275
   Morris Edward 275
   Virginia 292
PACKINEAU, Warren 254

PAGE
   Delonais Thelma 276
   Dophine 249
   Fillian Albany 244
   Frank 269
   Josette 173
   Mary Ethel 252
   Nancy 288
   Raymond 264
PAGO, Gertrude 127
PAPAIS, Elaine 84
PARISIEN
   Alice 276
   Beulah 244
   Charles Arthur 264
   Charley 271
   Charlie 244
   Clemance 131
   Dora May 285
   Eliza 224
   Elmer John 252
   Emily 17,112
   Ernest Melvin 276
   Ezear 290
   Francois Martin 241
   Irene Mae 244
   Joan O'Arc 257
   Josephine 43
   Julius Melvin 269
   Justine 18
   Louis 284
   Malain 116
   Mary 50
   Mary Ann 191
   Mary Emily 285
   Mary Lillian 257
   Mary M 184
   Mary Madeline 264
   Michael George 257
   Phillip Jerome 253
   Ralph Oliver 257
   Roy 290
   Stella May 285
   Verne S 249
PARISIEN (CHAMPAGNE), William
   288
PARISIEN (HAYES), Joseph 288
PARISIEN (LAGIMODIERE),

Index

Mary Dorothy..................244
PARISIEN.BONNEAU, Justine...186
PARKES, Sarah......................198
PATENAUD, Malvina...................96
PATNAUD
   Agnes Laverne 257
   Betsey 7
   Charlotte................................203
   Ernest....................................249
   Francis...................................264
   Gertrude E 276
   James.....................................276
   Joseph B 264
   Josephine...............................117
   Marguerite..............................276
   Mary..............................220,244
   Sam Eugene 244
   Stanilaus................................257
   Virginia.............................23,40
   Willie 244
PAUL
   Agnes 79
   Barton 40
   Clemence 157
   Evelyn 70
   Marie.......................................58
   Mary Madeline......................264
PAUL (JEANNOTT), Mary Madeline
  257
PELTIER
   Abraham................................282
   Albert 46
   Delia......................................142
   Eliza......................................232
   Elizabeth 32
   Ellen......................................190
   Emerize.................................159
   Emily......................................55
   Emma....................................142
   Florestine 227
   Gabriel 276
   Joseph 281
   Joseph Gilbert 276
   Julia...12
   Louise 41,253
   Margaret................................125
   Mary............22,68,99,202,208,290
   Mary Ann..............................241

   Mary Emma..................... 287,288
   Mary Laura 288
   Mary Rose 207
   Paul.. 281
   Robert.................................... 275
   Rose.. 60
   St Ann................................... 113
PELTIER.AZURE, Eliza............. 101
PELTIER.HENRY, Rosine 195
PELTIER.JOHNSON, Florence ... 217
PELTIER.STANDING, Adele 220
PEPIN
   Josephine................................ 13
   Margaret 100
PERMEAU, Mary Ida 73
PERRONTEAU
   Adele 41
   Alex Peter............................. 260
   Anna..................................... 163
   Caroline 127
   Clara 79
   Louise 276
   Marie Cecile 269
   Mary Jane 41
   Rosalie.................................. 210
   Rose...................................... 121
PETERSON
   Annie Pauline 269
   Dolores Elaine 257
   Mary 287
PEWAPACOMAWAT, Iron Bear
   285
PIGG, Mamie B........................... 151
PIPPENGER
   Albert Andrew 269
   Paul Eugene.......................... 253
   Robert Brown 241
   Viola Phoebe 264
   Violet.................................... 281
PIPPINGER, David Gregor 249
PLANT, Emma............................. 55
PLANTE
   Albert Edward 253
   Alfred 249,264
   Alice Rose 241
   Antoinette............................... 46
   Daniel Francis....................... 249
   Dora....................................... 46

Index

Francis James 264
George James 269
Lola 253
Louis 290
Mary Angeline 257
Mary Teresa 276
Virginia 122
PLUMMER, Zilda 113
POINTRA
    Arthur Archie 249
    Francis Albert 249
    Oscar Clenoy 249
    Phillip Albert 249
    Redempta Louise 249
    Wallace Lawrence 249
POITRA
    Adele 43
    Adeline 77
    Albert 253
    Alfred Raymond 253
    Angela 245,284
    Arline Jos 264
    Beatrice 173
    Catherine 44
    Celina 169,188
    Clara 245
    Clifford J 276
    David John 258,287
    David Lloyd 245
    Delima 264,270
    Dorothy 264
    Dorothy Ann 276
    Eleanor 253
    Elise 234
    Elizabeth 83,234
    Elnora 245
    Ernestine 264
    Flora 174
    Floyd 244
    Fred Elmer 244
    Henry 281
    Herman 245
    Ida May 162
    Ina 258
    Irene 292
    Irene Bernice 276
    Irene Mabel 254
    Irene May 269

J Alphonse 290
James 276
John Ernest 258
John Jos Clarence 264
John Warren 244
Joseph 257
Joseph Martin 241
Joseph Norman 264
Josephine 244,285,287
Josephine R. 244
Julia 215
Julianne 115
Julius Maxim 264
Laura 264
Lillian 58,264
Louis Paul 276
M R Alvina 173
Mabel Irene 287
Marie 30,44
Marion 264
Martin 173,241
Mary 82,96,216
Mary Aurelia 253
Mary Corinne 277
Mary Emily 141
Mary Jane 140
Mary P 73
Mary Roe 96
Mary Rose 44
Mary Stella 276
Mary Verna 276
Melvin Francis 264
Mildred Marie 276
Norine 245
Olympia B 276
Rachel Sylvia 257
Ray Stephen 276
Raymond 264,270
Raymond Sylvester 269
Rita E 192
Rosalie 211
Rose 241
Rose E 24
Rosella 270
Stanley Michael 269
Stella 264
Stella A 290
Stella Mae 245

Index

Stephen 292
Theresa 264
Veronica 275
Veronica V 277
Viola 245
Violet Nora 270
Wallace 285
Zilda 56
PORTRA
   Ernest 282
   Francois 282
   Irene 282
PREMEAU
   Arthur Roger 258
   Eliza 136
   Ida Jean 241
   Joseph William 270
   Louise 215
   Mary 135
   Mary Jane 153
   No Name 264
   Olympia 249,290
   Sarah 25
   Theresa 249
   Theresa Dolores 258
   Winifred 67
PRING, Dora 148
PURDY
   Clarence Wm 258
   Clinton James 249
   Elizabeth J 241
   Lucille 113
PURVIS, Christine 275
RAKES, Edward, Jr 276
RARDON, Cosette Pauline 258
REARDEN, Patricia Dean 276
REARDON
   Abraham 284
   Gabriel 241
   James Michael 258
   Louise Patricia 249
RED THUNDER
   Fred 290
   Tom 169
REFLECTION MAN
   Blue Thunder 258
   Mary 276
REINDEAU, Serena 245

RENAULT
   Benjamin 285
   Elalie 288
   Eliza 287
   Grace 258,288
   Grant 258
   Regina 290
RENVILLE
   Fred 282
   Harry Joseph 241
   John Francis 253
   Joseph 282
   Mary 215
   Octave 284
   Rose Myrtle 258
   Virginia June 270
RENVILLE.GOSSLINE, Celina .. 106
RENVILLE.POITRA, Josephine 43
RICHARD
   Bernice Marie 253
   Clemence 172
   Delia 201
   Florestine 214
   Francis Elmer 276
   Gladys Grace 249
   Justine 156
   Willard Hubert 258
RICHWINE
   Lucille 287
   Shirley Ann 270
RIENDEAU
   Adolph 276
   Alice Mae 249
   Cecelia 264
   Luciana 258
ROBERT
   Edgar Norbert 258
   Marion 108
   Ophelia 264
ROBINSON, Christine 61
ROLETTE
   Anna Jane 181
   Emily 145
   Jane 285
   Josephine 205
   Margaret 35
   Nora E 181
   Virginia 211

Index

RONDEAU
  Geneva Olive 245
  Muriel Marie 253
ROSSKNECHT
  Annie Mary 106
  Ralph 258
ROUSSIN
  Charley Raymond 276
  John 253
  Leonard 264
  Louis Joseph 258
  Roger 292
  Roger Raymond 270
  Wm Bruno 245
ROY
  Madeline 11
  Minerva 276
  Mont Delia Iris Elaine 264
  Theodore Albert 253
RUSSELL, James, Jr. 270
RYAN
  Richard Lee 276
  Wm Howard 270
SAGER, Teda 266
SAICE.ROLETTE, Annie 224
SALMONSON
  Florestine 281
  Glenn 245
SALO
  Donald Martin 276
  Francis Michael 264
SAMPION, Margaret 15
SAN GRAIT
  Caroline 290
  Casper 276
  Joseph 264,290
  Madeline 258
  Mary 114
  Mary V 249
SAUNDERS, Lillie 131
SAYER
  Clara 119
  Francis 119
  Mary Jane 176
SAYERS
  Ellen 31
  Jean 129
  Mary Ann 46

  Mary Florence 129
SCHINDLER
  Adrine Frances 253
  Beatrice 192
  Clara 103
  Edna Patricia 264,270
  Elaine M 276
  Emma 218
  Ernestine E 249
  Evelyn 119
  Fred William 245
  Hattie 179
  Winifred 21
SCOTT
  Elizabeth 151
  Eva L 177
SEDEVIK, Darrell 276
SENECAL, Mary Rose 284
SHAFER
  Ilene Agnes 249
  Leonard Palmer 258
SHANKS, Marie Lyda 258
SHEFFERT, Muriel 150
SHEPERD, Margaret 19
SHINING CLOUD 288
SHIREBACK
  James Edward 258
  Mary Belgarde 245
  Richard Mark 276
  Robert Paul 249
SHORT
  Evelyn 270
  Fabian 245
  Francis 264
  Josephine 183
  Lizzie 114
  Mary Vivian 264
  Philomeme 114
SINDT
  Gladys Agnes 264
  Grace 276
  Wesley Leroy 249
SKINNER
  Amelia 249
  Angeline 245
  Flora 253
  Madeline 288,290
  Mebel 276

Index

Mrs 282
Olive 253
Puyat 282
Stanley 245
Theresa 171
SLATER
   Albina 258
   Eleanor 253
   Emma 222
   Frances 270
   Louise 155
   Rose 54
   William John 265
SMIGIEL
   Betty Jane 253
   Carrie Joyce 265
   Robert Joseph 241
SMITH
   Arthur Ben 276
   Barbara Mae 253
   Beverly Ann 276
   Cecelia Mae 290
   Cecelia May 265
   Clarence Louie 249
   Delia Jane 245
   Elizabeth 39
   Emma 125
   Francis Sylvester 253
   Israel 281
   Judith 54
   Julienne 290
   Martha 186
   Mary Florestine 249
   Matilda 39
   Michael 253
   Rose Ann 11
   Ruth Adele M 265
ST ARNAUD
   Albert 266
   Anna 181
   Elmer 249
   Eva 163,230
   Josephine 69
   Julia 199
   Leona 230
   Mary 204
   Raphael 276
ST ARNAUD. DUCEPT, Margaret...
   148
ST CLAIR, Lucille Alvina 265
ST CLAIRE
   Doris May 253
   Flora 171
   Lloyd Edward 245
   Marion 276
   Mary 69
   Priscilla Rose 249
   Rachel 224
   Rose 47
ST GERMAIN
   Irene Dolores 241
   John Findley 249
   Marie 130
   Maynard Sylvester 258
   Rosalie 60
ST GERMAINE, Marie Rose 214
ST PEIRRE, Celine 245
ST PIERRE
   Adeline 115
   Delia 38
   Francois 290
   Laura 25
   Marie 56,285
   Mary Adeline 180
   Rose 249
   Seraphine 253
STALEY
   Davidf 258
   Jennie 245
   Richard Abraham 276
STANDING
   Edna May 63
   Evelyn 107
STANDING ACROSS, Maggie ... 157
STANDING CHIEF, Minerva 171
STEVENSON (HENRY), Mary Louise
.... 285
STEWART, Angeline 284
STOEN, Joyce Marjory 241
STOFIEL
   Maxine 270
   Robert 276
SWAIN
   Adele 58
   Marie Zelma 285
   Zelma 245

Index

Zilda 139
SWAN, Mary 22
TALIMENTES, Frank 38
TETRAULT
   Cecelia 258
   Dorothea Mae 265
   Gilbert Wm 253
   Lucille Bernice 245
   Margaret 270
   Margaret B 277
THIBERT
   Adolph Peter 253
   Amelia 127
   Arthur Lawrence 245
   Dorothy Margaret 265
   Flora 201
   Pauline Marcella 258
   Vernon Stephen 241
   Wanelda Jeannette 258
THIFAULT
   Adeline 68
   Harry 253
   Josephine 31
   Norbert 282
   Wallace 270
THOMAS
   Alex 249
   Allen Edward 249
   Angeline M 134
   Catherine 287
   Celina 64
   Claudia 40
   Ernest Allen 253
   Jero Francis 265
   Marie 92
   Nora 241,245
   Rose 67
   St Ann 195
THOMAS.BERCIER, Alvina 130
THORNE, Bertha Loma 277
TINKAY
   Laverne Leo 245
   Rosella Evelyn 270
   Violet Mar 258
TIPPS, Dorothy 178
TOBINESS, Iron Feather 245
TOM, Joseph 114
TORGERSON, Glenn Allen 277

TOUPIN, Virginia 31
TOUPIN.FREDERICK, Veronica 119
TRESTER, Clara 282
TROTHIER
   Betty 258
   Doris 249,287
   Eugene 265,270
   Gerald 277
   Helen 25
   Isabel 121
   Lillian 139
   Louise 18
   Mary 102,245
   Mary Louise 265
   Maxine Rosella 258
   Patrick Everett 245
   Rose 91
   Rosine 225
   Sylvia 258
   Wayne Sanford 265,270
   William 282
TURCOTT
   Alfred 249
   Alvina 258
   Evelyn Agnes 245
   Flora 253
   Georgeline Rita 245
   Henry 265
   Irene 241,245
   Josephine 285
   June Marvena 265,270
   Louis Patrick 253
   Lucy 80
   Mary 40
   Michael Richard 253
   Rita 277
   Rose Lena 270
   Sarah 20
   Stanley Roger 249
   Viola Margaret 265
   Vitaline 277
TURCOTTE
   Angelique 50
   Celina 19
   Claudia 205
   Flora 287
   Josephine 75
   Lena 233

Index

Mary L 59
Michael 287
Susan 79
Wilhelmina 109
TURCOTTE.HOULE, Henrietta 90
VALLIE
    Caroline 178
    Cecelia 270
    Eliza 54
    Helen 258
    Jane 29
    John 290
    Julia 121,282
    Louis 253
    Margaret 122
    Marie 155
    Mary 35
    Mary Jane 245
    Victoria 44
VALLIE.DECOTEAU, Emma 194
VANDAL
    Edmund Francis 258
    Esther Beulah 253
    John Ernest 241
    Lorene 258
    Lucille 265,288
    Marie Evelyn 249
    Mary 16,290
    Mary Jane 55
    Rose 277
    Rosina 74
    William 290
VANDAL.GOUMEAU, Rose 137
VANDAL.MORIN, Mary L 74
VANERAL, Erma D 270
VILLENEUVE
    Alfred Louis 283
    Eliza 170
    Emilia 249
    Evangeline 260
    Josephine 170
    Leona Christine 270
    Mary Agnes 199
    Mary Alice 199
    Sarah 84
VIVIER
    Archie Cx 277
    Catherine Inez 258

Ellen 65
Emily 11
Ernestine 117
Esther 253
Flora 168
Fred 245
Gladys 277
James Stephen 277
Leona Vilma 253
Mary E 204
Mary Jane 105
Napoleon 245
Norbert 258
Patrice Sylvester 249
Philomeme 26
Rosalie 135
Rose 230
Rosina 200
St Ann 8,103
Stella Mae 249
Vincent 270
WALLETT
    Adeline 147
    Alexander 249
    Alvina 258
    Cecelia Gladys 258
    David 277
    Emma 249
    Francis 253,285
    Gertrude 266
    Henry 249
    John Baptiste 258
    Lillian 260
    Melanie 288
    Moses 249
    Patrick 245
    Ruth 242
    Sarah 277
WALSH
    Arlene 253
    Mary Louise 245,285
    Virginia 253
WARREN
    Agnes 3
    Angeline 124
    Delphine 28
    Joseph John 265,270
    Mary 63

Index

Philomeme 108
William 285
Wm Belgarde 258
WATROUS, Myrtle 105
WEEKLY, Ellen 165
WEEKS, Leila Mae 265
WELSH, Arline 285
WEST, Bernice 242
WESTFALL
   Frank Edward 270
   Harold Joel 277
WILBURN
   Marian Edna 229
   Mary Edna 270
WILCOX
   Cecilia 287
   Hillie Harry 250
WILKIE
   Adele 57
   Adeline M E 265
   Agnes 193
   Amelia Alice 277
   Bertha 246
   Cecile 27
   Clara 65
   Doris 246
   Dorothy 242
   Elizabeth 113,270
   Elizabeth C 265
   Elzear 250
   Emil 290
   Euvene David 250
   Eva 56
   Florestine 265,270
   Francis 282
   Fred Louis 250
   John Israel 245
   Josephine 290
   Leona 250
   Lillian 258
   Margaret 56,184
   Marie 290
   Marie Clara 265
   Martha 258
   Mary 146,154
   Mary Ann 171,246
   Mary Delia 285
   Mary Edna 283

   Mary Rose 100
   Michael Stephen 265
   Morris 253,287
   Name Unknown 258
   Nora 53
   Patrick 250,265
   Peamelia 277
   Rose 143
   Susan Marie 277
   Unknown 287
   Veronica 245
   Victoria 144
   Virginia 229
WILKIE.AZURE, Virginia 111
WILLIAMS, Mamie 145
WOLGAST, Annie 151
WOND, Herbert 259
WONG, Jennie 250
WORMBECKER, Phyllis 45
YEPSON, Virginia Ann 265
YOUNG, Oskine 172
ZACHE, Alvina 25
ZURA
   Leon 277
   Margaret 265
   Robert Norman 253

www.ingramcontent.com/pod-product-compliance
Lightning Source LLC
Chambersburg PA
CBHW020245030426
42336CB00010B/617